# Lecture Notes in Artificial Intelligence 11352

Subseries of Lecture Notes in Computer Science

More information about this series at http://www.springer.com/series/1244

Jaap van den Herik · Ana Paula Rocha (Eds.)

# Agents and Artificial Intelligence

## 10th International Conference, ICAART 2018
## Funchal, Madeira, Portugal, January 16–18, 2018
## Revised Selected Papers

*Editors*
Jaap van den Herik
Leiden University
Leiden, The Netherlands

Ana Paula Rocha
University of Porto
Porto, Portugal

ISSN 0302-9743 ISSN 1611-3349 (electronic)
Lecture Notes in Artificial Intelligence
ISBN 978-3-030-05452-6 ISBN 978-3-030-05453-3 (eBook)
https://doi.org/10.1007/978-3-030-05453-3

Library of Congress Control Number: 2018947333

LNCS Sublibrary: SL7 – Artificial Intelligence



This Springer imprint is published by the registered company Springer Nature Switzerland AG
The registered company address is: Gewerbestrasse 11, 6330 Cham, Switzerland

# Preface

The present book includes extended and revised versions of a set of selected papers from the 10th International Conference on Agents and Artificial Intelligence (ICAART 2018), held in Funchal, Madeira, Portugal, during January 16–18.

ICAART 2018 received 161 paper submissions from 35 countries, of which 14% are included in this book. The papers were selected by the event chairs and their selection is based on a number of criteria that include the classifications and comments provided by the Program Committee members, the session chairs' assessment, and also the program chairs' global view of all papers included in the technical program. The authors of selected papers were then invited to submit a revised and extended version of their papers having at least 30% innovative material.

The purpose of the International Conference on Agents and Artificial Intelligence is to bring together researchers, engineers, and practitioners interested in the theory and applications in the areas of agents and artificial intelligence. Two simultaneous related tracks were held, covering both applications and current research work. One track focused on agents, multi-agent systems and software platforms, distributed problem solving and distributed AI in general. The other track focused mainly on artificial intelligence, knowledge representation, planning, learning, scheduling, perception reactive AI systems, and evolutionary computing and other topics related to intelligent systems and computational intelligence.

The book consists of 23 contributions of high quality. For a list of the papers, we refer the reader to the Table of Contents. In general, the ICAART 2018 topics covered in this book are as follows: natural language processing (4, 2 of which are from the Special Session on Natural Language Processing in Artificial Intelligence), neural networks (4), multi-agent systems (4), planning and scheduling (2), intelligent user interfaces (2), knowledge representation and reasoning (2), machine learning (2), Semantic Web (1), soft computing (1), uncertainty in AI (1).

We would like to thank all the authors for their contributions and also the reviewers who helped ensure the quality of this publication.

January 2018

Jaap van den Herik
Ana Rocha

# Organization

## Conference Chair

| | |
|---|---|
| Jaap van den Herik | Leiden University, The Netherlands |

## Program Chair

| | |
|---|---|
| Ana Rocha | LIACC/FEUP, Portugal |

## Program Committee

| | |
|---|---|
| Suzanne Barber | The University of Texas, USA |
| Cees Witteveen | Delft University of Technology, The Netherlands |
| Thomas Ågotnes | University of Bergen, Norway |
| Varol Akman | Bilkent University, Turkey |
| Vicki Allan | Utah State University, USA |
| Klaus-Dieter Althoff | German Research Center for Artificial Intelligence/University of Hildesheim, Germany |
| Frédéric Amblard | Toulouse 1 University Capitole, France |
| Cesar Analide | University of Minho, Portugal |
| Andreas Andreou | Cyprus University of Technology, Cyprus |
| Alla Anohina-Naumeca | Riga Technical University, Latvia |
| Antonio Arauzo-Azofra | University of Cordoba, Spain |
| Marcelo Armentano | ISISTAN Research Institute (CONICET- UNICEN), Argentina |
| Jean-Michel Auberlet | IFSTTAR (French Institute of Science and Technology for Transport, Development and Networks), France |
| Snorre Aunet | Norwegian University of Science and Technology, Norway |
| Federico Barber | Polytechnic University of Valencia, Spain |
| John Barnden | University of Birmingham, UK |
| Teresa Basile | University of Bari, Italy |
| Montserrat Batet | Rovira i Virgili University, Spain |
| Bernhard Bauer | University of Augsburg, Germany |
| Nabil Belacel | National Research Council of Canada, Canada |
| Carole Bernon | University of Toulouse III, France |
| Daniel Berrar | Tokyo Institute of Technology, Japan |
| El Bezzazi | Faculté Droit Lille, France |
| Jérémy Boes | Toulouse 1 University Capitole, France |
| Marco Botta | University of Turin, Italy |
| Vicente Botti | Polytechnic University of Valencia, Spain |

| | |
|---|---|
| Bruno Bouchard | LIARA Laboratory, Université du Québec à Chicoutimi, Canada |
| Lars Braubach | Universität Hamburg, Germany |
| Joerg Bremer | University of Oldenburg, Germany |
| Ramon Brena | Tecnologico de Monterrey, Mexico |
| Paolo Bresciani | Fondazione Bruno Kessler, Italy |
| Daniela Briola | University of Milano-Bicocca, Italy |
| Renato Bruni | University of Rome La Sapienza, Italy |
| Lucian Busoniu | Technical University of Cluj-Napoca, Romania |
| Aleksander Byrski | AGH University of Science and Technology, Poland |
| Giacomo Cabri | University of Modena and Reggio Emilia, Italy |
| Silvia Calegari | University of Milano-Bicocca, Italy |
| Valérie Camps | IRIT - Université Paul Sabatier, France |
| Javier Carbó Rubiera | Carlos III University of Madrid, Spain |
| Amilcar Cardoso | University of Coimbra, Portugal |
| John Cartlidge | University of Bristol, UK |
| Matteo Casadei | University of Bologna, Italy |
| Cristiano Castelfranchi | Institute of Cognitive Sciences and Technologies, National Research Council, Italy |
| Brahim Chaib-draa | Université Laval, Canada |
| Wen-Chung Chang | National Taipei University of Technology, Taiwan |
| Amitava Chatterjee | Jadavpur University, India |
| Mu-Song Chen | Da-Yeh University, Taiwan |
| Rung-Ching Chen | Chao-Yang University of Technology, Taiwan |
| Flavio Correa Da Silva | University of Sao Paulo, Brazil |
| Gabriella Cortellessa | ISTC-CNR, Italy |
| Paulo Cortez | University of Minho, Portugal |
| Anna Costa | Universidade de São Paulo, Brazil |
| Matteo Cristani | University of Verona, Italy |
| Fernando Da Souza | Universidade Federal de Pernambuco, Brazil |
| Mehdi Dastani | Utrecht University, The Netherlands |
| Darryl Davis | University of Hull, UK |
| Arthur Dempster | Harvard University, USA |
| Andreas Dengel | German Research Center for Artificial Intelligence (DFKI GmbH), Germany |
| Enrico Denti | University of Bologna, Italy |
| Sebastien Destercke | Université de Technologie de Compiègne/CNRS, France |
| Nicola Di Mauro | University of Bari, Italy |
| Bruno Di Stefano | Nuptek Systems Ltd., Canada |
| Irene Diaz | University of Oviedo, Spain |
| Dragan Doder | Université Paul Sabatier, France |
| Francisco Domínguez Mayo | University of Seville, Spain |
| Julie Dugdale | Laboratoire d'Informatique de Grenoble, France |
| Béatrice Duval | LERIA, France |
| Wolfgang Dvorak | Vienna University of Technology (TU Wien), Austria |

| | |
|---|---|
| Thomas Eiter | Technische Universität Wien, Austria |
| Fabrício Enembreck | Pontifical Catholic University of Paraná, Brazil |
| Floriana Esposito | University of Bari, Italy |
| Savo Fabio | University of Rome La Sapienza, Italy |
| Fabrizio Falchi | ISTI-CNR, Italy |
| Stefano Ferilli | University of Bari, Italy |
| Edilson Ferneda | Catholic University of Brasília, Brazil |
| Alexander Ferrein | MASCOR Institute, FH Aachen University of Applied Sciences, Germany |
| Roberto Flores | Christopher Newport University, USA |
| Agostino Forestiero | ICAR-CNR, Italy |
| Claude Frasson | University of Montreal, Canada |
| Muhammad Fuad | Technical University of Denmark, Denmark |
| Katsuhide Fujita | Tokyo University of Agriculture and Technology, Japan |
| Naoki Fukuta | Shizuoka University, Japan |
| Catherine Garbay | CNRS, France |
| Leonardo Garrido | Tecnológico de Monterrey, Campus Monterrey, Mexico |
| Andrey Gavrilov | Novosibirsk State Technical University, Russian Federation |
| Jean-Pierre Georgé | Toulouse 1 University Capitole, France |
| Herman Gomes | Universidade Federal de Campina Grande, Brazil |
| Jorge Gomez-Sanz | Complutense University of Madrid, Spain |
| Charles Gouin-Vallerand | TELUQ, Canada |
| Madhu Goyal | University of Technology, Sydney, Australia |
| Emmanuelle Grislin-Le Strugeon | LAMIH, Université de Valenciennes, France |
| Perry Groot | Radboud University Nijmegen, The Netherlands |
| Hisashi Hayashi | Advanced Institute of Industrial Technology, Japan |
| Vincent Hilaire | UTBM, France |
| Hanno Hildmann | Carlos III University of Madrid, Spain |
| Rolf Hoffmann | Darmstadt University of Technology, Germany |
| Wladyslaw Homenda | Warsaw University of Technology, Poland |
| Wei-Chiang Hong | Jiangsu Normal University, China |
| Mark Hoogendoorn | Vrije Universiteit Amsterdam, The Netherlands |
| Ales Horak | Masaryk University, Czech Republic |
| Marc-Philippe Huget | University of Savoie Mont-Blanc, France |
| Luke Hunsberger | Vassar College, USA |
| Dieter Hutter | German Research Centre for Artificial Intelligence, Germany |
| Carlos Iglesias | Polytechnic University of Madrid, Spain |
| Hiroyuki Iida | JAIST, Japan |
| Jun-ichi Imai | Chiba Institute of Technology, Japan |
| Thomas Ioerger | Texas A&M University, USA |
| Luis Iribarne | University of Almería, Spain |
| Jan Jakubuv | Czech Technical University in Prague, Czech Republic |

| | |
|---|---|
| Vahid Jalali | Indiana University, USA |
| Michael Jenkin | York University, Canada |
| Luis Jiménez Linares | University of Castilla-La Mancha, Spain |
| Yasushi Kambayashi | Nippon Institute of Technology, Japan |
| Norihiro Kamide | Teikyo University, Japan |
| Geylani Kardas | Ege University International Computer Institute, Turkey |
| Petros Kefalas | CITY College, International Faculty of the University of Sheffield, Greece |
| Sung-Dong Kim | Hansung University, South Korea |
| Matthias Klusch | German Research Center for Artificial Intelligence (DFKI) GmbH, Germany |
| Mare Koit | University of Tartu, Estonia |
| Martin Kollingbaum | University of Aberdeen, UK |
| Ah-Lian Kor | Leeds Beckett University, UK |
| Hristo Koshutanski | Atos, Spain |
| Igor Kotenko | St. Petersburg Institute for Informatics and Automation of the Russian Academy of Sciences (SPIIRAS), Russian Federation |
| Jaroslaw Kozlak | AGH University of Science and Technology, Poland |
| Pavel Kral | University of West Bohemia, Czech Republic |
| Rudolf Kruse | Otto von Guericke University Magdeburg, Germany |
| Lun-Wei Ku | Academia Sinica, Taiwan |
| Amruth Kumar | Ramapo College of New Jersey, USA |
| Divesh Lala | Kyoto University, Japan |
| Ramoni Lasisi | Virginia Military Institute, USA |
| Nuno Lau | Universidade de Aveiro, Portugal |
| Egons Lavendelis | Riga Technical University, Latvia |
| Marc Le Goc | Laboratory for Systems and Information Sciences, UMR CNRS 7296, France |
| Ladislav Lenc | University of West Bohemia, Czech Republic |
| Letizia Leonardi | University of Modena and Reggio Emilia, Italy |
| Churn-Jung Liau | Academia Sinica, Taiwan |
| Francesca Lisi | University of Bari, Italy |
| António Lopes | ISCTE-Instituto Universitário de Lisboa, Portugal |
| Noel Lopes | IPG, Portugal |
| Henrique Lopes Cardoso | Universidade do Porto, Portugal |
| Daniela Lopéz De Luise | CIIS Lab, Argentina |
| Adolfo Lozano-Tello | University of Extremadura, Spain |
| Bernd Ludwig | University of Regensburg, Germany |
| Xudong Luo | Guangxi Normal Universty, China |
| Audrone Lupeikiene | VU Institute of Mathematics and Informatics, Lithuania |
| José Machado | University of Minho, Portugal |
| Letizia Marchegiani | Oxford University, UK |
| Jerusa Marchi | Universidade Federal de Santa Catarina, Brazil |
| Francisco Martínez Álvarez | University of Seville, Spain |

| | |
|---|---|
| Philippe Mathieu | University of Lille 1, France |
| Eric Matson | Purdue University, USA |
| Toshihiro Matsui | Nagoya Institute of Technology, Japan |
| Fiona McNeill | Heriot-Watt University, UK |
| Paola Mello | University of Bologna, Italy |
| Eduardo Mena | University of Zaragoza, Spain |
| Daniel Merkle | University of Southern Denmark, Denmark |
| Marjan Mernik | University of Maribor, Slovenia |
| Elena Messina | National Institute of Standards and Technology, USA |
| Tamás Mészáros | Budapest University of Technology and Economics, Hungary |
| Ambra Molesini | University of Bologna, Italy |
| Raul Monroy | Tec de Monterrey in Mexico, Mexico |
| Ariel Monteserin | ISISTAN Research Institute (CONICET- UNICEN), Argentina |
| José Moreira | Universidade de Aveiro, Portugal |
| Pedro Moreira | Escola Superior de Tecnologia e Gestão - Instituto Politécnico de Viana do Castelo, Portugal |
| Maxime Morge | Université de Lille, France |
| Bernard Moulin | Université Laval, Canada |
| Juan Carlos Nieves | Umeå Universitet, Sweden |
| Jens Nimis | Hochschule Karlsruhe - Technik und Wirtschaft, Germany |
| Antoine Nongaillard | Lille University, France |
| Farid Nouioua | Aix-Marseille University, France |
| Houssem Nouri | Université de la Manouba, Tunisia |
| Luis Nunes | Instituto Universitário de Lisboa (ISCTE-IUL) and Instituto de Telecomunicações (IT), Portugal |
| Andreas Oberweis | Karlsruhe Institute of Technology (KIT), Germany |
| Michel Occello | Université Grenoble Alpes, France |
| Akihiko Ohsuga | The University of Electro-Communications (UEC), Japan |
| Haldur Õim | University of Tartu, Estonia |
| Andrei Olaru | University Politehnica of Bucharest, Romania |
| Joanna Isabelle Olszewska | University of West Scotland, UK |
| Stanislaw Osowski | Warsaw University of Technology, Poland |
| Nandan Parameswaran | University of New South Wales, Australia |
| Hong-Seok Park | University of Ulsan, South Korea |
| Andrew Parkes | University of Nottingham, UK |
| Krzysztof Patan | University of Zielona Gora, Poland |
| Manuel G. Penedo | University of A Coruña, Spain |
| Loris Penserini | TTP Technology, Italy |
| Célia Pereira | Université de Nice Sophia Antipolis, France |
| Gauthier Picard | Hubert Curien CNRS Laboratory, France |
| Sébastien Picault | University of Lille, CNRS, France |
| Marcin Pietron | University of Science and Technology in Cracow, Poland |
| Agostino Poggi | University of Parma, Italy |

| | |
|---|---|
| Ramalingam Ponnusamy | CVR College of Engineering-Hyderabad, India |
| Enrico Pontelli | New Mexico State University, USA |
| Filipe Portela | University of Minho, Portugal |
| Roberto Posenato | University of Verona, Italy |
| Mariachiara Puviani | University of Modena and Reggio Emilia, Italy |
| David Pynadath | University of Southern California, USA |
| Badran Raddaoui | University of Poitiers, France |
| Riccardo Rasconi | National Research Council of Italy, Italy |
| Luís Reis | University of Porto, Portugal |
| Lluís Ribas-Xirgo | Autonomous University of Barcelona, Spain |
| Patrizia Ribino | ICAR- CNR, Italy |
| Alessandro Ricci | University of Bologna, Italy |
| Ana Rocha | LIACC/FEUP, Portugal |
| Fátima Rodrigues | Instituto Superior de Engenharia do Porto (ISEP/IPP), Portugal |
| Daniel Rodriguez | University of Alcalá, Spain |
| Juha Röning | University of Oulu, Finland |
| Silvia Rossi | University of Naples Federico II, Italy |
| Danielle Rousy Silva | UFPB, Brazil |
| Alvaro Rubio-Largo | University of Extremadura, Spain |
| Ruben Ruiz | Polytechnic University of Valencia, Spain |
| Luca Sabatucci | ICAR-CNR, Italy |
| Fariba Sadri | Imperial College London, UK |
| Lorenza Saitta | University of Piemonte Orientale Amedeo Avogadro, Italy |
| Manuel Santos | University of Minho, Portugal |
| Jurek Sasiadek | Carleton University, Canada |
| Stefan Schiffer | RWTH Aachen University, Germany |
| Christoph Schommer | University Luxembourg, Luxembourg |
| Michael Schumacher | University of Applied Sciences and Arts Western Switzerland (HES-SO), Switzerland |
| Frank Schweitzer | ETH Zurich, Switzerland |
| Valeria Seidita | University of Palermo, Italy |
| Emilio Serrano | Polytechnic University of Madrid, Spain |
| Huma Shah | Coventry University, UK |
| Denis Shikhalev | The State Fire Academy of EMERCOM of Russia, Russian Federation |
| Mohammad Shojafar | University of Rome La Sapienza, Italy |
| Peer-Olaf Siebers | Nottingham University, UK |
| Marius Silaghi | Florida Institute of Technology, USA |
| Ricardo Silveira | Universidade Federal de Santa Catarina, Brazil |
| Guillermo Simari | Universidad Nacional del Sur in Bahia Blanca, Argentina |
| David Sislak | Czech Technical University in Prague, Czech Republic |
| Alexander Smirnov | SPIIRAS, Russian Federation |
| Pavel Smrz | Brno University of Technology, Czech Republic |
| Armando Sousa | Inesc Tec and FEUP, Portugal |

| | |
|---|---|
| Gerasimos Spanakis | Maastricht University, The Netherlands |
| Efstathios Stamatatos | University of the Aegean, Greece |
| Bernd Steinbach | Freiberg University of Mining and Technology, Germany |
| Thomas Stützle | Université Libre de Bruxelles, Belgium |
| Toshiharu Sugawara | Waseda University, Japan |
| Zhaohao Sun | PNG University of Technology; Federation University Australia, Papua New Guinea |
| Pavel Surynek | Czech Technical University, Czech Republic |
| Ryszard Tadeusiewicz | AGH University of Science and Technology, Poland |
| Nick Taylor | Heriot-Watt University, UK |
| Mark Terwilliger | University of North Alabama, USA |
| Michele Tomaiuolo | University of Parma, Italy |
| José Torres | Universidade Fernando Pessoa, Portugal |
| Viviane Torres da Silva | IBM Research, Brazil |
| Jan Tozicka | CTU in Prague, Czech Republic |
| Miroslaw Truszczynski | University of Kentucky, USA |
| Franco Turini | KDD Lab, University of Pisa, Italy |
| Paulo Urbano | Universidade de Lisboa, Portugal |
| Marina V. Sokolova | Orel State University named after Turgenev, Russian Federation |
| Egon L. van den Broek | Utrecht University, The Netherlands |
| Leo van Moergestel | HU Utrecht University of Applied Sciences, Netherlands |
| Eloisa Vargiu | EURECAT, Spain |
| Srdjan Vesic | CNRS, France |
| Jørgen Villadsen | Technical University of Denmark, Denmark |
| Serena Villata | CNRS, France |
| Emilio Vivancos | Polytechnic University of Valencia, Spain |
| Marin Vlada | University of Bucharest, Romania |
| Wojciech Waloszek | Gdansk University of Technology, Poland |
| Yves Wautelet | KU Leuven, Belgium |
| Rosina Weber | Drexel University, USA |
| Gerhard Weiss | University of Maasticht, The Netherlands |
| Jianshu Weng | HP Labs Singapore, Singapore |
| Mark Winands | Maastricht University, The Netherlands |
| Bozena Wozna-Szczesniak | Jan Dlugosz University in Czestochowa, Poland |
| Fusun Yaman | Raytheon BBN Technologies, USA |
| Kristina Yordanova | University of Rostock, Germany |
| Neil Yorke-Smith | TU Delft, The Netherlands |
| Jing Zhao | ECNU, China |
| Haibin Zhu | Nipissing University, Canada |

## Additional Reviewers

| | |
|---|---|
| Quentin Baert | Université de Lille, France |
| Davide Calvaresi | Scuola Superiore Sant'Anna, Italy |

| | |
|---|---|
| Claudia Di Napoli | Istituto di Calcolo e Reti ad Alte Prestazioni - C.N.R., Italy |
| Dario Dotti | Maastricht University, The Netherlands |
| Andrea Pazienza | University of Bari, Italy |
| Felipe Leno da Silva | University of São Paulo, Brazil |
| Paolo Torroni | University of Bologna, Italy |
| Luis Trejo | ITESM, Mexico |
| Razieh Zaeem | UT Austin, USA |

## Invited Speakers

| | |
|---|---|
| Luc Steels | ICREA, Institute of Evolutionary Biology Barcelona, Spain |
| Virginia Dignum | Delft University of Technology, The Netherlands |
| Eduard Hovy | Carnegie Mellon University, USA |
| Luís Antunes | Universidade de Lisboa, Portugal |

# Contents

# Agents

# A Unified Comparative Study of Heuristic Algorithms for Double Combinatorial Auctions: Locality-Constrained Resource Allocation Problems

Diana Gudu(✉), Marcus Hardt, and Achim Streit

Karlsruhe Institute of Technology, Karlsruhe, Germany
{diana.gudu,marcus.hardt,achim.streit}@kit.edu

**Abstract.** Market-oriented resource allocation in cloud computing is driven by increasingly stringent needs for flexibility, fine-grained allocation, and more critically, revenue maximization. Double combinatorial auctions aptly address these demands, but their $\mathcal{NP}$-hardness has hindered them from being widely adopted. Heuristic algorithms, with their input-dependent performance and solution quality, have failed to offer a robust alternative. We posit that a unifying approach for evaluating all existing algorithms, under the umbrella of a consistent problem formulation and a variety of common test cases, can propel combinatorial auctions towards real-world usage.

In this paper, we performed an extensive empirical evaluation of a portfolio of heuristic algorithms for double combinatorial auctions, applied to problems with hard resource locality constraints. We found that there is no single algorithm that outperforms the others in all test scenarios. However, we offer insights into the behavior of the algorithms, and provide methods to explore the portfolio's performance over a wide range of input scenarios.

**Keywords:** Combinatorial auction · Resource allocation
Cloud computing · Heuristic algorithm · Benchmarking

## 1 Introduction

In the ever-growing [1], dynamic landscape of cloud computing [2], combinatorial auctions [3] can add flexibility and appropriate economic incentives to a currently rigid resource provisioning approach.

Recent trends [4] in cloud computing are driving the field towards market-driven resource allocation and pricing, with some commercial cloud providers already adopting the concept of dynamic pricing. For example, Amazon is auctioning off unused resources on the so-called spot market [5], in order to increase their revenue. However, the mechanisms used are single-good: fast but simple.


J. van den Herik and A. P. Rocha (Eds.): ICAART 2018, LNAI 11352, pp. 3–22, 2019.
https://doi.org/10.1007/978-3-030-05453-3_1

A combinatorial approach, where customers are able to bid on various combinations of resources, would significantly increase flexibility and provide fine-grained control to cloud customers. However, the use of combinatorial auctions in practice is hindered by their computational complexity: they are $\mathcal{NP}$-hard problems [3]. Fast, approximate algorithms must be employed, but they incur a certain monetary loss that needs to be bounded.

Although there is a plethora of approximate algorithms for combinatorial auctions in the literature [6–14], a systematic and comprehensive comparison was lacking.

In [15], we performed the first such comparison in order to lay the groundwork for a unified and consistent benchmarking approach. We created a portfolio of algorithms based on existing work or well-known optimization methods. We then introduced a flexible tool for generating artificial datasets for combinatorial auctions, which was used to perform an extensive empirical comparison of the algorithms in the portfolio over a large input space. We found that there is no algorithm that outperforms all the other algorithms in the portfolio in all cases. Furthermore, we found that this effect was more pronounced when soft resource locality constraints were considered.

In this paper, we reformulate the resource allocation problem in [15] to enforce hard locality constraints. The most significant change concerns the sellers, which now offer pre-packaged resource bundles that can each be allocated to a single bidder, instead of individual resources that can be combined with other seller's resources to fulfill a user request. This is more in line with current cloud computing provisioning strategies and is technically feasible with current cloud technologies, whereas implementing the formulation proposed in [15] in the real world would need to address performance issues that can arise from on-the-fly provisioning of custom VMs or inter-cloud data transfers, as well as SLA compatibility issues inherent to multi-cloud applications.

Furthermore, we provide a detailed account of how the algorithms in the portfolio were adapted to this formulation. We then extensively evaluate the portfolio on several datasets, containing larger problems, generated using a wider range of parameters for the input generator. The trade-off between solution quality and execution time is also considered: the algorithms in the portfolio are compared from the perspective of variable preferences regarding this trade-off.

The rest of the paper is organized as follows. In Sect. 2, we present related work on heuristic algorithms for combinatorial auctions, and benchmarking efforts in this area. Section 3 details the theoretical formulation for the resource allocation problem as a two-sided combinatorial auction, with a special consideration to economic properties. Section 4 provides an in-depth look into a portfolio of heuristic algorithms for combinatorial auctions. In Sect. 5, we present our comprehensive evaluation over a variety of test scenarios. Finally, in Sect. 6, we summarize our results, together with the possible directions for future research opened up by our analysis.

## 2 Related Work

There is a rich literature on heuristic algorithms for solving the WDP [6–14]. While each work compares its newly introduced algorithm to other existing algorithms, there is no attempt, to our knowledge, to experimentally compare all the existing algorithms in a more systematic and consistent manner.

CATS [16] is a "universal test suite" for combinatorial auctions which tries to unify benchmarking efforts by offering a range of economically-driven artificially-generated scenarios, but the focus of the evaluation is on optimal algorithms and their execution time, or hardness.

In [15], we performed an extensive evaluation of a portfolio of approximate algorithms for combinatorial auctions, built upon a consistent problem formulation. Moreover, we introduced an artificial input generator, which enabled comprehensive benchmarking over a wide range of input problems. However, the problem formulation did not support hard resource locality constraints.

## 3 Combinatorial Auctions

To incorporate resource locality requirements, we reformulate the resource allocation problem [15] for cloud computing below. The participants of a double, or two-sided, combinatorial auction are:

- a set of $n$ bidders $U = \{1, \ldots, n\}$,
- a set of $m$ sellers $P = \{1, \ldots, m\}$,
- and an auctioneer that decides upon the allocation and pricing of resources based on the bids and asks it receives.

The object of the exchange is a set of $l$ resource types, or goods, $G = \{1, \ldots, l\}$, which can be traded in various integer amounts, packaged in bundles. Therefore, each bid or ask can be expressed as a vector of quantities and an associated bundle value, as described in Eqs. 1 and 2, respectively.

$$\text{bid}\, i : (\langle r_{i1}, \ldots, r_{il} \rangle, b_i) \tag{1}$$

$$\text{ask}\, j : (\langle s_{j1}, \ldots, s_{jl} \rangle, a_j) \tag{2}$$

More specifically, $r_{ik}$ and $s_{jk}$ are the amounts of resource type $k$ requested or offered by bidder $i$ or seller $j$, respectively. Bidder $i$ bids a value $b_i$ on the bundle—the maximum amount it is willing to pay. Similarly, seller $j$ offers its bundle of resources at a price $a_j$.

After collecting the bids and asks, the auctioneer computes the resource allocation and pricing according to two rules:

1. Allocation rule: the auctioneer solves the Winner Determination Problem (WDP) [17] by deciding which bidders and sellers will trade goods such that the social welfare is maximized.
2. Payment rule: the auctioneer computes the prices at which the bundles are traded by using a payment scheme that satisfies certain economic properties.

The social welfare is defined [18] as the sum of all the trade participants' utilities, where utility is a measure of a trader's satisfaction. We assume that both bidders and sellers are single-minded, which means that they are only interested in buying or selling the full bundle, and have 0 utility for any other bundle.

As a result, a bidder $i$'s utility for a requested bundle $S$ is defined in Eq. 3, where $v_i(S)$ (valuation) is the true value bidder $i$ is willing to pay for bundle $S$, and $p_i$ is the actual price paid at the end of the auction. When a bidder is truthful, $v_i(S) = b_i$. A seller's utility is defined in a similar way.

$$u_i(S) = \begin{cases} v_i(S) - p_i, & \text{if } i \text{ wins bundle } S \text{ in the auction} \\ 0, & \text{otherwise.} \end{cases} \tag{3}$$

### 3.1 Allocation Rule

The WDP is defined as the following integer program:

$$\max_{x,y} \left( \sum_{i=1}^{n} b_i x_i - \sum_{j=1}^{m} \sum_{i=1}^{n} a_j y_{ij} \right) \tag{4}$$

subject to constraints:

$$x_i, y_{ij} \in \{0, 1\}, \forall i \in U, \forall j \in P \tag{5}$$

$$\sum_{i=1}^{n} y_{ij} \leq 1, \forall j \in P \tag{6}$$

$$\sum_{j=1}^{m} y_{ij} = x_i, \forall i \in U \tag{7}$$

$$r_{ik} x_i \leq \sum_{j=1}^{m} s_{jk} y_{ij}, \forall i \in U, \forall k \in G. \tag{8}$$

Constraint (5) expresses the single-mindedness of bidders and sellers and forbids partial bundle allocations. Constraint (6) ensures that a seller allocates its bundle to at most one bidder, while Constraint (7) ensures that each bidder receives the resources in its bundle from a single provider. Finally, Constraint (8) ensures that, in the eventuality of a trade, a seller's bundle contains at least the quantity of resources requested by the bidder for each resource type.

### 3.2 Payment Rule

With the new problem formulation where each bidder and seller is involved in at most one exchange, the payment scheme is vastly simplified.

Similar to [15], we use the $\kappa-$pricing scheme [19], which distributes the trade surplus between the trade participants, in a proportion given by the factor $\kappa$. Thus the surplus resulting from a trade between a buyer $i$ and seller $j$ is:

$$\delta_{ij} = b_i - a_j, \forall y_{ij} = 1 \tag{9}$$

Bidder $i$ will thus receive a discount of a $\kappa$-th part of this surplus, resulting in the following payment:

$$p_i = b_i - \kappa\delta_{ij} = (1 - \kappa)b_i + \kappa a_j \tag{10}$$

Similarly, seller $j$ will receive the following payment:

$$p_j = a_j + (1 - \kappa)\delta_{ij} = (1 - \kappa)b_i + \kappa a_j \tag{11}$$

Throughout the experiments in this paper, we use $\kappa = 0.5$ and thus equally distribute the trade surplus between winning buyers and sellers.

### 3.3 Mechanism Properties

In auction mechanism design, there are four essential economic properties which need to be considered when formulating the allocation rule and the payment rule: incentive compatibility, individual rationality, economic efficiency and budget-balance. Nevertheless, as proven by [20], no mechanism can simultaneously satisfy all four properties. It is left to the mechanism designer to choose the properties that can be satisfied, and put them in accordance with other constraints, such as tractability, auctioneer profit, etc.

The auction mechanism proposed in this paper is **budget-balanced**, since the trade surplus is distributed among the trade participants, and therefore the auctioneer neither makes a profit, nor subsidizes the trade.

The mechanism is also **individually rational**, since no agent loses by participating in the trade: cf. Eq. 3, an agent's utility is always positive or zero at the end of the auction.

The economic efficiency property is satisfied only when an optimal algorithm is used to solve the WDP. However, tractability is typically desired for cloud resource allocation, i.e. the algorithm should execute in polynomial time. Heuristic algorithms do not always yield the optimal solution, but it was shown for algorithms such as Greedy [8] that a solution within a factor of $\sqrt{l}$ of the optimal solution can be guaranteed. Thus, the proposed mechanism is **asymptotically economically efficient**.

Finally, due to the chosen $\kappa-$pricing scheme, the mechanism is **not truthful** or incentive compatible. This means that agents are not motivated to reveal their true valuations and might try to game the system to their advantage. However, in [19] it was shown that non-truthful bidding increases the risk of no allocation due to the competition in the market. Thus, in practice, agents are truthful.

Classic payment schemes such as Vickrey-Clarke-Groves (VCG) [21] were not used in this work: even though VCG can guarantee truthfulness, it is computationally expensive, and it would violate the budget-balanced property by forcing the auctioneer to subsidize the trade. Both issues are not acceptable in a real-world scenario for cloud resource allocation.

## 4 Algorithm Portfolio

We built a portfolio of heuristic algorithms for solving the WDP. In this section, we give a detailed account of the algorithms, the optimization methods used, as well as our specific contributions.

The algorithms are based on our previous work [15]. However, the new problem formulation led to significant changes in the algorithms and, in some cases, a complete rethinking of the approach. Generally, the algorithms are based on the vast literature on approximate algorithms for combinatorial auctions or optimization algorithms, but they are normalized to a single problem formulation. This enables a fair and consistent comparison.

Note that algorithms based on the relaxed linear problem [22] were not included in the current portfolio, due to their exponential time complexity, combined with poor solution quality as observed in [15].

### 4.1 Optimal Algorithm

We include the optimal algorithm in the portfolio, to be used as a reference throughout the evaluation. The optimal algorithm treats the WDP as a mixed-integer linear program (MILP) [23], a class of problems which is typically solved using branch-and-cut techniques [24]. We implemented the optimal algorithm using IBM's commercial software CPLEX [25], hailed as the most performant solver for MILPs.

### 4.2 Greedy Algorithms

Greedy algorithms are heuristics that make the locally optimal choice at every step, aiming for a globally optimal solution [26]. The rich literature of greedy algorithms for the WDP [7,8,22] hinges on a common idea: the bids (and asks for the two-sided case) are sorted according to a certain criterion, and then they are greedily allocated as long as there are no conflicts.

We use bid and ask densities as sorting criteria, which are defined for buyer $i$ and seller $j$ in Eqs. 12 and 13, respectively.

$$d_i = \frac{b_i}{\sqrt{\sum_{k=1}^{l} f_k^b r_{ik}}}, \forall i \in U \tag{12}$$

$$d_j = \frac{a_j}{\sqrt{\sum_{k=1}^{l} f_k^a s_{jk}}}, \forall j \in P \tag{13}$$

Compared to the average price per unit, the density gives priority to smaller customer requests and was shown to yield higher welfare [8].

Based on [7], we introduced the relevance factors $f_k$, defined as the relative weight of resource type $k$, which can be used to express differences in value for the different resource types. In [15], we proposed using different weights for bids and asks, $f_k^b$ and $f_k^a$, respectively. We extended the three calculation methods proposed by [7] to the two-sided case as follows.

1. Uniform weights, as a generalization of the one-sided case [8]:
$$f_k^b = f_k^a = 1, \forall k \in G \tag{14}$$
2. Weights based on the absolute scarcity of each resource, defined as the inverse of the supply of the resource on the market (for bids) or the inverse of the demand for the respective resource (for asks):
$$f_k^b = \frac{1}{\sum_{j=1}^{m} s_{jk}}, f_k^a = \frac{1}{\sum_{i=1}^{n} r_{ik}}, \forall k \in G \tag{15}$$
3. Weights based on the relative scarcity of each resource, defined as the difference between demand and supply, normalized by the demand (for bids), and normalized by the supply (for asks):
$$f_k^b = \frac{\left|\sum_{i=1}^{n} r_{ik} - \sum_{j=1}^{m} s_{jk}\right|}{\sum_{i=1}^{n} r_{ik}}, f_k^a = \frac{\left|\sum_{i=1}^{n} r_{ik} - \sum_{j=1}^{m} s_{jk}\right|}{\sum_{j=1}^{m} s_{jk}}, \forall k \in G \tag{16}$$

In this paper, we will refer to the greedy algorithms for each method of calculating the relevance factors as: GREEDY1, GREEDY2, and GREEDY3. The pseudocode is shown in Algorithm 1.

**Algorithm 1.** Greedy algorithms for different calculation methods of relevance factors.

```
function GREEDYX(n, m, l, b, r, a, s)
    compute relevance factors f_k^a, f_k^b, ∀k ∈ G with method X
    compute bid and ask densities
    sort bids descendingly by bid density d_i, ∀i ∈ U
    sort asks ascendingly by ask density d_j, ∀j ∈ P
    i ← 1; j ← 1
    while i ≤ n and j ≤ m do
        if r_ik ≤ s_jk, ∀k ∈ G and b_i ≥ a_j then     ▷ if ask j can satisfy bid i
            x_i ← 1; y_ij ← 1                         ▷ allocate resources offered
                                                        by seller j to bidder i
            i ← i + 1                                 ▷ move to next bidder
        end if
        j ← j + 1                                     ▷ move to next seller
    end while
    return (x, y)
end function
```

Additionally, due to the two-sided aspect, we implemented a greedy algorithm that gives priority to sellers and moves through the list of bids until one that satisfies the considered ask is found. In Algorithm 1, this is achieved by simply swapping lines 10 and 12. Throughout this work, the naming convention is to add an "'-s" prefix for algorithms that prioritize asks, in this case GREEDY1S.

### 4.3 Hill Climbing Algorithms

Hill climbing algorithms [9,27] typically perform a local search in the solution space by starting off at a random point and moving to a neighboring solution if the new solution is better. The algorithm stops when it finds a (local) optimum. This is depicted in Algorithm 2, where the initial solution is determined using a greedy algorithm. We devised two different methods of exploring the neighborhood of a solution in the solution space.

Firstly, as shown in Algorithm 3, a neighboring solution is found by changing the ordering of bids or asks, and applying a greedy algorithm onto this ordering. Based on [10], an unallocated bid is moved to the beginning of the bid list to generate a neighboring solution, starting with the first bid after the critical bid (or first unallocated bid in the ordered list) and then going through the sorted list. We call this algorithm HILL1. The version that prioritizes sellers, HILL1S, changes the ordering of asks to explore the neighborhood of a solution and uses GREEDY1S.

A more generic hill climbing algorithm, where neighboring solutions are generated by toggling the $x_i$ variables, as proposed by [14] for the multiknapsack problem, is depicted in Algorithm 4. This means that a single bid in the current solution is allocated or removed from the allocation. The corresponding $y_{ij}$ variable is adjusted, in order to produce a feasible solution. We call this algorithm HILL2. A hill climbing algorithm that prioritizes sellers, HILL2S, was also implemented. Algorithm HILL2S explores the neighborhood of a solution by toggling the allocation of a random ask $j$, and uses GREEDY1S for allocation.

**Algorithm 2.** Hill Climbing algorithms.

```
function HILL(n, m, l, b, r, a, s)
    (x, y) ←GREEDY1(n, m, l, b, r, a, s)                ▷ generate initial solution
    while solution improves do
        while solution has unexplored neighbors do
            (x', y') ←NEIGHBOR(x, y)                     ▷ get neighboring solution
            if welfare(x', y') > welfare(x, y) then      ▷ if new solution is better
                (x, y) ← (x', y')                        ▷ move to new solution
                break
            end if
        end while
    end while
    return (x, y)
end function
```

**Algorithm 3.** Function that returns the neighbor in the solution space of a given solution, by changing the bid.

**function** NEIGHBOR1$(x, y)$
    move bid $i$ to beginning of list ▷ $i \leftarrow$ *critical* $i+1, n$
    **return** GREEDY1$(n, m, l, b, r, a, s)$ ▷ *apply on new ordering*
**end function**

### 4.4 Simulated Annealing Algorithms

Simulated annealing [28] is an optimization method that tries to mitigate the issues of gradient-based methods (such as hill climbing) of being stuck in local optima. To that end, it accepts worse solutions during the search process, with a probability that is decreasing over time. The algorithm is shown in Algorithm 5. In our implementation, the so-called temperature decreases at a constant rate $\alpha = 0.9$, and a fixed number of iterations is executed for each temperature. The acceptance probability is computed using the formula in Eq. 17, where $(x, y)$ is the current solution in the search space, while $(x', y')$ is the explored neighboring solution. As a result, better solutions are always accepted (the probability is always higher or equal to 1), while for worse solutions, the probability that they are accepted is in $[0, 1]$ but decreases with the temperature variable $T$, ultimately allowing the search to converge.

$$ap = \mathrm{e}^{\frac{\mathrm{welfare}(x', y') - \mathrm{welfare}(x, y)}{T \cdot \mathrm{welfare}(x, y)}} \tag{17}$$

Similar to HILL2, the initial solution is generated using GREEDY1, and a neighboring solution is generated using the NEIGHBOR2 function (cf. Algorithm 4). We implemented two algorithms, SA and SAS, by giving priority to bidders and sellers, respectively, and using the appropriate greedy algorithm.

### 4.5 Casanova Algorithms

Based on [11], we included in the portfolio a stochastic local search algorithm named CASANOVA which, similar to SA, uses randomization to escape from local optima. The pseudocode is shown in Algorithm 6. The search starts with an empty allocation and adds a bid to the solution to reach a neighbor in the search space: with a walk probability $wp$, a random bid is chosen for allocation; with a probability of $1 - wp$, a bid is selected greedily by ranking the bids according to their score (the average bid price). From the sorted bids, the highest-ranked one is selected if its age is higher than that of the second highest ranked bid; otherwise, we select the highest ranked bid with a novelty probability $np$ and the second highest one with a probability of $1 - np$. The age of a bid is defined as the number of steps since it was last selected. The search is restarted $maxTries = 10$ times and the best solution from all runs is chosen. As [11], we set $wp = 0.15$ and $np = 0.5$.

Algorithm 7 shows how a bid is added to a partial solution: a greedy-like algorithm is used to find an unallocated ask that can satisfy it. If no ask is

**Algorithm 4.** Function that returns the neighbor in the solution space of a given solution, by toggling a random $x_i$.

```
function NEIGHBOR2(x, y)
    i ← random(1, n)                                      ▷ randomly select bid
    if x_i = 1 then
        x_i ← 0; y_{i,j} ← 0, ∀j ∈ P                      ▷ undo allocation of bid i
    else
        j ← 1
        while j ≤ m do                                    ▷ greedy-like search for ask
            if y_{qj} = 0, ∀q ∈ U then                    ▷ j not allocated
                if r_{ik} ≤ s_{jk}, ∀k ∈ G and b_i ≥ a_j then   ▷ if ask j can satisfy bid i
                    x_i ← 1; y_{ij} ← 1                   ▷ match bid i and ask j
                    break
                end if
            end if
            j ← j + 1                                     ▷ move to next ask
        end while
    end if
    return (x, y)
end function
```

**Algorithm 5.** Simulated annealing.

```
function SA(n, m, l, b, r, a, s)
    (x, y) ← GREEDY1(n, m, l, b, r, a, s)                 ▷ generate initial solution
    while T > T_min do                                    ▷ decreasing temperature
        for i ← 1, it do                                  ▷ fixed number of iterations
            (x', y') ← NEIGHBOR2(x, y)                    ▷ get neighboring solution
            ap = e^((welfare(x',y') − welfare(x,y)) / (T·welfare(x,y)))   ▷ acceptance probability
            if ap > rand(0, 1) then                       ▷ with probability ap...
                (x, y) ← (x', y')                         ▷ ... move to new solution
            end if
        end for
        T ← αT                                            ▷ fixed rate α = 0.9
    end while
    return (x, y)
end function
```

found, the search continues with the already allocated asks, but the bid can replace an already allocated bid only if it improves the social welfare.

An algorithm that prioritizes sellers, CASANOVAS, was also implemented, with the following differences: asks are sorted by their score, while bids are sorted by density; the insert function takes an ask $j$ and tries to find a matching bid $i$.

## 5 Evaluation

We performed an extensive and systematic evaluation of the algorithm portfolio, and we present the results in the rest of this section.

**Algorithm 6.** Casanova algorithms, based on stochastic local search.

```
function CASANOVA(n, m, l, b, r, a, s)
    for try ← 1, maxTries do                              ▷ restart search try times
        (x, y) ← 0                                        ▷ empty allocation
        sort bids descendingly by score
        sort asks ascendingly by density
        for step ← 1, maxSteps do
            if wp > rand(0, 1) then                       ▷ with walk probability wp
                (x, y) ←INSERT(random unallocated bid i, x, y)
            else
                if age(first bid) > age(second bid) then
                    (x, y) ←INSERT(first unallocated bid, x, y)
                else
                    if np > rand(0, 1) then               ▷ with novelty probability np
                        (x, y) ←INSERT(first unallocated bid, x, y)
                    else
                        (x, y) ←INSERT(second unallocated bid, x, y)
                    end if
                end if
            end if
        end for
    end for
    return best (x, y) found
end function
```

Since real-world auction data for cloud resources is difficult to find, we use artificial data in all our tests, a common practice in the area of combinatorial auctions [3, 16, 29]. This also affords a coverage of a wider scope of scenarios, while providing full control over the input. In [15], we introduced a novel tool for generating artificial data for multi-good multi-unit double combinatorial auctions, compatible with legacy distributions [16], named CAGE (Combinatorial Auctions input GEnerator). We adapted it to the new problem formulation for the purpose of this paper.

Using CAGE, we created two different datasets:

D1: comprising 20438 instances, with a fixed number of bids and asks ($n = m = 512$); the number of resource types was varied ($l \in \{16, 32\}$), as were all parameters of random distributions used by CAGE to generate the bundle size, relative resource scarcity and resource valuations (e.g. mean and standard deviation for normal distribution of bundle sizes); three different additivity parameters were used to compute bid and ask values. All combinations of available distributions with varied parameters were used to generate the dataset; infeasible problems (where no match is possible) were filtered out.

D2: comprising 2961 instances, with a fixed number of bids and asks ($n = m = 1024$) and varied number of resource types ($l \in \{16, 32\}$); three different additivity parameters were also used for this dataset, while the parameters

**Algorithm 7.** Function which adds an unallocated bid and best matching ask to the current solution.

```
function INSERT(i, x, y)
    j ← 1
    while j ≤ m do                                      ▷ greedy-like search for ask
        if y_qj = 0, ∀q ∈ U then                        ▷ j not allocated
            if r_ik ≤ s_jk, ∀k ∈ G and b_i ≥ a_j then   ▷ if ask j can satisfy bid i
                x_i ← 1; y_ij ← 1                       ▷ match bid i and ask j
                reset age(i)
                return (x, y)                           ▷ match found
            end if
        end if
        j ← j + 1                                       ▷ move to next ask
    end while
    j ← 1                                               ▷ no match, restart search
    while j ≤ m do                                      ▷ greedy-like search for ask
        if ∃q ∈ U, y_qj = 1 then                        ▷ j already allocated
            if r_ik ≤ s_jk, ∀k ∈ G and b_i ≥ a_j then   ▷ if ask j can satisfy bid i
                if b_i > b_q then                       ▷ if bid i improves allocation
                    x_i ← 1; y_ij ← 1                   ▷ match bid i and ask j
                    x_q ← 0; y_qj ← 0                   ▷ undo allocation of bid q
                    reset age(i)
                    return (x, y)                       ▷ match found
                end if
            end if
        end if
        j ← j + 1                                       ▷ move to next ask
    end while
    return (x, y)                                       ▷ no match found
end function
```

of the random distributions were set to their default values. All combinations of the available distributions in CAGE were used; infeasible instances were removed.

Therefore, D1 contains a larger number of more diverse instances, while D2 consists of larger problem instances. Nevertheless, both datasets consist of larger auction instances than we used in [15].

### 5.1 Average Case

First, we studied the average behavior of the algorithm portfolio on each dataset. We measured the execution time and recorded the computed welfare, with the results depicted in Figs. 1 and 2.

Figure 1 shows that there are large differences between the algorithms in terms of computed welfare (normalized to the optimal welfare): the greedy algorithms generally yield a low welfare (≈14%), but have a large variation over the dataset; algorithms HILL2(S) and SA(S) compute the highest welfare in the portfolio, with averages of $84\% - 94\%$ and lower standard deviations. The remaining algorithms, CASANOVA(S) and HILL1(S) have inconclusive results: they compute a social welfare at a half or a third of the optimal one, and have the highest standard deviation of all algorithms.

Moreover, this behavior is consistent over the two datasets, with two notable exceptions: the simulated annealing algorithms perform worse on D2 (dataset with larger problems), suggesting that, for SA(S), the welfare does not scale linearly with the problem size; the HILL2(S) algorithms, on the other hand, have a reduced standard deviation on D2, thus improving with problem size.

The immediate conclusion of the results in Fig. 1 is that the HILL2(S) algorithms are the best in the portfolio, but the execution time analysis in Fig. 2 paints a different picture.

Figure 2 shows that the greedy algorithms are $3 - 4$ orders of magnitude faster than any other algorithm in the portfolio. Furthermore, while HILL2(S) and SA(S) all have an average time of $\approx$9% of CPLEX's time on dataset D1, they scale differently with the problem size: as expected, simulated annealing algorithms are faster on D2 (by a factor of $\approx$2.4). Similarly, CASANOVA(S) algorithms use stochastic search to speed up the optimization process, and are thus faster on the larger problems in dataset D2.

Nevertheless, the average case behavior is consistent with our findings in [15] for a problem formulation with soft or no locality constraints. The evaluation confirms our hypothesis that algorithm performance and solution quality are highly dependent on the input, and thus there is no clear portfolio winner—each algorithm has its strengths and weaknesses.

### 5.2 Effect of Randomization

The CASANOVA(S) and SA(S) algorithms are stochastic, causing them to yield different results for different runs on the same input. For a reliable usage, it is desirable to minimize welfare variations between runs. Thus, we evaluated the robustness of the four algorithms with respect to randomness. We used the D2 dataset and performed 100 runs on each problem instance.

Figure 3 shows the percentual variations for each algorithm with respect to the mean of the 100 runs. We performed this normalization in order to have a comparative overview over all the instances and algorithms. For all the evaluated algorithms, we observed a variation in a similar range to the one we observed in [15] for soft locality-constrained algorithms: the lower and upper quartile are inside the interval $(-3.5\%, 3.6\%)$ with respect to the mean, with 5% to 95% of the data in $(-19\%, 33\%)$. However, outliers can vary as much as $\pm 100\%$. Furthermore, higher variations were observed for the algorithms that prioritize bidders (SA and CASANOVA), which also compute a lower welfare than the seller-prioritizing variants, cf. Fig. 1.

Therefore, even though the variation is small in most cases, in order to use these algorithms more reliably, multiple runs are necessary, and the best solution can be used in the end. This would, however, increase the execution time.

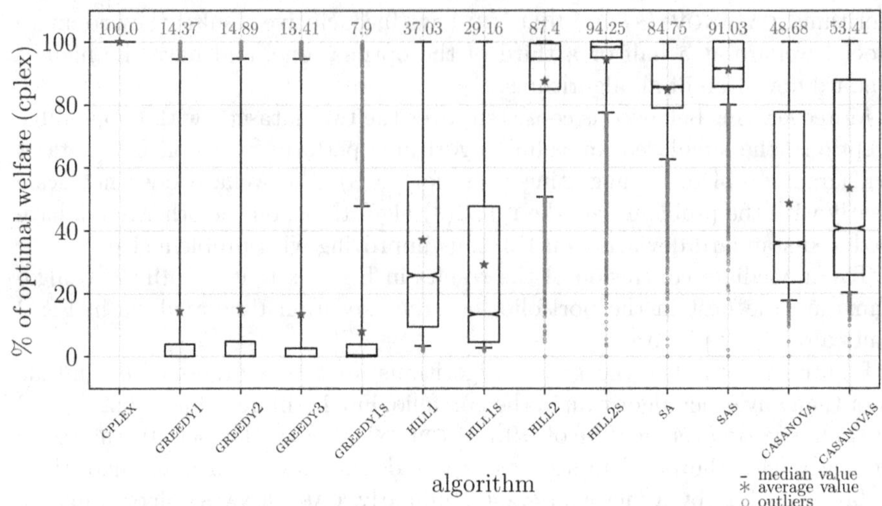


(a) Dataset D1: Social welfare, normalized by the optimal welfare computed with CPLEX

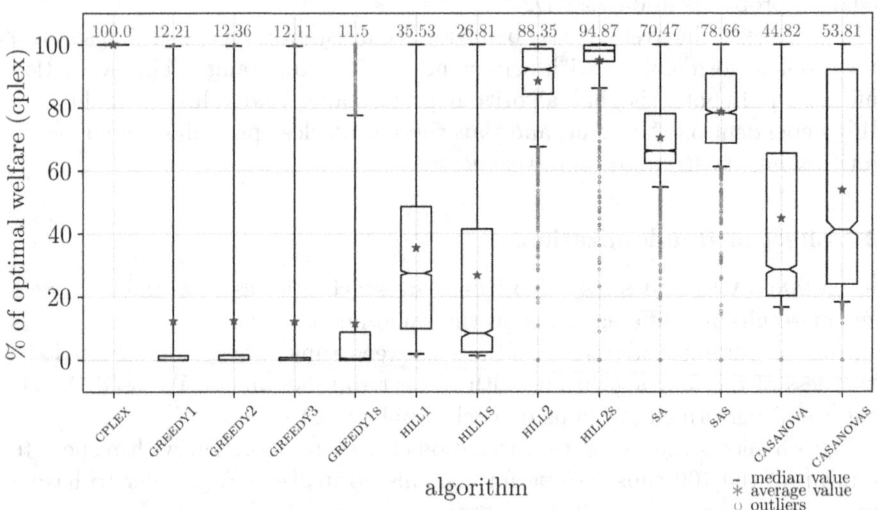


(b) Dataset D2: Social welfare, normalized by the optimal welfare computed with CPLEX

**Fig. 1.** Social welfare results for two datasets. The average value for each algorithm is represented by a red star, with the actual value attached at the top of each box. The boxes extend from the lower to the upper quartile values of the data, with a blue line at the median. The notches around the median represent the confidence interval around the median. The whiskers reach from 5% to 95% of the data. The remaining data are represented as outliers with gray circles. (Color figure online)

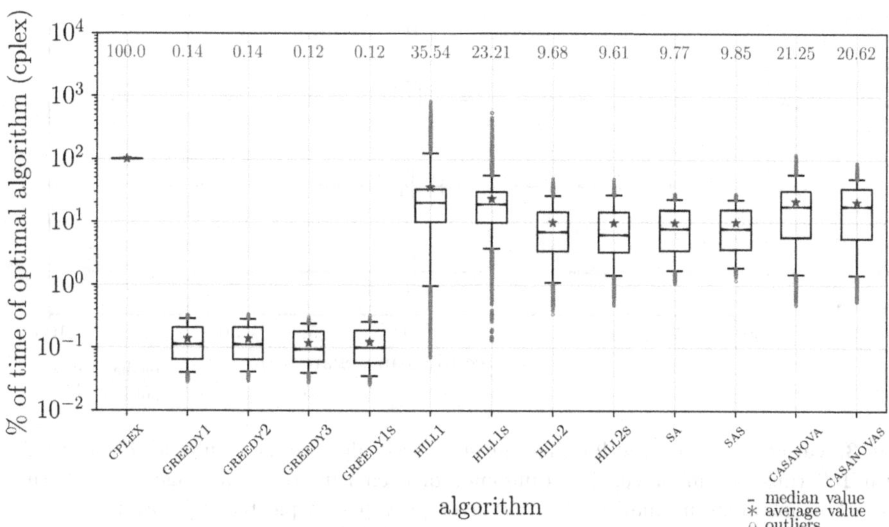


(a) Dataset D1: Execution time, normalized by the execution time of the optimal algorithm CPLEX

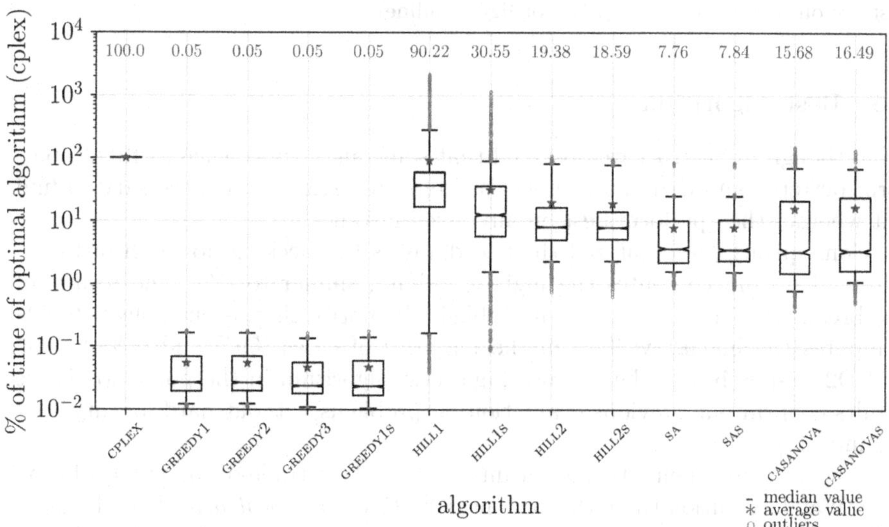


(b) Dataset D2: Execution time, normalized by the execution time of the optimal algorithm CPLEX

**Fig. 2.** Execution time results for two datasets. The average value for each algorithm is represented by a red star, with the actual value attached at the top of each box. The boxes extend from the lower to the upper quartile values of the data, with a blue line at the median. The notches around the median represent the confidence interval around the median. The whiskers reach from 5% to 95% of the data. The remaining data are represented as outliers with gray circles. A logarithmic scale was used for the $y$-axis for better readability. (Color figure online)

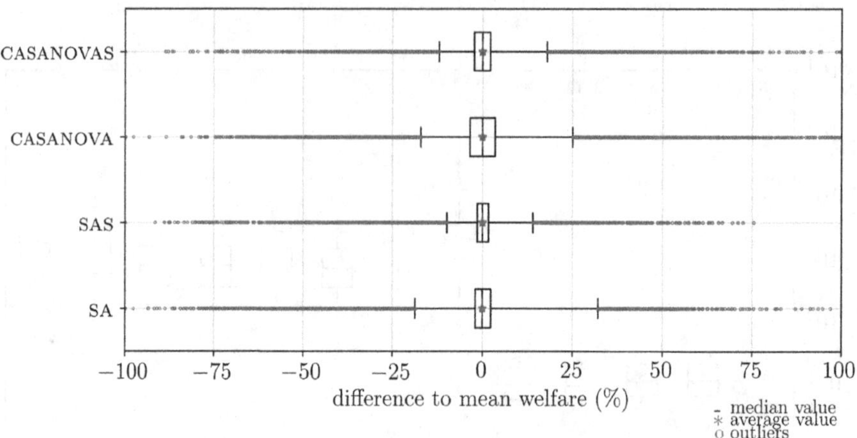


**Fig. 3.** Variation in social welfare for the stochastic algorithms: results for dataset D2, with 100 runs per instance. The difference of each run to the average value of the respective instance, normalized by that average value, is plotted. The average value (red star) is always at 0. The boxes extend from the lower to the upper quartile, with a blue line at the median. The whiskers reach from 5% to 95% of the data, and the rest are outliers (gray circles). (Color figure online)

### 5.3 Best Algorithm

Even though in Sect. 5.1 we observed that some algorithms, such as HILL2, perform better than others on average, a deeper investigation is necessary to find out whether they perform best on any given instance.

Consequently, we analyzed the two datasets by checking, for each instance, which algorithm computes the highest welfare, similar to [15]. The results of the breakdown are summarized in Table 1. We notice that, even though HILL2S computes the highest welfare in the majority of cases (59% and 66% for D1 and D2, respectively), there is no single best algorithm in the portfolio. These results confirm our previous evaluation on problems without hard locality constraints [15].

However, since heuristic algorithms give rise to a trade-off between solution quality and execution time, the current definition for *best algorithm* as the algorithm with the highest welfare is inadequate. A more complex definition of what *best algorithm* means in the context of heuristic algorithms is required, which takes into account variable preferences for the time-quality trade-off.

We model the best algorithm selection as a multi-objective optimization problem [30], whose objectives are a maximum social welfare and a minimum execution time. A Pareto optimal solution is given by the algorithm which minimizes the distance to origin in the objective space.

We first normalize the social welfare and execution time, in order to obtain non-dimensional objective functions. The normalized welfare objective is called welfare cost $c_{\mathrm{w}}(o, a)$, as defined in Eq. 18, where $w(o, a)$ is the welfare computed

**Table 1.** Breakdown of datasets D1 and D2 by best algorithm: number of instances where each heuristic algorithm computes the highest welfare in the portfolio (excluding CPLEX)—absolute numbers and percentage of total instances on which the portfolio was run.

| | D1 | | D2 | |
|---|---|---|---|---|
| | # instances | % instances | # instances | % instances |
| GREEDY1 | 103 | 0.50% | 15 | 0.51% |
| GREEDY2 | 6 | 0.03% | 2 | 0.07% |
| GREEDY3 | 20 | 0.10% | 4 | 0.14% |
| GREEDY1S | 95 | 0.46% | 19 | 0.64% |
| HILL1 | 1413 | 6.91% | 167 | 5.64% |
| HILL1S | 242 | 1.18% | 25 | 0.84% |
| HILL2 | 4124 | 20.18% | 355 | 11.99% |
| HILL2S | 12138 | 59.39% | 1972 | 66.60% |
| SA | 364 | 1.78% | 16 | 0.54% |
| SAS | 1224 | 5.99% | 43 | 1.45% |
| CASANOVA | 577 | 2.82% | 197 | 6.65% |
| CASANOVAS | 132 | 0.65% | 146 | 4.93% |

by algorithm $a$ on instance $o$, while $w(o, \text{CPLEX})$ is the optimal welfare.

$$c_{\mathrm{w}}(o,a) = 1 - \frac{w(o,a)}{w(o,\text{CPLEX})} \tag{18}$$

Similarly, in Eq. 19 we define the time cost $c_{\mathrm{t}}(o,a)$ as the normalized time objective, where $t(o,a)$ is the execution time of algorithm $a$ on instance $o$, and $t(o, \text{CPLEX})$ is the execution time of the optimal algorithm on instance $o$.

$$c_{\mathrm{t}}(o,a) = \frac{t(o,a)}{t(o,\text{CPLEX})} \tag{19}$$

Thus, CPLEX has minimum welfare cost, but maximum time cost.

For more control over the quality-time trade-off, we introduce a user-defined preference parameter $\lambda \in [0,1]$ that reflects the relative importance of the two objectives: $\lambda = 1$ implies that solely the welfare objective should be considered, $\lambda = 0$ only considers speed, while $\lambda = 0.5$ places equal importance on welfare and time. Finally, we define the *best algorithm* as the one closest to the origin of the objective space ($c_{\mathrm{w}} = c_{\mathrm{t}} = 0$). We use the Euclidean distance, as defined in Eq. 20.

$$c_{\lambda}(o,a) = \sqrt{\left(\lambda c_{\mathrm{w}}\left(o,a\right)\right)^2 + \left(\left(1-\lambda\right) c_{\mathrm{t}}\left(o,a\right)\right)^2} \tag{20}$$

In Fig. 4, we analyze the same datasets for 5 values of $\lambda$, equidistantly distributed across $[0,1]$. For each $\lambda$, the instances in each dataset are categorized by the best algorithm for the respective $\lambda$, i.e. with a minimum $c_{\lambda}$.

Note that, while for $\lambda = 1$, HILL2S is the best algorithm in most cases—since it computes a higher welfare on average—, the breakdown is more balanced for smaller $\lambda$ values, where SAS is the best algorithm more often. A small $\lambda$ means that algorithms that are fast are preferred to more accurate ones, as long as the welfare loss is reasonably small compared to the time decrease. Therefore, simulated annealing algorithms might be preferred, since they are fast and compute good solutions. Similarly, for $\lambda = 0$, execution speed is the most important objective, which leads to greedy algorithms being considered *best*.

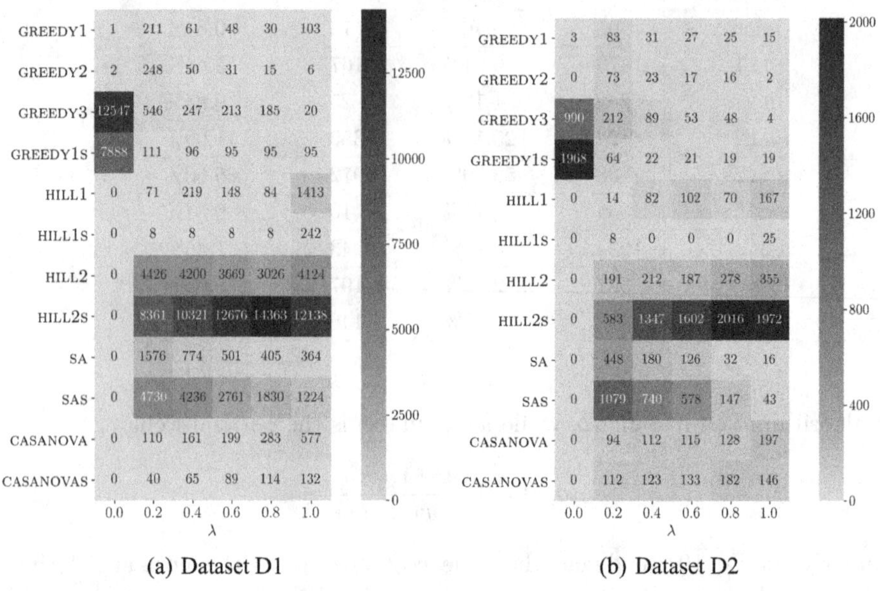


(a) Dataset D1 (b) Dataset D2

**Fig. 4.** Breakdown of each dataset by best algorithm for several $\lambda$ values. A value $\lambda = 0$ means that execution time is the most important when defining the *best* algorithm, while $\lambda = 1$ only considers social welfare.

This result reinforces the idea that there is no clear winner of the algorithm portfolio, especially when preferences for the time-quality trade-off are considered. Even though our $\lambda$-based analysis of the best algorithm adds a certain complexity, it also provides more control and a deeper understanding of the algorithms.

## 6 Conclusion

In this paper, we argued for the need to unify benchmarking efforts for heuristic algorithms for combinatorial auctions. Building upon our work in [15], the first one, to our knowledge, to consistently compare a plethora of approximate auction algorithms under the same problem definition and test cases, we investigated a locality-constrained resource allocation problem for cloud computing.

We built a portfolio of algorithms tailored to this type of problems, and performed a comprehensive evaluation over multiple datasets and test cases. Our analysis revealed that there is no clear portfolio winner, and the algorithms' performance highly depends on the input. Furthermore, we explored the speed-quality trade-off to quantify the definition of a best algorithm, given a variable preference for this trade-off. We then used this definition to further evaluate our portfolio over the two datasets.

In the future, we will employ machine learning methods to identify the input characteristics that differentiate the algorithms in terms of solution quality and execution time, and then predict the best algorithm for each given input.

## References


1. Smith, D.M.: Predicts 2017: cloud computing enters its second decade. Gartner Special Report (2017)
2. Rappa, M.A.: The utility business model and the future of computing services. IBM Syst. J. **43**, 32–42 (2004). https://doi.org/10.1147/sj.431.0032
3. De Vries, S., Vohra, R.V.: Combinatorial auctions: a survey. INFORMS J. Comput. **15**, 284–309 (2003). https://doi.org/10.1287/ijoc.15.3.284.16077
4. Buyya, R., Yeo, C.S., Venugopal, S.: Market-oriented cloud computing: vision, hype, and reality for delivering it services as computing utilities. In: 2008 10th IEEE International Conference on High Performance Computing and Communications. HPCC 2008, pp. 5–13. IEEE (2008). https://doi.org/10.1109/HPCC.2008.172
5. Amazon: Amazon EC2 pricing (2017). https://aws.amazon.com/ec2/pricing. Accessed 3 Nov 2018
6. Fujishima, Y., Leyton-Brown, K., Shoham, Y.: Taming the computational complexity of combinatorial auctions: optimal and approximate approaches. IJCAI **99**, 548–553 (1999)
7. Nejad, M.M., Mashayekhy, L., Grosu, D.: Truthful greedy mechanisms for dynamic virtual machine provisioning and allocation in clouds. IEEE Trans. Parallel Distrib. Syst. **26**, 594–603 (2015). https://doi.org/10.1109/TPDS.2014.2308224
8. Lehmann, D., Oćallaghan, L.I., Shoham, Y.: Truth revelation in approximately efficient combinatorial auctions. J. ACM (JACM) **49**, 577–602 (2002). https://doi.org/10.1145/585265.585266
9. Holte, R.C.: Combinatorial auctions, knapsack problems, and hill-climbing search. In: Stroulia, E., Matwin, S. (eds.) AI 2001. LNCS (LNAI), vol. 2056, pp. 57–66. Springer, Heidelberg (2001). https://doi.org/10.1007/3-540-45153-6_6
10. Zurel, E., Nisan, N.: An efficient approximate allocation algorithm for combinatorial auctions. In: Proceedings of the 3rd ACM Conference on Electronic Commerce, pp. 125–136. ACM (2001). https://doi.org/10.1145/501158.501172
11. Hoos, H.H., Boutilier, C.: Solving combinatorial auctions using stochastic local search. In: AAAI/IAAI, pp. 22–29 (2000)
12. Chu, P.C., Beasley, J.E.: A genetic algorithm for the multidimensional knapsack problem. J. Heuristics **4**, 63–86 (1998). https://doi.org/10.1023/A:1009642405419
13. Khuri, S., Bäck, T., Heitkötter, J.: The zero/one multiple knapsack problem and genetic algorithms. In: Proceedings of the 1994 ACM Symposium on Applied Computing, pp. 188–193. ACM (1994). https://doi.org/10.1145/326619.326694

14. Bertocchi, M., Butti, A., Słomiñ ski, L., Sobczynska, J.: Probabilistic and deterministic local search for solving the binary multiknapsack problem. Optimization **33**, 155–166 (1995). https://doi.org/10.1080/02331939508844072
15. Gudu, D., Zachmann, G., Hardt, M., Streit, A.: Approximate algorithms for double combinatorial auctions for resource allocation in clouds: an empirical comparison. In: Proceedings of the 10th International Conference on Agents and Artificial Intelligence - ICAART, INSTICC, vol. 1, pp. 58–69. SciTePress (2018). https://doi.org/10.5220/0006593900580069
16. Leyton-Brown, K., Pearson, M., Shoham, Y.: Towards a universal test suite for combinatorial auction algorithms. In: Proceedings of the 2nd ACM Conference on Electronic Commerce, pp. 66–76. ACM (2000). https://doi.org/10.1145/352871.352879
17. Lehmann, D., Müller, R., Sandholm, T.: The winner determination problem. In: Combinatorial Auctions, pp. 297–318 (2006). https://doi.org/10.7551/mitpress/9780262033428.003.0013
18. Shoham, Y., Leyton-Brown, K.: Multiagent Systems: Algorithmic, Game-Theoretic, and Logical Foundations. Cambridge University Press, Cambridge (2008). https://doi.org/10.1145/1753171.1753181
19. Schnizler, B., Neumann, D., Veit, D., Weinhardt, C.: Trading grid services-a multi-attribute combinatorial approach. Eur. J. Oper. Res. **187**, 943–961 (2008). https://doi.org/10.1016/j.ejor.2006.05.049
20. Myerson, R.B., Satterthwaite, M.A.: Efficient mechanisms for bilateral trading. J. Econ. Theory **29**, 265–281 (1983). https://doi.org/10.1016/0022-0531(83)90048-0
21. Nisan, N., et al.: Introduction to mechanism design (for computer scientists). Algorithmic Game Theory **9**, 209–242 (2007)
22. Pfeiffer, J., Rothlauf, F.: Greedy heuristics and weight-coded eas for multidimensional knapsack problems and multi-unit combinatorial auctions. In: Kalcsics, J., Nickel, S. (eds.) Operations Research Proceedings 2007, pp. 153–158. Springer, Heidelberg (2008). https://doi.org/10.1007/978-3-540-77903-2_24
23. Gonen, R., Lehmann, D.: Optimal solutions for multi-unit combinatorial auctions: branch and bound heuristics. In: Proceedings of the 2nd ACM Conference on Electronic Commerce, pp. 13–20. ACM (2000). https://doi.org/10.1145/352871.352873
24. Padberg, M., Rinaldi, G.: A branch-and-cut algorithm for the resolution of large-scale symmetric traveling salesman problems. SIAM Rev. **33**, 60–100 (1991). https://doi.org/10.1137/1033004
25. IBM: ILOG CPLEX 12.6.3 (2017). http://www-03.ibm.com/software/products/en/ibmilogcpleoptistud. Accessed 3 Nov 2018
26. Cormen, T.H., Leiserson, C.E., Rivest, R.L., Stein, C.: Greedy algorithms. In: Introduction to Algorithms, vol. 1, pp. 329–355 (2001)
27. Russell, S., Norvig, P.: Beyond classical search. In: Artificial Intelligence, A Modern Approach, pp. 125–128 (2010)
28. Kirkpatrick, S., Gelatt, C.D., Vecchi, M.P., et al.: Optimization by simulated annealing. Science **220**, 671–680 (1983). https://doi.org/10.1126/science.220.4598.671
29. Sandholm, T.: An algorithm for optimal winner determination in combinatorial auctions. Artif. Intell. **135**, 1–54 (2002). https://doi.org/10.1016/S0004-3702(01)00159-X
30. Deb, K.: Multi-objective optimization. In: Burke, E.K., Kendall, G. (eds.) Search Methodologies, pp. 403–449 (2014). https://doi.org/10.1007/978-1-4614-6940-7_15

# An Approach for Detecting and Resolving Indirect Normative Conflicts in Multi-agent Systems

Jéssica S. Santos[1,2(✉)], Mairon Belchior[1], and Viviane T. Silva[2]

[1] Universidade Federal Fluminense, Niterói, RJ, Brazil
{jsoares,mbelchior}@ic.uff.br, jessica.soares@ibm.com
[2] IBM Research, Rio de Janeiro, RJ, Brazil
vivianet@br.ibm.com

**Abstract.** In Multi-agent systems (MAS), norms can be adopt as a strategy to regulate and guide the behavior of software agents and avoid that unexpected actions occur in the system. In order to guarantee that the MAS runs properly, the set of norms must be free of conflict. Two norms are in conflict when the agent automatically violates a norm when adopts the other one. In this paper, we present an approach for detecting and resolving indirect conflicts among norms that regulate a multi-agent system. Indirect conflicts are those who arise among norms whose elements being regulated are not the same but are related. Our approach uses a lexical database and a domain ontology to detect indirect conflicts and the conflicts detected are resolved by manipulating the activation/deactivation conditions of the conflicting norms taking into account the relationships identified among the elements of the conflicting norms.

**Keywords:** Multi-agent systems · Norms · Conflict detection
Conflict resolution · Ontology and WordNet

## 1 Introduction

Multi-agent Systems (MAS) are systems composed of several software agents that cooperate in order to achieve their own goals and the goal of the whole system. Those software agents are entities endowed with autonomy that can be designed independently. In order to avoid that undesirable actions/states occur in MAS, norms specifying prohibitions, obligations and permissions can be applied in the system. In this context, MAS regulated by norms must ensure that their set of norms is free of conflict. We say that there is a normative conflict in the system, when an agent is not able to comply with a norm addressed to him without violate another one automatically. A normative conflict can be classified, as follows: (i) direct conflict: it is a conflict that involves two norms regulating the *same* elements and that have contradictory or opposite modalities, i.e., one norm prohibits the agent to perform an action while the other permits or obliges


J. van den Herik and A. P. Rocha (Eds.): ICAART 2018, LNAI 11352, pp. 23–45, 2019.
https://doi.org/10.1007/978-3-030-05453-3_2

the same agent to perform that action and both norms are active at the same time; or as an (ii) indirect conflict: it is a conflict that involves two norms whose elements are not the same but are *related*. For instance, we say that there is an indirect conflict when there are two norms that are active at the same time and are obliging the same agent to perform opposite actions. Note that for detecting direct conflicts we need to verify if two norms addressed to the same entity and regulating the same behavior are active at the same time and have opposite or contradictory modalities. On the other hand, the detection of indirect normative conflicts is not an easy task since we need to identify relationships among the elements of the norms. Although there are several lines of research in the literature presenting a means to detect normative conflicts, the approaches surveyed can only detect indirect conflicts when the system designer specifies previously the relationships existing among the elements of the norms in a document or an axiom (see Sect. 2). For this reason, in a previous research [14] we presented a means to detect conflicts among norms even when the system designer does not specify relationships among the elements of the norms. Our approach uses a lexical database called WordNet [10] in order to identify relationships among the elements of the norms. This is possible because the WordNet stores semantic relationships between words, for instance, if one norm is obliging an agent *to move* and other is obliging the same agent *to stop*, an indirect conflict can be detected because, according to the WordNet, these words denote opposite actions in the real world. Then, by adopting WordNet as a source of information, the system designer does not need to specify relationships that are valid in the real world (domain-independent relationships). Additionally, in order to consider specific relationships that are valid inside a MAS, our approach analyzes a domain ontology previously defined by the system designer describing relationships between norm elements (domain-dependent relationships).

This research is an extension of the work described in [14]. While in that work we describe the steps performed by our approach to detect indirect normative conflicts in MAS, in the present paper we present a way of resolving the normative conflicts detected and present a case study to illustrate the detection and resolution mechanisms. In our approach, normative conflicts are resolved by restricting the period in which the conflicting norms are active based on relationships identified by using the WordNet and a domain ontology. Additionally, we also extended the related work presented in [14] by surveying different approaches that present a means for resolving conflicts among norms.

The remainder of this paper is organized as follows: Sect. 2 describes lines of research that were proposed to detect and resolve indirect conflicts among norms in MAS. Section 3 presents all background information needed to the understanding of our research. Section 4 describes the steps performed by our approach to detect and resolve normative conflicts. Section 5 presents a case study in order to demonstrate the execution of our mechanism. In Sect. 6, we conclude the paper and point out limitations and suggestions for future work.

## 2 Related Work

In the literature, many approaches were proposed to deal with normative conflicts. One difference between the approaches surveyed is that some of them detect and resolve conflicts before the execution of the MAS (design time strategies), as for example presented in [1–3,18]; and others detect and resolve normative conflicts during the execution of the MAS (runtime strategies), as for instance, described in [5,8,16].

Most of approaches for detecting normative conflicts in MAS can detect direct conflicts [4,11,12,17], but other approaches can detect some kinds of indirect conflicts [1–3,5,8,16,18]. In order to detect indirect conflicts, the work described in [1,2,8] and in [16] verify which are the side-effects of the performance of actions. The work presented in [18] and the work in [16] take into account a composition relationship between actions. The approaches described in [3,5] and in [18] consider a relationship of mutual exclusion (orthogonality) between actions, that is, actions that cannot be performed simultaneously. Although most approaches only consider relationships among actions in order to detect indirect conflicts, the work in [18] also takes into account relationships of hierarchy among entities, relationships that relate an entity to the role it plays, and relationships that relate an entity to the environment that it inhabits, for instance.

The different strategies for conflict resolution are basically divided into [15]: (i) norm prioritization: an order is established between the conflicting norms stating which norm is more relevant. In this case there are three classical strategies that are commonly adopted: *lex posterior* (the most recent norm is prioritized); *lex specialis* (the most specific norm is prioritized); and *lex superior* (the norm issued by the most important authority is prioritized); and (ii) norm update: the scope of influence of one of the conflicting norms is reduced or extended in order to eliminate the conflict.

The work presented in [4,16,17], considers that norms can have variable terms in their definition in order to allows that actions are associated with constraints. In [16], a conflict occurs when the variables of a prohibition overlap with the variables of an obligation or permission. The algorithm presented for conflict resolution manipulates the constraints of norms to eliminate overlapping values of variables, i.e., constraints are added restricting the scope of influence of one of the norms. In the approaches in [4,17], the scope of influence of the norms are restricted after determining which values the norms cannot assume to avoid the conflict. In these two approaches, prohibitions are curtailed but the authors state that the same mechanism can be applied to curtail obligations.

The research described in [1] resolves normative conflicts based on norm refinement strategies (*lex posterior*, *lex superior* and *lex specialis*). In the norm refinement step, an automated planner searches for a plan that implies a state of the world in which the expiration condition of one of the norms in conflict holds. In the work in [6], prohibitions and obligations are represented through commitments and conflicts are solved by changing the activation conditions of the commitments.

In this paper we describe a mechanism for dealing with indirect conflicts taking into account relationships that are also considered by other approaches, such as, *specialization* and *hierarchy* and others that have not been considered such as *antonymy* and *synonymy* (all relationships considered are detailed in Sect. 3). Additionally, our approach can identify those relationships not only analyzing relationships previously defined (in a ontology, for instance) but it also can identify relationships that were not specified by the system designer but that are valid in the real world (by using the WordNet). After detecting the indirect conflicts, our mechanism resolve them taking into account the relationships identified. The resolution consists in manipulating the activation/deactivation conditions of the norms.

In [15], we present a survey about different techniques to detect and resolve normative conflicts in MAS, pointing out advantages and disadvantages of each approach.

## 3 Background

In this section, we present the essential aspects of our proposal. First, we present the norm definition adopted. The norm definition is an important factor, since all kinds of conflicts that can be detected depend on the norm expressivity, i.e., the elements that a norm can represent. After that, we list the relationships that the mechanism to detect conflicts will investigate between the elements of the norms. Our research combines two different approaches of conflict detection whose relationships are listed separately.

### 3.1 Norm Definition

We assume that a norm obliges, permits or prohibits an entity to perform an action that can be applied to a specific object. For instance, a norm can say that an agent is obliged *to drive* a *car*, where *drive* is the action and *car* is the object. The object is an optional element of our norm definition, i.e., a norm can regulate an action that is not associated with an object.

**Definition:** A norm is a tuple in the form

$$n = \langle id, deoC, c, e, act(obj), ac, dc \rangle$$

where *id* is the norm identifier; *deoC* is the deontic concept that determines the modality of the norm $deoC \in \{obligation, permission, prohibition\}$; $c \in C$ is the context where the norm is defined (it can be an organization $o \in O$ or an environment $env \in Env$); $e \in E$ is the entity being regulated by the norm. An entity $e$ may be an agent $a \in A$, an organization $o \in Org$ or a role $r \in R$; $act \in Act$ is the action being regulated; $obj \in Obj$ is the object associated with the action. The object is an optional field; and $ac \in Cd$ and $dc \in Cd$ are dates that, respectively, activate and deactivate the norm. The symbol "_" can be used to determine that a norm regulates all entities of a specific context.

### 3.2 Domain Ontology Relationships

The mechanism proposed to detect conflicts is able to receive an ontology as input, specifying the relationships of the application domain. The relationships that can be specified in the ontology by the application designer are listed below, as follows:

**Inhabit:** It relates an entity to the environment that it inhabits. This relationship indicates that if a norm regulates an environment, the norm also regulates the entities that inhabit such an environment.

**Play:** It relates an entity to the roles it can assume. This relationship indicates that if a norm regulates a role, the norm also regulates the entities that play such a role.

**Ownership:** It defines the roles that belong to a given organization. This relationship indicates that if a norm regulates an organization, the norm also regulates the roles that belong to the organization.

**Hierarchy:** It defines that an element is super element of another one. This relationship indicates that if there is a norm regulating a super context/entity, the norm also regulates their sub contexts/entities.

**Refinement:** It defines that an action is the specialization of another one.

**Composition:** It defines that an action (called *whole action*) is composed of other actions (called *part actions*).

**Orthogonality:** It defines actions that cannot be performed at the same time by the same entity or related entities.

**Dependency:** It determines that an action (called *client action*) is a precondition to the performance of another one (called *dependent action*).

### 3.3 WordNet Relationships

Our approach uses the WordNet database to find relationships between contexts, entities, actions and objects (associated with actions).

**Synonymy:** Words that denote the same concept are grouped in a same set (called synset) in the WordNet and are related by the relationship *Synonymy.* We map the contexts described in the norms to nouns and verify if they are related through the relationship *Synonymy.* For instance, if there is a norm whose context is *United States of America* and other one whose context is *USA*, the algorithm will conclude that both contexts are equivalents and that both norms are applied to the same context. Similarly, by using the relationship *Synonymy* we can infer that two norms that are, in principle, addressed to different entities, in fact, refer to the same entity. For instance, *physician* and *doctor* are nouns that denote a *licensed medical practitioner.* We also use the relationship *Synonymy* to map the actions to verbs and objects to nouns, and identify that the actions/objects of two norms are equivalent. For instance, the actions *to collaborate* and *to cooperate* are related by the relationship *Synonymy.*

**Specialization:** It is described in the WordNet as "*Hyponymy/Hypernymy*" and relate a noun that denotes an element to its respective sub-elements contexts and super-contexts. For instance, the context *hospital* is a sub context of *medical institution*, since a *hospital* is a *medical institution.* Similarly, this relationship can be used to detect that a sub-entity is related to a super-entity. When a norm is applied to a super-entity, such a norm is propagated to its sub-entities. For instance, if a norm is applied to the role *doctor*, supposing that there is the role *angiologist* in the domain, the norm also is applied to all entities that are playing the role *angiologist.* We also use this relationship to detect relationships among objects. For instance, the object *train* is a specialization of the object *public transport*, because a *train* is a kind of *public transport.* The relationship *Specialization* among verbs is defined as "*Troponymy/Hypernymy*" in the WordNet and is used to identify that a sub-action is related to a super-action. For instance, in the WordNet the verbs *to move* and *to walk* are related by this relationship since *to walk* is a way of *to move.*

**Part-Whole:** It is described in the WordNet as "*Meronymy/Holonymy*" and relates an element that denotes a part to an element that denotes a whole. Usually, this relationship is used to relate geographic areas in the WordNet. For instance, the context *USA* is part of the context *North America.* Similarly, the *intensive care unit* is part of the *hospital* and *sacristy* is a part of *church.* This relationship can be applied to detect related objects, for instance, the objects *window* and *car* are related by the relationship *Part-Whole* because a *window* is part of a *car.*

**Entailment:** It relates an action that entails another one. For instance, when someone *buy* something it must *pay* for it. Then, the verbs *to buy* and *to pay* are related in the WordNet by the relationship *Entailment.*

**Antonymy:** It relates an action to its opposite. For instance, *to move* and *to stop* are verbs related in the WordNet by the relationship *Antonymy* because they denote opposite actions.

## 4 Detecting and Resolving Indirect Conflicts

In this section, we describe the mechanisms proposed for detecting and resolving normative conflicts in MAS.

### 4.1 Conflict Detection

Our algorithm receives as input a domain ontology that describes domain elements (contexts, entities, actions, objects), the set of norms and, optionally, domain-dependent relationships. After that, it combines two approaches of conflict detection and is divided into two steps, as follows:

1. Detection of domain-dependent conflicts by using relationships described in the domain ontology (*Domain Conflict Checker*);
2. Detection of domain-independent conflicts by using relationships described in the WordNet (*WordNet Conflict Checker*).

Both approaches are divided into the following sub-steps:

a. Propagation of norms according to the relationships;
b. Grouping norms in sets according to their similarity;
c. Verification of time intersection between each pair of norms belonging to the same set;
d. Application of rules to identify conflict patterns;

After receiving the domain ontology describing the relationships, entities, contexts, actions, objects and the norms considered by the MAS, the algorithm performs a propagation of norms. During propagation, norms addressed to general entities and contexts are addressed to specific entities and contexts of the domain (sub-step a). For instance, let us consider that there are two agents called *agent1* and *agent2* that are playing the role *physician* in the MAS (relationship *play*). Then, if the application designer specifies a norm *n1* that is addressed to the role *physician*, the propagation process will create two new norms *n1.1* and *n1.2* that will be composed of the same elements of *n1* but will be addressed to the agents *agent1* and *agent2* (see Fig. 1). However, the propagation of norms according to domain-dependent relationships can generate inconsistent norms if it contradicts other relationships defined in the domain ontology. When it occurs, such norms must be discarded. The rules to discard inconsistent norms are described in Table 1. Since the propagation of contexts and entities can generate multiple norms, to reduce the number of comparisons needed, norms that have the same entity and context are grouped in the same group (sub-step b). For instance, suppose that exists a set of norms: *n3*, *n4*, *n5*, *n6*, *n7* and *n8*. The norms *n3*, *n6* and *n8* are associated with the context *Brazil* and regulate the entity *agent3*; the norm *n5* is associated with the context *Argentina* and regulates the entity *agent4*; and the norms *n4* and *n7* are addressed to the *agent5* and to the context *USA* and *United States of America*, respectively. Note that the contexts *USA* and *United States of America* are synonyms. Then, in this example, the sub-step of grouping norms will create three sets of norms (see Fig. 2) and only norms belonging to a same set will be compared in the next sub-step. Only norms addressed to the same (or equivalent) entities and applied to the same (or equivalent) contexts can conflict. Next, for each pair of norms of a same group, the algorithm verifies if there is an intersection between the activation and deactivation conditions of the given two norms (sub-step c) and, if so, the algorithm analyzes the actions, objects and the deontic concepts of the norms in order to verify if the pair of norms is conflicting (sub-step d). The norms that were propagated and the conflicts detected are passed to the second step as an input parameter. The algorithm performs norm propagation considering relationships described in the WordNet (sub-step a). Norms are grouped together in sets when they are addressed to the same or to a synonym entities and contexts (sub-step b). The algorithm verifies if there is a time intersection to each pair of norms of the same set (sub-step c). The algorithm applies the conflict rules to detect conflicting patterns considering the relationships of WordNet (sub-step d). To conclude that two norms are in conflict, the actions defined in the norms must be analyzed with their objects (when the action involves objects). The objects of norms are mapped to WordNet nouns and their relationships are analyzed. Finally, the algorithm exhibits all conflicts detected and the domain-dependent and domain-independent relationships that were identified. Note that in Sect. 5, we exhibit some conflicting patterns, that is, patterns that indicate that two norms cannot be adopted at the same time and for this reason are in conflict. The complete list of conflicting patterns that have been defined involving domain-independent/domain-dependent relationships are described in [13] and [18], respectively.

**n1 = ⟨O, hospital, physician, attend, patient, _, _⟩**

**n1.1= ⟨O, hospital, agent1, attend, patient, _, _⟩**

**n1.2= ⟨O, hospital, agent2, attend, patient, _, _⟩**

**Fig. 1.** Example of norm propagation [14].

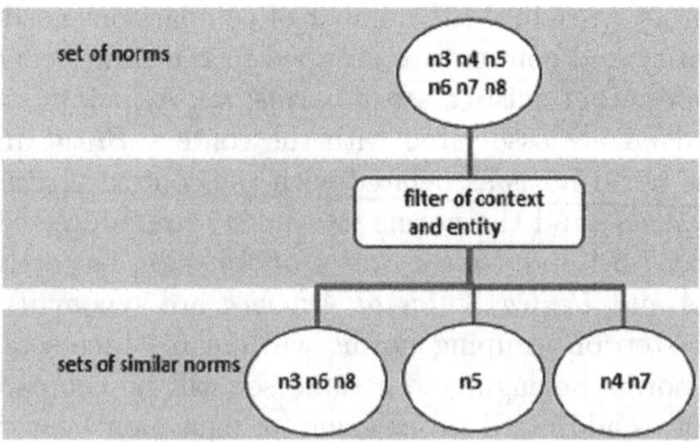


**Fig. 2.** Example of grouping norms according to their similarity [14].

## 4.2 Conflict Resolution

The detection mechanism described in Sect. 4.1 does the conflict identification between each pair of norms belonging to the same set. Once those conflicts were

**Table 1.** Rules to discard inconsistent norms generated by the propagation process [14].

| Kind of propagation | Discard rule |
|---|---|
| *Hierarchy* among contexts that are environments | The entity of the original norm is an organization/agent and is not defined in the domain ontology that such entity inhabits the environment of the propagated norm (*inhabit*) |
| *Hierarchy* among contexts that are organizations | (i) the entity of the original norm is an organization that is not a suborganization (*hierarchy*) of the context of the propagated norm and is not the context of the propagated norm<br>(ii) the entity of the original norm is a role that is not related to the organization that is the context of the propagated norm (*ownership*) |
| *Inhabit* between contexts that are environments and contexts that are organizations | (i) the entity of the original norm is an organization that is not a suborganization (*hierarchy*) of the context of the propagated norm and is not equal to the context of the propagated norm<br>(ii) the entity of the original norm is a role that is not related (*ownership*) to the context of the propagated norm (that is an organization) |
| *Inhabit* between contexts that are environments and entities that are organizations | The entity of the propagated norm is not a suborganization (*hierarchy*) of the entity of the original norm |

detected, a resolution approach must be performed in order to eliminate the conflict. We propose to reduce the scope of influence of the pair of conflicting norms by restricting the period in which these norms are active. In other words, the resolution mechanism manipulates the activation/deactivation conditions of one of the conflicting norms in order to eliminate the overlaps between the two norms in conflict. The activation condition determines the moment from which a norm will be activated and the deactivation condition defines when the norm will be deactivated. In this paper, the activation and deactivation conditions of a norm are represented by a date, as detailed in Sect. 3.1.

A norm can have one activation condition, one deactivation condition, both of them or no condition. Therefore, a norm *n1* can have one of the four types of activation intervals illustrated in Fig. 3 based on its activation/deactivation conditions. The first type is when *n1* has no activation/deactivation condition and is always active. Its activation interval starts at time zero and lasts until +infinite, i.e., the norm is always active until the ending of the system execution. The second type refers to *n1* associated with only one activation condition represented by *date1*. Therefore, the activation interval of *n1* starts from *date1* and lasts until *+infinite*. The third type represents *n1* with only one deactivation condition, which is defined by *date2*, and its activation interval starts from zero and lasts until *date2*. Finally, the fourth type refers to *n1* associated with one activation condition (*date3*) and one deactivation condition (*date4*). Thus, the activation interval of *n1* starts from *date3* until *date4*.

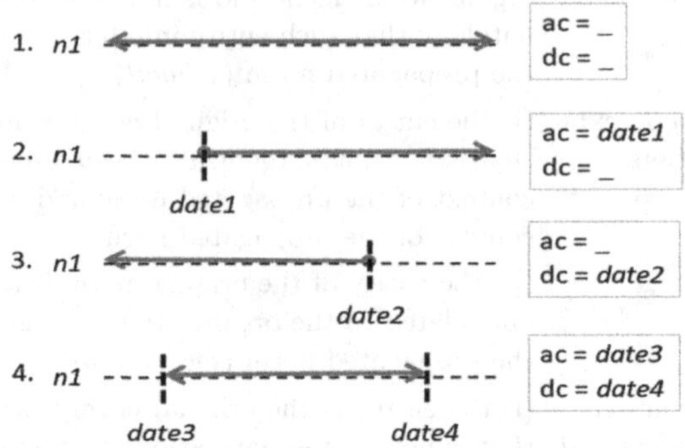


**Fig. 3.** Types of activation intervals based on activation/deactivation conditions.

The resolution mechanism proposed in this paper resolves normative conflicts between pair of norms based on four strategies. Let *n1* and *n2* be a pair of norms in conflict. Each strategy, except the first one, changes somehow the activation/deactivation conditions of the norms in conflict. The four strategies are defined as follows.

- Strategy 0: One of the norms in conflict is removed. When a relationship that denotes some kind of specialization among norm elements is detected (*refinement*, *composition*, *dependency*, *specialization*, *part-whole*, *entailment*), the most specific norm is prioritized (*lex specialis*) and consequently the other one is chosen to be removed. If no specialization relationship is identified, our resolution mechanism chooses one of the norms in conflict to be removed based on its modality. We assume in this paper that when a conflict involves a prohibition and a permission, the permission is removed; and when a conflict involves a prohibition and an obligation, the prohibition is removed. However, we consider that this decision is up to the system designer [4]. In case that the modality of both norms in conflict are the same (for instance, two norms obligating orthogonal actions), the decision of what norm to remove is arbitrary.
- Strategy 1: Norm *n1* is removed and a new norm *n1'* is included in the set of norms. The norm *n1'* is a copy of *n1*, but its activation condition is going to be one day after the deactivation condition of *n2* (or empty if *n2* does not have deactivation condition) and its deactivation condition is going to be one day before the activation condition of *n2* (or empty if *n2* does not have activation condition).
- Strategy 2: Norm *n1* is removed and a new norm *n1'* is added in the set of norms, which is a copy of *n1*, but its deactivation condition is changed to be one day before the activation condition of *n2*.

- Strategy 3: Norm *n1* is removed and a new norm *n1′* is included in the set of norms, which is a copy of *n1*, but its activation condition is changed to be one day after the deactivation condition of *n2*.

The resolution mechanism applies Strategy 0 when the pair of norms in conflict has the same types of activation intervals and also the same activation/deactivation conditions. For example, suppose that there is a norm *n1* = ⟨*N1,P,home,John,eat(pasta),date1,_*⟩ and a norm *n2* = ⟨*N2,F,home,John,eat(spaghetti),date1,_*⟩. Norms *n1* and *n2* are in conflict because one allows (*P*) *John* to *eat pasta* and the other prohibits (*F*) the same agent to *eat spaghetti*, which is a specialization of *pasta*. Also, they are active at the same period of time since their activation and deactivation conditions are exactly the same. Therefore, according to Strategy 0, our resolution mechanism chooses to remove the less specific norm, which is norm *n1*. If we replace *pasta* to spaghetti in norm *n1*, then no specialization relationship would be identified between *n1* and *n2*. Therefore, according to Strategy 0, when a conflict involves a prohibition and a permission, the permission is removed. In this case, norm *n1* is a permission and then it is removed from the set of norms.

We propose the following criteria in order to select which norm is to be changed in Strategies 1, 2 and 3. First, our resolution mechanism chooses to change the norm where the result does not eliminate the entire norm. In other words, it tries to save as much as possible both norms when the resolution mechanism eliminates the intersections between activation periods of the norms in conflict. If the choice does not matter, i.e., the result does not eliminate entirely either norm in conflict, our resolution mechanism uses *lex specialis* in order to select which norm is to be changed. If no specialization relationship is detected, the selection is based on their modality, according to Strategy 0. We will show examples of those strategies throughout this section.

The resolution mechanism applies one or more strategies, depending on the types of activation intervals of the pair of norms in conflict, detailed as follows. We consider a combination of all possible types of activation intervals (Fig. 3) to decide how to change the activation and deactivation conditions of the norms.

When a conflict involves a norm *n1* whose activation interval is type 1 and a norm *n2* whose activation interval is type 2, Strategy 2 can be used to solve the conflict. As mentioned, the resolution mechanism chooses to change the norm where the result does not eliminate the entire norm. Thus, norm *n1* whose activation interval is type 1 is chosen to be modified. Strategy 2 removes norm *n1* and adds a new norm *n1′* in the set of norms, which is a copy of *n1*, but its deactivation condition is changed to be one day before the activation condition of *n2* (see Fig. 4). When the conflict involves a norm *n1* whose activation interval is type 1 and a norm *n2* whose activation interval is type 3, the resolution mechanism uses Strategy 3 (see Fig. 5).

When the conflict involves a norm *n1* whose activation interval is type 1 and a norm *n2* whose activation interval is type 4, the resolution mechanism uses Strategy 2 and Strategy 3 to resolve the conflict. By using Strategy 2, a new norm *n1′* is created, which is a copy of *n1*, but its deactivation condition is

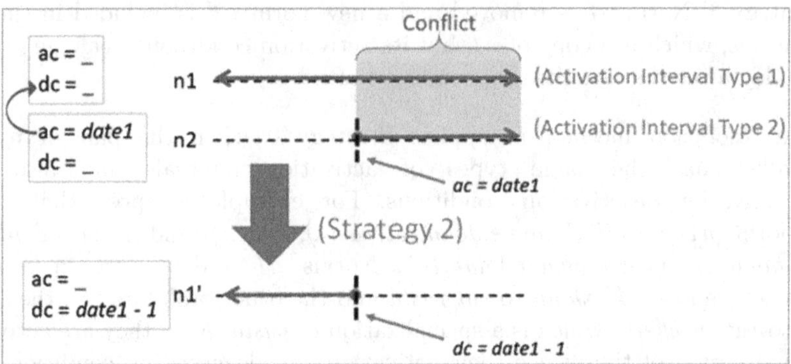


**Fig. 4.** Conflict resolution involving activation interval type 1 and type 2 by using Strategy 2.

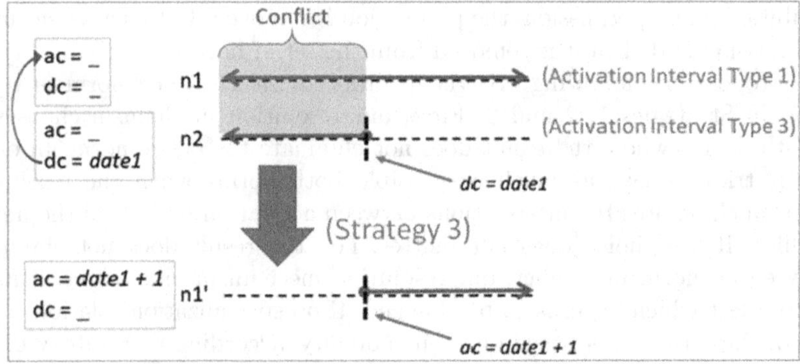


**Fig. 5.** Conflict resolution involving activation interval type 1 and type 3 by using Strategy 3.

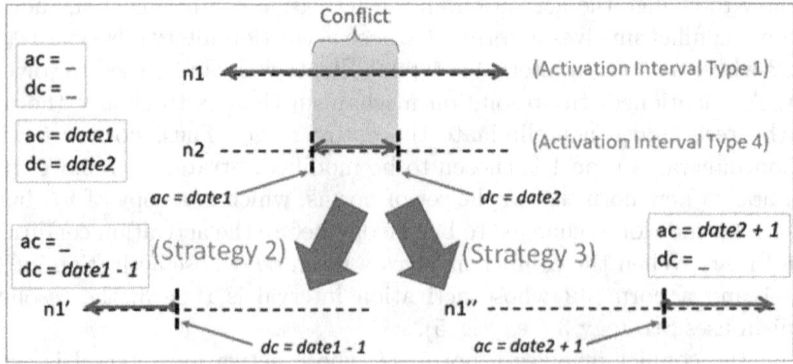


**Fig. 6.** Conflict resolution involving activation interval type 1 and type 4 by using Strategy 2 and 3.

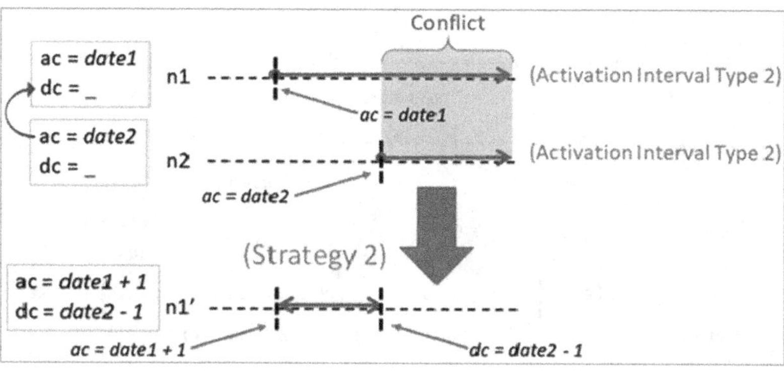


**Fig. 7.** Conflict resolution involving activation interval type 2 and type 2 by using Strategy 2.

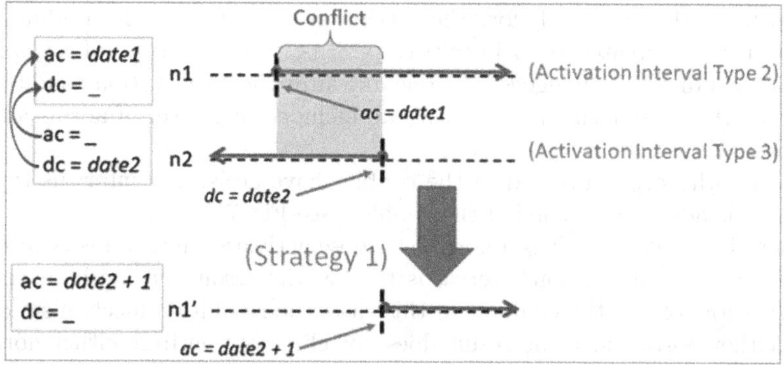


**Fig. 8.** Conflict resolution involving activation interval type 2 and type 3 by using Strategy 1.

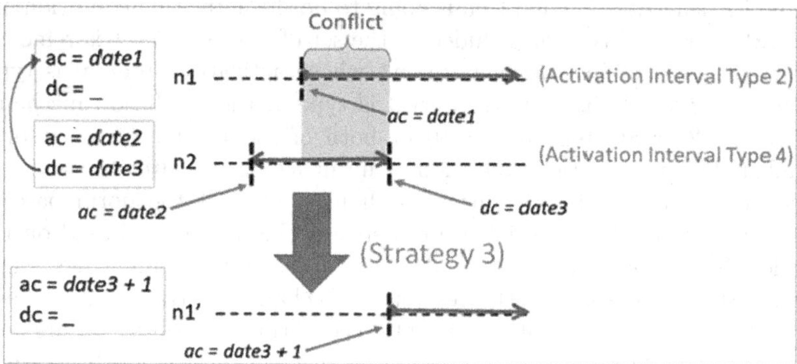


**Fig. 9.** Conflict resolution involving activation interval type 2 and type 4 by using Strategy 3.

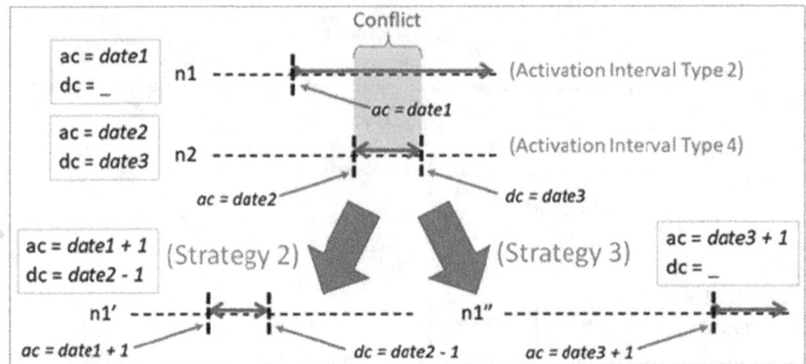


**Fig. 10.** Conflict resolution involving activation interval type 2 and type 4 by using Strategy 2 and Strategy 3.

changed to be the one day before the activation condition of *n2*. In addition, a new norm *n1″* is created by using Strategy 3, i.e., *n1″* is a copy of *n1*, but its activation condition is changed to be one day after the deactivation condition of *n2* (see Fig. 6). The norms *n1′* and *n1″* are included in the set of norms and *n1* is removed.

When both norms involved in the conflict have activation intervals type 2, Strategy 2 is adopted for solving the conflict (see Fig. 7).

When the conflict involves a norm *n1* whose activation interval is type 2 and a norm *n2* whose activation interval is type 3, the resolution mechanism uses Strategy 1 for solving the conflict. In this case, the resolution mechanism could choose either norm, since the result does not eliminate entirely either norm in conflict. This way, our resolution mechanism uses *lex specialis* in order to select which norm is to be changed. For example, if the resolution mechanism chooses to change norm *n1*, according to Strategy 1, a copy of *n1*, called *n1′*, is created but its activation condition is going to be one day after the deactivation condition of *n2* and its deactivation condition is going to be the activation condition of *n2* (see Fig. 8). Norm *n1′* is then included in the set of norms and *n1* is removed.

When the conflict involves a norm *n1* whose activation interval is type 2 and a norm *n2* whose activation interval is type 4, the resolution mechanism uses Strategy 2 or Strategy 3 (Fig. 9) or both of them (Fig. 10) for resolving the conflict. If the activation condition of norm *n1* occurs after the activation condition of norm *n2*, the resolution mechanism chooses the norm based on *lex specialis* (if there is a specialization between the norms) or based on their modalities. If *n1* is chosen, Strategy 3 is used to solve the conflict (see Fig. 9). Otherwise, if *n2* is chosen by the resolution mechanism, Strategy 2 is used to resolve the conflict. However, if the activation condition of norm *n1* occurs before the activation condition of *n2*, the resolution mechanism uses both Strategy 2 and Strategy 3 to solve the conflict (Fig. 10).

When both conflicting norms *n1* and *n2* have activation intervals type 3, the resolution mechanism uses Strategy 3 for solving the conflict (Fig. 11). When

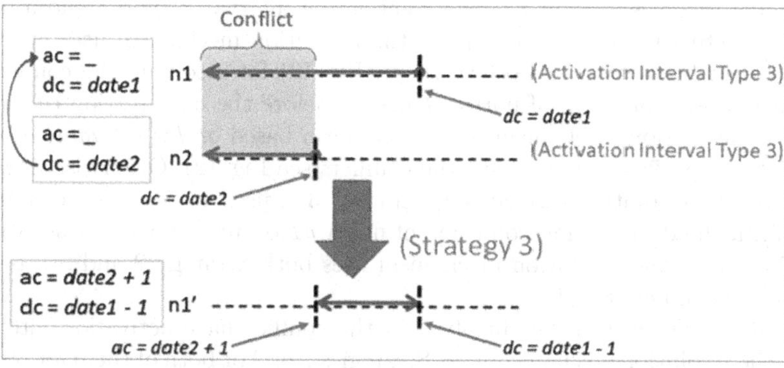


**Fig. 11.** Conflict resolution involving activation interval type 3 and type 3 by using Strategy 3.

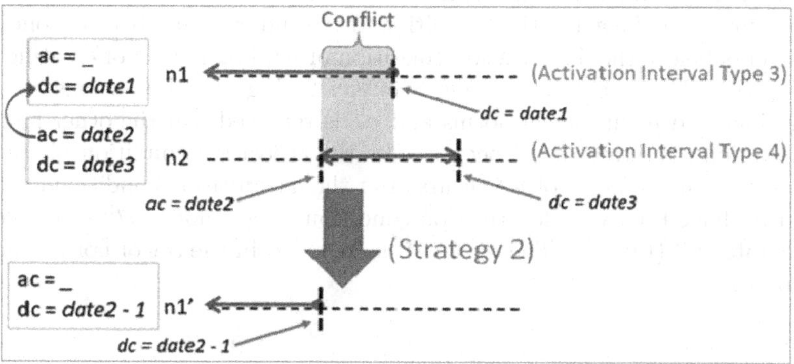


**Fig. 12.** Conflict resolution involving activation interval type 3 and type 4 by using Strategy 2.

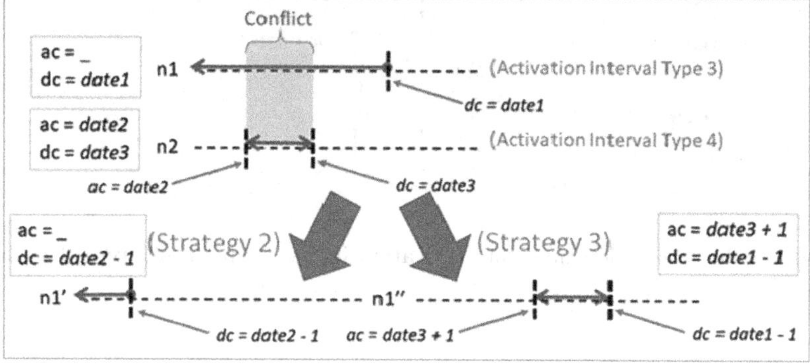


**Fig. 13.** Conflict resolution involving activation interval type 3 and type 4 by using Strategy 2 and Strategy 3.

the conflict involves a norm *n1* whose activation interval is type 3 and a norm *n2* whose activation interval is type 4, the resolution mechanism uses Strategy 2 (Fig. 12) or Strategy 3 or both of them (Fig. 13) for resolving the conflict. If the deactivation condition of norm *n1* occurs before the deactivation condition of *n2*, the resolution mechanism selects the norm based on *lex specialis*. If *n1* is chosen, Strategy 2 is used to solve the conflict (see Fig. 12). Otherwise, if *n2* is chosen by the resolution mechanism, Strategy 3 is used to resolve the conflict. However, if the deactivation condition of norm *n1* occurs after the deactivation condition of *n2*, the resolution mechanism uses both Strategy 2 and Strategy 3 to solve the conflict (Fig. 13).

Finally, when both norms involved in the conflict have activation intervals type 4, the resolution mechanism uses Strategies 2 or 3 or both of them for resolving the conflict. If the deactivation condition of *n1* occurs after the deactivation condition of *n2* and the activation condition of *n1* occurs after the activation condition of *n2* or *n1* and *n2* have the same activation condition, a new norm *n1′* is created by using Strategy 3 (Fig. 14). Otherwise, if the activation condition of *n2* occurs after the activation condition of *n1* and the deactivation condition of *n2* occurs before the deactivation condition of *n1*, in addition of creating *n1′*, a new norm *n1″* is created by using Strategy 2 (Fig. 15). The norms *n1′* and *n1″* are included in the set of norms and *n1* is removed. On the other hand, if the activation condition of *n2* occurs after the activation condition of *n1* and the deactivation condition of *n2* occurs after the deactivation condition of *n1* or *n1* and *n2* have the same deactivation condition, a new norm *n1′* is created by using Strategy 2 (Fig. 16). The norm *n1′* is included in the set of norms and *n1* is removed.

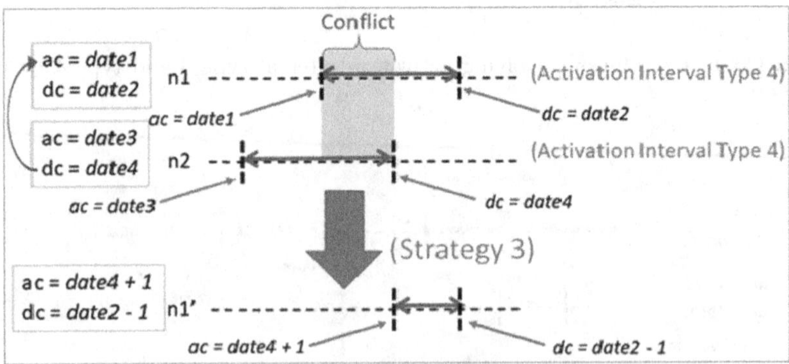


**Fig. 14.** Conflict resolution involving activation interval type 4 and type 4 by using Strategy 3.

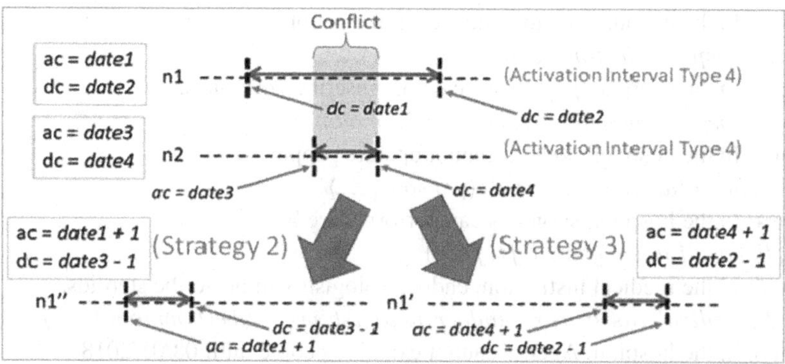


**Fig. 15.** Conflict resolution involving activation interval type 4 and type 4 by using Strategy 2 and 3.

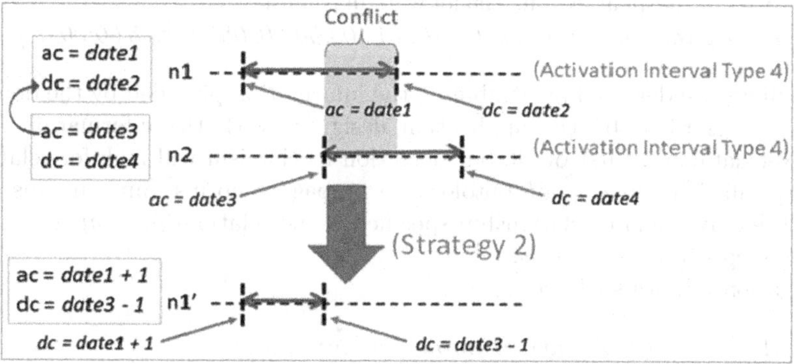


**Fig. 16.** Conflict resolution involving activation interval type 4 and type 4 by using Strategy 2.

## 5 Case Study

In this section, we demonstrate how our approach deals with normative conflicts that can only be detected when the relations among the elements of the norms are identified. Note that in this case study some conflicts occur among norms apparently not related, i.e., among norms associated with different contexts, entities, actions or objects. Our case study is based on some norms of a medical scenario which describe which actions doctors can perform in relation to their patients. In this scenario, there are two organizations: *hospital* and *medical institution* and five roles: *doctor*, *physician*, *surgeon*, *endocrinologist*, *nurse*. In this case study, the domain ontology specifies that an agent called *Agent1* plays the role *doctor* and an agent called *Agent2* plays the role *nurse*. Let's consider the following norms:

Norm 1: In the hospital, doctors must examine people.
$\langle N1, O, hospital, doctor, examine(person), \_, \_\rangle$
Norm 2: In the hospital, physicians cannot prescribe hormones.
$\langle N2, F, hospital, physician, prescribe(hormone), \_, \_\rangle$
Norm 3: In the hospital, doctors cannot operate people.
$\langle N3, F, hospital, doctor, operate(person), \_, \_\rangle$
Norm 4: In the hospital, surgeons can perform face lift.
$\langle N4, P, hospital, surgeon, lift(face), \_, \_\rangle$
Norm 5: In the medical institution, endocrinologists can prescribe steroids.
$\langle N5, P, medical\_institution, endocrinologist, prescribe(hormone), \_, \_\rangle$
Norm 6: In the hospital, Agent1 cannot examine people until 08/01/2018.
$\langle N6, F, hospital, Agent1, examine(person), \_,$ *08/01/2018 00:00:00* $\rangle$
Norm 7: In the hospital, nurses must work between January and December of 2018.
$\langle N7, O, hospital, nurse, work,$ *01/01/2018 00:00:00, 12/31/2018 00:00:00*$\rangle$
Norm 8: In the hospital, Agent2 cannot work in August.
$\langle N8, F, hospital, Agent1, work,$ *08/01/2018 00:00:00, 08/31/2018 00:00:00*$\rangle$

Conflicts are detected by combining the information provided by the domain ontology (described by the application designer) with the information from WordNet database. First of all, our detection mechanism will look for relationships specified in the domain ontology to propagate norms. Since in this case study the only domain relationship specified is the relationship *Play*, the propagation step will be as follows:
Propagation of norms - Entity:

$\langle N1.1, O, hospital, Agent1, examine(person), \_, \_\rangle$
$\langle N3.2, F, hospital, Agent1, operate(person), \_, \_$
$\langle N7.3, O, hospital, Agent2, work,$ *01/01/2018 00:00:00, 12/31/2018 00:00:00*$\rangle$

After propagation and domain-dependent processing, the original norms are joined to the propagated norms and independent domain processing is performed, i.e., the detection mechanism will look for relationships using the WordNet database and it will find that: (i) *hospital* is a sub organization of *medical institution*; (ii) *physician* and *doctor* are synonyms that are in a same "synset" whose meaning is "a licensed medical practitioner"; and (iii) *surgeon* and *endocrinologist* are specializations of *doctor* and *physician*. The norms addressed to *doctor* and *physician* will be propagated to *surgeon* and *endocrinologist*:
Propagation of norms - Entity:

$\langle N1.1, O, hospital, endocrinologist, examine(person), \_, \_\rangle$
$\langle N1.2, O, hospital, surgeon, examine(person), \_, \_\rangle$
$\langle N2.3, F, hospital, endocrinologist, prescribe(hormone), \_, \_\rangle$
$\langle N2.4, F, hospital, surgeon, prescribe(hormone), \_, \_\rangle$

$\langle N3.5, F, hospital, endocrinologist, operate(person), \_, \_\rangle$
$\langle N3.6, F, hospital, surgeon, operate(person), \_, \_\rangle$

Propagation of norms - Context:

$\langle N5.1, P, medical\_institution, hospital, prescribe(steroid), \_, \_\rangle$
$\langle N5.11, P, hospital, endocrinologist, prescribe(steroid), \_, \_\rangle$

The conflicts detected are presented in Table 2.

**Table 2.** Conflicts detected in the case study presented.

| Conflict | Conflict Pattern | Norms |
|---|---|---|
| (N1, N6) | -Time intersection<br>-Same Action<br>-Same Object<br>- O x F | $(\langle N1.1, O, hospital, Agent1, examine(person), \_, \_\rangle$,<br>$\langle N6, F, hospital, Agent1, examine(person), \_,$<br>*08/01/2018 00:00:00*$\rangle)$ |
| (N3, N4) | -Time intersection<br>-Action *Specialization*<br>(operate, lift)<br>-Object *Part-Whole*<br>(face, person)<br>- F x P | $(\langle N3.6, F, hospital, surgeon, operate(person), \_, \_\rangle$,<br>$\langle N4, P, hospital, surgeon, lift(face), \_, \_\rangle)$ |
| (N2, N5) | -Time intersection<br>-Same Action<br>-Object *Specialization*<br>(steroid, hormone)<br>-F x P | $(\langle N2.3, F, hospital, endocrinologist, prescribe(hormone), \_, \_\rangle$,<br>$\langle N5.11, P, hospital, endocrinologist, prescribe(steroid), \_, \_\rangle)$ |
| (N7, N8) | -Time intersection<br>-Same Action<br>-Same object<br>-O x F | $(\langle N8, F, hospital, Agent2, work,$<br>*08/01/2018 00:00:00, 08/31/2018 00:00:00*$\rangle$,<br>$\langle N7.3, O, hospital, Agent2, work,$<br>*01/01/2018 00:00:00, 12/31/2018 00:00:00*$\rangle)$ |

The normative conflict involving norms *N1.1* and *N6* is a conflict between norms of type 1 and type 3, respectively. Then, the conflict will be solved by applying Strategy 3 to N1.1. A new norm *N1.1′* will be created, where *N1.1′* is a copy of *N1.1* but its activation condition is one day after the deactivation condition of *N6* as follows:

$\langle N1.1', O, hospital, Agent1, examine(person),$ *08/02/2018 00:00:00*$, \_\rangle$

The normative conflict involving norms *N2.3* and *N5.11* is a conflict between norms of type 1. Then, the conflict will be solved by applying Strategy 0. Since there is a specialization relationship indicating that norm *N5.11* is more specific, this norm is prioritized (*lex specialis*) and norm *N2.3* is excluded of the set of norms. Similarly, Strategy 0 is also chosen for solving conflict between norms *N3.6* and *N4*, i.e., norm *N4* is prioritized and norm *3.6* is excluded.

The normative conflict involving norms *N7.3* and *N8* is a conflict between norms of type 4. As explained in the previous section, this kind of conflict will be solved by applying Strategy 3 and Strategy 2 to norm *N7.3*. Then, a new norm *N7.3'* is created, which is a copy of *N7.3* but its deactivation condition is changed to be one day before the activation condition of *N8*. Additionally, a new norm *N7.3''* is created, which is a copy of *N7.3* but its activation condition is changed to be one day after the deactivation condition of *N8*. The new norms *N7.3'* and *N7.3''* are as follows:

$\langle N7.3', O, hospital, Agent2, work, 01/01/2018\ 00{:}00{:}00,\ 07/31/2018\ 00{:}00{:}00\rangle$
$\langle N7.3'', O, hospital, Agent2, work, 09/01/2018\ 00{:}00{:}00,\ 12/31/2018\ 00{:}00{:}00\rangle$

## 6 Conclusions

Regulation mechanisms, such as norms, are commonly applied in MAS to coordinate agents' interactions. In MAS regulated by multiple norms it is essential to ensure if the set of norms is free of conflict. The ability of dealing with normative conflicts is a topic that must be considered in MAS. This is because the process of verification/revision of a large and/or complex set of norms is not simple and is a task that demands a lot of time and that is prone to errors. Once a normative conflict is detected, it must be solved to guarantee that software agents can be norm-compliant.

In this context, our research aims to automate the processes of conflict detection and resolution, providing a mechanism able to deal with direct and indirect normative conflicts in MAS. Different of other approaches, our research presents a means to detect indirect normative conflicts even when the system designer does not previously specify the relationships among the elements of the norms. This is possible by performing a semantic mapping based on relationship information extracted from the WordNet. Our approach considers cases of conflict that may occur due to relationships that have not yet been considered in any proposal of other authors, such as: synonyms and antonyms. The resolution process also takes into account some of the relationships identified.

During the detection process, the mechanism does not consider only relationships that exist in the real world. It also considers specific information of the MAS (a domain ontology predefined by the system designer containing relationships that are valid in the MAS) to detect conflicts. In order to do that, we have combined our approach with the research presented in [18] and have developed a robust mechanism to detect normative conflicts in MAS.

The detection of normative conflicts is made according to three steps, as follows. The first step consists in creating a mechanism that maps the elements that compose the norms to words and after that, search for relationships between words. In this step, several cases of normative conflicts were defined that can be inferred using WordNet as source of information. This step is responsible for detecting domain-independent conflicts. The second step extends the approach presented in [18] so that it can be integrated with the mechanism created in the first step in order to detect domain-dependent conflicts. The third step consists of integrating the first and second steps and creating a tool for checking indirect conflicts involving relationships that depend or not of the domain.

In addition of detecting normative conflicts, the mechanism proposed is also able to solve conflicts. The resolution mechanism resolves normative conflicts between pair of norms based on four strategies. Each strategy, except the first one, changes somehow the activation/deactivation conditions of one of the conflicting norms in order to eliminate the overlap between the periods in which these norms are active. In order to select which norm is to be changed we proposed the following criteria. First, our resolution mechanism chooses to change the norm where the result does not eliminate the entire norm. In other words, it tries to save as much as possible both norms when the resolution mechanism eliminates the intersections between activation periods of the norms in conflict. If the choice does not matter, i.e., the result does not eliminate entirely either norm in conflict, our resolution mechanism uses *lex specialis* in order to select which norm is to be changed. If no specialization relationship is detected, the selection is based on their modality. The first strategy simply removes one of the norms in conflict. The resolution mechanism applies it when both norms are active at the same period of time (their activation and deactivation conditions are exactly the same). The same criteria based on relationships identified (*lex specialis*) or norm modality are used to select which norm is to be removed. The result is a set of norms free of conflict.

One limitation of our approach is that the proposed mechanism cannot distinguish words that are homonymous, that is, words whose spelling is the same, but have different meanings when inserted in different contexts. For example, the word *doctor* may refer to *a person graduated in medicine* (medical context) or *a person who holds a doctorate degree* (academic context). This problem is known as Lexical Disambiguation of Meaning (LDM) or Word Sense Disambiguation (WSD) in Artificial Intelligence (AI) [7]. The lexical disambiguation could be done by analyzing the grammatical class of the word and perform an analysis involving all the elements that compose the norm (context, entity, action, object). Other possible strategy could investigate the semantic similarity between two words, that is, it could use metrics to calculate numerical values that determine the proximity between a word and a concept that contains a certain word or simply analyze the words contained in the description (called "gloss") of each WordNet synset. However, since most existing LDM methods require high computational complexity and do not provide a guarantee of certainty we did not address lexical disambiguation. Additionally, in practice, such ambiguities are unlikely to occur during conflict detection because, in general, norms are related to the same domain or related ones. We adopt a heuristic of disambiguation that consists in adopting the most common sense of the language (this is possible because the WordNet sorts the synsets according to their frequency of use). Other known approaches to address the disambiguation problem are presented in [9].

The research presented in this paper provided a mechanism that can help software engineers to design/include norms in a MAS in a consistent way. Software engineers/system designers only need to specify in a domain ontology relationships that do not occur in the real world. We consider that this mechanism represents a great contribution to the area of MAS since a large set of norms can be verified automatically in order to find conflicts/inconsistencies and the conflicts found can also be resolved automatically. As future work we will focus on the detection of other kinds of conflicts, such as, cases of domain-independent conflicts between norms that regulate states. This can be implemented by using the majority of relationships defined between actions, but by referring to another grammar class, i.e., states could be mapped to adjectives. Other possible direction for future research is to receive as input of the algorithm norms and description of relationships in natural language. We also intend to improve our mechanism including other kinds of strategies for solving conflicts and to allow that the user (system designer/software engineer) chooses the most appropriate resolution method among different strategies.

## References

1. Aphale, M.S., Norman, T.J., Şensoy, M.: Goal-directed policy conflict detection and prioritisation. In: Aldewereld, H., Sichman, J.S. (eds.) COIN 2012. LNCS (LNAI), vol. 7756, pp. 87–104. Springer, Heidelberg (2013). https://doi.org/10.1007/978-3-642-37756-3_6
2. Şensoy, M., Norman, T.J., Vasconcelos, W.W., Sycara, K.: OWL-POLAR: a framework for semantic policy representation and reasoning. Web Semant. Sci. Serv. Agents World Wide Web **12–13**, 148–160 (2012)
3. Fenech, S., Pace, G.J., Schneider, G.: Detection of conflicts in electronic contracts. In: NWPT 2008, p. 34 (2008)
4. Gaertner, D., Garcia-Camino, A., Noriega, P., Rodriguez-Aguilar, J.A., Vasconcelos, W.W.: Distributed norm management in regulated multiagent systems. In: Proceedings of the 6th International Joint Conference on Autonomous Agents and Multiagent Systems, AAMAS 2007, pp. 90:1–90:8. ACM, New York (2007)
5. Giannikis, G.K., Daskalopulu, A.: Normative conflicts in electronic contracts. Electron. Commer. Res. Appl. **10**(2), 247–267 (2011)
6. Günay, A., Yolum, P.: Engineering conflict-free multiagent systems. In: First International Workshop on Engineering Multiagent Systems (EMAS) (2013)
7. Ide, N., Véronis, J.: Introduction to the special issue on word sense disambiguation: the state of the art. Comput. Linguist. **24**(1), 2–40 (1998)
8. Kollingbaum, M.J., Norman, T.J., Preece, A., Sleeman, D.: Norm conflicts and inconsistencies in virtual organisations. In: Noriega, P., et al. (eds.) COIN -2006. LNCS (LNAI), vol. 4386, pp. 245–258. Springer, Heidelberg (2007). https://doi.org/10.1007/978-3-540-74459-7_16
9. Mihalcea, R.: Knowledge-based methods for WSD. In: Agirre, E., Edmonds, P. (eds.) Word Sense Disambiguation. Text, Speech and Language Technology, vol. 33, pp. 107–131. Springer, Dordrecht (2007). https://doi.org/10.1007/978-1-4020-4809-8_5
10. Miller, G.A.: WordNet: a lexical database for English. Commun. ACM **38**(11), 39–41 (1995)
11. dos Santos Neto, B.F., da Silva, V.T., de Lucena, C.J.P.: An architectural model for autonomous normative agents. In: Barros, L.N., Finger, M., Pozo, A.T., Gimenénez-Lugo, G.A., Castilho, M. (eds.) SBIA 2012. LNCS (LNAI), pp. 152–161. Springer, Heidelberg (2012). https://doi.org/10.1007/978-3-642-34459-6_16

12. dos Santos Neto, B.F., da Silva, V.T., de Lucena, C.J.P.: Developing goal-oriented normative agents: the NBDI architecture. In: Filipe, J., Fred, A. (eds.) ICAART 2011. CCIS, vol. 271, pp. 176–191. Springer, Heidelberg (2013). https://doi.org/10.1007/978-3-642-29966-7_12
13. Santos, J.S., Silva, V.T.: Identifying domain-independent normative indirect conflicts. In: 2016 IEEE 28th International Conference on Tools with Artificial Intelligence (ICTAI), 2016, San Jose, p. 536 (2016)
14. Santos, J.S., Silva, V.T.: A novel tool for detecting indirect normative conflicts in multi-agent systems. In: 10th International Conference on Agents and Artificial Intelligence, 2018, Funchal. Proceedings of the 10th International Conference on Agents and Artificial Intelligence, p. 70 (2018)
15. Santos, J.S., Zahn, J.O., Silvestre, E.A., Silva, V.T., Vasconcelos, W.W.: Detection and resolution of normative conflicts in multi-agent systems: a literature survey. Auton. Agents Multi-Agent Syst. 1–47 (2017). https://doi.org/10.1007/S10458-017-9362-Z
16. Vasconcelos, W.W., Kollingbaum, M.J., Norman, T.J.: Normative conflict resolution in multiagent systems. Auton. Agents Multi-Agent Syst. **19**(2), 124–152 (2009)
17. Vasconcelos, W.W., García-Camino, A., Gaertner, D., Rodríguez-Aguilar, J.A., Noriega, P.: Distributed norm management for multi-agent systems. Expert. Syst. Appl. **39**(5), 5990–5999 (2012)
18. Zahn, J.O.: Um Mecanismo de Verificação de Conflitos Normativos Indiretos. Master's thesis, Instituto de Computação - Universidade Federal Fluminense (IC/UFF), Niterói, Brasil (2015)

# Comparative Quantitative Evaluation of Distributed Methods for Explanation Generation and Validation of Floor Plan Recommendations

Christian Espinoza-Stapelfeld[1], Viktor Eisenstadt[1(✉)], and Klaus-Dieter Althoff[1,2]

[1] Institute of Computer Science, Intelligent Information Systems Lab (IIS), University of Hildesheim, Samelsonplatz 1, 31141 Hildesheim, Germany
{christian.espinoza-stapelfeld,viktor.eisenstadt}@uni-hildesheim.de, klaus-dieter.althoff@dfki.de

[2] German Research Center for Artificial Intelligence, Trippstadter Strasse 122, 67663 Kaiserslautern, Germany

**Abstract.** In this work, we compare different explanation generation and validation methods for semantic search pattern-based retrieval results returned by a case-based framework for support of early conceptual design phases in architecture. Compared methods include two case- and rule-based explanation engines, the third one is the discriminant analysis-based method for explanation and validation prediction and estimation. All of the explanation methods use the same data set for retrieval and subsequent explainability operations for results. We describe the main structure of each method and evaluate their quantitative validation performance against each other. The goal of this work is to examine which method performs better under which circumstances, at which point in time, and how good the potential explanation ant its validation can be predicted in general. To evaluate these issues, we compare not only the general performance, i.e., the average rate of valid explanations but also how the validation rate changes over time using a number of time steps for this comparison. We also show for which search pattern type which methods perform better.

**Keywords:** Case-based design
Ditributed artificial intelligence · Explainable agents
Comparative evaluation · Discriminant analysis · Validation
Semantic search

## 1 Introduction

Explainability of artificial intelligence systems (also known as Explainable AI or XAI) is currently a much discussed topic in the area of AI research. Many approaches were started and new trends of this research topic are discussed,


J. van den Herik and A. P. Rocha (Eds.): ICAART 2018, LNAI 11352, pp. 46–63, 2019.
https://doi.org/10.1007/978-3-030-05453-3_3

for example, at the XAI Workshop. For distributed AI systems, that rely on case-based reasoning (CBR) as its main underlying reasoning means, a number of approaches, but even more general theoretical foundations, were presented. However, in the combined research area of computer-aided architectural design (CAAD), multi-agent systems (MAS), and CBR no such approach has been presented to date (except our approach [1]) and no comparative evaluation between the approaches was conducted. In this paper, we present such a comparative evaluation between three explanation approaches implemented in MetisCBR, a distributed case-based framework for support of early phases in architectural conceptual design. The framework prototype was developed during the activities of Metis[1], a joint basic research project for the research domains of CBR, MAS, and CAAD.

The initial core functionality of MetisCBR was the retrieval of possibly helpful building design recommendations that could provide inspiration for the user (architect) during his or her conceptualization process. However, the growing interest of the AI community in XAI, user experience requirements for modern recommendation engines, and the absence of a versatile working explanation generation approach for retrieval results among the CAAD support software, lead to the idea of conceptualization and implementation of an explanation module for MetisCBR, whose first version [1] was based on explanation patterns and a ruleset for their detection. The explanation engine of MetisCBR is aimed at answering the questions of how the framework was able to find the results presented, what is the purpose of presenting exactly this set of results (i.e., why they are recommended), and which semantic and relational differences and similarities between the query and each of the single results are crucial and lead to inclusion of this result in the final result set.

After the first version of the explanation module, also called *the Explainer*, two other versions were conceptualized and implemented: an advanced version of the Explainer *(Explainer-2)* and an explanation estimation approach based on discriminant analysis (*DA-Explainer*, currently still in the early stage of development). In this paper, we compare all three approaches with each other in terms of their functionality for estimation of an explanation to be correctly produced, i.e., to contain a valid explanation expression.

This paper is structured as follows: related work for XAI in CBR and MAS will be presented in Sect. 2. In the next section, we give a short description of the MetisCBR framework: its main functionalities, including semantic search patterns, will be briefly described. In Sect. 4, we in detail present the explanation approaches implemented in MetisCBR. The comparative evaluation of these approaches will be described in detail in Sect. 5. The last section concludes this work and provides an outlook of our future research.

[1] http://ksd.ai.ar.tum.de/?page_id=240&lang=en.

## 2 Related Work

In this section we present work related to the purposes of this paper, i.e., work released in the research domains of (explainable) CBR and MAS, and the CBR-based approaches for support of architectural design phases.

### 2.1 Explainable CBR and MAS

CBR has a long and rich history in conceptualization and implementation of explainability features in the corresponding case-based systems. Early work on explanations for CBR approaches [2] was one of the precursors for the development of theoretical foundations for this area. Later, Roth-Berghofer [3] presented general questions of CBR-based explainability and examined a number of future research directions. The theoretical foundations of explanation problem frames for intelligent systems (see Sect. 4.2) were discussed by Cassens and Kofod-Petersen [4]. On the practical side, an explanation-aware system module for the CBR software myCBR was presented [3].

For the MAS research area, the most notable explainability approach is an explainable BDI (belief, desire, intention) agent [5,6]. These research contributions describe an explanation module inside a BDI architecture-based agent that contains a so-called *behavior log* that is parsed by an explanation algorithm for finding beliefs and goals for the current explanation of actions.

### 2.2 CBR-Based Architectural Design Support

CBR was one of the first AI areas to support the conceptual design phases by means of applying case-based decision support approaches, such as FABEL [7], PRECEDENTS [8], SEED [9], DIM [10], VAT (Visual Architectural Topology, a semantic representation method) [11], or CaseBook [12]. The latter approach CaseBook is the only one known to contain an explicit explainability feature, the *similarity explanation report*, but information available in [12] does not provide a sufficient amount of insight into this feature.

A comprehensive review of these and other CBR-based architectural design support approaches is available in [13]. Another seminal work [14] contains a detailed review of CBR's current state, influence, and history in CAAD. Current issues of CBR in CAAD are published in a short review [15].

## 3 MetisCBR

The MetisCBR framework prototype for support of early design phases of the architectural conceptualization process is based on a distributed structure where the agents of the system perform a case-based search for similar architectural designs in a database (case base) of previous designs. After the search the system automatically applies an explanation process for each single result in the result set and enriches the result, if possible, with explanations. The available explanation methods, that are the evaluated in this paper, are described in Sect. 4.

The actual search for similar architectural designs is performed by means of applying a number of semantic search patterns *(semantic fingerprints)* – (graph-based) abstractions of established architectural room configuration concepts, such as adjacency of rooms, or availability of natural light for the rooms. The list of fingerpints (FPs) currently implemented in MetisCBR is shown in Fig. 1.

Fingerprints can be divided into graph-based (FP3, FP5, FP6, FP7) and metadata-based, i.e., use an abstract summarizing attribute, such as count of available rooms, for comparison (FP1, FP2, FP4). Multiple fingerpints can be applied for each query/request to the system, result sets of each particular fingerprint search are then combined/amalgamated and presented to the user. For graph-based FPs, a pre-selection step is applied during retrieval, that governs the exclusion of the non-similar atomic parts of a floor plan (such as rooms and room connections) from the search process.

MetisCBR has been object of different comparative evaluations of retrieval methods for search of architectural designs. Examples of such evaluations are the perfomance comparison and qualitative evaluation with graph-based methods of the Metis project [16], and the comparison with the rule-based retrieval coordination software KSD Coordinator [17].

## 4 Explanation Generation Methods

In this section, we present the explanation generation and validation methods of MetisCBR that were used in the comparative evaluation presented in Sect. 5. Each of the methods will be presented including the description of its general structure and functionality, how the explanation patterns are applied, and how the validation of generated explanations is performed. Before the actual description of the methods, we give a short review of general requirements for explanation methods to be used for MetisCBR.

### 4.1 General Explainability Requirements for MetisCBR

Generally, MetisCBR can use every compatible explanation method that can interpret the agent messages constructed with the FIPA-SL language. The main requirement for explanation methods to be used in MetisCBR, however, is that it should be able not only to produce/generate explanations but also validate them. The validation step is an essential one as it ensures the general quality of explanations and can exclude explanations that make no sense to the user. Which validation method is used is a decision of the method's developers, however, it is advisable to make the validation process transparent to be able to compare it to other methods.

For explanations themselves, *explanation patterns* (see Sect. 4.2) should be used. Alternatively the explanations should be able to answer the why-, how-, purpose-questions as described by Roth-Berghofer [3]. This ensures the common explanation structure for all explainable recommendations and provides the user with a familiar structure of expressions.

| Fingerprint | Name / Specifics | Fingerprint | Name / Specifics |
|---|---|---|---|
| FP1 | **Room Count** No connections between rooms and no labels specified | FP5 | **Adjacency** Rooms information is complete, no edge labels |
| FP2 | **Relation Count** No room information specified | FP6 | **Accessibility** Edge information is complete, no room labels |
| FP3 | **Room Graph** Anonymous representation (no labels) of rooms & edges | FP7 | **Full Graph** All information about rooms and edges available |
| FP4 | **Room Types** No room connections, only room labels are specified | FP8 | **Natural Light** Light condition attributes |

**Fig. 1.** Semantic search patterns (FPs) currently implemented in MetisCBR. Figure from [1].

### 4.2 Explanation Problem Frames and Patterns

A framework for *explanation patterns* for intelligent information systems and applications was conceptualized by Cassens and Kofod-Petersen [4] to provide such systems with a possibility to make the behaviour of such systems more transparent and traceable for their users. Initially conceptualized for case-based reasoning applications, the patterns can be used for almost every type of an intelligent AI system that follows their structure, i.e., uses the patterns with their initially conceptualized structure and purpose. Explanation patterns themselves are based on *Problem Frames* conceptualized by Jackson [18]. Thus, the patterns enhance the problem frames for use for explainability problems. A number of different patterns was conceptualized that provide different explanation functions. The most important of them, and implemented in all our examined explanation methods are *Justification*, *Transparency*, and *Relevance*. The adaptation of explanation patterns for MetisCBR is shown in Fig. 3.

**Relevance Pattern.** The Relevance pattern is aimed at explaining why the question that the systems asks the user is relevant in the current context. For the purposes of our design support framework, this means that the system may ask the user (an architect) for more relevant data for proper comparison of case and query if the structural and relational connections provided in the query

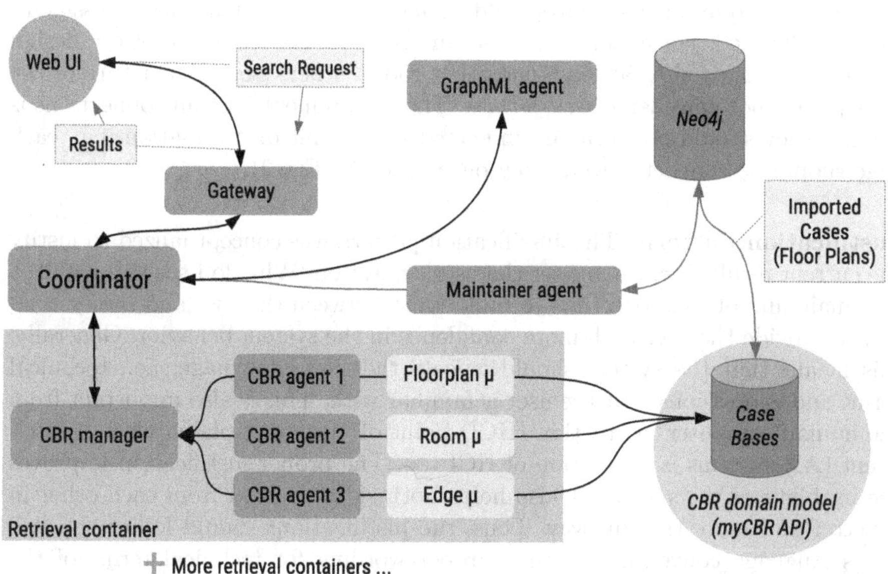


**Fig. 2.** Overview over the retrieval component of MetisCBR. Figure from [16].

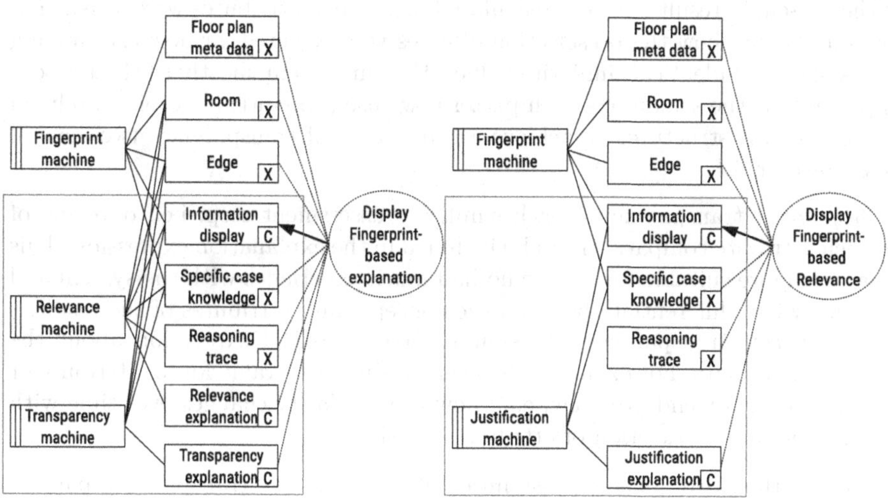


**Fig. 3.** Explanation patterns in MetisCBR. Highlighted in blue rectangles are the original patterns [4]. `C` denotes the goal of explanation, `X` is the system knowledge. Figure adapted from [1]. (Colour figure online)

did not contain sufficient amount of information. Usually, this is the case when some of the requirements, that should be met for proper similarity assessment, were not fulfilled. For example, a room in the room configuration of the design should be connected to at least one other room, otherwise the structure of the floor plan is not considered *well-formed*. The requirement for rom connections is similar, they should not have an undefined start point or destination, i.e., each edge should be connected to a room on both ends (Fig. 2).

**Justification Pattern.** The Justification pattern was conceptualized to justify the current results, i.e., to answer the user's question 'Why do I see this result?'. The main aim of this pattern is to build trust between the user and the system, i.e., to provide the user with more confidence in the system behavior. Generally, this means that the system should 'speak' the user's language, i.e., technical terms and expressions that the user is familiar with. This is also important from the human-computer interaction (HCI) point of view as explainability of intelligent (AI) systems is a question of HCI too. The proper justification improves the usability of the system, it also helps both sides to learn from each other in a better and more trustful way. Thus, the justifications should follow the system's language conventions with a proper wording for technical terms of the explanation expression.

**Transparency Pattern.** The Transparency pattern's goal is to provide the user with information of *how* the result was reached by the system. That is, it should be made transparent, for example, how exactly the final similarity value of the presented result has been calculated, i.e., which attributes were considered for comparison, how the preselection of cases was executed, or how the ranking works in case of identical similarity values. For our system, mostly the first case is important, as the semantic search patterns we use (semantic fingerpints) rely on attribute-value-structure. To achieve a good grade of transparency, two general possibilities exist:

- *Sequential* transparency – each similarity assessment step, i.e., outcome of each attribute comparison can be included in the explanation expression. This way is more suitable for users who had much experience with the system and quickly can differentiate between the concepts and attributes of the result.
- *Cumulative* transparency – a summarized statistical expression about the assessment data. For example, the average similarity value for an attribute or concept, or a trend overview, e.g., how the similarity changes over time with addition and/or deletion of attributes considered.

Beside this, two general possibilities of assigning the transparency pattern expression to the retrieval results are available:

- *Global* transparency that is assigned to the complete result set and can be placed over all of the single results to provide a general transparency expression about the results. The above mentioned cumulative transparency is usually used for this global expression.

– *Local* transparency that is provided for a single result to enrich it with insights for its own similarity assessment only. Cumulative as well as sequential transparency can be used for this type of transparency assignment.

### 4.3 CBR-Explainer-1

The first version of the explanation module for MetisCBR, the Explainer, was created to initially implement the explanation patterns for retrieval of architectural designs. This version implemented pattern detection based on a common ruleset for all patterns, however, it did not use the particular attributes of rooms and edges and relied on floor plan metadata only. Following exemplary rules can be applied (rules form our paper on the first version of the Explainer [1]):

– `FP 1, 2, 4, 8`: The pattern 'Transparency' is detected if 2/3 properties from {`Room Count, Edge Count, Room Types`} could be detected in the meta data of the query floor plan.
– `FP 1, 2, 4, 8`: The pattern 'Justification' is detected if the similarity grade of the result floor plan is better than *unsimilar.*
– `FP 6`: The pattern 'Transparency' is detected if *all* properties from {`Room Count, Edge Count, Edge Types`} could be detected in the meta data of the query floor plan.
– `FP 7`: The pattern 'Justification' is detected if the similarity grade of the result floor plan is better than *unsimilar* and all properties from {`Room Count, Edge Count, Room Types, Edge Types`} could be detected in the meta data of the query floor plan.

The first version of the Explainer (CBR-Explainer-1) employed two agents responsible for creation and validation of explanation expressions: the *Explanation Deliverer* agent, who is responsible for receiving of the query and result to be explained and sending the results enriched with explanations back for displaying in the user interface; and the *Explanation Creator* agent responsible for generation and validation of actual explanation expressions. In Fig. 4, the general structure of the CBR-Explainer-1 is shown.

The validation process in the CBR-Explainer-1 is implemented as a case-based validation process. That is, each produced explanation is handled as a case and gets validated against the case base of ground-truth explanations provided by an expert in the architectural domain/CAAD. The maximum similarity value from the comparison with each of the ground-truth explanations becomes then the *validation similarity* $v_{max}$. If $v_{max}$ exceeds a specified threshold, then the produced explanation is considered valid. The similarity measure for validation determination is a dynamically adapted weighted sum, i.e., the weights get adapted with increasing/decreasing of the number of detected patterns. Attributes used for the dynamically weighted sum are shown in Table 1.

After the validation process, the *Explanation Creator* adds the explanation, if valid, to the result object and sends it to the *Explanation Deliverer*, which in turn sends it to the *Result Collector* agent that is responsible for collection of results for all FPs of the current query.

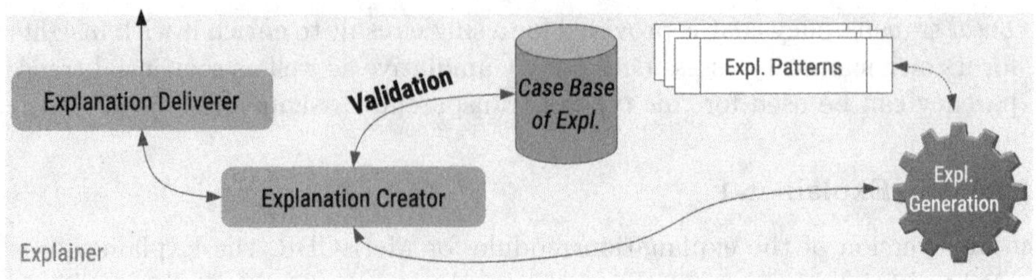


**Fig. 4.** General structure of the first version of the MetisCBR explanation module (Figure adapted from [1]).

**Table 1.** Attributes for validation in the CBR-Explainer-1 (Table from [1]).

| Attribute | Type | Description | Similarity Func. |
|---|---|---|---|
| `id` | `string` | Internal Explanation ID | *not in use* |
| `Case` | `string` | Reference to the case (result) | *not in use* |
| `Query` | `string` | Reference to the query | *not in use* |
| `Text` | `string` | Text of the explanation | Levenshtein dist. sim |
| `PatternJustification` | `boolean` | Justification pattern available? | boolean comparison |
| `PatternRelevance` | `boolean` | Relevance pattern available? | boolean comparison |
| `PatternTransparency` | `boolean` | Transparency pattern available? | boolean comparison |

### 4.4 CBR-Explainer-2

The second version of the Explainer, the CBR-Explainer-2, is an advanced version of the CBR-Explainer-1 and is intended to provide a more detailed, and thus restricted, explanation approach which also takes the particular attribute values of the room and room connection concepts into account. Structurally, the tasks of the agents of the Explainer remained the same, however, for each explanation pattern a special *pattern agent* was created that works with its assigned pattern only and communicates with the Creator. In Fig. 5, the general structure of CBR-Explainer-2 is shown.

The detection of patterns is different for almost all patterns. For the Relevance pattern, the CBR-Explainer-2 analyzes all rooms and room connections of the query and the currently compared case for availability of specific requirements. If the required features are not available, e.g., a room does not have connections or its label is unknown to the system, or an edge does not have a source or target, then it is not considered for comparison. If a certain percent (determined by a special *Relevance score*) of rooms and edges does not provide a proper feature set, then the complete query is not considered for comparison and gets the *Relevanvce label* of `true`, otherwise this label is `false`.

If the Relevance label is `true`, the Justification and Transparency detection does not take place. Otherwise the pattern recognition continues with Justification, where the justification expression, like in the CBR-Explainer-1 depends on the *similarity grade* of the result. After Justification, Transparency is detected by means of applying a two-step reasoning process, where in the first step all available similarity data is collected for each room and room conection of the result. This data contains all historical comparison information in the context of the current query, including how often the room or edge has been used for each FP. The collected data is then cumulated (see also Sect. 4.4) and added as local transparency to each of the single results, for the complete result set this data is also cumulated and added as global transparency expression.

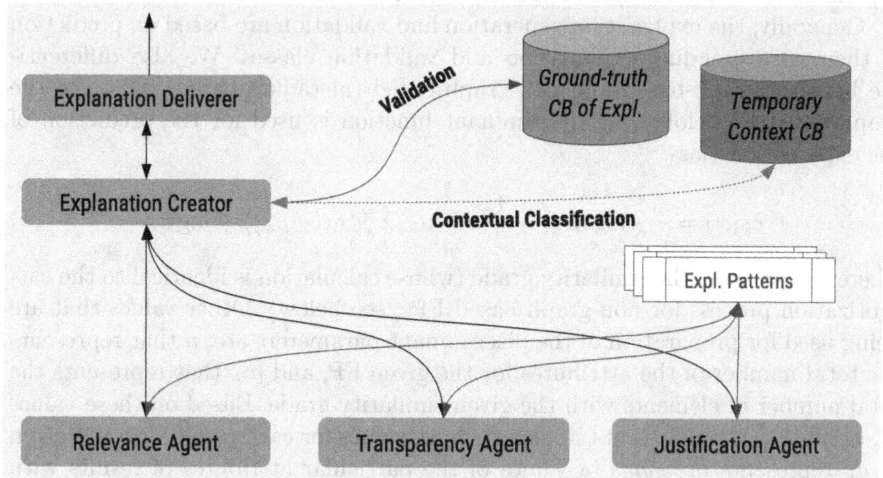


**Fig. 5.** General structure of the second version of the MetisCBR explanation module, the CBR-Explainer-2.

The validation process in the CBR-Explainer-2 is similar to that of the first version, however, the expression text similarity with Levenshtein distance has been replaced in the second version with the name of the semantic fingerprint and the overall similarity value of the result to provide a more exact comparison. The dynamic adaptation has also been replaced by a static weight distribution, as in the CBR-Explainer-2 the unrecognized explanation patterns are patrt of the similarity assessment as well. The mode of operation for determination of the validation similarity $v_{max}$ remained identical in the CBR-Explainer-2.

The special feature of the CBR-Explainer-2, which is however not part of the comparative evaluation, is the contextual classification of the results with valid explanations. That is, each result of each FP is parsed by a *feature extraction* engine and is decomposed in its main features such as room count, edge count, or room types set. All of these features are then analyzed for their potential to include the result in a specific context class. A context class is a category of results with special properties, such as RoomTypeDominace for *floor plans with a room type that dominates over all other room types*, i.e., takes more than 50% of the entire room type set. The main purpose of the contextual classification is automatic tagging of the result floor plans.

### 4.5 DA-Explainer

The third possibility of creation of explanations for floor plan retrieval results is based on *discriminant analysis* (DA), a well-known versatile classification method of machine learning. The adaptation of discriminant analysis for the purposes of the Explainer module of MetisCBR has been explored by Espinoza-Stapelfeld [19] where a detailed description of DA for each semantic fingerprint and explanation patterns is available. In this paper, like for the previous two explainers, we give only a description of the relevant features.

Generally, the explanation generation and validation are based on prediction of their corresponding explanation and validation classes. We also differentiate between graph-based and non-graph-based (metadata-based) FPs. For the graph-based FPs, following discriminant function is used for the prediction of the explanation class:

$$c_k(x) = -\frac{1}{2}\log|\Sigma_k| - \frac{1}{2}\langle x - \mu_k, \Sigma_k^{-1}(x - \mu_k)\rangle + \log \pi_k \tag{1}$$

where $k$ represents the similarity grade (whose calculation is identical to the categorization process for non-graph-based FPs, see below). Other values that are being used for preparation of the discriminant parameters are: $n$ that represents the total number of the attributes for the given FP, and $m_k$ that represents the total number of elements with the given similarity grade. Based on these values ($k$, $n$, and $m_k$), $x$ represents single attribute values for each result with the given $k$; $\mu_k$ represents *the sums* of values of the particular attributes of results with the given $k$ divided by $m_k$; $\Sigma_k$ represents the products of $(x - \mu_k)$ and $(x - \mu_k)^T$ with factor $m_k$, and $\pi_k = m_k/n$.

For non-graph-based fingerprints, a decision tree is used that categorizes the result into one of the explanation classes: A if result's overall similarity $Sim \geq 0.75$, B if $0.75 > Sim \geq 0.5$, C if $0.5 > Sim \geq 0.25$, and D if $Sim < 0.25$. After the predicted class is determined, the assignment of the explanation patterns, that are in turn assigned to the classes, takes place. Following explanation classes are available for the patterns:

1. A – High Justification, High Transparency, i.e., a sufficient amount of information is available in query and result to perform a similarity-based comparison between them.
2. B – Middle Justification, Middle Transparency.
3. C – Low Justification, Low Transparency, i.e., information in query and result is sufficient, but local similarity values are very low and do not allow for recommendation of this floor plan.
4. D – Relevance only, i.e., more information is required for a proper comparison between query and result.

After the assignment of explanation patterns, a validation estimation process takes place. The DA-Explainer does not use a case base for validation, instead, its validation process is intended to sort candidates for validation in the both above described explainers. Like in the assignment of explanation classes, we differentiate between graph-based and non-graph-based FPs. However, for the non-graph-based FPs, no explicit validation process is conducted, instead, the class determined in the explanation classification process is mapped to its corresponding validation estimation class $v$ (`A` to `V1`, `B` to `V2`, `C` to `V3`, `D` to `V4`). For graph-based FPs, following formula is used first to estimate the validation candidacy for the complete result set:

$$v_k(x) = -\frac{1}{2}\log|\Sigma_k| - \log|(x - \mu_k)| + \log\pi_k \tag{2}$$

The validation estimation class can then be one of the following:

1. `V1` – Highest category, the results with this class are most likely will produce a valid explanation.
2. `V2` – Middle category, the results with this class have a good probability to produce a valid explanation.
3. `V3` – Weak candidate, validation of its explanation can produce an insufficient value (below threshold).
4. `V4` – Not recommended for validation of explanation.

After that $v_k(x)$ is multiplied with the overall similarity value of each of the floor plans, so that an individual validation estimation value for each single result can be calculated.

## 5 Comparative Evaluation

To quantitatively compare the performance of all three above described explanation generation and validation methods we decided to conduct an experiment with all methods on the same data set and to answer three general questions (Q[n]):

1. Which method has a better validation performance for a common query set?
2. Which method performs validation better over time?
3. Which method has the best performance for which type of FPs?

For all questions, specific aspects of each method should be considered:

- CBR-Explainer-2 is a more advanced, however, also more restricted version of CBR-Explainer-1 in terms of the validation process, i.e., it uses more attributes for validation and does not adapt weights in favor of the number of detected explanation patterns. From a reversed point of view, the CBR-Explainer-1 is a light and more permissible method.
- DA-Explainer is a non-CBR method, that is, it is not fully adapted to the main distributed case-based paradigm of MetisCBR. However, it provides a different point of view at the validation problem as it is able to apply fuzzy validation estimation with different classes (see Sect. 4.5).

### 5.1 Setting

The evaluation was performed on a common set of 120 retrievable and explainable architectural designs constructed with a special web-based user interface [20]. The designs of the data set were available in different abstraction and complexity levels, see Fig. 6. For validation, the CBR-Explainer-1 and the CBR-Explainer-2 used their own validation base, however, cases in all of these bases referred to the same ground-truth cases provided in the very first validation base (of the CBR-Explainer-1).

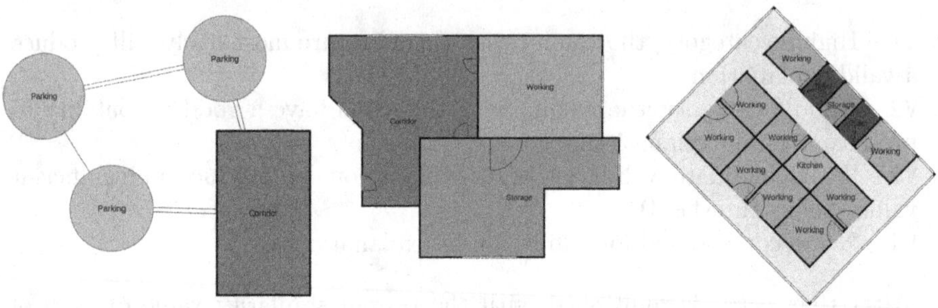


**Fig. 6.** Examples for different abstraction levels of the floor plans contained in the tested case base. From left to right: *abstract*, *semi-abstract*, *non-abstract* (complex).

### 5.2 Results for Q1

In Q1, we were interested in a general performance of each explanation method for a given, common for all three, amount of queries. To accomplish this, we sent 24 different queries for retrieval and subsequent explanation process for each of the methods. Each query included 2 FPs, i.e., consisted of 2 sub-queries, all FPs were the same for each method.

In Fig. 7, the total number of produced explanations is shown. In Fig. 14, the percent of valid explanations for each of the methods is shown. Following validity criteria were applied for the methods:

- `CBR-Explainer-1`, `CBR-Explainer-2`: the explanation is valid if its validation similarity value $v_{max}$ exceeds the threshold value of 0.5.
- `DA-Explainer`: the explanation is estimated valid if the result set's validation class *is not* `V4` and the validation estimation value of the single result is above the threshold of 1.5.

The results of Q1 showed that the DA-Explainer was generally able to predict the amount of possibly valid explanations for both CBR-Explainers, despite its very low total number of explanations produced (which however was developed/implemented on purpose using the discriminant analysis). The both CBR-Explainers also showed a good general rate of valid explanations (Fig. 8).

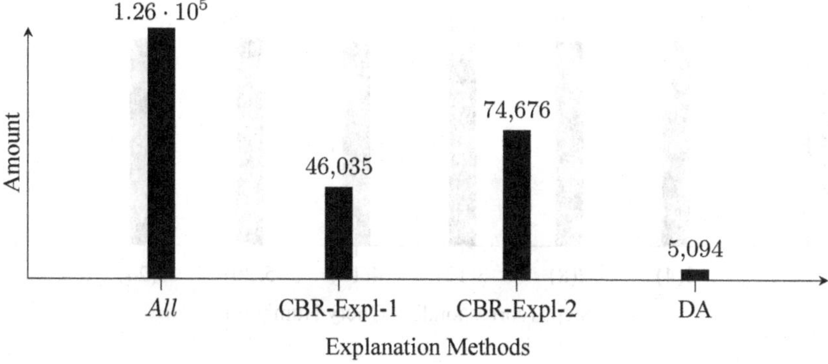


**Fig. 7.** The total numbers of explanations produced.

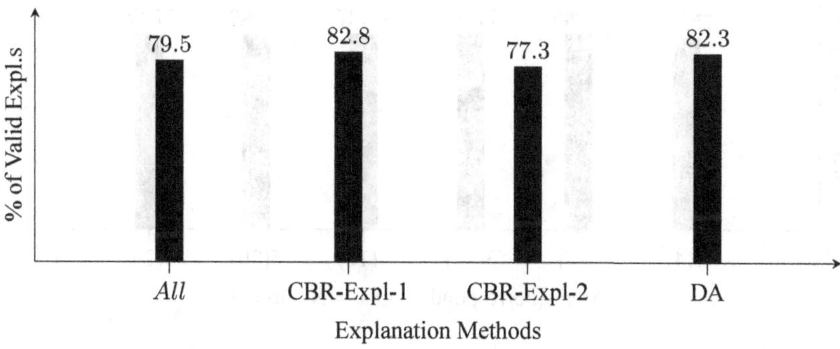


**Fig. 8.** The percent number of valid explanations.

### 5.3 Results for Q2

In Q2, we measured how each of the methods was performing over time, i.e., we also recorded the validation stepwise, after every 4th query (8th sub-query). The reason to perform this measurement was the question of how good or bad the validation percentage will be if the system will run for a longer time. A total number of 6 steps or sub-measurements of validation rate was produced, the results are shown in Figs. 9, 10, and 11.

As the results of Q2 show, the CBR-Explainer-1 shows the most constant performance in this measurement, only once its rate falls below the 82% rate, remaining between 82 – 83% for the other sub-measurements. CBR-Explainer-2 is constant as well, however, its start rate is lower. The most inconstant is the DA-Explainer, its final rate (and even the second) is much lower as its start rate.

### 5.4 Results for Q3

In Q3 we aimed at exploring the performance of the methods for different types of semantic fingerpints. The reason for this measurement is our intention to

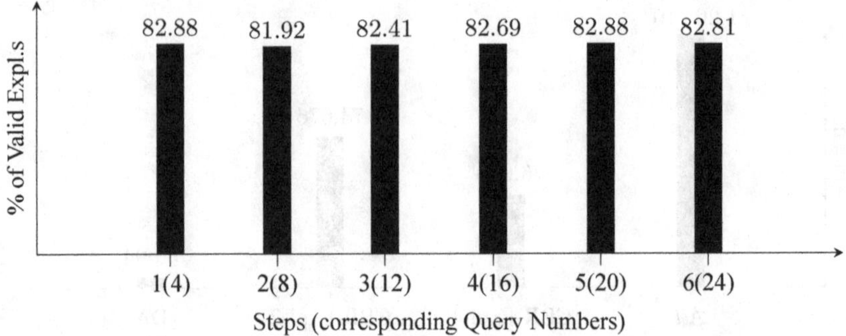


**Fig. 9.** The stepwise measurement of valid explanations for CBR-Explainer-1.

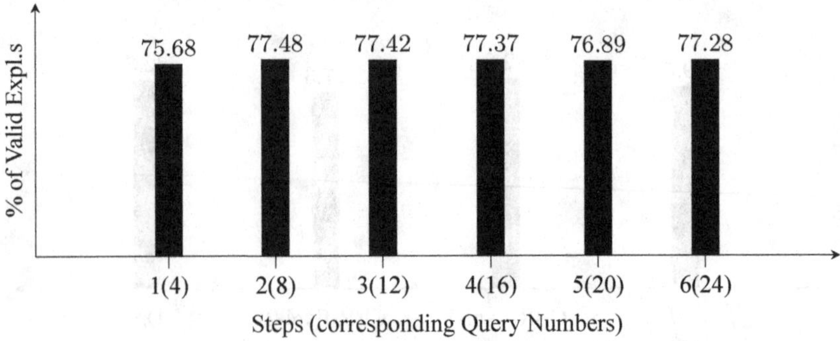


**Fig. 10.** The stepwise measurement of valid explanations for CBR-Explainer-2.

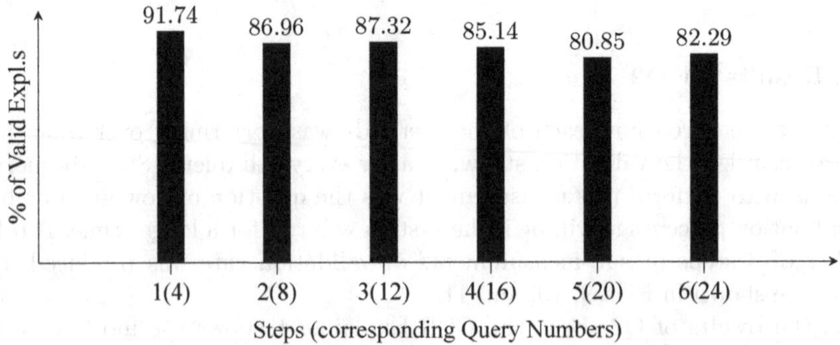


**Fig. 11.** The stepwise measurement of valid explanations for the DA-Explainer.

implement an automatic selection method for choosing the proper explanation method for the corresponding FP type. The results of Q3 for each method are shown below (Fig. 12).

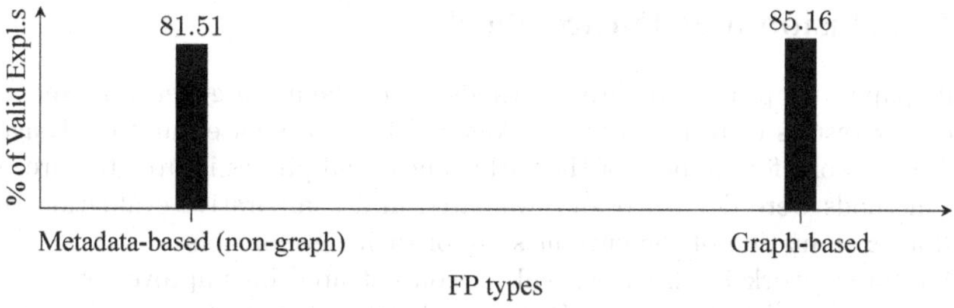


**Fig. 12.** The FP-type-wise measurement of valid explanations for the CBR-Explainer-1.

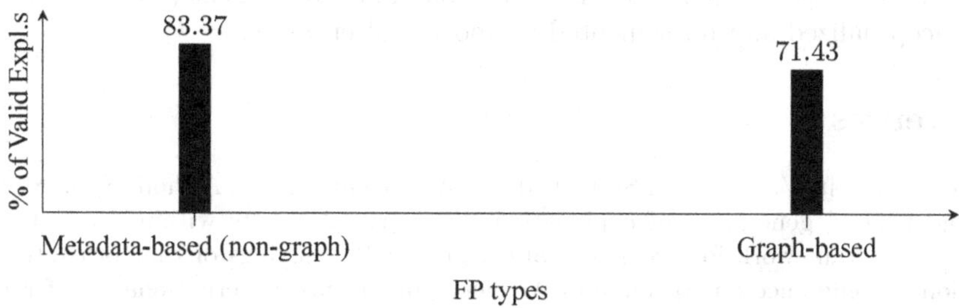


**Fig. 13.** The FP-type-wise measurement of valid explanations for the CBR-Explainer-2.

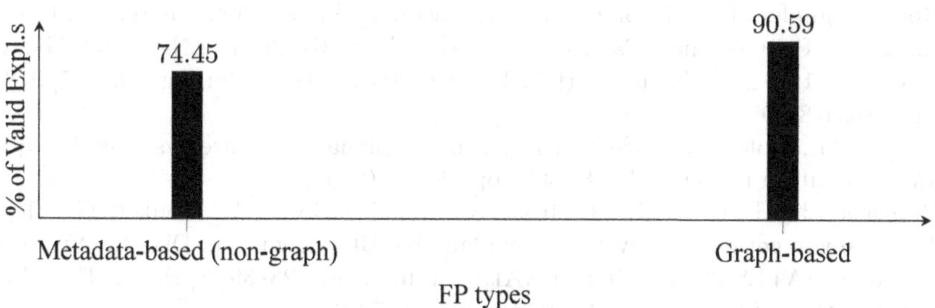


**Fig. 14.** The FP-type-wise measurement of valid explanations for the DA-Explainer.

The results of Q3 showed that for this measurement DA-Explainer performed better on graph-based FPs, that is, its prediction feature can be more trusted for this type of FPs and should be improved for non-graph-FPs. In contrast to the DA-Explainer, the CBR-Explainer-2 performed better on non-graph-based FPs, however the more strict behavior of this explainer is the most probable cause for its results. The CBR-Explainer-1 showed constant values in this measurement, however, for particular types, other explainers performed (slightly) better (Fig. 13).

## 6 Conclusion and Future Work

In this paper, we presented three methods for explanation generation and validation for results of retrieval within MetisCBR, a case-based and multi-agent based framework for support of the early conceptual phases in architecture. All three methods were described and evaluated in a comparative evaluation that aimed at examination of the current state of their development.

Our future work in this area will be concentrated on improvement of the methods presented in this work. For example, the next study we are planning is aimed at detailed examination of the prediction feature of the DA-Explainer to determine if the results and their explanations predicted valid are considered valid by case-based explainers. Also, an explainable BDI-Agent (see Sect. 2) will be conceptualized and implemented as another alternative.

## References


1. Ayzenshtadt, V., Espinoza-Stapelfeld, C.A., Langenhahn, C., Althoff, K.D.: Multi-agent-based generation of explanations for retrieval results within a case-based support framework for architectural design. In: Proceedings of the 10th International Conference on Agents and Artificial Intelligence. International Conference on Agents and Artificial Intelligence (ICAART-18), Scitepress (2018)
2. Aamodt, A.: Explanation-driven case-based reasoning. In: Wess, S., Althoff, K.-D., Richter, M.M. (eds.) EWCBR 1993. LNCS, vol. 837, pp. 274–288. Springer, Heidelberg (1994). https://doi.org/10.1007/3-540-58330-0_93
3. Roth-Berghofer, T.R.: Explanations and case-based reasoning: foundational issues. In: Funk, P., González Calero, P.A. (eds.) ECCBR 2004. LNCS (LNAI), vol. 3155, pp. 195–209. Springer, Heidelberg (2004). https://doi.org/10.1007/978-3-540-28631-8_29
4. Cassens, J., Kofod-Petersen, A.: Designing explanation aware systems: the quest for explanation patterns. In: ExaCt, pp. 20–27 (2007)
5. Broekens, J., Harbers, M., Hindriks, K., van den Bosch, K., Jonker, C., Meyer, J.-J.: Do you get it? user-evaluated explainable BDI agents. In: Dix, J., Witteveen, C. (eds.) MATES 2010. LNCS (LNAI), vol. 6251, pp. 28–39. Springer, Heidelberg (2010). https://doi.org/10.1007/978-3-642-16178-0_5
6. Harbers, M., van den Bosch, K., Meyer, J.J.: Design and evaluation of explainable BDI agents. In: 2010 IEEE/WIC/ACM International Conference on Web Intelligence and Intelligent Agent Technology (WI-IAT), vol. 2, pp. 125–132. IEEE (2010)
7. Voss, A.: Case design specialists in FABEL. In: Issues and Applications of Case-Based Reasoning in Design, pp. 301–335 (1997)
8. Oxman, R., Oxman, R.: Precedents: memory structure in design case libraries. In: CAAD Futures. vol. 93, pp. 273–287 (1993)
9. Flemming, U.: Case-based design in the SEED system. Autom. Constr. **3**, 123–133 (1994)
10. Lai, I.C.: Dynamic idea maps: a framework for linking ideas with cases during brainstorming. Int. J. Architectural Comput. **3**, 429–447 (2005)
11. Lin, C.J.: Visual architectural topology. In: Open Systems: Proceedings of the 18th International Conference on Computer-Aided Architectural Design Research in Asia, pp. 3–12 (2013)

12. Inanc, B.S.: Casebook. an information retrieval system for housing floor plans. In: The Proceedings of 5th Conference on Computer Aided Architectural Design Research (CAADRIA), pp. 389–398 (2000)
13. Richter, K., Heylighen, A., Donath, D.: Looking back to the future-an updated case base of case-based design tools for architecture. In: Knowledge Modelling-eCAADe (2007)
14. Richter, K.: Augmenting Designers' Memory: Case-based Reasoning in Architecture. Logos-Verlag, Berlin (2011)
15. Richter, K.: What a shame-why good ideas can't make it in architecture: a contemporary approach towards the case-based reasoning paradigm in architecture. In: FLAIRS Conference (2013)
16. Sabri, Q.U., Bayer, J., Ayzenshtadt, V., Bukhari, S.S., Althoff, K.D., Dengel, A.: Semantic pattern-based retrieval of architectural floor plans with case-based and graph-based searching techniques and their evaluation and visualization. In: ICPRAM, pp. 50–60 (2017)
17. Ayzenshtadt, V., et al.: Comparative evaluation of rule-based and case-based retrieval coordination for search of architectural building designs. In: Goel, A., Díaz-Agudo, M.B., Roth-Berghofer, T. (eds.) ICCBR 2016. LNCS (LNAI), vol. 9969, pp. 16–31. Springer, Cham (2016). https://doi.org/10.1007/978-3-319-47096-2_2
18. Jackson, M.: Problem analysis using small problem frames. S. Afr. Comput. J. 47–60 (1999)
19. Espinoza, C.: Case-based classification of explanation expressions in search results of a retrieval system for Support of the early conceptual design phase in architecture. Bachelor Thesis. University of Hildesheim (2018)
20. Bayer, J., et al.: Migrating the classical pen-and-paper based conceptual sketching of architecture plans towards computer tools - prototype design and evaluation. In: Lamiroy, B., Dueire Lins, R. (eds.) GREC 2015. LNCS, vol. 9657, pp. 47–59. Springer, Cham (2017). https://doi.org/10.1007/978-3-319-52159-6_4

# Population Dynamics Necessary to Avert Unpopular Norms

Arshad Muhammad[(✉)], Kashif Zia, and Dinesh Kumar Saini

Faculty of Computing and Information Technology, Sohar University, Sohar, Oman
{amuhammad,kzia,dinesh}@su.edu.om

**Abstract.** People lives in the society abide by different norms and sometime these norms are unpopular. Usually, these norms develop within small local community, but later spread out to entire population. It is evidenced that the people not only abide by these norms but also start enforcing in certain situations. It is imperative to know why people enforce a norm they privately oppose. Furthermore, for the overall societal good, many a times, it is necessary to oppose and possibly avert unpopular norms. To achieve this goal, it is necessary to know the conditions, which enable persistence of the unpopular norms and models that support possible aversion of them. This study attempts to elaborate the conditions and reasons for the emergence, spreading and aversion of unpopular norms in society, using theory-driven agent-based simulation. The simulation results reveal that in addition to agents actively participating in averting the unpopular norm, incorporating a rational decision-making model in the population of agents is necessary to achieve a dominant norm aversion.

**Keywords:** Agent-based modeling · Unpopular norms
Emperors dilemma · Norm aversion · Population dynamics

## 1 Introduction

Norms, practices and processes in a society develop over a period of time [25]. Each society has its own norms and behavior and level of acceptance. Social norms have a historical perspective, which evolves into traditions and standards to which a society can relate and act. Societal norms, such as, way of doing things, greetings, festivals celebrations, dressing and code of conduct have a pivotal role in development of social order [27]. An individual in a community is expected to behave according to the societal norms. However, following a norm and believing in it are two different things. There may be other conditions and incentives that force an individual to follow a social norm [23], even when one does not believe in it.

Social norms can be unpopular; a situation in which majority of people do not agree. In fact, people personally do not conform to these so-called "unpopular norms", but follow them and sometimes unintentionally enforce others to


J. van den Herik and A. P. Rocha (Eds.): ICAART 2018, LNAI 11352, pp. 64–75, 2019.
https://doi.org/10.1007/978-3-030-05453-3_4

follow them as well. In a sociology, such situations are dealt through a dilemma, named as **Emperor's Dilemma** as given in [26]. It relates to a tale in which everyone shows fake admiration for the new gown worn by an emperor even though the emperor was naked. The cunning gown designers announced that the (non-existent) gown would not be visible to those who are not loyal to the emperor or who are dumb. The fear of being punished, and identified as having inferior societal traits, no one spoke the truth, but in fact, the emperor was naked.

Unpopular Norm (UN) can be classified into three types; the classification is based on three different causal mechanism [34] - herd behavior (mainly studied by economists), pluralistic ignorance (mainly studied by psychologists) [22,28] and false enforcement.

**Herd behavior** [2,3] is a reaction to widespread uncertainty that lead people to follow others' decision assuming that they have more accurate and/or reliable information, but in reality they are following the herd believing that "this many people cannot be wrong" [21]. Other examples of herd behavior can be observed in financial markets, such as bubbles and crashes [15] and bank runs [1]. **Pluralistic ignorance** term first used by Katz [10], describes the situation where majority of people reject the norm privately, but assume (incorrectly) that the majority accept it. Like herd behavior, pluralistic ignorance is based on false belief resulted in self-reinforcing. In herd behavior, people copy others behavior assuming (wrongly) to have better information, while in pluralistic ignorance people suppress their disagreement and copy others behavior assumed (again wrongly) to follow the majority.

Silently following an unpopular norm at an individual level is one thing. But, when a large population adopts it, following an unpopular norm becomes a kind of default behavior and influence the section of the population, which does not follow or remains neutral. As a consequence, it has been observed that people even start enforcing unpopular norm to which they personally disapprove. This behavior can be termed as **false enforcement** [20,34] have focused on discovering the reason of wrong enforcement. The authors opinion that people falsely enforce unpopular norms to create an illusion of sincerity rather than conviction. The study has been tested in two experiments of wine tasting and text evaluation. Both experiments reveal that people who enforced a norm, even against their actual belief, in fact, criticized deviants of the norm (the alternates of the unpopular norm). These outcomes indicate how social pressure can lead to false enforcement of an unpopular norm.

In many places around the world, manifestations of Emperor's dilemma are evident. Whether it is foot-binding in neo-Confucian China or inter-cousin marriages and dowry in Asia (indicated by Blake in [4] and Hughes in [9], respectively). People do not reveal what they believe due to the fear of being identified as ignorant or anti-social. However, there are evidences that a minority of activists can make a big difference if the environment is conducive as indicated by Khondker in [11]. Hence, the question *"Can a minority of activists change an unpopular norm adopted by the majority?"* becomes relevant.

Essentially, norms propagation and transformation are co-relate to each other. Norms propagate through diffused influence. Since the subjects being influenced may have their perspective, they may decide to adhere or reject it. As a consequence, reciprocating influence of the subjects may transform the norm itself. Exploration of the scenarios of such nature ("being influenced and influencing reciprocally") has been a subject of complex adaptive systems using agent-based modeling as given by Macy and Flache in [16,17]. Understanding the emergence of norms in a society of agents is a challenge and an area of ongoing research [33].

To avert unpopular norms, it is necessary to understand the conditions that help to stop propagation of these norms. Especially, it is imperative to find the conditions necessary to establish the **alternative norm** (a reciprocal norm of prevailing unpopular norm) and the conditions that enforce others (people other than activists) to follow the alternative norm. Towards this, the social interaction model of unpopular norm, proposed in [6] is customized and extended.

Studying norms in society has been one of the research focus of agent-based modeling community. However, there is limited work on how unpopular norms can be averted. To the best our knowledge, we found not a single agent-based model on this topic except for our previous work [35]. In this paper, we propose a model of (unpopular) norm aversion. The agent-based model is simulated asking important "what-if" questions to elaborate the conditions and reasons for the emergence, spreading and aversion of unpopular norms.

The rest of the paper is organized as follows. Section 2 presents background work related to the research area, followed by Sect. 3 presents the motivation of the proposed model, followed by the proposed and extended model. In Sect. 4, the simulation scenarios and analysis of simulation results is presented. The paper ends with conclusions of the study presented in Sect. 5.

## 2 Background Work

Studying norms in a society has been one of the research focus of agent-based modeling community. Theoretical studies on norms such as those conducted by Conte and Castelfranchi [7] and Meneguzzi et al. [19] explored that agent are supposed to comply with social norms. The sense of punishment from the society is evident as the predominant factor behind compliance of norms [5]. Studies conducted by Sanchez-Anguix et al. [29] and Sato and Hashimoto [30] focused on the emergence of norms and they described strategies show how norms prevail in a society. This is basically governed by societal influence. Agents set their goals and frequently change their behavior based on societal influence until a global equilibrium in achieved [33]. In [8] argued that norms implementation in some expert system such as norm-based reasoners are commonly used. Also, social norms have received considerable attention in other similar domains such as social and logical philosophy. Norms can be views as emergent properties of agents' behaviors, which do not depend on their goals and beliefs. In [32] have studied the implementation of norm enforcement and issues that highly affect such enforcement and how these norms should be operationally implemented in MAS.

Willer et al. have pointed out many "empirical cases in which individuals are persuaded to publicly support behaviors or beliefs that they privately question" [34]. The term, Preference falsification, coined by Kuran [14] is defined as "the act of misrepresenting one's genius wants under perceived social pressures". According to him, an equilibrium is the sum of three utilities namely, intrinsic, expressive, and reputation. The intrinsic utility is about individual's personal satisfaction being part of the society. The expressive utility is about an individual gain in response of presenting himself/herself to be what is expected. The utility that is acquired through the reaction of others is termed as reputation utility.

The concept of unpopular norm is very close to the concept of preference falsification, in which individuals publicly lie about their privately held preferences [13]. According to Makowsky and Rubin [18], such societies are "prone to cascades of preference revelation if preferences are interconnected - where individuals derive utility from conforming to the actions of others". Further, "ICTs and preference falsification complement each other in the production of revolutionary activity. The former facilitates the transmission of shock while the latter increases the magnitude of change that arises after a shock." Utility acts in two different ways in the propagation of unpopular norms. At one end, it can force an individual to follow an unpopular norm, or even falsely enforce it. On the other end, it can propagate an opposite sentiment as a result of private preference revelation. There are evidences that a minority of activists (capable of revealing their private preferences on will) can make a big difference, but in a conducive environment [11].

## 3 The Proposed Extended Model

To avert UN, it is important to understand conditions that might help to stop the propagation of these norms. Particularly, it is imperative to find the conditions necessary to establish an alternative norm - a reciprocal norm of prevailing UN, and the conditions that enforce people other than activists to follow the alternate norm. This section first introduces the social interaction model for following UN proposed by Centola et al. [6]. It, then, provides briefly our previous extension to this model followed by the proposed extension in this paper.

### 3.1 Centola's Model of Norm Aversion

In Centola model [6], agents decide whether to comply or follow the norm, which is supported by few individuals while majority opposed it. Depending on agents' horizon, if it is limited to immediate neighbors, resulting in emergence of an unpopular norm locally and later spread. Such examples can be seen in our daily lives; where work carried out by the prestigious scholars are widely acceptable publicly, and cannot be criticized due to the fear of being labeled as "unfit for office"/"incorrigibly stupid", while privately people find them entirely inappropriate. This is true in case of naked emperor, where majority can see him naked, but due to fear prefer to go along with the charade and admire the emperor, hence reinforcing the same false belief.

Centola used agent-based modeling to study the consequences of false enforcement as a signal of sincerity on the population level. Using theory driven approach, this model is capable of elaborating the conditions behind the emergence, spreading, and the aversion of UN. A majority of agents who do not believe in the UN and can be represented as Dis-Believers (DB's), while agents believe in the UN can be represented as True Believer (TB's). Each agent let say $i$ has a binary private belief (Bi) and defines agent either as TB or DB. In case of TB (Bi = 1), while for DB (Bi = −1). Irrespective of the social pressure not to comply, a small group of TB's always comply with the norm. When these agents are not satisfied with the compliance level by the others, they may enforce them, and this is called "true enforcement", because the agent is enforcing compliance with its true belief i.e. Bi = 1. The rest of the population (DB's), who opposed the norm in private, but less conviction in comparisons with TB's. This opposition can result in deviating from the norm and even convenience other to deviate as well. This is again "true enforcement". Due to the weak strength of this convocations as compared to the TB, DB may be pressurized to support the norm in public. This support not only includes to comply with the norm, but also to pressurize others to comply as well. This is "false enforcement" because the agent enforcing the norm contradict with agent's private belief.

Initially, all TB's comply with the UN represented as compliance = 1, while DB's not complying with the UN represented as compliance = −1. The compliance is based on the level and the direction of the social pressure, which is relative to the strength of an agent's conviction i.e. how truly agent believe in norm. Social pressure is the sum of enforcement decisions by the $i$*'s* neighbor i.e. each neighbor $j$ enforcement of the norm increases pressure on $i$ to comply and vice versa. A positive value means that more pressure on the agent to comply and a negative value results in encouraging deviation. By default, TB's alway comply even if all their neighbors enforce deviation. In case of DB's, due to the weak conviction may change subject to the sufficient positive social pressure. More formally, An agent $i$'s belief is a static value. The value of compliance may change using Eq. 1.

$$compliance_i = \begin{cases} -belief_i \;\; if \; (\frac{-belief_i}{N_i} \times NE_i) > strength_i \\ belief_i \qquad\qquad\qquad\qquad\qquad otherwise \end{cases} \tag{1}$$

Where, $NE_i$ = count of (Moore's) neighbors enforcing opposite belief and $N_i$ = count of (Moore's) neighbors. This means that an agent's decision to comply with UN or not is dependent on enforcement of opposite belief by the neighborhood. If $NE_i$ is greater than the strength of a DB, the agent would comply against its belief. Since, TBs compliance (which equals their belief about a UN) and strength are already equal to 1, Eq. 1 would not change the compliance value of TBs.

$$enforcement_i = \begin{cases} -belief_i, \ if \ (\frac{-belief_i}{N_i} \times NE_i) > (strength_i + k) \bigwedge (belief_i \neq compliance_i) \\ belief_i, \ if \ (strength_i \times enforcement\_need_i > k) \bigwedge (belief_i = compliance_i) \\ 0, \ otherwise \end{cases} \quad (2)$$

Enforcement is an agent influence on the neighborhood and it could be true or false, starting with a default value of 0, it can be either 1 or −1. In case of false believers, who secretly opposed the norm, they do not pressurize others to comply with the norm, but in case of true believers who support to promote compliance. The propensity to falsely enforce is directly propositional to increase in social pressure to support the norm and decreases with increased conviction, same in case with the decision to comply.

Equation 3 is used to compute $enforcement\_need_i$ - that is the need of enforcement reflecting influence of neighborhood compliance.

$$enforcement\_need_i = \frac{(1 - \frac{belief_i}{N_i}) \times NC_i}{2} \quad (3)$$

Where, $NC_i$ = number of (Moore's) neighbors whose compliance is different than agent's belief.

### 3.2 Our Previous Extension

Since, DBs compliance in basic centolla's model is undesirable, in our previous work [35], published in recent conference [24] we extended it and introduced a special kind of DBs (called Activists (ACTs)) with more desire to avert (act against) a UN. These ACTs are triggered by the presence of TBs in the surrounding, particularly who are enforcing. Their strength is progressively incremented proportional to the intensity of enforcement from TBs. The strength of an ACTs is calculated using Eq. 4.

$$strength_i = strength_i + (\frac{E_{jb}}{N_i}) \quad (4)$$

where, $E_{jb}$ = is the number of enforcing TBs.

### 3.3 The Model Extension

In this paper, the model is further extended to incorporate the decision-making of a DBs as a result of neighborhood condition. It is proposed that TBs (who are not ACTs) should not be considered as entirely a numb entity. We propose a decision-making model represented in Eq. 5. In this model, the strength of DBs (who are not ACTs) is changed (increased or decreased) based on its type being either "optimistic" or "pessimistic". The difference between percentage of enforcing TBs (termed as, $P_{jb}$) and percentage of complying DBs (termed as, $P_{jd}$) is

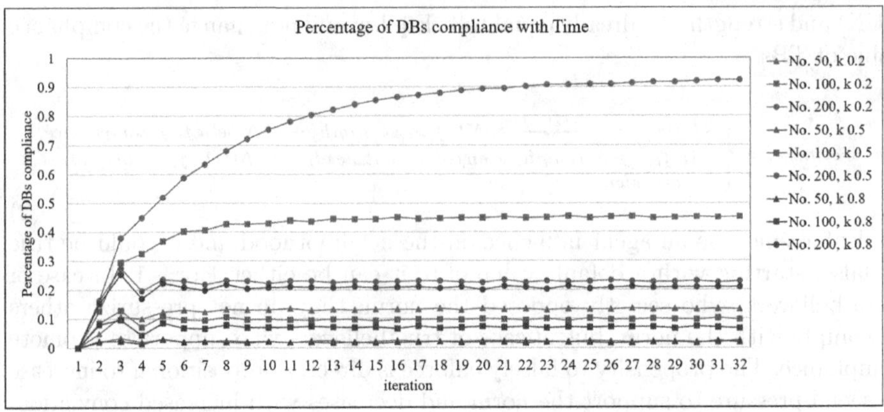


**Fig. 1.** Simulation results of the basic Centolla's model for various scenarios based on number of agents (considered 50, 100, and 200) and threshold value k - showing an agent's desire to comply (considered 0.2, 0.5, and 0.8).

divided by neighborhood density ($N_i$) times the fraction of DBs of that type (consider *opt* for an optimistic and "1−*opt*″ for a pessimistic DBs). If an agent belongs to the optimistic category, its strength would be increased/decreased based on the difference of "true enforcement" (represented as $P_{jb}$) and "false compliance" (represented as $P_{jd}$). When fast compliance is more then the strength will decrease. On the other hand, when true enforcement is more then the strength will increase.

$$strength_i = \begin{cases} strength_i + (P_{jb} - P_{jd})/(N_i \times opt), & if\ i\ is\ optimistic \\ strength_i + (P_{jb} - P_{jd})/(N_i \times (1 - opt)), & otherwise \end{cases} \quad (5)$$

## 4 Simulations and Results

### 4.1 Simulation Environment

Netlogo [31] - a popular agent-based simulation tool with a support for grid based spaces, is used to simulate the work presented in this paper. The agents reside on cells of a spatial grid. We have used the concept of Moore's neighborhood to represent the surrounding of an agent - a very popular strategy in many cell-based spatial configurations [12]. For a coarse grained evaluation, we used a simulation space consisting of a torus of 17 × 17 cells.

### 4.2 Results and Discussion

**Previous Findings.** Due to the spatial nature of neighborhood, it was expected that a more dense population is susceptible to more DBs compliance. This fact is evident from the results shown in Fig. 1. Further, DBs compliance is inversely

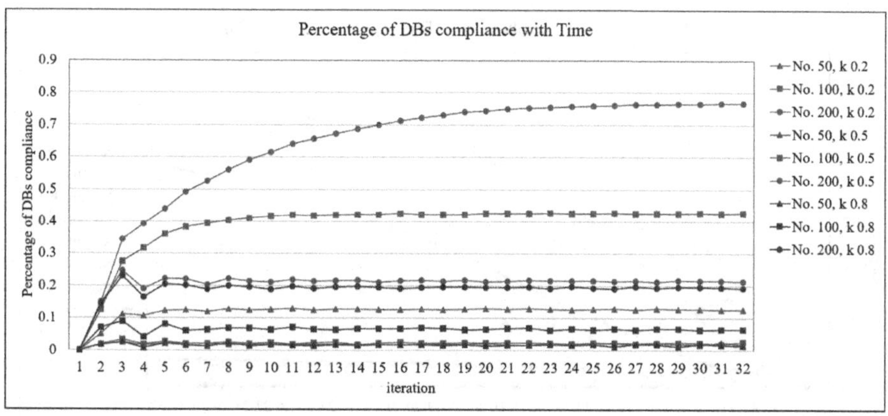


**Fig. 2.** Simulation results of our previous extension to Centolla's model for various scenarios based on number of agents (considered 50, 100, and 200) and threshold value k - showing an agent's desire to comply (considered 0.2, 0.5, and 0.8).

proportional to the value of k - an agent's desire to comply. Ironically, in all cases depicted in Fig. 1, the population achieves stability always being attracted towards various fixed points. In our previous work [35], it was observed that in highly dense conditions with a large number of norm aversion ACTs, the aversion of unpopular norms can be achieved. This fact is highlighted in Fig. 2. There is a striking similarity between the basic model and our previously extended model whose results are presented in Figs. 1 and 2 in corresponding order. It is learnt that the cases comprises of smaller values of k and large number of agents are worst than the rest of the cases. A marginal improvement was achieved by introducing the ACTs where comparatively less number of DBs were witnessed complying with a UN.

**Current Findings: A Brief Analysis.** This model uses optimistic DBs that are intrinsically believing in averting the UN. Simulation work conducted in this paper uses three different numbers of these optimistic DBs which are counted as 10, 20 and 30% of the total population. It is learnt that the proposed model significantly reduces the number of DBs complying with a UN. Even the scenario considered as a worst one (the one comprises of 200 agent and a threshold value k = 0.2) achieved a 100% improvement by dropping compliance rate from 70% to 35%. This is illustrated in Figs. 2 and 3.

When the proposed model is compared with previous model, it was noted that DBs compliance comparatively get worse as the number of agents' increases irrespective of the value of k. The cases where the number of agents are 200 always perform worst than other cases (comprising of 50 or 100 agents). This can be noticed while comparing the results presented in Fig. 2 with 3). Overall, with an increase in the number of optimistic DBs, the results get improved as witnessed by comparing the results given in Figs. 3, 4, and 5).

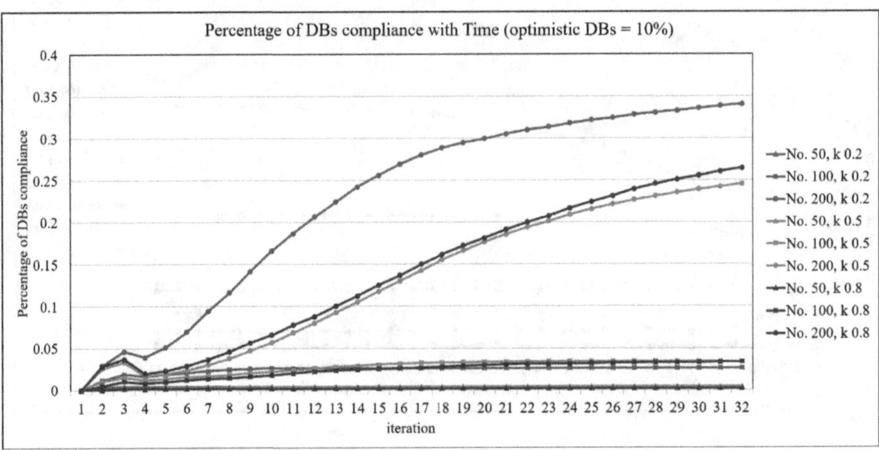


**Fig. 3.** Simulation results of the proposed extension (with 10% agents of total population being optimistic) to Centolla's model for various scenarios based on number of agents (considered 50, 100, and 200) and threshold value k - showing an agent's desire to comply (considered 0.2, 0.5, and 0.8).

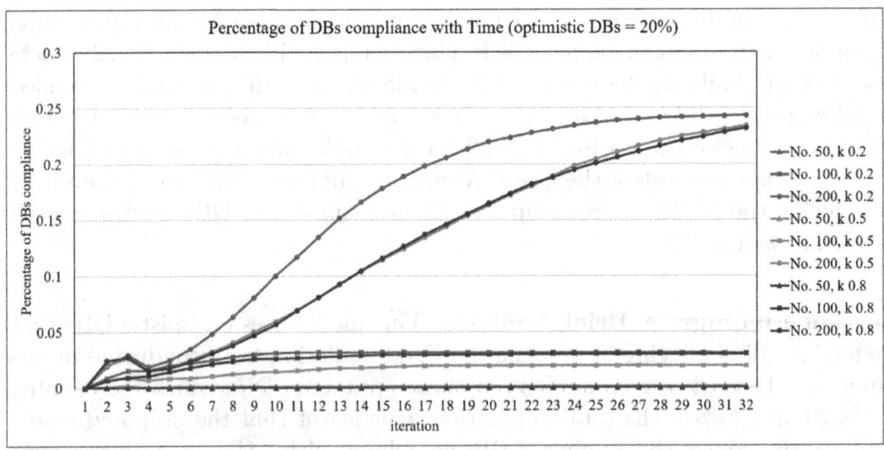


**Fig. 4.** Simulation results of the proposed extension (with 20% agents of total population being optimistic) to Centolla's model for various scenarios based on number of agents (considered 50, 100, and 200) and threshold value k - showing an agent's desire to comply (considered 0.2, 0.5, and 0.8).

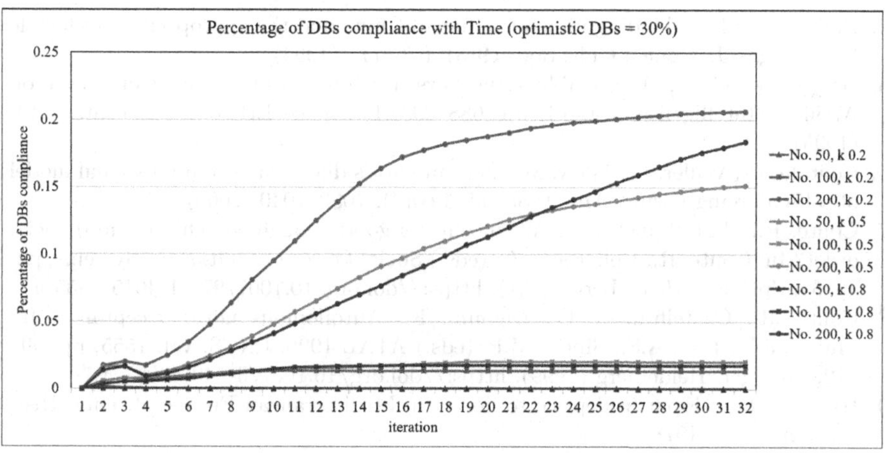


**Fig. 5.** Simulation results of the proposed extension (with 30% agents of total population being optimistic) to Centolla's model for various scenarios based on number of agents (considered 50, 100, and 200) and threshold value k - showing an agent's desire to comply (considered 0.2, 0.5, and 0.8).

## 5 Conclusion

It is argued that for societal good, it is necessary to oppose and possibly avert unpopular norms. This work is an attempt to realise the conditions that result in the emergence of unpopular norms, and define situations under which these norms can be changed and averted. It presented an agent-based simulation for unpopular norm aversion. It utilised the reciprocal nature of persistence and aversion of norms to define situations under which these norms can be changed and averted. The simulation results revealed that, in addition to agents actively participating in averting the unpopular norm, incorporating a rational decision making model for normal agents is necessary to achieve a dominant norm aversion. Further, it is learnt that the inclusion of true believers and activists play a significant role in norm aversion dynamics. In short, this study revealed that more educated and socially active individuals are key to reduce undesirable norms in a society. The significance of this fact is also applicable to digital societies primarily created by social networking applications now-a-days.

## References


1. Aizenman, J., Lee, J.: International reserves: precautionary versus mercantilist views, theory and evidence. Open Econ. Rev. **18**(2), 191–214 (2007)
2. Banerjee, A.V.: A simple model of herd behavior. Q. J. Econ. **107**(3), 797–817 (1992)
3. Bikhchandani, S., Sharma, S.: Herd behavior in financial markets. IMF Staff Pap. **47**(3), 279–310 (2000)

4. Blake, C.F.: Foot-binding in neo-Confucian China and the appropriation of female labor. Signs J. Women Cult. Soc. **19**(3), 676–712 (1994)
5. Briggs, W., Cook, D.: Flexible social laws. In: International Joint Conference on Artificial Intelligence, vol. 14, pp. 688–693. Lawrence Erlbaum Associates Ltd. (1995)
6. Centola, D., Willer, R., Macy, M.: The emperor's dilemma: a computational model of self-enforcing norms. Am. J. Sociol. **110**(4), 1009–1040 (2005)
7. Conte, R., Castelfranchi, C.: Are incentives good enough to achieve (info) social order? In: Conte, R., Dellarocas, C. (eds.) Social Order in Multiagent Systems, pp. 45–61. Springer, Heidelberg (2001). https://doi.org/10.1007/978-1-4615-1555-5_3
8. Conte, R., Castelfranchi, C., Dignum, F.: Autonomous norm acceptance. In: Müller, J.P., Rao, A.S., Singh, M.P. (eds.) ATAL 1998. LNCS, vol. 1555, pp. 99–112. Springer, Heidelberg (1999). https://doi.org/10.1007/3-540-49057-4_7
9. Hughes, D.O.: From brideprice to dowry in Mediterranean Europe. J. Fam. Hist. **3**(3), 262–296 (1978)
10. Katz, D., Allport, F.H., Jenness, M.B.: Students' attitudes; a report of the Syracuse University reaction study (1931)
11. Khondker, H.H.: Role of the new media in the Arab spring. Globalizations **8**(5), 675–679 (2011)
12. Kretz, T., Schreckenberg, M.: Moore and more and symmetry. In: Waldau, N., Gattermann, P., Knoflacher, H., Schreckenberg, M. (eds.) Pedestrian and Evacuation Dynamics 2005, pp. 297–308. Springer, Heidelberg (2007). https://doi.org/10.1007/978-3-540-47064-9_26
13. Kuran, T.: The inevitability of future revolutionary surprises. Am. J. Sociol. **100**(6), 1528–1551 (1995)
14. Kuran, T.: Private Truths, Public Lies: The Social Consequences of Preference Falsification. Harvard University Press, Cambridge (1997)
15. Lux, T.: Herd behaviour, bubbles and crashes. Econ. J. 881–896 (1995)
16. Macal, C., North, M.: Introductory tutorial: agent-based modeling and simulation. In: Proceedings of the 2014 Winter Simulation Conference, pp. 6–20. IEEE Press (2014)
17. Macy, M., Flache, A.: Social dynamics from the bottom up: agent-based models of social interaction. In: The Oxford Handbook of Analytical Sociology, pp. 245–268 (2009)
18. Makowsky, M.D., Rubin, J.: An agent-based model of centralized institutions, social network technology, and revolution. PloS one **8**(11), e80380 (2013)
19. Meneguzzi, F., Rodrigues, O., Oren, N., Vasconcelos, W.W., Luck, M.: BDI reasoning with normative considerations. Eng. Appl. Artif. Intell. **43**, 127–146 (2015)
20. Merdes, C., et al.: Growing unpopular norms. J. Artif. Soc. Soc. Simul. **20**(3), 1–5 (2017)
21. Merton, R.K.: The matthew effect in science: the reward and communication systems of science are considered. Science **159**(3810), 56–63 (1968)
22. Miller, D.T., McFarland, C.: Pluralistic ignorance: when similarity is interpreted as dissimilarity. J. Pers. Soc. Psychol. **53**(2), 298 (1987)
23. Morrow, P.: The thesis of norm transformation in the theory of mass atrocity. Genocide Stud. Prev. Int. J. **9**(1), 8 (2015)
24. Muhammad, A., Zia, K., Saini, D.K.: Agent-based simulation of socially-inspired model of resistance against unpopular norms. In: Proceedings of the 10th International Conference on Agents and Artificial Intelligence, ICAART, vol. 1, pp. 133–139. INSTICC, SciTePress (2018). https://doi.org/10.5220/0006735501330139

25. Neighbors, C., et al.: Injunctive norms, deviance regulation, and social norms interventions. Alcohol. Clin. Exp. Res. **39**, 292A (2015)
26. Nkomo, S.M.: The emperor has no clothes: rewriting "race in organizations". Acad. Manag. Rev. **17**(3), 487–513 (1992)
27. Ostrom, E.: Collective action and the evolution of social norms. J. Nat. Resour. Policy Res. **6**(4), 235–252 (2014)
28. Prentice, D.A., Miller, D.T.: Pluralistic ignorance and alcohol use on campus: some consequences of misperceiving the social norm. J. Pers. Soc. Psychol. **64**(2), 243 (1993)
29. Sanchez-Anguix, V., Julian, V., Botti, V., García-Fornes, A.: Tasks for agent-based negotiation teams: analysis, review, and challenges. Eng. Appl. Artif. Intell. **26**(10), 2480–2494 (2013)
30. Sato, T., Hashimoto, T.: Dynamic social simulation with multi-agents having internal dynamics. In: Sakurai, A., Hasida, K., Nitta, K. (eds.) JSAI 2003-2004. LNCS (LNAI), vol. 3609, pp. 237–251. Springer, Heidelberg (2007). https://doi.org/10.1007/978-3-540-71009-7_21
31. Tisue, S., Wilensky, U.: NetLogo: a simple environment for modeling complexity. In: International Conference on Complex Systems, Boston, MA, vol. 21, pp. 16–21 (2004)
32. Vázquez-Salceda, J., Aldewereld, H., Dignum, F.: Implementing norms in multiagent systems. In: Lindemann, G., Denzinger, J., Timm, I.J., Unland, R. (eds.) MATES 2004. LNCS (LNAI), vol. 3187, pp. 313–327. Springer, Heidelberg (2004). https://doi.org/10.1007/978-3-540-30082-3_23
33. Vouros, G.A.: The emergence of norms via contextual agreements in open societies. In: Koch, F., Guttmann, C., Busquets, D. (eds.) Advances in Social Computing and Multiagent Systems. CCIS, vol. 541, pp. 185–201. Springer, Cham (2015). https://doi.org/10.1007/978-3-319-24804-2_12
34. Willer, R., Kuwabara, K., Macy, M.W.: The false enforcement of unpopular norms. Am. J. Sociol. **115**(2), 451–490 (2009)
35. Zareen, Z., Zafar, M., Zia, K.: Conditions facilitating the aversion of unpopular norms: an agent-based simulation study. Int. J. Adv. Comput. Sci. Appl. **7**(7), 499–505 (2016)

# Artificial Intelligence

# Modelling and Simulating Extreme Opinion Diffusion

Enzo Battistella and Laurence Cholvy(✉)

ONERA, Toulouse, France
cholvy@onera.fr

**Abstract.** This paper focuses on modelling and simulating diffusion of extreme opinions among agents. In this work, opinions are modelled as formulas of the propositional logic. Moreover, agents influence each other and any agent changes its current opinion by merging the opinions of its influencers, taking into account the strength of their influence. We propose several definitions of extreme opinions and extremism. Formal studies of these definitions are made as well as some simulations.

## 1 Introduction

Understanding the dynamics of opinion diffusion and especially of extremism is a tremendous question in Multi-Agent System and Artificial Intelligence communities. See for instance [1–8] for the study of opinion diffusion and [9–11] for the study of extremism diffusion.

Opinions are usually represented by a single real value between 0 (or −1) and 1 corresponding to the position of an agent regarding a given question. The closer to 1 an agent's opinion is, the more this agent positively answers the question. For instance, if the question is "Do you think that the cafeteria serves GMO food ?", an agent whose opinion is 0.9 strongly believes that GMO food is served; an agent whose opinion is 0.2 rather thinks that GMO food is not served. If the question is now "Do you agree with serving GMO food at the cafeteria ?", an agent whose opinion is 0.9 strongly agrees in serving GMO food while an agent whose opinion is 0.2 is rather against serving GMO food. As for extremism, it is obviously defined there by having an opinion which is close to 0 (or −1) or to 1. Moreover, in such models, agents can easily be classified from most to least extremist. Recently, some works in Artificial Intelligence community [4,8] have adopted a different way of modelling opinions and represent an opinion by a single binary vector whose values correspond to answers to several questions. For instance, if the two questions are "Do you think that the cafeteria must be open until 4pm?" and "Do you think that vegan food should be served at the cafeteria ?" then the vector $(0, 1)$ represents the opinion of an agent which thinks that the cafeteria must not to open until 4pm but has to serve vegan food.

Following [12], we have recently adopted an even more general approach [3,13] and we consider that an opinion is modelled by a set of binary vectors, or equivalently, by a propositional formula. For instance, in such a model, the set of


J. van den Herik and A. P. Rocha (Eds.): ICAART 2018, LNAI 11352, pp. 79–104, 2019.
https://doi.org/10.1007/978-3-030-05453-3_5

binary vectors $\{(1,1),(0,1),(0,0)\}$, which is equivalent to the formula $F \rightarrow V$, represents the opinion of an agent who thinks that, if the cafeteria is open until 4 then it has to serve vegan food. The set of binary vectors $\{(1,1),(0,1)\}$, which is equivalent to the formula $V$ represents the opinion of an agent who thinks that, whatever the open hours are, the cafeteria has to serve vegan food. As for the diffusion process, we consider a model in which any agent is influenced by some other agents called its influencers. There, an agent regularly updates its opinion by merging the opinions of its influencers according to the strenght of their influence. For this, we introduced the notion of Importance-Based Merging Opinion Structures (IODS).

In [14], we have started studying extremism diffusion in IODS. We proposed a definition of extreme opinions which could be called "precise opinions" and we studied their diffusion in IODS.

The present paper extends this work by proposing several definitions and studying their diffusion in IODS. We recall precise opinions definition but we also define extreme opinions based on selected topics and extreme opinions based on selected agents. Moreover we study and compare their diffusion in IODS.

This paper is organized as follows. Section 2 recalls the notion of Importance-Based Opinion Diffusion Structures (IODS). The different definitions of extreme opinions are given in Sect. 3 and their diffusion in IODS is studied in Sect. 4. Sections 5 and 6 focus on experiments. Section 5 shows how to generate graphs corresponding to real social networks. Section 6 presents experiments for the diffusion od some extreme opinions. Section 7 concludes this paper. The proofs of the different propositions given in the paper are gathered in Sect. 8.

## 2 Importance-Based Opinion Diffusion Structures

This section presents Importance-Based Opinion Diffusion Structures.

We consider a finite propositional langage $L$. The set of interpretations of $L$ is $Mod(L)$ with $\mid Mod(L) \mid = 2^{|L|}$. An element $w$ of $Mod(L)$ is denoted $\{p_1, ..., p_n, \neg q_1, ..., \neg q_m\}$ where $p_1...p_n$ are the propositional letters satisfied in $w$ and $q_1...q_m$ are the propositional letters which are not satisfied in $w$. If $\varphi$ is a propositional formula of language $L$, $Mod(\varphi)$ is the set of its models (i.e., the set of the interpretation which satisfy it). A multi-set of formulas is a set with possible repeted occurrences of formulas. An ordered multi-set of formulas is a multi-set of formulas in which formulas are ranked with a total ranking. It is denoted $\varphi_1 \prec .. \prec \varphi_n$. The distance between an interpretation $w$ and a formula $\varphi$ is defined by: $D(w, \varphi) = min_{w' \in Mod(\varphi)} d(w, w')$, where $d$ is a pseudo-distance between interpretations (i.e., $\forall w \forall w' \; d(w, w') = d(w', w)$ and $d(w, w') = 0 \implies w = w'$). Some simple pseudo-distances $d$ are $d_D$, the drastic pseudo-distance, ($d_D(w, w') = 0$ iff $w = w', 1$ otherwise); $d_H$, the Hamming pseudo-distance ($d_H(w, w') = m$ iff $w$ and $w'$ differ on $m$ propositional letters).

**Definition 1.** *An Importance-Based Merging Operator is a function $\Delta$ which associates a formula $\mu$ and a non-empty ordered multi-set of consistent formulas*

$\varphi_1 \prec ... \prec \varphi_n$ *with a formula denoted* $\Delta_\mu(\varphi_1 \prec ... \prec \varphi_n)$ *so that:* $Mod(\Delta_\mu(\varphi_1 \prec ... \prec \varphi_n)) = Min^d_{\leq_{\varphi_1 \prec ... \prec \varphi_n}} Mod(\mu)$ *with:*

- $w \leq^d_{\varphi_1 \prec ... \prec \varphi_n} w'$ *iff* $[D(w, \varphi_1), ..., D(w, \varphi_n)] \leq_{lex} [D(w', \varphi_1), ..., D(w', \varphi_n)]$
- $[D(w, \varphi_1), ..., D(w, \varphi_n)]$ *is a vector which* $k^{th}$ *element is* $D(w, \varphi_k)$
- $\leq_{lex}$ *is a lexicographic comparison of vectors of reals defined by:* $[v_1, ..., v_n] \leq_{lex} [v'_1, ..., v'_n]$ *iff (i)* $\forall k\ v_k = v'_k$ *or (ii)* $\exists k\ v_k < v'_k$ *and* $\forall j < k\ v_j = v'_j$

**Definition 2.** *An Importance-Based Opinion Diffusion Structure (IODS) is a quadruplet* $DS = (A, \mu, B, Inf)$ *where:* $A = \{1, ..., n\}$ *is a finite set of agents.* $\mu$ *is a consistent formula of* $L$*.* $B$ *is a function which associates any agent* $i$ *of* $A$ *with a consistent formula of* $L$ *denoted for short* $B_i$ *such that* $B_i \models \mu$*.* $Inf$ *is a function which associates any agent* $i$ *of* $A$ *with a non-empty set of agents* $\{i_1, ..., i_{n_i}\}$ *equipped with a total order* $\prec_i$ *s.t.* $i_k \prec_i i_{k+1}$ *for* $k = 1...(n_i - 1)$*. The agents of* $Inf(i)$ *will be called influencers of* $i$*. The influencer* $i_1$ *will be called the main influencer of* $i$*. For short, we denote* $Inf(i) = \{i_1 \prec_i ... \prec_i i_{n_i}\}$*.*

In an IODS any agent updates its opinion by applying an Importance-based Merging Operator on the opinions of its influencers as shown below.

**Definition 3 (Opinion Sequence).** *Let* $DS = (A, \mu, B, Inf)$ *be an IODS and* $i \in A$ *with* $Inf(i) = \{i_1 \prec_i ... \prec_i i_{n_i}\}$*. The Opinion Sequence of* $i$ *in* $DS$ *is denoted* $(B^s_i)_{s \in \mathbb{N}}$ *and is defined by* $(B^s_i)_{s \in \mathbb{N}}$*, is defined by:* $B^0_i = B_i$ *and* $\forall s > 0$*,* $B^s_i = \Delta_\mu(B^{s-1}_{i_1} \prec ... \prec B^{s-1}_{i_{n_i}})$

*Example 1.* Consider a language with propositional letters $a$ and $b$. Let $S = (A, \mu, B, Inf)$ be an IODS with: $A = \{1, 2, 3\}$, $\mu$ is a tautology, $B_1 = \neg a$, $B_2 = a \vee b$, $B_3 = \neg b$, $Inf_1 = \{1\}$, $Inf_2 = \{2 \prec_2 1\}$, $Inf_3 = \{3 \prec_3 2\}$. The graph of influence is represented in Fig. 1. Moreover, Table 1 shows the evolution of the agents opinions.

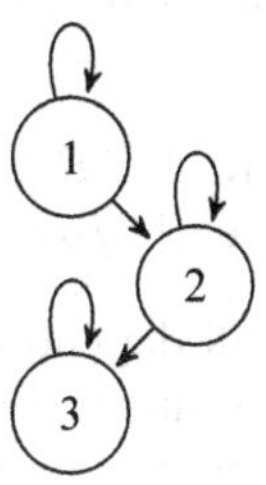


**Fig. 1.** Graph of influence of Example 1.

Let us finally introduce some interesting definitions.

**Table 1.** Opinion evolution in Example 1 (extracted from [14]).

| | $s = 0$ | $s = 1$ | $s \geq 2$ |
|---|---|---|---|
| $i = 1$ | $\neg a$ | $\neg a$ | $\neg a$ |
| $i = 2$ | $a \vee b$ | $\neg a \wedge b$ | $\neg a \wedge b$ |
| $i = 3$ | $\neg b$ | $a \wedge \neg b$ | $a \wedge \neg b$ |

**Definition 4 (dogmatic and self-confident agents).** *Let $DS = (A, \mu, B, Inf)$ be an IODS, and $i \in A$.*
*$i$ dogmatic iff $Inf(i) = \{i\}$.*
*$i$ is self-confident iff $Inf(i) = \{i \prec_i i_2 \prec_i ... \prec_i i_{n_i}\}$ with $n_i \geq 1$.*

**Definition 5 (Sphere of Influence of an Agent).** *Let $DS = (A, \mu, B, Inf)$ be an IODS and $i \in A$. The sphere of influence of $i$ is defined by: $Sphere(i) = \bigcup_{k \geq 1} Sphere^k(i)$ with*
*$Sphere^1(i) = \{j_1 : Inf(j_1) = \{i \prec ...\}\}$*
*$Sphere^k(i) = \{j_k : Inf(j_k) = \{j_{k-1} \prec ...\}$ and $j_{k-1} \in Sphere^{k-1}(i)\}$*

An agent is *dogmatic* when it is not influenced by other agents. As a consequence, a dogmatic agent $i$ will never change its opinion i.e., $\forall s \geq 0\ B_i^s = B_i^0$. An agent is *self-confident* when it is its main influencer. Notice that dogmatic agents in IODS are self-confident. Moreover if $i$ is self-confident then $i \in Sphere(i)$.

## 3 Definitions of Extreme Opinions

This section presents several definitions of extreme opinions. Notice that precise opinions have been introduced in [14].

### 3.1 Extreme Opinions as Precise Opinions

Here we consider that extreme opinions are precise opinions i.e. formulas which have "few" models.

**Definition 6 (Precise Opinions).** *Let $R$ be a given integer closer to 1 than to $2^{|L|}$. An opinion $o$ is extreme iff $1 \leq |Mod(o)| \leq R$.*

The choice of the threshold $R$ will depend on the application. But $R$ has to be much smaller than the number of interpretations in the language. Moreover, inconsistent opinions are not considered as extreme. For instance, consider that the two letters of the language are $a, b$. If $R = 1$ then $a \wedge b$, $a \wedge \neg b$, $\neg a \wedge b$, $\neg a \wedge \neg b$ are the extreme opinions. The following proposition gives a description of extreme opinions from a syntactical point of view. More precisely, it shows that an extreme opinion is equivalent to a disjunction of less than $R$ conjunctions of all the literals.

**Proposition 1.** *Assume that the propositional letters are* $a_1, ..., a_n$. *Opinion* $o$ *is extreme iff* $o \equiv \bigvee_{k=1}^{N} l_{1,k} \wedge ... \wedge l_{n,k}$ *with* $\forall k \in [1, N]$, $\forall i \in [1, n]$, $l_i^k = a_i$ *or* $l_i^k \neg a_i$ *and* $N \leq R$.

*Proof.* Proofs are given in Sect. 8.

### 3.2 Extreme Opinions Based on Selected Topics

**Definition 7 (Selected Topics).** *A selected topic is a propositional letter of* $L$. *The set of selected topics is denoted* $S$ *with* $S \subseteq L$.

The choice of "selected topics" depends on the application we consider. For instance, in the context of food served at the cafeteria, GMO food is a controversial subject according to which we may want to measure polarization. On the other side, expressing a position towards serving potatoes or serving fresh fruits is usually not. Thus here we will consider $L = \{GMO, potatoes, fruits\}$ with $GMO$ meaning "I am ok with $GMO$ food", *potatoes* meaning "I am ok with serving potatoes", $fruits$ meaning "I am ok with serving fresh fruits" and $S = \{GMO\}$. But in winter, serving fresh fruits may become a controversial subject because of ecological reasons and expressing a positive position towards serving fresh fruits may become sensitive. In this context we will consider $S = \{GMO, fruits\}$.

In the following, we propose two definitions of extreme opinions. Each of them is based on a set of selected topics $S$ and also on an integer $\alpha \in [1, 2^{|L|}]$, used to quantify the level of extremism. We will call these opinions $S^1\alpha$-extreme and $S^2\alpha$-extreme respectively.

**Definition 8**

- *An opinion* $o$ *is* $S^1\alpha$*-extreme iff there is a subset of* $S$, $S_\alpha$, *whose size is* $\alpha$ *and so that* $Mod(o) \subseteq Mod(\bigwedge S_\alpha)$.
- *An opinion* $o$ *is* $S^2\alpha$*-extreme iff* $Mod(o) \subseteq \{w \in Mod(L) : S(w) \geq \alpha\}$, $S(w)$ *being the number of letters in* $S$ *which are true in* $w$.

Thus an opinion is $S^1\alpha$-extreme iff there are $\alpha$ selected topics each model of $o$ agrees on. An opinion is $S^2\alpha$-extreme iff its models agree on $\alpha$ selected topics at least. Moreover, we define $S^1$-not-extreme opinions and $S^2$-not-extreme opinions as follows.

**Definition 9.** *An opinion* $o$ *is* $S^1$*-not-extreme (resp* $S^2$*-not-extreme) iff* $\forall \alpha \in [1, 2^{|L|}]$, $o$ *is not* $S^1\alpha$*-extreme (resp* $S^2\alpha$*-extreme).*

The next proposition proves some results.

**Proposition 2**

- *If* $o$ *is* $S^1\alpha$*-extreme (resp* $S^2\alpha$*-extreme) then for any* $\beta$ *st* $1 \leq \beta \leq \alpha$, $o$ *is* $S^1\beta$*-extreme (resp,* $S^2\alpha$*-extreme).*

- $S^1\alpha$*-extreme* $\subseteq S^2\alpha$*-extreme but in general* $S^2\alpha$*-extreme* $\not\subseteq S^1\alpha$*-extreme*
- $S^2$*-not-extreme* $\subseteq S^1$*-not-extreme*
- $S^1 \mid S \mid$*-extreme* $= S^2 \mid S \mid$*-extreme*

**Proposition 3.** *Assume* $S = \{s_1, ..., s_n\}$.

- $o$ *is* $S^1$*-not-extreme iff for any* $S_\alpha = \{s_{i_1}, ...s_{i_\alpha}\} \subseteq S$, $\exists s_{i_j} \in S_\alpha$ *so that* $o \wedge \neg s_{i_j}$ *is consistent.*
- $o$ *is* $S^2$*-not-extreme iff* $o \wedge \neg s_1 ... \wedge \neg s_n$ *is consistent.*
- *There is an* $\alpha$ *so that* $o$ *is* $S^2\alpha$*-extreme iff* $o \models s_1 \vee ... \vee s_n$.
- $\alpha$ *is the highest value st* $o$ *is* $S^2\alpha$*-extreme iff there are* $S_1 \subseteq S$ ... $S_k \subseteq S$ *with* $\mid S_1 \mid = ... = \mid S_k \mid = \alpha$ *st* $o$ *equivalent to* $\bigvee_{i=1...k} (\bigwedge_{s \in S_i} s \ \bigwedge_{s \in S \setminus S_i} \neg s \ \bigwedge_{s \notin S} l_s)$, $l_s$ *being* $s$ *or* $\neg s$.

Let us give an example to illustrate these definitions.

*Example 2.* Suppose that $L = \{GMO, potatoes, fruits\}$ and $S = \{GMO, fruits\}$. Consider the following opinions: $GMO \wedge fruits$, $GMO$, $GMO \vee fruits$, $GMO \wedge potatoes$, $GMO \vee potatoes$, $potatoes$. Table 2 shows if they are extreme or not.

**Table 2.** Illustration of example 2.

| | $S^1\alpha$-extreme | $S^2\alpha$-extreme |
|---|---|---|
| $GMO \wedge fruits$ | $S^1 2$-extreme with $S_2 = \{GMO, fruits\}$ $S^1 1$-extreme with $S_1 = \{GMO\}$ or $S_1 = \{fruits\}$ | $S^2 2$-extreme $S^2 1$-extreme |
| $GMO$ | $S^1 1$-extreme with $S_1 = \{GMO\}$ | $S^2 1$-extreme |
| $GMO \vee fruits$ | $S^1$-not-extreme | $S^2 1$-extreme |
| $GMO \wedge potatoes$ | $S^1 1$-extreme with $S_1 = \{GMO\}$ | $S^2 1$-extreme |
| $GMO \vee potatoes$ | $S^1$-not-extreme | $S^2 1$-extreme |
| $potatoes$ | $S^1$-not-extreme | $S^2$-not-extreme |

### 3.3 Extreme Opinions Based on Selected Agents

The two definitions presented in the previous section are dependent on $S$ which is a subset of the language $L$. Here we propose a fourth definition which, assuming a set of agents $A$, depends on a subset $SA$ of $A$. Elements of $SA$ are called *selected agents* and are supposed to have extreme opinions. An opinion will then be considered extreme iff it is close to the current opinion of one of these selected agents.

In the following we consider $\delta$, a function which measures how close two opinions are. We also consider a threshold $\epsilon \geq 0$.

**Definition 10.** *Let $A$ be a set of agents. A selected agent is a particular agent in $A$. The set of selected agents is denoted $SA$ with $SA \subseteq A$.*

**Definition 11.** *Let $A$ be a set of agents and $SA \subseteq A$ a set of selected agents. An opinion $o$ is $SA\epsilon$-extreme at step $t$ iff $\exists i \in SA$ st $\delta(o, B_i^t) \leq \epsilon$ where $B_i^t$ denotes the opinion of $i$ at step $t$*

According to the definition of $SA\epsilon$-extreme opinions[1], an opinion is extreme iff it is close to the opinion of a selected agent. As written before, the choice of selected agents depends on the context. For instance, in the cafeteria context, we could select the secretaries of the different student unions, thus considering them as a reference for extremism. As for the threshold, it also depends on the application. The smaller it is, the less we get extreme opinions.

As for the measure $\delta$, there are many options. We could for instance consider some pseudo-distances [15].

- Sum of minimum distances:
  $\delta_{summin}(o_1, o_2) = \frac{1}{2}(\sum_{w \in Mod(o_1)} D(w, o_2) + \sum_{w \in Mod(o_2)} D(w, o_1))$
- Hausdorff distance:
  $\delta_{Hau}(o_1, o_2) = max(max_{w \in Mod(o_1)} D(w, o_2), max_{w \in Mod(o_2)} D(w, o_1))$
- Minimum of distances
  $\delta_{min}(o_1, o_2) = min_{w_1 \in Mod(o_1), w_2 \in Mod(o_2)} d(w_1, w_2)$
- Sum of distances
  $\delta_{sum}(o_1, o_2) = \sum_{w_1 \in Mod(o_1), w_2 \in Mod(o_2)} d(w_1, w_2)$

We could also consider the following measure:

- Agreement-disagreement distance: Assume that the propositional letters are $p_1, ..., p_n$. $\delta_{AD}(o_1, o_2) = asc(\delta_{AD}^1, ..., \delta_{AD}^n)$ such that:
  - $\forall i = 1..n$, $\delta_{AD}^i = 0$ iff $o_1$ and $o_2$ agree on $p_i$ (i.e., $o_1 \models p_i$ iff $o_2 \models p_i$ and $o_1 \models \neg p_i$ iff $o_2 \models \neg p_i$); $\delta_{AD}^i = 1$ iff $o_1$ and $o_2$ disagree on $p_i$ (i.e., $o_1 \models p_i$ iff $o_2 \models \neg p_i$ and $o_1 \models \neg p_i$ iff $o_2 \models p_i$); $\delta_{AD}^i = 0.5$ in the other case.
  - *cresc* is the function with orders a sequence of integers in the ascending order.

We could even define measure $\delta$ from an inconsistency measure as follows:

- $\delta_{Inc}(o_1, o_2) = Inc(\{o_1, o_2\})$ where $Inc$ is a measure of inconsistency [16–18].

Or we could consider sweaker functions than pseudo-distances like:

- $\delta_{max}(o_1, o_2) = max_{w_1 \in Mod(o_1), w_2 \in Mod(o_2)} d(w_1, w_2)$

Finally, since the relation of influence is not symmetric, we could also drop the property of symmetry and consider:

[1] Notice that we should index this definition with $\delta$ but we omit it for readability reasons.

- $\delta_{maxmin}(o_1, o_2) = \max_{w_1 \in Mod(o_1)} min_{w_2 \in Mod(o_2)} d(w_1, w_2)$

Since there are many options, we propose to consider a set of requirements on which the different measures can be compared. They are given below. Notice that these requirements are not minimal since (R5) is subsumed by (R1).

- (R1) $\delta$ is a pseudo-distance, i.e. $\delta(\varphi, \psi)$ is minimal iff $\models \varphi \leftrightarrow \psi$ and $\delta(\varphi, \psi) = \delta(\psi, \varphi)$.
- (R2) The more propositional letters $\varphi$ and $\psi$ agree on, the smaller $\delta(\varphi, \psi)$ is.
- (R3) The more propositional letters $\varphi$ and $\psi$ disagree on, the higher $\delta(\varphi, \psi)$ is.
- (R4) If $\varphi_1 \wedge \psi_1$ is inconsistent and if $\varphi_2 \wedge \psi_2$ is consistent then $\delta(\varphi_2, \psi_2) < \delta(\varphi_1, \psi_1)$.
- (R5) If $\models \varphi \leftrightarrow \psi$ then $\delta(\varphi, \psi)$ is minimal.
- (R6) If $\models \varphi \leftrightarrow \varphi'$ and $\models \psi \leftrightarrow \psi'$ then $\delta(\varphi, \psi) = \delta(\varphi', \psi')$
- (R7) If $\varphi_1 \models \varphi_2$ then $\delta(\varphi_1, \varphi) \leq \delta(\varphi_2, \varphi)$

**Proposition 4.** *Table 3 shows which requirements the previous measures satisfy.*

*Let us illustrate these definitions with an example.*

**Table 3.** Measures versus requirements.

| | $\delta_{summin}$ | $\delta_{Hau}$ | $\delta_{AD}$ | $\delta_{Inc}$ | $\delta_{max}$ | $\delta_{min}$ | $\delta_{sum}$ | $\delta_{maxmin}$ |
|---|---|---|---|---|---|---|---|---|
| (R1) | Yes | Yes | No | No | No | Yes | Yes | Yes |
| (R2) | No | No | Yes | No | No | No | No | No |
| (R3) | No | Yes | Yes | No | No | Yes | No | No |
| (R4) | No/yes | No | No | Yes | No | Yes | No | No |
| (R5) | Yes | Yes | No | Yes | No | Yes | Yes | Yes |
| (R6) | Yes | Yes | Yes | No | Yes | Yes | Yes | Yes |
| (R7) | Yes | Yes | No | No | Yes | Yes | Yes | Yes |

*Example 3.* Take again $L = \{GMO, potatoes, fruits\}$. Consider one selected agent *John* whose current opinion is $GMO \wedge \neg potatoes$. Consider the following opinions: $GMO$, $GMO \wedge fruits$, $potatoes$, $fruits$, $GMO \vee \neg potatoes$. Table 4 shows their distance to *John*'s opinion with $\delta_{summin}$, $\delta_{Hau}$ and $\delta_{AD}$ when the distance between interpretations is $d_H$.

Consider $\delta_{summin}$ and assume that $\epsilon = 3$. Then, the extreme opinions are $GMO$, $GMO \wedge fruits$ and $GMO \vee \neg potatoes$.

Consider $\delta_{Hau}$ and assume that $\epsilon = 3$. Then, the extreme opinions are $GMO$ and $GMO \wedge fruits$.

Consider $\delta_{AD}$ and assume that $\epsilon = [0, 0.5, 0.5]$. Then, the extreme opinions are $GMO$ and $GMO \wedge fruits$.

This example shows that depending on the distances used, the set of extreme opinions may vary.

**Table 4.** Illustration of example 3.

| | $\delta_{summin}$ | $\delta_{Hau}$ | $\delta_{AD}$ |
|---|---|---|---|
| $GMO$ | 1 | 1 | [0, 0.5, 0.5] |
| $GMO \wedge fruits$ | 1 | 1 | [0, 0.5, 0.5] |
| $potatoes$ | 4 | 6 | [0, 0.5, 1] |
| $fruits$ | 4 | 6 | [0.5, 0.5, 0.5] |
| $GMO \vee \neg potatoes$ | 2.5 | 5 | [0.5, 0.5, 0.5] |

# 4 Diffusion of Extreme Opinions in IODS

## 4.1 Diffusion of Precise Opinions

We first define extremist agents as agents whose opinions are extreme. Moreover, agent are moderate when they are not extremist.

**Definition 12 (Extremist, Moderate).** *An agent $i$ is extremist at step $s$ iff $B_i^s$ is an extreme opinion. Otherwise it is moderate.*

*Example 4.* Consider two propositional letters $a, b$ and assume that at a given step $s$ agents opinions are: $B_i^s = a \vee b$, $B_j^s = a$, $B_k^s = a \wedge b$. If $R = 1$ then only $k$ is extremist. If $R = 2$ then $j$ and $k$ are extremist.

By definition of extreme opinions, it is true that extremist agents are more certain of their opinions than moderate ones. Indeed, let $DS = (A, \mu, B, Inf)$ be an Opinion Diffusion Structure, then $\forall i \in A$, $\forall j \in A$, $\forall s \in \mathbb{N}$, if $i$ is extremist at $s$ and $j$ is moderate at $s$ then $\mid Mod(B_i^s) \mid < \mid Mod(B_j^s) \mid$. Moreover, due to the definition of dogmatic agents, it is true that in an Opinion Diffusion Structure, a dogmatic agent who initially is extremist will remain extremist.

In the following, we list some properties of diffusion of extreme opinions in *IODS*.

First we can show that an agent whose main influencer is extremist at some step will be extremist at the next step.

**Proposition 5.** *In an IODS $S = (A, \mu, B, Inf)$, for $i \in A$ with $Inf(i) = \{j \prec_i \ldots\}$, for $t \in \mathbb{N}$, if $j$ is extremist at step $s$, then $i$ is extremist at step $s + 1$.*

As a consequence, an agent whose all influencers are extremist will become extremist. Another consequence is that a self-confident agent which is extremist at some step will remain extremist ever after:

We can also show that even if all its influencers are moderate, an agent may become extremist. For instance, take $R = 1$ and consider an agent who is influenced by two agents whose opinions are respectively $a$ and $b$. The agent's opinion, got after merging these two opinions, is $a \wedge b$. That is, the agent's opinion is extreme, while the opinions of all of its influencers are not.

The following proposition states that an agent which $k$-th influencer has an opinion consistent with the merging of the ones of the previous influencers at step $s$ and which $k$-th influencer is extremist at step $s$ will be extremist at step $s+1$.

**Proposition 6.** *In an IODS $S = (A, \mu, B, Inf)$, for $i \in A$ with $Inf(i) = \{j_1 \prec_i ... \prec_i j_k \prec_i ... \prec_i j_n\}$, for $s \in \mathbb{N}$, if $\Delta_\mu(B^s_{j_1} \prec_i ... \prec_i B^s_{j_{k-1}}) \wedge B^s_{j_k}$ is consistent and $j_k$ is extremist at step $s$, then $i$ is extremist at step $s+1$.*

More generally, an agent will be extremist at step $s+1$ iff for some $k$, the merging of the $k$ first influencers' opinions at step $s$ has less than $R$ models.

**Proposition 7.** *In an IODS $S = (A, \mu, B, Inf)$, for $i \in A$ with $Inf(i) = \{j_1 \prec_i ... \prec_i j_k \prec_i ...\}$. Let $s \in \mathbb{N}$. If $\exists k \in \mathbb{N}$, such that $\mid Mod(\Delta_\mu(B^s_{j_1} \prec ... \prec B^s_{j_k})) \mid \leq R$ then, $i$ is extremist at $s+1$. Otherwise, it is moderate at step $s+1$.*

The following proposition states that a self-confident extremist agent spreads extremism in its sphere of influence.

**Proposition 8.** *Let $S = (A, \mu, B, Inf)$ an IODS and $i \in A$ extremist at step $s$ with $Inf(i) = \{i \prec_i ...\}$. $\exists s' \geq s$, $\forall s \geq s'$, $\forall j \in Sphere(i)$ $j$ is extremist at step $s$.*

### 4.2 Diffusion of $S^1\alpha$-extreme and $S^2\alpha$-extreme Opinions

**Definition 13.** *We consider an IODS $DS = (A, \mu, B, Inf)$, a set of selected topics $S$ and a value $\alpha$. Let $i \in A$ and $t > 0$. $i$ is $S^1\alpha$-extremist (resp $S^2\alpha$-extremist) at step $t$ iff $B^t_i$ is a $S^1\alpha$-extreme (resp $S^2\alpha$-extreme) opinion. $i$ is $S^1$-not-extremist (resp $S^2$-not-extremist) at step $t$ iff $B^t_i$ is a $S^1$-not-extreme opinion (resp, $S^2$-not-extreme opinion).*

We first show how important is the main influncer in the spreading of extremism.

**Proposition 9.** *Consider an IODS $DS = (A, \mu, B, Inf)$, a set of selected topics $S$ and a value $\alpha$. Let $i \in A$ with $Inf(i) = \{i_1 \prec_i ... \prec_i i_n\}$ and let $t \geq 0$. If $i_1$ is $S^1\alpha$-extremist (resp, $S^2\alpha$-extremist) at step $t$ then $i$ is $S^1\alpha$-extremist (resp, $S^2\alpha$-extremist) at step $t+1$.*

As a consequence, given a definition of extremism, a self-confident agent which is extremist at a given step remains extremist. Moreover, a self-confident agent which is extremist spreads extremism in its sphere of influence as shown in the proposition below.

**Proposition 10.** *Consider an IODS $DS = (A, \mu, B, Inf)$, a set of selected topics $S$, a value $\alpha$ and let $t \geq 0$. Let $i \in A$ a self-confident agent which is $S^1\alpha$-extremist (resp, $S^2\alpha$-extremist) at $t$. Then $\forall j \in Sphere(i)$ $\exists s \geq t$ $\forall s' \geq s$ st $j$ is $S^1\alpha$-extremist (resp, $S^2\alpha$-extremist) at $s'$.*

So the two types of extremism defined previously, spread with influence. However, the corresponding non-extremism generally do not: an agent may become $S^1\alpha$-extremist (resp, $S^2\alpha$-extremist) even if its main influencer is $S^1$-not-extremist (resp, $S^2$-not-extremist) or worst, even if its influencers are $S^1\alpha$-not-extremist (resp, $S^2\alpha$-not-extremist) as shown in the following example.

*Example 5.* Consider a language with letters $a, b, c$ and $S = \{a\}$. Take $\alpha = 1$. Assume $SD = (A, \mu, B, Inf)$ with $A = \{1, 2, 3\}$, $\mu$ being a tautology, $Inf(1) = \{1\}, Inf(2) = \{2\}, Inf(3) = \{1 \prec 2 \prec 3\}$ and $B_1^0 = b, B_2^0 = a \vee \neg b, B_3^0 = a \vee a$. We can show that $B_3^1 = a \wedge b$. This proves that, even 1 and 2 are $S^1$-not-extremist nor $S^2$-not-extremist, 3 becomes $S^1 1$-extremist and $S^2 1$-extremist.

In the following, we study a case when non-extremism spreads under influence. But before we introduce the notion of opposition, as a particular case of non-extremism.

**Definition 14.** *Consider an IODS $DS = (A, \mu, B, Inf)$, $i \in A$ and $S$ a set of $n$ selected topics. $i$ is $S$-opponent at $t$ iff $B_i^t$ is $\overline{S}^1 n$-extreme (or equivalently, $\overline{S}^2 n$-extreme).*

Thus $i$ is $S$-opponent at $t$ iff $B_i^t \models \bigwedge \overline{S}$, iff $B_i^t \models \bigwedge_{s_i \in S} \neg s_i$. Obviously, $S$-opposition is a particular case of non-extremism. i.e., if $i$ is $S$-opponent at $t$ then $i$ is $S^1$-not-extreme and $S^2$-not-extreme at $t$.

The following proposition shows that $S$-opposition spreads under influence.

**Proposition 11.** *Consider an IODS $DS = (A, \mu, B, Inf)$, a set of selected topics $S$. Let $i \in A$ with $Inf(i) = \{i_1 \prec_i ... \prec_i i_n\}$ and $t \geq 0$. If $i_1$ is $S$-opponent at $t$ then $i$ is $S$-opponent at $t+1$.*

Again this shows the importance of the main influencer.

*Example 6.* In Example 5, agent 1 is not $S$-opponent since $Mod(B_1^0) = \{\{a, b\}, \{\neg a, b\}\}$. Moreover in this case, the merging operator selectes the model $\{a, b\}$ which ensures that 3 becomes extremist. Consider now a modified version of Example 5 and supose now that 1 is $S$-opponent by assuming $B_1^0 = \neg a \wedge b$. Then $B_3^1 = \neg a \wedge b$ i.e. 3 is $S$-opponent.

### 4.3 Diffusion of $SA\epsilon$-extreme Opinions

In this section, we study the diffusion of extremism when extreme opinions are defined as $SA\epsilon$ extreme opinions. Thus we consider the following definition.

**Definition 15.** *Let $A$ be a set of agents and $SA \subseteq A$ a set of selected agents. An agent $i \in A$ is $SA\epsilon$-extremist at step $t$ iff $B_i^t$ is an $SA\epsilon$-extreme opinion.*

Moreover, we assume that the selected agents are dogmatic i.e., they are not influenced by others and thus they don't change their opinions. Under this assumption, we can prove the following propositions.

**Proposition 12.** *Consider an IODS $DS = (A, \mu, B, Inf)$, a set of selected agents $SA$, a value $\epsilon$. Let $i \in A$ so that $Inf(i) = \{i_1 \prec ....\}$. Suppose that the distance used to characterize the $SA\epsilon$ extremism satisfies (R6) and (R7). Then: If $i_1$ is $SA\epsilon$-extremist at step $t$ then $i$ is $SA\epsilon$-extremist at step $t+1$*

The following is a corollary.

**Proposition 13.** *Consider an IODS $DS = (A, \mu, B, Inf)$, a set of selected agents $SA$, a value $\epsilon$. Suppose that the distance used to characterize the $SA\epsilon$ extremism satisfies (R6) and (R7). Let $i \in A$ be a self-confident who becomes $SA\epsilon$-extremist at time $t$. Then:*

*(1) $\forall t' \geq t$ $i$ is $SA\epsilon$-extremist at time $t'$.*
*(2) $\forall j \in Sphere(i)$ $\forall t' \geq t$ $j$ is $SA\epsilon$-extremist at time $t'$.*

## 5 Generating Graphs for Experiments

In this section and the following, we focus on simulating with NetLogo the diffusion of some extreme opinions. More precisely, in this section, we address the question of generating graphs corresponding to real social networks. For that, we review some propositions made in graph theory during the last decades. Then, we adapt them to our context.

### 5.1 Graph Theory Bases

One of the most used models of graph is the one of Erdös-Rényi. It is a model of random graph (see [19]).

**Definition 16 (Erdös-Rényi Graph).** *Given a number of nodes $n$ and an integer $m$. An Erdös-Rényi Graph is any graph obtained by selecting randomly $m$ edges among the $2^n$ possible ones.*

Another model of graph that is widely used is the model of Watts-Strogatz. This model has been made to describe the phenomenon of Small-World or "six degrees of separation" highlighted by Milgram [20]. This psychologist established through an experiment the theory that a message can be transmitted from one person to one another by passing by an average of six friends. The Small-World theory is commonly formalized [19,21,22] as follows:

**Definition 17 (Small-World).** *A graph $G$ is said Small-World if it satisfies:*

1. *$G$ is connected.*
2. *$G$ is sparse: the average degree of the nodes $k$ is low compared to the number of nodes $n$, $k \ll n$.*
3. *$G$ is decentralized: the maximal degree of the nodes $k_{max}$ is low compared to the number of nodes $n$, $k_{max} \ll n$.*

4. *The characteristic path L (the average number of nodes traversed by a short path between two nodes) is close to the one of a random graph with the same number of nodes n and the same average degree k,* $L \approx L_{random} \sim \frac{ln(n)}{ln(k)}$.
5. *The clustering coefficient C (the probability that two nodes i and j are connected given that they share a common neighbor) is high compared to the one of a random graph with the same number of nodes n and the same average degree k,* $C \gg C_{random} \sim \frac{k}{n}$.

One can notice that Erdös-Rényi graphs as random graphs have low characteristic paths by definition.

The following model, from [19] and adapted from a model generally attributed to Watts and Strogatz, define Small-World graphs:

**Definition 18 (Rank-Based Friendship Graph).** *Given a number of nodes n, a threshold r, an exponent q and a dimension d, the nodes are randomly distributed in a space of dimension d. Rank-Based Friendship Graph is obtained by going as follows:*

*For each node i, we rank the other nodes according to their distances to i and we break ties with a chosen method. There will be an edge from a node j to the node i with probability* $\frac{1}{Z.rank_i(j)^q}$, $rank_i(j)$ *being the rank of j in i's neighbors and Z a coefficient of normalization,* $Z = \sum_{i=1}^{n} \frac{1}{rank_i(j)^q} = \sum_{i=1}^{n} \frac{1}{i^q}$.

## 5.2 Models

Here we adapt the previous models of graphs to IODS and explain how we construct them for the simulations. In the following we take an integrity constraint being a tautology.

The first model we adapt is the one of the random graph defined by Erdös and Rényi. The following definition shows how we construct Erdös and Rényi IODS. Notice that we add a parameter, the number of self-confident agents, which is an interesting variable to study.

**Definition 19 (Erdös-Rényi-Based IODS).** *Given the parameters num-letters, num-nodes, num-links and num-self-confident, the IODS is constructed as follows:*

*We begin by creating num-nodes agents, each of them has a random opinion in a language of num-letters letters. Then, we create num-links relations of influence by choosing randomly an influencer and an influenced agent (potentially the same). The influencers are ordered according to the order of creation of the relation of influence, the sooner a relation of influence would have been created the more influencing it is. Finally, each agent with no influencers will become dogmatic and, if necessary, we add relations of self-influence until we have num-self-confident self-confident agents (dogmatic agents included). We pick randomly an agent and if it does not already influence himself we make it self-confident by putting it as its main influencer (the order of the other influencers remains unchanged).*

This second model adapts the model of Rank-Based Friendship by considering a distance between opinions instead of a physical distance as for the graph model.

**Definition 20 (Rank-Based Influenceship IODS).** *Given the parameters num-letters, num-nodes, opinions-distance, q and num-self-confident, the IODS is constructed as follows:*

*We begin by creating num-nodes agents, each of them has a random opinion in a language of num-letters letters. Then, we fill a matrix with the distances between every couple of agents according to the distance between their opinions and computed with the distance opinions-distance. For each agent i we have a list $l_i$ of all the agents (i included) sorted according to their distances to i. If two agents $j_1$ and $j_2$ are at the same distance of i, then the tie will be randomly solved. Each agent j will be an influencer of i with probability $\frac{1}{Z.rank_i(j)^q}$, $rank_i(j)$ being the rank of j in $l_i$ and Z being a coefficient of normalization, $Z = \sum_{i=1}^{num-nodes} \frac{1}{rank_i(j)^q} = \sum_{i=1}^{num-nodes} \frac{1}{i^q}$. The influencers of i are ordered as in $l_i$. Finally, if necessary, we add relations of self-influence such as we have num-self-confident self-confident agents (dogmatic agents included). We pick randomly an agent and if it is not already self-confident we make it so by putting it as its main influencer (the order of the other influencers remains unchanged).*

The third model is a variant of the previous one, here an agent will be influenced by the $m$ agents that have the closest opinions from its own one for a given integer $m$.

**Definition 21 (Deterministic Rank-Based Influenceship IODS).** *Given the parameters num-letters, num-nodes, opinions-distance, m and num-self-confident, the IODS is constructed as follows:*

*We begin by creating num-nodes agents, each of them has a random opinion in a language of num-letters letters. Then, we fill a matrix with the distances between every couple of agents according to the distance between their opinions and computed with the distance opinions-distance. For each agent i, we conserve the m closest agents to i to be its influencers. If two agents $j_1$ and $j_2$ are at the same distance of i, then the tie will be randomly solved. The influencers of i are ordered according to their distances to i. Finally, we add relations of self-influence such as we have num-self-confident self-confident agents (dogmatic agents included). We pick randomly an agent and if it is not already self-confident we make it so by putting it as its main influencer (the order of the other influencers remains unchanged).*

The fourth model is a generalization of the Rank-Based Influenceship in which we have in addition to the distance between opinions a physical distance along a circle. The influencers of an agent $i$ are ordered according to the distance between their opinions and the one of $i$.

**Definition 22 (Opinions and Physical Rank-Based Influenceship IODS).** *Given the parameters num-letters, num-nodes, opinions-distance, r, q and num-self-confident, the IODS is constructed as follows:*

*We begin by creating num-nodes agents, each of them has a random opinion in a language of num-letters letters. We fill a matrix with the distances between every couple of agents according to the distance between their opinions and computed with the distance opinions-distance. For each agent i we have a list $l_i$ of all the agents (i included) sorted according to their distances to i. If two agents $j_1$ and $j_2$ are at the same distance of i, then the tie will be randomly solved. Each agent j will be an influencer of i with probability $\frac{1}{Z.rank_i(j)^q}$, $rank_i(j)$ being the rank of j in $l_i$ and Z a coefficient of normalization $Z = \sum_{i=1}^{num-nodes} \frac{1}{rank_i(j)^q} = \sum_{i=1}^{num-nodes} \frac{1}{i^q}$. At the previous influencers we add influencers that are physically close. Indeed, all the agents will be placed on a circle. The agents that are separated on the circle from an agent i by less than r agents will influence i. The influencers of i are ordered as in $l_i$ (according to the distance between opinions). Finally, if necessary, we add relations of self-influence such as we have num-self-confident self-confident agents (dogmatic agents included). We pick randomly an agent and if it is not already self-confident we make it so by putting it as its main influencer (the order of the other influencers remains unchanged).*

## 6 Some Experiments

In this section, we present simulations of precise opinion diffusion in the different graphs previously presented. Moreover, as for the distances between opinions, we focus on $\delta_{summin}$, $\delta_{Hau}$, $\delta_{max}$, $\delta_{min}$, $\delta_{maxmin}$, $\delta_{sum}$ with the drastic pseudo-distance between interpretations $d_D$.

To study and compare the results between the different models and distances, we carried out several simulations with the same settings. Furthermore, in order to do comparable and reproducible experiments we chose some values of seeds for the random operations in Netlogo. Seeds allow to have the same results in the same order for random operations when we repeat the simulations. The values we study are the number of extremist agents for $R = 1$, the average number of models per agents and the number of dogmatic agents.

In the simulations we present here, we have taken the following values: seed $\{0, 100, 200\}$, *num-letters* $\{3, 4, 5, 6\}$, *num-nodes* $\{10, 60, 110, 160, 210\}$, *num-self-confident* $\{0, 50, 100, 150, 200, 210\}$. For the three models using ranks we tested $\delta_{summin}$, $\delta_{Hau}$, $\delta_{max}$, $\delta_{min}$, $\delta_{maxmin}$, $\delta_{sum}$ with the drastic pseudo-distance between interpretations. For the Erdös-Rényi-Based model we took *num-links* varying from 10 to 2000 with an increment of 50. For the Rank-Based Influenceship and the Opinions and Physical Rank-Based Influenceship models we took the values $\{1, 2, 3, 4, 5\}$ for $q$, for the Deterministic Rank-Based Influenceship model we took $m$ in $\{1, 2, 3, 4\}$ and for the Opinions and Physical Rank-Based Influenceship model we took $r$ in $\{1, 2, 3, 4, 5\}$. The pseudo-distance between interpretations used to compute the Importance-based Merging operator is the drastic one.

First of all, *with the drastic pseudo-distance* $d_H$, we can notice that the different distances we used have particular behaviors. $\delta_{summin}(o_1, o_2) \in [0, 2^{num-letters}]$ and $\delta_{summin}(o_1, o_2) = 0$ iff $o_1 \equiv o_2$. $\delta_{summin}$ favors relations of influence between agents which opinions have models very close according to $D$, in average. $\delta_{Hau}(o_1, o_2)$ is 0 or 1 and $\delta_{Hau}(o_1, o_2) = 0$ iff $o_1 \equiv o_2$. $\delta_{Hau}$ favors relations of influence between agents which opinions have no models very far from one another. So, in the case of the drastic pseudo-distance, it favors relations between agents that have the same opinion. So, for the number of letters and agents we will consider, as such a case is unlikely the relations of influence will be mostly random. $\delta_{max}(o_1, o_2)$ is 0 or 1 and $\delta_{max}(o_1, o_2) = 0$ iff $\exists w$, $Mod(o_1) = Mod(o_2) = \{w\}$. So, as having two agents with only one model and the same model is very unlikely for the number of letters and agents we consider, $\delta_{max}$ favors random relations of influence and it will be interesting to compare the results obtained with this distance and the ones obtained with the other distances. $\delta_{min}(o_1, o_2)$ is 0 or 1 and $\delta_{min}(o_1, o_2) = 0$ iff $\exists w \in Mod(o_1) \cap Mod(o_2)$. Then, for a given agent $i$, $\delta_{min}$ favors relations of influence that are from agents that share a model with $i$'s opinion but that are otherwise random. $\delta_{maxmin}(o_1, o_2)$ is 0 or 1 and $\delta_{maxmin}(o_1, o_2) = 0$ iff $o_1 \models o_2$. So, $\delta_{maxmin}$ favors relations of influence from an agent $i$ to an agent $j$ such that all the models of $B_j$ are models of $B_i$. $\delta_{sum}(o_1, o_2) \in [0, 2^{num-letters}]$ and $\delta_{sum}(o_1, o_2) = 0$ iff $Mod(o_1) = Mod(o_2) = \{w\}$. $\delta_{sum}$ favors relations of influence from agents which opinions have the less models.

For the Erdös-Rényi-Based model (see Fig. 2), we have several peaks of the average number of models and of the number of dogmatic agents, corresponding to having low *num-links*. Indeed, in these cases, there are potentially more agents that are not influenced by other agents and that keep their initial opinions. Furthermore, we can see that the dogmatic agents are almost the only agents that are not extremist and thus contribute the more to the average number of models. So, the diffusion of extremism depends a lot on the ratio between *num-links* and *num-nodes*, the more there are relations of influence the more the agents will become extremist. We can only notice that the peaks of average number of models are higher and higher according to the increasing of the number of letters. Another experiment in which we took 200 agents and much more relations of influence (up to 7000) showed that for more than 2000 there are very few simulations with non-extremist agents.

For the Rank-Based Influenceship model (see Fig. 3), we have several plateaus higher and higher according to the increasing of the number of letters. Furthermore, there are cases with very low numbers of extremist agents and without very much dogmatic agents. Then, we can notice that there are big differences according to the distance we use. Indeed, a thorougher analysis highlights that the biggest peaks are with $\delta_{summin}$ and then with $\delta_{Haus}$ and $\delta_{maxmin}$. $\delta_{max}$ and $\delta_{min}$ cause some lesser peaks when $q$ gets bigger (more than 3) and $\delta_{sum}$ causes very small peaks for $q = 5$. For $q = 1$ almost all the agents are extremist

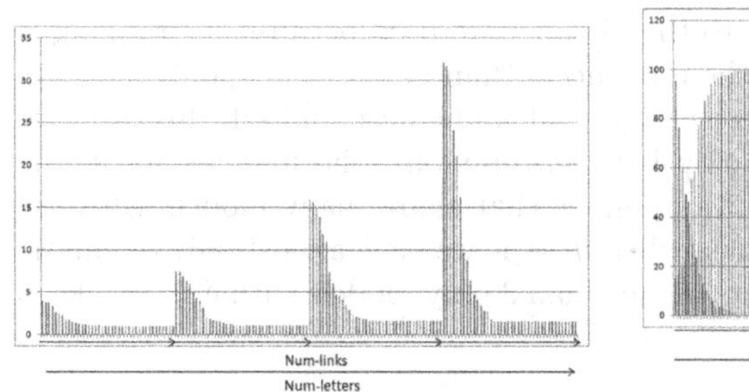


Average Number of Models per Agents

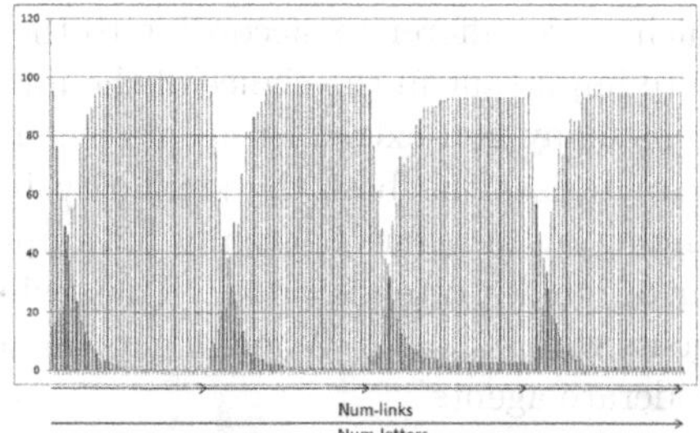


Proportion of extremist agents (blue) and dogmatic agents (red)

**Fig. 2.** Example: Erdös-Rényi-Based model *seed = 0, num-nodes = 210, num-self-confident = 0* (extracted from [14]).

whatever the distance we use. It can be explained by the fact that the lesser $q$ is the more likely relations of influence are to be created, furthermore for $q$ high enough the distance used matter less then even $\delta_{sum}$ that in the other cases spread extremism may be used to create an IODS where they may remain some moderate agents. But, according to [19] in the case of graphs, the Rank-Based Friendship generates graphs the closest of reality for $q = 1$. Furthermore, when the number of agents increases, the average number of models decreases because more relations of influence may be created. One can notice that with this model $\delta_{summin}$ and $\delta_{Haus}$ particularly favor moderation. So, having influencers with opinions for which each model is close of one of us model or for which each model is not far of any of our model favor moderation. But, we can notice that with $\delta_{Haus}$ agents are much less dogmatic than with $\delta_{summin}$.

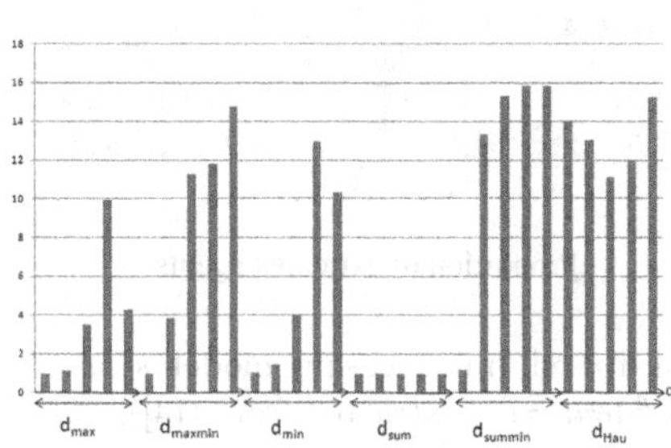


Average Number of Models per Agents

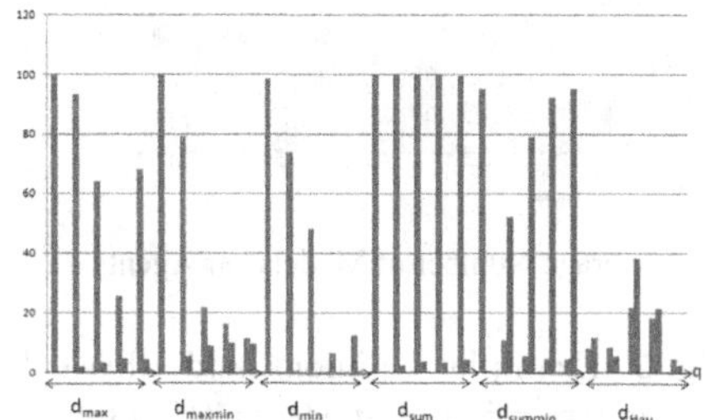


Proportion of extremist agents (blue) and dogmatic agents (red)

**Fig. 3.** Example: Rank-Based Influenceship model *seed = 0, num-letters = 5, num-nodes = 210, num-self-confident = 0* (extracted from [14]).

For the Deterministic Rank-Based Influenceship model (see Fig. 4), extremism spreads more and more when $m$ gets bigger. Moreover, this time there is much more differences according to the distance we used because the ranking is more important in the choice of the influencers than before. Then, only $\delta_{summin}$ keeps many non-extremist agents when $m$ is at its highest. Indeed, this distance characterizes the best the similarity between opinions, the first agents in the ranking of an agent $i$ actually have opinions that share many models with the one of $i$ and it often is $i$ itself. Thus, when $m = 1$, we have almost only dogmatic agents with $\delta_{summin}$. When $m$ gets higher than 3 only models with $\delta_{summin}$ keep moderate agents.

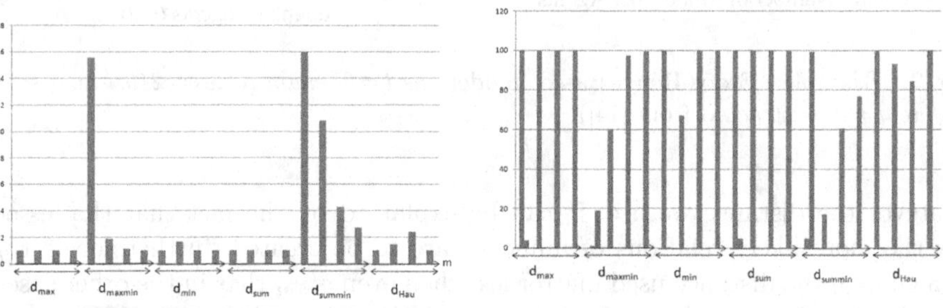


**Fig. 4.** Example: Deterministic Rank-Based Influenceship model *seed* = *0*, *num-nodes* = *210*, *num-self-confident* = *0* (extracted from [14]).

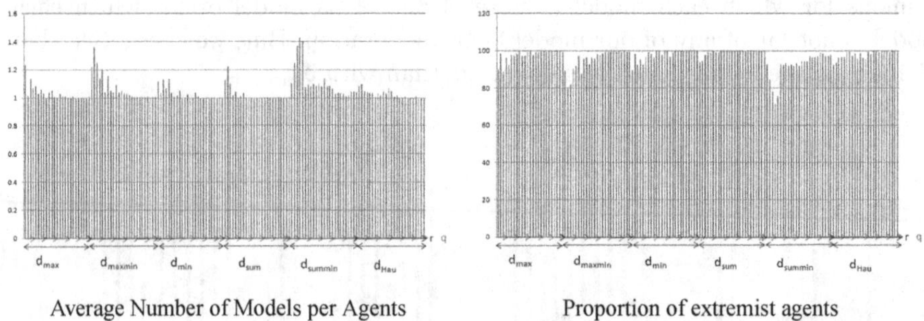


**Fig. 5.** Example: Opinions and Physical Rank-Based Influenceship model *seed* = *0*, *num-letters* = *5*, *num-nodes* = *210*, *num-self-confident* = *0* (extracted from [14]).

For the Opinions and Physical Rank-Based Influenceship model (see Fig. 5), we have very few non-extremist agents even with $\delta_{summin}$ and even less when $r$ increases. It is due to the fact that here there cannot be any dogmatic agent (contrary to the case of the Rank-Based Influenceship) and that an agent may have influencers with very different opinions (contrary to the case of the Deterministic Rank-Based Influenceship).

In all the simulations, the number of letters does not affect the proportion of extremist agents. The number of nodes affects the proportion of extremist agents for the Erdös-Rényi-Based model because of our definition of the model, in fact it is the ratio between the number of agents and the number of relations of influence that truly matters. It also has an influence for Rank-Based Influenceship model and the Opinions and Physical Rank-Based Influenceship model because it increases the average number of influencers.

For summarizing, among the different models of IODS, the ones which spread extremism the less are the Rank-Based Influenceship when $q$ is very high and the Erdös-Rényi-Based when *num-links* is much lower than *num-nodes*. But, those models have many dogmatic agents, on the other hand, the Deterministic Rank-Based Influenceship spreads extremism very little with $\delta_{summin}$ and a small $m$ and without many dogmatic agents. For the distances, it is $\delta_{summin}$ that spreads extremism the less because it favors relations of influence from agents with opinions sharing many models and it spreads extremism less than $\delta_{max}$ (the random one). At the opposite, $\delta_{sum}$ spreads extremism very well by creating hubs, agents with very few models that influence a lot of agents. $\delta_{min}$ spreads extremism a little less because it is less random, there is a constraint on one model. So, with the Importance-Based Merging Operator, the extremism spreads very well when the most extremist agents are very influential and much less when agents are influenced by agents with opinions similar to its own in the sense of they share many models. So, what makes that an agent remains moderate is the fact that he is influenced by agents which opinions share many models between them and that he does not have too many influencers. Having many self-confident agents favor extremism spreading with the Erdös-Rényi-Based model as it increases the average number of influencers but in the other models it favors moderation. Indeed, in this case the agents keep opinions close to their initial ones and so agents' influencers keep close opinions.

We can notice that, in every simulation, we reached the convergence very quickly in general in less than 5 updates.

It would have been interesting to test the models for much larger numbers of agents to increase the probabilities we have deemed negligible in our study of the distances for instance. Indeed, the Small-World phenomenon is considered interesting for very large number of nodes i.e. billions of nodes (see [23]) but the computation time that would be needed only for models of thousands of agents is very important.

Furthermore, other simulations with Hamming pseudo distance both for the computation of the distances between opinions and the update of the opinions gave similar results. Notwithstanding, extremism spreads slightly much, in average 0.8 less models per agents and 9% less extremist agents. This can mainly be explain by the fact that $Min_{\leq_{\delta_H,\varphi_1\prec\varphi_2}} Mod(\mu)$ contains generally less models than $Min_{\leq_{\delta_D,\varphi_1\prec\varphi_2}} Mod(\mu)$ as the second one keeps all the models of $\varphi_1$ if $\varphi_1$ and $\varphi_2$ are inconsistent. The only type of IODS that spreads less extremism in this case is the Rank-Based Influenceship model, in average there are 2 more models per agents and 10% less extremist agents. But, it can be explained by the fact that there are twice more (15% more) dogmatic agents, the hamming pseudo-distance allows a more accurate ranking of the agents and thus, it is less likely that agents with very different opinions influence an agent. It appears that this accuracy is all the more significant that the number of letters is important. However, the first agents in the rankings do not change a lot, so the Deterministic Rank-Based Influenceship model spreads more extremism. Another noticeable difference are for $\delta_{Hau}$ and $\delta_{summin}$ which spread extremism much less in the three Rank-Based Influenceship models.

What we can notice is that the more relations of influence there are, the more extremism spreads. And, the more influencers of agents have close opinions, the less extremism spreads. This result can be interpreted as follows: When someone makes its own mind by taking into account the opinions of many people it considers as reliable or experts on the matter and with different opinions then, it will be very sure of its new opinion as it is a compromised between the opinions of many experts. And so, this person will become extremist according to our definition.

## 7 Conclusion

This paper focused on extremism diffusion in IODS. Its main contributions are: a proposal of different definitions of extreme opinions and extremist agents; a formal study of diffusion of these different kinds of extreme opinions in IODS; a simulation in NetLogo of the diffusion of the first kind of extreme opinions.

This work could be continued according to several directions. Let us mention three of them. First, experiments for the other kinds of extreme opinions are to be made in a near future. Besides, we want to extend this study in the case when the procedure for updating opinions is not Importance-Based Merging but Majority-Based Merging Operator [24]. Finally, we plan to add a dynamic aspect by changing the relations of influence through time as it is often done in the usual models [1,2,9,10]. It will be especially interesting with the rank-based models where the ranking of the influencers is based on the distances between opinions. Since opinions change through time these distances also change and computing new rankings could be done.

## 8 Proofs

**Proof of Proposition 1**

Suppose that $o$ is extreme. Let $\{m_1, ...m_N\}$ (with $N \leq R$) be its models. By definition, each model $m_k$ of $o$ is of the form $\{l_1^k, ...l_n^k\}$ where $l_i^k$ is $a_i$ or $\neg a_i$. As a consequence, $o$ is equivalent to $\bigvee_{k=1}^{N} l_1^k \wedge ... \wedge l_n^k$ with $l_i^k$ being $a_i$ or $\neg a_i$.

**Proof of Proposition 2**

- If $o$ is $S^1\alpha$-extreme then there is $S_\alpha$ st $Mod(o) \subseteq Mod(\bigwedge S_\alpha)$. Consider $1 \leq \beta \leq \alpha$ and take $S_\beta \subseteq S_\alpha$ of size $\beta$. $S_\beta \subseteq S_\alpha$ implies $Mod(\bigwedge S_\alpha) \subseteq$

$Mod(\bigwedge S_\beta)$. As a consequence, $o$ is $S^1\beta$-extreme
Suppose now that $o$ is $S^2\alpha$-extreme. Then $Mod(o) \subseteq \{w : S(w) \geq \alpha\} \subseteq \{w : S(w) \geq \beta\}$ thus $o$ is $S^2\beta$-extreme.

- If $o$ is $S^1\alpha$-extreme then $\exists S_\alpha \subseteq S$ st$Mod(o) \subseteq Mod(\bigwedge S_\alpha)$. Thus any model of $o$ satisfies exactly $\alpha$ selected topics. Thus $Mod(o) \subseteq \{w \in Mod(L) : S(w) \geq \alpha\}$ (i.e. $o$ is $S^2\alpha$-extreme).
Moreover, the fifth line of Table 2 proves that $S^2\alpha$-extreme $\not\subseteq S^1\alpha$-extreme
- This is a corollary of the previous point.
- We notice that $\{w \in Mod(L) : S(w) \geq\mid S \mid\} = \{w : S(w) =\mid S \mid\} = Mod(S)$. Now suppose that $o$ is $S^1 \mid S \mid$-extreme. This means that $Mod(o) \subseteq Mod(\bigwedge S)$, i.e. $Mod(o) \subseteq \{w \in Mod(L) : S(w) \geq\mid S \mid\}$ i.e., $o$ is $S^2 \mid S \mid$-extreme

## Proof of Proposition 3

- $o$ is $S^1$-not-extreme iff for all $\alpha$ $o$ is not $S^1\alpha$-extreme i.e., for all $\alpha$, for any $S_\alpha = \{s_{i_1}, ..., s_{i_\alpha}\} \subseteq S$, $Mod(o) \not\subseteq Mod(S_\alpha)$ i.e., $\exists w \in Mod(o)$ such that $w \models \neg s_{i_1} \vee ... \vee \neg s_{i_\alpha}$ i.e. $\exists w \in Mod(o)$ and $\exists j$ such that $w \models \neg s_{i_j}$ i.e. $o \wedge \neg s_{i_j}$ is consistent.
- $o$ is $S^2$-not-extreme iff $\exists w \in Mod(o)$ st $S(w) = 0$ i.e., $\exists w \in Mod(o)$ st $w \models \neg s_1$ and... and $w \models \neg s_n$, i.e., $o \wedge \neg s_1 ... \wedge \neg s_n$ is consistent.
- There is an $\alpha$ so that $o$ is $S^2\alpha$-extreme iff $o$ is not not-extreme. I.e., $o \wedge \neg s_1 ... \wedge \neg s_n$ is inconsistent, i.e., $o \models s_1 \vee ... \vee s_n$.
- $\alpha$ is the highest value st $o$ is $S^2\alpha$-extreme iff each model of $o$ satisfies exactly $\alpha$ letters of $S$. Suppose that $Mod(o) = \{w_1, ...w_k\}$. Then for any $w_i$, there exists $S_i \subseteq S$ with $\mid S_i \mid= \alpha$ st $w_i \models \bigwedge_{s \in S_i} s \bigwedge_{s \in S \setminus S_i} \neg s \bigwedge_{s \notin S_i} l_s$, $l_s$ being $s$ ou $\neg s$.
Thus $o$ is equivalent to $\bigvee_{i=1...k} (\bigwedge_{s \in S_i} s \bigwedge_{s \in S \setminus S_i} \neg s \bigwedge_{s \notin S} l_s)$.

## Proof of Proposition 4

- $\delta_{summin}$ satisfies (R1). $\delta_{summin}$ does not satisfy (R2). Indeed if the distance between interpretations being $d_H$ Then $\delta_{summin}(c, a \wedge b) = 5/2$ and $\delta_{summin}(a \wedge c, a \wedge b) = 1$; if it is $d_D$, then $\delta_{summin}(c, a \wedge b) = 0$ and $\delta_{summin}(a \wedge c, a \wedge b) = 0$. $\delta_{summin}$ does not satisfy (R3). Indeed, if the distance between interpretations being $d_H$ then $\delta_{summin}(a, b \wedge c) = 2$ and $\delta_{summin}(a \wedge b \wedge c, \neg \wedge b \wedge c) = 1$; if it is $d_D$ then $\delta_{summin}(a, \neg a) = 1$ and $\delta_{summin}(a \wedge b, \neg a \wedge \neg b) = 1$. $\delta_{summin}$ does not satisfy (R4) when the distance between interpretations is $d_H$. Indeed $\delta_{summin}(a \wedge b \wedge c, \neg \wedge b \wedge c) = 1$ is not strictly less than $\delta_{summin}(a \wedge c, a \wedge b) = 1$. But it does when the distance between interpretations is $d_D$. Indeed, in this case, the distance between two consistent formulas is 0 while the distance between two inconsistent formulas is 1. $\delta_{summin}$ satisfies (R5) since it satisfies (R1). $\delta_{summin}$ satisfies (R6) since it is model-based. $\delta_{summin}$ satisfies (R7) because if $\varphi_1 \models \varphi_2$ then $Mod(\varphi_1) \subseteq Mod(\varphi_2)$ thus $\sum_{w \in Mod(\varphi_1)} D(w, \varphi) \leq \sum_{w \in Mod(\varphi_2)} D(w, \varphi)$.

- $\delta_{Hau}$ does not satisfy (R2). Indeed take $d_H$. $\delta_{Hau}(a \wedge b, a) = 1$ while $\delta_{Hau}(a \wedge b, a \wedge (a \rightarrow b)) = 0$. Now take $d_D$. $\delta_{Hau}(a, \neg a) = 0$ and $\delta_{Hau}(a \wedge b, \neg a \wedge b) = 0$ also. $\delta_{Hau}$ satisfies (R3). Indeed, if the number of letters $o_1$ and $o_2$ disagree on is less than the number of letters $o'_1$ and $o_2$ disagree on, then $max_{w \models o_1} D(w, o_2) \leq max_{w \models o'_1} D(w, o_2)$ thus $\delta_{Hau}(o_1, o_2) \leq \delta_{Hau}(o'_1, o_2)$. $\delta_{Hau}$ does not satisfy (R4). Take $d_H$, then $\delta_{Hau}(a \wedge b, c) = 2$ and $\delta_{Hau}(a \wedge b \wedge c, \neg a \wedge b \wedge c) = 1$. Take $d_D$, $\delta_{Hau}(a \wedge b, c) = 1$ and $\delta_{Hau}(a \wedge b, \neg a \wedge b) = 1$. Since $\delta_{Hau}$ satisfies (R1) it also satisfies (R5) $\delta_{Hau}$ satisfies (R6) since it is model-based. $\delta_{Hau}$ satisfies (R7). Indeed, if $\emptyset_1 \models \emptyset'_1$ then $Mod(\emptyset_1) \subseteq Mod(\emptyset'_1)$ thus $max_{w \models \emptyset_1} D(w, o_2) \leq max_{w \models \emptyset'_1} D(w, o_2)$ and $max_{w \models \emptyset_2} D(w, o_1) \leq max_{w \models \emptyset_2} D(w, o'_1)$. Thus $\delta_{Hau}(o_1, o_2) \leq \delta_{Hau}(o'_1, o_2)$.
- $\delta_{AD}$ does not satisfy (R1). Indeed, $\delta_{AD}$ is a less than a pseudo-distance. First, notice that $\delta_{AD}(\varphi, \varphi') = (0, ..., 0) \not\Longleftrightarrow \varphi \leftrightarrow \varphi'$. We only have $\delta_{AD}(\varphi, \varphi') = (0, ..., 0)$ iff they totally agree; However we have $\delta_{AD}(\varphi, \varphi') = \delta_{AD}(\varphi', \varphi)$. $\delta_{AD}$ satisfy (R2) and (R3). Indeed, if $\varphi$ and $\psi_1$ agree on more letters than $\varphi$ and $psi_2$ then $\delta_{AD}(\varphi, \psi_1) \leq_v \delta_{AD}(\varphi, \psi_2)$. If $\varphi$ and $\psi_1$ disagree on more letters than $\varphi$ and $\psi_2$ then $\delta_{AD}(\varphi, \psi_2) \leq_v \delta_{AD}(\varphi, \psi_1)$. $\delta_{AD}$ does not satisfy (R4). Take $a$ and $b$ on one side and $a \wedge b$ and $a \wedge \neg b$ on the other. The first two formulas are consistent while the second two are inconsistent. However $\delta_{AD}(a, b) = (0.5, 0.5)$ and $\delta_{AD}(a \wedge b, \neg a \wedge \neg b) = (0, 1)$. $\delta_{AD}$ does not satisfy (R5). Indeed, suppose that the language is $L = \{a, b, c\}$. Then $\delta_{AD}(a \wedge (b \vee c), a \wedge (a \rightarrow (b \vee c))) = (0, 0.5, 0.5)$. This proves that two equivalent formulas may not have the minimal $\delta_{AD}$-distance. $\delta_{AD}$ satisfy (R6). Indeed, if $\models \varphi \leftrightarrow \varphi'$ and $\models \psi \leftrightarrow \psi'$ then $\varphi$ and $\psi$ agree (resp disagree) on $p$ iff $\varphi'$ and $\psi'$ agree (resp disagree) on $p$. Thus $\delta(\varphi, \psi) = \delta(\varphi', \psi')$. $\delta_{AD}$ does not satisfy (R7). Take for instance $a \wedge \neg b \wedge \neg c \models a \wedge \neg b$ but $\delta_{AD}(a \wedge \neg b \wedge \neg c, a \wedge b \wedge c) = (0, 1, 1)$ and $\delta_{AD}(a \wedge \neg b, a \wedge b \wedge c) = (0, 0.5, 1)$.
- $\delta_{Inc}$ does not satisfy (R1). Take $a$ and $b$. $\delta_{Inc}(a, b) = 0$ even if $\not\models a \leftrightarrow b$. $\delta_{Inc}$ does not satisfy (R2). Indeed, we will have $\delta_{Inc}(\varphi, \psi) = 0$ as soon as $\varphi \wedge \psi$ is consistent. Take $a$ and $b$ on one side and $a$ and $a \wedge b$ on the other. Whatever the measure $Inc$ is, $\delta_{Inc}(a, b) = \delta_{Inc}(a, a \wedge b) = 0$, even if $a$ and $a \wedge b$ agree on more letter than $a$ and $b$. $\delta_{Inc}$ generally does not satisfy (R3). For instance $\delta_{Inc}$ where $Inc$ is the drastic inconsistency measure (defined by $Inc(S) = 1$ iff $S$ is inconsistent and $Inc(S) = 0$ iff $S$ is consistent) does not satisfy (R3). Indeed, even if $a \wedge b$ and $\neg a \wedge \neg b$ disagree on more letters than $a \wedge b$ and $\neg a$, $\delta_{Inc}(a \wedge b, \neg a) = \delta_{Inc}(a \wedge b, \neg a \wedge \neg b)$. $\delta_{Inc}$ satisfies (R4). Indeed, an inconsistency measure associates a set of formulas with a non negative real so that this real is 0 if and only if the set is consistent. As a consequence, if $\varphi_1 \wedge \psi_1$ is inconsistent, then $Inc(\{\varphi_1, \psi_1\}) > 0$ and if $\varphi_2 \wedge \psi_2$ is consistent, then $Inc(\{\varphi_2, \psi_2\}) = 0$. Thus $\delta_{Inc}(\varphi_2, \psi_2) < \delta_{Inc}(\varphi_1, \psi_1)$. $\delta_{Inc}$ satisfies (R5). Indeed, we only consider consistent formulas. Then, if $\models \varphi \leftrightarrow \psi$, $\varphi \wedge \psi$ is consistent thus $\delta_{Inc}(\varphi, \psi) = 0$. If $\delta_{Inc}$ is defined from a syntactical measure (such as the one which counts the minimal inconsistent subsets) then (R6) is not satisfied. $\delta_{Inc}$ does not satisfy (R7). For instance, indeed if $a \wedge \neg a \models b$, we have $\delta_{Inc}(a \wedge \neg a, a) > \delta_{Inc}(b, a)$. More generally, according to [16] any inconsistency measure $Inc$ satisfies the property of dominance i.e., $\varphi_1 \models \varphi_2$

implies $Inc(S \cup \{\varphi_1\}) \geq Inc(S \cup \{\varphi_2\})$. Thus $\varphi_1 \models \varphi_2$ implies $\delta_{Inc}(\varphi_1, \varphi) \geq \delta_{Inc}(\varphi_2, \varphi)$ i.e., $\delta_{Inc}$ never satisfies (R7).

- $\delta_{max}$ does not satisfy (R1). For instance if the letters are $a$ and $b$, $\delta_{max}(a, a) = 1$ (with $d_H$ and with $d_D$) which is not the minila value. $\delta_{max}$ does not satisfy (R2). Indeed, with $d_H$ we have: $\delta_{max}(a, a \wedge b) = 1$ and $\delta_{max}(a \wedge b, a \wedge b \wedge c) = 1$. With $d_D$ we have: $\delta_{max}(a, b) = 1$ and $\delta_{max}(a \wedge b, a \wedge b) = 0$. $\delta_{max}$ does not satisfy (R3). Indeed, with $d_H$ we have: $\delta_{max}(a, b \wedge c) = 3$ while $\delta_{max}(a \wedge b \wedge c, \neg a \wedge b \wedge c) = 1$. With $d_D$ we have: $\delta_{max}(a, b \wedge c) = 1$ while $\delta_{max}(a \wedge b \wedge c, \neg a \wedge b \wedge c) = 1$. $\delta_{max}$ does not satisfy (R4).Indeed, with $d_H$ or $d_D$ we have: $\delta_{max}(a \wedge b \wedge c, \neg a \wedge b \wedge c) = \delta_{max}(a \wedge b \wedge c, a \wedge b) = 1$. $\delta_{max}$ does not satisfy (R5). For instance,if the letters are $a$ and $b$ then with $d_H$ $\delta_{max}(a, a) = 2$ is not minimal; with $d_D$ $\delta_{max}(a, a) = 1$ is not minimal. $\delta_{max}$ satisfies (R6). $\delta_{max}$ satisfies (R7) since $\varphi_1 \models \varphi_2$ implies $Mod(\varphi_1) \subseteq Mod(\varphi_2)$.
- $\delta_{min}$ satisfies (R1). $\delta_{min}$ does not satisfy (R2). Indeed, $\delta_{min}(a, b) = 0$ (with $d_H$ or $d_D$) and $\delta_{min}(a \wedge b, \neg a \wedge b) = 1$
  $\delta_{min}$ satisfies (R3). Indeed $\delta_{min}(\varphi, \psi)$ is the number of letters on which $\varphi$ and $\psi$ disagree on. $\delta_{min}$ satisfies (R4). Indeed, if $\varphi_2 \wedge \psi_2$ is consistent then $\delta_{min}(\varphi_2, \psi_2) = 0$ and if $\varphi_1 \wedge \psi_1$ is inconsistent then $\delta_{min}(\varphi_2, \psi_2) > 0$ with $d_H$ and $d_D$. $\delta_{min}$ satisfies (R5), (R6) and (R7).
- $\delta_{sum}$ satisfies (R1). $\delta_{sum}$ does not satisfies (R2). Indeed, with $d_H$ (resp, $d_D$) $\delta_{sum}(a \wedge b \wedge c, a \vee b) = 7$ (resp, 5) and $\delta_{sum}((a \vee b) \wedge c, c) = 16$ (resp, 12). $\delta_{sum}$ does not satisfies (R3). Indeed, with $d_H$ (resp, $d_D$) $\delta_{sum}((a \vee b) \wedge c, c) = 16$ (resp, 12) while $\delta_{sum}(a \wedge b \wedge c, \neg a \wedge b \wedge \neg c) = 3$ (resp 1). This example also shows that $\delta_{sum}$ does not satisfies (R4). $\delta_{sum}$ satisfies (R5), (R6) and (R7).
- $\delta_{maxmin}$ satisfies (R1). $\delta_{sum}$ does not satisfies (R2). Indeed, with $d_H$ (resp, $d_D$) $\delta_{maxmin}(a, b) = 1$ (resp, 1) and $\delta_{maxmin}(a \wedge b \wedge c, a \wedge \neg b \wedge \neg c) = 2$ (resp, 1). $\delta_{sum}$ does not satisfies (R3). Indeed, with $d_H$ and $d_D$, $\delta_{maxmin}(a \vee b, a) = 1$ and $\delta_{maxmin}(a \wedge b, a \wedge \neg b) = 1$. This example also shows that $\delta_{maxmin}$ does not satisfies (R4). $\delta_{maxmin}$ satisfies (R5), (R6) and (R7).

**Proof of Proposition 5**

By definition of Importance-Based Merging Operator, we have $Mod(B_i^{s+1}) \subseteq Mod(B_j^s)$. Thus if $j$ is extremist at step $s$, then $\mid Mod(B_j^s) \mid \leq R$, is leading to $\mid Mod(B_i^{s+1}) \mid \leq R$ i.e., $i$ is extremist at $s+1$.

**Proof of Proposition 6**

As $\Delta_\mu(B_{j_1}^s \prec_i \ldots \prec_i B_{j_{k-1}}^s) \wedge B_{j_k}^s$ is consistent, $\exists w \in Mod(\Delta_\mu(B_{j_1}^s \prec_i \ldots \prec_i B_{j_{k-1}}^s)) \cap Mod(B_{j_k}^s)$. So, by definition of the Importance-Based Merging Operator, $w$ is such that $[D(w, B_{j_1}^s), \ldots, D(w, B_{j_{k-1}}^s)]$ is minimal according to $\leq_{lex}$. Furthermore, $D(w, B_{j_k}^s) = 0$. So, $[D(w, B_{j_1}^s), \ldots, D(w, B_{j_k}^s)]$ is minimal according to $\leq_{lex}$ and every $w \notin Mod(B_{j_k}^s)$ would not have such a property. By definition of $\leq_{lex}$, $\forall w' \in Mod(\Delta_\mu(B_{j_1}^s \prec_i \ldots \prec_i B_{j_n}^s))$, in particular, $[D(w', B_{j_1}^s), \ldots, D(w', B_{j_k}^s)]$ is minimal according to $\leq_{lex}$, thus $w' \in Mod(B_{j_k}^s)$. Then, as $j_k$ is extremist at step $s$, then $\mid Mod(B_{j_k}^s) \mid \leq R$, is leading to $\mid Mod(B_i^{s+1}) \mid \leq R$ i.e., $i$ is extremist at $s+1$.

**Proof of Proposition 7**

The proof is similar to the previous one. By definition of the Importance-Based Merging Operator, $\forall w \in Mod(B_i^{s+1})$, $w$ is such that $[D(w, B_{j_1}^s), ..., D(w, B_{j_n}^s)]$ is minimal according to $\leq_{lex}$. And, in particular by definition of $\leq_{lex}$, $[D(w, B_{j_1}^s), ..., D(w, B_{j_k}^s)]$ is minimal according to $\leq_{lex}$, thus $w \in Mod(\Delta_\mu(B_{j_1}^s \prec ... \prec B_{j_k}^s))$. Then, $\mid Mod(\Delta_\mu(B_{j_1}^s \prec ... \prec B_{j_k}^s)) \mid \leq R$, is leading to $\mid Mod(B_i^{s+1}) \mid \leq R$ i.e., $i$ is extremist at $s+1$.

**Proof of Proposition 8**

Let $j_k \in Sphere(i)$, then $\exists j_0 ... j_{k-1}\ \forall m = 1...(k-1)\ Inf(j_m) = \{j_{m-1} \prec_j ...\}$. We prove the proposition by induction on $k$. For $k = 1$, with $s' = s+1$, it comes from the Proposition 5. If we suppose the property for $k \in \mathbb{N}$, $\exists s' \geq t$, $\forall s \geq s'$, $j_{k-1}$ is extremist at step $s$. So, by Proposition 5, the property is satisfied at $s'+1$.

**Proof of Proposition 9**

First, we notice that $Mod(B_i^{t+1}) \subseteq Mod(B_i^t)$.

Suppose that $i_1$ is $S^1\alpha$-extremist at step $t$. Then there a subset $S_\alpha$ of $S$ st $Mod(B_{i_1}^t) \subseteq Mod(\bigwedge S_\alpha)$. Thus $Mod(B_i^{t+1}) \subseteq Mod(\bigwedge S_\alpha)$. Finally $i$ is $S^1\alpha$-extremist at step $t+1$

Suppose now that $i_1$ is $S^2\alpha$-extremist at step $t$. Then any $w$ in $Mod(B_{i_1}^t)$ satisfies $S(w) \geq \alpha$. Thus any $w$ in $Mod(B_i^{t+1})$ satisfies $S(w) \geq \alpha$. I.e., $i$ is $S^2\alpha$-extremist at step $t+1$.

**Proof of Proposition 10**

First we notice that if $j \in Sphere(i)$ then $\exists s \geq t\ \forall s' \geq s\ Mod(B_j^{s'}) \subseteq Mod(B_i^t)$.

Suppose that $i$ is a self-confident agent which is $S^1\alpha$-extremist (resp, $S^2\alpha$-extremist) at step $t$. Thus there is $S_\alpha$ st $Mod(B_i^t) \subseteq Mod(\bigwedge S_\alpha)$ (resp, any $w \in Mod(B_i^t)$ satisfies $S(w) \geq \alpha$). Thus there is $S_\alpha$ st $Mod(B_j^{s'}) \subseteq Mod(\bigwedge S_\alpha)$ (resp, ny $w$ in $Mod(B_j^{s'})$ satisfies $S(w) \geq \alpha$). This proves that $j$ is $S^1\alpha$-extremist (resp, $S^2\alpha$-extremist) at step $s'$.

**Proof of Proposition 11**

This is a corollary of Proposition 9.

**Proof of Proposition 12**

First, if $i_1$ is $SA\epsilon$-extremist at step $t$, then there exists a selected agent $a \in SA$ st $\delta(B_{i_1}^t, B_a^t) \leq \epsilon$. Secondly, if $i_1$ is the most influential influencer of $i$ then $B_i^{t+1} \models B_{i_1}^t$. Thirdly, if $\delta$ satisfies (R7) then $\delta(B_i^{t+1}, B_a^t) \leq \delta(B_{i_1}^t, B_a^t)$ thus $\delta(B_i^{t+1}, B_a^t) \leq \epsilon$. Moreover $a$ being dogmatic, we have $\models B_a^t \leftrightarrow B_a^{t+1}$. Finally, $\delta$ satisfying (R6), we conclude $\delta(B_i^{t+1}, B_a^{t+1}) \leq \epsilon$ i.e., $i$ is $SA\epsilon$-extremist at step $t+1$.

## References


1. Crawford, C., Brooks, L., Sen, S.: Opposites repel: the effect of incorporating repulsion on opinion dynamics in the bounded confidence model. In: International Conference on Agents and Multi-Agent Systems, AAMAS 2013, Saint Paul, MN, USA, 6–10 May 2013, vol. 6–10, pp. 1225–1226 (2013)
2. Christoff, Z., Hansen, J.U.: A logic for diffusion in social networks. J. Appl. Logic **13**, 48–77 (2015)
3. Cholvy, L.: Diffusion of opinion and influence. In: Schockaert, S., Senellart, P. (eds.) SUM 2016. LNCS (LNAI), vol. 9858, pp. 112–125. Springer, Cham (2016). https://doi.org/10.1007/978-3-319-45856-4_8
4. Grandi, U., Lorini, E., Perrussel, L.: Propositional opinion diffusion. In: Proceedings of the 2015 International Conference on Autonomous Agents and Multiagent Systems, AAMAS 2015, Istanbul, Turkey, 4–8 May 2015, pp. 989–997 (2015)
5. Hafızoğlu, F.M., Sen, S.: Analysis of opinion spread through migration and adoption in agent communities. In: Rahwan, I., Wobcke, W., Sen, S., Sugawara, T. (eds.) PRIMA 2012. LNCS (LNAI), vol. 7455, pp. 153–167. Springer, Heidelberg (2012). https://doi.org/10.1007/978-3-642-32729-2_11
6. Jager, W., Amblard, F.: A dynamical perspective on attitude change. In: Proceedings of NAACSOS (North American Association for Computational Social and Organizational Science) Conference, Pittsburgh, USA, 22–25 June 2004
7. Tsang, A., Larson, K.: Opinion dynamics of skeptical agents. In: International Conference on Autonomous Agents and Multi-Agent Systems, AAMAS 2014, Paris, France, 5–9 May 2014, pp. 277–284 (2014)
8. Christoff, Z., Grossi, D.: Stability in binary opinion diffusion. In: Baltag, A., Seligman, J., Yamada, T. (eds.) LORI 2017. LNCS, vol. 10455, pp. 166–180. Springer, Heidelberg (2017). https://doi.org/10.1007/978-3-662-55665-8_12
9. Chau, H., Wong, C., Chow, F., Fung, C.: Social judgment theory based model on opinion formation, polarization and evolution. Physica A **415**, 133–140 (2014)
10. Deffuant, G., Amblard, F., Weisbuch, G., Faure, T.: How can extremism prevail? A study based on the relative agreement interaction model. J. Artif. Soc. Soc. Simul. **5** (2002)
11. Sureda, C., Gaudou, B., Amblard, F.: An agent-based simulation of extremist network formation through radical behavior diffusion. In: Proceedings of the 9th International Conference on Agents and Artificial Intelligence, vol. 1, pp. 236–243. ICAART, INSTICC, ScitePress (2017)
12. Schwind, N., Inoue, K., Bourgne, G., Konieczny, S., Marquis, P.: Belief revision games. In: Proceedings of the Twenty-Ninth AAAI Conference on Artificial Intelligence, Austin, Texas, USA, 25–30 January 2015, pp. 1590–1596 (2015)
13. Cholvy, L.: Opinion diffusion and influence: a logical approach. Int. J. Approx. Reason. **93**, 24–39 (2018)
14. Battistella, E., Cholvy, L.: A logical approach to extreme opinion diffusion. In: Proceedings of the 10th International Conference on Agents and Artificial Intelligence, vol. 2, pp. 17–28. ICAART, SciTePress (2018)
15. Eiter, T., Mannila, H.: Distance measures for point sets and their computation. Acta Inf. **34**, 109–133 (1997)
16. Hunter, A., Konieczny, S.: On the measure of conflicts: shapley inconsistency values. Artif. Intell. **174**, 1007–1026 (2010)
17. Grant, J., Hunter, A.: Analysing inconsistent information using distance-based measures. Int. J. Approx. Reason. **89**, 3–26 (2017)

18. Xiao, G., Ma, Y.: Inconsistency measurement based on variables in minimal unsatisfiable subsets. In: 20th European Conference on Artificial Intelligence. Including Prestigious Applications of Artificial Intelligence (PAIS-2012) System Demonstrations Track, ECAI 2012, Montpellier, France, 27–31 August 2012, pp. 864–869 (2012)
19. Easley, D.A., Kleinberg, J.M.: Networks, Crowds, and Markets - Reasoning About a Highly Connected World. Cambridge University Press, Cambridge (2010)
20. Milgram, S.: The small world problem. Psychol. Today **2**, 60–67 (1967)
21. Prettejohn, B.J., Berryman, M.J., McDonnell, M.D.: Methods for generating complex networks with selected structural properties for simulations: a review and tutorial for neuroscientists. Front. Comput. Neurosci. **5**, 11 (2002)
22. Watts, D.J., Strogatz, S.H.: Collective dynamics of "small-world" networks. Nature **393**, 440–442 (1998)
23. Watts, D.J.: Networks, dynamics, and the small-world phenomenon. Am. J. Sociol. **105**, 493–527 (1999)
24. Konieczny, S., Pérez, R.P.: Merging information under constraints: a logical framework. J. Log. Comput. **12**, 773–808 (2002)

# Learning from Monte Carlo Rollouts with Opponent Models for Playing Tron

Stefan J. L. Knegt[1], Madalina M. Drugan[2], and Marco A. Wiering[1](✉)

[1] Institute of Artificial Intelligence and Cognitive Engineering, University of Groningen, Groningen, The Netherlands
stefanknegt@gmail.com, m.a.wiering@rug.nl
[2] ITLearns.Online, Utrecht, The Netherlands
madalina.drugan@gmail.com

**Abstract.** This paper describes a novel reinforcement learning system for learning to play the game of Tron. The system combines Q-learning, multi-layer perceptrons, vision grids, opponent modelling, and Monte Carlo rollouts in a novel way. By learning an opponent model, Monte Carlo rollouts can be effectively applied to generate state trajectories for all possible actions from which improved action estimates can be computed. This allows to extend experience replay by making it possible to update the state-action values of all actions in a given game state simultaneously. The results show that the use of experience replay that updates the Q-values of all actions simultaneously strongly outperforms the conventional experience replay that only updates the Q-value of the performed action. The results also show that using short or long rollout horizons during training lead to similar good performances against two fixed opponents.

**Keywords:** Reinforcement learning · Opponent modelling · Games
Monte Carlo rollouts · Multi-layer perceptrons

## 1 Introduction

Reinforcement learning (RL) algorithms [21] allow an agent to learn to play a game from trial and error by observing the result of each game. Often the result of a single game provides little information to learn from, as in many cases the game rules only return a value 1, 0, or −1 depending whether the game was won, ended in a draw, or was lost by the agent. Therefore, many games need to be played in order to learn which moves are optimal in each game state. Furthermore, games usually consist of very large state spaces and therefore appropriate function approximation techniques need to be used to generalize over the state space. The oldest self-learning program that learned to play a game is Samuel's checkers playing program [13]. It combined several machine learning methods and reached a decent amateur level in playing checkers. A very successful attempt to using reinforcement learning to play games is TD-Gammon


J. van den Herik and A. P. Rocha (Eds.): ICAART 2018, LNAI 11352, pp. 105–129, 2019.
https://doi.org/10.1007/978-3-030-05453-3_6

[22], that learned to play the game of Backgammon at human expert level using temporal difference learning [20] and multi-layer perceptrons. Although in the '90s, learning from 1.5 million games took multiple months, with the current computing power this can be done within several hours. A more recent and even more impressive system is AlphaGo Zero [18] which learned to play the complex game of Go from scratch and was able to beat its predecessor AlphaGo [16], which first learned from games played by human players and was able to beat the human Grandmaster Lee Sedol in 2016. AlphaGo Zero combines several techniques in a novel and effective manner: reinforcement learning, Monte Carlo tree search (MCTS) [8] and deep neural networks [14] by training a value function to predict the result of a game and a policy network on the frequency with which moves were selected in the MCTS rollout phase. AlphaGo Zero was later followed by AlphaZero [17] that learned to play chess and shogi from scratch according to the same principles as AlphaGo Zero and was able to strongly outperform the best previous computer programs for these games. This research has shown that learning from Monte Carlo tree search results is a very effective method for mastering different kinds of games.

Although in most game playing programs, no opponent model is learned, the optimal move in a game state can also depend on the opponent's playing style. This holds especially if a fixed opponent is used for playing the game. Therefore, for such games it would be useful to learn a model of the opponent in order to predict its moves. In most research on opponent modelling [5,6,19] the algorithm to learn the opponent model is problem specific and does not learn quickly. Therefore, in our previous work we developed a novel opponent modelling technique that learns to play the game of Tron and models the playing style of the fixed opponents simultaneously [7]. This technique was then combined with Monte Carlo rollouts, and the results of this system were much better than without using the opponent models.

In this paper, we extend our previous research on using reinforcement learning to play the game of Tron against two fixed opponents. We are primarily interested if learning from the outcomes of the Monte Carlo rollouts can increase the performances obtained in [7] even further. Although learning from the results of lookahead planning has been successfully applied in chess [1,17], Go [18], and other types of problems, this has not been integrated with learning a model of the opponent. To deal with the large state spaces of Tron, the learning algorithm combines Q-learning [24] with a multi-layer perceptron (MLP) [12]. This technique has already been successfully applied in games such as Backgammon [22], Ms. PacMan [2] and Starcraft [15]. Because the field of play in Tron is a $10 \times 10$ grid, there is no need to use deep reinforcement learning [10], however, as shown in [7], the use of vision grids to give a partial agent-centered representation of the game state was very effective and will also be used in this paper. Another extension is that in this paper experience replay [9] will be used in two different ways to learn from the estimates obtained through the Monte Carlo rollouts.

**Contributions:** We developed a novel system for learning to play the game of Tron that combines reinforcement learning, opponent models, and learning from lookahead planning with Monte Carlo rollouts. To speed-up learning, we examine two extensions compared to our work described in [7]: (1) Learning from lookahead planning, where the estimates obtained with Monte Carlo rollouts are used to train the Q-values of the actions, and (2) Using experience replay with a replay memory to learn from less games. Furthermore, we created two different methods in which the agent can learn from the Monte Carlo rollouts using experience replay: by only learning from the estimates obtained through the rollouts of the performed action, or learning from the estimates of all possible actions in a specific game state. By using the learned model of the opponent and the game rules, estimates are obtained for all actions in each game state that are used for selecting an action and that can be used for training the system. Therefore, learning from the rollout estimates of all actions does not require any computational overhead. Different experiments have been performed with different lookahead horizons and numbers of rollouts in order to examine if learning from the rollouts improves performance. The experiments are performed against two different fixed opponents and using two different game-state representation with different sizes of the vision grids. The results show that experience replay is very effective when training on the Monte Carlo rollout estimates of all actions. This leads to our new method attaining similar high win rates against the fixed opponents when learning from 150,000 games instead of the 1.5 million games used in our previous paper.

**Outline:** In the next section we explain the previous research we have done, including a description of the game of Tron and the RL system that was combined with opponent models and Monte Carlo rollouts. In Sect. 3, the novel method of learning from Monte Carlo Rollouts with experience replay is described. Section 4 describes the experiments and the results. In Sect. 5, the conclusions are presented together with possible future work directions.

## 2 Reinforcement Learning with Opponent Models for Playing Tron

In this section, we describe our previous approach [7] for learning to play Tron by self-play. Our RL-Tron system achieved remarkable successes against two different fixed opponent agents and consists of 3 elements: (1) Q-learning with multi-layer perceptrons are used to learn an approximation of the state-action value function, (2) The used multi-layer perceptron is combined with a novel algorithm for predicting which action the opponent selects in a game state (the opponent model), (3) The state-action value function and the opponent model are used in Monte Carlo rollouts to select an action in a game state based on future state trajectories during the final test games.

We will first describe the game of Tron. Then we describe the combination of Q-learning and multi-layer perceptrons. In Subsect. 2.3, we will describe three different state representations that were used in [7] for learning to play Tron. Finally, we will describe the opponent-model learning technique and how it was used in the Monte Carlo rollouts.

### 2.1 The Game of Tron

Tron is an arcade video game released in 1982 inspired by the Walt Disney motion picture Tron. In this game the player guides a light cycle in an arena against an opponent. The player has to do this, while avoiding the walls and the trails of light left behind by the opponent and the player itself. Figure 1 depicts an example game state played by two agents. For this research we developed a framework in order to use reinforcement learning in this game. This framework implements the game as a sequential decision problem, where two agents can play against each other and the environment is represented by a $10 \times 10$ grid.

At the beginning of a game the agents are randomly placed in either the top half or bottom half of the grid. At every game state there are four possible actions: moving up, down, right, or left. It is important to note that one of the four moves will always lead to the agent hitting its own trail of light. When both agents have selected a move, the new game state is determined. Whenever two agents move to the same location in the grid the game ends in a draw as well as when both agents hit a trail of light or the wall at the same time. In all other cases, the game continues until one of the two agents hits a trail of light or the wall. When looking at the possible amount of different game states, we estimate this to be in the order of $10^{20}$, which is similar to the game Othello that consists of a board of $7 \times 7$ cells.

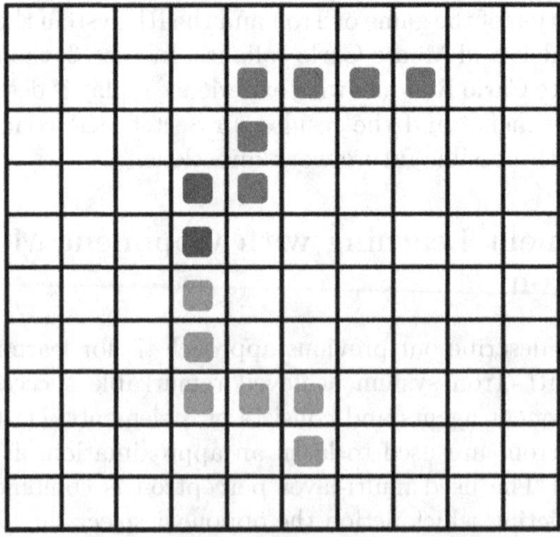

**Fig. 1.** Tron game environment with two agents, where their heads or current locations are in a darker colour (taken from [7]). (Color figure online)

In this research the agent always plays against one fixed opponent at a time and the opponents employ either a semi-random or semi-deterministic strategy. The semi-random opponent always randomly selects one of the four possible moves, unless that move results in an immediate collision. The semi-deterministic agent always tries to select its previous action and if that would result in a collision, it selects a random possible action. Therefore, both opponent strategies are constructed such that the opponent will never move to a location that is already visited or is a wall, unless there is no other possibility. Although both strategies seem quite basic, the semi-deterministic strategy can be a relatively good strategy for the game of Tron. By always selecting the previous action, if this is possible, the agent makes long trails of light and thereby easily closes the other agent in, which will eventually lead to this agent losing the game. We tested the performance of both opponent strategies by letting them play against each other for many games. The results of these matches showed that the semi-deterministic strategy (going straight as long as possible) wins in 55% of the games and loses in 25% of the games, while 20% of the games end in a draw. From here on we will refer to the agent employing the collision-avoiding random policy as the random opponent and the semi-deterministic opponent will be referred to as the deterministic opponent.

## 2.2 Reinforcement Learning

Reinforcement learning (RL) algorithms allow an agent to learn to optimize its behavior from its interaction with an environment. Each time-step, an agent observes the state of the environment and uses this information to select an action. Then the state is changed to a next state and the agent receives a scalar reward signal for this state transition. The aim of the agent is to learn an action-selection policy that maximizes the obtained future discounted sum of rewards. Reinforcement learning algorithms can be used to solve different kinds of sequential decision problems. Because the game of Tron is fully observable and the agent plays against a fixed (i.e. non-adaptive) opponent, the game can be modelled as a Markov Decision Process [11], which is defined by the following components:

- A set of states $S$, where $s_t \in S$ denotes the state at time $t$.
- A set of actions $A$, where $a_t \in A$ denotes the action selected at time $t$.
- A transition function $T(s, a, s')$, which specifies the probability of moving to state $s'$ after selecting action $a$ in state $s$.
- A reward function $R(s, a, s')$, which sends a reward signal to the agent for executing action $a$ in state $s$ and subsequently moving to state $s'$. $r_t$ denotes the reward obtained at time-step $t$.
- A discount factor $\gamma$ that makes rewards received further in the future less important, where $0 \leq \gamma \leq 1$.

In the game of Tron, the reward for winning a game is 1, for a draw the reward is 0, and if the RL agent loses it receives a reward of $-1$. There are no other rewards emitted while the game is not over. The environment is stochastic for the agent, because the agent selects an action and at the same time the opponent selects an action, after which the state of the game is updated. Because the agent learns to play against two different opponents that use a stochastic policy, the game is non-deterministic.

The agent needs to optimize its policy $\pi(s)$ which outputs an action $a$ given the current state $s$. Instead of directly optimizing this policy, value function based RL algorithms use state-value functions or state-action value functions. The state-action value function $Q^{\pi}(s,a)$ denotes the expected sum of discounted rewards obtained when the agent selects action $a$ in state $s$ and follows policy $\pi$ afterwards:

$$Q^{\pi}(s,a) = E\Big(\sum_{t=0}^{\infty} \gamma^t r_t | s_0 = s, a_0 = a, \pi\Big) \tag{1}$$

Where $E$ denotes the expectancy operator. This previous value is almost impossible to compute, because it involves an expectancy over all possible future state sequences which can be arbitrarily long. Instead, by using Bellman's equation the computation can be broken up into parts:

$$Q(s_t, a_t) = E(r_t) + \gamma \sum_{s_{t+1}} T(s_t, a_t, s_{t+1}) \max_a Q(s_{t+1}, a) \tag{2}$$

For general game-playing programs the transition model is not known, extremely large, or complex to combine with function approximation techniques. Furthermore, it is much more effective to use a reinforcement learning algorithm that learns to focus on parts of the state-space which are most rewarding for the agent. In many papers about learning to play games with reinforcement learning, the Q-learning algorithm [24] is used. Q-learning updates the approximation of the Q-value of a state-action pair denoted as $\widehat{Q}(s_t, a_t)$ after an experience $(s_t, a_t, r_t, s_{t+1})$ by:

$$\widehat{Q}(s_t, a_t) \leftarrow \widehat{Q}(s_t, a_t) + \alpha(r_t + \gamma \max_a \widehat{Q}(s_{t+1}, a) - \widehat{Q}(s_t, a_t)) \tag{3}$$

Where $0 \leq \alpha \leq 1$ denotes the learning rate. If state $s_{t+1}$ is a terminal state (i.e. the game is over), the following update is used:

$$\widehat{Q}(s_t, a_t) \leftarrow \widehat{Q}(s_t, a_t) + \alpha(r_t - \widehat{Q}(s_t, a_t)) \tag{4}$$

**Value-Function Approximation.** Because the state space in Tron is very large (around $10^{20}$ different states), we need to combine Q-learning with a function approximator. For this, we use a multi-layer perceptron (MLP) that receives as input the game-state representation and outputs the Q-values of the four different actions. The multi-layer perceptron consists of a single hidden layer and is trained with online backpropagation. After each experience $(s_t, a_t, r_t, s_{t+1})$ the target value for the MLP when executing action $a_t$ in state $s_t$ is:

$$Q^{target}(s_t, a_t) \leftarrow r_t + \gamma \max_a \widehat{Q}(s_{t+1}, a) \tag{5}$$

When a terminal state is reached, the target value is computed by only using the final reward of the game:

$$Q^{target}(s_t, a_t) \leftarrow r_t \tag{6}$$

These target values are then used by backpropagation to update the Q-value output of the selected action in the given state. Different activation functions can be used in the hidden layer of the multi-layer perceptron, while we use a linear activation unit for the output units representing the Q-values of the different actions. A commonly used activation function in the hidden layer of RL systems is the sigmoid function that transforms its weighted sum of inputs $a$ to a value between 0 and 1:

$$O(a) = \frac{1}{1 + e^{-a}} \tag{7}$$

Another possible activation function is the exponential linear unit, which has been shown to perform better when training deep neural networks on image recognition problems [4]. We therefore compared the performance of the agent using the sigmoid function and the exponential linear unit (Elu) in the hidden layer [7]. The exponential linear unit computes the activation of the hidden units with the following equation:

$$O(a) = \begin{cases} a & \text{if } a \geq 0 \\ \beta(e^a - 1) & \text{if } a < 0 \end{cases} \tag{8}$$

Where we set $\beta$ to 0.01 after performing some preliminary experiments.

### 2.3 State Representation

When applying Q-learning to the game of Tron, it is possible to use the entire game grid ($10 \times 10$) as input for the MLP. This would translate to 100 input variables, which have a value of one whenever a position has been visited by one of the agents and zero otherwise. In order to also assure that the agent is aware of its current position in the game, we supply another $10 \times 10$ grid in which the current position of the agent is equal to one. Finally, a $10 \times 10$ grid is used in which the head of the opponent has a value of one. Therefore, this representation consists of 300 input units.

In our previous work [7], we compared the use of this full-grid information method to the use of local vision grids. The results indicated that using vision grids is a very useful method to obtain information about the relevant parts of the environment and attain high performance scores. A vision grid can be seen as a local view of the environment taken from the position of the agent. This vision grid is a square rectangle with an uneven dimension. We used two different grid sizes: a small vision grid with an area of $3 \times 3$ and a large vision grid with a size of $5 \times 5$. To get all important information from the player and the opponent, 7 different vision grids are combined (in all these grids the standard value is zero):

- The player trail grid contains information about the locations visited by the agent itself: whenever the agent has visited the location it will have a value of one instead of zero.

- The player's opponent-trail grid contains information about the locations visited by the opponent: if the opponent or its tail is in the 'visual field' of the agent these locations are encoded with a one.
- The player's wall grid represents the walls: whenever the agent is close to a wall the wall locations will get a value of one.
- The player's opponent-head grid contains information about the current location of the head of the opponent. If the opponent's head is in the agent's visual field, this location will be encoded with a one.
- The opponent wall grid represents the walls for the opponent: whenever the opponent is close to a wall the wall locations will get a value of one.
- The opponent-trail grid contains information about the locations visited by the opponent: whenever the opponent has visited the location it will have a value of one instead of zero.
- The opponent's player grid encodes the locations visited by the player seen from the perspective of the opponent: if the player or its trail is in the 'visual field' of the opponent these locations are encoded with a one.

Because 7 vision grids are used, the total number of inputs for the small vision grid is 63 and for the large vision grid it is 175. This shows that the dimensionality of the input space is significantly reduced when using vision grids when compared to the full grid that used 300 inputs. An example game state and the seven associated (small) vision grids can be found in Fig. 2.

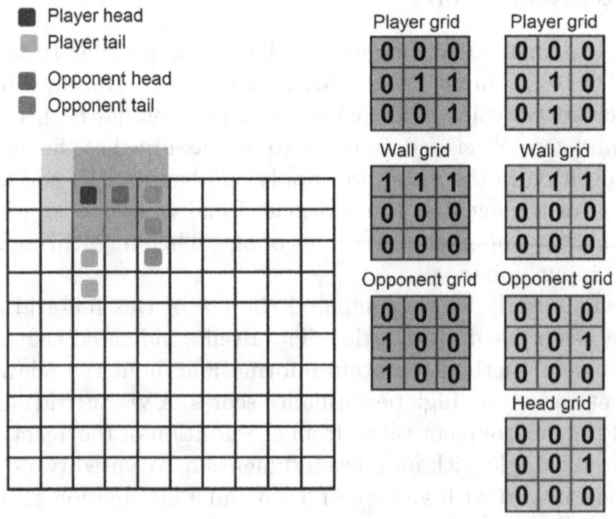


**Fig. 2.** An illustration of a game state and the associated values in the 7 vision grids.

### 2.4 Opponent Modelling and Monte Carlo Rollouts

The main contribution of our previous paper [7] was a novel opponent modelling technique, which allows an agent to learn a model of the opponent while at the same time learning to play the game. This learned opponent model was then used in Monte Carlo rollouts to select moves during the final test games.

In opponent modelling the task is to learn the opponent's behaviour in different states to predict what the opponent's next action will be. Opponent modelling techniques have mainly focused on imperfect information games [5,19] and are relatively problem specific. Our technique focuses on games in which the opponent's behaviour is fully observable. In our opponent modelling technique the agent learns a model of the opponent by learning to predict the opponent's next move using the same MLP as is used to learn to play the game. A possible benefit of incorporating opponent modelling in the same neural network is that the agent might learn hidden features regarding the opponent's behaviour, which could increase performance. The fact that the model can be learned using the same network and the backpropagation algorithm [12] is a reason that the method is widely applicable, as one only needs to slightly change the structure of the neural network. In fact, this opponent modelling technique can be used in many games in which the opponent's actions are observable. Another benefit of this technique is that the agent simultaneously learns a policy and a model of the opponent and no extra training phase is needed.

After the training phase has finished the agent's model of the opponent is reflected as a probability distribution over the opponent's next moves given the current state. This probability distribution can then be used in planning algorithms such as Monte Carlo rollouts.

In order to incorporate the opponent modelling technique we need to alter the structure of the neural network used. For this, we add four (as the action space consists of four actions) output units to the network, in which we will use a softmax activation function. By doing so, the output of these added nodes represent the probability distribution over the opponent's next action given the current game state. The softmax function is used to transform the vector $o$ containing the output modelling values for the next $K = 4$ possible actions of the opponent to values in the range $[0, 1]$ that add up to one:

$$P(s_t, o_i) = \frac{e^{o_i}}{\sum_{k=1}^{K} e^{o_k}} \tag{9}$$

After training these four output nodes with backpropagation, the output of each of these nodes represents the probability of the opponent conducting action $o_i$ in state $s_t$. When training the additional output nodes with backpropagation, we compute a target vector for the four output nodes. The target is one for the action conducted by the opponent and zero for all other actions given the previous game state. Whenever an agent follows a fully deterministic policy, this technique would allow the agent to learn to correctly predict all of the opponent's moves. Although in reality a policy is seldom entirely deterministic, players use certain rules to play a game and the agent can learn these rules with this opponent modelling technique.

So far we have explained how this opponent modelling technique can be incorporated in the neural network that is combined with Q-learning. In order to increase the performance of the agent, we can use the learned opponent model in a planning algorithm. In this research we will use the model in so-called Monte Carlo rollouts [23]. Such a rollout is used to estimate the value $\widehat{Q}_{sim}(s,a)$, the expected Q-value of performing action $a$ in state $s$ and subsequently performing the action suggested by the current policy for $n$ steps. This simulated Q-value is estimated by simulating the game ahead using the opponent model to determine the opponent's moves in this simulation. The number of rollouts to determine $\widehat{Q}_{sim}(s,a)$ can vary and this determines how the opponent's action is selected. If one rollout is used the opponent's move with the highest probability is carried out. When more than one rollout is performed, the opponent's action is selected based on the probability distribution. For every game state we can use a variable amount of rollouts $m$ with a horizon or length of $n$ actions to determine the expected or simulated Q-value of performing all actions in the given game state. Whenever more than one rollout is used ($m > 1$) we average the obtained simulated Q-values per action.

If a game ends before the horizon is reached, the simulated Q-value $\widehat{Q}_{sim}(s_t,a_t)$ for a single rollout equals the reward obtained in the simulated game (1 for winning, 0 for a draw, and $-1$ for losing) properly discounted by the number of moves $i$ until an end state is reached:

$$\widehat{Q}_{sim}(s_t,a_t) = \gamma^i r_{t+i} \tag{10}$$

If the game is not finished before reaching the rollout horizon the simulated Q-value is equal to the discounted Q-value of the last (greedy) action performed:

$$\widehat{Q}_{sim}(s_t,a_t) = \gamma^n \widehat{Q}(s_{t+n},a_{t+n}) \tag{11}$$

See Algorithm 1 for a detailed description. This kind of rollout is also called a truncated rollout as the game is not necessarily played to its conclusion [23]. In order to determine the importance of the number of rollouts $m$ and the length of the horizon $n$, we will perform different experiments with different amounts of rollouts and lengths of the horizon.

## 3 Learning from Monte Carlo Rollouts

In our previous paper [7], Monte Carlo rollouts using the model of the opponent were used to determine the optimal move given the current game state but they were only used in testing the final performances of the different systems. In this paper, we investigate whether it is beneficial to learn from the action estimates that are gathered in the rollouts while playing the game. In our novel approach, Monte Carlo rollouts will be used while training the RL system in two ways: for selecting actions in a game state while training and for computing target

Q-values in a game-state. Because using rollouts to select an action requires significantly more computations, we will combine this method with experience replay [9]. This could allow the agent to use significantly fewer training games to attain the same performances as in our previous paper. For learning from the Monte Carlo rollouts, the target values of the Q-values have to be adapted. With Q-learning the target is determined by the following formula:

$$\widehat{Q}^{target}(s_t, a_t) \leftarrow r_t + \gamma \max_a \widehat{Q}(s_{t+1}, a) \tag{12}$$

Now, we will use the action estimates obtained with the rollouts as targets, as they arguably reflect the expected future reward of performing an action more accurately. If a game finishes during a rollout, the target is equal to the reward obtained in the simulated game (1 for winning, 0 for a draw, and $-1$ for losing) with appropriate discounting using the length $i$ of the current rollout:

**Algorithm 1.** Monte Carlo rollout with Opponent Model (taken from [7]).

```
Input: Current game state s_t, starting action a_t, horizon N, number of rollouts M
Output: Average utility of performing action a_t at time t and subsequently following the policy
  over M rollouts
  for m = 1, 2, ..M do
     i = 0
     Perform starting action a_t
     if M = 1 then
        o_t ← argmax_o P(s_t, o)
     else if M > 1 then
        o_t ← sample P(s_t, o)
     end if
     Perform opponent action o_t
     Determine reward r_{t+i}
     rolloutReward_m = r_{t+i}
     while not game over do
        i = i + 1
        a_{t+i} ← argmax_a Q(s_{t+i}, a)
        Perform action a_{t+i}
        if M = 1 then
           o_{t+i} ← argmax_o P(s_{t+i}, o)
        else if M > 1 then
           o_{t+i} ← sample P(s_{t+i}, o)
        end if
        Perform opponent action o_{t+i}
        Determine reward r_{t+i}
        if Game over then
           rolloutReward_m = γ^i r_{t+i}
        end if
        if not Game over and i = N then
           game over ← True
           rolloutReward_m = γ^N Q(s_N, a_N)
        end if
     end while
     rewardSum = rewardSum + rolloutReward_m
     m = m + 1
  end for
  return rewardSum/M
```

$$\widehat{Q}^{target}(s_t, a_t) = \gamma^i r_{t+i} \tag{13}$$

If the game is not finished before reaching the rollout horizon, the target Q-value is equal to the discounted Q-value of the last (greedy) action performed:

$$\widehat{Q}^{target}(s_t, a_t) = \gamma^n \widehat{Q}(s_{t+n}, a_{t+n}) \tag{14}$$

where $n$ is the length of the horizon as before. Note that these targets are related to n-step backups [21], but here we use simulated experiences instead of real experiences. If multiple rollouts are used for selecting an action, these target values are averaged over all rollouts.

An interesting advantage of using the model of the game and the learned model of the opponent, is that estimates are collected for all actions. Therefore, instead of only training on the target of the selected action, it is also possible to train the multi-layer perceptron on estimates of all four actions obtained through the rollouts. Note that this is only possible because we have a model of the game and learn the model of the opponent, and this is quite different from most RL algorithms that only learn from the experience obtained with a single action: $(s_t, a_t, r_t, s_{t+1})$.

Experience replay does not only increase sample efficiency, in some cases it is needed to ensure stability (convergence to an optimal policy) in the learning process [3]. At first we implemented rollout learning without experience replay and experienced extreme difficulties when training the agents online in the rollouts, as the Q-values often exploded. This was caused by the fact that the back-propagation algorithm [25] assumes that training samples are independent. However, with online learning in the rollouts a lot of experiences are collected which were not independent as they were gathered sequentially. This is another reason why we used experience replay.

The implementation works as follows: at every state $s_t$ we store the current game state $s_t$, the action performed $a_t$, the opponent's action $o_t$ and the target Q-value computed with Eqs. 13 or 14, in the replay memory. We will let the system play 50 games (collecting around 1000 experiences in the replay memory), and we randomly select experiences from this pool to train on. The target values of the experiences are given by the multi-layer perceptron or the rewards during the rollouts as explained before. In case multiple rollouts are used, the targets are averages of the different rollout estimates. In total, we use 10 times the size of the replay memory to draw random experiences and train the MLP. Afterwards, the replay memory is emptied and the new MLP is used to play again 50 games and so on.

## 4 Experiments and Results

Previous results [7] showed that vision grids increase performance in most cases, as compared to using the full grid as state representation. Furthermore, that research showed that the Elu activation function outperforms the Sigmoid activation function. In the experiments conducted in our previous research the number of training games was set to 1.5 million. Their results are shown in Subsects. 4.1 to 4.3. In the new experiments, shown in Subsects. 4.4 to 4.6, 150,000 training games are used. The agent plays against the random and semi-deterministic opponent and the number of test games is equal to 10,000. In these test games, the agent makes no exploration actions. In order to obtain meaningful results, all experiments are conducted ten times. The performance is measured as the number of games won plus 0.5 times the number of games tied. This number is divided by the number of games to get a score between 0 and 1. In all experiments we use an MLP with the weights initialised between −0.5 and 0.5. In all experiments we use one hidden layer, as preliminary experiments indicated that this led to the best results. The state representation technique determines the number of input nodes and the number of hidden nodes varies from 200 to 400.

### 4.1 Learning Without Monte Carlo Rollouts

We performed many preliminary experiments to tune all hyperparameters. In these experiments concerning Q-learning without Monte Carlo rollouts, the number of input/hidden nodes are equal to 300/300, 175/400, and 63/200 for the full grid, large vision grids, and small vision grids respectively. In all experiments the MLP has eight output nodes, which represent the four Q-values for the different actions and the four outputs to model the opponent's probability of selecting that action. In all experiments $\epsilon$-greedy exploration is used. In most experiments the exploration rate $\epsilon$ decreases over the first 750,000 games from 10% to 0%. The exception to this rule is that with large vision grids and the sigmoid activation function against the random opponent, the exploration rate decreases from 10% to 0% over the first million games. The learning rate $\alpha$ and discount factor $\gamma$ are 0.005 and 0.95 respectively. The learning rate is 0.001 when using the full grid as state representation with the sigmoid activation function and set to 0.0025 with large vision grids and the sigmoid activation function against the random opponent. These changes were made to assure stable results. We note that in this experiment no rollouts are performed. Figures 3, 4, and 5 show the training performance for the three different state representations. Table 1 shows the performance over the final 10,000 test games.

The results show that the large vision grids with the Elu activation function obtain the best results against the two opponents. The worst results are obtained with the full-grid representation, which may need even more than 1.5 million training games to obtain good performances.

Although in these experiments, a model of the opponent is learned by the MLP at the same time as the Q-value function, the opponent model is not used during game play. Therefore, the only reason this might be beneficial is as having an auxiliary task while training the MLP. We therefore performed another experiment, where the MLP is not updated on the actions of the opponent and therefore does not learn an opponent model. Using the same setup as before, results of 10 simulations with 10,000 final test games were generated that can be found in Table 2.

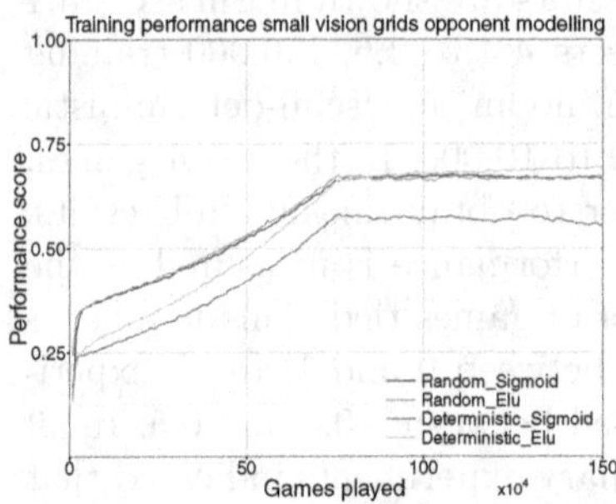


**Fig. 3.** Final performance score for small vision grids as state representation over 1.5 million training games with opponent modelling but without rollouts (taken from [7]).

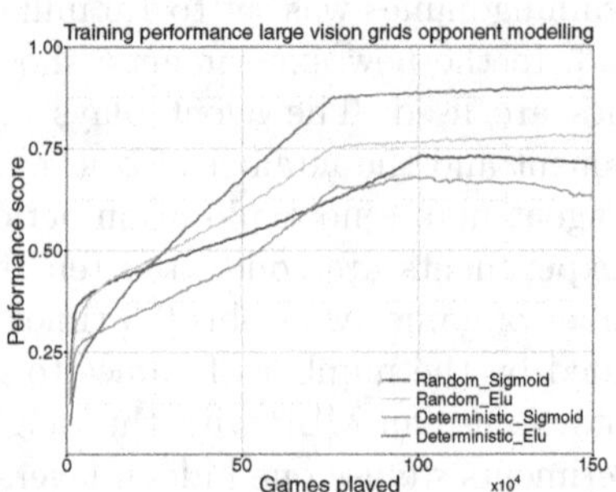


**Fig. 4.** Final performance score for large vision grids as state representation over 1.5 million training games with opponent modelling but without rollouts (taken from [7]).

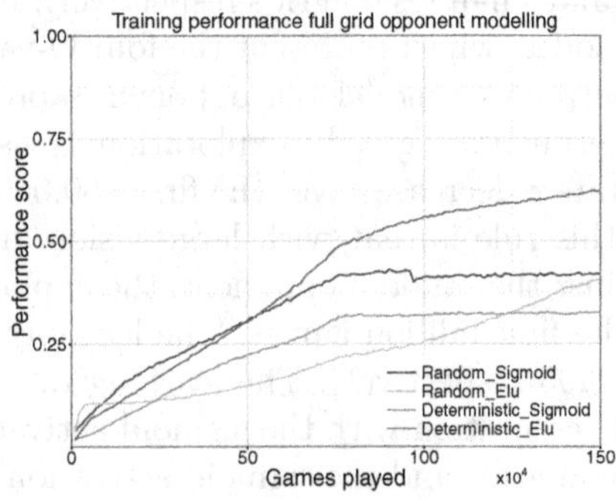


**Fig. 5.** Final performance score for the full grid as state representation over 1.5 million training games with opponent modelling but without rollouts (taken from [7]).

**Table 1.** Final performance score and standard errors with opponent modelling without rollouts.

| State representation | Opponent | Sigmoid | Elu |
|---|---|---|---|
| Small vision grids | Random | 0.67 (0.004) | 0.67 (0.009) |
| Large vision grids | Random | 0.72 (0.005) | **0.79 (0.003)** |
| Full grid | Random | 0.42 (0.016) | 0.40 (0.025) |
| Small vision grids | Deterministic | 0.57 (0.015) | 0.69 (0.005) |
| Large vision grids | Deterministic | 0.63 (0.019) | **0.90 (0.003)** |
| Full grid | Deterministic | 0.32 (0.023) | 0.62 (0.015) |

**Table 2.** Final performance score and standard errors with the Elu activation function and opponent vision grids, but without opponent modelling (taken from [7]).

| State representation | Random | Deterministic |
|---|---|---|
| Small vision grids | 0.69 (0.008) | 0.69 (0.003) |
| Large vision grids | **0.82 (0.009)** | **0.89 (0.003)** |

From these results we can conclude that the agent did not profit from learning an opponent model as there is no clear improvement when we compare Tables 1 and 2. The benefit of learning the opponent model is therefore researched in the next subsections, in which Monte Carlo rollouts are used that make use of the model of the game and the opponent model to generate simulated experiences before selecting an action.

### 4.2 Learning with Opponent Modelling and Monte Carlo Rollouts

By letting the agent learn a model of the opponent, this model can be used in Monte Carlo rollouts. The rollouts in this subsection are only used for selecting actions during the final test games. Here, the game is simulated ten steps into the future, as this was found to be the optimal amount of actions in the trade-off between looking far into the future and assuring that the predicted actions are correct in this rollout. In order to test the effect of the amount of rollouts per state action pair, we compare the agent's performance when one and ten rollouts are conducted. Since the opponent's actions within the rollouts are determined by the learned probability distribution, we plot the prediction accuracy of the agent against both opponents in Figs. 6 and 7 for the first 25,000 training games. These figures show that with the Elu activation function, which learns slightly faster than the sigmoid activation function, the agent correctly predicts 50% of the random opponent's moves and 90% of the semi-deterministic opponent's moves when we use vision grids. When the full grid is used, this accuracy is 40% and 80% respectively.

Now we turn to the agent's performance in 10,000 test games when using the rollouts after the agent was trained for 1.5 million games as before. The performance score and standard error using one rollout with a horizon of ten steps during 10,000 test games can be found in Table 3. From the results we can conclude that Monte Carlo rollouts increase the agent's performance in all scenarios, except for when large vision grids are used against the random opponent. A very high performance score of 0.98 is obtained using large vision grids and the Elu activation function against the semi-deterministic opponent, which shows that using this technique performance can be increased significantly. This increase is especially large when we use vision grids and play against the semi-deterministic opponent. When the opponent employs the collision-avoiding random policy, small vision grids lead to the highest performance and when comparing these results to the previous experiments we see that Monte Carlo rollouts also increase performance against the random opponent. This shows that although the policy of the opponent is far from deterministic, opponent modelling still significantly increases performance from 0.67 to 0.83 with the sigmoid activation function and from 0.67 to 0.84 with the Elu activation function when small vision grids are used as state representation.

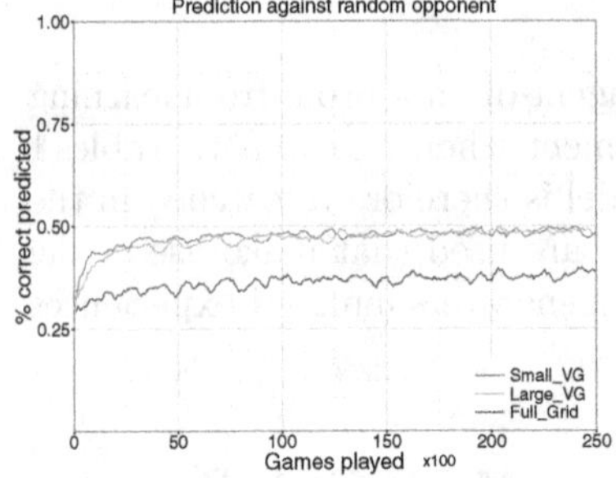


**Fig. 6.** Percentage of moves correctly predicted against the random opponent (taken from [7]).

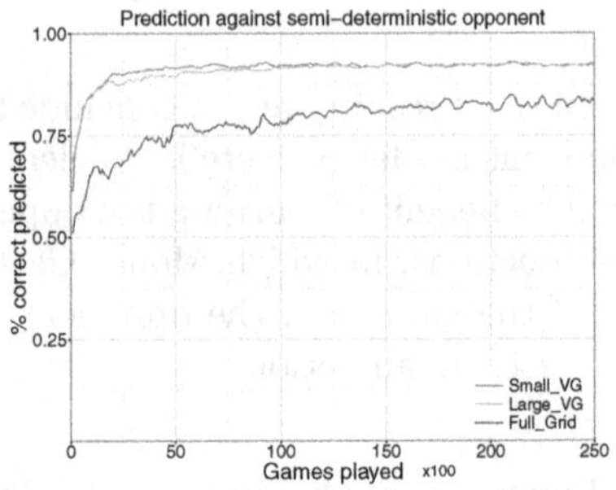

**Fig. 7.** Percentage of moves correctly predicted against the semi-deterministic opponent (taken from [7])

**Table 3.** Final performance score and standard errors with one rollout and a horizon of ten actions.

| State representation | Opponent | Sigmoid | Elu |
|---|---|---|---|
| Small vision grids | Random | 0.83 (0.002) | **0.84 (0.003)** |
| Large vision grids | Random | 0.66 (0.008) | 0.66 (0.004) |
| Full grid | Random | 0.65 (0.004) | 0.72 (0.007) |
| Small vision grids | Deterministic | 0.93 (0.002) | 0.96 (0.001) |
| Large vision grids | Deterministic | 0.95 (0.002) | **0.98 (0.001)** |
| Full grid | Deterministic | 0.54 (0.010) | 0.75 (0.010) |

After applying one rollout for each action in a given state, we also tested whether increasing the number of rollouts to ten would affect the agent's performance. The results are displayed in Table 4. We find one noteworthy difference in the agent's performance when using one or ten rollouts. The agent's performance against the random opponent considerably increases when we use ten instead of one rollout. Against the semi-deterministic opponent, increasing the number of rollouts has no noticeable effect. This is because the agent predicts the semi-deterministic opponent correctly in over 90% of the cases, causing the advantage of action sampling and multiple rollouts to be absent.

**Table 4.** Final performance score and standard errors with ten rollouts and a horizon of ten actions.

| State representation | Opponent | Sigmoid | Elu |
|---|---|---|---|
| Small vision grids | Random | 0.84 (0.016) | 0.88 (0.001) |
| Large vision grids | Random | 0.90 (0.001) | **0.91 (0.001)** |
| Full grid | Random | 0.72 (0.008) | 0.74 (0.009) |
| Small vision grids | Deterministic | 0.93 (0.002) | 0.96 (0.001) |
| Large vision grids | Deterministic | 0.96 (0.002) | **0.98 (0.001)** |
| Full grid | Deterministic | 0.55 (0.008) | 0.78 (0.010) |

### 4.3 Monte Carlo Rollouts Without Using the Learned Opponent Model

We observed that the agent's performance significantly increases when we use Monte Carlo rollouts. It is however not certain that without the opponent model but with Monte Carlo rollouts this performance would be lower. Therefore, we test the agent's performance when the moves in the rollouts are determined randomly instead of by the opponent model. The results of these experiments can be found in Table 5. The relatively low performance scores indicate that it is indeed the model of the opponent that increases the agent's performance when rollouts are used. Without a good opponent model, the results of Monte Carlo rollouts cannot be trusted for selecting an action, because the generated rollouts are not similar to how the game would actually be played.

**Table 5.** Final performance score and standard errors with one rollout and a horizon of ten actions without using the learned model of the opponent.

| State representation | Opponent | Sigmoid | Elu |
|---|---|---|---|
| Small vision grids | Random | 0.46 (0.007) | 0.50 (0.001) |
| Large vision grids | Random | 0.50 (0.001) | 0.51 (0.002) |
| Full grid | Random | 0.37 (0.010) | 0.35 (0.006) |
| Small vision grids | Deterministic | 0.34 (0.003) | 0.35 (0.001) |
| Large vision grids | Deterministic | 0.35 (0.001) | 0.36 (0.001) |
| Full grid | Deterministic | 0.21 (0.007) | 0.21 (0.005) |

### 4.4 Learning from Monte Carlo Rollouts

In this subsection, we will experiment with learning from the rollout estimates and lower the amount of training games to only 150,000. This can be done by either learning the Q-value of a single performed action using its rollout estimate or by updating the Q-values of all four actions simultaneously.

For this experiment the agent first plays 100,000 games without Monte Carlo rollouts and learns in an online manner as before. Afterwards, Monte Carlo rollouts are used for 50,000 training games in which the Q-values of the MLP are trained on the rollouts estimates (while the MLP is still trained on actions of the opponent). We want to note that during these 50,000 games experience replay is used, as explained in Sect. 3. Exploration decreases linearly from 10% to 0% over the first 100,000 games and the MLP now uses 400 hidden units for both the small and large vision grids. The learning rate is still set to 0.005 both for the initial 100,000 training games with online learning and for the later 50,000 training games where experience replay on the rollout estimates is used.

We again trained and tested against two opponents, but this time only using the Elu activation function and vision grids. We also compare the use of one rollout with a horizon of ten actions and five rollouts with a horizon of five actions. The previous results have shown that the first works better against the deterministic opponent, while the latter works better against the random opponent. We did not use 10 rollouts with a horizon of 10 actions, since such experiments are computationally very expensive. An experiment with the large vision grids and 5 rollouts with a horizon of 5 actions already took around 10 hours to complete on our CPUs. Note that all experiments have been conducted ten times to obtain meaningful results. The training performance against both opponents when learning only on the estimates of one action (the selected action) can be found in Figs. 8 and 9 and the performance score over the 10,000 final test games can be found in Table 6.

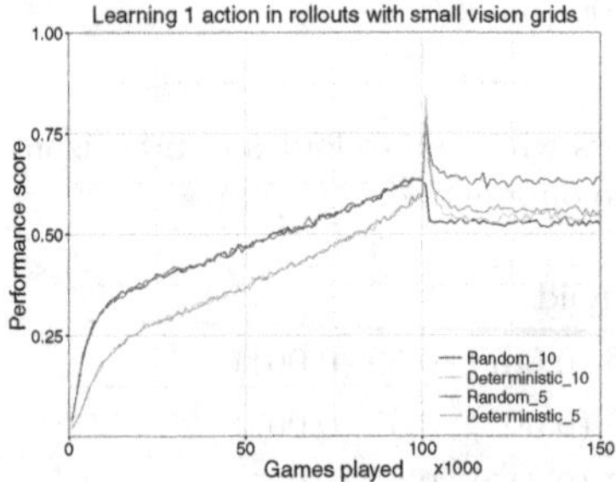


Fig. 8. Training performance with small vision grids when updating the Q-value of a single action. Random and deterministic indicate the opponent and 5 and 10 represent the horizon.

Fig. 9. Training performance with large vision grids when updating the Q-value of a single action. Random and deterministic indicate the opponent and 5 and 10 represent the horizon.

From the results we can conclude that when we update the Q-value of the single performed action, learning from the rollout estimates hinders performance. The peaks in Figs. 8 and 9 are caused by the onset of using Monte Carlo rollouts

**Table 6.** Final test performance for 10,000 games while training the Q-value of the single performed action on its rollout estimate.

| State representation | Opponent | 1 rollout 10 actions | 5 rollouts 5 actions |
|---|---|---|---|
| Small vision grids | Random | 0.45 (0.005) | 0.58 (0.006) |
| Large vision grids | Random | 0.43 (0.006) | 0.58 (0.010) |
| Small vision grids | Deterministic | 0.55 (0.006) | 0.57 (0.007) |
| Large vision grids | Deterministic | 0.54 (0.005) | 0.59 (0.008) |

for selecting actions after 100,000 games. The system's learning dynamics seem unstable and therefore the performance immediately drops with a large amount.

As mentioned in Sect. 3, the targets are determined by the simulated Q-values computed with the rollouts. However, since we determine a target for every possible action, it is possible to apply back-propagation on all four Q-values rather than only for the Q-value of the performed action. We believe that by updating the Q-values of all four actions, the agent can faster learn the correct Q-values and that this therefore should increase performance. We have conducted the same experiment as above, but now by updating the Q-values of all four actions using the rollout estimates. The results of training using small and large vision grids can be found in Figs. 10 and 11. The performance over the test games can be found in Table 7.

**Fig. 10.** Training performance with small vision grids when updating the Q-values of all actions. Random and deterministic indicate the opponent and 5 and 10 represent the horizon.

**Fig. 11.** Training performance with large vision grids when updating the Q-values of all actions. Random and deterministic indicate the opponent and 5 and 10 represent the horizon.

If we compare the results from training one action and training four actions, we can conclude that it is very beneficial to train four actions simultaneously, rather than only learning the Q-value of the performed action. Now we also see in the figures that the agent's performance increases over the last 50,000

**Table 7.** Final test performance for 10,000 games while training Q-values of 4 actions using the rollout estimates.

| State representation | Opponent | 1 rollout 10 actions | 5 rollouts 5 actions |
|---|---|---|---|
| Small vision grids | Random | 0.74 (0.002) | 0.82 (0.001) |
| Large vision grids | Random | 0.74 (0.002) | **0.84 (0.002)** |
| Small vision grids | Deterministic | 0.94 (0.001) | 0.88 (0.002) |
| Large vision grids | Deterministic | **0.96 (0.001)** | 0.93 (0.001) |

games but only against the deterministic opponent. This is most likely caused by the fact that the opponent model against this opponent is more accurate and therefore leads to more accurate targets in the rollouts. In addition, when we compare these results with the results after 1.5 million games in Table 3, where we also used one rollout with ten actions, we see that the results are slightly worse against the deterministic opponent. Against the random opponent the performance increases with large vision grids, but decreases with small vision grids. These results show that with the new proposed system good performances can already be obtained with 150,000 training games. From the results shown in Table 7 we can also conclude that it is better to use a horizon of 10 actions against the semi-deterministic opponent.

### 4.5 Learning from Monte Carlo Rollouts with Exploration

In the previous experiments, during the rollout learning phase no exploration was used. In this subsection, we want to explore if it would not be better to sometimes use an exploration action instead of the action proposed by the Monte Carlo rollouts. Therefore, we conducted the same experiments as in the previous section, however, now exploration decreases from 10% to 0% over the first 100,000 games and goes from 10% to 0% over the 50,000 games played using the rollouts. The training performances can be found in Figs. 12, 13, 14, and 15. The performance over the test games can be found in Tables 8 and 9.

**Table 8.** Final test performance for 10,000 games while learning the Q-value of 1 action from the rollout estimates with exploration during the rollout training phase.

| State representation | Opponent | 1 rollout 10 actions | 5 rollouts 5 actions |
|---|---|---|---|
| Small vision grids | Random | 0.47 (0.003) | 0.59 (0.011) |
| Large vision grids | Random | 0.43 (0.006) | 0.59 (0.006) |
| Small vision grids | Deterministic | 0.63 (0.020) | 0.60 (0.014) |
| Large vision grids | Deterministic | 0.62 (0.011) | 0.65 (0.009) |

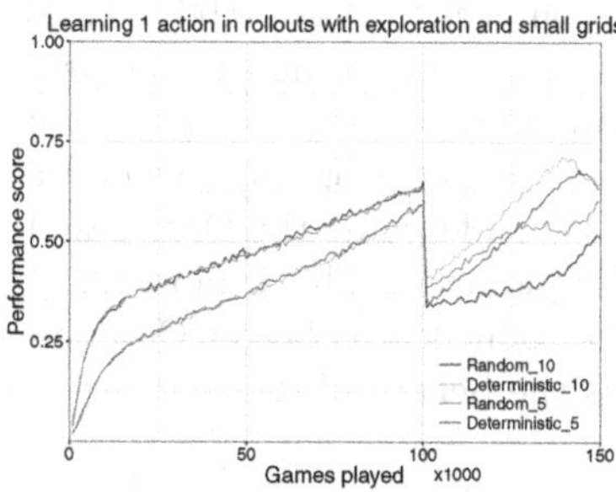


**Fig. 12.** Training performance with small vision grids and exploration in the rollouts when updating only the Q-value of 1 action. Random and deterministic indicate the opponent and 5 and 10 represent the horizon.

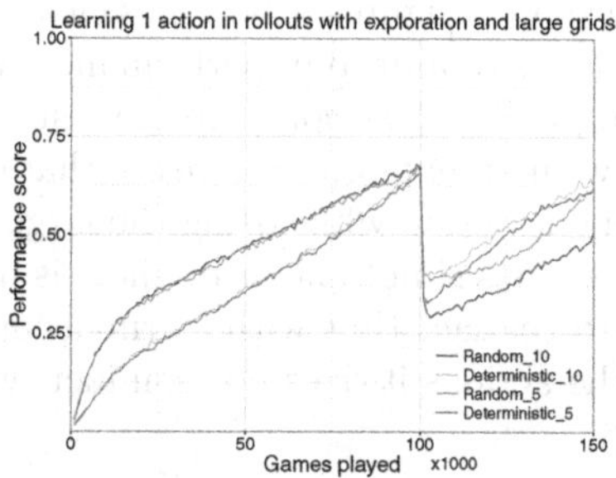


**Fig. 13.** Training performance with large vision grids and exploration in the rollouts when updating only the Q-value of 1 action. Random and deterministic indicate the opponent and 5 and 10 represent the horizon.

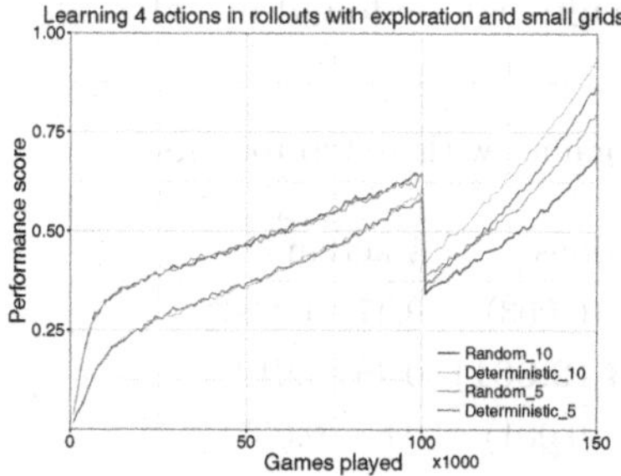


**Fig. 14.** Training performance with small vision grids and exploration in the rollouts when updating the Q-values of 4 actions. Random and deterministic indicate the opponent and 5 and 10 represent the horizon.

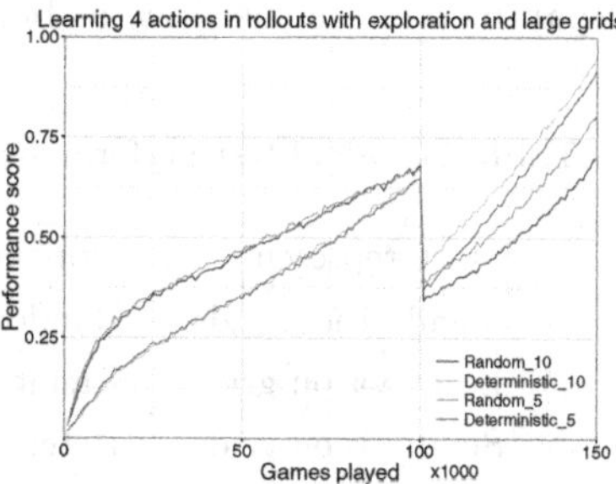


**Fig. 15.** Training performance with large vision grids and exploration in the rollouts when updating the Q-values of 4 actions. Random and deterministic indicate the opponent and 5 and 10 represent the horizon.

**Table 9.** Final test performance for 10,000 games while learning the Q-values of 4 actions from the rollout estimates with exploration during the rollout training phase.

| State representation | Opponent | 1 rollout 10 actions | 5 rollouts 5 actions |
|---|---|---|---|
| Small vision grids | Random | 0.73 (0.002) | 0.83 (0.002) |
| Large vision grids | Random | 0.74 (0.002) | **0.84 (0.002)** |
| Small vision grids | Deterministic | 0.94 (0.001) | 0.87 (0.004) |
| Large vision grids | Deterministic | **0.96 (0.001)** | 0.93 (0.002) |

From the figures it becomes clear that exploration over the last 50,000 games first leads to a drop in performance, while afterwards the performance increases strongly. When we compare the results from learning in rollouts with exploration and without exploration, we see that exploration increases performance when we train one action while using the large vision grid. When learning the Q-values of four actions simultaneously, there is no benefit of exploration. This is most likely due to the fact that with learning four actions the agent learns better Q-values for the actions it does not conduct, which reduces the benefit of exploration.

### 4.6 Using Experience Replay with 1-Step Rollouts

In order to determine the importance of using long horizons in the rollouts, we conducted experiments in which the agent uses experience replay but only used a rollout with 1 action. Therefore the horizon in the rollouts is reduced to 1 action, where the agent tries all possible actions and the model of the opponent is used to predict the next state. In these experiments we only perform one rollout per state during training. When playing the final test games, the agent still uses 1 rollout with a horizon of 10 actions. The exploration strategy and all other hyperparameters are the same as before. The results can be found in Table 10.

**Table 10.** Final test performance for 10,000 games with 1-step rollouts.

| State representation | Opponent | 4 actions | 1 action |
|---|---|---|---|
| Small vision grids | Random | 0.73 (0.003) | 0.47 (0.008) |
| Large vision grids | Random | **0.73 (0.001)** | 0.46 (0.012) |
| Small vision grids | Deterministic | 0.94 (0.001) | 0.65 (0.007) |
| Large vision grids | Deterministic | **0.95 (0.001)** | 0.65 (0.013) |

When we compare Table 10 to Tables 8 and 9 with 1 rollout, we notice no significant differences. Therefore, we can conclude that learning from the estimates of long rollouts is not necessary and actually costs more computing power. This is similar to learning from n-step backups [21] which can lead to a lower bias but suffers from a higher variance and is therefore not always fruitful.

Learning on the estimates of all actions using the Monte Carlo rollouts is however always much better than learning only on the estimate of a single action. Experience replay is general is always used to update the Q-value of a single action, because that action was the only one that was experienced in a state. However, with the model of the game and the opponent model, we have shown that experience replay can be improved by updating the Q-values of all actions simultaneously. This led to similar results as in our previous paper [7], but now by only learning from 150,000 games instead of from 1.5 million games.

## 5 Conclusion

This paper described a novel approach to learning to play the game of Tron. The proposed method combines reinforcement learning, multi-layer perceptrons, vision grids, opponent modelling and Monte Carlo rollouts in a novel way. Instead of only using Monte Carlo rollouts while playing test games, the new system uses Monte Carlo rollouts to select moves while training and learns from the estimates obtained with the Monte Carlo rollouts. We have extended the use of experience replay to make it possible to update the state-action values of all actions in a state simultaneously. This is possible due to the Monte Carlo rollouts that generate action estimates for all actions.

The results showed that the use of the novel experience replay method that updates all action values simultaneously strongly outperforms experience replay where only the performed action gets its action value updated. One reason is that experience replay on a single selected action requires a lot of exploration to compare the utilities of different actions in the same state. Furthermore, with the new method all action values are updated in the same state. The proposed system is able to perform similarly after training on 150,000 games to our previous system [7], which needed 1.5 million training games to obtain very good performances. The results also showed that while training the system, longer horizons in the Monte Carlo rollouts were not necessary to obtain good results, as with a horizon of a single action similar performances were obtained. Learning from longer horizons may reduce the bias due to bootstrapping, but also suffers from a higher variance. Against the semi-deterministic opponent the RL system profits from Monte Carlo rollouts with longer horizons, whereas against the random opponent the system profits from multiple rollouts.

This research opens up several interesting possibilities for future research. Instead of Monte Carlo rollouts, it would be interesting to also combine Monte Carlo tree search with opponent-model learning. Furthermore, from the different rollouts much more information is obtained than currently used for updating the state-action value function. It would be possible to update action values of each game state that was visited during one of the rollouts. Another direction is to combine the power of the vision grids with convolutional neural networks (CNNs). The vision grids summarize the most important local information, but lack more global information. By combining the vision grids with CNNs it should be possible to profit from the faster learning process using the local information, while still being able to integrate important global information. Finally, it would be interesting to examine if our extended experience replay algorithm that trains on simulated experiences of all actions in a given state would also be useful for learning to play other games.

## References

1. Baxter, J., Tridgell, A., Weaver, L.: Learning to play chess using temporal differences. Mach. Learn. **40**(3), 243–263 (2000)
2. Bom, L., Henken, R., Wiering, M.: Reinforcement learning to train Ms. Pac-Man using higher-order action-relative inputs. In: 2013 IEEE Symposium on Adaptive Dynamic Programming and Reinforcement Learning (ADPRL), pp. 156–163 (2013)
3. de Bruin, T., Kober, J., Tuyls, K., Babuška, R.: The importance of experience replay database composition in deep reinforcement learning. In: Deep Reinforcement Learning Workshop, NIPS (2015)
4. Clevert, D., Unterthiner, T., Hochreiter, S.: Fast and accurate deep network learning by exponential linear units (ELUs). CoRR abs/1511.07289 (2015)
5. Ganzfried, S., Sandholm, T.: Game theory-based opponent modeling in large imperfect-information games. In: the 10th International Conference on Autonomous Agents and Multiagent Systems-Volume 2, pp. 533–540. International Foundation for Autonomous Agents and Multiagent Systems (2011)
6. He, H., Boyd-Graber, J.L., Kwok, K., Daumé III, H.: Opponent modeling in deep reinforcement learning. CoRR abs/1609.05559 (2016)
7. Knegt, S., Drugan, M., Wiering, M.: Opponent modelling in the game of Tron using reinforcement learning. In: 10th International Conference on Agents and Artificial Intelligence, ICAART 2018, pp. 29–40 (2018)
8. Kocsis, L., Szepesvári, C.: Bandit based Monte-Carlo planning. In: Fürnkranz, J., Scheffer, T., Spiliopoulou, M. (eds.) ECML 2006. LNCS (LNAI), vol. 4212, pp. 282–293. Springer, Heidelberg (2006). https://doi.org/10.1007/11871842_29
9. Lin, L.J.: Reinforcement Learning for Robots Using Neural Networks. Ph.D. thesis, Carnegie Mellon University, Pittsburgh, January 1993
10. Mnih, V., et al.: Playing atari with deep reinforcement learning. arXiv preprint arXiv:1312.5602 (2013)
11. van Otterlo, M., Wiering, M.: Reinforcement learning and Markov decision processes. In: Wiering, M., van Otterlo, M. (eds.) Reinforcement Learning: State-of-the-Art, pp. 3–42. Springer, Heidelberg (2012). https://doi.org/10.1007/978-3-642-27645-3_1
12. Rumelhart, D.E., Hinton, G.E., Williams, R.J.: Learning internal representations by error propagation. In: Parallel Distributed Processing, vol. 1, pp. 318–362. MIT Press (1986)
13. Samuel, A.L.: Some studies in machine learning using the game of checkers. IBM J. Res. Dev. **3**, 210–229 (1959)
14. Schmidhuber, J.: Deep learning in neural networks: an overview. Neural Netw. **61**, 85–117 (2015)
15. Shantia, A., Begue, E., Wiering, M.: Connectionist reinforcement learning for intelligent unit micro management in Starcraft. In: The 2011 International Joint Conference on Neural Networks (IJCNN), pp. 1794–1801. IEEE (2011)
16. Silver, D., et al.: Mastering the game of Go with deep neural networks and tree search. Nature **529**(7587), 484–489 (2016)
17. Silver, D., et al.: Mastering chess and shogi by self-play with a general reinforcement learning algorithm. arXiv preprint arXiv:1712.01815 (2017)
18. Silver, D., et al.: Mastering the game of Go without human knowledge. Nature **550**, 354 (2017)
19. Southey, F., et al.: Bayes bluff: opponent modelling in poker. In: Proceedings of the 21st Annual Conference on Uncertainty in Artificial Intelligence (UAI), pp. 550–558 (2005)

20. Sutton, R.S.: Learning to predict by the methods of temporal differences. Mach. Learn. **3**(1), 9–44 (1988)
21. Sutton, R.S., Barto, A.G.: Introduction to Reinforcement Learning, 1st edn. MIT Press, Cambridge (1998)
22. Tesauro, G.: Temporal difference learning and TD-Gammon. Commun. ACM **38**(3), 58–68 (1995)
23. Tesauro, G., Galperin, G.R.: On-line policy improvement using Monte-Carlo search. In: Jordan, M.I., Petsche, T. (eds.) Advances in Neural Information Processing Systems 9, pp. 1068–1074. MIT Press (1997)
24. Watkins, C.J., Dayan, P.: Q-learning. Mach. Learn. **8**(3), 279–292 (1992)
25. Werbos, P.J.: Beyond regression: new tools for prediction and analysis in the behavioral sciences. Ph.D. thesis, Harvard University (1974)

# Conditional Uncertainty in Constraint Networks

Matteo Zavatteri[1(✉)] and Luca Viganò[2(✉)]

[1] Dipartimento di Informatica, Università di Verona, Verona, Italy
matteo.zavatteri@univr.it

[2] Department of Informatics, King's College London, London, UK
luca.vigano@kcl.ac.uk

**Abstract.** *Constraint Networks (CNs)* are a framework to model the *Constraint Satisfaction Problem (CSP)*, which is the problem of finding an assignment of values to a set of variables satisfying a set of given constraints. Therefore, CSP is a satisfiability problem. When the CSP turns conditional, consistency analysis extends to finding also an assignment to these conditions such that the relevant part of the initial CN is consistent. However, CNs fail to model CSPs expressing an *uncontrollable* conditional part (i.e., a conditional part that cannot be decided but merely observed as it occurs). To bridge this gap, in this paper we propose *Constraint Networks Under Conditional Uncertainty (CNCUs)*, and we define weak, strong and dynamic *controllability* of a CNCU. We provide algorithms to check each of these types of controllability and discuss how to synthesize (dynamic) execution strategies that drive the execution of a CNCU saying which value to assign to which variable depending on how the uncontrollable part behaves. We discuss Zeta, a tool that we developed for CNCUs to carry out an experimental evaluation. What we propose is fully automated from analysis to simulation.

**Keywords:** Constraint Networks Under Conditional Uncertainty CNCU · Directional consistency · Resource controllability · Zeta AI-based security

## 1 Introduction

Assume that we are given a resource-scheduling problem specifying a conditional part that is out of control, and that we are asked to schedule (some of the) resources in a way that meets all relevant constraints, or to prove that such a scheduling does not exist. We can also make our scheduling decisions as we like.

When facing uncontrollable parts we can in general act in three main different ways:

1. We assume that we know in advance how the uncontrollable part will behave and make sure that a (possibly different) strategy to operate on the controllable part exists.


J. van den Herik and A. P. Rocha (Eds.): ICAART 2018, LNAI 11352, pp. 130–160, 2019.
https://doi.org/10.1007/978-3-030-05453-3_7

2. We assume that we have a fixed strategy operating on the controllable part always in the same way no matter how the uncontrollable part will behave.
3. We assume that we have a strategy operating in real-time on the controllable part making (possibly different) decisions depending on how the uncontrollable part is behaving.

These are the intuitions behind the three main kinds of *controllability*: *weak* (for presumptuous designers/analysts), *strong* (for anxious ones) and *dynamic* (for grandmasters).

In recent years, a considerable amount of research has been carried out to investigate controllability analysis in order to deal with temporal and conditional uncertainty, either in isolation or simultaneously. In particular, a number of extensions of *Simple Temporal Networks* (*STNs*, [1]) have been proposed. For example, *Simple Temporal Networks with Uncertainty* (*STNUs*, [2]) add uncontrollable (but bounded) durations between pairs of temporal events, whereas *Conditional Simple Temporal Networks* (*CSTNs*, [3], and formerly *Conditional Temporal Problem, CTP*, [4]), extend STNs by turning the constraints conditional. Finally, *Conditional Simple Temporal Networks with Uncertainty* (*CSTNUs*, [5]) merge STNUs and CSTNs, whereas *Conditional Simple Temporal Networks with Uncertainty and Decisions* (*CSTNUDs*, [6]) encompass all previous formalisms.

Several algorithms have been proposed to check the controllability of a temporal network, e.g., constraint-propagation [3], timed game automata [6,7] and satisfiability modulo theory [8,9].

Research has also been carried out in the "discrete" world of classic *Constraint Networks* (*CNs*, [10]) in order to address different kinds of uncertainty. For example, a *Mixed Constraint Satisfaction Problem* (*Mixed CSP*, [11]) divides the set of variables in controllable and uncontrollable, whereas a *Dynamic Constraint Satisfaction Problem* (*DCSP*, [12]) introduces activity constraints saying when variables are relevant depending on what values some other variables have been previously assigned. Probabilistic approaches such as [13] aim instead at finding the most probable working solution.

Despite all this, a formal model to extend classic CNs [10] with conditional uncertainty adhering to the modeling ideas employed by CSTNs is still missing. In a CSTN, for instance, time points (variables) and linear inequalities (constraints) are labeled by conjunctions of literals where the truth value assignments to the embedded Boolean propositions are out of control. Every proposition has an associated *observation time point*, a special kind of time point that reveals the truth value assignment to the associated proposition upon its execution (i.e., as soon as it is assigned a real value). Equivalently, this truth value assignment can be thought of as being under the control of the environment.

To give an example of conditional uncertainty, consider a patient coming to the ER. The severity of the patient's condition is not known a priori but it is established by a physician *while* the workflow is being executed. Since the result of this condition discriminates what tasks have, or have not, to be executed, the system must be able to complete the workflow by executing all relevant tasks and satisfying all relevant constraints regardless of the result of (any combination) of uncontrollable conditions.

When the assignment of users to task is generated while the workflow executes we must never backtrack. In the real world, this means that we must avoid situations in which, if a patient is urgent, no doctor is available because we chose to assign the wrong doctor to some previous task. That is, one who will violate some constraint during execution.

In [14], Zavatteri et al. defined and investigated weak, strong and dynamic controllability of access controlled workflows for the first time by encoding workflow paths into CNs and reasoning on the intersection of common parts. After that, *Constraint Networks Under Conditional Uncertainty* (*CNCU*, [15]) were proposed as an underlying, more abstract, formalism to handle resource scheduling (a.k.a. resource allocation) problems under conditional uncertainty.

Towards the validation and runtime management of resource scheduling problems, our contributions in this paper are three-fold:

1. We define CNCUs as an extension of classic constraint networks and give the semantics for weak, strong and dynamic controllability of a CNCU.
2. We provide algorithms to check each of these types of controllability and to execute a controllable CNCU.
3. We provide ZETA, a tool we developed for CNCUs along with an experimental evaluation.

This paper revises and extends all the material in [15] (which was presented at ICAART 2018) and provides a more accurate experimental evaluation.

We proceed as follows. Section 2 provides essential background on CNs and the adaptive consistency algorithm. Section 3 introduces our main contribution: CNCUs. Section 4 defines the semantics for weak, strong and dynamic controllability and Sect. 5 addresses the related algorithms. Section 6 discusses the correctness of our approach. Section 7 discusses our tool ZETA for CNCUs along with an experimental evaluation. Section 8 discusses related work. Section 9 draws conclusions and discusses future work.

## 2 Background

In this section, we give essential background on CNs and the *adaptive consistency algorithm* for the related consistency checking [10].

**Definition 1.** *A* Constraint Network (CN) *is a triple* $\mathcal{Z} = \langle \mathcal{V}, \mathcal{D}, \mathcal{C} \rangle$*, where:*

- $\mathcal{V} = \{V_1, \ldots, V_n\}$ *is a finite set of variables,*
- $\mathcal{D} = \{D_1, \ldots, D_n\}$ *is a set of discrete domains* $D_i = \{v_1, \ldots, v_j\}$ *(one for each variable),*
- $\mathcal{C} = \{R_{S_1}, \ldots, R_{S_n}\}$ *is a finite set of constraints each one represented as a relation* $R_S$ *defined over a* scope *of variables* $S \subseteq \mathcal{V}$ *such that if* $S = \{V_i, \ldots, V_r\}$*, then* $R \subseteq D_i \times \cdots \times D_r$*.*

**Algorithm 1.** ADC($\mathcal{Z}, d$) from [15].

**Input:** A CN $\mathcal{Z} = \langle \mathcal{V}, \mathcal{D}, \mathcal{C} \rangle$ and an ordering $d = V_1 \prec \cdots \prec V_n$
**Output:** A set *Buckets* of buckets (one for each variable) if $\mathcal{Z}$ is consistent, inconsistent otherwise.

**for** $i \leftarrow n$ **downto** 1 **do** ▷ Partition the constraints as follows:
  Put in $Bucket(V_i)$ all unplaced constraints mentioning $V_i$
**for** $p \leftarrow n$ **downto** 1 **do**
  Let $j \leftarrow |Bucket(V_p)|$ and $S_i$ be the scope of $R_{S_i} \in Bucket(V_p)$
  $S' \leftarrow \bigcup_{i=1}^{j} S_i \setminus \{V_p\}$
  $R_{S'} \leftarrow \pi_{S'}(\bowtie_{i=1}^{j} R_{S_i})$
  **if** $R_{S'} \neq \emptyset$ **then**
    $Bucket(V') \leftarrow Bucket(V') \cup \{R_{S'}\}$, where $V' \in S'$ is the "latest" variable in $d$.
  **else**
    **return** inconsistent
$Buckets = \{\{Bucket(V)\} \mid V \in \mathcal{V}\}$
**return** *Buckets*

*A CN is* consistent *if each variable* $V_i \in \mathcal{V}$ *can be assigned a value* $v_i \in D_i$ *such that* all *constraints are satisfied.*

The *Constraint Satisfaction Problem* (*CSP*) is NP-hard [10]. A CN is $k$-ary if all constraints have scope cardinality $\leq k$ and therefore *binary* when $k = 2$ [10,16]. Let $R_{ij}$ be a shortcut to represent a binary relation having scope $S = \{V_i, V_j\}$. A binary CN is *minimal* if any tuple $(v_i, v_j) \in R_{ij} \in \mathcal{C}$ belongs to at least one global solution for the underlying CSP [16]. Thus, a minimal CN models an $n$-ary relation whose scope is $\mathcal{V}$ and whose tuples represent the set of all solutions. Besides for a few restricted classes of CNs, the general process of computing a minimal network is NP-hard [16]. Furthermore, even considering a binary minimal network, the problem of generating an arbitrary solution is NP-hard if there is no total order on the variables [17].

Therefore, a first crude technique is that of searching for a solution by exhaustively enumerating and testing all possible solutions and stopping as soon as one satisfies all constraints in $\mathcal{C}$. To speed up the search, we can combine techniques such as backtracking with pruning techniques such as *node*, *arc* and *path consistency* [18]. A variable $V_i$ is *node-consistent* if $v \in R_{S_i}$ for each $v \in D_i$. A CN is node-consistent if each variable is node-consistent. A variable $V_i$ is *arc-consistent* with respect to a second variable $V_j$ if for each $v \in D_i$, there exists $u \in D_j$ such that $(v, u) \in R_{ij}$. A CN is arc-consistent if every variable is arc-consistent with respect to any other second variable. A pair of variables $(V_i, V_j)$ is *path-consistent* with respect to a third variable $V_k$ if for any assignment $V_i = v, V_j = u$, where $v \in D_i$ and $u \in D_j$, there exists $k \in D_k$ such that $(v, k) \in R_{ik}$ and $(k, u) \in R_{kj}$. A CN is path-consistent if any pair of variables is path-consistent with respect to any other third variable. Path consistency is not enough for a backtrack free search [10] (i.e., it is an incomplete inference approach).

*k-consistency* guarantees that any (locally consistent) assignment to any subset of $(k-1)$-variables can be extended to a $k^{\text{th}}$ (still unassigned) variable such that all constraints between these $k$-variables are satisfied. *Strong k-consistency* is $k$-consistency for each $j$ such that $1 \leq j \leq k$ [19]. As a result, 1, 2 and 3-consistency are node, arc and path consistency.

*Directional consistency* has been introduced to speed up the process of synthesizing a solution for a constraint network limiting backtracking [20]. In a nutshell, given a total order on the variables of a CN, the network is *directional-consistent* if it is consistent with respect to the given order that dictates the assignment order of variables. In [20], an *adaptive-consistency (ADC) algorithm* was provided as a directional consistency algorithm adapting the level of $k$-consistency needed to guarantee a backtrack-free search once the algorithm terminates, if the network admits a solution (see Algorithm 1). The input of ADC is a CN $\mathcal{Z} = \langle \mathcal{V}, \mathcal{D}, \mathcal{C} \rangle$ along with an order $d$ for $\mathcal{V}$. At each step the algorithm *adapts* the level of consistency to guarantee that if the network passes the test, any solution satisfying all constraints can be generated without backtracking. If the network is inconsistent, the algorithm detects it before the solution generation process starts. ADC initializes a $\mathit{Bucket}(V)$ for each variable $V \in \mathcal{V}$ and first processes all the variables top-down (i.e., from last to first following the ordering $d$) by filling each bucket with all (still unplaced) constraints $R_S \in \mathcal{C}$ such that $V \in S$. Then, it processes again the variables top-down and, for each variable $V$, it computes a new scope $S'$ consisting of the union of all scopes of the relations in $\mathit{Bucket}(V)$ neglecting $V$ itself. After that, it computes a new relation $R_{S'}$ by joining all $R_S \in \mathit{Bucket}(V)$ and projecting with respect to $S'$ ($\bowtie$ and $\pi$ are the join and projection operators of relational algebra). In this way, it enforces the sufficient level of consistency which is needed not to backtrack when generating any solution. If the resulting relation is empty, then $\mathcal{Z}$ is inconsistent; otherwise, the algorithm adds $R_{S'}$ to the bucket of the *latest* variable in $S'$ (with respect to the ordering $d$), and goes on with the next variable. Finally, it returns the set of *Buckets* (we slightly modified the return statement of ADC). Note that ADC takes as input a $k$-ary CN $\mathcal{Z}$ and returns a $k'$-ary CN $\mathcal{Z}'$, where $k' \geq k$ (see [10, Chap. 4] for a binary CN turned into a ternary one).

Time and space complexity of ADC are $\mathcal{O}(n(2z)^{w^*+1})$ and $\mathcal{O}(nz^{w^*})$, respectively, where $n = |\mathcal{V}|$, $z = \max_{i=1,\dots,n} |D_i|$ is the maximal cardinality of variables domains, and $w^*$ is the induced width of the graph along the order of processing [10, Chap. 4]. Informally, $w^*$ represents the maximum number of variables that can be affected by the value assumed by another variable; i.e., a characterization of the topology of the CN.

Any binary CN can be represented as a *constraint graph* where the set of nodes coincides with $\mathcal{V}$ and the set of edges represents the constraints in $\mathcal{C}$. Furthermore, nodes are labeled by their domains. Each (undirected) edge between two variables $V_1$ and $V_2$ is labeled by the corresponding $R_{12} \in \mathcal{C}$. As an example, consider the *constraint graph* in Fig. 1a representing $\mathcal{Z} = \langle \mathcal{V}, \mathcal{D}, \mathcal{C} \rangle$, where:

- $\mathcal{V} = \{V_1, V_2, V_3, V_4\}$,
- $\mathcal{D} = \{D_1, D_2, D_3, D_4\}$ with $D_1 = D_2 = D_3 = D_4 = \{\mathtt{a}, \mathtt{b}, \mathtt{c}\}$,

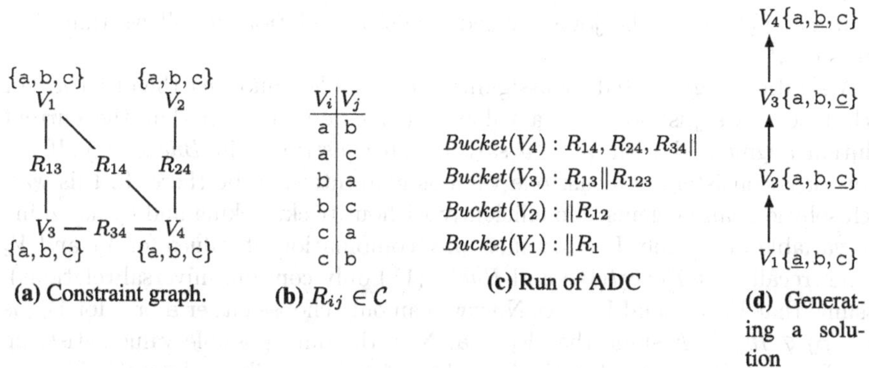


**Fig. 1.** Graphical representation of a binary CN (a) Relational constraint (b) Run of ADC (c) Solution generation without backtracking (d) Subfigures (a) and (c) are taken from [15].

- $\mathcal{C} = \{R_{13}, R_{14}, R_{24}, R_{34}\}$.

All $R_{ij} \in \mathcal{C}$ contain the same tuples; actually, they all specify the $\neq$ constraint between the pair of variables they connect (Fig. 1b). That is,

$$R_{13} = R_{14} = R_{24} = R_{34} = \{(\mathtt{a},\mathtt{b}), (\mathtt{a},\mathtt{c}), (\mathtt{b},\mathtt{a}), (\mathtt{b},\mathtt{c}), (\mathtt{c},\mathtt{a}), (\mathtt{c},\mathtt{b})\}$$

The CN in Fig. 1a is consistent. To prove that, we choose, without loss of generality (recall that *any* order is fine for this algorithm [10]), the order $d = V_1 \prec V_2 \prec V_3 \prec V_4$ and run ADC$(\mathcal{Z}, d)$ on the CN. We show the output of the algorithm in Fig. 1d.

ADC first processes $V_4$ by filling *Bucket*$(V_4)$ with $R_{14}$, $R_{24}$ and $R_{34}$ (as they all mention $V_4$ in their scope and are still unplaced). Then, it processes $V_3$ by filling *Bucket*$(V_3)$ with $R_{13}$ (but not $R_{34}$). Finally, it leaves *Bucket*$(V_2)$ and *Bucket*$(V_1)$ empty as all relations mentioning $V_2$ and $V_1$ in their scope have already been put in some other bucket. Therefore, the initialization phase fills the buckets in Fig. 1d with all relations on the left of $\|$ (the newly generated ones will appear on the right). When we add a relation in a bucket containing another relation with the same scope we keep the intersection of these relations (tightening).

In the second phase, the algorithm computes $R_{123} = \pi_{123}(R_{14} \bowtie R_{24} \bowtie R_{34}) = \{(\mathtt{a},\mathtt{a},\mathtt{a}), (\mathtt{a},\mathtt{a},\mathtt{b}), (\mathtt{a},\mathtt{a},\mathtt{c}), (\mathtt{a},\mathtt{b},\mathtt{a}), (\mathtt{a},\mathtt{b},\mathtt{b}), (\mathtt{a},\mathtt{c},\mathtt{a}), (\mathtt{a},\mathtt{c},\mathtt{c}), (\mathtt{b},\mathtt{a},\mathtt{a}), (\mathtt{b},\mathtt{a},\mathtt{b}), (\mathtt{b},\mathtt{b},\mathtt{a}), (\mathtt{b},\mathtt{b},\mathtt{b}), (\mathtt{b},\mathtt{b},\mathtt{c}), (\mathtt{b},\mathtt{c},\mathtt{b}), (\mathtt{b},\mathtt{c},\mathtt{c}), (\mathtt{c},\mathtt{a},\mathtt{a}), (\mathtt{c},\mathtt{a},\mathtt{c}), (\mathtt{c},\mathtt{b},\mathtt{b}), (\mathtt{c},\mathtt{b},\mathtt{c}), (\mathtt{c},\mathtt{c},\mathtt{a}), (\mathtt{c},\mathtt{c},\mathtt{b}), (\mathtt{c},\mathtt{c},\mathtt{c})\}$ and adds it to *Bucket*$(V_3)$ (the latest variable in the scope $\{V_1, V_2, V_3\}$). Then, it goes ahead by processing *Bucket*$(V_3)$ generating in a similar way $R_{12}$ and adding it to *Bucket*$(V_2)$. Finally, it processes *Bucket*$(V_2)$ by computing $R_1$ and adding it to $Bucket(V_1)$. Since the joins yielded no empty relation, it follows that $\mathcal{Z}$ is consistent.[1]

A solution is generated by assigning the variables following the order $d$. For each $V \in d$ we just look for a value $v$ in its domain such that the current solution augmented with $V = v$ satisfies all constraints in $Bucket(V)$. If the network is consistent, at least one value is guaranteed to be there. In this way, each solution can be generated efficiently without backtracking and by assigning one variable at a time. For instance, any combination of values for $V_1$ and $V_2$ is fine (recall that $Bucket(V_1)$ and $Bucket(V_2)$ only contain universal relations). Assume that $V_1 = \mathtt{a}$ and $V_2 = \mathtt{c}$. Now we can only choose either $\mathtt{a}$ or $\mathtt{c}$ for $V_3$ (as $(\mathtt{a}, \mathtt{c}, \underline{\mathtt{b}}) \notin R_{123}$). Assume that $V_3 = \mathtt{a}$. Now the only possible value satisfying $R_{14}$, $R_{24}$ and $R_{34}$ in $Bucket(V_4)$ is $\mathtt{b}$. Therefore, a possible solution is $V_1 = \mathtt{a}$, $V_2 = \mathtt{c}$, $V_3 = \mathtt{c}$ and $V_4 = \mathtt{b}$ (Fig. 1d).

## 3 Constraint Networks Under Conditional Uncertainty

In this section, we extend CNs to address conditional uncertainty. We call this new kind of network *Constraint Network under Conditional Uncertainty (CNCU)*. CNCUs are obtained by extending CNs with

- a set of Boolean *propositions* whose truth value assignments are out of control (or, equivalently, can be thought of as being under the control of the environment),
- *observation variables* to observe such truth value assignments, and
- *labels* to enable or disable a subset of variables and constraints, and therefore introduce an (implicit) notion of partial order among the variables.

We will also talk about *execution* meaning that we *execute a variable* by assigning it a value and we *execute a CNCU* by executing all relevant variables. Variables and constraints are *relevant* if they must be considered during execution.

Given a set $\mathcal{P} = \{p, q, \dots\}$ of Boolean propositions, a *label* $\ell = l_1 \wedge \dots \wedge l_n$ is a finite conjunction of literals $l_i$, where a literal is either a proposition $p \in \mathcal{P}$ (positive literal) or its negation $\neg p$ (negative literal). The *empty label* is denoted by $\boxdot$. The *label universe of* $\mathcal{P}$, denoted by $\mathcal{P}^*$, is the set of all possible labels drawn from $\mathcal{P}$; e.g., if $\mathcal{P} = \{p, q\}$, then $\mathcal{P}^* = \{\boxdot, p, q, \neg p, \neg q, p \wedge q, p \wedge \neg q, \neg p \wedge q, \neg p \wedge \neg q, p \wedge \neg p, q \wedge \neg q\}$. A label $\ell_1 \in \mathcal{P}^*$ is *consistent* iff $\ell_1$ is satisfiable, *entails* a label $\ell_2$ (written $\ell_1 \Rightarrow \ell_2$) iff all literals in $\ell_2$ appear in $\ell_1$ too (i.e., if $\ell_1$ is more *specific* than $\ell_2$) and *falsifies* a label $\ell_2$ iff $\ell_1 \wedge \ell_2$ is not consistent. The *difference* of two labels $\ell_1$ and $\ell_2$ is a new label $\ell_3 = \ell_1 - \ell_2$ consisting of all literals of $\ell_1$ minus those shared with $\ell_2$. For instance, if $\ell_1 = p \wedge \neg q$ and $\ell_2 = p$, then $\ell_1$ and $\ell_2$ are consistent, $\ell_1 \Rightarrow \ell_2$, $\ell_1 - \ell_2 = \neg q$ and $\ell_2 - \ell_1 = \boxdot$.

[1] Note that $R_{12}$ and $R_1$ should not be recorded in $Bucket(V_2)$ and $Bucket(V_1)$ as they represent the universal relations $R_{12} = D_1 \times D_2$ and $R_1 = D_1$. However, doing so is superfluous but not wrong.

**Definition 2.** *A Constraint Network Under Conditional Uncertainty (CNCU) is a tuple* $\langle \mathcal{V}, \mathcal{D}, D, \mathcal{OV}, \mathcal{P}, O, L, \prec, \mathcal{C} \rangle$*, where:*

- $\mathcal{V} = \{V_1, V_2, \dots\}$ *is a finite set of variables.*
- $\mathcal{D} = \{D_1, D_2, \dots\}$ *is a set of discrete domains.*
- $D \colon \mathcal{V} \to \mathcal{D}$ *is a mapping assigning a domain to each variable, where more variables can share the same domain.*
- $\mathcal{OV} \subseteq \mathcal{V} = \{P?, Q?, \dots\}$ *is a set of* observation variables.
- $\mathcal{P} = \{p, q, \dots\}$ *is a set of Boolean* propositions *whose truth values are all initially unknown.*
- $O \colon \mathcal{P} \to \mathcal{OV}$ *is a bijection assigning a unique observation variable* $P?$ *to each proposition* $p$*. When* $P?$ *executes, the truth value of* $p$ *becomes known and no longer changes.*
- $L \colon \mathcal{V} \to \mathcal{P}^*$ *is a mapping assigning a label* $\ell$ *to each variable* $V$ *saying when* $V$ *is relevant.*
- $\prec \subseteq \mathcal{V} \times \mathcal{V}$ *is a precedence relation on the variables. We write* $(V_1, V_2) \in \prec$ *(or* $V_1 \prec V_2$*) to express that* $V_1$ *is assigned* before $V_2$.
- $\mathcal{C}$ *is a finite set of* labeled relational constraints *of the form* $(R_S, \ell)$*, where* $S \subseteq \mathcal{V}$ *and* $\ell \in \mathcal{P}^*$*. If* $S = \{V_1, \dots, V_n\}$*, then* $R_S \subseteq D(V_1) \times \cdots \times D(V_n)$.

We graphically represent a (binary) CNCU by extending the constraint graph discussed for CNs into a *labeled constraint (multi)graph*, where each variable is also labeled by its label $L(V)$, and the edges are of two kinds: *order edges* (directed unlabeled edges) and *constraint edges* (undirected labeled edges). An order edge $V_1 \to V_2$ models $V_1 \prec V_2$. A constraint edge between $V_1$ and $V_2$ models $(R_{12}, \ell)$. Many constraint edges may possibly be specified between the same pair of variables, as long as $\ell$ is different (e.g., $(R_1, \boxdot)$ and $(R_1, \neg p)$ between `ProcR` and `LogR` in Fig. 2).

Consider now the CNCU in Fig. 2 modeling an access controlled workflow under conditional uncertainty describing a loan origination process (LOP) for customers whose financial records have already been approved. The LOP starts by processing a request (`ProcR`) with Alice, Bob and Charlie being the only authorized users. After that, the request is logged for future accountability purposes (`LogR`) with the same users of `ProcR` authorized for this task. The flow of execution then splits into two (mutually-exclusive) branches upon the execution of the observation variable $P?$ acting as a "conditional split connector" which sets the truth value of $p$ according to the *discovered* type of loan. A workflow engine (`wf`) is authorized to execute this conditional split connector. If $p$ is true, it means that the workflow will handle a *personal loan* and that the flow of the execution continues by preparing a personal contract (`PersC`), with Alice and Bob the only authorized users. Moreover, when processing personal loans, different security policies hold depending on what truth value a second Boolean variable ($q$) is assigned (see below). The truth value of $q$ is set upon the execution of the observation variable $Q?$ (acting as a second "conditional split connector") whose authorized user is again `wf`. Note that no variable will be prevented from executing depending on the value of $q$, only the users assigned to them will. Instead, if $p$ is false, the workflow will handle a *business loan* and

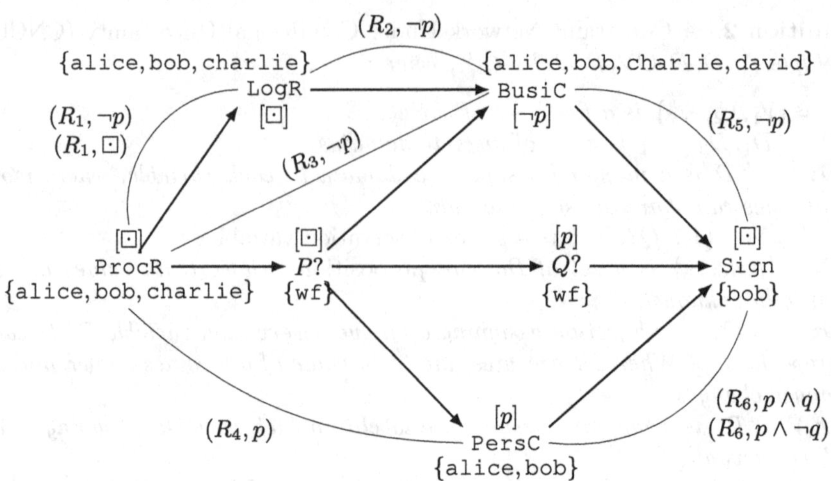


**Fig. 2.** Binary CNCU modeling the loan origination process [15].

the flow of execution continues by preparing a business contract (`BusiC`) with Alice, Bob, Charlie and David authorized users. Regardless of the truth values of $p$ and $q$ the LOP concludes with the signing of the contract (`Sign`) with Bob the only authorized user. Finally, the labeled constraints enforce the following security policies, where we recall that a *separation of duties (SoD)* (resp., *binding of duties (BoD)*) between two tasks says that the users executing such tasks must be different (resp., equal).

- $(R_1, \boxdot)$ calls for a SoD between `ProcR` and `LogR` (always, Table 1a), whereas $(R_1, \neg p)$ requires that the users executing `ProcR` and `LogR` are not relatives whenever $p$ turns out to be false (Table 1b).
- $(R_2, \neg p)$ calls for a SoD between `LogR` and `BusiC` (implicitly when $p$ is false, Table 1c).
- $(R_3, \neg p)$ calls for a SoD between `ProcR` and `BusiC` (implicitly when $p$ is false, Table 1d).
- $(R_4, p)$ calls for a SoD between `ProcR` and `PersC` *and* also requires that the users executing these two tasks must not be relatives (implicitly when $p$ is true, Table 1e).
- $(R_5, \neg p)$ calls for a SoD between `BusiC` and `Sign` (implicitly when $p$ is false, Table 1f).
- $(R_6, p \wedge q)$ calls for a SoD between `PersC` and `Sign` if $p$ and $q$ are both true (Table 1g), whereas $(R_6, p \wedge \neg q)$ calls for a BoD between the same variables if $p$ is true and $q$ is false (Table 1h).

In this example, Alice and Bob are married and thus the only relatives.

We conclude this section by saying when CNCUs are well-defined. We inherit the notions of label honesty and coherence from [3,6].

**Table 1.** Labeled relational constraints of the CNCU in Fig. 2 [15].

**(a)** $(R_1, \boxdot)$

| ProcR | LogR |
|---|---|
| alice | bob |
| alice | charlie |
| bob | alice |
| bob | charlie |
| charlie | alice |
| charlie | bob |

**(b)** $(R_1, \neg p)$

| ProcR | LogR |
|---|---|
| alice | alice |
| alice | charlie |
| bob | bob |
| bob | charlie |
| charlie | alice |
| charlie | bob |
| charlie | charlie |

**(c)** $(R_2, \neg p)$

| LogR | BusiC |
|---|---|
| alice | bob |
| alice | charlie |
| alice | david |
| bob | alice |
| bob | charlie |
| bob | david |
| charlie | alice |
| charlie | bob |
| charlie | david |

**(d)** $(R_3, \neg p)$

| ProcR | BusiC |
|---|---|
| alice | bob |
| alice | charlie |
| alice | david |
| bob | alice |
| bob | charlie |
| bob | david |
| charlie | alice |
| charlie | bob |
| charlie | david |

**(e)** $(R_4, p)$

| ProcR | PersC |
|---|---|
| charlie | alice |
| charlie | bob |

**(f)** $(R_5, \neg p)$

| BusiC | Sign |
|---|---|
| alice | bob |
| charlie | bob |
| david | bob |

**(g)** $(R_6, p \wedge q)$

| PersC | Sign |
|---|---|
| alice | bob |

**(h)** $(R_6, p \wedge \neg q)$

| PersC | Sign |
|---|---|
| bob | bob |

**Definition 3.** *A CNCU* $\langle \mathcal{V}, \mathcal{D}, D, \mathcal{OV}, \mathcal{P}, O, L, \prec, \mathcal{C} \rangle$ *is* well defined *iff all labels are consistent and the following properties hold.*

- Variable Label Honesty. *$L(V)$ is honest for any $V \in \mathcal{V}$, and $O(p) \prec V$ for any $p$ or $\neg p$ belonging to $L(V)$. That is, $V$ only executes when the honest $L(V)$ becomes completely known and evaluates to true; e.g.,* `BusiC` after $P?$ if $\neg p$ *in Fig. 2.*
- Constraint Label Honesty. *$\ell$ is honest for any $(R_S, \ell) \in \mathcal{C}$. That is, $R_S$ only applies when the honest $\ell$ becomes completely known and evaluates to true; e.g., $(R_6, p \wedge q)$ in Fig. 2 if* after $P?$ *and* $Q?$, $p$ *and* $q$ are observed *true.*
- Constraint Label Coherence. *$\ell \Rightarrow L(V)$ for any $(R_S, \ell) \in \mathcal{C}$ and any $V \in S$. That is, the label of a constraint is at least as specific as any label of the variables in its scope; e.g., $(R_6, p \wedge q)$ in Fig. 2.*
- Precedence Relation Coherence. *For any $V_1, V_2 \in \mathcal{V}$, if $V_1 \prec V_2$ then $L(V_1) \wedge L(V_2)$ is consistent. That is, no partial order can be specified between variables not taking part together in any execution; e.g.* `PersC` *and* `BusiC` *in Fig. 2.*

The CNCU in Fig. 2 is well-defined.

## 4 Semantics

In this section, we give the semantics for weak, strong and dynamic controllability of CNCUs. Our goal is to synthesize execution strategies saying which value to assign to which variable (and in which order) so that in the arising projection (see below) the execution satisfies both the partial order and all constraints.

**Definition 4.** *A* scenario $s\colon \mathcal{P} \to \{\bot, \top\}$ *is a complete truth value assignment to the Boolean propositions in* $\mathcal{P}$. *A scenario* $s$ *satisfies a label* $\ell$ *(in symbols,* $s \models \ell$*), if* $\ell$ *is true under the interpretation given by* $s$. $\Sigma$ *models the set of all scenarios.*

Consider Fig. 2 and $s(p) = \top$ and $s(q) = \bot$. We have that $s \models L(\texttt{PersC})$ and $s \not\models L(\texttt{BusiC})$ (as $L(\texttt{BusiC}) = \neg p$ would require $s(p) = \bot$).

**Definition 5.** *Let* $\mathcal{Z} = \langle \mathcal{V}, \mathcal{D}, D, \mathcal{OV}, \mathcal{P}, O, L, \prec, \mathcal{C}\rangle$ *be a CNCU and* $s$ *any scenario. The* projection *of* $\mathcal{Z}$ *onto* $s$ *is a CN* $\mathcal{Z}_s = \langle \mathcal{V}_s, \mathcal{D}, \mathcal{C}_s\rangle$ *such that:*

- $\mathcal{V}_s = \{V \mid V \in \mathcal{V} \land s \models L(V)\}$
- $\mathcal{C}_s = \{R_S \mid (R_S, \ell) \in \mathcal{C} \land s \models \ell\}$

For example, the projection of Fig. 2 with respect to $s(p) = \top$ and $s(q) = \bot$ results in a CN, where $\mathcal{V}_s = \{\texttt{ProcR}, \texttt{LogR}, P?, \texttt{PersC}, \texttt{Sign}\}$ and $\mathcal{C}_s = \{R_1, R_4, R_6\}$, where $R_1$ is the relation of the original $(R_1, \boxdot) \in \mathcal{C}$ (Table 1a), $R_4$ is $(R_4, p)$ (Table 1e), whereas $R_6$ is $(R_6, p \land \neg q)$ and not $(R_6, p \land q)$ or the intersection of the two (Table 1h).

**Definition 6.** *A* schedule *for a subset of variables* $\mathcal{V}' \subseteq \mathcal{V}$ *is a mapping* $\psi\colon \mathcal{V}' \to \bigcup_{V \in \mathcal{V}'} D(V)$ *from variables to values saying which values are assigned to which variables. A schedule is* consistent *if the assignments it makes satisfy all constraints.* $\Psi$ *represents the set of all schedules.*

Consider $\mathcal{V}' = \{\texttt{ProcR}, \texttt{LogR}, P?, \texttt{Sign}\}$ containing the relevant variables when the truth values of $p$ and $q$ are still unknown. A consistent schedule is

$$\psi(\texttt{ProcR}) = \texttt{charlie}, \quad \psi(\texttt{LogR}) = \texttt{alice}, \quad \psi(P?) = \texttt{wf}, \quad \psi(\texttt{Sign}) = \texttt{bob}$$

satisfying the only relevant constraint $(R_1, \boxdot)$ (Table 1a). However, a schedule is nothing but a fixed plan for executing a bunch of variables (not even saying in which order). The interesting part is how we generate it. To do so, we need a *strategy*. Let $\Delta$ be the set of all possible orderings on the variables of a CNCU.

**Definition 7.** *An* execution strategy *is a pair* $\sigma = (\sigma^v, \sigma^o)$ *where* $\sigma^v\colon \Sigma \to \Psi$ *is a* value strategy *mapping scenarios to schedules, whereas* $\sigma^o\colon \Sigma \to \Delta$ *is an* order strategy *mapping scenarios to total orderings on the variables. An execution strategy is* viable *if for any* $s \in \Sigma$, *there exists an ordering* $\sigma^o(s)$ *such that the schedule* $\sigma^v(s)$ *is consistent.*

We write $[\sigma^v(s)]_V$ (instead of $\sigma^v(s)(V)$) to denote the value assigned to $V$ and $[\sigma^o(s)]_V$ (instead of $\sigma^o(s)(V)$) to denote the index of $V$ in the order $\sigma^o(s)$.

The first kind of controllability is *weak controllability* which ensures that each projection is consistent.

**Definition 8.** *A CNCU is* weakly controllable *(WC) if there exists a viable execution strategy.*

Figure 2 is weakly controllable. We prove that at the end of Sect. 5.1. Dealing with weak controllability is quite complex as it always requires one to predict what the truth value assignments to the Boolean propositions will be before starting the execution. This leads us to consider the opposite case in which we want to synthesize a strategy working for all possible scenarios (or in other words, a solution which is not influenced by the uncontrollable part). Thus, the second kind of controllability is *strong controllability.*

**Definition 9.** *A CNCU is* strongly controllable *(SC) if there exists a viable execution strategy $\sigma$ working for all scenarios.*

Figure 2 is not strongly controllable. We discuss why that at the end of Sect. 5.2. Strong controllability is, however, "too strong". If a CNCU is not strongly controllable, it could be still executable by refining the schedule in real time depending on the scenario being generated. To achieve this purpose, we introduce *dynamic controllability.* Since the truth values of propositions are revealed incrementally, we first introduce the formal definition of history that we use to define dynamic controllability.

**Definition 10.** *Given a strategy $\sigma$, a scenario $s$ and a variable $V$, the* scenario history *$\mathcal{H}(V, s, \sigma)$ of $V$ in $s$ with respect to $\sigma$ is the set of truth value assignments observed before $V$ upon the execution of the corresponding observation variables $P?$ in the schedule $\sigma(s)$. Formally,*

$$\mathcal{H}(V, s, \sigma) = \{(p, s(p)) \mid [\sigma^o(s)]_{P?} < [\sigma^o(s)]_V\}$$

*for any $P? \in \mathcal{OV}$.*

Consider the ordering $\texttt{ProcR} \prec \texttt{LogR} \prec P? \prec Q? \prec \texttt{BusiC} \prec \texttt{PersC} \prec \texttt{Sign}$, the scenario $s(p) = s(q) = \top$, a strategy $\sigma$ and the variable $\texttt{Sign}$. Then $\mathcal{H}(\texttt{Sign}, s, \sigma) = \emptyset$ before $P?$ and $Q?$ execute, $\mathcal{H}(\texttt{Sign}, s, \sigma) = \{(p, \top)\}$ after $P?$ and before $Q?$ executes, and $\mathcal{H}(\texttt{Sign}, s, \sigma) = \{(p, \top), (q, \top)\}$ after $P?$ and $Q?$ execute.

**Definition 11.** *An execution strategy $\sigma = (\sigma^v, \sigma^o)$ is* dynamic *if $\sigma^v$ and $\sigma^o$ are dynamic, where:*

- *A value strategy $\sigma^v$ is dynamic if whenever the scenario history looks the same, then the strategy assigns the same values to the same variables. That is, for all $s_1, s_2 \in \Sigma$ and any $V \in \mathcal{V}$, if $\mathcal{H}(V, s_1, \sigma) = \mathcal{H}(V, s_2, \sigma)$, then $[\sigma^v(s_1)]_V = [\sigma^v(s_2)]_V$.*
- *An order strategy $\sigma^o$ is dynamic if whenever the scenario history looks the same, then the strategy orders the variables always in the same way. That is, for all $s_1, s_2 \in \Sigma$ and any $V \in \mathcal{V}$, if $\mathcal{H}(V, s_1, \sigma) = \mathcal{H}(V, s_2, \sigma)$, then $[\sigma^o(s_1)] = [\sigma^o(s_2)]$.*

**Definition 12.** *A CNCU is* dynamically controllable *if there exists a dynamic and viable execution strategy.*

Figure 2 is dynamically controllable. We prove that at the end of Sect. 5.3.

Abusing grammar, we use WC, SC and DC as both nouns and adjectives (the use will be clear from the context). As for temporal networks [2], it is easy to see that SC $\Rightarrow$ DC $\Rightarrow$ WC.

# 5 Controllability Checking Algorithms

In this section, we provide the algorithms to check the three kinds of controllability introduced in Sect. 4. Since we are going to exploit directional consistency (thus relying on total orderings), we first need to address how to get a suitable total order for the variables meeting the restrictions specified by $\prec$. We will always classify as uncontrollable those CNCUs for which no total order exists. Although for weak and strong controllability the problem of getting an order is important up to a certain extent (we only need to make sure that one exists), it is absolutely necessary to get the *most conservative order* when dealing with dynamic controllability since otherwise the algorithm would for sure face incompleteness (see Sect. 5.3).

Given a CNCU, to get a possible total order coherent with $\prec$, we build a directed graph $G$ where the set of nodes is $\mathcal{V}$ and the set of edges is such that there exists a directed edge $V_1 \to V_2$ in $G$ for any $(V_1, V_2) \in \prec$. We refer to this graph as $G = \langle \mathcal{V}, \prec \rangle$. For example, in Fig. 2, $G$ is the graph that remains after removing all labels and constraint edges.

From graph theory, we know that an ordering of the vertexes of a directed acyclic graph (DAG) meeting a given restriction $\prec$ can be found in polynomial time by running the TopologicalSort algorithm on $G$ [21]. At every step, TopologicalSort chooses a vertex $V$ without any predecessor (i.e., one without incoming edges), outputs $V$ and removes $V$ and all directed edges from $V$ to any other vertex (equivalently, removes every $(V, V_2) \in \prec$). Then, TopologicalSort recursively applies to the reduced graph until the set of vertexes becomes empty. If no total order exists, TopologicalSort gets stuck in some iteration because of a cycle $V_1 \to \cdots \to V_1$, which makes it impossible to find a vertex without any predecessor.

## 5.1 Weak Controllability Checking

The idea behind the *weak controllability checking (WC-checking)* is quite simple: *every projection must have a total order and a solution.* Given a CNCU $\mathcal{Z} = \langle \mathcal{V}, \mathcal{D}, D, \mathcal{OV}, \mathcal{P}, O, L, \prec, \mathcal{C} \rangle$, we run the classic ADC on each projection $\mathcal{Z}_s$ according to a complete scenario $s$. Since each $\mathcal{Z}_s$ is a classic CN, any ordering (meeting the relevant part of $\prec$ for $\mathcal{Z}_s$) will be fine. We get one by running TopologicalSort on $G_s = \langle \mathcal{V}_s, \prec_s \rangle$, where $\prec_s = \{(V_1, V_2) \mid (V_1, V_2) \in \prec \wedge V_1, V_2 \in \mathcal{V}_s\}$ (this is the relevant part of $\prec$). After that, we synthesize a strategy $\sigma(s)$ by generating a solution for the projection $\mathcal{Z}_s$ following the ordering $d$ computed initially (Algorithm 2, line 4). Although Definition 8 says that one strategy is enough, our approach is able to handle all possible strategies for each scenario $s$ as during the solution-generation process the value assignments do not depend on any uncontrollable part. WC-checking (Algorithm 2) shows the pseudo-code of the algorithm.

The CNCU in Fig. 2 is WC. To prove that, we give an assignment of values to variables for each scenario.

- If $s(p) = \bot$, $s(q) = \{\bot, \top\}$, then $\psi(\texttt{ProcR}) = \texttt{alice}, \psi(P?) = \texttt{wf}, \psi(\texttt{LogR}) = \texttt{charlie}, \psi(\texttt{BusiC}) = \texttt{david}, \psi(\texttt{Sign}) = \texttt{bob}$ with $\texttt{ProcR} \prec P? \prec \texttt{LogR} \prec \texttt{BusiC} \prec \texttt{Sign}$.
- If $s(p) = \top, s(q) = \top$, then $\psi(\texttt{ProcR}) = \texttt{charlie}, \psi(P?) = \texttt{wf}, \psi(\texttt{PersC}) = \texttt{alice}, \psi(Q?) = \texttt{wf}, \psi(\texttt{Sign}) = \texttt{bob}, \psi(\texttt{LogR}) = \texttt{alice}$ and $\texttt{ProcR} \prec P? \prec \texttt{PersC} \prec Q? \prec \texttt{Sign} \prec \texttt{LogR}$.
- If $s(p) = \top, s(q) = \bot$, then $\psi(\texttt{ProcR}) = \texttt{charlie}, \psi(P?) = \texttt{wf}, \psi(\texttt{PersC}) = \texttt{bob}, \psi(Q?) = \texttt{wf}, \psi(\texttt{Sign}) = \texttt{bob}, \psi(\texttt{LogR}) = \texttt{bob}$ and $\texttt{ProcR} \prec P? \prec \texttt{PersC} \prec Q? \prec \texttt{Sign} \prec \texttt{LogR}$.

**Algorithm 2.** WC-CHECKING ($\mathcal{Z}$). The original version is in [15].

**Input:** A CNCU $\mathcal{Z} = \langle \mathcal{V}, \mathcal{D}, D, \mathcal{OV}, \mathcal{P}, O, L, \prec, \mathcal{C} \rangle$
**Output:** A set of solutions each one having the form $\langle s, d, \mathit{Buckets} \rangle$, where $s$ is a scenario, $d$ an ordering for $\mathcal{V}_s$ and *Buckets* is a set of buckets (one for each variable in $\mathcal{V}_s$) if $\mathcal{Z}_s$ is WC, uncontrollable otherwise.

*Solutions* $\leftarrow \emptyset$
**foreach** $s \in \Sigma$ **do** ▷ for each scenario
    Let $\mathcal{Z}_s$ be the projection of $\mathcal{Z}$ onto $s$
    $d \leftarrow$ TOPOLOGICALSORT($G$) ▷ where $G \leftarrow \langle \mathcal{V}_s, \prec_s \rangle$
    **if** *no order is possible* **then**
        **return** *uncontrollable*
    *Buckets* $\leftarrow$ ADC($\mathcal{Z}_s, d$)
    **if** $\mathcal{Z}_s$ *is inconsistent* **then**
        **return** uncontrollable
    *Solutions* $\leftarrow$ *Solutions* $\cup \{\langle s, d, \mathit{Buckets} \rangle\}$
**return** *Solutions*

Note that in the first scenario, the value of $s(q)$ is not important because $Q?$ is not executed when $s(p) = \bot$. Therefore, the first case holds for both $s(p) = \bot$, $s(q) = \bot$ and $s(p) = \bot$, $s(q) = \top$.

The relevant part of the complexity of WC-CHECKING is $2^{|\mathcal{P}|} \times$ *Complexity*(*ADC*) as the worst case is a CNCU specifying $2^{|\mathcal{P}|}$ complete scenarios (all other sub-algorithms run in polynomial time).

### 5.2 Strong Controllability Checking

The *strong controllability checking (SC-checking)* does not need to unfold all honest scenarios at all. From an algorithmic point of view it is even easier to understand: *a single ordering and a single solution must work for all projections.* To achieve this purpose, we start with a simple operation: *we wipe out all the labels in the CNCU.* Then, we run ADC on this "super-projection" by choosing an order obtained by TOPOLOGICALSORT run on the related $G$ (Algorithm 3). Strong controllability forces solutions (if any) to also satisfy constraints that are inconsistent one another. If the buckets survive to the filling phase (i.e., no empty relation is added), ADC tries to hunt down an empty relation enforcing the adequate level of $k$-consistency. If this resulting network is consistent, it means that there exists (at least) a solution which is so strong that it does not depend on any uncontrollable part (i.e., a solution that just works).

The CNCU in Fig. 2 is *not* SC. Although a total order exists once we have wiped out all the labels ($d = \texttt{ProcR} \prec P? \prec \texttt{PersC} \prec Q? \prec \texttt{LogR} \prec \texttt{BusiC} \prec \texttt{Sign}$), there is no way to find a consistent assignment to Sign that always works for the initial CNCU. It is not difficult to see that the problem lies in the constraints of the original CNCU shown in Table 1. In the first phase, when ADC fills the buckets, each original constraint $(R_S, \ell)$ is deprived of its label $\ell$ (becoming $(R_S, \boxdot)$) and added to the bucket of the latest variable in $S$.

**Algorithm 3.** SC-CHECKING ($\mathcal{Z}$) from [15].

**Input:** A CNCU $\mathcal{Z} = \langle \mathcal{V}, \mathcal{D}, D, \mathcal{OV}, \mathcal{P}, O, L, \prec, \mathcal{C} \rangle$

**Output:** A tuple $\langle d, \mathit{Buckets} \rangle$, where $d$ is a total ordering for $\mathcal{V}$ and *Buckets* is a set of buckets (one for each variable) if $\mathcal{Z}$ is SC, uncontrollable otherwise.

```
Compute a CN Z* ← ⟨V, D, C*⟩ where C* ← {R_S | (R_S, ℓ) ∈ C}
d ← TopologicalSort(G)                         ▷ where G ← ⟨V, ≺⟩
if no order is possible then
    return uncontrollable
return ADC(Z*, d)
```

Consider the original $(R_6, p \wedge q)$ (Table 1g) and $(R_6, p \wedge \neg q)$ (Table 1h). ADC transforms them into (two) *unlabeled* constraints $(R_6, \boxdot)$ and then adds both to *Bucket*($S$). Since the labels of the two relations are the same, *Bucket*(Sign) actually contains the intersection of the two (as both must hold). However, $(\{(\mathtt{a}, \mathtt{b})\}, \boxdot) \cap (\{(\mathtt{b}, \mathtt{b})\}, \boxdot) = (\emptyset, \boxdot)$.

In other words, in Fig. 2 Bob always does the signing. The problem is that the user who prepares the personal contract must be different according to which truth value $q$ will be assigned. If the system calls for a SoD (i.e., $s(q) = \top$), then Alice prepares the contract, else Bob does it. However, the intersection of the users allowed to carry out this task according to $q$ is empty, which means that the user who prepares the contract for a personal loan *cannot* be decided before the execution starts.

The complexity of SC-CHECKING is $|\mathcal{C}| + \mathit{Complexity}(\text{ADC})$. Despite computing a total ordering and wiping out the labels on variables run in polynomial time, we recall that in the worst case $\mathcal{C}$ may specify $K - 1$ relational constraints (where $K$ is the number of all subsets of $\mathcal{V}$) and each relation may in turn appear $(2^{|\mathcal{P}|} + 1)$ times according to all possible different labels.

**Algorithm 4.** CCLOSURE(*Labels*) from [15].

**Input:** A set of labels *Labels*
**Output:** The closure of all possible consistent conjunctions
*Closure* ← *Labels*
**do**
  Pick two labels $\ell_1$ and $\ell_2$ from *Closure*
  **if** $\ell_1 \wedge \ell_2$ *is consistent and* $\ell_1 \wedge \ell_2 \notin$ *Closure* **then**
    *Closure* ← *Closure* $\cup \{\ell_1 \wedge \ell_2\}$
**while** *Any adding is possible*
**return** *Closure*

### 5.3 Dynamic Controllability Checking

The *dynamic controllability checking (DC-checking)* addresses the most appealing type of controllability. If a CNCU is not SC, it could be DC by deciding which value to assign to which variable depending on how the uncontrollable part behaves. This subsection discusses this algorithm. We start with LABELEDADC (Algorithm 5), a main sub-algorithm we make use of, which extends ADC to address the conditional part by refining the adding or tightening of constraints to the buckets and the constraint-propagation.

When we add a constraint $(R_S, \ell)$ to a $Bucket(V)$, we *lighten* $\ell$ by removing all literals $p$ or $\neg p$ in $\ell$ that will still be *unknown* by the time $V$ executes. That is, those whose related observation variables are either $V$ itself or will be assigned after $V$ according to $d$.

When propagating constraints, LABELEDADC enforces the adequate level of $k$-consistency for all combinations of relevant (partial) scenarios arising from the conjunctions of all labels related to the constraints in the buckets. That is, for each $V$, it runs CCLOSURE on the set $Closure = \{\ell \mid (R_S, \ell) \in Bucket(V)\}$. After that, it generates a new constraint $(R_{S_n}, \ell_n)$ for each $\ell_n \in Closure$, where $S_n$ is the union of the scopes of the constraints in $Bucket(V)$ (whose labels are entailed by $\ell_n$) deprived of $V$. $R_{S_n}$ contains all tuples surviving the join of the entailed constraints projected onto $S_n$ (as in the classic ADC). If no empty relation is computed, then the new constraint is added to the bucket of the latest variable in $S_n$ (if any). If $S_n = \emptyset$, then it means that the algorithm computed a (implicit) unary constraint for $V$.

Finally, LABELEDADC returns the set of buckets from which any solution can be built *according to d* (or inconsistent if no solution exists).

However, given an ordering $d$, if LABELEDADC "says no", it could be a matter of wrong ordering. Consider `PersC`, $Q?$ and `Sign` in Fig. 2, and assume that those three variables are ordered as `PersC` $\prec Q? \prec$ `Sign`. Furthermore, consider Fig. 1 and suppose that `PersC` = `alice`. When $Q?$ is executed ($Q?$ = `wf`), the truth value of $q$ becomes known (recall that in this partial scenario $s(p) = \top$). If $s(q) = \top$, then `Sign` = `bob` and (`alice`, `bob`) $\in (R_6, p \wedge q)$ (Table 1g), but if $s(q) = \bot$, then `Sign` = `bob` and (`alice`, `bob`) $\notin (R_6, p \wedge \neg q)$ (Table 1h).

**Algorithm 5.** LabeledADC($\mathcal{Z}, d$) from [15].

**Input:** A CNCU $\mathcal{Z} = \langle \mathcal{V}, \mathcal{D}, D, \mathcal{OV}, \mathcal{P}, O, L, \prec, \mathcal{C} \rangle$ and an ordering $d = V_1 \prec \cdots \prec V_n$
**Output:** A set *Buckets* of buckets (one for each variable) if $\mathcal{Z}$ is consistent *along* $d$, inconsistent otherwise.

**foreach** $(R_S, \ell) \in \mathcal{C}$ **do** ▷ Partition constraints as follows
  Let $V$ be the latest variable in $S$ according to $d$
  Let $\ell_{Rem}$ be the conjunction of all literals $p$ or $\neg p$ in $\ell$ such that either $V = P?$ or $V \prec P?$ in $d$, where $P? = O(p)$ ▷ Remove unknown literals
  Add $(R_S, \ell - \ell_{Rem})$ to $Bucket(V)$
**foreach** $V$ *in* $d$ *taken in reverse order* **do** ▷ Process buckets
  $Closure \leftarrow$ CClosure($\{\ell \mid (R_S, \ell) \in Bucket(V)\}$)
  **for** $\ell_n \in Closure$ **do** ▷ new constraint's label
    $Entailed \leftarrow \{R_S \mid (R_S, \ell) \in Bucket(V) \wedge \ell_n \Rightarrow \ell\}$
    $S_n \leftarrow \bigcup_{R_S \in Entailed} S \setminus \{V\}$ ▷ new constraint's scope
    Compute $R_{tmp} \leftarrow \bowtie_{R_S \in Entailed} R_S$ ▷ enforce $k$-consistency
    **if** $R_{tmp} = \emptyset$ **then**
      **return** inconsistent
    **if** $S_n \neq \emptyset$ **then** ▷ propagate the new constraint
      $R_{S_n} \leftarrow \pi_{S_n}(R_{tmp})$ ▷ Project onto the new scope
      Let $V_n$ be the latest variable in $S_n$ according to $d$
      Compute $\ell_{Rem}$ as before but w.r.t. $\ell_n$
      Add $(R_{S_n}, \ell_n - \ell_{Rem})$ to $Bucket(V_n)$
$Buckets \leftarrow \{\{Bucket(V)\} \mid V \in \mathcal{V}\}$
**return** *Buckets*

**Algorithm 6.** DC-checking ($\mathcal{Z}$). The original version is in [15].

**Input:** A CNCU $\mathcal{Z} = \langle \mathcal{V}, \mathcal{D}, D, \mathcal{OV}, \mathcal{P}, O, L, \prec, \mathcal{C} \rangle$
**Output:** A tuple $\langle d, Buckets \rangle$, where $d$ is an ordering for $\mathcal{V}$ and *Buckets* is a set of buckets (one for each variable) if $\mathcal{Z}$ is DC along $d$, uncontrollable otherwise.

$G \leftarrow \langle \mathcal{V}, \prec \rangle$ ▷ All variables, whole partial order
**foreach** *ordering* $d \in$ AllTopologicalSorts($G$) **do**
  $Buckets \leftarrow$ LabeledADC($\mathcal{Z}, d$)
  **if** $\mathcal{Z}$ *is consistent (along* $d$*)* **then**
    **return** $\langle d, Buckets \rangle$
**return** uncontrollable

More simply, if Alice executes `PersC` and afterwards $s(q) = \bot$, then no valid user remains for `Sign` as our example calls for a binding of duties between the two tasks (Table 1h). If Bob executes `PersC` and afterwards $s(q) = \top$, then the problem is the same (so there is no user who can be assigned conservatively to `PersC` without any information on the truth value of $q$). Fortunately, `PersC` and $Q?$ are *unordered* (no precedence is specified between the two variables). This situation allows us to act in a more clever way: *What if we executed* $Q?$ *before executing* `PersC`? In such a case, we would have full information on $s(q)$ and our *strategy* would be: if $s(q) = \top$, then Alice, else Bob.

Formally, DC-CHECKING (Algorithm 6) works by looking for an ordering $d$ coherent with $\prec$ such that LABELEDADC "says yes" when analyzing $\mathcal{Z}$ along $d$. If no ordering works, then the network is uncontrollable. DC-CHECKING iterates on all possible orderings by using internally the ALLTOPOLOGICALSORTS algorithm [21]. Every time a total order is found, DC-CHECKING runs LABELEDADC on the CNCU with respect to that order. If the CNCU is consistent, then DC-CHECKING stops and returns the order and the sets of buckets.

For example, the CNCU in Fig. 2 is DC along the ordering $d_1 =$ `ProcR` $\prec$ `LogR` $\prec P? \prec Q? \prec$ `BusiC` $\prec$ `PersC` $\prec$ `Sign` and uncontrollable along $d_2 =$ `ProcR` $\prec$ `LogR` $\prec P? \prec$ `BusiC` $\prec$ `PersC` $\prec Q? \prec$ `Sign` (as `PersC` is assigned before $Q?$).

We execute a CNCU proved to be DC as follows. Let $\ell_s$ be the label corresponding to the current scenario. Initially $\ell_s = \boxdot$. For each variable $V$ along the ordering $d$, if $V$ is relevant for $\ell_s$ (i.e., if $s \models L(V)$), then we look for a value $v$ in the domain of $V$ satisfying all relevant constraints in $Bucket(V)$. If $V$ is irrelevant (as $\ell_s$ falsifies $L(V)$), then we ignore $V$ and go ahead with the next variable (if any). Moreover, if $V$ is an observation variable, where $p$ is the associated proposition, then $\ell_s$ extends to $\ell_s \wedge p$ iff $p$ is assigned true (i.e., $s(p) = \top$), and to $\ell_s \wedge \neg p$ otherwise. In this way, a partial scenario extends to a complete one, one observation variable at a time.

A strategy to execute the CNCU in Fig. 2 is the following: Charlie executes `ProcR`, Alice `LogR` and the workflow engine executes the first conditional split connector (always). If $s(p) = \bot$, then David executes `BusiC`. If $s(p) = \top$, then the workflow engine executes the second split connector to have full information on $q$. If $s(q) = \top$, then Alice executes `PersC`, else Bob. Bob executes `Sign` (always).

The complexity of DC-CHECKING is $\mathcal{V}! \times Complexity($LABELEDADC$)$ as in the worst case there are $\mathcal{V}!$ orderings. We leave the investigation of the complexity of LABELEDADC as future work.

## 6 Correctness of the Algorithms

We discuss some correctness results of the algorithms we proposed in Sect. 5. We start by defining what *soundness* and *completeness* for a controllability checking algorithm are.

**Definition 13.** *A controllability algorithm is* sound *if, whenever it classifies a CNCUs as uncontrollable, the CNCU is really uncontrollable, and it is* complete *if, whenever a CNCU is uncontrollable, the algorithm classifies it as so. A controllability algorithm is correct if it is sound and complete.*

We sketch the proofs of the soundness and completeness of our algorithms. Given a CNCU $\mathcal{Z}$ and any scenario $s \in \Sigma$, WC-CHECKING runs TOPOLOGICALSORT and subsequently ADC on $\mathcal{Z}_s$. If no total order exists for $\mathcal{Z}_s$ or $\mathcal{Z}_s$ is inconsistent, then the original CNCU is uncontrollable as there is no way to satisfy the constraints if $s$ happens (regardless of whether we know it before starting the execution). Thus, WC-CHECKING is sound. WC-CHECKING is also complete because it does so for all possible scenarios guaranteeing that if some projection is inconsistent or no total order exists for that projection, WC-CHECKING will find out. Thus, WC-CHECKING is correct.

SC-CHECKING first wipes out the conditional part of the original CNCU obtaining a super-projection whose set of constraints corresponds to the intersection of all sets of constraints (even inconsistent with each other) related to all possible projections. Afterwards, SC-CHECKING runs TOPOLOGICALSORT and then ADC on the resulting super-projection. Hence, SC-CHECKING is sound and complete as it computes a total order in a correct way (provided one exists) with TOPOLOGICALSORT which is known to be correct [21, 22] and tests the resulting projection along that order with ADC which is known to be sound and complete [10]. Since all variables and constraints are kept, we are sure that a solution (if any) will satisfy the "for all scenarios"-part as requested by Definition 9.

Note that WC-CHECKING and SC-CHECKING carry out the analysis on (possibly many) *unconditional* CNs. We point out that the chosen ordering according to $\prec$ given in input to ADC never breaches soundness and completeness of ADC but might only affect its complexity (see the discussion on induced width in [10]).

LABELEDADC extends ADC to accommodate the propagation of labeled constraints. When it adds a constraint to the bucket of a variable $V$ it lightens the label of the constraint by removing all literals whose truth value will be still unknown by the time $V$ executes. This is because the observation variables associated to the propositions embedded in those literals will be executed *after* $V$ or coincide with $V$ itself. For this reason, we must be conservative and consider the constraint as if it just held, since we are unable to predict "what is going to be". LABELEDADC propagates the constraints enforcing the adequate level of $k$-consistency for all possible combinations of honest (partial) scenarios arising from the labels of the constraints in a bucket. If LABELEDADC detects an inconsistency, it means that there exists a (partial) scenario for which the value assignments to the variables of the CNCU (along with the ordering in input) will violate some constraint. We believe that DC-CHECKING is correct as it runs LABELEDADC on all possible orderings. If LABELEDADC detects inconsistency for all orders (or no total ordering exists), then the CNCU is uncontrollable (soundness), whereas if LABELEDADC finds an order for which LABELEDADC "says yes", then the CNCU is dynamically controllable with respect to that order (completeness). We leave a formal proof as future work.

## 7 ZETA: A Tool for CNCUs

We developed ZETA, a tool for CNCUs that takes in input a specification of a CNCU and acts both as a solver for weak, strong and dynamic controllability as well as an execution simulator. Listing 1.1 shows ZETA's help screen.

**Listing 1.1.** ZETA's help screen.

```
Usage: java -jar zeta.jar <network.cncu> ACTION <network.ob> [N] [--silent]

ACTION:
  --WCchecking performs weak controllability checking.
  --SCchecking performs strong controllability checking.
  --DCchecking performs dynamic controllability checking.
  --execute    performs [N] executions of a (weakly/strongly/dynamically)
               controllable network. If N is not specified , then the
               default value is 1.
  --silent     [--silent] suppresses the output (optional). If --silent is
               specified , then check the return value when doing --WC,
               --SC and --DCchecking. 0 means controllable, 1 means
               uncontrollable.

Examples:
---------
  java -jar zeta.jar Network.cncu --WCchecking Network.ob
  java -jar zeta.jar Network.cncu --SCchecking Network.ob
  java -jar zeta.jar Network.cncu --DCchecking Network.ob
  java -jar zeta.jar Network.cncu --execute Network.ob 1000
```

The input language of ZETA comprises five main sections. Listing 1.2 shows the specification of the CNCU in Fig. 2 written in ZETA's input language. There, the section `Domain` specifies the set $\mathcal{D}$, the section `Variables` specifies the sets $\mathcal{V}$ and $\mathcal{OV}$ as well as the mappings $O$, $D$ and $L$, the section `Precedence` specifies the precedence relation $\prec$, and the section `Constraints` specifies the set $\mathcal{C}$.

**Listing 1.2.** Specification of Figure 2 in ZETA's input language.

```
Domains {
  (D1 : alice bob charlie)
  (D2 : alice bob charlie david)
  (D3 : alice bob)
  (D4 : wf)
  (D5 : bob)
}

Propositions {
  p q
}

Variables {
  (ProcR : : D1 : )
  (LogR : : D1 : )
  (P : p : D4 : )
  (Q : q : D4 : p)
  (BusiC : : D2 : !p)
  (PersC : : D3 : p)
  (Sign : : D5 : )
```

```
}

Precedence {
  (ProcR < LogR)
  (ProcR < P)
  (P < Q)
  (P < BusiC)
  (P < PersC)
  (LogR < BusiC)
  (PersC < Sign)
  (BusiC < Sign)
  (Q < Sign)
}

Constraints {
  # (R1, )
  (ProcR LogR : (alice bob) (alice charlie) (bob alice) (bob charlie)
                (charlie alice) (charlie bob) : )
  # (R1, !p)
  (ProcR LogR : (alice alice) (alice charlie) (bob bob) (bob charlie)
                (charlie alice) (charlie bob) (charlie charlie) : !p)
  # (R2, !p)
  (LogR BusiC : (alice bob) (alice charlie) (alice david) (bob alice)
                (bob charlie) (bob david) (charlie alice) (charlie bob)
                (charlie david) : !p)
  # (R3, !p)
  (ProcR BusiC : (alice bob) (alice charlie) (alice david) (bob alice)
                (bob charlie) (bob david) (charlie alice) (charlie bob)
                (charlie david) : !p)
  # (R4, p)
  (ProcR PersC : (charlie alice) (charlie bob) : p)

  # (R5, !p)
  (BusiC Sign : (alice bob) (charlie bob) (david bob) : !p)

  # (R6, p q)
  (PersC Sign : (alice bob) : p q)

  # (R6, p !q)
  (PersC Sign : (bob bob) : p !q)
}
```

Given a CNCU specification file `network.cncu`, we check weak, strong and dynamic controllability by running

```
$ java -jar zeta.jar network.cncu --WCchecking network.ob
$ java -jar zeta.jar network.cncu --SCchecking network.ob
$ java -jar zeta.jar network.cncu --DCchecking network.ob
```

If the CNCU is proved controllable, ZETA saves to file the *order and buckets* needed to later generate any solution. For weak controllability, ZETA does so for any scenario and keeps the minimum set of scenarios. That is, considering Fig. 2, if $s(p) = \top$, then $s(q)$ is irrelevant, therefore ZETA keeps $s(p) = \top$ only. We execute a (controllable) CNCU by running

```
$ java -jar zeta.jar network.cncu --execute network.ob [N]
```

where `[N]` (default 1) is the number of simulations we want to carry out. For weak controllability, ZETA executes the CNCU with respect to each scenario, whereas for strong and dynamic controllability, it executes the CNCU generating a random scenario (that is why ZETA allows for multiple simulations).

We ran ZETA on the CNCU in Fig. 2. We used a FreeBSD virtual machine run on top of a VMWare ESXi Hypervisor using a physical machine equipped with an Intel i7 2.80 GHz and 20 GB of RAM. The VM was assigned 16 GB of RAM and full CPU power. ZETA proved in about 234 ms that the CNCU in Fig. 2 is weakly controllable (saving an ob-file of 12 Kb), is not strongly controllable (in about 200 ms) but is dynamically controllable in about 274 ms (saving an ob-file of 8 Kb). For weak and dynamic controllability, the CNCU was correctly executed. This example is available at http://regis.di.univr.it/LOP_LNAI2018.tar.bz2. Listing 1.3 shows the output of ZETA.

**Listing 1.3.** WC, SC and DC-checking of Figure 2 with ZETA.

```
$ java -jar zeta.jar Example.cncu --WCchecking Example.weak.ob
Weakly Controllable
$ java -jar zeta.jar Example.cncu --SCchecking Example.strong.ob
Uncontrollable
$ java -jar zeta.jar Example.cncu --DCchecking Example.dynamic.ob
Dynamically Controllable
```

Listing 1.4 shows one execution simulation for weak controllability. In the execution, ZETA provides a solution (i.e., a consistent schedule plus a total order) for each scenario. ZETA just picks up a random user for each variable among those valid for the specific projection.

**Listing 1.4.** Execution simulations for Figure 2 (weak controllability).

```
$ java -jar zeta.jar Example.cncu --execute Example.weak.ob
======================================
Scenario: !p
Order: ProcR -> P -> LogR -> BusiC -> Sign
--------------------------------------
ProcR = alice
P = wf
LogR = charlie
BusiC = david
Sign = bob
--------------------------------------
Verifying ... SAT!
```

```
==========================================
==========================================
Scenario: p q
Order: ProcR -> P -> PersC -> Q -> Sign -> LogR
------------------------------------------
ProcR = charlie
P = wf
PersC = alice
Q = wf
Sign = bob
LogR = alice
------------------------------------------
Verifying ... SAT!
==========================================
==========================================
Scenario: p !q
Order: ProcR -> P -> PersC -> Q -> Sign -> LogR
------------------------------------------
ProcR = charlie
P = wf
PersC = bob
Q = wf
Sign = bob
LogR = bob
------------------------------------------
Verifying ... SAT!
==========================================
```

Listing 1.5 shows three (random) execution simulations for dynamic controllability. In the execution, ZETA always provides a solution no matter which scenario will arise (we isolated the executions generating all scenarios).

**Listing 1.5.** Execution simulations for Figure 2 (dynamic controllability).

```
$ java -jar zeta.jar Example.cncu --execute Example.dynamic.ob 3
==========================================
Order: ProcR -> LogR -> P -> Q -> BusiC -> PersC -> Sign
------------------------------------------
ProcR = charlie
LogR = alice
P = wf, p = true
Q = wf, q = false
PersC = bob
Sign = bob
------------------------------------------
Verifying ... SAT!
==========================================
==========================================
Order: ProcR -> LogR -> P -> Q -> BusiC -> PersC -> Sign
------------------------------------------
ProcR = charlie
```

```
LogR = alice
P = wf, p = true
Q = wf, q = true
PersC = alice
Sign = bob
--------------------------------------
Verifying ... SAT!
======================================
======================================
Order: ProcR -> LogR -> P -> Q -> BusiC -> PersC -> Sign
--------------------------------------
ProcR = charlie
LogR = alice
P = wf, p = false
BusiC = david
Sign = bob
--------------------------------------
Verifying ... SAT!
======================================
```

Having ZETA allowed us to also carry out an automated experimental evaluation to compare the performances of WC-CHECKING, SC-CHECKING and DC-CHECKING. We summarize our findings in the following.

We generated 3000 CNCUs partitioned in 3 sets of benchmarks: `weak/`, `strong/` and `dynamic/`. Each set contains a directory `6vars/` specifying CNCUs with 6 variables and 5 sub-directories `2obs/`, `3obs/`, `4obs/`, `5obs/` and `6obs/` partitioning them by the number of observation variables, where each `Xobs` contains 2 further directories `controllable/` and `uncontrollable/`, each one containing 100 CNCUs. We generated the networks such that: (i) all weakly controllable CNCUs are neither strongly nor dynamically controllable and (ii) all dynamically controllable CNCUs are not strongly controllable. For example, `weak/6vars/3obs/controllable` contains weakly controllable CNCUs (only) with 6 variables, 3 of which are observation variables, `strong/6vars/4obs/uncontrollable` contains strongly uncontrollable CNCUs with 6 variables, 4 of which are observation variables, whereas `dynamic/6vars/6obs/controllable` contains dynamically (and not strongly) controllable CNCUs with 6 (observation) variables.

In this way, for each kind of controllability we have the same number of controllable and uncontrollable CNCUs specifying the same number of variables and variating the number of observation ones. These sets of benchmarks (along with the analysis that we are about to discuss) are available at http://regis.di.univr.it/EE_CNCU_LNAI2018.tar.bz2.

Regardless of the set, each CNCU has exactly 6 six variables, where each variable has the same 6 values in its domain. Each CNCU specifies a maximum number of relational constraints of 40% of $|\mathcal{V}| \times |\mathcal{OV}|$, where each (binary) relation $(R_{ij}, \ell)$ has a maximum number of tuples of 50% of $|D(V_i)| \times |D(V_j)|$ and the label $\ell$ is generated randomly. Furthermore, all variables are *unlabeled* and no partial order is specified. This contributes to generating "hard" instances for DC-CHECKING as it forces it to run on potentially all orders.

We proceed by discussing the graphical data of the experimental evaluation in Fig. 3 (time) and Fig. 4 (space), where x-axes always represent the number of observation variables (i.e., the set of benchmarks under analysis) and y-axes represent either the average time elapsed or the space consumed when saving the "order and buckets" of a controllable CNCU in the specific set.

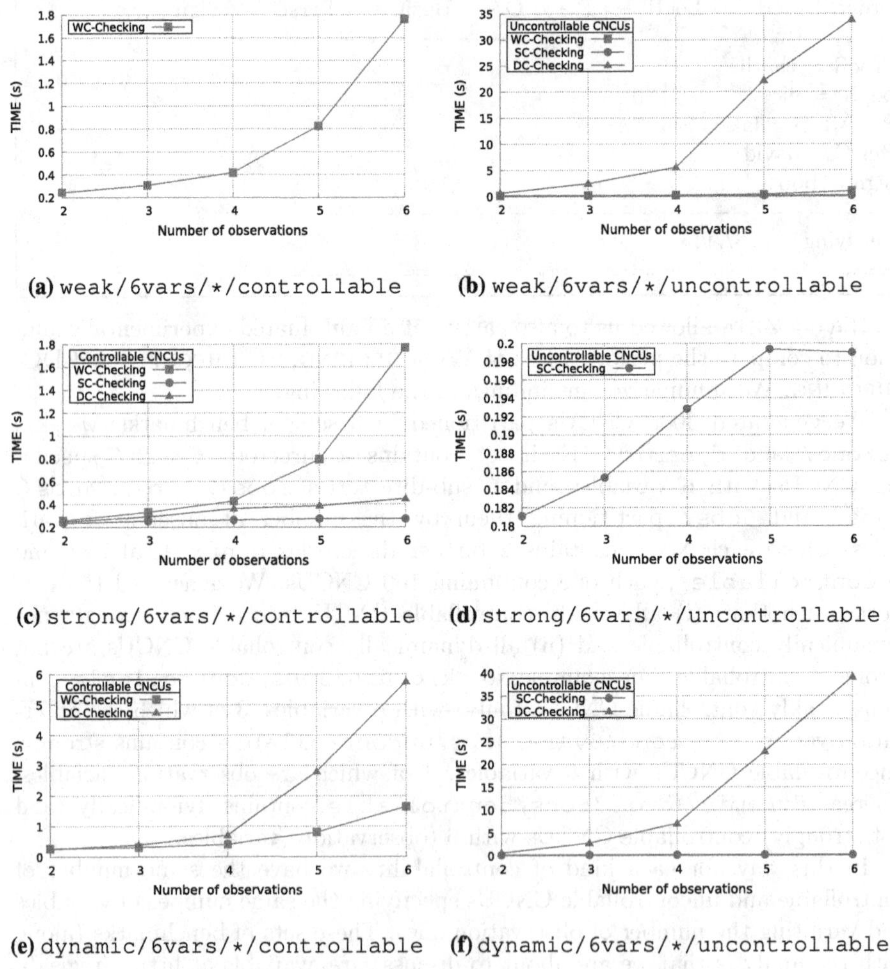


**(a)** weak/6vars/*/controllable **(b)** weak/6vars/*/uncontrollable

**(c)** strong/6vars/*/controllable **(d)** strong/6vars/*/uncontrollable

**(e)** dynamic/6vars/*/controllable **(f)** dynamic/6vars/*/uncontrollable

**Fig. 3.** Experimental evaluation with ZETA (time).

Figure 3a shows the time performance of WC-CHECKING on weakly controllable CNCUs only. The results confirm that augmenting observation variables worsens the time performance of the analysis. No other comparison is possible here since this set of benchmarks contains neither strongly nor dynamically controllable CNCUs.

Figure 3b shows the time performance of WC-CHECKING, SC-CHECKING and DC-CHECKING on weakly uncontrollable CNCUs. We recall that a weakly uncontrollable CNCU cannot be strongly controllable nor dynamically controllable. Therefore, when CNCUs are uncontrollable for all three kinds of controllability, SC-CHECKING is faster than WC-CHECKING which, in turn, is faster than DC-CHECKING to prove uncontrollability of the CNCUs.

Figure 3c shows the time performance of WC-CHECKING, SC-CHECKING and DC-CHECKING on strongly controllable CNCUs. We recall that a strongly controllable CNCU is also weakly and dynamically controllable. Therefore, when CNCUs are controllable for all three kinds of controllability, SC-CHECKING is faster than DC-CHECKING which, in turn, is faster than WC-CHECKING to validate the CNCUs (note that in this case any order is fine for DC-CHECKING).

Figure 3d shows the time performance of SC-CHECKING on strongly uncontrollable CNCUs. Note that a strongly uncontrollable CNCU could be weakly and/or dynamically controllable (that's why we excluded WC-CHECKING and DC-CHECKING from this comparison). The graph shows little difference on the average times, which is because of the conditional part that is wiped out.

Figure 3e shows the time performance of WC-CHECKING and DC-CHECKING on dynamically controllable CNCUs. We recall that a dynamically controllable CNCU is also weakly but in general can be *not* strongly controllable (in the sets we generated these networks so that they were not SC). Therefore, when CNCUs are dynamically but not strongly controllable, WC-CHECKING is faster than DC-CHECKING to validate them. This is because WC does not need to brute-force all the orders.

Figure 3f shows the time performance of SC-CHECKING and DC-CHECKING on dynamically uncontrollable CNCUs. We recall that a dynamically uncontrollable CNCU is also strongly uncontrollable (but could be weakly controllable, which is why WC-CHECKING was excluded from this comparison). Therefore when CNCUs are dynamically uncontrollable, SC-CHECKING is faster than DC-CHECKING to prove uncontrollability. This depends on the fact that the conditional part is wiped out but also that SC-CHECKING does not brute-force all the orders.

Figure 4a shows the space consumption of WC-CHECKING for weakly controllable CNCUs, confirming that augmenting the number of observations will augment the size of the saved strategy. We recall that all variables in any CNCU are unlabeled, therefore $K$ observation variables imply $2^K$ saved solutions.

Figure 4b shows the space consumption of WC-CHECKING, SC-CHECKING and DC-CHECKING for strongly controllable CNCUs (which are also weakly and dynamically controllable). SC-CHECKING saves strategies that are smaller than those saved by DC-CHECKING, which, in turn, are smaller than those saved by WC-CHECKING. This graph reveals that in a strategy, unfolding all scenarios (WC-CHECKING) is worse than keeping them compact (DC-CHECKING). This is also confirmed by Fig. 4c, which shows the difference in space consump-

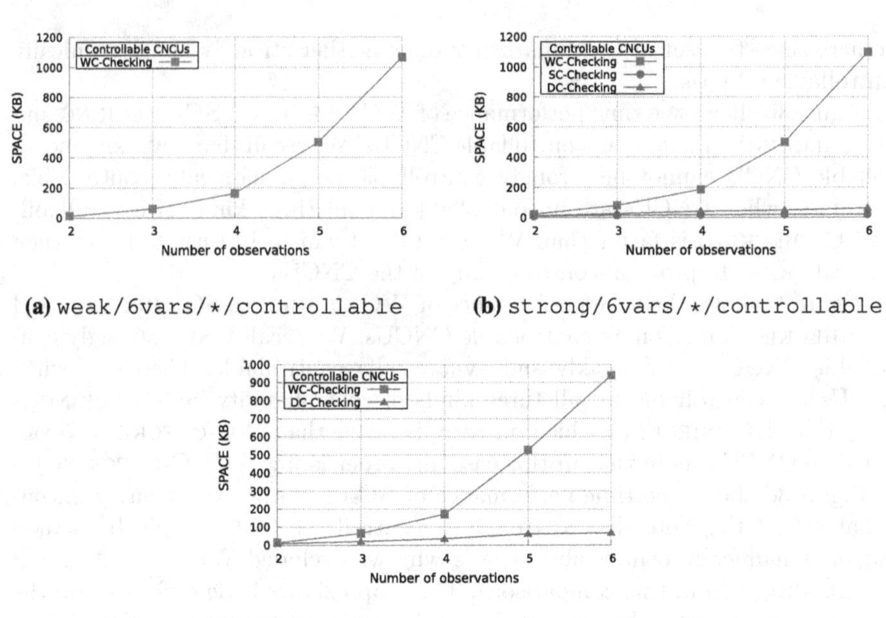


**(a)** `weak/6vars/*/controllable` **(b)** `strong/6vars/*/controllable`

**(c)** `dynamic/6vars/*/controllable`

**Fig. 4.** Experimental evaluation with ZETA (space).

tion between WC-CHECKING and DC-CHECKING for dynamically controllable CNCUs (which are also weakly but not strongly controllable).

Finally, we executed all controllable CNCUs 1000 times. No one crashed.

## 8 Related Work

We begin the discussion of related work by considering constraint network formalisms. A CN [10] specifies a finite set of variables, a set of finite discrete domains (one for each variable) and a set of relational constraints, and is a possible formalism to model the CSP (i.e., finding an assignment of values to variables satisfying all constraints). Solving the CSP is NP-hard [10]. Moreover, given a minimal network (i.e., a network where the inference of new constraints from the existing ones is no longer possible), generating an arbitrary solution is NP-hard as well [17]. Node, arc and path consistency are pruning algorithms that are know to be incomplete when looking for a minimal network [10]. *Directional consistency* has been introduced to generate any solution limiting backtracking [20]. Classic CNs in [10] do not address any uncontrollable parts. The work in this paper proposes CNCUs to address conditional uncertainty and strongly relies on directional consistency to deal with weak, strong and dynamic controllability, which supersede classic satisfiability.

A Mixed CSP partitions the set of variables in controllable and uncontrollable ones, and considers both full observability (FO) and no observability (NO). Full observability is when we get to known the uncontrollable part *before* making our decisions. In [11], Fargier et al. provide a consistency algorithm assuming full observability of the uncontrollable part. CNCUs do not have this restriction. Indeed, CNCUs deal with another kind of uncertainty and handle FO, NO and also partial observability (PO) via dynamic controllability.

Dynamic constraint satisfaction problems (DCSPs, [12]) introduce activity constraints saying when variables are relevant or not depending on the values assigned to some other variables. No uncontrollable parts are specified, therefore the approach in [12] deals with satisfiability only. CNCUs deal with controllability. Some probabilistic approaches (e.g., [13]) attempted to find the most probable working solution to a CSP under probabilistic uncertainty. Although probabilistic uncertainty is of interest, CNCUs address exact algorithms. As a result, CNCUs proved controllable will never break the execution if the corresponding control strategy is followed. In a Prioritized Fuzzy Constraint Satisfaction Problem (PFCSP) (e.g., [23]) a solution threshold states the overall satisfaction degree. CNCUs do not deal with satisfaction degrees.

We now turn to the subclass of CNs called temporal networks, where STNs [1], CSTNs [3], STNUs [2], CSTNUs [5] and CSTNUDs [6] only model temporal plans without any resource. However, some extensions of temporal network deal with resources. For example, in [24], STNUs are extended with security constraints in order to model temporal role-based access controlled workflows in which authorization constraints and temporal constraints mutually influence one another. Controllability checking has not been addressed for such an extension. *Access-Controlled Temporal Networks* (*ACTNs*, [25]) extend CSTNUs to represent a dynamic user assignment that also depends on temporal aspects, so ACTNs can address workflows under conditional and temporal uncertainty simultaneously. Weak and strong controllability are not addressed. Dynamic controllability is reduced to controller synthesis for a timed game automaton encoding the ACTN and synthesizes a memoryless execution strategy containing 1 action only for each uncontrollable behavior. CNCUs do not address temporal constraints for the good reason that directional consistency (CNs) allows for convergence when generating a solution only if a total ordering is followed. Most temporal networks do not have this restriction. ACTNs solve this problem by synthesizing memoryless execution strategies *before* starting. However, CNCUs allow one to handle all possible users assignments (with respect to the order of the variables) during execution.

Further related work has been carried out in the research communities focusing on security and on workflows (nowadays better known as business process), where the problem of verifying workflow features related to the assignment of agents to tasks is known as workflow satisfiability and resiliency [26]. More specifically, the *workflow satisfiability problem (WSP)* is the problem of finding an assignment of users to tasks (i.e., a plan) such that the execution of the workflow gets to the end satisfying all authorization constraints. The *workflow resiliency problem* is WSP under the uncertainty that a maximum number of users may become (temporally) absent before or during execution. If we think about a workflow context, then this paper dealt with a *dynamic* WSP by modeling an access controlled workflow with a CNCU for both checking controllability and executing such a workflow.

In [27], Cabanillas et al. deal with resource allocation for business processes. They consider a role-based environment and they do not impose any particular order on activities. They also address workflow loops (repeating subparts of the workflow) but their approach does not address *history-based allocation* of resources. Dynamic controllability of CNCUs is a history-based controllability.

In [14], Zavatteri et al., define weak, strong and dynamic controllability of access controlled workflows under conditional uncertainty. That work deals with structured workflows by unfolding and encoding workflow paths into CNs, and reasoning on the intersection of common parts. Furthermore, it considers binary constraints only (whose labels are the conjunction of the labels of the connected tasks) and assumes that a total order for the tasks is given in input. This paper overcomes all these limitations and paves the way for a formal encoding of access controlled workflows into CNCUs.

## 9 Concluding Remarks

CNCUs are a formalism to address conditional uncertainty in constraint networks. CNCUs implicitly embed classic CNs (if $\mathcal{OV} = \emptyset$ and $\prec = \emptyset$). We simplified the definition of weak, strong and dynamic controllability of CNCUs (as well as the provided algorithms to check each kind of controllability) in order to make them more understandable. The algorithms we provided rely on total orderings on the variables. CNCUs not admitting any are uncontrollable for all three kinds of controllability. We discussed the correctness and complexity of our algorithms and provided ZETA, a tool for CNCUs that acts as a solver for weak, strong and dynamic controllability as well as an execution simulator. In particular, we discussed the input language of ZETA and used the tool to validate the case study. We generated a set of benchmarks with which we carried out a more targeted experimental evaluation comparing time performance and space consumption of weak, strong and dynamic controllability. We made our tool, sets of benchmarks and results of the experiments available online. Our preliminary results suggest that strong controllability is the easiest type of controllability to check, followed by weak controllability and finally by dynamic controllability, which is currently the hardest one. Dynamic controllability is a matter of order, whereas weak and strong controllability are not. Strong and dynamic controllability provide usable strategies for executing workflows under conditional uncertainty. Weak controllability calls for predicting the future. However, weak controllability is important because a CNCU that is not weakly controllable will never be strongly controllable nor dynamically controllable.

As future work, we plan to work on the *all topological sort* phase of DC-CHECKING in order to contain the explosion of this step. We also plan to investigate if CNCUs classified as non-DC with respect to all possible total orderings might turn DC for some ordering that refines dynamically during execution, and determine the complexity of (deciding) dynamic controllability of a CNCU.

## References

1. Dechter, R., Meiri, I., Pearl, J.: Temporal constraint networks. Artif. Intell. **49**, 61–95 (1991)
2. Morris, P.H., Muscettola, N., Vidal, T.: Dynamic control of plans with temporal uncertainty. In: IJCAI 2001 (2001)
3. Hunsberger, L., Posenato, R., Combi, C.: A sound-and-complete propagation-based algorithm for checking the dynamic consistency of conditional simple temporal networks. In: TIME 2015 (2015)
4. Tsamardinos, I., Vidal, T., Pollack, M.E.: CTP: a new constraint-based formalism for conditional, temporal planning. Constraints **8**, 365–388 (2003)
5. Hunsberger, L., Posenato, R., Combi, C.: The dynamic controllability of conditional STNs with uncertainty. In: PlanEx 2012 (2012)
6. Zavatteri, M.: Conditional simple temporal networks with uncertainty and decisions. In: TIME 2017. LIPIcs (2017)
7. Cimatti, A., Hunsberger, L., Micheli, A., Posenato, R., Roveri, M.: Dynamic controllability via timed game automata. Acta Inf. **53**, 681–722 (2016)
8. Cimatti, A., Micheli, A., Roveri, M.: An SMT-based approach to weak controllability for disjunctive temporal problems with uncertainty. Artif. Intell. **224**, 1–27 (2015)
9. Cimatti, A., Micheli, A., Roveri, M.: Solving strong controllability of temporal problems with uncertainty using SMT. Constraints **20**, 1–29 (2015)
10. Dechter, R.: Constraint Processing. Elsevier, Amsterdam (2003)
11. Fargier, H., Lang, J., Schiex, T.: Mixed constraint satisfaction: a framework for decision problems under incomplete knowledge. In: IAAI 1996 (1996)
12. Mittal, S., Falkenhainer, B.: Dynamic constraint satisfaction problems. In: AAAI 1990 (1990)
13. Fargier, H., Lang, J.: Uncertainty in constraint satisfaction problems: a probabilistic approach. In: Clarke, M., Kruse, R., Moral, S. (eds.) ECSQARU 1993. LNCS, vol. 747, pp. 97–104. Springer, Heidelberg (1993). https://doi.org/10.1007/BFb0028188
14. Zavatteri, M., Combi, C., Posenato, R., Viganò, L.: Weak, strong and dynamic controllability of access-controlled workflows under conditional uncertainty. In: Carmona, J., Engels, G., Kumar, A. (eds.) BPM 2017. LNCS, vol. 10445, pp. 235–251. Springer, Cham (2017). https://doi.org/10.1007/978-3-319-65000-5_14
15. Zavatteri, M., Viganò, L.: Constraint networks under conditional uncertainty. In: 10th International Conference on Agents and Artificial Intelligence (ICAART 2018), vol. 2, pp. 41–52. INSTICC, SciTePress (2018)
16. Montanari, U.: Networks of constraints: fundamental properties and applications to picture processing. Inf. Sci. **7**, 95–132 (1974)
17. Gottlob, G.: On minimal constraint networks. Artif. Intell. **191–192**, 42–60 (2012)
18. Mackworth, A.K.: Consistency in networks of relations. Artif. Intell. **8**, 99–118 (1977)
19. Freuder, E.C.: A sufficient condition for backtrack-free search. J. ACM **29**, 24–32 (1982)
20. Dechter, R., Pearl, J.: Network-based heuristics for constraint-satisfaction problems. Artif. Int. **34**, 1–38 (1987)
21. Knuth, D.E.: The Art of Computer Programming, Volume I: Fundamental Algorithms. Addison-Wesley, Boston (1968)

22. Cormen, T.H., Leiserson, C.E., Rivest, R.L., Stein, C.: Introduction to Algorithms, 3rd edn. The MIT Press, Cambridge (2009)
23. Luo, X., Lee, J.H.M., Leung, H.F., Jennings, N.R.: Prioritised fuzzy constraint satisfaction problems: axioms, instantiation and validation. Fuzzy Sets Syst. **136**, 155–188 (2003)
24. Combi, C., Viganò, L., Zavatteri, M.: Security constraints in temporal role-based access-controlled workflows. In: Proceedings of the Sixth ACM Conference on Data and Application Security and Privacy, CODASPY 2016. ACM (2016)
25. Combi, C., Posenato, R., Viganò, L., Zavatteri, M.: Access controlled temporal networks. In: ICAART 2017. INSTICC, ScitePress (2017)
26. Wang, Q., Li, N.: Satisfiability and resiliency in workflow authorization systems. ACM Trans. Inf. Syst. Secur. **13**, 40:1–40:35 (2010). https://dl.acm.org/citation.cfm?id=1880034
27. Cabanillas, C., Resinas, M., del-Río-Ortega, A., Cortés, A.R.: Specification and automated design-time analysis of the business process human resource perspective. Inf. Syst. **52**, 55–82 (2015)

# Safe Deep Reinforcement Learning Hybrid Electric Vehicle Energy Management

Roman Liessner[(✉)], Ansgar Malte Dietermann, and Bernard Bäker

Dresden Institute of Automobile Engineering, Technische Universität Dresden, George-Bähr-Straße 1c, 01069 Dresden, Germany
roman.liessner@mailbox.tu-dresden.de

**Abstract.** The optimality-based design of the energy management of a hybrid electric vehicle is a challenging task due to the extensive and complex nonlinear reciprocal effects in the system, as well as the unknown vehicle use in real traffic. The optimization has to consider multiple continuous values of sensor and control variables and has to handle uncertain knowledge. The resulting decision making agent directly influences the objectives like fuel consumption. This contribution presents a concept which solves the energy management using a *Deep Reinforcement Learning* algorithm which simultaneously permits inadmissible actions during the learning process. Additionally, this approach can include further state variables like the battery temperature, which is not considered in classic energy management approaches. The contribution focuses on the used environment and the interaction with the *Deep Reinforcement Learning* algorithm.

**Keywords:** Energy management · Deep learning
Safe reinforcement learning · Hybrid electric vehicle

## 1 Introduction

Hybrid electric vehicles have gained increased attention due to their ability to positively contribute to fuel reduction comparing to conventional combustion vehicles. However, the development and operation of hybrid power trains poses additional challenges regarding the coordination of multiple drive units and energy storages. As introduction, this chapter outlines these challenges and the resulting need for an energy management strategy. Furthermore, currently applicated methods for solving the energy management are analyzed, resulting in an overview of their weaknesses and the hypothesis, how the proposed *Safe Reinforcement Learning* strategy can solve these.

### 1.1 Hybrid Electric Vehicles

*Hybrid Electric Vehicles* (HEV) are classified as vehicles which have at least two energy storages and two energy converters for locomotion. Today, the most


J. van den Herik and A. P. Rocha (Eds.): ICAART 2018, LNAI 11352, pp. 161–181, 2019.
https://doi.org/10.1007/978-3-030-05453-3_8

widely spread implementation is the combination of a conventional internal combustion engine (ICE) with an electric machine (EM) in combination with an extended electrical energy storage (battery). With the EM assisting the ICE in times of high loads, up to 30% of fuel can be saved, especially in urban environments, where the efficiency of vehicles operated solely by ICE is typically low [1]. Also, the vehicle deceleration can be exploited for energy recuperation, meaning the conversion of braking energy into electric energy for recharging the electric energy storage, further improving energy efficiency. Further information on the varieties of hybrid drive configurations can be found in [1]. Nevertheless, the additional drive unit increases the degree of freedom in the power train. A decision making entity has to be established to decide if both drive units or only one of the two units are used for locomotion given the current drive scenario and regarding the optimization objective of energy efficiency. How the EM is used to recharge the electrical energy storage is also part of this decision making process. This process is called the *Energy Management.*

The goal of the energy management is to decide the division of the amount of energy extracted out of each energy source in the vehicle at every moment of driving, while considering multiple constraints. The vehicle control/operation can be derived into two levels. The lower level – or component level – controls the drive train components using classic feedback-control strategies. The higher level – or supervisory level – controls the energy flows throughout the vehicle with regard to the state of charge of the battery. The higher level is understood as energy management or operating strategy and processes vehicle information in its execution. This information includes i.a. rotation speeds and torques of the energy converters, driver demands as velocity and acceleration, environmental influences like the slope. The goal of this level is the optimal usage of the actuators, which is then realized by the lower level.

## 1.2 Existing Energy Management Approaches

The basic goal of the energy management is to define the use of the additional drive units in the hybrid electrical vehicle, which is especially challenging due to the huge amount of different traffic scenarios the vehicle can be exposed to. Also, the control of the electric machine is continuous in contrast to boolean use – full activation or deactivation. This vastly increases the solution space for solving each traffic scenario. Thus, in a large number of publications, a fixed controller structure is defined for which a parameter variation is performed. The *Electric Assist Control Strategy* (EACS) [2] differentiates into operation modes – boost, recuperation, load point shifting and electric drive. Threshold values are defined for mode activation. Fuzzy approaches like [3] define fixed rules, whose quality depends on the experts defining them. The *Equivalent Consumption Minimization Strategy* (ECMS) [4] calculates the energy consumption of both storages by merging them into one general consumption value using the equivalence factor lambda ($P_{equi} = P_{fuel} + \lambda \cdot P_{elec}$) and then solving this simplified problem. Especially due to the fixed controller structure as well as the dependence on simplifications and constraints, the described strategies cannot ensure a global optimization of the energy management in all possible traffic scenarios.

The *Dynamic Programming* (DP) is a strategy which also optimizes the controller structure as well as its parameters [5]. Nevertheless, solving continuous problems with DP is only possible in special cases [6]. Thus, to enhance the problem solving for high dimensional continuous problems, an established practice is the discretization of state and action spaces. However, a wide discretization decreases the optimization quality. A fine discretization decreases application performance. Additionally, the DP needs perfect system models. In the context of vehicle driving, this includes the driver model as well as the vehicle model. A realistic model representing all possible stochastic situations occurring in real traffic, cannot be derived. Nevertheless, the DP with a pre-defined velocity profile can be used as benchmarking algorithm [7].

### 1.3 Safe Reinforcement Learning

According to [6] and [8], a solution of the previously described dilemmas are *Reinforcement Learning* (RL) approaches. These do not need perfect models and modern approaches like the DDPG [9] use artificial neural networks to approximate the state space. Also, as RL approaches are learning-based strategies, they can adapt to real world traffic scenarios.

Reinforcement Learning algorithms consist of an decision-maker (*Agent*), which directly influences the system (*Environment*). The agents receives feedback about the quality of its decisions getting *Rewards*, which are processed in the learning procedure. Additionally, further control variables like the battery cooling can be considered by the RL approaches, which are not part of classic strategies.

One significant objection to the use of RL approaches in safety critical applications, is the unpredictability of future decisions of the agent based on the learning process. In order to still ensure the application safety, *Safe Reinforcement Learning* introduces a separate validation subalgorithm *Shield* [10] following the agent, which verifies the decisions regarding pre-defined boundary conditions and which can override these in case of occurring harm.

### 1.4 Structure of the Contribution

As the *Safe Reinforcement Learning* algorithm is proposed to solve the energy management problem in this paper, chapter two gives detailed background about this algorithm. Chapter three describes the vehicle model (*Environment*) in which the algorithm is used. Chapter four details the implementation of the algorithm and the interaction with the environment. In chapter five the results of the energy management optimization are discussed and concluded in chapter six.

## 2 Background

In the first section of this chapter, the basic concept of *Reinforcement Learning* an *Q-Learning* are described. Thereafter, this is extended to *Deep Reinforcement Learning* and a discourse about the handling of continuous parameters is provided. Finally the chapter concludes with the introduction of the *Safe RL* algorithm.

### 2.1 Reinforcement Learning (RL)

*Reinforcement Learning* [6] is an interactive process inspired by the means human beings and animals learn. Thereby, an agent is interacting with its environment using the trial-and-error principle to learn how to maximize a numerical value representing its actions in order to gain a maximum return. The structure of this procedure is shown in Fig. 1. In each discrete time step $t$, the agent is confronted with a state $s_t \in S$ by the environment, for which it must choose an action $a_t \in A$. Here, $S$ is the entirety of all possible states and $A = A(s_t)$ are all possible actions at the state $s_t$. For each performed action, a new state $s_{t+1}$ and a numerical feedback $r_{t+1}$ as the reward are handed to the agent. The reward is calculated by the environment according to the reward function considering the chosen action. A learning process occurs, if the agent maximizes his return $G_t$ with continued interaction based on its chosen actions. The return is a weighted sum of all future rewards and therefore is also called a *cumulative reward*:

$$G_t = R_{t+1} + \gamma R_{t+2} + \gamma^2 R_{t+3} + \ldots = \sum_{k=0}^{\infty} \gamma^k R_{t+k+1} \tag{1}$$

The weighting $\gamma \in [0, 1]$ is called *discount factor* and indicates the impact of future rewards on the return in time step $t$. In contrast to explicitly learn this *Policy*, a variety of RL algorithms use an implicit learning procedure in which states and actions are related to the value of the expected return. This is done using value functions, which can be distinguished into the.

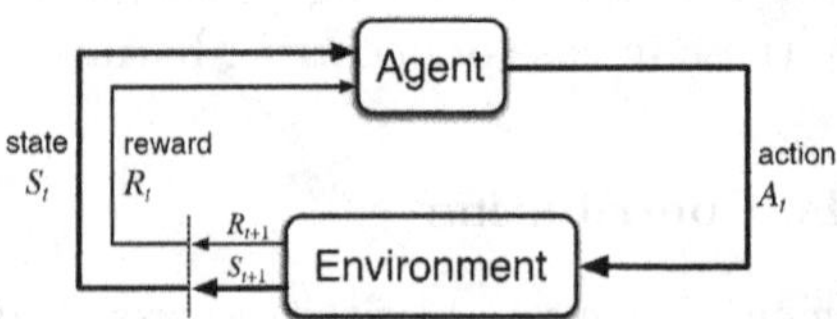


**Fig. 1.** Agent-environment interaction [6].

**State-Value-Function** $V_\pi(s)$
The expected return when beginning in state $s$ and following the policy from thereon, with $E_\pi$ as expected value of the policy for an arbitrary time step $t$.

$$V_\pi(s) = E_\pi[G_t|s_t = s] = E_\pi\left[\sum_{k=0}^{\infty} \gamma^k r_{t+k+1}|s_t = s\right] \tag{2}$$

**State-Action-Value-Function** $Q_\pi(s,a)$
The expected return when beginning in state $s$, choosing action $a$ and following the policy from thereon.

$$Q_\pi(s,a) = E_\pi[G_t|s_t = s, a_t = a] = E_\pi\left[\sum_{k=0}^{\infty}\gamma^k r_{t+k+1}|s_t = s, a_t = a\right] \quad (3)$$

Both functions can be learned by the agent during interaction with its environment using various algorithms in an iterative adaption process, resulting in an optimal policy. For example, if the state-action-value (also Q-Value) is known for each action in each state, the optimal policy choses the action with the highest value for each state, which automatically leads to the highest return:

$$\pi_*(s) = \arg\max_{a \in A(s)} Q(s,a) \quad (4)$$

To explain the iterative learning process, the Q-Learning shall be introduced next. Because of its simplicity and effectivity it is easy to use and also is the fundament of modern approaches like Deep Reinforcement Learning.

**Q-Learning:** is a model-free algorithm in which the agent does not need any knowledge about the environment or the reward function. The agent learns through experience gained after the execution of an action in its environment in each time step. Using this experience, the agent can constantly perform an assessment of the Q-Value function (see above). The iterative adaption of such an assessment is called a *Temporal Difference* (TD) procedure, which is of high importance in solving RL problems. For each experienced state $s_t$ and related action $a_t$, the current assessment $Q_\pi(s_t, a_t)$ can be updated by the experienced reward $r_{t+1}$ and the Q-Value of the next state $s_{t+1}$:

$$Q_\pi(s,a) := Q_\pi(s,a) + \alpha\left[r_{t+1} + \gamma \max_{a_t+1} Q_\pi(s_{t+1}, a_{t+1}) - Q_\pi(s_t, a_t)\right] \quad (5)$$

with $\alpha \in (0, 1]$ as the learning rate. $Q_\pi(s_{t+1}, a_{t+1})$ represents the best possible assessment of the future at time step $t$. An assessment based on other assessments is called *Bootstrapping* and is one of the core ideas of TD procedures. As $S$ and $A(s)$ are discrete quantities of states and actions, the learned Q-Values can be stored in a solution table named *Q-Table*. Therefore, Q-Learning is categorized as a Table-Look-Up procedure.

Linear function approximations as extension to Q-Tables have been a widely used approach to reduce the calculation time at increasing parameter numbers. Only a few lasting successes are known as the instability and sensitivity of the learning procedure increase. Only recently the advances in Deep Learning with neuronal networks have enabled RL for high dimensional problems, which is known as Deep Reinforcement Learning. These methods shall be explained in the next subchapter.

### 2.2 Deep Reinforcement Learning

*Deep Reinforcement Learning* uses deep neural networks [11] as Q-Value function approximatora, which is called a *Deep-Q-Network* (DQN) [12], instead of a Q-Table. The neural networks with its trainable parameters $\theta$ outputs a Q-Value $Q(s, a|\theta)$ for each of the $n$ possible actions. In contrast to Q-Learning, however, the agent does not try to iteratively evaluate all possible actions in the entire state space, but instead learns through the training to approximate the true Q-Value function $Q(s, a)$ with the neural network. Stability of the algorithm is mainly achieved by the following two measures.

**Experience Replay:** A limited data buffer is used, which stores the state $s_t$, the selected action $a_t$, the successor state $s_{t+1}$ and the obtained reward $r_{t+1}$ for a certain number of preceding time steps. Rather than always training with the most up-to-date data, the iterative update of network parameters $\theta$ is realized using minibatches, a sample of $N$ randomly selected state-action reward combinations from the data buffer. Since it is possible in principle for samples to be selected several times for the training, the efficiency in handling the data is increased at the same time.

**Target Networks:** The Loss function determines the current network output error to the desired output for training the DQN. Similar to Q-Learning and Eq. 5, the future rewards must be estimated with bootstrapping to find a difference. The costs $L$ of a Q-Value approximation in time step $t$ are also calculated in the DQN algorithm with:

$$L_t(\theta_t) = E[(y_t - Q(s_t, a_t|\theta_t))^2] \tag{6}$$

Here, $y_t$ is the current target value, which is estimated via the received reward $r_{t+1}$ and the highest Q-Value in the state $s_{t+1}$. Since a corresponding optimization of the network parameters $\theta$ to minimize the cost $L$ changes not only $Q(s_t, a_t|\theta)$ but also $Q(s_{t+1}, a_{t+1}|\theta)$, the stability of the learning process can be strongly influenced. To prevent this, Mnih et al. [12] introduce a second neural network with the parameters $\theta'$, the target network. Using this, the estimation of the target value can be done independent of the DQN for the training process:

$$y_t = E[r_{t+1} + \gamma \max_{a_{t+1}} Q(s_{t+1}, a_{t+1}|\theta')] \tag{7}$$

After a certain number of $C$ time steps, the network parameters are transmitted $\theta' \leftarrow \theta$, which synchronizes the target network with the DQN and allows a slow but stable adaptation of the two networks. A more detailed description of the process and a presentation of the results can be found in the related publications in [12] and [13].

**Actions with Continuous Parameters**

The *Deep Deterministic Policy Gradient* (DDPG) from [9] is based on an actor-critic-approach already known from [6] and is supplemented with the modern methods of Deep-RL. Actor-Critic methods consist of two independent components. The actor represents a policy $\mu$ that assigns an action a to each state

s. The critic, on the other hand, uses an estimate of the action value function $Q(s, a)$ to criticize or evaluate the decision made by the actor.

The training of a DDPG agent consists of two parallel learning processes. On the one hand, the critic has to learn about the closest possible approximation of the Q-Value function via continuous interaction with the environment. Second, the actor uses the current approximation of the Q-Values to adjust its policy to maximize the cumulative reward. For the critic, Silver et al. build on recent successes in *Deep Learning* and use Deep-Q networks with customizable parameters $\theta^Q$ to approximate the Q-Value function $Q(s, a)$. The learning process then is realized in accordance with the approaches explained in Sect. 1.3. At each time step $t$, the agent selects, through *Experience Replay*, a minibatch of $N$ random samples $(s_t, a_t, r_{t+1}, s_{t+1})$ of the data buffer $R$. The costs of the current approximation $Q(s_i, a_i|\theta^Q)$ with respect to a target value $y_i$ are determined by the mean square error:

$$L = \frac{1}{N}\sum_{i}^{N}(y_i - Q(s_i, a_i|\theta^Q))^2 \tag{8}$$

Since the target values $y_i$ consist of an estimate of future rewards, a second target network with parameters $\theta^{Q'}$ is used to ensure the stability of the learning process. The action $a_{i+1}$ chosen for $s_{i+1}$ is determined via the target network of the actor $\mu'$ with the parameters $\theta^{Q'}$:

$$y_i = E[r_{i+1} + \gamma Q'(s_{i+1}, \mu'(s_{i+1}|\theta^{\mu'})|\theta^{Q'})] \tag{9}$$

Unlike the original DQN algorithm, the DQN and target network are synchronized

$$\theta^{Q'} \leftarrow \tau\theta^Q + (1-\tau)\theta^{Q'} \tag{10}$$

with $\tau << 1$ at each time step. With the loss function and a common optimization method, the parameters of the DQN can then be updated in a simplified way using

$$\theta^Q \leftarrow \tau\theta^Q + \alpha\nabla_\theta L \tag{11}$$

in the direction of lower cost, where $\nabla_\theta L$ is the gradient of $L$ to the parameters $\theta$ and $\alpha$ the step size (learning rate) of the learning process. There are a lot more complex optimization methods for the learning process of neural networks and Eq. 11 is only intended to clarify the basic procedure.

In the second step, the actor uses the evaluation of his selected action by the critic for the iterative improvement of the policy $\mu$, which is also represented by a neural network. For this it uses the deterministic policy gradient $\nabla_{\theta\mu} J$ which is derived in [14] as the border case of a stochastic policy gradient and which can be understood as a gradient of the Q-Value to the parameters of the policy network $\nabla_{\theta\mu} Q$. With the help of the chain rule the gradient calculates as follows:

$$\nabla_{\theta^\mu} J = E_\mu[\nabla_{\theta^\mu} Q(s, \mu(s|\theta^\mu))|\theta^Q] = E_\mu[\nabla_a Q(s, a|\theta^Q) \cdot \nabla_{\theta^\mu}(s|\theta^\mu)] \tag{12}$$

The policy gradient indicates the performance of the currently pursued strategy and points towards higher Q-Values. If the actor updates its network parameters according to the gradient, as in Eq. 11, it also increases its yield.

Finally, the *Deep RL* algorithm is expanded to the *Safe Deep RL*. The basic concept is described in Sect. 1.3. The detailed implementation can be found in Sect. 4.6.

## 3 Environment

The overall goal is to implement the *Deep RL* agent into real vehicles as the energy management, where it can adapt to the occurring traffic scenarios. But as proof of concept in this contribution, the agent is executed using simulative models first. This also gives the opportunity to provide a learning advance for real world usage. Therefore, the environment described in this chapter consists of a vehicle model which is influenced by the agent, as well as a driver model which provides the demanded velocity profiles as input to the vehicle model (see Fig. 2). The most pragmatic approaches to provide said velocity profiles, are previously defined profiles like the *New European Drive Cycle*. Nevertheless, providing only one fixed cycle can lead to overfitting of the learning procedure, which has to be avoided. As a result, a driver model which can provide a limitless amount of stochastic velocity profiles is used in this contribution.

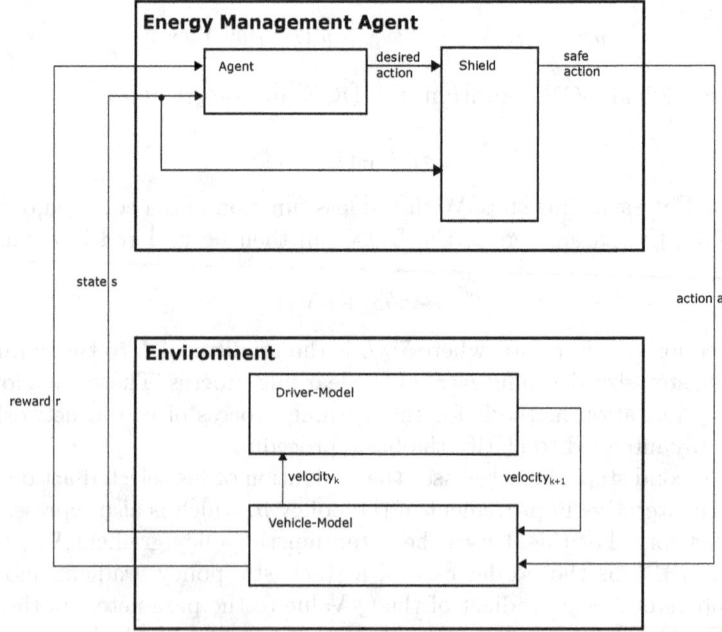


**Fig. 2.** Agent-environment interaction HEV.

### 3.1 Driver Model

The stochastic driver model from [15] already implicitly contains the driving environment (city, country, altitude profile) in which the vehicle is driven by the driver. Also, by selecting a specific database (market, traffic situation and driving style), the calibration purpose can be set. The tuning of operating strategies towards special features in real-world driving scenarios can be seen as a major benefit for customers concerning fuel efficiency of their vehicles since it can be assumed that e.g. an operating strategy derived with European driving data will not work as efficient in India or China. As the driver model is not influenced by the optimization proposed in this paper, it is not discussed in full detail. How the derivation of the real world driving cycles is realized, can be found in detail in [15] and [16].

### 3.2 Vehicle Model

This section describes the vehicle model as part of the environment, which is a reverse-oriented model. This quasi-static approach depends on the assumption that the drive cycle is precisely fulfilled by the vehicle. To realize this, the drive cycle is divided into small time intervals for which a constant velocity, torque, and acceleration are assumed. This is equivalent to the neglect of internal drive train dynamics [17]. Each drive unit component is modeled describing the relation of the inputs and outputs. This relation is realized by modern approaches like polynomial models or artificial neural networks.

$$[V_{fuel}, SOC, T_{bat}] = f(v_{hev}, \alpha_{slope}, P_{aux}, Trq_{em}, C_{cool}, Gear) \tag{13}$$

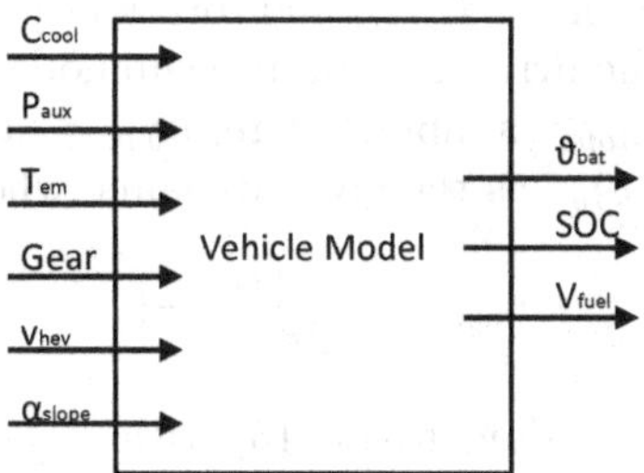


**Fig. 3.** Vehicle model system function.

The necessary data originates from dynamometer test series, onboard measurements (e.g. for the battery cooling), as well as component test benches. Because of this empirical modeling, there have to be no assumptions about the degree of efficiency of the components. Also, the resulting models offer short executions times in contrast to physical models, which is especially advantageous for optimization purposes [18]. The complete vehicle model represents the functional relation as described in Eq. 13 and visualized in Fig. 3. It includes the battery temperature and cooling in contrast to classic energy management approaches. The vehicle velocity $v_{hev}$, slope $\alpha_{slope}$, and gear are influences by the driver. The target torque of the elecrtic machine $T_{em}$ and the control of the battery cooling $C_{cool}$ are controlled by the energy management. The electric power of the auxiliary components $P_{aux}$ currently is a constant value but will be extended to a dynamic input in future contributions. Figures 4, 5 and 6 extend step by step the content of the vehicle model by necessary submodels.

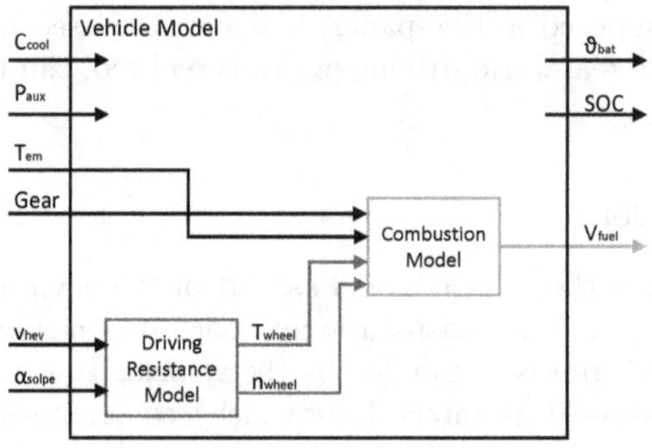


**Fig. 4.** Vehicle model combustion submodels.

In Fig. 4 the vehicle model is extended by the combustion model, which calculates the fuel consumption output $V_{fuel}$. The submodel is realized using an empirically trained *Multi-Layer-Perceptron Model.* Besides the torque of the electric machine $T_{em}$ and the gear as given inputs to the overall vehicle model, the submodel requires the torque $T_{wheel}$ and rotation speed $n_{wheel}$ at the wheels. These are calculated by the driving resistance submodel, with the given vehicle velocity $v_{hev}$ and slope $\alpha_{slope}$ as inputs. Here, $n_{wheel}$ can directly be calculated according to Eq. 14, with $r_{dyn}$ as the given dynamic wheel radius.

$$n_{wheel} = \frac{v_{hev}}{2\pi \cdot r_{dyn}} \tag{14}$$

$T_{wheel}$ is calculated according to Eq. 15, with $F_{pp}$ as the propulsion force which is calculated according to Eq. 16, with the acceleration force $F_{acc}$, roll resistance force $F_{rr}$, air resistance force $F_{air}$, and the slope force $F_{slope}$.

$$T_{wheel} = F_{pp} \cdot r_{dyn} \tag{15}$$

$$F_{pp} = F_{acc} + F_{rr} + F_{air} + F_{slope} \tag{16}$$

The acceleration force $F_{acc}$ is the multiplication of the vehicle mass $m_{hev}$ and the vehicle acceleration $a_{hev}$, which is the derivation of the given vehicle speed $v_{hev}$.

$$F_{acc} = m_{hev} \cdot a_{hev} \tag{17}$$

The roll $F_{rr}$ and the air resistance $F_{air}$ are substituted by a polynomial function of second degree according to Eq. 18 [19]. The polynomial values $R_0$, $R_1$, and $R_2$ are empirically measured. $F_{slope}$ as final part for the calculation of $T_{wheel}$ is determined according to Eq. 19, with the vehicle mass $m_{hev}$, gravitational acceleration $g$ and the vehicle model input slope $\alpha_{slope}$.

$$F_{rr} + F_{air} = R_0 + R_1 \cdot v_{hev} + R_2 \cdot v_{hev}^2 \tag{18}$$

$$F_{slope} = m_{hev} \cdot g \cdot sin(\alpha_{slope}) \tag{19}$$

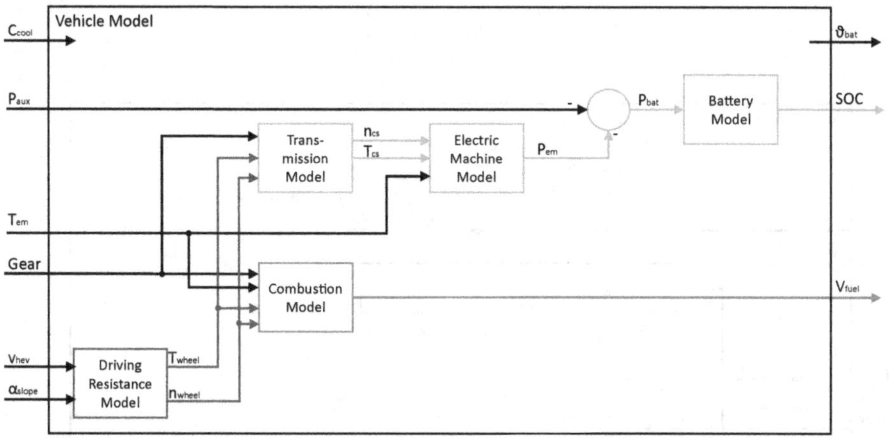


**Fig. 5.** Vehicle model electric machine submodels.

Figure 5 extends the vehicle model with the electric machine submodels, which calculate the *State of Charge SOC* as vehicle model output. The battery model itself is the last entity in this combination of submodels and calculates the final $SOC$, using the requested electrical power $P_{bat}$ as input, which has a positive value when delivering and a negative value when recuperating energy. The model is basically a dipole substitute model with the power $I_{bat}$ calculating according to Eq. 20, with the battery resistance $R_{bat}$ and battery voltage $U_{bat,0}$. Using $I_{bat}$, the $SOC$ can be determined according Eq. 21, with the electrical charge of the battery $Q_{bat,max}$.

$$I_{bat} = \frac{U_{bat,0} - \sqrt{U_{bat,0}^2 - 4 \cdot P_{bat} \cdot R_{bat}}}{2 \cdot R_{bat}} \tag{20}$$

$$I_{bat}(t) = -\frac{\Delta SOC(t) \cdot Q_{bat,max}}{\Delta t} \tag{21}$$

The requested power $P_{bat}$ at the battery is the sum of the auxiliary power demand $P_{aux}$ and the electrical machine power demand $P_{em}$, which can be positive or negative depending on the operation mode. The electric machine submodel is realized using an polynomical model, which is derived empirically and calculates the power demand $P_{em}$. The inputs for this calculation are the rotation speed of the crankshaft $n_{cs}$, torque at the crankshaft $T_{cs}$, and requested electric machine torque $T_{em}$.

Crankshaft torque $T_{cs}$ and rotation speed $n_{cs}$ are provided by the transmission submodel, which transmits the wheel torque $T_{wheel}$ and rotation speed $n_{wheel}$ provided by the driving resistance submodel according to Eqs. 22 and 23 using the current transmission gear ratio $g_{tm}$.

$$n_{cs} = g_{tm} \cdot n_{wheel} \tag{22}$$

$$T_{cs} = \frac{1}{g_{tm}} \cdot T_{wheel} \tag{23}$$

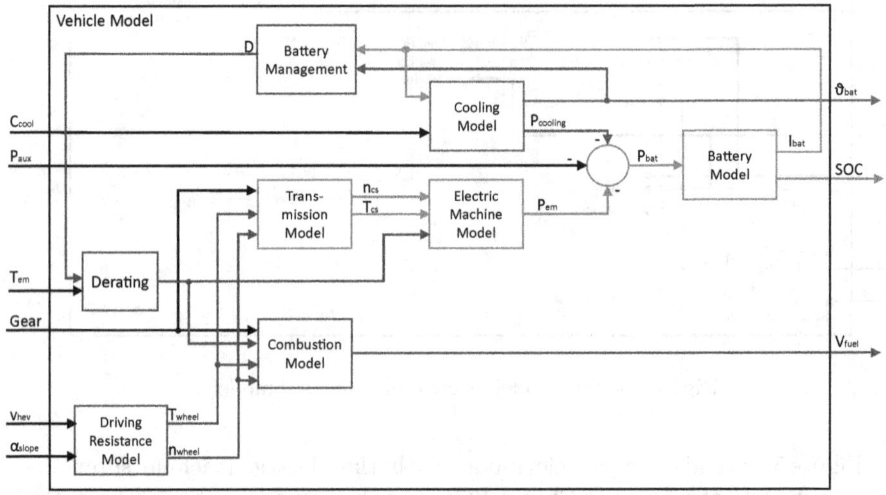


**Fig. 6.** Vehicle model battery cooling and derating submodels

Figure 6 finalizes the vehicle model with the cooling, battery management, and derating submodel. The cooling submodel calculates the power demand of the cooling system $P_{cooling}$, which is added to the calculation of the requested battery power $P_{bat}$. Also, it calculates the vehicle model output battery temperature $\vartheta_{bat}$. The global input cooling control $C_{cool}$, which is a percentage value in between $-100\%$ and $100\%$ (cooling and heating), and the battery current $I_{bat}$ are used as inputs. The battery management submodel calculates the derating factor, which is processed by the derating submodel. The battery temperature $\vartheta_{bat}$ and current $I_{bat}$ are used as inputs. As these submodel structures are protected by non-disclosure, further details cannot be provided here about the internal model structures.

The battery temperature is a critical factor influencing the lifespan of the battery [21]. Therefore, a consideration in the context of the battery model is reasonable. High charge and decharge currents increase the cell temperature, which can exceed the allowed limits, and thus lead to damage and accelerated aging of the battery. To prevent these, the power output is reduced if a temperature threshold is reached. This procedure is called *derating* [20]. Experienced-based derating diagrams punish high currents and excessive deviation from the optimal battery temperature. The power output reduction is achieved by influencing the requested electric machine torque $T_{em}$.

### 3.3 Driver and Vehicle Model Interaction

In each time step, the driver model receives the velocity in the current state $k$ from the vehicle model, on which the driver model chooses an acceleration. As described in Sect. 3.1, the driver is realized by representative drive cycles, which include the environmental data like the slope. Based on the current velocity, the velocity for the next state $k+1$ is derived, as well as the slope and gear. These are delivered to the vehicle model as inputs.

## 4 Energy Management Agent

This chapter describes the implemented agent as well as its interaction with the environment described in Chap. 3 and visualized in Fig. 2. As introduced in Sect. 1.3, the Agent executes actions $a$ onto the environment. To constantly increase its decision-making process leading to the choice of actions $a$, the agent learns and adapts using the environment state $s$ and a reward $r$ which represents the feedback about the quality of the results of the actions $a$. The structure of this chapter orientates at this procedure first describing the actions $a$ which can be understood as the agent outputs. Thereafter, the environment states $s$ and rewards $r$, which can be understood as input to the agent, are detailed. Next, the agent algorithm itself and the learning procedure are detailed. Finally the *Shield* is introduced in between the agent output and the environment, which extends the *Deep Reinforcement Learning* to the *Safe Deep RL* by validating and possibly overwriting bad actions of the agent and thus safeguarding the environment.

### 4.1 Agent Actions

The agent controls the torque demand of the electric machine $T_{em}$, as well as the cooling control variable $C_{cool}$, which are both direct inputs to the vehicle model of the environment. Thus, the set actions in each time step are defined according to Eq. 24.

$$a = [T_{em}, C_{Cool}] \tag{24}$$

### 4.2 Environment States

As described before, the objective of the energy management is the minimization of the vehicle energy consumption. To achieve this, the agent influences the vehicle model part of the environment as shown in Fig. 2. Nevertheless, the biggest influence factor to the vehicle consumption is the velocity demand by the driver given by the driver model of the environment. Although it is possible to influence the velocity by the agent, in this contribution the driver is still independent. Optimizing the velocity profile is a different kind of task, which is not the goal of the research here. Nevertheless, as the velocity demand of the driver is still the largest influence on the optimization goal, the agent has to consider this. Thus, the rotation speed at the wheel $n_{wheel}$, torque at the wheel $T_{wheel}$, and gear are part of the state vector $s$. In the model application in this contribution, the gear is a direct output of the driver model, whereas $n_{wheel}$ and $T_{wheel}$ are calculated by the driving resistance submodel of the vehicle model. Although technically part of the vehicle model, $n_{wheel}$ and $T_{wheel}$ are directly influenced only by the driver model and not by the agent (compare to the action description in the previous subschapter).

Besides the driver influence, the vehicle state includes the state of charge $SOC$ and battery temperature $\vartheta_{bat}$ outputs of the vehicle model as described in Sect. 3.2. Additionally, the internal vehicle model derating variable $D$ is included in the state vector. These last three states are influenced by the agent. Thus, the environment state $s$ is defined according to Eq. 25.

$$s = [\underbrace{n_{wheel}, T_{wheel}, gear}_{\textbf{Drivers influence}}, \underbrace{SOC, T_{bat}, D}_{\textbf{Agents influence}}] \tag{25}$$

### 4.3 Rewards

The reward $r$ is the combined energy conversion of both energy storages, chemical $E_{che}$ and electrical $E_{el}$, in each time step. As *RL* algorithms typically try to maximize the reward, the inverse annotation for the rewards is defined according to Eq. 26. The vehicle model output fuel consumption $V_{fuel}$ is converted to the chemical energy consumption $E_{che}$, whereas the electrical energy consumption is calculated by the multiplication of battery current $I_{bat}$ and voltage $U_{bat,0}$.

$$r = -(E_{che} + E_{el}) \tag{26}$$

### 4.4 Agent Implementation

The chosen *Deep RL* agent is the *Deep Deterministic Policy Gradient* (DDPG) algorithm [9]. In [22], nine different continuous control *Deep RL* approaches have been compared according to various benchmarks. Compared to the others, the DDPG algorithm was particularly outstanding due to its fast convergence during the demanding Half-Cheetah benchmark. Introduced by Lillicrap in 2015, the DDPG is an actor critic, model-free algorithm working with continuous actions. This algorithm was able to solve more than 20 simulated physical tasks in a robust manner in [22]. The simulations were based on the same learning algorithm, the same neural network architecture and utilized the same hyper parameters for all tasks. This strategy qualified the *DDPG* algorithm as an approach for solving the *HEV* energy management problem.

Details on the structure of the *DDPG* can be found in [9]. In the implementation of this contribution, the training of the neural networks is performed using the *Adam Optimizer* [24] with a learning rate of $10^{-5}$ for the actor, and $10^{-4}$ for the critic. The discount factor is $\gamma = 1.0$. The soft target update is performed with $\tau = 0.001$. Rectified non-linearities [25] were used for all hidden layers. The actor's final output layer was a tanh layer to bind the actions. The low-dimensional networks had 2 hidden layers of 400 and 300 units. Actions were included in the second hidden layer of Q. Mini batch sizes of 64 are used. The replay buffer has a size of $10^6$.

An additional challenge for *Deep RL* implementations is the conflict between exploitation and exploration. To achieve a large reward, the agent has to prefer actions which have achieved good results in the past (exploitation). On the other hand, the agent has to try new actions in order to enlarge the gained knowledge about the environment (exploration) [6]. To solve this conflict, the Ornstein-Uhlenbeck process [26] is suitable especially for continuous environments [23]. This procedure generates temporal correlated random samples of a Gaussian distribution. The samples influence each other in that two consecutive samples are likely to be closer together. Thus, smooth transitions are generated, which are advantageous especially for the control of engines.

### 4.5 Training

The training is achieved by processing a series of velocity profiles. In order to avoid overfitting and achieve a good generalization, the velocity profiles and initial vehicle states (state of charge, battery temperature, derating) vary for each episode. This can be understood as representing different vehicle trips, even if the same route is chosen. During training, a fixed reference velocity profile is processed every ten stochastic profiles to supervise the learning process. This procedure is necessary, as the quality of the achieved results in each stochastic profile is also influenced by the initial values and specifics of the profiles. Thus, a reference is needed to exclude this influence for evaluation purposes.

### 4.6 Shield

As introduced in Sect. 1.3 and shown in Fig. 2, the shield is implemented between the agent and the environment. Its purpose is the safeguarding of the environment by overwriting damaging actions from the agent. Thus, the shield converts the desired action of the agent into a safe action for the environment. The desired action is only altered, if violating the safety rule in the shield.

In the implementation in this contribution, the shield constraints the maximum and minimum battery power. As the shield is informed about the current vehicle state $s$, the currently possibly battery power influenced by the derating of the battery management is known and can be compared to the requested electric machine performance by the agent. If the agent action leads to a violated battery power constraint, the action is altered according to the possible power output. Also, the maximum and minimum battery power is limited to the state of charge, which also affects the battery cooling.

# 5 Results

In the related contribution [27], the successful use of *Deep RL* for energy management has been proven, approximating the optimum. The current contribution extends the content by including the battery temperature and cooling, as well as the derating in the energy management. The achieved results by the *Deep RL* are described using two scenarios. First a constant downhill drive is discussed, which is suitable to verify the correct behavior of the agent, as the wheel rotation speed $n_{wheel}$, torque $T_{wheel}$, and gear are constant. The second scenario is a mixed real drive, consisting of urban, country, and highway parts. This is used to validate the energy management purpose of energy consumption reduction.

## 5.1 Constant Downhill Drive Scenario

The constant downhill scenario illustrates the difficulty of manually defining suitable control strategies for the electric motor and the battery cooling, without the derating entirely limiting the performance of the system. Even at constant values for wheel speed, wheel torque and gear, finding a suitable control cannot be determined intuitively or by a few tests.

The negative slope in this scenario is chosen, so that the vehicle could potentially use full recuperation in each time step, with the electric machine in generator mode recharging the battery. Generally, the energy management tries to increase the state of charge as quick as possible. All manually defined strategies, which could potentially be applicated operation strategies, trigger full derating. The next step could be to determine threshold values to avoid full derating. On the other hand, this process could be completely left to the *Deep RL* agent.

The agent has to prevent the derating of the power consumption capability of the battery, while simultaneously using the cooling to keep the battery temperature in the best operation point, and while trying to reduce the energy consumption. The initial state of charge is $SOC_{t_0} = 0.1$, battery temperature $T_{bat,t_0} = 35°C$, and derating $DR_{t_0} = 0$.

**Conventional Results**

Figure 7 visualizes the resulting time diagrams of the state of charge $SOC$, battery temperature $\vartheta_{bat}$, derating $D$, battery power $P_{bat}$, and control of the cooling, for multiple conventional solutions of the energy management. In every manually defined strategy, the derating is fully utilized, so that the battery cannot gain any more energy after half of the scenario. The best final state of charge is about $SOC_{t_{end}} = 0.16$. Note, to increase the visuability of the relevant effect, the battery capacity in this example has been enlarged by a factor of ten.

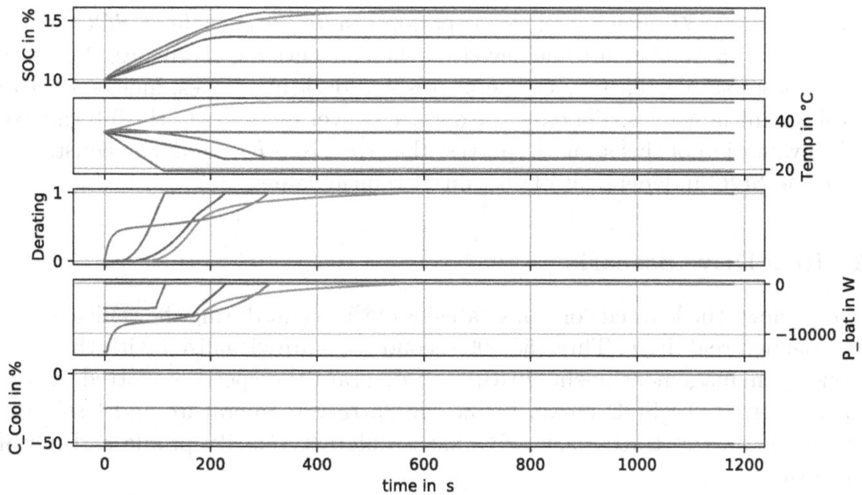


**Fig. 7.** Conventional results of the downhill scenario for multiple operation rules.

## Deep RL Results

Regarding the *Deep RL*, Fig. 8 shows the parameters analogically to the evaluation of the conventional results. The time curves represent variating initial states of the vehicle, which the trained *Deep RL* agent is confronted with in this evaluation.

The blue lines represent a scenario execution using the same initial states for the vehicle as used in the conventional results derivation (Fig. 7). Comparing

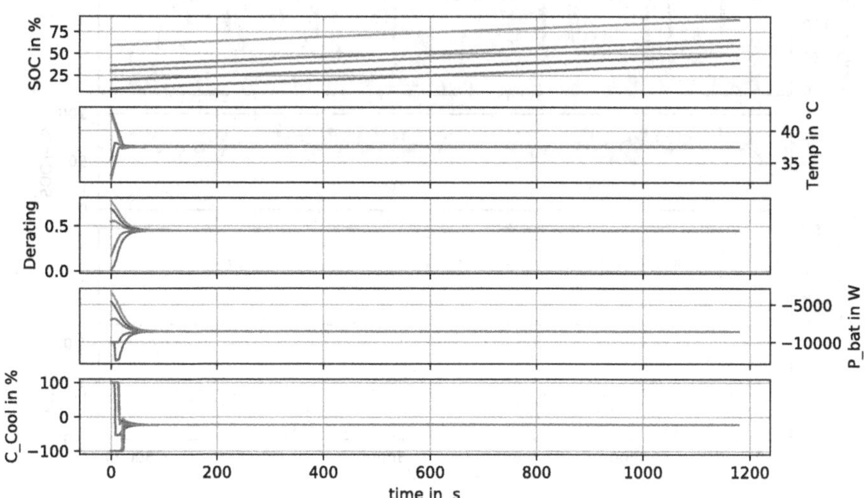


**Fig. 8.** Deep RL results of the downhill scenario for multiple initial vehicle states.

these, the *Deep RL* agent achieves superior results with an final *SOC* of 0.4 in contrast to a SOC of 0.16 achieved by the conventional strategies. Also, the agent chooses similar battery temperatures and derating values, independent of the vehicle initial values. Thereby, the derating never increases to the full value of 1. The evaluation of this scenario proves, that the *Deep RL* agent can constantly charge the *SOC* independent of the initial vehicle values.

## 5.2 Real Drive Scenario

Figure 9 shows the learned control strategies of the agent during the vehicle usage in the defined real drive. Three 50,000 second trips are visualized with the *Deep RL* energy management agent. In the top diagram the speed is plotted, in the second diagram the SOC curve, below the battery temperature and lastly the derating curve over time. Each drive has a different velocity profile and initial vehicle values.

The agent keeps the SOC in a range of about 50 to 90% regardless of the initial SOC value. The agent automatically keeps the battery temperature within the temperature range that is most suitable regarding derating. The agent identifies this by itself through interaction with the environment. The value for derating is always kept below a value of about 0.6. The full control of derating, which would result in a full restriction of the use of the electric motor, is not triggered at any time.

The progression of the values of the parameters influenced by the *Deep RL* agent are in plausible ranges. It can be summarized that the agent is able to understand the extended energy management problem and to independently set

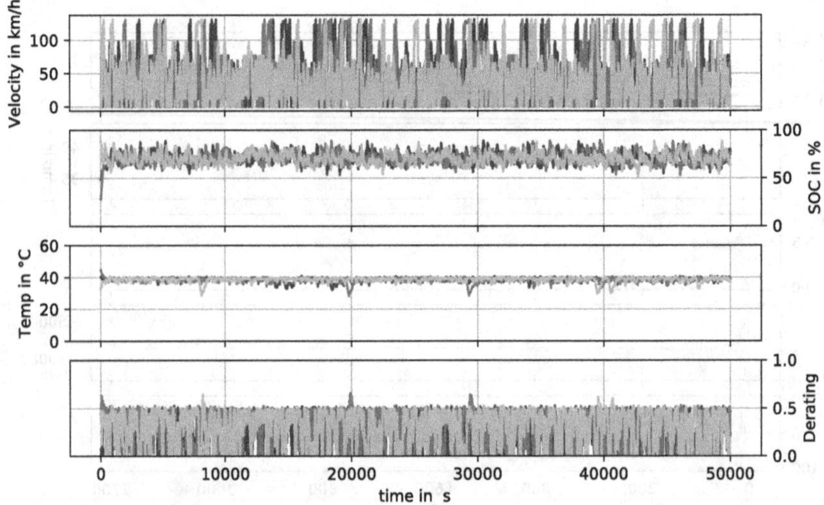


**Fig. 9.** Deep RL results of the real drive scenario for multiple initial vehicle states.

all relevant condition and action variables in such a way that the overall goal, the reduction of energy consumption, is achieved.

## 6 Summary and Further Work

The objective of this contribution is to present a *Safe Deep RL* implementation for solving continuous energy management problems in hybrid electric vehicles and to evaluate its potential in comparison to conventional rule-based strategies. To achieve this goal, the contribution gives a short introduction into *Deep RL* algorithms, and describes the vehicle and driver model as environment in which the *Deep RL* agent is deployed. After detailing the relations and work flows, the *Deep RL* results are discussed at two scenarios.

In the constant downhill scenario, the performance of the *Deep RL* agent in contrast to multiple conventional strategies is shown. With an state of charge increase as objective in this scenario, the *Deep RL* agent performed above expectations, being able to increase the *SOC* 250% of the best of the tested conventional methods. The real drive scenario showed the plausible adaptation of the agent to multiple drives and can be understood as the proof of concept of using *Deep RL* agents for solving continuous energy management problems of hybrid electric vehicles.

Meanwhile, apart from the *DDPG* algorithm, other *Deep RL* algorithms have been introduced. On the one hand, it is planned to draw comparisons with the *A2C* [28], *A3C* [29], and *PPO* [30] algorithms. On the other hand, hyperparameter optimizations represent a further goal of the investigation.

Furthermore, the state space shall be expanded. E.g. the power of the auxiliary users is planned to be used as a dynamic state variable in the future, as well as further variables with influence on energy consumption. In the long-term perspective, including the variables influencing the vehicle emissions is a reasonable goal. Also, it is planned to fine tune agents, which are trained in simulation, on power train test benches.

Finally, the authors conclude that *Deep RL* is perfectly suitable for the application in the *HEV* energy management and presents a large potential for future demands and extensions.

## References

1. Guzzella, L., Sciarretta, A.: Vehicle Propulsion Systems: Introduction to Modeling and Optimization, 3rd edn. Springer, Heidelberg (2013). https://doi.org/10.1007/978-3-642-35913-2
2. Banvait, H., Anwar, S., Chen, Y.: A rule-based energy management strategy for plugin hybrid electric vehicle (PHEV). In: American Control Conference (2009)
3. Lee, H.-D., Koo, E.-S., Sul, S.-K., Kim, J.-S.: Torque control strategy for a parallel-hybrid vehicle using fuzzy logic. In: IEEE Industry Applications Magazine (2000)
4. Sivertsson, M., Sundström, C., Eriksson, L.: Adaptive control of a hybrid powertrain with map-based ECMS. In: IFAC World Congress (2011)

5. Foellinger, O.: Optimale Regelung und Steuerung. Oldenbourg (1994). ISBN: 3486231162
6. Sutton, R.: Reinforcement Learning: An Introduction, 2nd edn. MIT Press, Cambridge (2018)
7. Kirschbaum, F., Back, M., Hart, M.: Determination of the fuel-optimal trajectory for a vehicle along a known route. IFAC Proc. Vol. **35**(1), 235–239 (2002)
8. Bertsekas, D.P., Tsitsiklis, J.N.: Neuro-dynamic programming (1996). ISBN: 1886529108
9. Lillicrap, T.P., et al.: Continuous control with deep reinforcement learning. CoRR, abs/1509.02971 (2015)
10. Alshiekh, M., Bloem, R., Ehlers, R., Könighofer, B., Niekum, S., Topcu, U.: Safe Reinforcement Learning via Shielding, CoRR, abs/1708.08611 (2017)
11. LeCun, Y., Bengio, Y., Hinton, G.: Deep learning. Nature **521**, 436–444 (2015)
12. Mnih, V., et al.: Human-level control through deep reinforcement learning. Nature **518**(7540), 529–533 (2015)
13. Mnih, V., et al.: Playing Atari with deep reinforcement learning. In: NIPS Deep Learning Workshop (2013)
14. Silver, D., Lever, G., Heess, N., Degris, T., Wierstra, D., Riedmiller, M.: Deterministic policy gradient algorithms. In: Proceedings of the 31st International Conference on Machine Learning (ICML 2014). Hrsg. von Tony Jebara und Eric P. Xing. JMLR Workshop und Conference Proceedings, pp. 387–395 (2014)
15. Liessner, R., Dietermann, A., Bäker, B., Lüpkes, K.: Generation of replacement vehicle speed cycles based on extensive customer data by means of Markov models and threshold accepting. SAE Int. J. Altern. Powertrains **6**(1), 165–173 (2017)
16. Liessner, R., Dietermann, A., Bäker, B., Lüpkes, K.: Derivation of real-world driving cycles corresponding to traffic situation and driving style on the basis of Markov models and cluster analyses. In: 6th Conference on Hybrid and Electric Vehicles, (HEVC 2016) (2016)
17. Onori, S., Serrao, L., Rizzoni, G.: Hybrid Electric Vehicles: Energy Management Strategies. Springer, London (2016)
18. Helbing, M., Bäker, B., Schiffer, S.: Total vehicle concept design using computational intelligence. In: 6th Conference on Future Automotive Technology, Fürstenfeldbruck (2017)
19. Pillas, J.: Modellbasierte Optimierung dynamischer Fahrmanöver mittels Prüfständen, Dissertation, Technischen Universität Darmstadt (2017)
20. Engelhardt, T.: Derating-Strategien für elektrisch angetriebene Sportwagen, Wissenschaftliche Reihe Fahrzeugtchnik Universität Stuttgart (2017)
21. Wei, L.: Introduction to Hybrid Vehicle System Modeling and Control. Wiley, Hoboken (2013). ISBN 978-1-118-30840-0
22. Duan, Y.: Benchmarking deep reinforcement learning for continuous control. In: Proceedings of the 33rd International Conference on Machine Learning (ICML) (2016)
23. Plappert, M., et al.: Parameter Space Noise for Exploration, CoRR, abs/1706.01905 (2017)
24. Kingma, D., Ba, J.: Adam: a method for stochastic optimization, CoRR, abs/1412.6980 (2014)
25. Glorot, X., Bordes, A., Bengio, Y.: Deep sparse rectifier networks. In: Proceedings of the 14th International Conference on Artificial Intelligence and Statistics. JMLR W and CP Volume, vol. 15, pp. 315–323 (2011)
26. Uhlenbeck, G., Ornstein, L.: On the theory of the brownian motion. Phys. Rev. **36**(5), 823 (1930)

27. Liessner, R., Dietermann, A., Schroer C., Bäker, B.: Deep reinforcement learning for advanced energy management of hybrid electric vehicles. In: Proceedings of the 10th International Conference on Agents and Artificial Intelligence - (Volume 2) (2018)
28. Wu, Y., Mansimov, E., Liao, S., Grosse, R., Ba, J.: Scalable trust-region method for deep reinforcement learning using Kronecker-factored approximation, CoRR, abs/1708.05144 (2017)
29. Mnih, V., et al.: Asynchronous Methods for Deep Reinforcement Learning, CoRR, abs/1602.01783 (2016)
30. Schulman, J., Wolski, F., Dhariwal, P., Radford, A., Klimov, O.: Proximal Policy Optimization Algorithms, CoRR, abs/1707.06347 (2017)

# Planning Under Uncertainty Through Goal-Driven Action Selection

Juan Carlos Saborío[1(✉)] and Joachim Hertzberg[1,2]

[1] Institute of Computer Science, University of Osnabrück, Wachsbleiche 27, Osnabrück, Germany
jcsaborio@uos.de

[2] DFKI Robotics Innovation Center (Osnabrück), Albert-Einstein-Straße 1, Osnabrück, Germany

**Abstract.** Online planning in domains with uncertainty and partial observability conveys a series of performance challenges: agents must obtain information about the environment, quickly select actions with high reward prospects and avoid very expensive mistakes, while interleaving planning and execution in highly variable and uncertain domains. In order to reduce the amount of mistakes and help an agent focus on directly relevant actions, we propose a goal-driven, action selection method for planning in (PO)MDP's. This method introduces a reward bonus and a rollout policy for MCTS planners, both of which depend almost exclusively on a clear specification of the goal and produced promising results when planning in large domains of interest to cognitive and mobile robotics.

## 1 Introduction

Planning under uncertainty requires deliberating over actions, their effects, and computing values that reflect a combination of some form of utility or reward and their probability. Uncertainty in planning domains may come from non-deterministic actions or from incomplete knowledge about the environment and the agent's current state. These planning problems are often modelled as Markov Decision Processes (MDP's) or Partially Observable MDP's (POMDP's), and solved using many well known methods among which Monte-Carlo Tree Search (MCTS) is a popular choice, especially in the online planning community. UCT is the modern MCTS standard [1], and it guarantees asymptotic convergence and solutions that minimize regret by expanding a tree of states and selecting actions following the UCB1 formula [2]. An extension of UCT for partially observable domains, called POMCP [3], constitutes the (arguably) most general Monte-Carlo POMDP solver. As such POMCP is a basic starting point for online POMDP planning and the most obvious alternative to traditional, point-based POMDP solvers, most of which are simply incapable of solving moderately large problems.

We are interested in problems that can be modelled as POMDP's for several reasons: POMDP's explicitly represent the effect of information-gathering


J. van den Herik and A. P. Rocha (Eds.): ICAART 2018, LNAI 11352, pp. 182–201, 2019.
https://doi.org/10.1007/978-3-030-05453-3_9

actions, actions are assumed to be non-deterministic, and policies depend on a correct representation and estimation of the agent's true state. In other words, POMDP's correctly model the full extent of robotic task-planning in a mathematical framework with a strong analytical background. We are also interested in transferring these methods to planning onboard robots, but unlike many common AI problems, robot planning domains tend to be orders of magnitude more complex. Often, planning problems are reduced to their minimal and necessary elements and, while still potentially large, do not address the challenges that robots face when planning in the "real world": a massive amount of states that are reachable by the algorithm and yet, mostly irrelevant for any given goal. This means robot planning using POMDP's must follow a very strict, guided, goal-driven mechanism to avoid excessive computation.

The challenge to overcome in planning under uncertainty then becomes that of avoiding a very large number of states that contribute little to reaching the goal state, and identifying those that provide a significant contribution. This amounts to producing satisficing behavior, potentially overlooking parts of an optimal policy but generating visible results more quickly in very large planning domains. This approach responds to our attempts to provide a formal interpretation of the intuitive concept of "relevance", which in planning terms may be seen as a reliable (albeit imperfect) attentional filter guiding action selection, which may open up ways of handling problems with high dimensionality. Planning algorithms should be able to quickly identify promising (high expected value) states and focus on getting there. State values represent a weighted average of future rewards, so the problem reduces to quickly locating these sources of future rewards. One relatively simple idea is preferring actions that lead to subgoals (subsets of some terminal state) while avoiding those that don't, and encouraging these actions by providing additional, positive rewards. Achieving a subgoal objectively brings the agent a step closer to achieving a larger goal, and so we use this idea to formalize a metric of state-to-goal proximity.

We propose *partial goal satisfaction* as a way to compute the proximity of states to goals and provide a reward bonus in action selection, which easily becomes an action selection policy for Monte-Carlo rollouts. This is by no means a complete solution to online planning onboard robots, but rather a contribution towards the improvement of action selection in planning algorithms, when information about the goal is available. The effect is that the planning agent is encouraged to pursue certain promising actions, and receives optimistic value initializations in newly discovered states. This is a way of implicitly helping an agent or robot *do the right thing* by avoiding less promising alternatives during planning.

Existing approaches that address large planning spaces include value approximation and state aggregation, but these work under the assumption that there are large groups of states that can be clustered together (due to similarity or other reasons) using fixed criteria. At the moment we are interested in how agents may use knowledge of their goal(s) to improve their action selection criteria, in particular by focusing on only a few good alternatives when many options are available, as is the case of domains with high variability and large branching factor.

In the following sections we discuss previous related work, and proceed to explain our proposal. We then provide a simple example in a fully observable MDP and two examples of large POMDP's, as well as an analysis of experimental results. We finalize by discussing the challenges of online POMDP planning and comment on future directions.

Please note that this is an extended version of a conference paper (see [4]). We introduce a new planning domain, test our proposed method in this new domain, and provide further analysis and considerations not present in our previous, related publication.

## 2 Notation

We rely on the standard notation for an MDP: let $S$ and $A$ be finite sets of states and actions respectively and $T(s, a, s') = P(s'|s, a)$ the probability of reaching state $s'$ when executing $a$ in $s$, which yields a real-valued reward $R(s, a, s')$. An MDP is the tuple $\langle S, A, T, R\rangle$, with discount factor $\gamma$.

In a POMDP, an agent receives an observation $\omega \in \Omega$ with probability $O(s, a, \omega) = P(\omega|s, a)$ and maintains an internal belief state $b \in B$, where $b$ is a probability distribution over states and $b(s)$ is the probability of $s$ being the current state. A POMDP is therefore $\langle S, A, T, R, \Omega, O\rangle$. The sequence $h_t = (a_0, \omega_1, \ldots, a_{t-1}, \omega_t)$ is the *history* at time $t$. Notice the complexity of planning in belief space, a $|S|$-dimensional hyperplane.

Many POMDP planning algorithms directly search over a tree of beliefs, explicitly reasoning about and choosing valuable (informative) beliefs, producing policies that are also given in terms of beliefs. We will however present our action selection bias in terms of states with mixed observability (states that contain both fully and partially observable features). This responds to two core principles: (1) Exploiting the structure of problems to simplify POMDP planning is possible and necessary, and in robotic task planning one simple and fair assumption is that there are some fully-observable features. (2) A state with fully-observable features can be sampled at any given point, using an approximator that provably approaches the true belief state, greatly reducing the complexity of planning.

## 3 Previous Work

POMDP planning has a very extensive literature that spans decades. Important highlights include the realization that value functions are piecewise-linear and convex (PWLC) and can thus be approximated by a PWLC function [5]. Algorithms such as Witness [6] or Incremental Pruning [7] actively select and discard vectors that correctly approximate the optimal value function. Anytime algorithms include HSVI [8], which follows heuristics derived from upper and lower bounds of the value function, PBVI [9], which carefully selects belief update points and SARSOP [10], that avoids non-reachable beliefs. PBVI and SARSOP were actually tested in limited robotic applications or similar scenarios, but all of these algorithms are restricted to POMDP's so small, they fail to represent most robot planning scenarios.

Instead, POMCP follows a generative model approach through a POMDP simulator and an adapted version of UCT [3]. Its key contributions are approximating the current belief state using an unweighted particle filter, and expanding a tree of histories instead of a tree of states. This combination successfully addresses the *curse of dimensionality* and makes it possible to perform online planning in large POMDP's. Because this is a key improvement, this paper assumes a belief-state approximator and focuses on states with partially observable elements, instead of explicit belief states. The concept of mixed observability has produced positive results even outside of MCTS algorithms [11]. A similar Partially Observable UCT-based algorithm with more detailed belief selection also exists [12].

In order to address the state-space complexity of large POMDP's, well known techniques include clustering states and generalizing state or belief values [9, 13], function approximation [14] and random forest model learning [15]. These methods are based on fixed aggregation criteria that do not respond to the connection between states and goals, and despite (some of them) being anytime algorithms they still follow the slow belief tree search approach.

It is also possible to generate abstractions for planning and learning over hierarchies of actions [16,17]. This is inconvenient for general planning, as relatively detailed, prior knowledge of the domain is required to manually create these hierarchies. Recent work however shows a promising way to automatically construct action hierarchies [18].

Planning algorithms for MDP's and POMDP's often overlap with reinforcement learning (RL) methods, with the difference that in RL the agent must find an optimal policy while discovering and learning the transition dynamics. Reward shaping is commonly used in RL to improve an agent's performance by awarding additional rewards for certain preferred actions, implicitly defining subgoals. This generates a decision process with a different reward distribution and therefore different convergence properties, but potential-based reward shaping (PBRS) has been shown to preserve policy optimality [19]. A study of PBRS in the context of online POMDP planning can be found in [20].

Building on these arguments, this paper reflects our efforts to provide a general-purpose, PBRS bias for action selection under uncertainty, in order to address the complexity of planning in large domains using only partial information, as is the case of robotics.

## 4 Measuring Goal Proximity

An ideally efficient planning algorithm should quickly separate *good* or promising states from *bad* or unwanted states. In other words, it should quickly prefer states that lead to the goal and avoid a large number of those that don't. Most planning domains, even those without clearly specified goals (eg. pure RL tasks), have terminal states or conditions that specify what must be accomplished and, to some extent, what subgoals the agent should pursue. In robotics, it is reasonable to assume planning agents are somewhat informed and aware of at least part of their goal(s). Any sufficiently detailed state description (such as a feature vector) provides information to compute, for any given state, some numerical score representing how many features in the terminal state have already been accomplished. The larger this number is, the closer this state is to being a terminal or a goal state. We call this idea *partial goal satisfaction* (PGS), formalized in Eq. 1. A previous version of this section, including equations, was published in [4].

PGS is simple to implement for fully observable features, which can be easily counted in meaningful ways (Eq. 2). For partially observable features, information gathering actions should increase the probability that their current, estimated value is correct, thus also affecting the probability of an agent being in some given state ($b(s)$). In other words, collecting information about a given set of partially-observable features yields a better estimate of the world's current, true state. The simplest, most general approach is therefore measuring some form of uncertainty or entropy and providing rewards as this uncertainty is reduced (Eq. 3). Let $s \in S$ be a state, decomposed into countable discrete features $s_i$, $G_+$ be the set containing the observable features present in the goal, $G_-$ the set of observable restrictions, $\Delta(s)$ the set of states reachable from $s$ (similar to the transitive closure of $T(s, \cdot)$) and $G_p$ the set of partially or non-observable elements, then:

$$\text{pgs}(s) = \sum_{s_i \notin G_p} v(s_i) + \sum_{s_j \in G_p} w(s_j) \tag{1}$$

where:

$$v(s_i) = \begin{cases} 1 & \text{iff } s_i \in G_+ \\ x \in (0,1) & \text{iff } \exists s' \in \Delta(s) \text{ s.t.:} \\ & \quad s'_k \in s' \wedge s'_k \in G_+ \\ 0 & \text{iff } s_i \notin \{G_+ \cup G_-\} \\ -1 & \text{iff } s_i \in G_- \end{cases} \tag{2}$$

and

$$w(s_j) = \begin{cases} 0 & \text{iff } H(s_j) \leqslant T_H \\ -1 & \text{otherwise} \end{cases} \tag{3}$$

This means the different features in each state are evaluated depending on whether they are partially observable ($s_j \in G_p$) or not. Positive, observable features add points and negative features deduct points. State changes that lead to a positive feature ($s'_k \in G_+$) in a future state ($s' \in \Delta(s)$) yield a fraction of a point and help implicitly define subgoals (eg. interacting with an object referenced in the goal, such as picking up the coffee cup that goes on the table), and if no relevant features are present no points are awarded or taken. Partially-observable features are scored based on the entropy of their underlying distribution, punishing features or states with high entropy. Whenever enough information is gathered and the entropy is reduced below some threshold $T_H$, this punishment is removed. This encourages the agent to quickly get rid of this penalty by executing a number of information gathering actions, which in turn may lead to discovering new reward sources (eg. interacting with relevant but previously unrecognized elements). In principle any combination of the individual elements in the goal may be considered a subgoal for scoring purposes, and only completing all of them simultaneously yields the total, problem-defined terminal reward. This scoring is derived from a clearly specified goal, which should always available to a planning agent or robot. Some very specific problems, however, might also benefit from introducing some amount of domain information.

PGS may be useful in different contexts, but it is intended as an optimistic value initialization method that allows an agent to identify subgoals and exploit immediate opportunities if available. As such, it addresses action selection under uncertainty, not the full planning problem. Using PGS directly to solve classical planning problems, such as some Blocks World configuration, may result in overly greedy actions. As explained in the next subsections, PGS is intended to be used as a reward bonus in planning algorithms, and as a rollout policy in the context of Monte-Carlo or similar planning algorithms, where optimistic assumptions will eventually be corrected (if they're wrong) and the problem solved properly.

### 4.1 PGS in Reward Shaping

Reward shaping is a well-known technique used to improve the performance of (PO)MDP algorithms and RL problems. It works by adding a small, additional reward to some state transitions, encouraging the agent to choose certain *implicitly* preferred actions. In practice, the amount of reward bonus often comes from an in-depth analysis of the structure of the problem and provides some form of heuristic bias in action selection. In our case, instead of providing explicit, domain-dependent knowledge to shape rewards, we use the PGS function to encourage the agent to pursue courses of action leading to the completion of subgoals. The reward bonus produces a new reward distribution and therefore a potentially different problem, one with additional reward sources. Following the PBRS form however, guarantees the introduction of implicit subgoals doesn't affect the algorithm's convergence and, therefore, policies are transferable to the original problem.

Reward shaping substitutes the usual reward function in an MDP with:

$$R(s, a, s') + F(s, a, s') \tag{4}$$

where $R$ is the problem-defined reward distribution and $F$ is a reward bonus. If $F$ has the form

$$F(s, a, s') = \gamma\phi(s') - \phi(s) \tag{5}$$

then it is a potential function and Eq. 4 is potential-based. We now define $\phi(s)$ for PGS as

$$\phi(s) = \alpha \mathrm{pgs}(s) \tag{6}$$

where $\alpha$ a scaling factor. Because most (PO)MDP algorithms already use $\gamma$ to refer to the discount factor, from now on we will refer to $\gamma_{\text{PGS}}$ when in the context of PBRS. In practice, transitions to states that are *closer* to a subgoal (positive reward source) will produce a positive difference, transitions to states that are farther from subgoals generate a negative difference, and other transitions cancel each other out. Normally reward shaping functions are highly specific for particular problems, but PGS manages to attain simplicity and generality.

### 4.2 PGS as a Rollout Policy

Monte-Carlo Tree Search algorithms, such as UCT and POMCP, work by sampling sequences of states from a probabilistic transition model. A tree of states (or in the case of POMCP a tree of histories) is progressively expanded and the average returns and visit counts are maintained per tree node. When enough statistics are available (eg. all known successors of a state have been visited) the UCB1 rule is used to select an action. When a new state is discovered, a rollout or random simulation is performed and its outcome used as an initial value estimation. Rollout policies are therefore largely responsible for the performance of MCTS online planning algorithms. Using PGS as a rollout policy, the agent quickly focuses on actions that directly contribute to the completion of (sub)goals and, likewise, avoids undesirable actions. Selecting actions that maximize state-to-goal proximity can implicitly summarize a very rich array of knowledge and heuristics, that must otherwise be given explicitly. To the best of our knowledge, the effect of evaluating goal proximity within the context of Monte-Carlo rollouts hasn't yet been systematically studied.

Using PGS as a rollout policy is very simple: Let $s$ be the current state and $\mathcal{A}$ a set of actions. Then select the action $a \in \mathcal{A}$ leading to the state $s' \leftarrow (s, a)$ that satisfies the largest amount of subgoals, where ties are broken randomly. The action selection policy is formalized in Eq. 7:

$$\mathcal{A}(s) = \arg\max_{a} \text{pgs}(s' \leftarrow (s, a)) \tag{7}$$

In line with the goal-based approach, $\mathcal{A}$ could be defined as the action set consisting of legal actions and uncertainty reducing actions, avoiding information gathering actions if their effects do not provide more information (eg. if feature $j \in s$ affected by such action already satisfies $H(s_j) \leqslant T_H$). For example, avoid action "*scan object* 3" during rollouts if there is enough information to assume it is a cup.

Because PGS is computed as a difference between the current and previous states (Eq. 5), when $\gamma_{\text{PGS}} = 1$ only newly completed subgoals produce positive values. For example imagine a robot tasked with collecting and delivering a cup of coffee: during planning, standing next to the cup offers the possibility of picking it up, satisfying a subgoal that yields a reward bonus, therefore becoming the preferred action of the rollout policy. Once holding it, dropping the cup in any place other than the correct location reverts this condition and produces a negative reward, meaning it will never be chosen in a rollout (albeit eventually during simulation, if all actions are systematically sampled). Online Monte-Carlo planning produces an action recommendation only after arbitrarily many simulations have been carried out, but starting out with the (seemingly) right action greatly improves performance. Unlike with PGS, improved rollout policies often rely on manually designed heuristics and explicit preferred actions.

# 5 Results

We tested PGS in two well-known and commonly used benchmark problems, as well as a new problem introduced in this paper. The first one is known as the "Taxi domain", and it defines a fully observable MDP useful to test basic functionality. The second is Rocksample, a POMDP that can be scaled up to fairly large state spaces. The third problem, explained in more detail below, is called Cellar and is a derivation of Rocksample with additional objects, observations and a different reward distribution, in an attempt to more closely resemble robotic planning. For the taxi problem we implemented our own version of UCT, and for the last two we modified the POMCP source code. All tests ran on a desktop workstation with an Intel i7-4790 CPU, 20 GB RAM and Debian GNU/Linux, and both planners are programmed in C++.

The challenge for robot planning under uncertainty is achieving good performance within a finite horizon, fast enough, even in large problems. These scenarios show the performance of PGS using limited resources (very few or relatively few Monte-Carlo simulations) and how it scales in considerably large POMDP's.

Some of the results presented in this section were previously published in [4]. Subsection 5.1, however, contains additional experiments and Subsect. 5.3 (Cellar domain) is completely new.

## 5.1 Taxi Domain

The taxi domain, first proposed in [17], is a simple, fully-observable MDP often used to test planning and learning algorithms. The taxi agent moves in any of four directions in a $5 \times 5$ grid and must pick up a passenger located in one of four possible depots, and bring it to another depot. A slight variation is the "fickle taxi" in which movement is non-deterministic: with a small probability (eg. $p = 0.1$) the taxi will end up East or West of its intended direction. Possible actions are moving North, East, South or West, collecting a passenger when standing on the same grid cell or dropping the passenger (when carrying one). Rewards are $-1$ for each regular move, $-10$ for dropping the passenger in the wrong location and 20 for delivering a passenger correctly, which also terminates the episode. We chose one instance of the taxi domain and obtained the total discounted reward of its optimal policy, 8.652 (with $\gamma = 0.95$), in order to compare it with the experimental results. This particular configuration and in general the taxi domain are illustrated in Fig. 1, where the dark cell at the top left corner is the goal depot where the passenger must be dropped. The walls shown in the picture are also included in the experiment which means the agent's movement is restricted, in cells next to walls, to only open, adjacent cells.

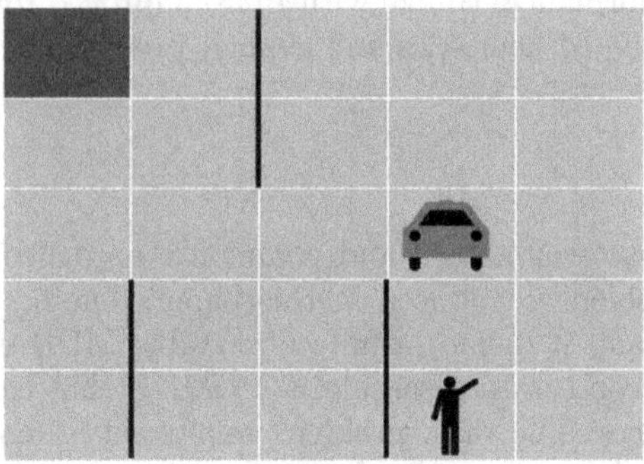

**Fig. 1.** The taxi domain. Source: [4].

Because all elements are fully observable, PGS in the taxi domain is easy to formalize. We simply award 0.25 points for picking up the passenger and 1 point for dropping it at the correct depot ($G_+$). There are no restrictions ($G_- = \emptyset$). The terminal state reward is preserved but PGS reward substitution is used for the rest, with $\gamma_{\text{PGS}} = 1$ and $\alpha = 10$ to reflect the punishment for illegally dropping a passenger. Finally, a discount factor of $\gamma = 0.95$ and search depth of 90 steps were used within UCT. It is common to allow the taxi to start only over a depot, but in our experiments it could be anywhere on the grid. We ran UCT with PGS in both (regular and fickle) versions of the taxi domain, and obtained the average discounted rewards and running times over 1000 runs. Table 1 shows the result of repeated runs on the fixed task (Fig. 1) and a set of randomly generated episodes (randomized origin and destination depots, and taxi starting location) using 1024 simulations, extremely few for Monte-Carlo standards.

**Table 1.** Performance in the taxi domain with 1024 simulations. Source: [4].

| Transition | Episodes | Avg. return | Time |
|---|---|---|---|
| Normal | Fixed | 6.161 | 3.049 |
| | Random | 4.257 | 3.531 |
| Fickle | Fixed | 3.275 | 4.410 |
| | Random | 2.138 | 4.176 |

Results are promising if we compare the average discounted reward with the optimal policy in the fixed (non fickle) task (8.652). Restricting the amount of computation to only 256 simulations per move (≈1.6 s. per episode), the PGS-based planner achieved an average discounted reward of 5.089. On random tasks it is important to mention that episodes were terminated after 5 s., but their (negative) reward still averaged.

Averaging performance, especially in stochastic domains, may hide interesting details of particularly good runs. We ran a separate batch of 1000 episodes using 1024 simulations, of which 616 finished in 2 s. or less and 797 in 3 s. or less. In these test the statistical mode was the maximum discounted reward (8.652), meaning most runs found the optimal policy.

Finally, Fig. 2 shows how the PGS method scaled in the Taxi domain. Performance was averaged over 1000 randomly generated runs, with a more strict acting budget of 35 steps but a more generous timeout per episode of 30 s. to allow for enough planning time with up to 8192 simulations. PGS quickly achieved satisfactory performance, even with very few simulations which translates into a very short planning time (shown at the top). We don't include comparative results with plain UCT (without PGS) because, in practice, it required (comparatively) excessive amounts of time and simulations to achieve even little improvements in performance.

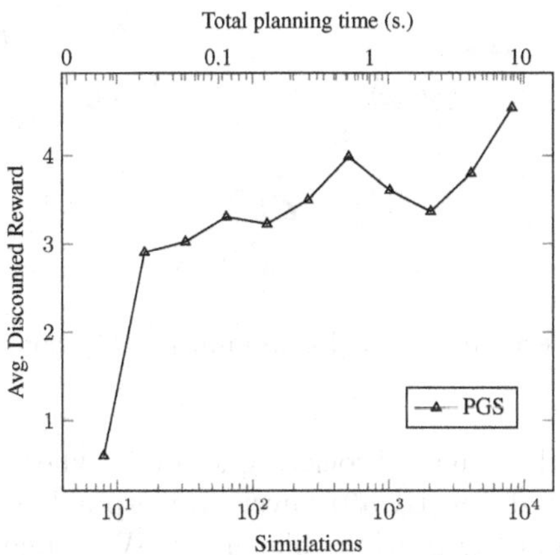


**Fig. 2.** Performance in the Taxi domain.

These results show how performance can be substantially improved in fully observable tasks by following a goal-driven, action selection method that implicitly exploits the problem structure. In the following subsections, we present results in problems with partial observability.

## 5.2 Rocksample

*Rocksample*, originally found in [8], is a commonly used problem that roughly simulates a Mars rover tasked with collecting valuable rocks. This problem corresponds to a POMDP in which the location of the agent and the rocks are known, but the value of these rocks is initially unknown and must be determined by the use of a noisy sensor that returns one of two observations, *good* or *bad*, with a given reliability. *Rocksample*$[n, k]$ defines an $n \times n$ grid with $k$ rocks, where the agent may move in any of four directions, sample a rock if standing directly on top of it, or use the sensor on any rock (action $check_i$ for rock $i$) for a total of $5 + k$ actions (see Fig. 3). Rewards are 10 for sampling good rocks, $-10$ for sampling bad rocks, 10 for exiting (East) and $-100$ for leaving the grid in any other direction [8]. We used POMCP as a POMDP solver [3], but modified it to test our proposal.

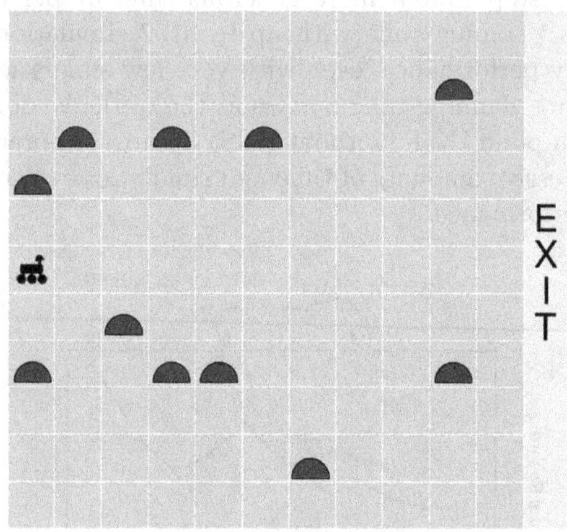


**Fig. 3.** Special layout for Rocksample[11, 11]. Source: [4].

POMCP uses slightly enhanced rocksample states, where the probability that a rock is good is updated directly after every corresponding *check* action, using the sensor efficiency and the previous likelihood. We defined $C = G_+ \cap G_-$ to be the set of collected rocks, and $G_p$ the remaining rocks. Scoring function $v(s_i)$ returns 1 for good rocks with good observations ($G_+$) and $-1$ for bad rocks ($G_-$). Function $w(s_j)$ returns $-1$ if $H_b(p_r) > 0.5$, that is, if the binary entropy of rock $r$ ($s_j$) is higher than 0.5. POMCP comes with a preferred actions policy, which uses manually encoded heuristics such as "head North if there are rocks with more positive observations" or "check rocks that have been measured less than five times and have less than two positive observations". Clearly, PGS succeeds in avoiding this level of over specification.

We used $\gamma_{\text{PGS}} = 1$ and $\alpha = 10$ (to reflect the difference in rewards received when sampling good and bad rocks). This scoring function deducts points for undesirable states (eg. collecting bad rocks, high entropy for any rock) and only adds points when collecting good rocks, but further negative points are withdrawn once the knowledge about any particular rock increases (i.e. entropy $< 0.5$). In practice this means that during rollouts *check* will be preferred if it reduces entropy for some rock, that *sample* will be preferred when standing over a promising rock, and that otherwise movement actions will be considered.

We compared three different policies: uniformly random with legal moves ("legal" in POMCP), explicit preferred actions ("smart" in POMCP) and our own, "PGS". Figure 4 shows the discounted rewards averaged over 1000 runs for all three policies in *rocksample* [11, 11], [15, 15], and the large [25, 25] and [12, 25], with up to 2048 Monte-Carlo simulations per move.

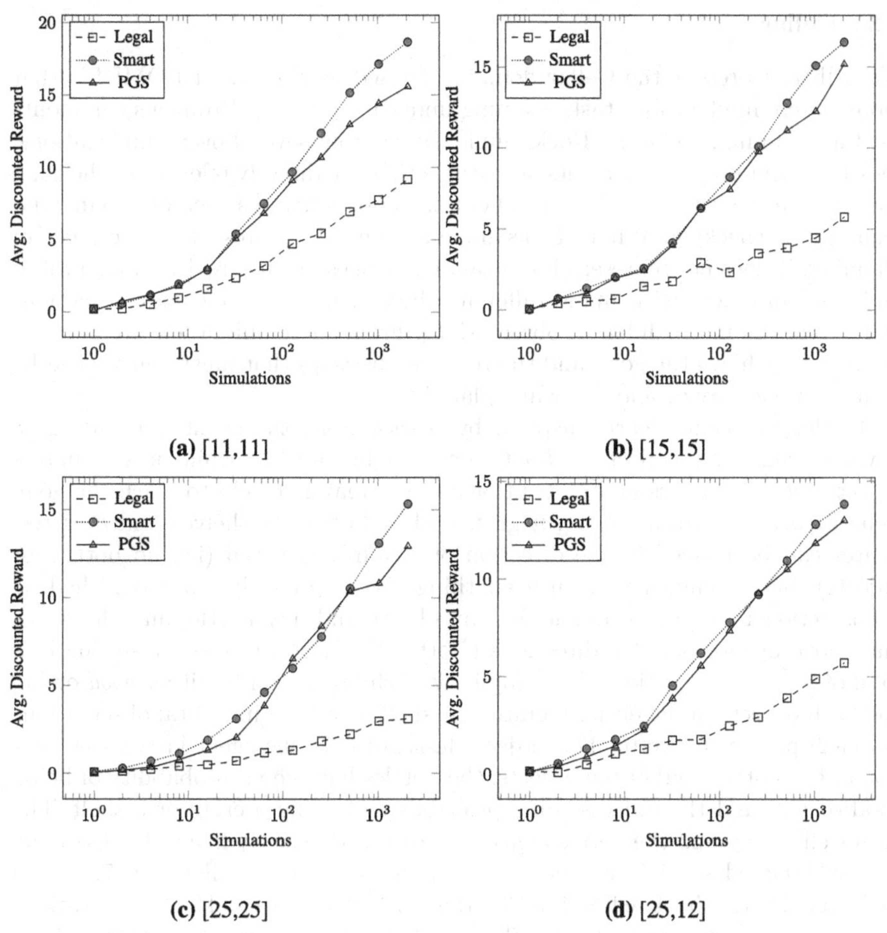


**Fig. 4.** Performance in Rocksample. Source: [4].

PGS clearly outperforms the legal policy and is only slightly outmatched by the smart policy. This difference however reduces as the problem size increases, particularly in [25, 25], a very large problem for *rocksample* standards and in [25, 12], an equally large grid but with fewer reward sources. Estimating the PGS value of derived states for every action in our rollout policy may be somewhat computationally expensive, particularly when all or many actions are available, since it trades off simulations for runtime. Results show, however, this pays off compared to the random policy: with $\approx 2.5$ s of computation in *rocksample*[25, 12], the legal rollout policy achieves a discounted reward of 5.713 with 2048 simulations, whereas PGS collects 7.35 with only 128 simulations. A faster implementation for planning onboard robots might be necessary, but also a shallower planning depth may be used (the experiments used a depth of 90 steps).

### 5.3 Cellar

We will now present the Cellar domain, devised as a series of POMDP's that more closely model robot task-planning under uncertainty. Problems commonly used in planning, including Rocksample, suffer from several oversimplifications: they represent only the elements or features that are directly relevant to the goal, and make unrealistic assumptions about the cost of actions such of moving and scanning or checking. While Rocksample succeeds at representing the goals of planning, it does not represent important challenges: in the "real world", a robot finds and interacts with many different objects, it has many possible actions and it receives many different observations. From these only a few are actually relevant to achieve the goal, and the rest are obstacles that must nonetheless be addressed one way or another while planning.

In this problem, clearly inspired by Rocksample, the agent must navigate a wine cellar and collect *at least one* valuable bottle, while it encounters objects such as shelves and crates that may or may not help to reach the goal. Cellar$[n, k, s, c]$ defines an $n \times n$ grid, with $k$ bottles, $s$ shelves and $c$ crates. Crates can be pushed in the direction of any free grid cell (i.e. no bottles or objects), but attempting to push anything else is (more heavily) punished. A *check* action is always available for any object and any bottle, and the agent may move in four possible directions (North, West, South, East) resulting in a total of $9 + k + s + c$ actions. For simplicity, each bottle can be either *good* or *bad* and each object can be either a crate or a shelf, resulting in 4 total observations but each pair exclusive to their object class. Initially the agent knows the location of the bottles and of the objects, the bottles have equal probability of being good or bad and the objects equal probability of being a crate or a shelf. The sensor efficiency and the derived *check* actions work exactly like in Rocksample.

We designed special layouts for two cases of interest: Cellar[7, 8, 7, 8] and Cellar[11, 11, 15, 15]. The first is a POMDP with 32 actions and $2 \times 2$ observations resulting in a state space of more than $10^{15}$ states. The second problem defines a POMDP with 50 actions, $2 \times 2$ observations, and a seriously large state space: approximately $10^{31}$. In comparison, Rocksample[11, 11] has 247,808 states and Rocksample[25, 25], approximately $10^{10}$ states. The larger Cellar problem is illustrated in Fig. 5, where the tall rectangles represent shelves, the short squares represent crates, and the bottles are shown in dark red.

The reward distribution for the Cellar problem is +10 for collecting a good bottle, −10 for collecting a bad bottle, +10 for the terminal state (leaving the

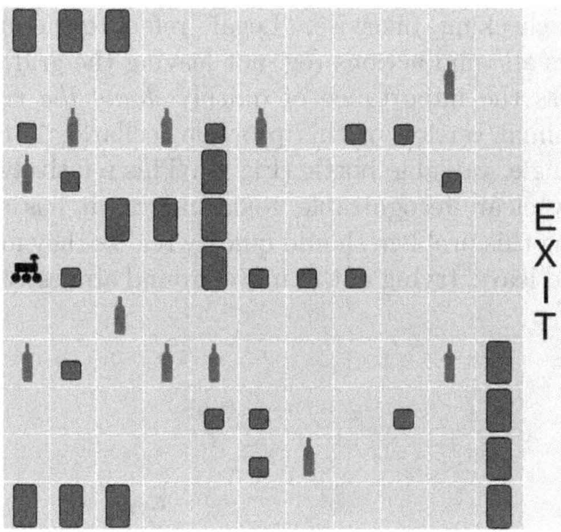


**Fig. 5.** Layout of Cellar[11, 11, 15, 15]. (Color figure online)

grid to the East with at least one good bottle), −0.5 for checking, −1 per movement step, −2 for pushing crates and −10 for pushing anything else. This distribution reflects our attempts to better capture robot planning, where no action is truly free and some actions (such as pushing) can be relatively expensive even if they are necessary. Additionally, rewards implicitly relate to the goal and in domains as complex as this one, time restrictions with free actions can lead to undesirable (yet rational) behavior such as spending the allotted time performing only *check* actions and not moving or sampling, thus minimizing the loss in the total cumulative reward but not actually reaching a terminal state. This type of behavior may result in very poor policies with deceivingly acceptable performance (not much reward loss), a detail lost when presenting only average performance tables.

PGS scoring in Cellar is equivalent to its Rocksample counterpart: collecting valuable or non-valuable bottles yields its respective fully-observable points, and uncertainty about bottles yields equivalent punishments. Uncertainty about objects such as shelves and crates should not be punished however, because they do not form part of the goal. Rewarding (or lifting the punishment) for *checking* objects encourages the agent to acquire potentially unnecessary knowledge and to execute many, relatively expensive actions. An interesting challenge, to be addressed in future work, is deciding when to gather information about surrounding objects. That is, identifying which non goal-related, information-gathering actions actually contribute to increasing the total reward.

Unlike in Rocksample, however, during rollouts we consider only movement, sampling, pushing and uncertainty-reducing *checks*, meaning we don't check objects that already meet the entropy requirements. We adapted the preferred actions in the "Smart" Rocksample policy (included with POMCP) so that the same movement, checking and sampling heuristics apply, and added equivalent heuristics for object checking. Likewise, "Legal" refers to the uniformly random policy that considers all valid actions (eg. not leaving the grid).

In order to stress the importance of quickly *doing the right thing*, let us first consider a minimal version of this problem, cellar[5, 1, 0, 4], where four crates surround a single, valuable bottle (Fig. 6). This relatively straightforward POMDP has a very clear, recognizable goal, and yet it has around 6 million states. Agents solving this problem should quickly realize they must push a crate, collect the bottle and leave, trying not to move around aimlessly or unnecessarily checking and pushing.

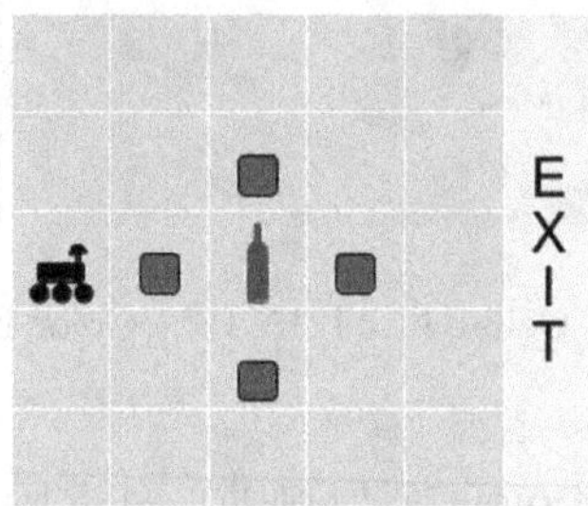


**Fig. 6.** Minimal Cellar example.

Figure 7 shows the performance of all three policies in the minimal version of the Cellar domain. The total discounted return was averaged over 100 runs with up to 2048 Monte-Carlo simulations per step and discount $\gamma = 0.99$, t. In this problem, after 128 simulations PGS dramatically outperformed the two other action selection policies. Out of the 100 runs, PGS reached the terminal state in 97 of them with only 512 simulations, and with 1024 simulations or more, 99 runs reached the terminal state. Non-terminal runs ended when the agent spent its allotted *acting* budget, set to a generous 100 steps. The heuristic policy was capable of terminating a maximum of 64 times, whereas the random policy a maximum of only 37 despite having a similar mean discounted reward. In this configuration the low bar set by the terminal state is actually informative given that there is exactly one bottle to collect.

The comparative performance of PGS in the larger Cellar problems is shown in Fig. 8, averaged over 100 runs with up to 8192 Monte-Carlo simulations per move, with a large acting budget of 500 steps. In cellar[7, 8, 7, 8] we used a discount factor of $\gamma = 0.99$, but chose a discount factor of $\gamma = 0.95$ in cellar[11, 11, 15, 15] in order to make the problem slightly more manageable by reducing the search horizon (which also results in a different range of rewards).

These results in the full Cellar problems show how PGS scaled in very large, task-planning POMDP's. In the first case (Fig. 8a) with very few simulations PGS already performed slightly better than two other policies, and with more simulations it clearly outperformed the random and the heuristic policies by a fair margin. Interestingly, PGS was also faster than Smart: in less than half the

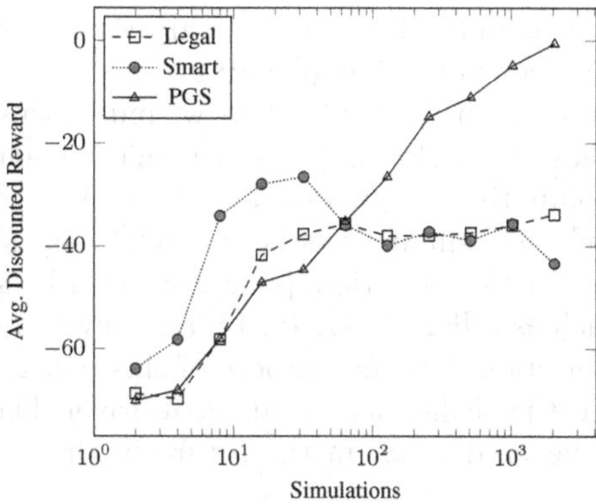


**Fig. 7.** Performance in cellar[5, 1, 0, 4].

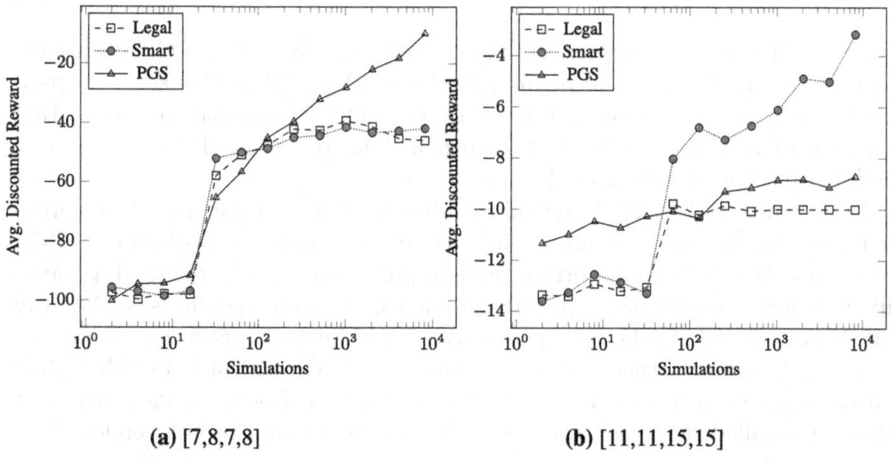


**(a)** [7,8,7,8] **(b)** [11,11,15,15]

**Fig. 8.** Performance in the Cellar domain.

time, it gathered more discounted reward and achieved a much higher terminal state count.

In the second case (Fig. 8b), PGS improved upon the overall performance achieved by the random policy and, with very few simulations, achieved comparatively better performance than both competing policies. However, due to the extremely large state-space and branching factor of this POMDP, it didn't scale as well as the manually designed, heuristic policy. The Legal policy, on the other hand, quickly settled on a low, local maximum performance possibly limited by its uninformed, uniformly random sampling. It must be noted that due to the size of the second problem there's little difference in the total discounted reward across the three policies, up to the maximum amount of simulations used, which suggests we might essentially be looking at the beginning of the plot. Perhaps if significantly more simulations were used, sizable differences in performance would appear, but that amount of computational resources and response times are already outside the scope of *online* planning.

In order to transfer these methods to robots we must focus on quickly achieving a significant increase in performance, since we're attempting to minimize response time (and computing resources). This type of reasonably satisfactory behavior with relatively few simulations is precisely what should be expected from a more informed action-selection policy. Efficiently solving large task-planning problems, such as cellar[11, 11, 15, 15] and beyond, requires more than "just" better action selection. For the purpose of this paper, the Cellar domain allowed us to measure the scalability of our goal-driven bias in very complex scenarios, but it will be used again in the future in the context of managing state complexity.

## 6 Conclusions and Discussion

Our experimental results show that despite its simplicity, PGS effectively improves the performance of planning in large (PO)MDP's, thanks to its goal-driven approach to action selection. In the fully observable problem (Taxi domain), PGS achieved a level of performance far out of reach for a uniformly random policy in standard UCT.

In domains with partial and mixed observability and particularly in problems with scarce reward sources, such as larger versions of Rocksample, PGS easily outperformed the uniformly random policy and closely followed a manually designed, heuristic policy. In such problems, the random policy scaled poorly and domain knowledge became necessary to achieve good performance quickly. We showed, however, that with barely any domain-dependent knowledge, PGS can be competitive with a manually designed action-selection policy even if it relies on detailed, heuristic knowledge. This type of domain-independent bias is essential for planning and acting in complex domains, and estimating the information gain of uncertainty-reducing actions may be necessary to correctly address large robotic planning domains, avoiding less useful choices.

The second partially observable domain, Cellar, showed the performance of a goal-driven bias in action selection when planning in very large domains with obstacles, unnecessary actions and a more realistic reward distribution. The minimalistic version of this domain underlines the importance of quickly identifying reward sources and choosing actions that lead to them, which both the uniform and heuristic policies failed to do. The larger problems constitute a much more complicated optimization challenge that nonetheless benefits from goal-oriented behavior, as shown by the performance of PGS in cellar[7, 8, 7, 8]. As mentioned in the previous section, the largest of these problems requires more refined mechanisms that directly address the state complexity. In principle for any given planning problem it is possible to design a detailed and extremely efficient heuristic rollout policy using domain knowledge, in the spirit of "Smart", and it should perform and scale relatively well. However general-purpose planning under uncertainty, especially onboard robots, cannot rely on manually designed, domain-dependent heuristics. When solving practical, well-understood problems in controlled scenarios, the combination of both domain-knowledge and goal-driven action selection might produce very promising results.

In general we can identify three main approaches for speeding up planning in large stochastic domains: (1) Action hierarchies that produce smaller, abstract MDP's and then transfer these solutions to the base MDP. a minimal version of (2) State abstractions that group states together so their values are shared and the values of unknown states, approximated. a minimal version of (3) PBRS, that forces an agent to focus on good action prospects, avoiding potentially costly choices. Current techniques for both action and state abstraction rely on fixed criteria that might cause a planner to traverse many unique states anyway, which is the challenge addressed by PGS. We attempt to quickly identify reward sources and back propagate scaled partial rewards, using as little domain knowledge as possible but exploiting an agent's knowledge of its own goals.

As previously stated, this work is only part of our efforts to introduce the notion of relevance in task planning. Future work includes designing *dynamic* value approximation and/or state aggregation methods derived from this methodology, as well as limiting the amount of reachable states to those that directly contribute to the goal. In order to transfer these methods to real-world robotic tasks, it will also be necessary to map continuous to discrete state representation. We argue that similar to PGS, dimensionality reduction techniques should consider criteria derived from the goal (something that, as far as we know, hasn't been tried yet).

In order to obtain the results presented in this paper we experimented extensively on the three domains, using different parameters and observing different types of behavior when such parameters were modified. It is very well known that UCT is sensitive to certain important variables, such as the number of simulations per step, the search horizon or discount factor, and the exploration rate in UCB1 action selection. The really significant leap in performance for any kind of planning agent (human, program or robot) however, comes from an appropriate modeling or understanding of the domain, including available actions and goals. In problems such as cellar[5, 1, 0, 4] we can as humans intuitively understand, very quickly, what needs to be done and promptly suggest a sufficiently good plan (maybe even optimal), despite the almost 6 million possible states and the much, much larger belief space. Similar problems in larger grids (eg. imagine cellar[50, 1, 0, 4]) have exponentially larger state and belief spaces (approximately $10^{17}$ states) and yet the problem structure is essentially the same. The agent must "simply" focus on a few good states and actions, and avoid the rest (large empty grids can in fact be simplified with state aggregation and action hierarchies). It seems, then, that efficient planning requires more than just evaluating many reachable states and beliefs.

Often the perceived complexity of planning problems is justified based on their worst-case computational complexity, which is a direct function of the number of states. Planning problems however are defined not only in terms of their transition dynamics, but also in terms of some implicit or explicit goal, so the intrinsic relationship between the values of states and their proximity to the goal (or subgoals) must be considered. An efficient planning algorithm should quickly identify the gaps in the different state values, in order to separate good states from bad states, and focus on the good ones. These values come uniquely from perceived (or simulated) rewards. Because the value of a state is the average discounted return of its children, it might be difficult to differentiate promising states from less promising ones early on, when the agent is simply too far (in terms of state or belief transitions) from any source of reward and doesn't have enough knowledge or statistics to decide. However, if an agent finds itself initially "close" to its goal or a reward source (eg. a few actions away), the problem should be simple to address or even solve if the appropriate actions are chosen, regardless of the number of reachable states and beliefs.

We designed PGS, a simple and straightforward action selection bias, as an attempt to exploit these observations. Experimental results indicate that it performs and scales well even in large domains, and underline the importance of goal-oriented behavior. We expect this type of relevance-driven methodology to improve the performance of online planning under uncertainty in robots and similar agents, that must quickly act with only limited information despite the complexity of "real-world" problems.

**Acknowledgements.** We would like to thank our colleagues Sebastian Pütz and Felix Igelbrink for their suggested reward distribution in the Cellar domain, and the DAAD for supporting this work with a research grant.

## References

1. Kocsis, L., Szepesvári, C.: Bandit based Monte-Carlo planning. In: Fürnkranz, J., Scheffer, T., Spiliopoulou, M. (eds.) ECML 2006. LNCS (LNAI), vol. 4212, pp. 282–293. Springer, Heidelberg (2006). https://doi.org/10.1007/11871842_29
2. Auer, P., Cesa-Bianchi, N., Fischer, P.: Finite-time analysis of the multiarmed bandit problem. Mach. Learn. **47**, 235–256 (2002)
3. Silver, D., Veness, J.: Monte-Carlo planning in large POMDPs. Adv. Neural Inf. Process. Syst. **23**, 2164–2172 (2010)
4. Saborío, J.C., Hertzberg, J.: Towards domain-independent biases for action selection in robotic task-planning under uncertainty. In: Proceedings of the 10th International Conference on Agents and Artificial Intelligence, ICAART, INSTICC, vol. 2, pp. 85–93. SciTePress (2018)
5. Smallwood, R.D., Sondik, E.J.: The optimal control of partially observable Markov processes over a finite Horizon. Oper. Res. **21**, 1071–1088 (1973)
6. Cassandra, A.R., Kaelbling, L.P., Littman, M.L.: Acting optimally in partially observable stochastic domains. In: Proceedings of the 12th National Conference on Artificial Intelligence, Seattle, WA, USA, 31 July – 4 August, vol. 2, pp. 1023–1028 (1994)
7. Cassandra, A.R., Littman, M.L., Zhang, N.L.: Incremental pruning: a simple, fast, exact method for partially observable markov decision processes. In: Proceedings of the Thirteenth Conference on Uncertainty in Artificial Intelligence, UAI 1997, Brown University, Providence, Rhode Island, USA, 1–3 August 1997, pp. 54–61 (1997)

8. Smith, T., Simmons, R.: Heuristic search value iteration for POMDPs. In: Proceedings of the 20th Conference on Uncertainty in Artificial Intelligence, UAI 2004, pp. 520–527. AUAI Press, Arlington (2004)
9. Pineau, J., Gordon, G.J., Thrun, S.: Anytime point-based approximations for large POMDPs. J. Artif. Intell. Res. **27**, 335–380 (2006)
10. Kurniawati, H., Hsu, D., Lee, W.S.: SARSOP: efficient point-based POMDP planning by approximating optimally reachable belief spaces. In: Robotics: Science and Systems IV, Eidgenössische Technische Hochschule Zürich, Zurich, Switzerland, 25–28 June 2008 (2008)
11. Ong, S.C.W., Png, S.W., Hsu, D., Lee, W.S.: Planning under uncertainty for robotic tasks with mixed observability. Int. J. Rob. Res. **29**, 1053–1068 (2010)
12. Somani, A., Ye, N., Hsu, D., Lee, W.S.: DESPOT: online POMDP planning with regularization. In: Burges, C.J.C., Bottou, L., Welling, M., Ghahramani, Z., Weinberger, K.Q. (eds.) Advances in Neural Information Processing Systems, vol. 26, pp. 1772–1780. Curran Associates, Inc. (2013)
13. Pineau, J., Gordon, G., Thrun, S.: Policy-contingent abstraction for robust robot control. In: Proceedings of the Nineteenth Conference on Uncertainty in Artificial Intelligence, UAI 2003, pp. 477–484. Morgan Kaufmann Publishers Inc., San Francisco (2003)
14. Sutton, R.S., Barto, A.G.: Reinforcement Learning: An Introduction, 2nd edn. MIT Press, Cambridge (2012). (to be published)
15. Hester, T., Stone, P.: TEXPLORE: real-time sample-efficient reinforcement learning for robots. Mach. Learn. **90**, 385–429 (2013)
16. Sutton, R., Precup, D., Singh, S.: Between MDPs and semi-MDPs: a framework for temporal abstraction in reinforcement learning. Artif. Intell. **112**, 181–211 (1999)
17. Dietterich, T.G.: Hierarchical reinforcement learning with the MAXQ value function decomposition. J. Artif. Intell. Res. **13**, 227–303 (2000)
18. Konidaris, G.: Constructing abstraction hierarchies using a skill-symbol loop. In: Proceedings of the Twenty-Fifth International Joint Conference on Artificial Intelligence, IJCAI 2016, New York, NY, USA, 9–15 July 2016, pp. 1648–1654 (2016)
19. Ng, A.Y., Harada, D., Russell, S.: Policy invariance under reward transformations: theory and application to reward shaping. In: Proceedings of the Sixteenth International Conference on Machine Learning, pp. 278–287. Morgan Kaufmann (1999)
20. Eck, A., Soh, L.K., Devlin, S., Kudenko, D.: Potential-based reward shaping for finite Horizon online POMDP planning. Auton. Agents Multi-agent Syst. **30**, 403–445 (2016)

# Personalized Sentiment Analysis and a Framework with Attention-Based Hawkes Process Model

Siwen Guo[1(✉)], Sviatlana Höhn[1], Feiyu Xu[2], and Christoph Schommer[1]

[1] ILIAS Research Lab, CSC, University of Luxembourg, Esch-sur-Alzette, Luxembourg
siwen.guo@uni.lu
[2] AI Lab, Lenovo, Beijing, China

**Abstract.** People use different words when expressing their opinions. Sentiment analysis as a way to automatically detect and categorize people's opinions in text, needs to reflect this diversity and individuality. One possible approach to analyze such traits is to take a person's past opinions into consideration. In practice, such a model can suffer from the data sparsity issue, thus it is difficult to develop. In this article, we take texts from social platforms and propose a preliminary model for evaluating the effectiveness of including user information from the past, and offer a solution for the data sparsity. Furthermore, we present a finer-designed, enhanced model that focuses on frequent users and offers to capture the decay of past opinions using various gaps between the creation time of the text. An attention-based Hawkes process on top of a recurrent neural network is applied for this purpose, and the performance of the model is evaluated with Twitter data. With the proposed framework, positive results are shown which opens up new perspectives for future research.

**Keywords:** Sentiment analysis · Hawkes process
Personalized model · Attention network · Recurrent neural networks

## 1 Introduction

Sentiment analysis is defined in Oxford dictionaries[1] as 'the process of computationally identifying and categorizing opinions expressed in a piece of text, especially in order to determine whether the writer's attitude towards a particular topic, product, etc. is positive, negative, or neutral.'. This definition outlines three types of information that are essential to the study: the text, the target (topic, product, etc.) and the writer. It also reflects the evolvement of this field from document- or sentence-level [1,2] to aspect-level [3,4] which considers various aspects of a target, and later to an advanced level where the text is not

[1] https://en.oxforddictionaries.com/definition/sentiment_analysis, last seen on April 19, 2018.


J. van den Herik and A. P. Rocha (Eds.): ICAART 2018, LNAI 11352, pp. 202–222, 2019.
https://doi.org/10.1007/978-3-030-05453-3_10

the only source for determining sentiments and the diversity among the writers (or speakers, users depending on the application) is considered as well. However, the writer of a text is not necessarily the person who holds the sentiment. As in [5], the situation is elaborated with an example that a review of product (target) 'Canon G12 camera' by John Smith contains a piece of text *'I simply love it .... my wife thinks it is too heavy for her.'*. The example shows different opinions from two persons published by John Smith who thinks positively towards the target while his wife holds a negative opinion. An accurate research should involve a study that identifies the holder of a sentiment before generating a sentiment score for it. The negligence of this aspect in sentiment analysis is caused by the lack of demand in most applications where opinions are desired regardless of which persons expressing them. Nevertheless, exceptions exist for the task of establishing user groups or for security reasons where locating the holders is as prioritized as extracting opinions. To simplify the task, sentiment holder or opinion holder is mostly used to indicate the person who publishes the text when it comes to analyze individual behaviors through short messages posted on social platforms.

The significance of considering the sentiment holder is based on the observation that people are diverse and they express their sentiments in distinct ways [6]. Such diversity is caused by many factors such as linguistic and cultural background, expertise and experience. While different lexical choices are made by sentiment holders, a model that is tailored by the individual differences should be built accordingly. We name a model that includes individual differences in sentiment analysis *personalized sentiment model*. Note that we distinguish this task from personality modeling [7] where such diversity is also considered in form of linguistic features in discovering users' personality. On social platforms, another phenomenon is that the entity behind a user account is not necessarily one particular individual—it could be a public account run by a person or a group of persons who represent an organization. It is also possible for a person to have more than one account, e.g. a private account and a work account. In our work, we argue that a person may act or express himself/herself differently while using different accounts, but the way of expressing opinions by the person(s) behind one account tends to be consistent.

One critical issue of generating a model for each user individually is the data sparsity. There is an inconsistency in the frequency of posting messages on social platforms per user. For instance, it is reported in 2016 that Twitter has 700 million annually active users, of which 420 million are quarterly active and 317 million are monthly active[2]. The gap between the numbers shows that the amount of messages (also called 'tweets') published per user is normally in the range of a few to a few thousand with roughly 500 million tweets sent per day[3], and the frequency of the postings varies from user to user. In this

[2] https://www.fool.com/investing/2016/11/06/twitter-has-700-million-yearly-active-users.aspx, last seen on April 19, 2018.

[3] http://www.internetlivestats.com/twitter-statistics/#trend, last seen on April 19, 2018.

article, we introduce a framework with neural networks to model individualities in expressing opinions, which intrinsically offers a solution for the data sparsity in the setting of social networks. This framework is developed based on the first-stage results of PERSEUS [8] which evaluates the effectiveness of including users' historical text for determining the sentiment of the current text. Twitter data was used for the evaluation in the first stage and was used in the improved framework as well. However, different datasets were applied in the experiments that one was manually labeled and the other was automatically labeled and associated with more frequent users.

Major modifications are done after the first stage of PERSEUS. First, each tweet is represented by a sequence that consists of the concepts, the entities, the negation cues and the user identifier. Instead of using user identifier as a separate node, such a combination of features unifies the input structure for neural networks to extract information easier. Second, the embeddings of the tweets are learned directly through a stacked network with sentiment labels, therefore only one learning process is required. Third, an attention model is used after the recurrent layers to enhance the influence of related content from the past. Finally, the output from the attention model is shaped by Hawkes process that is used to capture the decay of information caused by various gaps between the tweets of a user. Hawkes process [9] is a special kind of point process with a 'self-exciting' character, which is widely used for modeling 'arrivals' of events over time. The usage of Hawkes process varies from earthquake modeling [10] to crime prediction [11], and to financial analysis [12]. As an example close to our study, Hawkes process is also used to predict retweets on Twitter for popularity analysis [13,14]. In our work, we argue that the chance that a user's opinion 'arrives' at a specific time point is affected by the time points at which the user expressed past opinions. While the recurrent network is used to find relations between the content of the tweets from the past, the Hawkes process is used to model the decay of such relations with time. Evaluated with a larger number of tweets of frequent users in a period of time, more comprehensive results are given using this framework.

This article is organized as follows: Sect. 2 gives discussions of related work; Sect. 3 introduces the structure of the preliminary personalized sentiment model and the enhanced model, mainly on the design of their input sequences and the description of the recurrent neural network used in the models; in Sect. 4, we discuss the attention mechanism and Hawkes process, and the possibility to combine them in order to model information decay in personalized sentiment analysis; Sect. 5 presents the technical setup of our experiments, the datasets used to evaluate the models, and the baselines for the model comparison; evaluation results and findings are reported and discussed in Sect. 6; we conclude our work in Sect. 7 and give an outlook on future research.

## 2 Related Work

Most academic contributions in sentiment analysis focus on population-level approaches [15,16]. Nevertheless, there are a number of studies that consider the diversity of people and apply such traits in distinct ways to improve the performance. Gong et al. [17] propose an adaptation from a global sentiment model to personalized models assuming that people's opinions are shaped by 'social norms'. By using such a global model, the issue with data sparsity is alleviated while individualities are included by performing a series of linear transformations based on the shared model. Later on, Gong et al. argue that like-minded people tend to form groups and conjointly establish group norms even when there are no interactions between the people in the same group [18]. This argument shifts their study from per-user basis to per-group. The concept of user groups is also explored in another work by Song et al. [19], where user following information is infused in the representation to enhance personalization. Moreover, a modified latent factor model is applied to map users and posts into a shared low-dimensional space while the posts are decomposed into words to handle the data sparsity issue. The consideration of user groups is able to capture individuality to a certain extent and can potentially enrich the sparse data. However, an alternative is discovered in our work that is unconstrained by the user group assumption.

Similarly to our approach, several studies have used neural networks to analyze individualities in sentiment analysis. Targeting product reviews, Chen et al. [20] utilize two separate recurrent neural networks to generate user and product representations in order to model the individual differences in assigning rating scores and to obtain the consistencies in receiving rating scores of the same product. A convolutional neural network is used to generate embeddings for the review text. Finally, the representations from the three parties are combined using a traditional machine learning classifier. Another work on product reviews is done by Chen et al. [21] who employ a hierarchical network with Long Short-Term Memory (LSTM) on word-level and sentence-level representations. Additionally, an attention mechanism based on user and product information is used on each level after the LSTM layer. By doing that, user preferences and product characteristics are introduced in the network to produce a finer-represented document embeddings. There are similar works that consider individual differences related to sentiment [22,23], but very few have explicitly modeled the evolvement of sentiments of an individual over time. In our work, earlier posted texts are concerned in determining the sentiment of the current text. In addition, we propose a method towards an evaluation of the influence of gaps between texts generated at different time points.

## 3 Personalized Model with Recurrent Neural Network

In this section, we introduce a basic structure of the *personalized sentiment model*. We explain how it has evolved from the preliminary model, where the effectiveness of considering opinion holders and historical texts is evaluated, to an enhanced version, where the information from the opinion holders and the texts is better represented and learned.

### 3.1 The Preliminary Model

In [8], we have proposed a personalized model which aims at investigating the effectiveness of including individualities in sentiment analysis. With respect to individualities, the following assumptions were considered:
**Assumption I:** Different individuals make different lexical choices to express their opinions.
**Assumption II:** An individual's opinion towards a topic is likely to be consistent within a period of time, and opinions on related topics are potentially influential to each other.
**Assumption III:** There are connections between an individual's opinion and the public opinion.

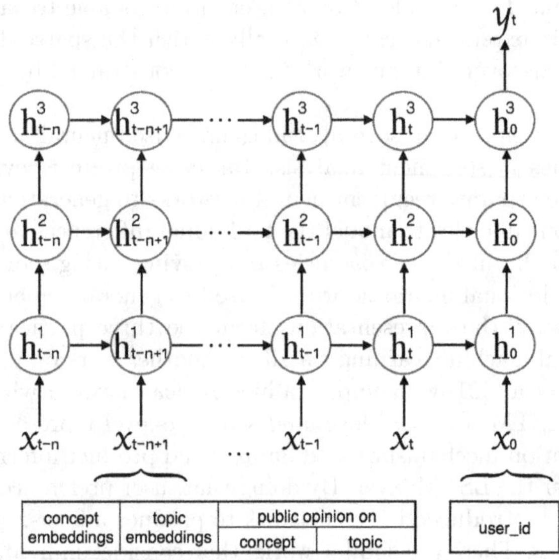


**Fig. 1.** Personalized sentiment model with a recurrent neural network and two types of neurones at the input layer: the user index ($x_O$) and the tweet of the user at a specific time point ($x_{t*}$) [24]. The latter is represented by a concatenation of four components $x_{t*} = [E_{concept}\ E_{topic}\ P_{concept}\ P_{topic}]_*$.

To leverage these assumptions, a many-to-one recurrent network with three hidden layers ($h^1$, $h^2$ and $h^3$) is built to preserve and extract related information from historical data (Fig. 1). Each layer contains a number of LSTM cells as defined in [25] without peephole connections. Let $(i_k, f_k, C_k, o_k, h_k)$ denote respectively the input gate, forget gate, cell memory, output gate, and hidden states of the LSTM cell. The update of the cell state and the output of the cell are then described with the following equations:

$$i_k = \sigma(W_i[x_k, h_{k-1}] + b_i) \quad (1)$$
$$f_k = \sigma(W_f[x_k, h_{k-1}] + b_f) \quad (2)$$
$$C_k = f_k \odot C_{k-1} + i_t \odot \tanh(W_C[x_k, h_{k-1}] + b_C) \quad (3)$$
$$o_k = \sigma(W_o[x_k, h_{k-1}] + b_o) \quad (4)$$
$$h_k = o_k \odot \tanh(C_k) \quad (5)$$

where $\sigma$ denotes the sigmoid activation function. With Eqs. 1, 2 and 3, the cell $k$ selects new information and discards outdated information to update the cell memory $C_k$. For the output of the cell, $o_k$ selects information from the current input and the hidden state (Eq. 4), and $h_k$ combines the information with the cell state (Eq. 5). This memory network is beneficial for understanding implicit or isolated expressions such as *'I have changed my mind about it'*.

Each input sequence consists of two parts: one is the user identifier $x_0$ of the current tweet, and the other is the representation of the current tweet and a number of past tweets.

**User Identifier.** The use of the user identifier is inspired by [26] who add a language index in the input sequence to enable zero-shot translation in a multilingual neural machine translation system. By adding this identifier in the input, our proposed network is able to learn user-related information and to compare between users. More importantly, the data sparsity issue is resolved since only one model is required.

**Tweet Representation.** Each tweet is represented by a concatenation of four components $x_{t*} = [E_{concept}\ E_{topic}\ P_{concept}\ P_{topic}]_*$, where $E_{concept}$ is the concept embedding of the tweet $t*$, $E_{topic}$ is the topic embedding of the tweet $t*$, $P_{concept}$ is the public opinion on the concepts, and $P_{topic}$ is the public opinion on the topic. Here, the concepts are taken from SenticNet[4] [27] and contain conceptual and affective information of the text. Topics are provided in the used corpus. The embeddings for concepts and topics are learned using a fully connected shallow network similar to Word2Vec [28]. Concept embeddings are the weights at the output layer trained with the target concept at the output layer and its context concepts at the input layer. Topic embeddings are trained by setting the target topic at the output layer and its associated concepts at the input layer. Such embeddings are generated based on the co-occurrences of terms, so that terms with greater similarity are located closer in the vector space. Furthermore, public opinions are Sentic values extracted from the SenticNet, and the values are static.

In Fig. 1, the input sequence $X$ is a matrix of $[x_{t-n}, x_{t-n+1}, ..., x_{t-1}, x_t, x_0]$ where $x_t$ is the current tweet, $x_{t-*}$ are the tweets published before it by the same user $x_0$, and $n$ is the number of past tweets considered. Zero-padding is performed before the earliest tweet for users with less than $n+1$ tweets. The

[4] http://sentic.net/, last seen on April 19, 2018.

output $y_t$ is the sentiment orientation of the current tweet. Both $x_*$ and $y_t$ are vectors and $n$ is a constant. For training and testing, the tweets are first sorted by the user index, and then by the creation time of the tweets.

The preliminary model is a simplified network that is used for evaluating the effectiveness of introducing the mentioned assumptions in determining sentiment. Although experiments have shown positive results (Sect. 6.1), there are several aspects that can be modified to improve the performance. First, the input of the network takes two different types of information – the user index and the tweet representation – at different nodes, and the network has to react with the same set of parameters. This setting makes the network harder to train. Second, the representation of a tweet is not sufficient to include necessary information in the text. Negation cues, as signal terms, can invert the polarity of sentiment, hence they should be added in the representation [29]. Moreover, the single topic given for each tweet can be unilateral since multiple entities are mentioned in some cases. Furthermore, the influence of past opinions can be affected by time, i.e. the gap between the tweets of a user can be a reflector of the importance of the past opinions.

### 3.2 Stacked Neural Network

Stacked networks are popular for tasks that require representations from different levels [21,30]. Here, we consider a tweet-level representation and a user-level representation, and merge the embedding networks in the preliminary model with the recurrent network so that the representations of the tweets are learned automatically through the network by the sentiment label $y_t$ (Fig. 2).

In the input sequence of the stacked network, each tweet $x_*$ is represented by a set of concepts, entities, negation cues and the user identifier. The concepts are from the same knowledge base as the preliminary model, whereas entities are extracted from the text instead of using the single topic so that the relation between the concept and the target can be more flexible. Additionally, explicit negations are included in the input based on a pre-defined list of rules. As a better alternative, the user identifier is placed in the tweet representation instead of occupying an individual node at the input layer of the recurrent network to obtain a consistency in the inputs. There are also a number of tweets with no explicit concepts, entities or negation cues mentioned in the text, and such tweets are represented by the appeared components. In an extreme case, it is also possible that a tweet is simply represented by the user identifier, and historical tweets will play an important role in predicting the sentiment of the current tweet. Public opinions are redundant, because the opinions of majorities can be learned automatically given enough training samples from a sufficient number of users. Meanwhile, the tendency of whether a person's opinions align with the public can be learned directly. Since the representation is concept-based, the order of words appeared in the text does not play a role in the representation. As a result, a single embedding layer is applied to map the terms into a dense, low-dimensional space.

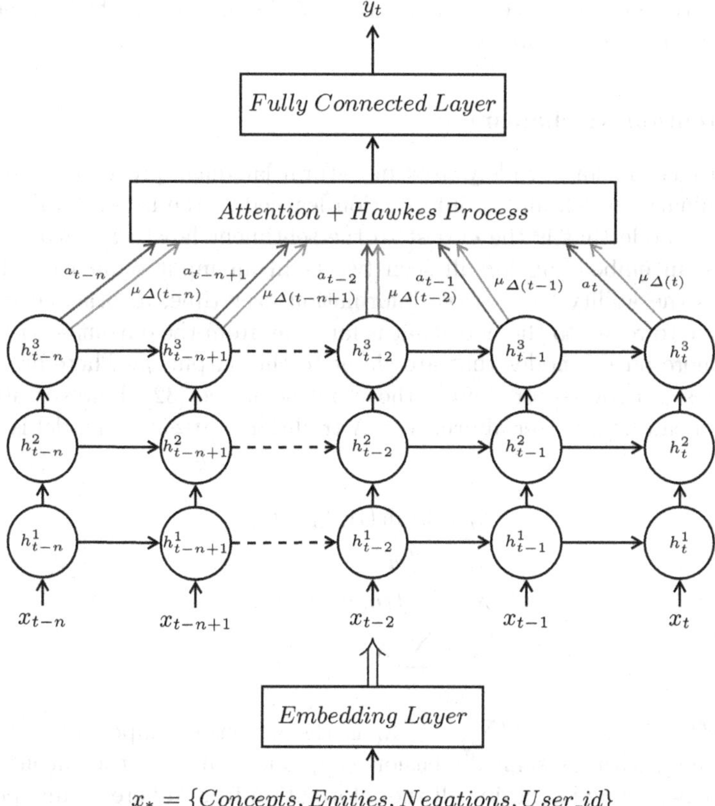


**Fig. 2.** Stacked personalized sentiment model with a recurrent neural network that is shaped by an attention-based Hawkes process. The input sequence of the network is sets of concepts, entities, negation cues, and the user identifier at different time points.

The stacking of networks happens between the generation of the tweet embeddings and the construction of the input sequence for the recurrent neural network. Similarly, a recurrent network with LSTM cells is used in the model. With a consistent formulation of the representation at each input node, the network can be trained efficiently. Again, the input sequences are first sorted by the user identifier and afterwards by the creation time of the text.

## 4 Attention-Based Hawkes Process

As shown in Fig. 2, we employ an attention-based Hawkes process at the output of the recurrent network. This layer models time gaps of different lengths between the publishing dates of the texts. Attention is given to the past tweets that are related to the current tweet content-wise, while the decay of the relation is modeled by the Hawkes process.

### 4.1 Attention Mechanism

Attention mechanism is widely used in natural language processing [30,31]. In the preliminary model, all the information learned in the network are accumulated at the node that is the closest to the sentiment label ($h_0^3$), which can be treated as an embedding for all seen tweets in an input sequence. Although LSTM has the ability to preserve information over time, in practice it is still problematic to relate to the node that is far away from the output. LSTM tends to focus more on the nodes that are closer to the output $y_t$. There are studies that propose to reverse or double the input sequence [32], however attention mechanism can be a better alternative. A traditional attention model is defined as:

$$u_i = \tanh(W_t h_i + b_t) \tag{6}$$

$$a_i = u_i^T w_s \tag{7}$$

$$\lambda_i = softmax(a_i) h_i \tag{8}$$

$$v = \sum_i \lambda_i \tag{9}$$

where $softmax(x_i) = e^{x_i} / \sum_j e^{x_j}$. $\lambda_i$ is the attention-shaped output at the specific time $t_i$ with the same dimension as $h_i$, and $v$ sums up the output at each $t_i$ dimension-wise and contains all the information from different time points of a given sequence. The context vector $w_s$ can be randomly initialized and jointly learned with other weights in the network during the training phase.

### 4.2 Hawkes Process

Hawkes Process is a one-dimensional *self-exciting* point process. A process is said to be *self-exciting* if an 'arrival' causes the conditional intensity function to increase (Fig. 3) [33]. Hawkes Process models a sequence of arrivals of events over time, and each arrival excites the process and increases the possibility of a future arrival in a period of time.

As in [33], the conditional intensity function of Hawkes process is:

$$\lambda^*(t) = \lambda + \sum_{t_i<t} \mu(t - t_i) = \lambda + \sum_{t_i<t} \alpha e^{-\beta(t-t_i)} \tag{10}$$

where $\lambda$ is the background intensity and should always be a positive value, and $\mu(\cdot)$ is the excitation function. Here, we use exponential decay as the excitation function because it is a common choice for many tasks. The value of $\alpha$ and $\beta$ are positive constants where $\alpha$ describes how much each arrival lifts the intensity of the system and $\beta$ describes how fast the influence of an arrival decays.

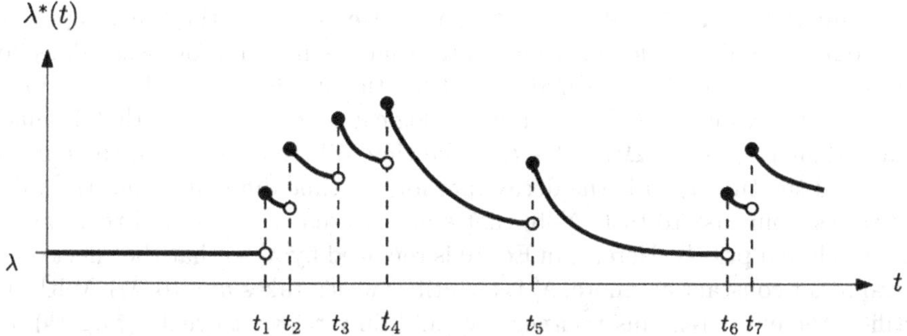


**Fig. 3.** An example conditional intensity function for a self-exciting process [33].

**Hawkes Process in Sentiment.** Traditional Hawkes process models the influence of the past events on the future event which assumes that these are the same events (or similar in nature). For that reason, the value of $\alpha$ is constant, i.e. each arrival affects the system in the same way. As a heuristic study, we see an opinion as an 'event' that positively influences future opinions, and such influence decreases with time. However, people's opinion may be affected by their past opinions when there are some connections between the targets (topics or entities) of the opinions. In our setting, the preceding opinion can be irrelevant to the current one, in which case the influence from the preceding opinion should not be boosted.

### 4.3 Hawkes Process with Attention

In order to apply Hawkes process on opinions, we shape the effect of past opinions with attention mechanism. The exponential decay factor is added at each time point based on the attention output, so that the historical text which contains more relevant content affects the current opinion more intensively than those with less relevant content. The following two equations describe the shaped output with the attention mechanism and the Hawkes process:

$$v'(t) = v + \varepsilon \sum_{i:\Delta t_i > 0} \lambda'_i e^{-\beta \Delta t_i} \tag{11}$$

$$= \sum_{i:\Delta t_i \geq 0} (\lambda_i + \varepsilon \lambda'_i e^{-\beta \Delta t_i}) \tag{12}$$

where

$$\lambda'_i = \begin{cases} \lambda_i & \text{if } \lambda_i > 0 \\ 0 & \text{otherwise} \end{cases}$$

In Eq. 11, the first element $v$ is the background intensity which acts as a base factor and describes the content in the text throughout the time. $\varepsilon$ represents a decay impact factor and balances the importance of adding the Hawkes process in the output, and a value of zero indicates that the information decay does not play any part in the decision making. Theoretically, there should be no upper bound for the value of $\varepsilon$, however it is illogical to take a value that is much greater than 1 ($\varepsilon \not\gg 1$). $\Delta t_i = t - t_i$ is the time difference between the current time $t$ and the time $t_i$. $\beta$ is the decay rate for the time difference, and the value of $\beta$ varies from task to task. Note that $\varepsilon$ and $\beta$ are constants, and their values must be chosen priorly. Here, $\alpha$ in Eq. 10 is replaced by $\lambda_i'$ so that the effect of an arrival is not constant anymore. $\lambda_i'$ is a rectifier which takes $max(0, \lambda_i)$. With the rectifier, the effect remains non-negative and only relevant events (targets) are considered. $\lambda_i$ is calculated according to Eq. 8. Given Eqs. 9 and 12 is deduced so that at each time point in the past, the attention output is boosted by the process factor when it is a positive value. The final output $v'(t)$ is the sum of the modified attention outputs over time for the current tweet created at time $t$. Additionally, a fully connected layer is added after applying the Hawkes process in order to regularize the output for the network to train.

## 5 Implementation

In this section, we present the implementation of both the preliminary model and the enhanced model. The former is referred to as 'P-model' (**P**reliminary model) throughout this text and the latter as 'AHP model' (**A**ttention-based **H**awkes **P**rocess model). The models are evaluated using different datasets which are labeled in distinct ways.

### 5.1 Technical Setup

The concepts used as a part of the text representation are taken from SenticNet and are 50,000 in total. The implementation of both models is conducted using Keras[5] with the Tensorflow[6] back-end. In the P-model, topics are embedded with 32-dimensional vectors and concepts are embedded with 128-dimensional vectors. In contrast, all the terms are embedded with 128-dimensional vectors in the embedding layer of the AHP model. The first two layers in the recurrent network are equipped with 64 LSTM cells each while the last layer has 32 cells. Moreover, dropout is used for both models to prevent overfitting [34].

### 5.2 Datasets

There are a number of datasets for Twitter sentiment analysis, and they differ mainly by the annotation technique. The labeling of sentiment can be performed in two ways: manually and automatically. Manual labeling is mostly done by the 'Wisdom of Crowd' [35], which is time consuming and only applicable for a

5 https://keras.io/, last seen on April 19, 2018.

6 https://www.tensorflow.org/, last seen on April 19, 2018.

**Table 1.** Statistics of the datasets used for the P-model and the AHP model.

| Model | Dataset | Polarity | | | | # Topic/Entity | User frequency | |
|---|---|---|---|---|---|---|---|---|
| | | Pos. | Neg. | Neu. | Total | | #Tweets p.User | #User |
| P- | Sanders | 424 | 474 | 2,008 | 2,906 | 4 | >5 | 51 |
| | SemEval | 6,758 | 1,858 | 8,330 | 16,946 | 100 | >=2 | 971 |
| AHP | Sentiment140 | 79,009 | 42,991 | – | 122,000 | 311 | >=20 | 2,369 |

small amount of data. For the text from social platforms, an automatic labeling mechanism is possible by categorizing the emoticons appeared in the text. The emoticons are employed in a distant supervision approach. As discussed in [36], such labeling can be quite noisy but effective. Furthermore, these two methods can be seen as annotations from different standpoints [37], which is a separate research direction that may be focus of a separate study. For a personalized sentiment analysis, manually labeled data do not contain sufficient user information to explore the individualities. For that reason, we use manually labeled data for the P-model in our experiments so that an universal comparison can be made to evaluate the effectiveness of including user data, while automatically labeled data are used for the AHP model so that a more comprehensive evaluation on the personalization can be provided.

The statistics of the datasets used for the models is shown in Table 1. Sanders Twitter Sentiment Corpus[7] and the development set of SemEval-2017 Task 4-C Corpus[8] are manually labeled datasets and are used for the evaluation of the P-model. For the SemEval corpus, germane labels are merged into three classes (positive, negative and neutral) in order to combine the corpus with the Sanders corpus. These two datasets are combined since there are no sufficient frequent users (only 51 users have tweeted more than 5 times). It is also to show the independency of the topic-concept relation between different datasets. Sentiment140[9] is automatically labeled with two classes (positive and negative) and is used in the AHP model. Originally, Sentiment140 contains 1,600,000 training tweets, however we extract tweets published by users who have tweeted at least 20 times before a pre-defined date so that only frequent users are considered in this model. The extracted subset contains 122,000 tweets in total. As explained in Sect. 3.2, entities are used instead of topics which results in 15,305 entities extracted from the text.

Furthermore, each dataset is split into a training set, a validation set and a test set for training and evaluation. The original test sets from the mentioned corpora are not suitable for our experiments because for the P-model, the topic-opinion relations are to be examined while the provided test set contains only unseen topics; for the AHP model, the provided test set contains only unseen users which is unable to verify the user preferences learned by the network.

[7] http://www.sananalytics.com/lab/twitter-sentiment/, last seen on April 19, 2018.
[8] http://alt.qcri.org/semeval2017/task4/, last seen on April 19, 2018.
[9] http://help.sentiment140.com/for-students/, last seen on April 19, 2018.

### 5.3 Baselines

**Sanders + SemEval.** To evaluate the effectiveness of introducing user information in sentiment analysis, we use the original, manually labeled datasets and compare the P-model with five baselines. The first one is the Sentic values which are sentiment scores between $-1$ (extreme negativity) and 1 (extreme positivity) from SenticNet. For each tweet, the Sentic values are combined, and afterwards the result and the number of concepts appeared in the tweet are fed to a shallow fully connected network for training.

To compare the P-model with the traditional machine learning technique, we choose to apply the Support Vector Machine (SVM) which is a prominent method in this field. Two SVM classifiers are built that one is trained with the concepts and the topic in the text (named Generalized SVM) while the other one is trained with the same features of the Generalized SVM together with the user index and public opinions (named Personalized SVM). Implemented with scikit-learn [38], the radial basis function kernel and the parameters $C = 0.01$ and $\gamma = 1/N\_features$ are set by 10-fold cross-validation.

Convolutional neural network (CNN) as another widely used neural network structure, has been shown to provide competitive results on several sentence classification tasks compared to various approaches. We use a network similar to the simple CNN proposed by Kim [39] with concepts as inputs instead of words that are used in the original work. Such a network highlights the relations between adjacent elements, however it may be difficult to explore since the order of concepts does not necessarily convey useful information.

The last one is a generalized recurrent neural network (named Generalized RNN) which uses the same network with the P-model but without the user index and the public opinions. As a result, $x_{t*} = [E_{concept}\ E_{topic}]_*$ is set at each input node, and the input sequence is ordered by the creation time of the tweets.

**Sentiment140.** With the larger, automatically labeled dataset, we are able to train the AHP model with frequent users. We compare the performance of the following models:

1. A model with the output layer applied directly after the recurrent network (named Basic model);
2. A model with the output layer applied after adding the attention layer to the recurrent network but without Hawkes process (named Attention model);
3. The AHP model as in Fig. 2.

The same input sequences are given to the AHP model and its substitutions, thus the effect of applying the attention and Hawkes process layer can be evaluated.

## 6 Results and Discussion

In this section, we report the evaluation results of the P-model compared with five baselines, and discover the effects of the key factors for personalization. The performance of the AHP model will be discussed as well.

### 6.1 Evaluation of the P-Model

We compare the P-model with the baselines introduced in Sect. 5.3. Accuracy is used as the primary evaluation metric, and macro-averaged recall is used to demonstrate the balance of the prediction over classes which is more intuitive than displaying the recall value for each class. Note that we do not compare the performance of the P-model with the reported results of SemEval because different test data are used for the evaluation, as explained in Sect. 5.2. The comparison is shown in Table 2 as in our earlier publication [8].

**Table 2.** Comparison of the performance between the P-model and the chosen baselines.

| Dataset | Model | Accuracy | Avg. Recall |
|---|---|---|---|
| Sanders + SemEval | Sentic | 0.3769 | 0.4408 |
| | Generalized SVM | 0.6113 | 0.5847 |
| | Personalized SVM | 0.6147 | 0.5862 |
| | CNN | 0.5481 | 0.5360 |
| | Generalized RNN | 0.6382 | 0.6587 |
| | P-model | **0.6569** | **0.6859** |

In the same way as for the P-model, concept-based representation is used for the baseline models. The Sentic scores reflect an interpretation of the concepts from a general point of view; they are used as public opinions in the P-model. Without integrating any additional information, it performs the worst implying that no implicit knowledge is captured from the text. Reasonable results are achieved by the generalized and personalized SVM models. The personalized model offers a slightly better performance given additional user-related features, however the improvement is not significant enough to serve the purpose of modeling individuality. The CNN model, which follows the work by Kim [39], makes use of the dependencies between contiguous terms. Such dependencies are rather vague in the concepts, because the words are already shuffled while extracting concepts from the text. Thus, the performance of the CNN model is comparatively worse than the SVM- and RNN-based models.

The generalized RNN captures the trend in public opinions by comparing the concepts and the associated topic from different time points in the past. This model outperforms the personalized SVM, which reveals the significance of considering the dependencies between tweets. By adding the user-related information in the P-model, the performance is further improved with $p < 0.05$ for the $t$-test. The improvement indicates that individuality is a crucial factor in analyzing sentiment and is able to positively influence the prediction.

### 6.2 Key Factors for Personalization

To explore the influential factors in the personalized sentiment model, we conduct experiments from three different angles. More evidence is shown for the effectiveness of including user diversity in the model.

**Topic-Opinion Relation.** To evaluate the effect of considering topic-opinion relations, we exclude the topic-related components from the input sequence and set $x_{t*} = [E_{concept}\ P_{concept}]_*$ for the input nodes before the user identifier. The resulting model gives an accuracy of 0.5536 and an average recall of 0.5429, which is significantly worse than the P-model (Table 2). The gap between the results reveals the advantage of associating sentiment with topics and adding the components $E_{topic}$ and $P_{topic}$ in the system.

**User Frequency.** As shown in Table 1, there are 714 users who have tweeted twice and 51 users who have tweeted more than 5 times. In fact, most users in the combined dataset have only one tweet. While targeting users with different frequencies, the P-model achieves an accuracy of 0.6282 for the users who have tweeted twice, and the accuracy rises to 0.7425 for the users who have more than 5 tweets. As expected, the model is able to provide a better prediction for more frequent users.

**Length of the History.** An experiment is conducted with different numbers of past tweets added in the input sequence. Results are shown in Table 3 as reported in our previous work [8]. The performance is poor while considering one past tweet, because the possibility of having meaningful relations between two consecutive tweets is relatively low. By taking more past tweets into account, the performance of the model keeps improving. Note that when associating 10 past tweets, the performance is competitive with the generalized RNN model, which is associated with 20 past tweets as reported in Table 2. This shows the importance of integrating user information and historical text in sentiment analysis.

**Table 3.** Performance of the P-model considering different numbers of past tweets in the input sequence.

| Number of past tweets | Accuracy | Avg. recall |
|---|---|---|
| 1 | 0.5680 | 0.5481 |
| 5 | 0.6216 | 0.6346 |
| 10 | 0.6305 | 0.6671 |
| 15 | 0.6461 | 0.6688 |
| 20 | 0.6569 | 0.6859 |

### 6.3 Evaluation of the AHP Model

Based on the results from the last two sections, we enhance the model and verify its performance by experimenting with a larger dataset and comparing with its substitutions. For the AHP model, accuracy is used as the primary evaluation metric as well, and F1-score is calculated for each class to demonstrate the balance of the prediction since only two classes are concerned.

**Table 4.** Comparison of the performance between the AHP model and its substitutions.

| Dataset | Model | Accuracy | Pos. F1 | Neg. F1 |
|---|---|---|---|---|
| Sentiment140 | Basic model | 0.7287 | 0.7344 | 0.7223 |
| | Attention model | 0.7491 | 0.7464 | 0.7516 |
| | AHP model | **0.7596** | **0.7534** | **0.7652** |

In Table 4, we can see improvements after adding the attention layer and after shaping the attention outputs with Hawkes process. The Attention model compensates the loss of focus of the Basic model with distant nodes, and the AHP model tightens or loosens the relations of the nodes according to the gaps between them. To implement the AHP model, the values of $\varepsilon$ and $\beta$ in Eq. 11 must be set beforehand. We take $\varepsilon = 0.7$ and $\beta = 0.01$ which give the best performance in the experiment, and the corresponding results are shown in Table 4.

### 6.4 Key Factors for Information Decay

**Decay Impact Factor $\varepsilon$ and Decay Rate $\beta$.** The values for $\varepsilon$ and $\beta$ are found experimentally by grid search given an empirical range. The results are illustrated in Fig. 4. Because $\varepsilon$ and $\beta$ interact with each other on the rectified attention output, it is difficult to find a significant trend between these two values and the accuracy of the prediction. However, there is a slight tendency to offer better results with a smaller $\beta$. Comparing to the best results in Table 4 which are given by $\varepsilon = 0.7$ and $\beta = 0.01$, the worst result in the set range is 0.7270 (accuracy) given by $\varepsilon = 0.9$ and $\beta = 0.1$ which is worse than the accuracy of the Basic model. Such a performance shows the importance of setting suitable parameters in the excitation function.

**Excitation Function.** The advantages of using exponential kernels in Hawkes process descend from a Markov property as explained in [12], which motivates the use of this excitation function in our model. The property can be extended to the case where the value of $\beta$ is non-constant, which is useful in assigning different decay rates for different users or for different levels of intensity (attention outputs). The effect of using these variants or applying other excitation functions for Hawkes process is to be discovered.

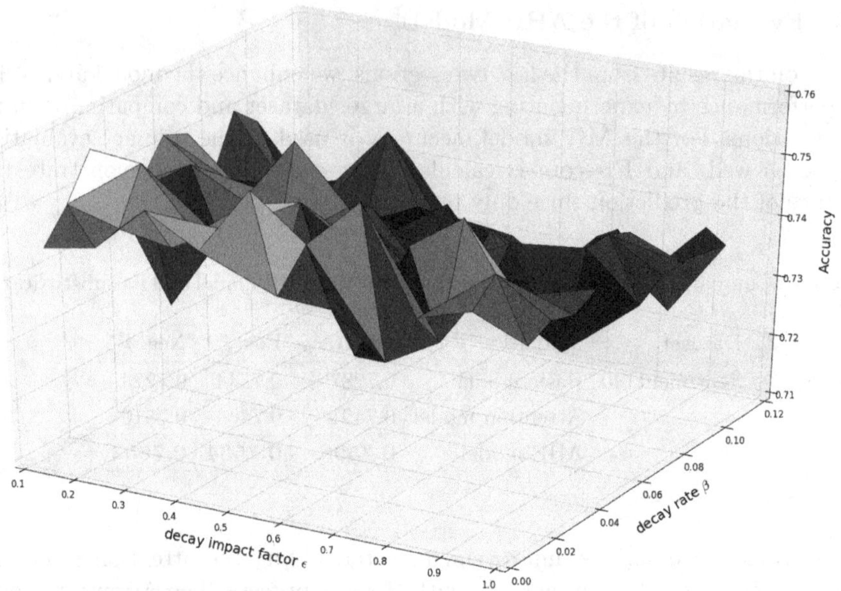


**Fig. 4.** A grid search on the parameters $\varepsilon$ and $\beta$ for the attention-based Hawkes process.

## 7 Conclusion and Future Work

In this article, we focused on developing a *personalized sentiment model* that is able to capture users' individualities in expressing sentiment on social platforms. To evaluate the effectiveness of including user information in sentiment analysis, we built a preliminary model based on three assumptions and conducted a series of experiments with Twitter data. The assumptions reflect the individuality from different aspects and the model is designed accordingly. We use concepts appeared in the text to represent people's lexical choices; we add the topic in the text representation to include the topic-opinion relations; public opinions are used in the input in order to find connections between individual and public opinions. A simple recurrent neural network is built for this task which is able to relate the information of the current tweet with historical tweets. The issue of data sparsity is handled by adding a user identifier in each input sequence. The preliminary model is evaluated with a combined, manually labeled Twitter dataset, and the effectiveness of introducing user data in the model is verified by comparing to five baseline models. Moreover, the key factors of a personalized sentiment model are discovered. We believe that the topic-opinion relation, the user frequency and the number of the historical tweets considered in the network are the major factors that nfluence the performance of the model.

Given the positive results of the preliminary model, we proposed an enhanced model that focuses on frequent users. The enhanced model is a stacked network that takes concepts, entities, negation cues and user identifier to represent each tweet and applies an embedding layer to generate inputs for the recurrent network. Furthermore, attention mechanism is used on the output of the recurrent network which helps the network to concentrate on related and distant tweets. To consider the different gaps between the tweets, we introduce a novel approach that is to shape the attention output with Hawkes process. By using this approach, the attention on the related tweets is boosted and the effect fades by a certain decay rate on the distance between these tweets and the current tweet. Thus, a decay of information with time can be modeled in the network. This model is tested on a larger dataset with users who have tweeted at least 20 times before a pre-defined timestamp, and improvements are shown after adding the attention layer with Hawkes process.

The results from these two models bring us significant meanings of applying a personalized sentiment model. We have learned that the individualities have substantial influence on sentiment analysis and can be easily captured by models like the ones we have proposed in this article. Moreover, traditional recurrent neural networks neglect the effect of various gaps between the nodes which can be an important factor in many tasks. As we have shown, the Hawkes process can be combined with recurrent networks to compensate such lack of information, and the effect of using different variants of Hawkes process has yet to explore.

The improvements of the preliminary model and the enhanced model have opened up new opportunities for future research. To generalize the use of the proposed models, we can test the performance by evaluating with finer-labeled sentiments or emotions. It is also possible to use these models on existing sentiment models that do not concern user information in the prediction in order to enhance the performance. As a heuristic research, the attention mechanism can be combined with the Hawkes process in different ways. For instance, Cao et al. [40] proposed an approach of non-parametric time decay effect, which takes different time intervals and learns discrete variables for the intervals as the decay effect $\mu$. As a result, no pre-defined decay functions are needed for the modeling, and the effect can be flexible based on different time intervals. Such a technique can also be beneficial for our task, and the decay effect and the attention model can be applied on the output of the recurrent network separately. As an extension on the field of application, the personalized model can be used in an artificial companion that is adapted under a multi-user scenario to improve communication experience by offering user-tailored responses.

## References


1. Meena, A., Prabhakar, T.V.: Sentence level sentiment analysis in the presence of conjuncts using linguistic analysis. In: Amati, G., Carpineto, C., Romano, G. (eds.) ECIR 2007. LNCS, vol. 4425, pp. 573–580. Springer, Heidelberg (2007). https://doi.org/10.1007/978-3-540-71496-5_53
2. Wiebe, J., Wilson, T., Bell, M.: Identifying collocations for recognizing opinions. In: Proceedings of the ACL Workshop on Collocation: Computational Extraction, Analysis, and Exploitation, pp. 24–31 (2001)

3. Cheng, X., Xu, F.: Fine-grained opinion topic and polarity identification. In: LREC, pp. 2710–2714 (2008)
4. Pontiki, M., Galanis, D., Pavlopoulos, J., Papageorgiou, H., Androutsopoulos, I., Manandhar, S.: SemEval-2014 task 4: aspect based sentiment analysis. In: Proceedings of SemEval, pp. 27–35 (2014)
5. Liu, B.: Sentiment Analysis: Mining Opinions, Sentiments and Emotions. Cambridge University Press, Cambridge (2015)
6. Reiter, E., Sripada, S.: Human variation and lexical choice. Comput. Linguist. **28**, 545–553 (2002)
7. Markovikj, D., Gievska, S., Kosinski, M., Stillwell, D.: Mining Facebook data for predictive personality modeling. In: Proceedings of the 7th international AAAI conference on Weblogsand Social Media (ICWSM 2013), Boston, pp. 23–26 (2013)
8. Guo, S., Höhn, S., Xu, F., Schommer, C.: PERSEUS: a personalization framework for sentiment categorization with recurrent neural network. In: International Conference on Agents and Artificial Intelligence, p. 9, 16–18 January 2018, Funchal (2018)
9. Hawkes, A.G.: Spectra of some self-exciting and mutually exciting point processes. Biometrika **58**, 83–90 (1971)
10. Ogata, Y.: Space-time point-process models for earthquake occurrences. Ann. Inst. Stat. Math. **50**, 379–402 (1998)
11. Mohler, G.O., Short, M.B., Brantingham, P.J., Schoenberg, F.P., Tita, G.E.: Self-exciting point process modeling of crime. J. Am. Stat. Assoc. **106**, 100–108 (2011)
12. Bacry, E., Mastromatteo, I., Muzy, J.F.: Hawkes processes in finance. Mark. Microstruct. Liq. **1**, 1550005 (2015)
13. Kobayashi, R., Lambiotte, R.: TiDeH: Time-dependent Hawkes process for predicting retweet dynamics. In: ICWSM, pp. 191–200 (2016)
14. Zhao, Q., Erdogdu, M.A., He, H.Y., Rajaraman, A., Leskovec, J.:Seismic: A self-exciting point process model for predicting tweetpopularity. In: Proceedings of the 21th ACM SIGKDD International Conference on Knowledge Discovery and Data Mining, pp. 1513–1522. ACM (2015)
15. Gilbert, C.H.E.: Vader: a parsimonious rule-based model for sentiment analysis of social media text. In: Eighth International Conference on Weblogs and Social Media (ICWSM 2014) (2014). http://comp.social.gatech.edu/papers/icwsm14.vader.hutto.pdf. Accessed 20 Apr 2016
16. Saif, H., He, Y., Fernandez, M., Alani, H.: Contextual semantics for sentiment analysis of Twitter. Inf. Process. Manag. **52**, 5–19 (2016)
17. Gong, L., Al Boni, M., Wang, H.: Modeling social norms evolution for personalized sentiment classification. In: Proceedings of the 54th Annual Meeting of the Association for Computational Linguistics, (Volume 1: Long Papers), vol. 1, pp. 855–865 (2016)
18. Gong, L., Haines, B., Wang, H.: Clustered model adaption for personalized sentiment analysis. In: Proceedings of the 26th International Conference on World Wide Web, International World Wide Web Conferences Steering Committee, pp. 937–946 (2017)
19. Song, K., Feng, S., Gao, W., Wang, D., Yu, G., Wong, K.F.: Personalized sentiment classification based on latent individuality of microblog users. In: IJCA, pp. 2277–2283 (2015)
20. Chen, T., Xu, R., He, Y., Xia, Y., Wang, X.: Learning user and product distributed representations using a sequence model for sentiment analysis. IEEE Comput. Intell. Mag. **11**, 34–44 (2016)

21. Chen, H., Sun, M., Tu, C., Lin, Y., Liu, Z.: Neural sentiment classification with user and product attention. In: Proceedings of the 2016 Conference on Empirical Methods in Natural Language Processing, pp. 1650–1659 (2016)
22. Dou, Z.Y.: Capturing user and product information for document level sentiment analysis with deep memory network. In: Proceedings of the 2017 Conference on Empirical Methods in Natural Language Processing, pp. 521–526 (2017)
23. Tang, D., Qin, B., Liu, T.: Learning semantic representations of users and products for document level sentiment classification. In: Proceedings of the 53rd Annual Meeting of the Association for Computational Linguistics and the 7th International Joint Conference on Natural Language Processing, (Volume 1: Long Papers), pp. 1014–1023 (2015)
24. Guo, S., Schommer, C.: Embedding of the personalized sentiment engine PERSEUS in an artificial companion. In: International Conference on Companion Technology, Ulm, 11–13 September 2017. IEEE (2017)
25. Graves, A., Mohamed, A.R., Hinton, G.: Speech recognition with deep recurrent neural networks. In: 2013 ieeeinternational conference on Acoustics, speech and signal processing (ICASSP), pp. 6645–6649. IEEE (2013)
26. Johnson, M., et al.: Google's multilingual neural machine translation system: enabling zero-shot translation. arXiv preprint arXiv:1611.04558 (2016)
27. Cambria, E., Poria, S., Bajpai, R., Schuller, B.W.: SenticNet 4: a semantic resource for sentiment analysis based on conceptual primitives. In: COLING, pp. 2666–2677 (2016)
28. Mikolov, T., Chen, K., Corrado, G., Dean, J.: Efficient estimation of word representations in vector space. arXiv preprint arXiv:1301.3781 (2013)
29. Jia, L., Yu, C., Meng, W.: The effect of negation on sentiment analysis and retrieval effectiveness. In: Proceedings of the 18th ACM Conference on Information and Knowledge Management, pp. 1827–1830. ACM (2009)
30. Yang, Z., Yang, D., Dyer, C., He, X., Smola, A., Hovy, E.: Hierarchical attention networks for document classification. In: Proceedings of the 2016 Conference of the North American Chapter of the Association for Computational Linguistics: Human Language Technologies, pp. 1480–1489 (2016)
31. Vaswani, A., et al.: Attention is all you need. In: Advances in Neural Information Processing Systems, pp. 6000–6010 (2017)
32. Zaremba, W., Sutskever, I.: Learning to execute. arXiv preprint arXiv:1410.4615 (2014)
33. Laub, P.J., Taimre, T., Pollett, P.K.: Hawkes processes. arXiv preprint arXiv:1507.02822 (2015)
34. Srivastava, N., Hinton, G.E., Krizhevsky, A., Sutskever, I., Salakhutdinov, R.: Dropout: a simple way to prevent neural networks from overfitting. J. Mach. Learn. Res. **15**, 1929–1958 (2014)
35. Surowiecki, J.: The wisdom of crowds: Why the many are smarter than the few and how collective wisdom shapes business. Econ. Soc. Nat. **296** (2004)
36. Go, A., Bhayani, R., Huang, L.: Twitter sentiment classification using distant supervision. CS224N Project Report, Stanford 1 (2009)
37. Schommer, C., Kampas, D., Bersan, R.: A prospect on how to find the polarity of a financial news by keeping an objective standpoint. In: Proceedings ICAART 2013 (2013)
38. Pedregosa, F., Varoquaux, G., Gramfort, A., Michel, V., Thirion, B., Grisel, O., Blondel, M., Prettenhofer, P., Weiss, R., Dubourg, V., et al.: Scikit-learn: machine learning in Python. J. Mach. Learn. Res. **12**, 2825–2830 (2011)

39. Kim, Y.: Convolutional neural networks for sentence classification. arXiv preprint arXiv:1408.5882 (2014)
40. Cao, Q., Shen, H., Cen, K., Ouyang, W., Cheng, X.: DeepHawkes: bridging the gap between prediction and understanding of information cascades. In: Proceedings of the 2017 ACM on Conference on Information and Knowledge Management, pp. 1149–1158. ACM (2017)

# Using Generic Ontologies to Infer the Geographic Focus of Text

Christos Rodosthenous(✉) and Loizos Michael

Open University of Cyprus, P.O. Box 12794, Latsia, Nicosia, Cyprus
christos.rodosthenous@ouc.ac.cy, loizos@ouc.ac.cy

**Abstract.** Certain documents are naturally associated with a country as their geographic focus. Some past work has sought to develop systems that *identify* this focus, under the assumption that the target country is explicitly mentioned in the document. When this assumption is not met, the task becomes one of *inferring* the focus based on the available context provided by the document. Although some existing work has considered this variant of the task, that work typically relies on the use of specialized geographic resources. In this work we seek to demonstrate that this inference task can be tackled by using generic ontologies, like ConceptNet and YAGO, that have been developed independently of the particular task. We describe GeoMantis, our developed system for inferring the geographic focus of a document, and we undertake a comparative evaluation against two freely-available open-source systems. Our results show that GeoMantis performs better than these two systems when the comparison is made on news stories whose target country is either not explicitly mentioned, or has been artificially obscured, in the story text.

**Keywords:** Information retrieval · Geographic focus identification
Ontologies · Natural language processing
Geographic information systems

## 1 Introduction

In this work we tackle the problem of identifying the geographic focus of a text document. Humans are able to read a document and identify its geographic focus [1]. According to Silva et al. [2], "Geographic scope or focus of a document is the region, if it exists, whose readers find it more relevant than average". Narratives are examples of such documents, that human readers can identify the location where the story takes place, along with other properties (e.g., the protagonist, the timeline, etc.) [3].

---

An earlier version of this work was presented at the 10th International Conference on Agents and Artificial Intelligence (ICAART 2018). In this article, compared to the conference paper we give a more extensive evaluation of the GeoMantis system with different datasets and comparisons with more systems. Furthermore, we updated the GeoMantis system with new knowledge from ontologies and present details on the structure of the ontologies and the way they are used.


J. van den Herik and A. P. Rocha (Eds.): ICAART 2018, LNAI 11352, pp. 223–246, 2019.
https://doi.org/10.1007/978-3-030-05453-3_11

For a machine to perform this task, it needs to process the text, identify location mentions from the text, and then try to identify its geographic focus. The majority of systems developed in this line of research rely on gazetteers, atlases, and dictionaries with geographic-related content, that identify the geographic focus of the text. In this work, we investigate whether generic ontologies can be exploited for tackling this problem with a special focus on cases where no explicit mention of the target country exists in the text.

We present **GeoMantis**, a system developed to identify the country-level focus of a text document or a web page using knowledge from generic ontologies. In particular, the system takes as input any type of document, processes it, and it stores the contents of the document in a database. Independently of the previous process, the system retrieves triples from ontologies about countries, processes each triple, filters it using its internal mechanisms, and stores it in a database. In this workflow, a full-text search algorithm is used for matching each search text of the document against the search text of each triple in the country's knowledge base set. A number of filtering options are also available during this process.

The outcome of the above-mentioned search process is the set of country triples that are activated by the document text. This outcome is used in the query answering process to produce a list of countries in order of confidence. The ordering of this list is performed using one of the four supported by the system strategies presented in detail later in this work.

In the following sections, we present the current state in geographic focus identification, along with systems developed to perform this task. Next, the GeoMantis system is presented, followed by a detailed presentation of the generic ontologies employed by it. The penultimate section, presents the results of the parameter selection process and the comparative evaluation of the system. In the final section, new features and possible extensions to the GeoMantis system are discussed as part of our ongoing work.

## 2 Problem Definition and Related Work

The geographic focus of a document can be defined as the geographic location the document is related to. In this work, we limit this area to locations on earth that have administrative boundaries. For example, the text snippet "*A letter to creditors says Mr Tsipras is prepared to accept most conditions that were on the table before talks collapsed and he called a referendum.*"[1] has a geographic focus in Greece, Europe.

The task of identifying the geographic focus of text goes back to the 90's and the research in this area [4] led to the development of several systems. Many of these systems rely on geoparsers, i.e., systems for extracting places from text [5,6], for identifying locations, disambiguating them, and finally for identifying the geographic focus of the text. These systems, perform well when documents include place mentions for geoparsers to work, but leave open the

[1] http://www.bbc.com/news/.

case of documents that have none or very few place mentions. It is common for a document to also contain references to geographic locations in the form of historical dates, monuments, ethnicity, typical food, traditional dances and others [7]. These references can be used to infer the geographic focus of a text document.

In the 90's, the Geo-referenced Information Processing SYstem **GIPSY** [8] was created. This system was able to perform geocoding on documents related to the region of California. Geocoding was applied using a subset of the US Geological Survey's Geographic Names Information System (GNIS) database. GIPSY's document geocoding pipeline included three steps. First, the system extracts keywords and phrases from each document according to their spatial relatedness. Each of these phrases are weighted according to a heuristic algorithm. Second, the system identifies the spatial locations for the keywords and phrases extracted in the first step using synonyms and hierarchical containment relations. Third, geographic reasoning is applied and after extracting all the possible locations for all the terms and phrases denoting places in a given document, the final step presents the geospatial footprints as a three-dimensional polyhedron.

In the 00's, the **Web-a-Where** system [9] was introduced, which can identify a place name in a document, disambiguate it, and determine its geographic focus. This system detects mentions of places in a document or a webpage and determines the location each place name refers to. Moreover, it assigns a geographic focus to it by using a similar workflow with the GIPSY system and it also has a specific approach for disambiguating locations for both geo/non-geo and geo/geo ambiguity. When a place name has the same name as a non-place (e.g., Turkey the country and Turkey the bird), a geo/non-geo ambiguity is identified. When two or more places have the same name (e.g., Athens in Greece and Athens in the USA), a geo/geo ambiguity is identified. Furthermore, the system can assign a geographic focus to a document, even though its location is not explicitly mentioned in it, but it is inferred from other locations. The Web-a-Where system was evaluated using two different pre-annotated datasets. The authors report that their system detects a geographic focus in 75% of the documents and report a score of 91% accuracy in detecting the correct country.

A more recent attempt is the geo-referencing system developed within the **MyMose project** framework [10]. This system, performs a city-level focus identification using dictionary search and a multistage method for assigning a geographic focus to web pages, using several heuristics for toponym disambiguation and a scoring function for focus determination. The authors report an accuracy of over 70% with a city-level resolution in English and Spanish web pages.

A similar to the Web-a-Where system workflow was used in the **CLIFF-CLAVIN** system [11], which identifies the geographic focus of news stories. This system uses a three step workflow to identify the geographic focus. First, it recognizes toponyms in each story, then, it disambiguates each toponym, and finally, it determines the focus using the "most mentioned toponym" strategy.

This system relies on "CLAVIN"[2], an opensource geoparser that was modified to facilitate the specific needs of news story focus detection. The authors report an accuracy of 90–95% for detecting the geographic focus when tested on various datasets. This system is freely available under an opensource license. It is also integrated in the MediaMeter[3] suite of tools for quantitative text analysis of media coverage.

Related to this line of research, is the work on **SPIRIT** [12], a spatially aware search engine which is capable of accepting spatial queries in the form of <theme><spatial relationship><location>. Relevant research is also found in the work of Yu [13] on how the geographic focus of a named entity can be resolved at a location (e.g. city or country).

Furthermore, work done on a system called **Newstand** [14], monitors RSS feeds from online news sources, retrieves the articles in realtime and then extracts geographic content using a geotagger. These articles are grouped into story clusters and are presented on a map interface, where users can retrieve stories based on both topical significance and geographic region.

More relevant work, mainly concentrated in using knowledge bases extracted from Wikipedia, is presented in work of de Alencar and Davis Jr, and Quercini et al. [15,16]. de Alencar and Davis Jr, presented a strategy for tagging documents with place names according to the geographical context of their textual content by using a topic indexing technique that considers Wikipedia articles as a controlled vocabulary. Quercini et al., discussed techniques to automatically generate the local lexicon of a location by using the link structure of Wikipedia.

A system called **Newsmap** [17], uses a semi-supervised machine learning classifier to label news stories without human involvement. Furthermore, the system identifies multi-word names to automatically reduce the ambiguity of the geographical traits. The authors evaluated their system's classification accuracy against 5000 human-created news summaries. Results show that the Newsmap system outperforms the geographical information extraction systems in overall accuracy, but authors report that simple keyword matching suffers from ambiguity of place names in countries with ambiguous place names.

Imani et al. [18], proposed a mechanism that utilizes the named entities for identifying potential sentences containing focus locations and then uses a supervised classification mechanism over sentence embedding to predict the primary focused geographic location. The unavailability of ground truth (i.e., whether words in a sentence is focus or non-focus) suggests a major challenge for training a classifier and an adaptation mechanism is proposed to overcome sampling bias in training data. This mechanism was evaluated against baseline approaches on datasets that contain news articles.

Silva et al. [2], presented a system for automatically identifying the geographic scope of web documents, using an ontology of geographical concepts and a component for extracting geographic information from large collections of web documents. Their approach involves a mechanism for identifying geographic

[2] https://clavin.bericotechnologies.com/.

[3] http://mediameter.org/.

references over the documents and a graph ranking algorithm for assigning geographic scope. Initial evaluation of the system, suggests that this is a viable approach.

A system called **TEXTOMAP** [19], aims to design the geographic window of the text, based on the notion of important toponyms. Toponym selection is based on spatial, linguistic or semantic indicators.

A relatively new system called **Mordecai** [20], performs full text geoparsing and infers the country focus of each place name in a document. The system's workflow extracts the place names from a piece of text, resolves them to the correct place, and then returns their coordinates and structured geographic information. This system utilizes a number of natural language processing techniques and neural networks to perform these tasks.

## 3 The GeoMantis System

GeoMantis (from the Greek words Geo that means earth and Mantis, which means oracle or guesser), is a web application designed for identifying the geographic focus of documents and web pages at a country-level.

Users can add a document to the system using a web-interface. The document enters the processing pipeline depicted in Fig. 1 and gets processed.

The system uses factual knowledge in the form of Resource Description Framework (RDF) [21] triples retrieved from ontologies (e.g., ConceptNet and YAGO). These triples are of the form <`Subject`><`Predicate`><`Object`>, where the `Subject` has a relationship `Predicate` with the `Object`. Detailed information on the RDF semantics can be found in the W3C specification document [22]. Triples are stored locally in the system's geographic knowledge database. This database can be updated at any time by querying the corresponding knowledge source online.

Retrieved triples from ontologies are used for searching in each document and generate the predicted geographic focus. Instead of returning only one prediction for the target country, the system returns a list of countries in order of confidence for each prediction. Countries in the first places have a higher confidence score.

The system can be tuned using a number of parameters such as the selected ontology, the query answering strategy (see Sect. 3.3), and text filtering options (e.g., stopwords and named entities).

In the next paragraphs, we present how the GeoMantis system pipeline works.

### 3.1 Text Input Parsing

First, users upload a text document or type a webpage URL through a web interface. This text is firstly cleaned from HTML tags (e.g., <br>, <b>, <p>, <div>) and wiki specific format (e.g., [[Link title]]). Then, the text is parsed using a Natural Language Processing (NLP) system, the Stanford CoreNLP [24]; extracted lemmas, part of speech, and named-entity labels extracted by the Named Entities Recognition (NER) process, are stored and indexed in the

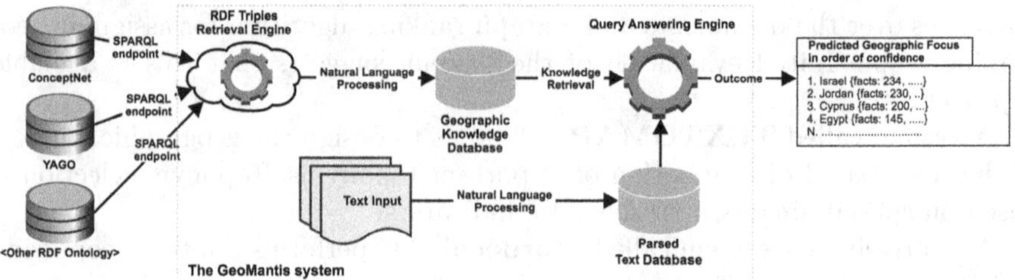


**Fig. 1.** The GeoMantis system processing workflow. The workflow includes the RDF Triples Retrieval and Processing Engine (left), the Text Processing mechanism and the Query Answering Engine. The outcome of the system appears on the right. Figure adapted from [23].

system's database. The NER system can identify named entities of type location, person, organization, money, number, percent, date and time, duration, and miscellaneous (misc).

### 3.2 Knowledge Retrieval

The RDF triple retrieval process starts by identifying each country's official name and alternate names from the GeoNames database[4]. Geonames is a geographical database that includes more than 10 million geographical names. It also contains over 9 million unique features where 2.8 million are populated places and 5.5 million are alternate names. The database is integrating geographical data such as names of places, alternate names in various languages, elevation, population, and others from various sources. Sources include, among others, the National Geospatial-Intelligence Agency's (NGA), the U.S. Board on Geographic Names and the Ordnance Survey OpenData.

The system retrieves triples by using an available SPARQL endpoint for every ontology integrated with the system. SPARQL [25] is a query language for RDF that can be used to express queries across diverse data sources. SPARQL contains capabilities for querying RDF graph patterns and supports extensible value testing and constraining queries by source RDF graph. The outcome of a SPARQL query can be result sets or RDF graphs. In Fig. 1 (left part), the integration of the system with a number of ontologies is presented. GeoMantis is capable of retrieving RDF triples from any ontology that exposes a SPARQL endpoint and represents factual knowledge in RDF triples.

The final step in the knowledge retrieval workflow, is the processing of the retrieved RDF triples using the CoreNLP system. The object part of the triple is tokenized and lemmatized, and common stopwords are removed. For each RDF triple in the system's geographic knowledge base, a search string is created with lemmatized words.

[4] http://www.geonames.org.

Algorithm 1 presents the knowledge retrieval process. The SPARQL query created in line 6 of Algorithm 1 is used to retrieve the RDF triples and it is of the form: `SELECT * WHERE { <Countryname> ?p ?o }` when the country name is in the subject of the triple, and `SELECT * WHERE { ?p ?o <Countryname> }` when the country name is in the object of the triple.

From each retrieved RDF triple, a search text is created using tokenization, lemmatization, and stopword removing techniques. The search text is stored in the GeoMantis local database.

### 3.3 Query Answering

For each country, a case-insensitive full-text search is executed for each unique word in the text against the search text of each triple in the country's knowledge base. A triple is activated by the text if any of the document's words matches any of the triple's search text words (excluding common stopwords). For example, a document containing the sentence "They had a really nice dish with halloumi while watching the Aegean blue." should activate the RDF triples: `<halloumi> <RelatedTo> <Cyprus>` and `<Greece> <linksTo> <Aegean_Sea>`. To maximize the search capabilities, the GeoMantis system uses lemmatized words. Full-text searching takes advantage of the MariaDB's[5] search functionality, using full-text indexing for better search performance.

The final step in the query answering process, involves the ordering of the list of countries and the generation of the predicted geographic focus. Ordering is performed using one of the following strategies:

**Percentage of Triples Applied (PERCR):** List of countries is ordered according to the fraction of each country's total number of activated triples over the total number of triples for that country that exist in the geographic knowledge bases, in descending order.

**Number of Triples Applied (NUMR):** List of countries is ordered according to each country's total number of activated triples, in descending order.

**Term Frequency - Inverse Document Frequency (TF-IDF):** List of countries is ordered according to the TF - IDF algorithm [26], which is applied as follows:

$D_c$ is a document created by taking the triples of a country $c$
$TF_t$ = (Number of times term t appears in $D_c$)/(Total number of terms in $D_c$)
$IDF_t = \log_e$(Total number of $D_c$/Number of $D_c$ with term $t$ in it).

**Most Triples per Country Ordering (ORDR):** List of countries is ordered according to the number of triples that are retrieved for each country, in descending order.

[5] https://mariadb.org/.

**Algorithm 1.** Knowledge retrieval from ontologies.

```
procedure RetrieveKnowledge(KB)
// Use the ISO two-letter country code
    for each countryCode in countryCodes do
        countryNames ← RetrieveNames(countryCode)
        for each countryName in countryNames do
            while N ∈ {subject, object} do
                SPARQLquery ← CreateQuery(countryName,N)
                triples ← RetrieveRDFTriples(SPARQLquery)
                for each triple in triples do
                    if N="subject" then
                        arg1 ← GetPart(subject,triple)
                        arg2 ← GetPart(object,triple)
                    else
                        arg1 ← GetPart(object,triple)
                        arg2 ← GetPart(subject,triple)
                    end if
                    relation ← GetPart(predicate,triple)
                    searchText ← arg2
                end for
// Use NLP to tokenize and lemmatize
                searchText ← NLP(searchText)
// Use a common stopwords list
                searchText ← ClearStopWords(searchText)
            end while
        end for
        SaveGeoDatabase(searchText,countryCode)
    end for
end procedure
```

### 3.4 System Implementation

The GeoMantis system is built using the PHP web scripting language and the MariaDB database for storing data. The system is designed using an extendable architecture which allows the addition of new functionality.

GeoMantis also exposes a number of its services using a REST API, based on JavaScript Object Notation (JSON)[6] for data interchange and integration with other systems. Knowledge can be updated at any time by querying the corresponding ontology SPARQL endpoint.

Furthermore, the system has a separate module for producing statistics on documents, datasets, and RDF triples and for visualizing them using a powerful graph library based on Chart.js[7]. For each processed document, a detailed log of activated triples is kept for debugging purposes and better understanding of the query answering process.

[6] http://www.json.org/.
[7] http://www.chartjs.org/.

# 4 Empirical Material

The extended evaluation of the GeoMantis system, required three inputs: (i) a list of countries, (ii) generic knowledge from ontologies about each of these countries, and (iii) datasets where the geographic focus of the text is known.

For the first input, we chose countries which are members of the United Nations (UN). The UN is the world's largest intergovernmental organization and has 193 member states. For the other two inputs we provide information in the following sections.

## 4.1 Use of Generic Ontologies

A large amount of general-purpose knowledge is stored in databases in the form of ontologies. This knowledge is gathered from various sources using human workers, game players, volunteers, and contributors in general. We chose two popular ontologies: ConceptNet [27] and YAGO [28–30] which include generic knowledge for countries instead of only geographic knowledge that exist in a gazetteer. A brief overview of these ontologies is presented in the following paragraphs.

**Table 1.** Information on triples retrieved from ConceptNet and YAGO ontologies for UN countries. The filtered YAGO ontology (YAGO_Fil) is also depicted in this table and is described in Sect. 5.1.

| Property | ConceptNet | YAGO | YAGO_Fil |
|---|---|---|---|
| Total number of triples | 51,771 | 2,966,765 | 2,903,186 |
| Number of unique relations | 33 | 373 | 300 |
| Country with highest number of triples | China | USA | USA |
| Number of UN countries with triples | 193 | 192 | 192 |

**ConceptNet** is a freely-available semantic network that contains data from a number of sources such as crowdsourcing projects, Games With A Purpose (GWAPs) [31], online dictionaries, and manually coded rules. In ConceptNet, data are stored in the form of edges or assertions. An edge is the basic unit of knowledge in ConceptNet and contains a relation between two nodes (or terms). Nodes represent words or short natural language phrases. ConceptNet version 5.6 includes 37 relations, such as "AtLocation", "isA", "PartOf", "Causes" etc. The following are examples of edges available in ConceptNet: `<cat>` `<RelatedTo>` `<meow>`, `<statue>` `<AtLocation>` `<museum>`. ConceptNet is not represented in an RDF format, but there is relevant work that suggests such a conversion [32]. ConceptNet's version 4 ability to answer IQ questions using simple test-answering algorithms was evaluated and the results showed that the system has the Verbal IQ of an average four-year-old child [33].

For each UN country, its name along with its alternate names are extracted and the ConceptNet 5.6 API[8] is queried for returning the proper Uniform

[8] http://api.conceptnet.io/.

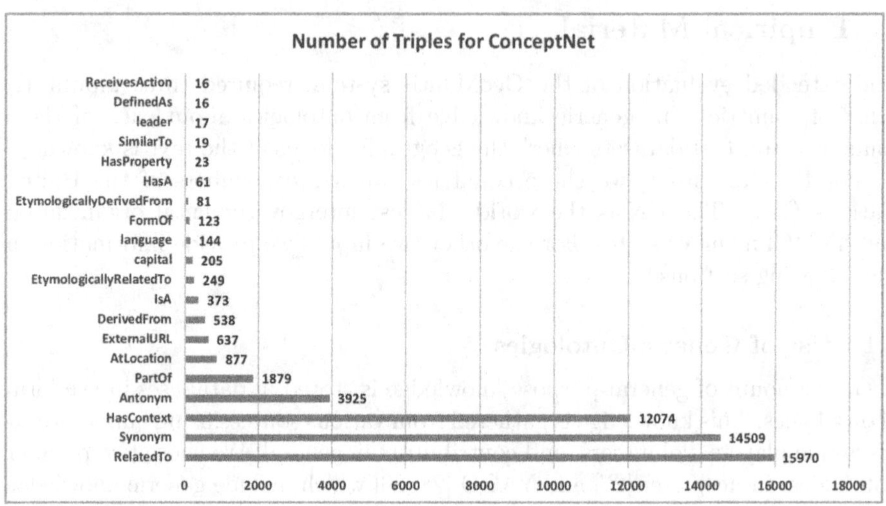


**Fig. 2.** The 20 most frequent relations in triples retrieved from ConceptNet ontology about UN countries.

Resource Identifier (URI) in the database. In ConceptNet, each URI includes the language (e.g., "en") and the term. This is an example of a complete URI:"`/c/en/peru`". When the term includes spaces (e.g., "United Kingdom"), these are substituted by underscores, i.e.,"`c/en/united_kingdom`".

For each obtained URI, all facts are retrieved in the form of triples `<Arg1>` `<Relation>` `<Arg2>` and are stored in the GeoMantis geographic knowledge database. In ConceptNet, the country name can appear either in `<Arg1>` or `<Arg2>` and an additional check is needed to capture the appropriate search string. For example, when a search for "Greece" is performed, facts like the ones presented in Fig. 3 are returned, which after processing (see Algorithm 1) result to the search strings: `europe` and `ithaka`. In Fig. 2, the 20 most frequent relations in the retrieved knowledge are depicted.

**YAGO (Yet Another Great Ontology)** is a semantic knowledge base built from sources like Wikipedia, WordNet [34] and GeoNames (See footnote 4). More specifically, information from Wikipedia is extracted from categories, redirects and infoboxes available in each wikipedia page. Also, there is a number

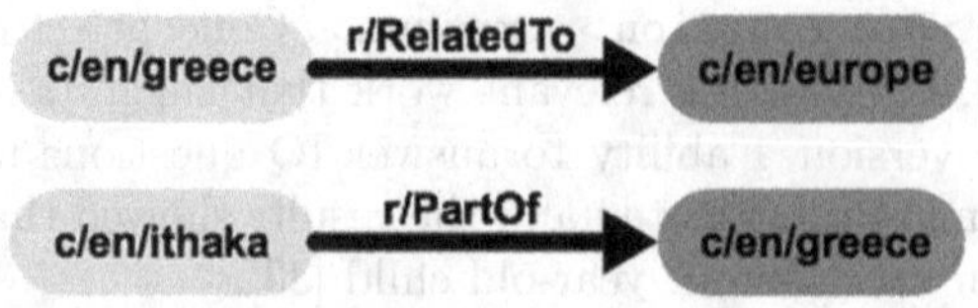


**Fig. 3.** Examples of facts retrieved from ConceptNet when the search term "Greece" is used.

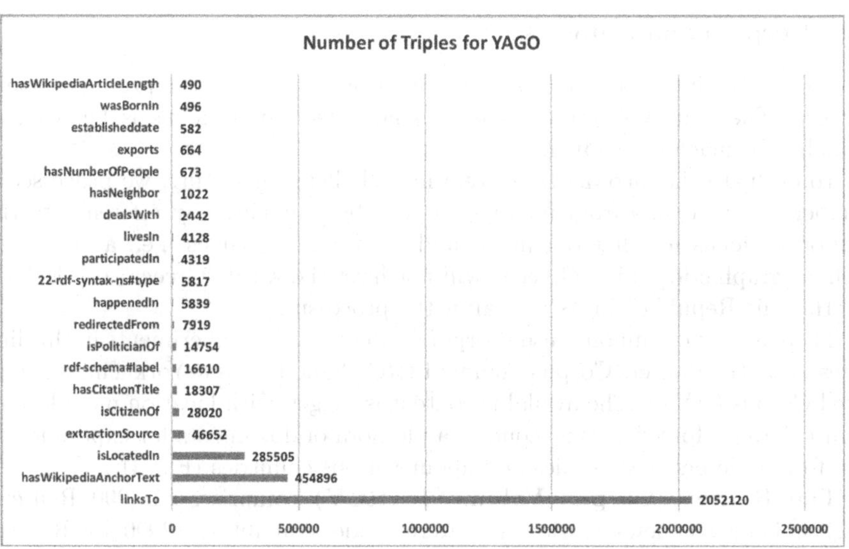


**Fig. 4.** The 20 most frequent relations in triples retrieved from YAGO ontology about UN countries.

of relations between facts that are described in detail in the work of Hoffart et al. [28]. Currently, YAGO contains 447 million facts and about 9,800,000 entities. Facts in YAGO were evaluated by humans, reporting an accuracy of 95%.

Relations in YAGO are both semantic (e.g., "`wasBornOnDate`", "`locatedIn`" and "`hasPopulation`") and technical oriented (e.g., "`hasWikipediaAnchorText`", "`hasCitationTitle`"). A search for "Greece" in YAGO returns facts like the ones presented in Fig. 5.

Moreover, YAGO has a number of spatial relations that place an object in a specific location (i.e., country, city, administrative region, etc.). For example, relations "`wasBornIn`", "`diedIn`", "`worksAt`" place an entity of type `Person` in a location, e.g., `<Isaac_Asimov> <wasBornIn> <Petrovichi>`.

For retrieving facts, the YAGO SPARQL endpoint[9] was queried for each UN country name along with its alternate names.

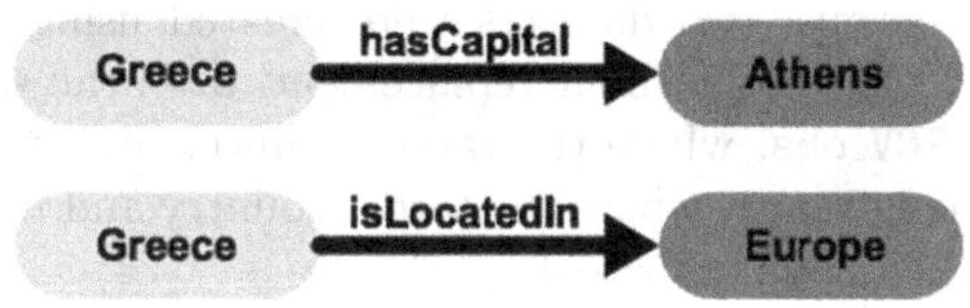


**Fig. 5.** Examples of facts retrieved from YAGO when the search term "Greece" is used.

[9] https://linkeddata1.calcul.u-psud.fr/sparql.

### 4.2 Corpora and Datasets

The last of the inputs needed for the evaluation process are the pre-tagged text corpora. These are collections of texts whose geographic focus is known and available for machine reading.

To evaluate the GeoMantis system in a challenging setting, we processed a number of documents from popular corpora by removing any reference to the country of focus for that document and its alternate names, i.e., a document with geographic focus in "Greece" will not have the word "Greece" or "Hellas" or "Hellenic Republic" in its text after the processing.

There are two commonly used corpora for conducting experiments in this line of research; the Reuters Corpus Volume 1 (RCV) and the New York Times Annotated Corpus (NYT). The available content is tagged with location metadata at country-level. Moreover, they contain a plethora of documents for experimentation from different news topics and about various countries (Fig. 4).

**The Reuters Corpus Volume 1 (RCV)** comprises 810,000 Reuters, English language news stories that were made available in 2000 by Reuters Ltd. Each story is in English and the corpus contains stories from 20/08/1996 to 19/08/1997, tagged with information on where the story is geographically located [35]. Tagging was performed by a combination of automatic categorizing techniques, manual editing, and manual correction.

**The New York Times Annotated Corpus (NYT)** has in its collection over 1,800,000 articles, written and published by the New York Times between 1987 and 2007. Most articles are tagged with location metadata [36]. The NYT corpus categorization allows a news story to be tagged with more than one locations. Tagging was performed by humans.

From the above two corpora we created six datasets to use in the evaluation of the GeoMantis system. These datasets had either the target country and its alternate names obscured, i.e., substituted with the word "unknown" or not present at all. To the best of our knowledge, there is no corpus that guarantees that there is no mention of the target country inside the document. For that reason, we used corpora that are frequently used in this line of research and we constructed datasets either by obscuring or by selecting texts that do not have a mention of the target country to evaluate GeoMantis. The alternate names of the countries were retrieved from the GeoNames database and were limited to english alternate names only.

From the RCV corpus, two datasets were created using 1000 documents, uniformly randomly selected, without replacement, from the set of news stories in the dataset: the `RCV_obs`, where the target country and its alternate names are obscured and the `RCV_npr`, where the target country and its alternate names are not present in the document's text.

From the NYT corpus, two datasets were created using 1000 news stories, uniformly randomly selected, without replacement, from the set of news stories in the dataset that belong to the "Top/News/World/ Countries and Territories/" category with a single country tag: the `NYT_obs`, where the target country and its alternate names are obscured, and the `NYT_npr`, where the target country and its alternate names are not present in the document's text.

The majority of stories in the NYT corpus are geographically focused on the United States of America and Russia, and the majority of stories in the RCV1 corpus are geographically focused on the United States of America and the United Kingdom. For each of the four datasets, we tried to have a balanced distribution of news stories per target country of focus, hence five news stories were uniformly randomly selected, without replacement (if they were available), for each UN member country from the respective corpus. The remaining documents were uniformly randomly selected, without replacement, from the whole pool of documents of that corpus.

We also created two new datasets for the comparison of GeoMantis with other systems and two baseline metrics, the `EVA_obs` and the `EVA_npr`.

The `EVA_obs` dataset included 500 uniformly randomly selected without replacement news stories from the RCV corpus and 500 uniformly randomly selected without replacement news stories from the NYT corpus categorized under the "Top/News/ World/Countries and Territories/" category with a single country tag, in a similar way as with the rest of the datasets. Every occurrence of the target country was substituted with the word "unknown". For the `EVA_npr` dataset the same procedure was followed, but each story in the dataset did not have any occurrence of the target country or its alternate names.

For uniformity, from each of the two corpora, two documents were uniformly randomly selected without replacement (if they were available) for each UN member country. The remaining documents were uniformly randomly selected without replacement from the whole pool of documents. As before, this process allowed a balanced distribution of stories per country in the dataset.

**Table 2.** Characteristics of the six datasets, including number of documents, number of tagged countries, total and mean number of words and the percentage of the NER labels. Details on the identified named entities are presented as the percentage of words tagged with NER labels in each dataset along with the five labels used in our experiments which are presented as the fraction of the words tagged with each label over the total number of NER labels, converted to a percentage.

| Dataset | RCV_obs | RCV_npr | NYT_obs | NYT_npr | EVA_obs | EVA_npr |
|---|---|---|---|---|---|---|
| Number of documents in dataset | 1000 | 1000 | 1000 | 1000 | 1000 | 1000 |
| Number of countries in dataset | 180 | 125 | 171 | 117 | 186 | 138 |
| Number of words in dataset | 174347 | 166373 | 393531 | 362228 | 283896 | 216014 |
| Mean number of words per document | 174 | 166 | 394 | 362 | 284 | 216 |
| Percentage of named entities | 23.19% | 31.76% | 29.36% | 24.37% | 25.51% | 27.86% |
| [location] | 10.97% | 9.83% | 15.14% | 14.68% | 14.25% | 12.66% |
| [organization] | 21.78% | 19.40% | 15.08% | 17.44% | 17.16% | 17.49% |
| [money] | 2.63% | 2.62% | 1.49% | 1.83% | 1.69% | 1.86% |
| [person] | 20.25% | 18.88% | 23.59% | 24.36% | 22.31% | 22.63% |
| [misc] | 6.39% | 6.36% | 10.88% | 9.93% | 9.28% | 8.69% |

## 5 Evaluation and Analysis

The GeoMantis system is evaluated on whether it can identify the geographic focus of a text document, when the country name in that text is obscured or does not exist, using only knowledge from generic ontologies. The process followed, the metrics, and the results of the evaluation are presented in this section.

A two phase evaluation was conducted: the 1st phase measured the system's performance for each of the parameters (parameter selection) in identifying the geographic focus of a document at a country-level, and the 2nd phase compared the GeoMantis system using the prevailing strategy from the 1st phase, with two opensource freely available systems and two common baseline metrics (comparative evaluation). For these experiments, general-purpose knowledge was retrieved for countries that are members of the United Nations (UN)[10] as described in Sect. 4.1 (Table 2).

### 5.1 Parameter Selection

The 1st phase of the evaluation was conducted using the four datasets described in Sect. 4.2. We evaluated every combination of values for the ontology, and the PERC and TF-IDF query answering strategies.

A similar evaluation was conducted and described in detail in our previous work [23]. That evaluation included three datasets (two from the same sources as with this evaluation and one manually created from the WikiTravel[11] website) and knowledge from Conceptnet and YAGO. The results of that evaluation suggested that the best performing parameters were the YAGO ontology, the application of NER filtering, and the PERC query answering strategy, even though the TF-IDF strategy was also performing very well. Those datasets were processed by just obscuring the reference country name from the document, as opposed to the extensive filtering of both the name and alternate names we performed in this evaluation.

Parameters like NER filtering, were tested thoroughly in the previous evaluation of GeoMantis and found to increase the performance of the system when used, hence it was always enabled in this evaluation. NER filtering includes the use of words that were labeled as location, person, organization, and money by the NER process. Although not reported here, the application of the NER filter also significantly reduces the processing time. Furthermore, the *Number of triples activated (NUMR)* and *Most triples per country ordering (ORDC)* query answering strategies, were found not to perform well and were not tested in this evaluation.

For the evaluation process, the datasets were imported to the GeoMantis database and processed with the Stanford CoreNLP. Then, the system's knowledge retrieval engine was directed to ConceptNet and YAGO ontologies

[10] http://www.un.org.

[11] https://wikitravel.org.

to retrieve RDF triples. These triples were processed using the NLP system. Table 1 depicts the properties for the ontologies used.

The performance of each combination of parameters, was evaluated using the mean position metric and the accuracy. The mean position ($\bar{P}$) denotes the position of the target country in the ordered list of countries over the number of countries available in the dataset. For comparison purposes, this number is converted to a percentage.

The accuracy($A_i$) of the system is defined as $A_i = \frac{N_i}{C}$, where $i \in \{1, 2, 3, \ldots, M\}$ and $M$ is the number of countries in the dataset, $N_i$ denotes the number of correct assignments of the target country when the target country's position is $\leq i$ in the ordered list of countries and $C$ denotes the number of available documents in the dataset.

The parameter selection process was applied on the RCV_obs, RCV_npr, NYT_obs and NYT_npr datasets.

In Table 3, we present the results of the parameter selection process after the chosen ontology and the query answering strategy followed (see Sect. 3.3) are tested. These results are also depicted graphically in Fig. 6.

Comparing the results in terms of ontology used, knowledge from YAGO yields better results than that of ConceptNet. Further analysis of the two ontologies, shows a huge gap in the amount of facts retrieved for each country. In particular, YAGO includes 2,966,765 triples against 51,771 triples in ConceptNet.

The results indicate that the common prevailing strategy for all four datasets is **TF-IDF** when the **YAGO** knowledge base is used. These results are inline with the results from our previous experiments, since the TF-IDF strategy performed almost equally well with the PERC startegy in that evaluation. Furthermore, we speculate that the increase in the amount of triples from the YAGO ontology required a more refined method of selecting the activated triple than the simple PERC strategy.

The results propose that further tuning of the selected parameters could increase the accuracy and minimize the mean position. Instead of using the "money" NER tag, we chose the "misc" tag that actually contains named entities that do not exist in any other tags. The "money" tag included words like "billion", "4,678,909" that do not offer much in the query answering process.

Furthermore, we created a filtered version of the YAGO ontology (`YAGO_Fil`), by removing triples with relations that identify and contain technical information (e.g., "`owl#sameAs`", "`extractionSource`", "`hasWikipediaArticleLength`") and relations like "`imageflag`" and "`populationestimaterank`", that do not include useful information.

Results presented in Table 4, suggest that the usage of the **YAGO_Fil** ontology with the "**misc**" tag, minimize $\bar{P}$ and maximize the accuracy of both $A_1$ and $A_2$ for all four datasets. In fact, the $\bar{P}$ is decreased by two positions in three out of four datasets and $A_1$ and $A_2$ were increased for all datasets.

**Table 3.** Results from the parameter selection phase of the GeoMantis system evaluation. The query answering strategies and ontologies, when the NER filtering option is used, were evaluated. Rows highlighted in light blue, identify the best performing set of parameters in terms of minimum value for $\bar{P}$ and maximum value for $A_1$ and $A_2$.

| # | Dataset | Ontology | Strategy | $A_1$ | $A_2$ | $\bar{P}$ |
|---|---|---|---|---|---|---|
| YP1 | RCV_obs | YAGO | PERCR | 23.70 | 39.80 | 8 |
| YT1 | RCV_obs | YAGO | TF-IDF | 41.10 | 61.60 | 6 |
| CP1 | RCV_obs | ConceptNet | PERCR | 18.70 | 27.7 | 16 |
| CT1 | RCV_obs | ConceptNet | TF-IDF | 19.80 | 29.30 | 16 |
| YP2 | RCV_npr | YAGO | PERC | 36.30 | 48.80 | 8 |
| YT2 | RCV_npr | YAGO | TF-IDF | 45.40 | 58.60 | 8 |
| CP2 | RCV_npr | ConceptNet | PERCR | 29.40 | 42.80 | 12 |
| CT2 | RCV_npr | ConceptNet | TF-IDF | 27.50 | 37.90 | 13 |
| YP3 | NYT_obs | YAGO | PERCR | 18.60 | 31.20 | 11 |
| YT3 | NYT_obs | YAGO | TF-IDF | 34.00 | 52.40 | 7 |
| CP3 | NYT_obs | ConceptNet | PERCR | 11.60 | 22.20 | 14 |
| CT3 | NYT_obs | ConceptNet | TF-IDF | 15.10 | 27.00 | 13 |
| YP4 | NYT_npr | YAGO | PERCR | 36.40 | 50.70 | 10 |
| YT4 | NYT_npr | YAGO | TF-IDF | 49.80 | 65.50 | 7 |
| CP4 | NYT_npr | ConceptNet | PERCR | 26.50 | 44.00 | 11 |
| CT4 | NYT_npr | ConceptNet | TF-IDF | 28.80 | 43.70 | 11 |

**Table 4.** Results from fine-tuning the parameter selection phase of the GeoMantis system evaluation. We examined the performance when using the "misc" NER tag instead of "money" and the use of the filtered YAGO ontology (`YAGO_Fil`).

| # | Dataset | Ontology | Strategy | $A_1$ | $A_2$ | $\bar{P}$ |
|---|---|---|---|---|---|---|
| YFT1 | RCV_obs | YAGO_Fil | TF-IDF | 42.80 | 61.60 | 5 |
| YFT2 | RCV_npr | YAGO_Fil | TF-IDF | 49.60 | 62.20 | 6 |
| YFT3 | NYT_obs | YAGO_Fil | TF-IDF | 36.60 | 55.20 | 5 |
| YFT4 | NYT_npr | YAGO_Fil | TF-IDF | 52.90 | 67.90 | 5 |

### 5.2 Comparative Evaluation

In the 2nd phase of the evaluation, the GeoMantis system, using the prevailing strategy identified in the 1st phase of the evaluation, was compared with two freely available opensource systems, CLIFF-CLAVIN and Mordecai, and two common baseline metrics. These metrics included the random selection of countries (RAND) and the ordering of countries based on their frequency of appearance in the dataset (ORDC) for ordering the list of countries.

Two additional independent datasets were used comprising previously unseen documents from the same sources used for the 1st phase.

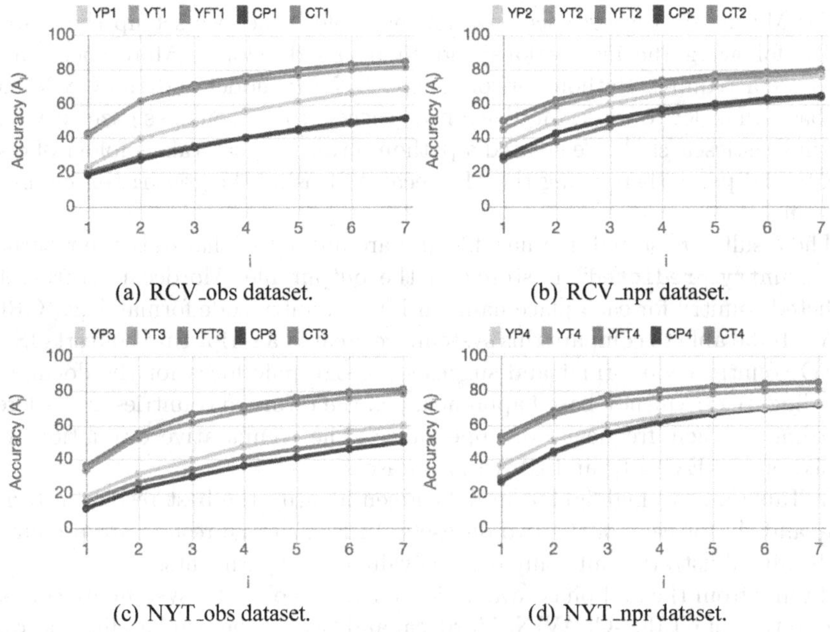


(a) RCV_obs dataset.

(b) RCV_npr dataset.

(c) NYT_obs dataset.

(d) NYT_npr dataset.

**Fig. 6.** Graphical representation of the results when the four datasets are used. On the x-axis, $i$ gets values from 1 to 7 and the values on the y-axis present $A_i$, that is the percent of the correct assignments of the target country in the first $i$ responses of the system.

For the comparative evaluation, we used the accuracy metric and the unanswered metric. The unanswered metric $U$ denotes the percentage of the number of documents processed without the system returning a result.

To conduct the comparative evaluation, the CLIFF-CLAVIN geolocation service was set up and a script was used to read the JSON output of the system. More specifically, the "places/focus/countries" array of the JSON results was used.

Results returned from the CLIFF-CLAVIN system are not ordered, so for comparison reasons with the GeoMantis system, the $A_1$ and $A_7$ metrics are used, where $A_1$ is the accuracy of the system when only one result is returned and it is the correct target country assignment and $A_7$ is the accuracy of the system when up to 7 results are returned and the correct target country assignment is in this set. The reason 7 was chosen is that it corresponds to the maximum number of predicted countries CLIFF-CLAVIN returns when executed on both the `EVAL_obs` and the `EVAL_npr` datasets and the target country is identified by any one of them. This weakness of the CLIFF-CLAVIN system is also stressed by other researchers [18] who used this system for comparison purposes.

For Mordecai, a webservice was not available, hence we set up the system locally, following the instructions[12] given by its developer. More specifically, this system requires Python version 3, spaCy NLP model and the GeoNames database. In order to work, Mordecai needs access to a Geonames gazetteer running in Elasticsearch[13]. We created a python script that can take a folder of documents and parse them using the Mordecai API using the `geo.infer_country` function.

The results are stored in a new file and are filtered so that only the returned tag "`country_predicted`" is stored in the output file. Mordecai returns the predicted country for each place name in ISO3 country code format (e.g., GRC, BGR). To be able to compare this system, we created a script that converts ISO3 to ISO country code format and suggests a geographic focus for the document according to a frequency-based approach, i.e., the returned countries are ordered according to their frequency of appearance. The comparative evaluation was applied on the EVA_obs and EVA_npr datasets.

In Table 5, rows highlighted in light green identify the best results in terms of $A_1$ and $A_7$ for each of the two datasets. In Fig. 7 these results are presented graphically, illustrating all comparative evaluation experiments.

Results from the 2nd phase evaluation for the GeoMantis system are comparable to that of CLIFF-CLAVIN, Mordecai and that of the two baseline metrics. In cases where the target country is obscured or not present in the dataset, the GeoMantis system outperforms both CLIFF-CLAVIN and Mordecai, and the two baseline metrics.

The `EVA_npr` dataset presents better results in terms of accuracy, since the information present in this dataset is unaffected by the obscuring process. The way stories are written probably includes other type of information to identify the country without an explicit mention of it in the text. On the other hand, stories in the `EVA_obs` dataset have an explicit mention of the target country in the document text that was obscured. This led to fewer references left in the story text and hence, made it more difficult to identify the target country.

Furthermore, the comparison of C1 with M1 and C2 with M2 shows that CLIFF-CLAVIN performs marginally better than Mordecai, when the target country is obscured or not present in the document. This was also tested in work of Imani et al. [18], on sentences without the target country obscured and the results show that the CLIFF-CLAVIN system outperformed Mordecai in terms of accuracy.

In terms of the $U$ metric, CLIFF-CLAVIN and Mordecai have a relatively high percentage of unanswered documents. More specifically, CLIFF-CLAVIN was not able to identify the geographic focus of 179 documents in the `EVA_npr` dataset and 107 documents in the `EVA_obs`.

[12] https://github.com/openeventdata/mordecai.
[13] https://www.elastic.co/.

**Table 5.** Comparison of the GeoMantis system with CLIFF-CLAVIN, Mordecai and the Baseline. Rows highlighted in light green identify the results that are comparable.

| # | Dataset | System | Parameters | $A_1(\%)$ | $A_2(\%)$ | $A_7(\%)$ | $U(\%)$ |
|---|---|---|---|---|---|---|---|
| G1 | EVA_obs | Geomantis | YAGO_Fil, TF-IDF | 46.60 | 64.60 | 87.02 | 0 |
| C1 | EVA_obs | CLIFF-CLAVIN | default | 42.50 | - | 50.00 | 10.70 |
| M1 | EVA_obs | Mordecai | default | 41.10 | 51.50 | 64.00 | 7.20 |
| B1 | EVA_obs | Baseline | RAND | 0.50 | 1.10 | 3.90 | 0 |
| B2 | EVA_obs | Baseline | ORDC | 2.00 | 3.80 | 11.00 | 0 |
| G2 | EVA_npr | Geomantis | YAGO_Fil, TF-IDF | 55.40 | 68.20 | 86.10 | 0 |
| C2 | EVA_npr | CLIFF-CLAVIN | default | 52.70 | - | 59.50 | 17.90 |
| M2 | EVA_npr | Mordecai | default | 52.10 | 62.20 | 66.90 | 14.80 |
| B3 | EVA_npr | Baseline | RAND | 0.80 | 1.30 | 5.10 | 0 |
| B4 | EVA_npr | Baseline | ORDC | 3.30 | 5.50 | 15.70 | 0 |

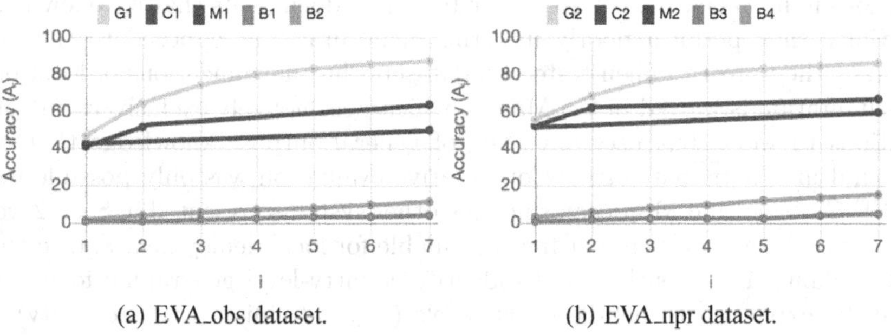


(a) EVA_obs dataset. (b) EVA_npr dataset.

**Fig. 7.** Graphical representation of the comparative evaluation results when the EVA_obs and EVA_npr datasets are used. On the x-axis, $i$ gets values from 1 to 7 and the values on the y-axis present $A_i$, that is the percent of the correct assignments of the target country in the first $i$ responses of the system.

## 6 Discussion

The evaluation process results, show that the methodology chosen, i.e., using general purpose ontologies, is applicable and well suited for the problem of identifying the geographic focus of documents that do not explicitly mention the target country. In this work, a number of strategies were tested and the one that presents better results, is the ordering of the list of countries according to the TF-IDF algorithm, in descending order (TF-IDF). In terms of knowledge source, the YAGO ontology results present a greater accuracy than the ConceptNet ontology results. Moreover, the usage of named entities filtering on the document text increases the performance and the accuracy of target country identification.

The field of text comprehension can benefit from the recent advances in Artificial Intelligence [37]. Researchers started growing concern in algorithm transparency and accountability, since most newly developed "intelligent" systems and algorithms are opaque black boxes where you give an input and the output is presented without actually presenting their "thinking" process. Algorithms should provide transparency [38] on their methods, results, and explanations. The system we designed is inline with that direction, since it exposes its query answering strategy and can provide explanations on why a specific geographic focus of a document was chosen, i.e., the facts that were activated from the ontology. The explanatory role of such systems, with respect to the target natural cognitive systems they take as source of inspiration, is highlighted in work of Lieto and Radicioni [39].

Currently, there are not many systems dedicated for the task of identifying the geographic focus of a text document. The majority of the available systems are basically geoparsers that offer focus identification as an additional feature of their primary purpose and they rely on text that has a good amount of place mentions in it. When these systems are tested on documents that have few place mentions, they perform poorly in terms of accuracy, as opposed to the high accuracy they present when tested on datasets that have mentions of locations. This limitation is waived in GeoMantis, which does not rely exclusively on place mentions to work, but uses any type of general-purpose knowledge that can be found in generic ontologies. Comparative evaluation was only possible with CLIFF-CLAVIN and Mordecai, since the other systems presented in Sect. 2 were not accessible or they were not freely available for local deployment and testing.

GeoMantis is currently able to identify country-level geographic focus, but it can be expanded to handle other levels (e.g., administrative area, city), as long as the relevant knowledge triples exist in the selected ontologies. The techniques used for news stories, could also apply to other types of documents such as myths, novels, legal documents, etc. This line of research can also find applications for document classification and geographic knowledge extraction from text. Moreover, it can be used with techniques for linking image and text-based contents together, for document management tasks [40].

## 7 Conclusion and Future Work

In this work we tried to tackle the problem of identifying the geographic focus of text that does not explicitly mention the target country, making our problem one of inference or prediction, rather than one of identification. General-purpose ontologies were used, instead of gazetteers, atlases or other purposed built geographic bases, to address this problem. More specifically, we demonstrated a methodology that retrieves general-purpose knowledge in the form of RDF triples, processes it and identifies the geographic focus of a document. This methodology and the GeoMantis system, were evaluated in various scenarios using "gold standard" annotated datasets and metrics, and results showed that the GeoMantis system outperforms the other two systems tested and the two baseline metrics, when certain conditions apply.

GeoMantis can be extended to utilize paths of various lengths between a geographical entity (e.g., country) and other entities. An example of a length 2 relation path is depicted in Fig. 8. In such a scenario, if a document contains the word "Florence", facts related to `Greece` will be activated. Results from this approach will be compared with results from using direct connections between the entities (length 1 relation path). Early experiments suggest that this will decrease the performance of the system, as it ends up connecting countries to entities, spatial or not, that are conceptually remote (see Fig. 8).

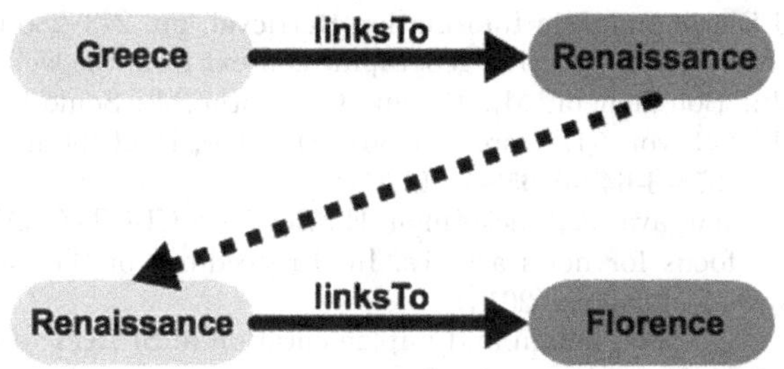


**Fig. 8.** An example of a length 2 relation path from YAGO.

Crowdsourcing approaches like GWAPs or hybrid solutions [41], could also be applied in future versions of the system for fact disambiguation. The integration of other ontologies or knowledge bases with GeoMantis, like the one generated from the Never Ending Language Learner [42], DBpedia [43], Wikidata [44] or their combination, could also be explored.

We believe that the GeoMantis system can be used in several application scenarios, such as document searching and tagging, games (e.g., taboo game challenges), and news categorization. Its extendable architecture enables the addition of new functionality and new sources of knowledge and also the integration with other systems. GeoMantis could also be used in conjunction with other systems to return results in cases where the other systems are not able to return any.

## References

1. Tversky, B.: Cognitive maps, cognitive collages, and spatial mental models. In: Frank, A.U., Campari, I. (eds.) COSIT 1993. LNCS, vol. 716, pp. 14–24. Springer, Heidelberg (1993). https://doi.org/10.1007/3-540-57207-4_2
2. Silva, M.J., Martins, B., Chaves, M., Afonso, A.P., Cardoso, N.: Adding geographic scopes to web resources. Comput. Environ. Urban Syst. **30**(4), 378–399 (2006)
3. Bower, G.H.: Experiments on story understanding and recall. Q. J. Exp. Psychol. **28**(4), 511–534 (1976)

4. Andogah, G., Bouma, G., Nerbonne, J.: Every document has a geographical scope. Data Knowl. Eng. **81–82**, 1–20 (2012)
5. Leidner, J.L., Lieberman, M.D.: Detecting Geographical References in the Form of Place Names and Associated Spatial Natural Language. SIGSPATIAL Special **3**, 5–11 (2011)
6. Melo, F., Martins, B.: Automated geocoding of textual documents: a survey of current approaches. Trans. GIS **21**(1), 3–38 (2016)
7. Monteiro, B.R., Davis, C.A., Fonseca, F.: A survey on the geographic scope of textual documents. Comput. Geosci. **96**, 23–34 (2016)
8. Woodruff, A.G., Plaunt, C.: GIPSY: georeferenced information processing system. J. Am. Soc. Inf. Sci. **45**, 645–655 (1994)
9. Amitay, E., Har'El, N., Sivan, R., Soffer, A.: Web-a-where: geotagging web content. In: Proceedings of the 27th Annual International ACM SIGIR Conferenceon Research and Development in Information Retrieval, pp. 273–280 (2004)
10. Zubizarreta, Á., et al.: Extracting geographic context from the web: georeferencing in mymose. In: Boughanem, M., Berrut, C., Mothe, J., Soule-Dupuy, C. (eds.) ECIR 2009. LNCS, vol. 5478, pp. 554–561. Springer, Heidelberg (2009). https://doi.org/10.1007/978-3-642-00958-7_50
11. D'Ignazio, C., Bhargava, R., Zuckerman, E., Beck, L.: CLIFF-CLAVIN: determining geographic focus for news articles. In: Proceedings of the NewsKDD: Data Science for News Publishing (2014)
12. Purves, R.S., et al.: The design and implementation of SPIRIT: a spatially aware search engine for information retrieval on the internet. Int. J. Geogr. Inf. Sci. **21**(7), 717–745 (2007)
13. Yu, J.: Geotagging named entities in news and online documents. In: Proceedings of the 25th ACM International Conference on Information and Knowledge Management, pp. 1321–1330 (2016)
14. Teitler, B.E., Lieberman, M.D., Panozzo, D., Sankaranarayanan, J., Samet, H., Sperling, J.: NewsStand: a new view on news. In: Proceedings of the 16th ACM SIGSPATIAL International Conference on Advances in Geographic Information Systems, pp. 1–18 (2008)
15. de Alencar, R.O., Davis Jr., C.A.: Geotagging aided by topic detection with wikipedia. In: Geertman, S., Reinhardt, W., Toppen, F. (eds.) Advancing Geoinformation Science for a Changing World. Lecture Notes in Geoinformation and Cartography, vol. 1, pp. 461–477. Springer, Heidelberg (2011). https://doi.org/10.1007/978-3-642-19789-5_23
16. Quercini, G., Samet, H., Sankaranarayanan, J., Lieberman, M.D.: Determining the spatial reader scopes of news sources using local lexicons. In: Proceedings of the 18th SIGSPATIAL International Conference on Advances in Geographic Information Systems - GIS 2010, pp. 43–52 (2010)
17. Watanabe, K.: Newsmap. Digit. Journal. **6**(3), 294–309 (2018)
18. Imani, M.B., Chandra, S., Ma, S., Khan, L., Thuraisingham, B.: Focus location extraction from political news reports with bias correction. In: 2017 IEEE International Conference on Big Data (Big Data), pp. 1956–1964 (2017)
19. Brun, G., Dominguès, C., Paris-est, U.: TEXTOMAP: determining geographical window for texts. In: Proceedings of the 9th Workshop on Geographic Information Retrieval, GIR 2015, pp. 7–8. ACM, New York (2015)
20. Halterman, A.: Mordecai: full text geoparsing and event geocoding. J. Open Source Softw. **2**(9), 91 (2017)
21. Lassila, O., Swick, R.R.: Resource Description Framework (RDF) Model and Syntax Specification. W3C Recommendation (1999)

22. Hayes, P., McBride, B.: RDF Semantics. W3C Recommendation. World Wide Web Consortium (2004)
23. Rodosthenous, C.T., Michael, L.: GeoMantis: inferring the geographic focus of text using knowledge bases. In: Proceedings of the 10th International Conference on Agents and Artificial Intelligence, ICAART, INSTICC, vol. 2, pp. 111–121. SciTePress (2018)
24. Manning, C.D., Bauer, J., Finkel, J., Bethard, S.J., Surdeanu, M., McClosky, D.: The stanford CoreNLP natural language processing toolkit. In: Proceedings of the 52nd Annual Meeting of the Association for Computational Linguistics: System Demonstrations, pp. 55–60 (2014)
25. Quilitz, B., Leser, U.: Querying distributed RDF data sources with SPARQL. In: Bechhofer, S., Hauswirth, M., Hoffmann, J., Koubarakis, M. (eds.) ESWC 2008. LNCS, vol. 5021, pp. 524–538. Springer, Heidelberg (2008). https://doi.org/10.1007/978-3-540-68234-9_39
26. Manning, C.D., Raghavan, P., Schütze, H.: An Introduction to Information Retrieval, vol. 1. Cambridge University Press, Cambridge (2008)
27. Speer, R., Havasi, C.: ConceptNet 5: a large semantic network for relational knowledge. In: Gurevych, I., Kim, J. (eds.) The Peoples Web Meets NLP. Theory and Applications of Natural Language Processing, pp. 161–176. Springer, Heidelberg (2013). https://doi.org/10.1007/978-3-642-35085-6_6
28. Hoffart, J., Suchanek, F.M., Berberich, K., Lewis-kelham, E., Melo, G.D., Weikum, G.: YAGO2 : exploring and querying world knowledge in time, space, context, and many languages. In: Proceedings of the 20th International Conference on World WideWeb, pp. 229–232 (2011)
29. Suchanek, F.M., Kasneci, G., Weikum, G.: Yago: a core of semantic knowledge. In: Proceedings of the 16th International Conference on World Wide Web, pp. 697–706 (2007)
30. Suchanek, F.M., Kasneci, G., Weikum, G.: YAGO: a large ontology from wikipedia and wordnet. Web Semant.: Sci. Serv. Agents World Wide Web **6**(3), 203–217 (2008)
31. von Ahn, L., Dabbish, L.: Designing games with a purpose. Commun. ACM **51**(8), 57 (2008)
32. Najmi, E., Malik, Z., Hashmi, K., Rezgui, A.: ConceptRDF: an RDF presentation of conceptnet knowledge base. In: 2016 7th International Conference on Information and Communication Systems (ICICS), pp. 145–150 (2016)
33. Ohlsson, S., Sloan, R.H., Turán, G., Urasky, A.: Verbal IQ of a four-year old achieved by an AI System. In: Proceedings of the 17th AAAI Conference on Late-Breaking Developments in the Field of Artificial Intelligence, pp. 89–91 (2013)
34. Fellbaum, C.: WordNet. In: Poli, R., Healy, M., Kameas, A. (eds.) Theory and Applications of Ontology: Computer Applications, pp. 231–243. Springer, Netherlands (2010). https://doi.org/10.1007/978-90-481-8847-5_10
35. Lewis, D.D., Yang, Y., Rose, T.G., Li, F.: RCV1: a new benchmark collection for text categorization research. J. Mach. Learn. Res. **5**, 361–397 (2004)
36. Sandhaus, E.: The New York Times Annotated Corpus LDC2008T19. DVD. Linguistic Data Consortium, Philadelphia (2008)
37. Hermann, K.M., et al.: Teaching machines to read and comprehend. In: Advances in Neural Information Processing Systems (NIPS 2015), vol. 28, pp. 1–13 (2015)
38. Dignum, V.: Responsible autonomy. In: Proceedings of the Twenty-Sixth International Joint Conference on Artificial Intelligence (IJCAI2017), pp. 4698–4704 (2017)

39. Lieto, A., Radicioni, D.P.: From human to artificial cognition and back: new perspectives on cognitively inspired AI systems. Cogn. Syst. Res. **39**, 1–3 (2016)
40. Cristani, M., Tomazzoli, C.: A multimodal approach to relevance and pertinence of documents. In: Fujita, H., Ali, M., Selamat, A., Sasaki, J., Kurematsu, M. (eds.) IEA/AIE 2016. LNCS (LNAI), vol. 9799, pp. 157–168. Springer, Cham (2016). https://doi.org/10.1007/978-3-319-42007-3_14
41. Rodosthenous, C., Michael, L.: A hybrid approach to commonsense knowledge acquisition. In: Proceedings of the 8th European Starting AI Researcher Symposium, pp. 111–122 (2016)
42. Mitchell, T., et al.: Never-ending learning. In: AAAI Conference on Artificial Intelligence, pp. 2302–2310 (2015)
43. Lehmann, J., et al.: Others: DBpedia-a large-scale, multilingual knowledge base extracted from wikipedia. Semant. Web **6**(2), 167–195 (2015)
44. Erxleben, F., Günther, M., Krötzsch, M., Mendez, J., Vrandečić, D.: Introducing wikidata to the linked data web. In: Mika, P., et al. (eds.) ISWC 2014. LNCS, vol. 8796, pp. 50–65. Springer, Cham (2014). https://doi.org/10.1007/978-3-319-11964-9_4

# Smart Device Stealing and CANDIES

Martin Jänicke[1(✉)], Viktor Schmidt[1], Bernhard Sick[1], Sven Tomforde[1], Paul Lukowicz[2], and Jörn Schmeißing[3]

[1] Intelligent Embedded Systems, University of Kassel, Wilhelmshöher Allee 73, 34121 Kassel, Germany
jaenicke@uni-kassel.de, schmidt.viktor@gmail.com, {bsick,stomforde}@uni-kassel.de

[2] German Research Center for Artificial Intelligence, Trippstadter Straße 122, 67663 Kaiserslautern, Germany
paul.lukowicz@dfki.de

[3] University of Kassel, Wilhelmshöher Allee 73, 34121 Kassel, Germany
joern@schmeissing.org
https://www.ies-research.de
https://www.dfki.de

**Abstract.** Personal devices such as smart phones are increasingly utilized in everyday life. Frequently, activity recognition is performed on these devices to estimate the current user status and trigger automated actions according to the user's needs. In this article, we focus on improving the self-awareness of such systems in terms of detecting theft: We equip devices with the capabilities to model their own user and to, e.g., alarm the legal owner if an unexpected other person is carrying the device. We gathered 24 h of data in a case study with 14 persons using a Nokia N97 and trained an activity recognition system. Using the data from this study, we investigated several autonomous novelty detection techniques, that ultimately led to the development of CANDIES. The algorithm is able to continuously check if the observed user behavior corresponds to the initial model, triggering an alarm if not. Our evaluations show that the presented methods are highly successful with a theft detection rate of over 85% for the trained set of persons. Comparing the experiments with state of the art techniques support the strong practicality of our approach.

**Keywords:** Smart devices · Gaussian mixture model
Organic computing · Self-awareness · CANDIES
Probabilistic theft detection

## 1 Introduction

More and more smart devices are available nowadays, interconnected and always trying to improve our daily lives. Their automated support ranges from reminders for meetings via navigational assistance to analyzing and improving our running style. Their ubiquitous assistance is completely pervading our


J. van den Herik and A. P. Rocha (Eds.): ICAART 2018, LNAI 11352, pp. 247–273, 2019.
https://doi.org/10.1007/978-3-030-05453-3_12

personal environments. It is also common that users have more than one smart device, as old ones are rarely disposed or sold. Unfortunately, the monetary value of such devices is also very high, so that thefts are quite common, especially in urban areas. Even though it is possible to track a stolen device afterwards, an active involvement of the user in particular is necessary – and often happens when it is already too late. The major challenge with such approaches is that theft and the discovery of the theft might be hours apart. So, we envision an approach where the device itself recognizes whether it was stolen or not autonomously and only based on internal sensors. Such self-aware systems can then trigger counteractions or alarms timely, even before the legitimate user misses the device. In terms of developing such self-* properties, the proposed approach augments the concept of initiatives such as Autonomic Computing [20] or Organic Computing [28,32]. In particular, we aim at providing capabilities to autonomously observe the user behavior and estimate whether the device itself is still carried by the owner or not. In case a severe deviation between actual and expected behavior is observed, the owner can be notified immediately using a backup-channel or sensible information can be secured even stronger. Our proposal uses methods from the field of Activity Recognition (AR) to model the characteristics of users activities. Methods from the field of Novelty Detection (ND) are then used to detect whether a carrier's activities still match that model or deviate from the expected behavior. So far, such a combination of approaches from these different research directions does not exist. We see our approach as an important step towards creating self-awareness in technical systems, as the detection of environmental changes is integral to such a task.

In this article, we use a probabilistic, generative approach based on Gaussian Mixture Models (GMMs) to classify daily activities from smartphone data. The evaluation of our method involves a case study with activity data from 14 users and 5 sessions of approximately 20 min each, so the overall database comprises roughly 24 h of user data. Even though the data covers very basic daily activities, our approach is not limited to them. The used GMM captures structure in arbitrary data, so it is not confined to a predefined set of activities. Based on the trained models, the detection of novel activities is investigated and discussed in depth. By detecting novel/previously unknown data, it is possible to realize an autonomous theft detection that works well, even with data from very simple activities. Figure 1 gives an idea of the architecture of such a system, how such a system can be designed.

The **key contributions** of our work are 1. the introduction of methods to realize an unobtrusive security feature for body-worn smart devices and 2. to realize a theft detection with a very simple and common sensor, along with easily computable features of very basic, daily activities. It is worth pointing out, that we used a very simple device for our evaluations, however, current technology has much more computing power available, so that the overall detection and modeling process can be embettered with low overhead.

This article is a refined and extended version of a conference article [18]. Most importantly, we added novel parts in comparison to the initial article as follows: (a) investigated alternative novelty detection techniques, (b) extended

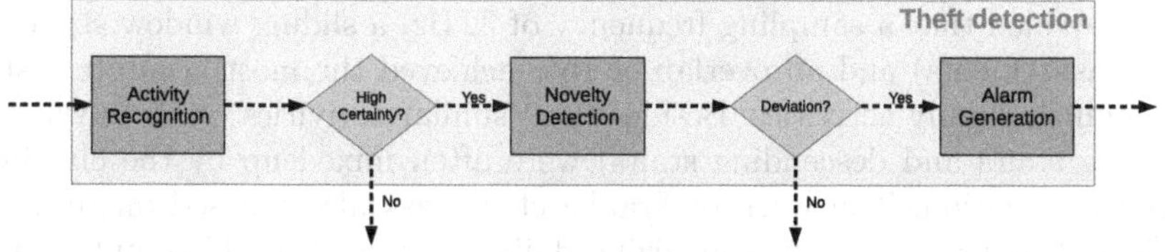


**Fig. 1.** System parts involved in a theft detection that run on smart devices. With input being processed by the AR component (see Sect. 3 for details), output with high certainty (regarding the type of activity) is forwarded to an ND component (see Sects. 4 and 5 for details). If a deviation to a pre-learned model is measured, an alarm can be generated and further actions can be taken [18].

the evaluation of the classification results incorporating further success measures, (c) compared the results of different techniques, and (d) extended the discussion of the state of the art.

The remainder of this article is structured as follows: In Sect. 2, our approach is put into perspective with the work from other groups in the area of ND and AR. In Sect. 3, the solution for the AR task based on acceleration data is presented. Based on optimized AR-models, one approach towards the problem of ND is addressed in Sect. 4. A further development is discussed and investigated afterwards in Sect. 5. Both approaches are put into perspective and compared to the state of the art method in depth in the following Sect. 6. Afterwards, in Sect. 7, a realization of a smart device with theft detection capabilities is sketched. This work is then concluded with a summary and outlook on further research in Sect. 8.

## 2 Related Work

Our related work briefly touches the field of Activity Recognition (AR), but mostly focuses on Novelty Detection (ND). The term AR was first publicly discussed nearly 20 years ago by Abowd et al. [1] and has since then gained a lot of popularity among researchers. The greatest challenge of inferring a user's activity from body-worn devices was pursued since day one, c.f. e.g. [9,15]. A first step moved research from visual data (i.e. probands were filmed) to movement data from body worn sensors. Those sensors were packed in sensor-nodes and strapped to the body, on arms, torso, thighs, etc. Later, smartphones became more popular in research, due to the sensors of interest being integrated and their increasing computing power. Those two properties led to Machine Learning (ML) techniques being implemented on the devices, so that the recognition could happen effortlessly.

Addressing preparations for ML algorithms, Lau et al. [23] focused on various parameters that have an influence on feature computation. They investigated different sensor sampling frequencies (8 Hz, 16 Hz, 32 Hz) along with different sliding window sizes (0.5 s, 1 s, 2 s, 4 s) and different sliding window overlaps (25%, 50%, 75%), with features being calculated from each sliding window. The results revealed that a sampling frequency of 32 Hz, a sliding window size of 4 s (128 measurements) and an overlap of 75% achieved the most accurate results for recognizing daily activities. Besides that, similar activities (such as walking, ascending stairs and descending stairs) were often mixed up by the classifiers under investigation. The work of Franke et al. was also focused on technical details and preprocessing in recognizing daily activities [14]. They put a lot of effort into recognizing user activities based on sound samples of a smartphone's microphone, that itself was carried in different pockets. However, they did not investigate advanced ML techniques in depth.

The question of how to build a model with recorded data is the following: *Which modeling technique(s) should be used to represent the data?* In [8], the authors give an overview of different methods, as well as approaches based on prior problem knowledge (so called "knowledge driven"). They did not discuss inconsistencies and missing values in training data, however, both effects are very common in real life datasets. An explicit distinction between discriminative approaches, e.g. Support Vector Machines (SVMs), and generative approaches, e.g. Hidden Markov Models, is made and discussed in depth. Despite their discussion of different approaches that were tried for AR scenarios, the authors neglect the heavy influence of chosen training algorithms. Our experience showed that a classifier can perform somewhere between excellent and very bad, only depending on the training algorithm; sometimes even only the initialization of the very same training algorithm. Even though classifiers of various kinds are investigated, in practical applications most solutions prefer discriminative techniques, completely neglecting the information that can be extracted when using generative models (e.g., structural information of training data). While often superior in terms of classification performance, no further information other than the class prediction can be extracted from discriminative models. Contrarily, generative models approximate the structure of the data and thus allow the detection of data points that do not fit to that structure: *outliers*. With this huge advantage, we decided to use a generative representation over a discriminative one.

Outlier detection or Novelty Detection (ND) focuses on the detection of data, that does not fit a specific data-model. With a trained model at hand, observed data is expected to fit that model, because an implicit assumption usually is that training data is representative and thus the model trained on it is a good representation of expected data to come. However, over time or due to changes in the observed environment, the distribution of observed data may change and that assumption is violated. Suppose an input space with several clusters and, at some point in time, a new cluster arising, which is not covered by the data-model. Those data points can be seen as outliers with respect to the model or, as *novel*, if never before observations were made in that region. A first categorization of ND approaches was done by Markou et al. resulting in two groups of detection mechanisms. One group included statistical methods, relying on trained models [25]. Data points were depicted as novel, if they differed too much from that model. According to the authors, statistical approaches involved non-parametric models (e.g., $k$ nearest neighbor approaches or density estimators), as well as parametric models, for which certain assumptions on the data distribution are made. The second group was associated with neural network based approaches [26], however, should not be discussed further, as our method clearly is a group one approach. The authors put a common technique in the second group, namely the detection of outliers via one-class SVMs, but to our understanding the approach is not neural network based. The approach was first suggested by [29] and later applied to the problem of object recognition based on image data by [31]. The authors used an artificial dataset with artificially added outliers, as well as images from handwritten digits with artificially added outliers. Even though a certain feasibility was shown, the authors had no real life dataset to proof their concept. Apart from that, the approach was accepted for outlier detection among researchers and later applied to, e.g., intrusion detection scenarios [24] or the detection of abnormal nodes in wireless sensor networks [33]. In both cases, training data representing a *normal* situation were used to train one-class SVMs and the goal was to detect deviations from it.

The novelty detection mechanism we propose is based on a Gaussian Mixture Model (GMM) and uses a state variable to define the current status of data fitting the model. The parameters associated with the measure then enable users to influence the tradeoff between detection-accuracy and time-to-detection. The technique was introduced and first used by Fisch et al. in [12] and further investigated in [13]. It is quite obvious, that data in the form of outliers/novel data points with respect to modelled user behaviour can help to identify device theft.

**Related Work in a Nutshell:** As noted at the beginning of this section, AR based on body worn sensors, such as smartphones, smart watches, or other wearables, is a promising field for research. Even though preprocessing steps have heavily been researched, detection algorithms mostly ignore usable information available in the dataset. So, with respect to information gained from datasets, there is room for improvement. Secondly, the field of novelty detection has a broad field of techniques at hand, however, only few were investigated on real life datasets.

Furthermore it should be noted, that theft detection based on inertial measurement units (or just acceleration signals) has never been done to our knowledge. A related work from Mitra et al. [27] focusses on theft detection, but by means of tagged objects and infrastructure elements (so call anchors). The algorithmic realization happens on a server, not on the devices/tags themselves. This is a clear disadvantage, compared to the techniques we propose, which require no additional hardware, just the smart device itself.

To address the first point, we see big potential in the use of probabilistic, generative approaches and thus investigated the usage of classifiers based on Gaussian Mixture Models and present results in Sect. 3. Building on top of that, we are first in the field of theft detection based on such models and discuss our proposals in depth in Sect. 4 and based on that, a evolutionary step of the algorithm in Sect. 5.

## 3 Activity Recognition

In Sect. 1 the overall approach with all necessary steps for a theft detection (AR followed by ND) were introduced (Fig. 1). In this section, all experiments that were performed to reach a most accurate activity prediction are discussed.

The used dataset was recorded at our institute and comprises the data of 14 different users. Each user followed a script that described which activity should be performed, how long, and in which order. This process was repeated five times for every user, with a maximum of two sessions on the same day, to reduce day specific similarities in the data. The activities under investigation were *walking*, *ascending stairs*, *descending stairs*, *standing*, and *sitting*. Please note that, while these activities are very basic, our techniques are not confined to them and, as will be explained, GMM are rather powerful modeling approaches that can capture all kinds of data. The five basic activities are chosen as examples for comparison with other studies, cf., e.g., [21,22]. All data were three-dimensional acceleration data recorded on a Nokia N97 with a highest possible frequency of 182 Hz. Overall 70 sessions with an overall length of approximately 1400 min were recorded and labeled.

Preprocessing steps included a resampling to 32 Hz (cf. Sect. 2), a linear interpolation of missing values, a feature extraction, and a standardization. To train an optimal classifier for the activity recognition, we assessed the influence of (1) an additional value, (2) different features, (3) optimize parameters and (4) aggregated classifier outputs.

The first step towards improving AR performance was the addition of the *magnitude* as additional value. The values of this new "dimension" were calculated as the length of the acceleration vector by using the Euclidean norm:

$$mag = \sqrt{x^2 + y^2 + z^2}. \tag{1}$$

Afterwards, for every dimension the following of the acceleration signal, four features were extracted:

- mean

$$\mu = \frac{1}{N} \sum_{n=1}^{N} x_n, \tag{2}$$

- standard deviation

$$\sigma = \sqrt{\frac{1}{N-1} \sum_{n=1}^{N} (x_n - \mu)^2}, \tag{3}$$

- energy of Fourier transformation

$$energy = \sum_{n=1}^{N} {fft_n}^2, \tag{4}$$

– normalized information entropy of Fourier transformation

$$entropy = \frac{-1}{\log(N)} \sum_{n=1}^{N} \mathit{fft}_n \cdot \log(\mathit{fft}_n), \tag{5}$$

with $\mathit{fft}_n$ being the magnitude of the $n$-th Fourier coefficient. Please note that the energy (Eq. (4)) could also be computed on the sliding window directly, following Parseval's theorem (cf., e.g., [6]).

All features are extracted with a sliding window approach which is quite common in AR, cf., e.g., [23, 30] with a size of 128 values and an offset of 32 (i.e. 75% overlap); aggregating 4 s of data for one classification prediction every second.

The generative approach we used as a classifier is also used as a basis for the novelty detection mechanism later (see Sect. 4), as the detailed modeling of data enables a reliable outlier detection. Generative approaches model the given data by means of a density model; so that after training, data generated by this model would underly the same distribution as the original training data. Given $C$ different activities, the trained classifier should be used to compute $p(c|\mathbf{x}')$; the probability for a class $c \in C$, given a sample $\mathbf{x}'$. With an overall set of $J$ Normal distributions (*components*) in the model and class labels (*conclusions*) associated with each component, the posterior distribution to predict a class, given an input sample $\mathbf{x}$, can be formulated in a Bayesian manner as follows:

$$\begin{aligned} p(c|\mathbf{x}) &= \frac{p(\mathbf{x}|c)p(c)}{p(\mathbf{x})} \\ &= p(c) \sum_{j=1}^{J} \frac{p(\mathbf{x}|c,j)p(j)}{p(\mathbf{x})}. \end{aligned} \tag{6}$$

With that notation, $p(c)$ is the probability for class $c$, the *class prior*, the term $p(\mathbf{x}|c,j)$ describes the probability for a sample $\mathbf{x}$, given component $j$ and its associated class $c$. $p(j)$ also underlies a multinomial distribution, with each parameter $\pi_j$ being a so called *mixture coefficient* that represents the weight, component $j$ has in the model. Note that all mixture coefficients are greater than 0.0 and sum up to 1.0. Finally, the term $p(\mathbf{x})$ is the probability of sample $\mathbf{x}$ given the current GMM. Derived from that, the *responsibility* $p(\mathbf{x}|j)$, is defined as follows:

$$p(\mathbf{x}|j) = \frac{p(\mathbf{x}|j)p(j)}{p(\mathbf{x})}. \tag{7}$$

Considering the generative nature of GMMs, this expression shows how responsible a component can be held for the generation of sample $\mathbf{x}$. We focus on a Classifier based on Gaussian Mixture Models (CMM) as previously defined in, e.g., [13], trained by a realization of Variational Bayesian Inference (VI), a method proposed in [4].

The second optimization step was a better computation of features to allow a better discrimination between *ascending stairs*, *descending stairs*, and *walking*.

It turned out, that the most vivid combination was formed by the replacement of the Fourier transformation based features (Eqs. (4) and (5)). They were replaced by mean and standard deviation of the fourier coefficients, that were computed on a highpass-filtered fourier transformation (cut-off frequency: 18 Hz). The great performance of this replacements is no coincidence, but was previously observed by others, cf. [19], stating that "simple" features (mean and standard deviation) perform very well most of the time. It should also be noted, that using additional features does not necessarily mean that the models perform better. Considering the fact that using more features usually needs more resources and takes a longer computation time, feature combinations where features are replaced, should be preferred.

The third optimization step was the optimization of classifier parameters. A popular method from the domain of ML is a parameter grid search, so that an optimal configuration for the classifier can be used in a practical application. However, a detailed grid search is exhaustive, since it tests every possible parameter combination. It also comes at very high computational costs, with respect to time and resources. The parameter search was carried out in a five-fold cross-validation, with four parts being used for training and the fifth part being used for parameter-validation. This leads to 70 (14 users, 5 sessions each) different models, each one with the need for a grid search on three of the four VI-parameters, cf. [4]. To find optimized parameters for the CMM, we use an initialization heuristic with initial centers being placed farthest apart from each other as described by Bishop [5], with an initial number of 50 components. Convergence criterion for the training algorithm was a likelihood function, with a convergence threshold of 0.01 between two consecutive steps. Following the parameter-naming as in [5], the parameter $\alpha$ was varied between 0.1–0.5, $\beta$ between 0.1–1.0 and $w$ between 0.01–1.0. As known from comparable scenarios, these regions are most interesting. Parameter combinations were chosen from these intervals and evaluated in a five-fold cross-validation (overall 17920 classifier trainings), with the classification error of the validation data being the comparison measure and the lowest error denoting the best fitting model.

As a last, fourth, optimization step to improve the classification performance, a short term memory is added right after the classifier. This is motivated by the fact that users are unlikely to change their current activity for just a short period of time. E.g. with our preprocessing, every second a class prediction is made; but *sit*, *ascending stairs*, *sit* is a highly implausible chain of activities, given one prediction per second. The size of this memory, which was realized as a FIFO buffer, had varying sizes between 2 and 10, storing the last activity predictions. The classifier as we used it before, is not affected in any way. The final system prediction is determined by a simple majority vote on the buffer. If there is no majority, the last majority decided value will be taken and, if the buffer is not filled yet, the classifier output is used. Please note that with each actual activity transition, there is a delay in system output. However, numbers clearly indicate that those few misclassifications (which only occur on activity transitions) compensate the greater number of (otherwise misclassified) "outliers" during normal operation.

Buffer sizes 2, 3, 5 and 7 are favorable (depending on whether recognition speed is important to an application or not, while buffer sizes 4, 6 and 8–10 performed worse for each user. In our case, a buffer size of 7 implies a prediction delay of 4 s between activities.

Optimizations were done for each user separately, while the results are aggregated and summarized in Table 1.

**Table 1.** CMM classification accuracies and f1-scores of test data with one additional optimization added in each step, showing one step per line. The last line represents the setting with all optimizations active. Mean ± Standard Deviation are evaluated by five-fold cross-validations and aggregated across all 14 users. The best results are shaded gray.

| Optimization | Accuracy (Test) [%] | $F_1$-score (Test) [%] |
|---|---|---|
| baseline | 85.38 ± 5.00 | 85.45 ± 9.91 |
| + additional value | 87.48 ± 5.06 | 87.58 ± 8.83 |
| + better features | 91.03 ± 3.20 | 91.13 ± 6.32 |
| + grid search | 91.20 ± 3.15 | 91.30 ± 2.90 |
| + short term memory | 93.01 ± 2.69 | 93.16 ± 2.49 |

The overall improvement based on five-fold cross-validations, leads to an average classification error of 6.99% ± 2.79% standard deviation, which is an error reduction of 7.63%. It is also worth mentioning, that wisely chosen features lead to the greatest improvement (3.55%), whereas a parameter optimization of the training algorithm reveals a surprisingly low improvement (0.17%).

## 4 $\chi^2$-Novelty Detection

A simple novelty detection mechanism is described in this section, along with the performed parameter optimization and experiments. The measure is based on CMMs and was first proposed by Fisch et al. in [12]. It is bound to [0.0, 1.0] and based on a penalty/rewards scheme, i.e., with each new observation a variable is either increased (data point fits the model) or decreased (data point seems to be an outlier). The term novelty stems from the first applications of this measure, where data (that is unknown to a generative model, cf. Sect. 2) represented novel processes in the input space. Hence, a "dissatisfaction" of the measure with the current model was the result: There were more penalties than rewards for the observations and thus the measure fell, eventually below a predefined threshold. Please note that the detection mechanism can be applied to GMMs of any kind. Here, the pretrained models from Sect. 3, that are based on basic daily activities, are used for all evaluations.

### 4.1 Parameter Optimization

The novelty detection mechanism has two parameters ($\alpha$, $\eta$) and a threshold $\gamma$. Once the measure falls below $\gamma$, it indicates a difference between observations and data-model. The parameter $\alpha$ describes the fraction of data points that should be seen as "normal" with respect to the model, with $1 - \alpha$ denoting the fraction of outliers that is acceptable. Values from the interval [0.75, 0.95] were chosen in steps of 0.05. Other values were not investigated, as data with more than 25% outliers ($\alpha = 0.75$) or less than 5% outliers ($\alpha = 0.95$) might appear in data – but to our understanding, would only be so extreme due to bad models. The parameter $\eta$ describes a kind of sensitivity, i.e., the magnitude of the measure's punishment and reward factors. As in comparable datasets, tested values were chosen from the interval [0.001, 0.1] in 100 equidistant steps. Finally, the threshold $\gamma$ allows for statements about data-to-model fitment: If the measure stays above that threshold for every data point (more reward than punishment), the current data and the training data seem to underly the same distribution. Hence, the model covers the data well and the novelty measure stays up. In contrast, data that underly a different distribution than the training data, will reduce the novelty value until it falls below $\gamma$.

It is obvious that $\eta$ and $\gamma$ are connected: a lower threshold can be reached within the same number of data points as a higher one, if the sensitivity is increased. Furthermore, the adaption of one parameter can be compensated by changing the value of the other parameter, resulting in the same effects. Due to this, $\gamma$ was fixed before $\eta$ was adjusted independently for each user.

In our experiments, the goal is to find an $\eta$ for each investigated $\alpha$, so that no novelty is detected for the own user, but for all other users (i.e., low misclasification rate), as fast as possible. For $\gamma$, 8 equidistant values from the interval [0.0, 0.7] were investigated. If more than one $\eta$ fulfilling the condition during validation was found, it was averaged for final testing. For a detailed description of the parameters please refer to [12].

For all evaluation scenarios two graphs were generated. The figures for success rates show the reached values, illustrated by a bar for each $\alpha$ and $\gamma$ combination for a fitting $\eta$, which was determined by the respective method. The success rate is composed of user data (bottom), where no novelty should be detected and data from other users (top), for which the measure should fall below $\gamma$ for success.

Because there is more data from other users than from the actual user (Ratio 13 to 1), the results are weighted accordingly to have a maximum af 50% each, so that the overall maximum is 100%. The average time needed for a novelty detection is displayed by a line chart. This time is only determined by the number of successfully detected novelties. Displayed values of both graphs are averaged results of five-fold cross-validations from each user.

When looking at working combinations of $\alpha$ and $\gamma$, successful detections mean that a fitting $\eta$ was found during our experiments.

One way to configure the $\eta$ parameter for each user, would be the usage of the training data to optimize the parameters. In other words, the optimization takes place with data, which "is known" to the models. However, a major concern for this scenario is overfitting: If the data was used to create the model, how representative would an optimization on its basis be?

As we wanted to use unknown, but user-fitting data to find a specific $\eta$, additional validation data was necessary. To address this issue, models were trained with only three out of five user-sessions, with one of the remaining sessions being a parameter validation set and the other one being the parameter test set (**V-VAL**). The model parameters themselves were optimized via grid search on $\alpha$ and $\eta$.

The optimization was aiming at an $\eta$, that made the novelty measure sensitive enough to reach a value in the interval [0.74, 0.76] for the correct user at least once, however, the measure was not allowed to fall below that interval. This specific interval can also be interpreted as follows: The target was to adjust the sensitivity, so that a 25% deviance on the current user's validation data was allowed with a tolerance of 1% ($0.75 \pm 0.01$). With that condition satisfied, all other test-users should be detected by the so parametrized measure.

Figure 2 visualizes the evaluation: The higher the demanded recognition threshold $\gamma$, the lower is the rate of successfully detected novelties. Everything considered, this means that for a predefined threshold ($\gamma$) the chance of finding a suitable sensitivity ($\eta$) decreases when the fraction of tolerated outliers is reduced ($\alpha$ is risen).

It can also be seen that for different $\gamma$ the success rate hardly differs, basically proving the dependence between $\gamma$ and $\eta$: for nearly every threshold, a sensitivity can be found. A first significant drop of the success rate can be recognized for a $\gamma$ of 0.60. The best average detection time was reached for $\alpha$-values of 0.75 and 0.80.

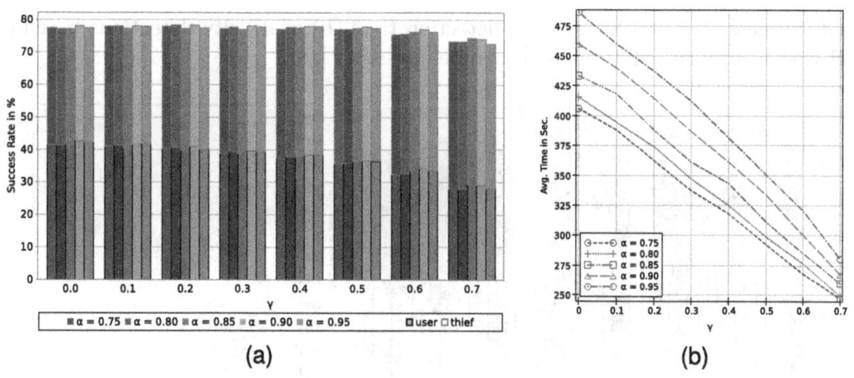


**Fig. 2.** Success rates (a) and average times (b) of a novelty detection with various configurations of the novelty measure (**V-VAL** [18]).

### 4.2 Ensemble-Based Approach

As three out of four training datasets are used to train the model on which novelty parameters are validated with the fourth session, four different models can also be stored and used as an ensemble for novelty detection. With several models, a number of ensemble members have to agree on the type of a data point (outlier or model-compatible), before the dataset under investigation can be identified as fraud.

Four novelty detections were run in parallel for one test session. Deviating data is detected, as soon as a predefined majority of the ensemble detects a novelty (**ENS**).

In Figs. 3, 4, 5 and 6 the evaluation results are visualized. A majority of one (Fig. 3a and b) results in a rather sensitive ensemble, that seems to be overcautious, the higher the detection threshold is selected.

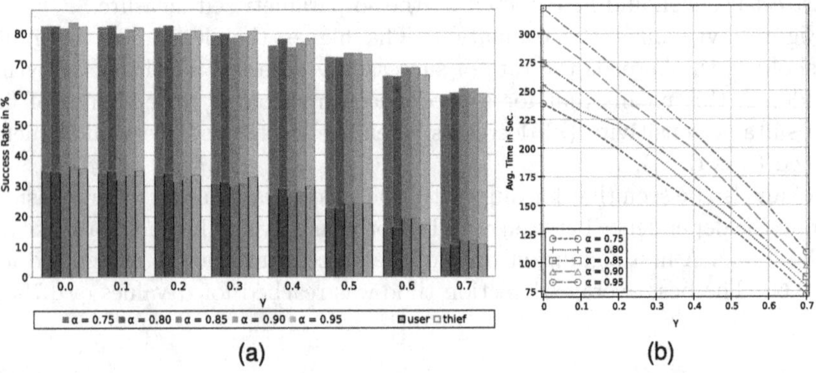


**Fig. 3.** Success rate (a) and average detection time (b) of novelty detections based on **ENS** with a majority of 1 out of 4 members ($ENS_1$) [18].

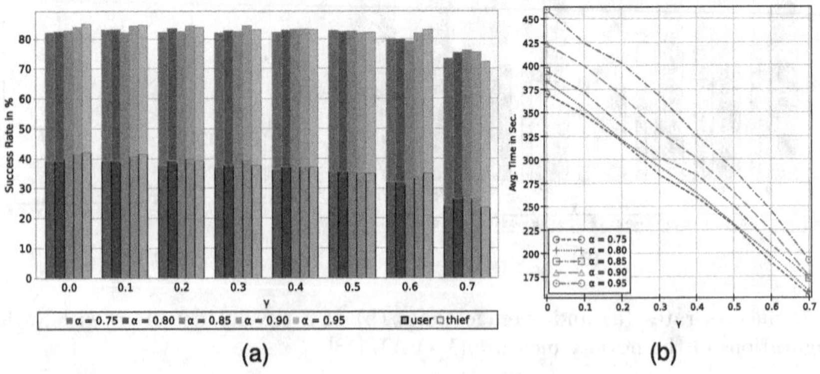


**Fig. 4.** Success rate (c) and average detection time (d) of novelty detections based on **ENS** with a majority of 2 out of 4 members ($ENS_2$) [18].

This means that novelty is easily detected, but also that the righteous user is more often falsely detected as non fitting the data. This can be seen in the success rate for data from other users, which is nearly at the maximum of 50% for each $\alpha$. However, in turn the success rate on legitimate user data is way below 50%; with $\gamma = 0.70$ even around 10% for each $\alpha$. A $\gamma$ of 0.20 seems to be a practical value, because the success rate on the user's data starts to drop from 0.30 onwards. With this low $\gamma$, an $\alpha$ of 0.80 reveals the best success rate and the second best detection time.

For each threshold, a majority of two increases the detection performance (Fig. 4a and b). A $\gamma$ of 0.60 and an $\alpha$ of 0.95 are a good choice here, as the success rate is high and the detection time fast.

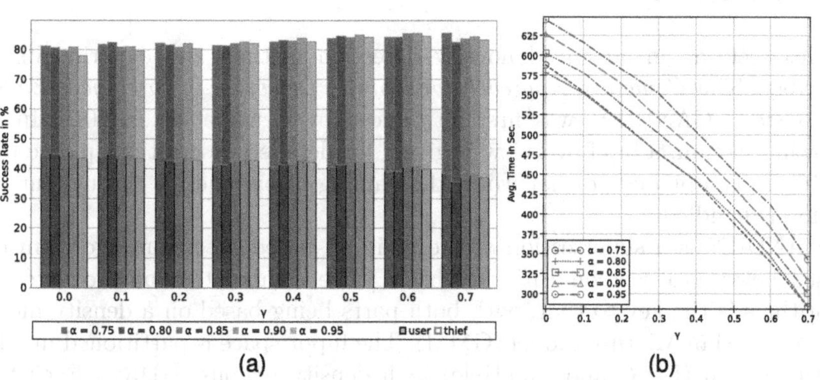


**Fig. 5.** Success rate (e) and average detection time (f) of novelty detections based on **ENS** with a majority of 3 out of 4 members ($ENS_3$) [18].

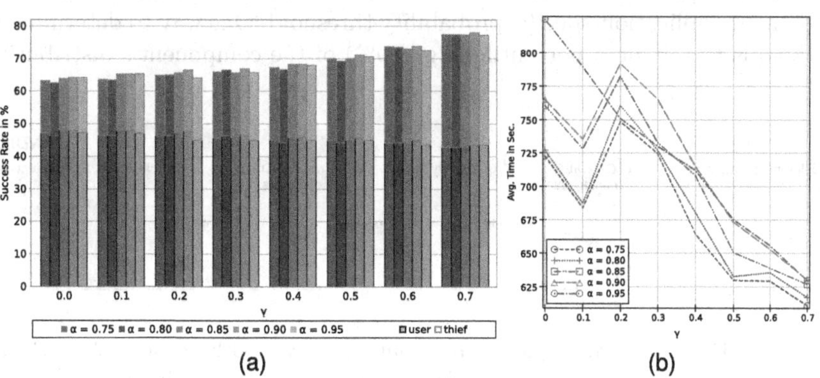


**Fig. 6.** Success rate (g) and average detection time (h) of novelty detections based on **ENS** with a majority of 4 out of 4 members ($ENS_4$) [18].

For a majority of three (Fig. 5a and b), the success rate for novelty detection is slightly rising with an increased $\gamma$, while the false alarm rate also increases (user success rate decreases). In order to keep the detection time low, a $\gamma$ of 0.7 and an $\alpha$ of 0.75 seem to be a good choice.

The majority of four is yet another special case (Fig. 6a and b). The insensitivity against deviating data is rather high and takes comparatively long, even with high thresholds (e.g. $\gamma = 0.60$ or 0.70). Output from this model can be interpreted as very reliable, however, successful detections take a very long time. A $\gamma$ of 0.70 is the only meaningful value here. Due to the lowest detection time with such an ensemble, an $\alpha$ of 0.75 would be an appropriate choice.

## 5 CANDIES

In this section, an advanced novelty detection method and experiments are described. The *Combined Approach for Novelty Detection in Intelligent Embedded Systems* CANDIES, was first introduced by Gruhl et al. in 2016. In the following section, a brief overview is given, for detailed descriptions please refer to [16]. In compliance to that work, the naming of parameters throughout this section is handled.

CANDIES is a supersession of the plain $\chi^2$-based detection algorithm discussed before, to overcome its drawbacks. The combination of two detection algorithms is the key to that, with both parts being based on a density model, e.g., a Gaussian Mixture Model (GMM). The input space is partitioned in a low density region (LDR) and (multiple) high density regions (HDRs). Each type of region then requires different detection methods. In the LDR, the detector searches for unexpected densities, more precisely, for accumulations of observations. This is done by a density based clustering algorithm. The HDR detection tries to identify deviations between observed data and modeled densities. This is achieved by means of a $\chi^2$ goodness of fit test. Each component of the GMM might be interpreted as a HDR, with the transition from HDR to LDR being based on an application-specific probability threshold. One way to determine the threshold is to rely on a percentile (e.g., 99%) of the component's distribution.

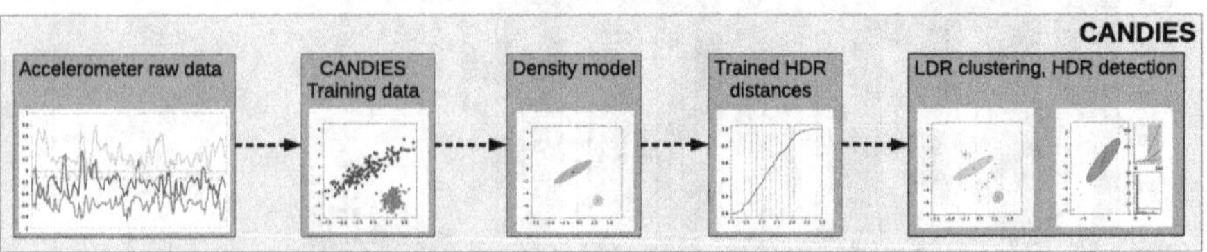


**Fig. 7.** CANDIES training sequence. Raw data is converted by means of a PCA and feature extraction, so that the training data can be used to train a density model. From that model, high density regions can be identified and $\chi^2$-detectors can be trained on a per-component-basis. Finally, a LDR-clustering, followed by a HDR-detection, are used to identify novelty.

A full process of CANDIES' training and detection is depicted in Fig. 7, with explanations for the most important part following in the remainder of this section. The current implementation works on a Principal Component Analysis (PCA)-transformed version of activity data, i.e., the raw training data has been transformed and the transformation-parameters were used to transform the test-data, too. That is why the density model for detection had to be trained from scratch and the models that were used for AR (cf. Sect. 3) could not be re-used in this specific application. After the PCA, the feature extraction happens as described previously.

The parameters for our experiments were found via grid search, similar to the search described in Sect. 4.1, on a user-to-user basis.

### 5.1 LDR Detection – Density Based Clustering

For LDR detection *2 Stage Novelty Detection and Reaction* 2SNDR is used (cf. [7]), which extends an existing GMM with novelty detection and model adaptation capabilities. In its first stage, 2SNDR identifies samples as "suspicious" if the predicted responsibilities (cf., [4]) of the model are below a given threshold, implying that the samples do not suit the model. Otherwise the sample is denoted as "normal" and therefore not considered for LDR detection, but for further processing by the HDR detector of CANDIES. Suspicious samples that occured in the input space are stored in a ring buffer. On that buffer, a nonparametric clustering algorithm (inspired by DBSCAN, cf. [10]) is run. A process is then recognized as novel, as soon as one of the clusters from the buffer reaches a sufficient size of at least two samples. Samples which are not affiliated with a cluster are denoted as noise. As soon as two noise samples are close enough to each other, a new cluster is formed. Samples belong to a cluster, if their distance is below a given threshold. Clusters may be fused if a suspicious sample lies close enough to both clusters. An example of such a situation is visualized in Fig. 8, where one new sample initiates the merge of two existent clusters. When the buffer is filled, the oldest samples are removed; so clusters can shrink and disappear over time as well.

### 5.2 HDR Detection – $\chi^2$ Goodness of Fit Test

The HDR novelty detection is based on a goodness of fit test and is performed by multiple detectors, namely one per GMM-component. Each detector must be initialized with training samples. The training samples for each component are affiliated with respect to the maximum responsibility (cf. Eq. (7)). From then on, instead of the actual feature space, only Mahalanobis distances (based on the component's covariance matrices) of the samples to the component's mean are used, reducing the dimensionality and thus the computational costs of each detector. Furthermore, each component stores a buffer of "normal" samples. Their distances are compared with the expected, trained distances, using a $\chi^2$-test. If the distributions of distances do not match, novelty is detected.

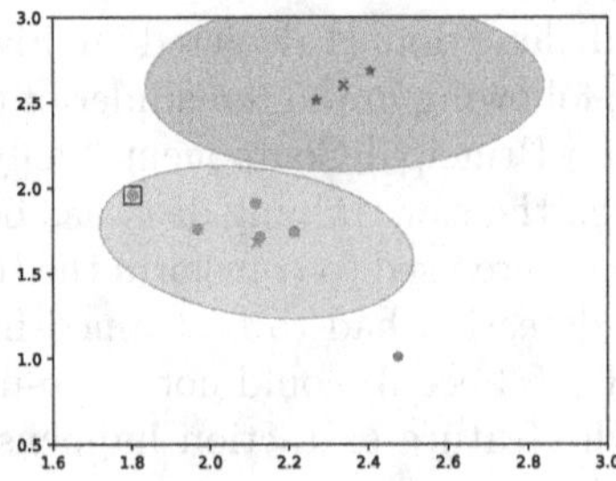


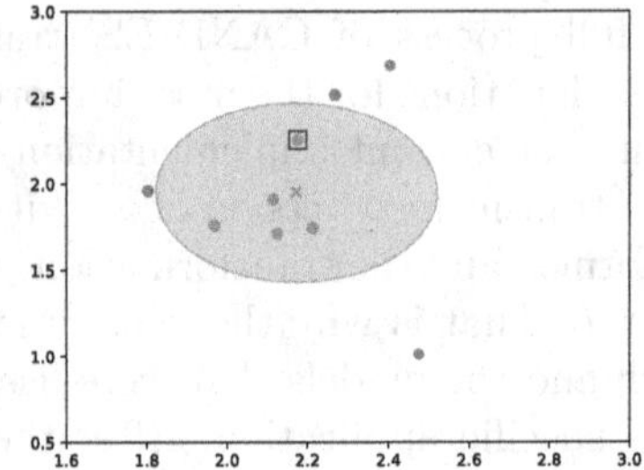


**Fig. 8.** Visualization of an examplary cluster-merge in the LDR with several suspicious samples. The **x** marks the center, the ellipse indicates the outline of the cluster, the newest sample is marked with a red box. On the left, two clusters can be seen, whereas on the right, a new sample occurs and connects both clusters, so that only one cluster remains. (Color figure online)

The results of our first evaluation on the dataset using CANDIES are displayed in Table 2. It can clearly be seen that the approach successfully detects theft-scenarios. However on some users, alerts are also generated on own-user-data and thus produce false positives.

**Table 2.** Comparison of the success rates and average detection times of all users based on CANDIES with LDR and HDR detection as described in Sects. 5.1 and 5.2 respectively. The average results are shaded grey in the form mean ± standard deviation.

| | ***Success Rate*** [%] | | | ***Avg.*** |
|---|---|---|---|---|
| User | user [%] | non-owner [%] | total [%] | [*s*] |
| **1** | 80.00 | 70.77 | 75.38 | 791 |
| **2** | 60.00 | 73.85 | 66.92 | 694 |
| **3** | 60.00 | 100.00 | 80.00 | 657 |
| **4** | 100.00 | 73.85 | 86.92 | 797 |
| **5** | 100.00 | 81.54 | 90.77 | 722 |
| **6** | 80.00 | 86.15 | 83.08 | 680 |
| **7** | 100.00 | 80.00 | 90.00 | 836 |
| **8** | 80.00 | 100.00 | 90.00 | 698 |
| **9** | 60.00 | 100.00 | 80.00 | 681 |
| **10** | 60.00 | 95.38 | 77.69 | 663 |
| **11** | 40.00 | 96.92 | 68.46 | 689 |
| **12** | 60.00 | 100.00 | 80.00 | 646 |
| **13** | 80.00 | 96.92 | 88.46 | 729 |
| **14** | 60.00 | 96.92 | 78.46 | 645 |
| **ø** | 72.86 ± 17.90 | 89.45 ± 10.85 | 81.15 ± 7.37 | 709 ± 58 |

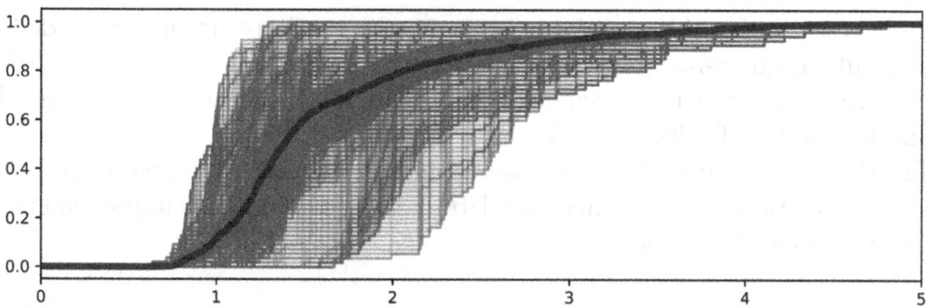


**Fig. 9.** Several ECDFs of a training dataset, depending on the content of the HDR buffer. Over time, due to different activities in the dataset, different distances are present in the buffer. The blue ECDF represents the distances, that occur in the overall dataset. (Color figure online)

### 5.3 HDR Detection – $\chi^2$-Ensembles

Activity data pose a special challenge when working with probabilistic models: Often overseen is the fact that such models assume data that is independent and identically distributed (i.i.d.). However, activity data are time-series and as such, the i.i.d.-assumption barely holds. The problem is that the distance-distribution of samples for one component are not consistent and vary over time. For a goodness of fit test, a changed distance-distribution is inseparable from the distance-distribution of novel data.

Ultimately, because of these variations, we observed situations, where the HDR detector reports novelty even on the training data. This problem is visualized in Fig. 9, where several, different empirical cumulative distribution functions (ECDFs) for distances of a training data set of a single component are visualized.

The blue ECDF is the ECDF that occurs, when the whole training dataset is taken into account. Please remember that the form of this curve is the basis for this component's $\chi^2$-test and the decision whether data fits the model or not, can be seen as a equivalency-check between two of these curves.

In other words, the different ECDFs are a result of the affiliation of samples from different activities with that very component. Using all available training samples to create just one ECDF proved to be imprecise, so we came up with three possible solutions, to counteract this flaw: (1) Disable HDR detection for components with large variety of distributions in the trainings data set, (2) Adjust the threshold of each HDR detector depending on the variety or (3) Train multiple detectors for the component, if the variety of the component is *too large*. As the first option would be a step back and a useful criterion for adjusting the threshold proved nearly impossible to find, we pursued option three. This lead to a HDR detector which is further referred as $\chi^2$-ensemble, as it is an ensemble of several $\chi^2$ detectors per component. To handle a variety that is "too large", CANDIES performs a HDR detection on the training data. If the detector reports novelty, another $\chi^2$ detector is added, based on the distances in the current buffer. After training, current observations are only regarded as novel, if all ensemble-members detect novelty.

A realization of this improvement was implemented and the evaluation results are summarized in Table 3.

The detection rate for the user itself could be increased by 2.86%, while the standard deviation could be decreased by 2.45%. Overall, an improvement of 1.32% in average was gained.

**Table 3.** Comparison of the success rates and average detection times of all users based on CANDIES with improved HDR detection, relying on $\chi^2$-ensembles per component. The LDR detection is left untouched and works as before. The average results are shaded grey in the form mean ± standard deviation.

| User | ***Success Rate*** [%] user [%] | non-owner [%] | total [%] | ***Avg.*** [*s*] |
|---|---|---|---|---|
| **1** | 80.00 | 66.15 | 73.08 | 795 |
| **2** | 60.00 | 72.31 | 66.15 | 710 |
| **3** | 60.00 | 100.00 | 80.00 | 657 |
| **4** | 80.00 | 95.38 | 87.69 | 698 |
| **5** | 100.00 | 80.00 | 90.00 | 723 |
| **6** | 80.00 | 83.08 | 81.54 | 669 |
| **7** | 100.00 | 80.00 | 90.00 | 836 |
| **8** | 80.00 | 98.46 | 89.23 | 687 |
| **9** | 80.00 | 95.38 | 87.69 | 680 |
| **10** | 60.00 | 95.38 | 77.69 | 663 |
| **11** | 60.00 | 92.31 | 76.15 | 677 |
| **12** | 60.00 | 100.00 | 80.00 | 642 |
| **13** | 100.00 | 92.31 | 96.15 | 773 |
| **14** | 60.00 | 98.46 | 79.23 | 667 |
| **ø** | 75.71 ± 15.45 | 89.23 ± 10.56 | 82.47 ± 7.75 | 705 ± 55 |

## 6 Discussion

The results presented so far involve innovative techniques, rely on generative models and goodness of fit tests. In the following discussion, a thorough investigation of our approaches is done, as well as a comparison to the most prominent outlier detection algorithm from the literature, based on a $\nu$-SVM.

### 6.1 One-Class SVM

For a meaningful comparison we decided to focus on one-class SVMs, which are commonly used for outlier/anomaly detection [2,11,17]. Positive data (in our case data from the actual user) is often used to train a discriminative function, which then outputs whether data belongs to the positive class ("+") or not ("−"). For that purpose, $\nu$-SVMs with a Radial Basis Function (RBF)-kernel ($\gamma_{\text{RBF}} = 0.10$) were trained in the same manner as before, i.e., three out of five sessions were used for training, a parameter-optimization was done on a fourth session (validation session) and the evaluation was done with the remaining session (test session). For the optimization step, the overall number of positive outputs from the validation set was used: The more positive predictions a certain parameter value caused, the better the trained SVM (and thus the current $\nu$) was considered.

As $\nu$ can be interpreted as a maximum accepted fraction of data points outside the region of interest, it is comparable to the parameter $\alpha$ from our novelty measure and thus, values $\{.05, .10, .15, .20, .25, .30\}$ were investigated. Cross-validated over all users, $\nu = 0.05$ turned out to be the best available parameter, i.e., the maximum number of accepted data points was reached for that parameter.

The next challenge on $\nu$-SVMs is the creation of a mechanism for novelty detection, so that outliers are recognized with a specific certainty: Our method of choice was the short term memory technique as introduced for the AR-task in Sect. 3.

**Table 4.** Comparison of the success rates and average detection times of all users using parameter optimized $\nu$-SVMs. The average results are shaded grey in the form mean ± standard deviation [18].

| | ***Success Rate*** [%] | | | ***Avg.*** |
|---|---|---|---|---|
| User | user [%] | non-owner [%] | total [%] | [$s$] |
| **1** | 80.00 | 13.85 | 46.93 | 1182 |
| **2** | 100.00 | 38.46 | 69.23 | 1262 |
| **3** | 80.00 | 60.00 | 70.00 | 1117 |
| **4** | 80.00 | 27.69 | 53.85 | 1114 |
| **5** | 60.00 | 27.69 | 43.85 | 1198 |
| **6** | 100.00 | 33.85 | 66.93 | 1075 |
| **7** | 80.00 | 80.00 | 80.00 | 858 |
| **8** | 80.00 | 33.85 | 56.93 | 1018 |
| **9** | 80.00 | 40.00 | 60.00 | 1109 |
| **10** | 80.00 | 27.69 | 53.85 | 901 |
| **11** | 100.00 | 16.92 | 58.46 | 1322 |
| **12** | 100.00 | 4.62 | 52.31 | 1032 |
| **13** | 80.00 | 3.08 | 41.54 | 1212 |
| **14** | 80.00 | 96.92 | 88.46 | 442 |
| **ø** | 84.29 ± 11.58 | 36.04 ± 26.87 | 60.17 ± 13.48 | 1060 ± 204 |

The necessary majority for outliers within a window was fixed to being greater than 50%. For each user, a specific window length was found. Starting with a window length of 3, the size was incremented up to the point, where all other users where recognized as being different (had more outliers in the sliding window than accepted data points), which corresponds to the fastest possible reaction time in terms of novelty detection.

Given an optimal sliding window length, the following criteria had to be met for a working configuration: (a) the dataset of the current user has to cause less than 50% outlier predictions, while (b) for each other user, the fraction of outlier predictions was greater than 50%.

Still, as a result, only 328 out of 930 (14 users with 13 datasets from other users and 5 sessions of each other user being tested) novelties were actually detected. Results are summarized in Table 4.

From the table can clearly be seen that the acceptance of user data by the trained $\nu$-SVM is rather high, however, the detection rate of non-owner-data is very bad: Out of 65 possible detections (13 other users, 5 sessions each) at most 62 (in the case of user 14th SVM) and at least 2 (in the case of user 13th SVM) were detected as not-fitting. Furthermore, the average detection time is quite high. Overall can be stated, that a one-class SVM seems unsuitable for novelty detection tasks in AR-scenarios. This statement is supported by the fact that the average detection accuracies have a very high standard deviation.

### 6.2 Comparison

In Table 5 a comparison of our new techniques along the commonly accepted one-class SVM approach is visualized.

Each entry comes from the most suitable, parameter-optimized configuration of novelty detection parameters. Whereas the SVM struggles most with an overall working detection, the $\chi^2$-based approaches are working and can even be parametrized to the user's needs: The tradeoff between accuracy and detection speed is the biggest issue and should be handled with care, depending on, e.g., whether false alarms are acceptable or not. In all investigated scenarios, the SVM delivers a mostly bad performance for novelty detection, while offering a rather acceptable performance for identifying the correct user. The influence of novel data however, leads to a seemingly random behavior. Furthermore, the SVM-based approach is completely inappropriate in terms of fast detections.

When false alarms (the actual user's data is detected as foreign) should be avoided at all costs, an ensemble with a majority of 4 out of 4 ($ENS_4$) seems to be the method of choice. It has the highest success rate (85.71%) for correctly identifying the owner, however, this comes (1) at the cost of the lowest detection rate for non-owner-data and (2) also a long detection time of more than 10 min (611 s). Approaches based on CANDIES also prove to be very reliable (approx. 82.47% success rate), however, at the cost of a long detection time (705 s, more than 11 min). It becomes obvious that the algorithm can be applied to activity data, but at the cost of inferior performance, as data distribution assumptions are not met. However, it should be noted that GMM-based approaches allow

**Table 5.** Comparison of the success rates and detection times for theft detection methods with suggested novelty configurations as described in Sects. 4.1 and 4.2 and a parameter optimized $\nu$-SVM. All values are given in the form mean ± standard deviation. Total success rate is calculated as the mean of user and thief success rates, time is calculated as the mean of successfully detected thefts. The best results are shaded gray.

| Method | *Success Rate* | | | *Time* |
|---|---|---|---|---|
| | user [%] | non-owner [%] | total [%] | [s] |
| **V-VAL** | 75.71 ± 11.32 | 79.45 ± 15.94 | 77.58 ± 13.95 | 325 ± 134 |
| **ENS$_1$** | 68.57 ± 18.07 | 96.59 ± 6.96 | 82.58 ± 19.59 | 219 ± 151 |
| **ENS$_2$** | 70.00 ± 18.13 | 96.04 ± 8.50 | 83.02 ± 19.24 | 246 ± 164 |
| **ENS$_3$** | 77.14 ± 12.78 | 93.96 ± 12.16 | 85.55 ± 15.04 | 284 ± 215 |
| **ENS$_4$** | 85.71 ± 9.04 | 69.34 ± 27.64 | 77.53 ± 22.13 | 611 ± 251 |
| **CANDIES$_{\chi^2}$** | 72.86 ± 17.90 | 89.45 ± 10.85 | 81.15 ± 7.37 | 709 ± 58 |
| **CANDIES$_{\chi^2-ens}$** | 75.71 ± 15.45 | 89.23 ± 10.56 | 82.47 ± 7.75 | 705 ± 55 |
| **One-Class SVM** | 84.29 ± 11.58 | 36.04 ± 26.87 | 60.17 ± 13.48 | 1060 ± 204 |

for a more precise statement, be it on user- or non-user-data, compared to techniques from the current state of the art. This seems to be a manifestation of the generative property those models possess.

If a good trade-off between success rates for user and novelty detection is targeted, an ensemble with a majority with 3 (ENS$_3$) is the best choice, with the highest total success rate of 85.55% and a rather acceptable detection time of 284 s in average. For increased flexibility, further parameters for CANDIES using $\chi^2$-ensembles are also a promising way and worth investigating. Another strong argument for CANDIES is the lower standard deviation in terms of success rate and detection time, seemingly the other approaches are more influenced by random effects.

## 7 Theft Detection

To train an autonomic theft detection for smart devices, it is necessary to train user models, that are as specific as possible. In terms of high quality data-descriptions, estimations via GMMs are very suitable. AR-datasets as used in this work can be collected explicitly or implicitly, while users follow their regular routine. With the goal of detecting unknown data (e.g., data from non-owners), please note that our modelling approach is not limited to a labeled dataset, but instead models the data distribution, no matter if classes are available or not. Labeled data just provides additional information, so that the false alarm rate can be minimized (see below). The techniques are also not limited to the simple activities chosen for this study, and the techniques can be adapted to more complex activities. Of course, several sessions of data, as used here, allow for

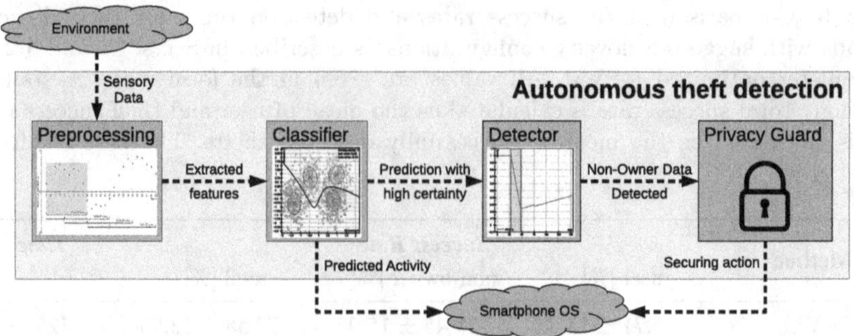


**Fig. 10.** Schematic visualization of theft detection on a smartphone. Sensors signals come from effects in the environment (acceleration, sound, etc.) and are preprocessed. Prepared features are put into a classifier for activity recognition and into a detection unit. While the classifier predicts the user's current activity only, the detector identifies foreign data (based on the data model of the classifier) and triggers a privacy protecting guard if necessary. As a result, sensible information on the smartphone can be locked and made inaccessible to a thief [18].

a better fine-tuning of the models and are thus advisable. In Fig. 10 a theft-detection system with all it's components is sketched. Visualized are involved components (dark gray rectangles), the data flow (dashed arrows), input source (the environment) and resulting output source (the smartphone's operating system).

Suppose that the overall system is consisting of a classification component and a detection component. Even though other algorithms might be eligible, the following explanations focus on a CMM as model in conjunction with a Novelty Detection in the same manner as described in Sect. 4 or Sect. 5. As the classifier is a probabilistic one, information about certainty for each output are available. Whenever the classifier is certain enough about an activity prediction, the observed sample can be forwarded to the detection part of the system. In that part, depending on the chosen technique, either the measure is updated and compared to the given threshold $\gamma$ – or the sample is analyzed by LDR and HDR detection algorithms. Whenever the measure calls for a reaction, the device could sample a soundclip and GPS-annotated picture (or video) footage and transmit it to a predefined location, server, backup- or rescue-address for the owner to review. Next actions could, e.g., be the shutdown of the device, the request for a pin, the activation of cryptographic code to secure sensible data or alike.

Two unknown numbers were just mentioned, one was a *certain enough* class prediction, the other one was a *given threshold* for novelty (or in this case theft-) detection. Concrete values are highly application specific, but usually a user would not want a hypersensitive smart device, but instead a very reliable theft detection (cf. Sect. 6.2). So one goal is a minimal false alarm rate, which can be achieved by defining a high class prediction certainty, along with a threshold, that matches the $\chi^2$-ND sensitivity parameter $\eta$. CANDIES on the other hand, needs an application specific tuning of the buffer size and the choice of a fitting HDR-technique, which can, e.g., be chosen by means of available computing power or complexity of the GMM in use.

All parameter estimations need data from non-owners, otherwise the adaptation to the user might not be specific enough (cf. Sect. 6.1, with a good detection of the rightful user but no more). Such data is usually not available on a user's device, but with cloud connected devices everywhere, it would be possible to push user-models into the cloud anonymously and make them available for other users. When you think of a new device generation, even if only a fraction of users participated in this setup, everyone would benefit, as novelty detection parameters could be adjusted very user-specific. In such a manner, every device of that new generation could be secured and autonomously react to detected thefts.

A technical implementation of the overall system needs to make sure that the following points are covered:

1. *Initialization.* The cold start phase of the system is crucial for correct functioning. While the personalization and adaptation to the user is important, an average model (e.g., data collected by the manufacturer prior to release) for detecting everyday activities can be used as a good starting point. For a correct initialization, the system should also occasionally question the user for feedback, as, e.g., done in the *Active Learning* domain (cf., e.g., [3]). During initialization, a set of activities that can be detected reliably for the device's user, should be fixed. Please note that the AR-part of the system is not limited to generative models, it is also thinkable to use, e.g., a SVM, if the uncertainty of activity predictions can be modeled.
2. *Online operation.* After a successful initialization, the theft detection can start to work. Parameter-tweaking can be done via, e.g., non-owner models that are provided via the manufacturers, or even a public cloud with movement models. To avoid confusion of the system, or a blurring of the model precision, the novelty detection should only receive data, when the classifying component is very certain. Again, this is a strong argument for the usage of simple activities, which can be detected very reliably.
3. *Detection action.* As soon as novelty is detected, the user action that was configured, should be taken. This could range from locking the device, via requesting a secure pin or answering a secret question to wiping all data, depending on the user's initial configuration and need for security.

## 8 Summary and Outlook

In this article, we based a Novelty Detection (ND) on top of an Activity Recognition (AR) process to realize a prototypical theft detection. Even though our experiments were based on five simple activities, the CMM is based on the structure of data and thus not confined to these exact activities. Hence, the exact classes only play a role for the activity recognition part, but not for modeling a user by means of his data. This is very advantageous, because no matter how precise how many activities can be recognized: thefts can be detected based on very simple activities, i.e. activities that can be predicted very well and for which a detection is nowadays included in every smartphone and fitness tracker from factory.

In Sect. 4 an established technique for investigating novel data in the input space was thoroughly investigated and optimized. Section 5 followed with a refined approach of the aforementioned and showed a very high reliability, while overcoming limitations of the plain $\chi^2$-based detection. A comparison with a one-class SVM approach in Sect. 6 revealed that there is no overall best technique, but that an implementation should be chosen with respect to an application-specific requirement: the always present trade-off between detection accuracy and detection speed. Even though one-class SVMs are commonly used for the task of anomaly detection, even with a parameter optimization, we were not able to get the SVM to function comparably well as our GMM based novelty detection approaches. One recommendation can be given out to ensemble based techniques due to several reasons: First, each part of the ensemble can be trained independently, which allows for a speed up by parallelization. Second, less data is necessary to train each competitive ensemble member. And finally, even small ensembles (three members) reveal a very good and robust performance, when compared to other models that were trained on larger datasets or with higher computational effort. A second recommendation can also be given out for CANDIES, which, even the current state of development, performed comparably well. Especially the lower standard deviations in experiment-results (cf. Table 5) show huge potential in creating more reliable monitoring techniques for generative models. Based on the ability to detect data that deviates from a learned model, we sketched the usage of an autonomous theft detection to secure user data in Sect. 7. Most remarkable are the facts, that even with just five daily activities, the detection works very well – and with only acceleration data from a quite simple smartphone.

In general, SVMs perform reasonably well in Activity Recognition scenarios and are a good approach that could be focused more intensively [23]. However, their usage always comes at the price of losing generative information, which can be very helpful when detecting outliers/deviations in data. Towards theft detection, an extended input space would be interesting, e.g. by incorporating more available sensors. Taking the theft detection towards a realization, it is necessary to conduct experiments with data not only from smartphones, but also from other smart devices (smart watches, smart infrastructure, ...). Regarding CANDIES, our research goes into two different directions and focusses on specific algorithmic parts. One part is the replacement of the HDR detection part by a Hidden Markov Model (HMM) detector, that is trained on distances in the feature space, that occur in time series. This would allow the detection of sequential motives, adding a transition matrix to find reappearing motives. Another part are improvements in the LDR part, i.e., the usage of Normal-Wishart distributions to model clusters of input-buffer-samples, which can be merged and integrated in a CMM more efficiently. Finally, as an alternative to our performed grid searches, better techniques such as Bayesian Optimization on training parameters are worth considering, due to much lower computational costs. A more effective parameter search will also help to overcome the additional step of performing a PCA, before a model for CANDIES can be trained.

**Acknowledgements.** The authors would like to thank the German research foundation (Deutsche Forschungsgemeinschaft, DFG) for the financial support in the context of the "Organic Computing Techniques for Runtime Self-Adaptation of Multi-Modal Activity Recognition Systems" project (SI 674/12-1, LU 1574/2-1).

## References

1. Abowd, G.D., Dey, A.K., Brown, P.J., Davies, N., Smith, M., Steggles, P.: Towards a better understanding of context and context-awareness. In: Gellersen, H.-W. (ed.) HUC 1999. LNCS, vol. 1707, pp. 304–307. Springer, Heidelberg (1999). https://doi.org/10.1007/3-540-48157-5_29
2. Amer, M., Goldstein, M., Abdennadher, S.: Enhancing one-class support vector machines for unsupervised anomaly detection. In: Proceedings of the ACM SIGKDD Workshop on Outlier Detection and Description, ODD 2013, pp. 8–15. ACM, New York (2013). https://doi.org/10.1145/2500853.2500857
3. Atlas, L.E., Cohn, D.A., Ladner, R.E.: Training connectionist networks with queries and selective sampling. In: Touretzky, D.S. (ed.) Advances in Neural Information Processing Systems 2, pp. 566–573. Morgan-Kaufmann (1990). http://papers.nips.cc/paper/261-training-connectionist-networks-with-queries-and-selective-sampling.pdf
4. Bishop, C.M.: Pattern Recognition and Machine Learning. In: Bishop, C.M. (ed.) Variational Inference, pp. 461–486. Springer, New York (2006)
5. Bishop, C.M.: Pattern Recognition and Machine Learning. Springer, New York (2006)
6. Boas, M.L.: Fourier series and transforms. In: Boas, M.L. (ed.) Mathematical Methods in the Physical Sciences, pp. 375–377. Wiley, Hoboken (2006)
7. Gruhl, C., Sick, B., Wacker, A., Tomforde, S., Hähner, J.: A building block for awareness in technical systems: online novelty detection and reaction with an application in intrusion detection. In: 2015 IEEE 7th International Conference on Awareness Science and Technology (iCAST), pp. 194–200 (2015)
8. Chen, L., Hoey, J., Nugent, C.D., Cook, D.J., Yu, Z.: Sensor-based activity recognition. IEEE Trans. Syst. Man Cybern. Part C (Appl. Rev.) **42**(6), 790–808 (2012). https://doi.org/10.1109/TSMCC.2012.2198883
9. Clarkson, B., Mase, K., Pentland, A.: Recognizing user context via wearable sensors. In: Proceedings of ISWC, pp. 69–75 (2000)
10. Ester, M., Kriegel, H.P., Sander, J., Xu, X., et al.: A density-based algorithm for discovering clusters in large spatial databases with noise. In: KDD, vol. 96, pp. 226–231 (1996)
11. Fernández-Francos, D., Martínez-Rego, D., Fontenla-Romero, O., Alonso-Betanzos, A.: Automatic bearing fault diagnosis based on one-class $\nu$-SVM. Comput. Ind. Eng. **64**(1), 357–365 (2013). https://doi.org/10.1016/j.cie.2012.10.013. http://www.sciencedirect.com/science/article/pii/S036083521200277X

12. Fisch, D., Jänicke, M., Kalkowski, E., Sick, B.: Learning by teaching versus learning by doing: knowledge exchange in organic agent systems. In: IEEE Symposium on Intelligent Agents, IA 2009, pp. 31–38. IEEE (2009)
13. Fisch, D., Jänicke, M., Kalkowski, E., Sick, B.: Learning from others: exchange of classification rules in intelligent distributed systems. Artif. Intell. **187–188**, 90–114 (2012). https://doi.org/10.1016/j.artint.2012.04.002. http://www.sciencedirect.com/science/article/pii/S0004370212000410
14. Franke, T., Lukowicz, P., Kunze, K., Bannach, D.: Can a mobile phone in a pocket reliably recognize ambient sounds? In: International Symposium on Wearable Computers, ISWC 2009, pp. 161–162. IEEE (2009)
15. Gellersen, H., Schmidt, A., Beigl, M.: Multi-sensor context-awareness in mobile devices and smart artifacts. Mob. Netw. Appl. **7**(5), 341–351 (2002)
16. Gruhl, C., Sick, B.: Detecting novel processes with CANDIES - an holistic novelty detection technique based on probabilistic models. CoRRabs/1605.05628 (2016). http://arxiv.org/abs/1605.05628
17. Guerbai, Y., Chibani, Y., Hadjadji, B.: The effective use of the one-class SVM classifier for handwritten signature verification based on writer-independent parameters. Pattern Recogn. **48**(1), 103–113 (2015). https://doi.org/10.1016/j.patcog.2014.07.016. http://www.sciencedirect.com/science/article/pii/S0031320314002751
18. Jänicke, M., Schmidt, V., Sick, B., Tomforde, S., Lukowicz, P.: Hijacked smart devices - methodical foundations for autonomous theft awareness based on activity recognition and novelty detection. In: Proceedings of the 10th International Conference on Agents and Artificial Intelligence - Volume 2: ICAART, pp. 131–142. INSTICC, SciTePress (2018). https://doi.org/10.5220/0006594901310142
19. Junker, H., Amft, O., Lukowicz, P., Tröster, G.: Gesture spotting with body-worn inertial sensors to detect user activities. Pattern Recogn. **41**(6), 2010–2024 (2008). https://doi.org/10.1016/j.patcog.2007.11.016. http://www.sciencedirect.com/science/article/pii/S0031320307005110
20. Kephart, J., Chess, D.: The vision of autonomic computing. IEEE Comput. **36**(1), 41–50 (2003)
21. Kwapisz, J., Weiss, G., Moore, S.: Activity recognition using cell phone accelerometers. ACM SIGKDD Explor. Newsl. **12**(2), 74–82 (2011)
22. Lau, S., David, K.: Movement recognition using the accelerometer in smartphones. In: Future Network and Mobile Summit, pp. 1–9. IEEE (2010)
23. Lau, S., König, I., David, K., Parandian, B., Carius-Düssel, C., Schultz, M.: Supporting patient monitoring using activity recognition with a smartphone. In: 2010 7th International Symposium on Wireless Communication Systems (ISWCS), pp. 810–814. IEEE (2010)
24. Li, K.L., Huang, H.K., Tian, S.F., Xu, W.: Improving one-class SVM for anomaly detection. In: 2003 International Conference on Machine Learning and Cybernetics, vol. 5, pp. 3077–3081. IEEE (2003)
25. Markou, M., Singh, S.: Novelty detection: a review - part 1: statistical approaches. Sig. Process. **83**, 2481–2497 (2003)
26. Markou, M., Singh, S.: Novelty detection: a review - part 2: neural network based approaches. Sig. Process. **83**, 2499–2521 (2003)
27. Mitra, S., et al.: An affordable, long-lasting, and autonomous theft detection and tracking system. In: Proceedings of the 7th ACM Conference on Embedded Networked Sensor Systems, SenSys 2009, pp. 351–352. ACM, New York (2009). https://doi.org/10.1145/1644038.1644096

28. Müller-Schloer, C., Tomforde, S.: Organic Computing - Technical Systems for Survival in the Real World. Autonomic Systems. Verlag, Birkhäuser (2017). https://doi.org/10.1007/978-3-319-68477-2. ISBN 978-3-319-68476-5
29. Schölkopf, B., Williamson, R.C., Smola, A.J., Shawe-Taylor, J., Platt, J.C., et al.: Support vector method for novelty detection. In: NIPS, vol. 12, pp. 582–588 (1999)
30. Sun, L., Zhang, D., Li, B., Guo, B., Li, S.: Activity recognition on an accelerometer embedded mobile phone with varying positions and orientations. In: Yu, Z., Liscano, R., Chen, G., Zhang, D., Zhou, X. (eds.) UIC 2010. LNCS, vol. 6406, pp. 548–562. Springer, Heidelberg (2010). https://doi.org/10.1007/978-3-642-16355-5_42
31. Tax, D., Duin, R.: Uniform object generation for optimizing one-class classifiers. J. Mach. Learn. Res. **2**, 155–173 (2002)
32. Tomforde, S., Sick, B., Müller-Schloer, C.: Organic Computing in the Spotlight, arXiv, January 2017. http://arxiv.org/abs/1701.08125
33. Zhang, Y., Meratnia, N., Havinga, P.: Adaptive and online one-class support vector machine-based outlier detection techniques for wireless sensor networks. In: 2009 International Conference on Advanced Information Networking and Applications Workshops, pp. 990–995, May 2009. https://doi.org/10.1109/WAINA.2009.200

# Integrated Route, Charging and Activity Planning for Whole Day Mobility with Electric Vehicles

Marek Cuchý, Michal Štolba(✉), and Michal Jakob

Department of Computer Science, Faculty of Electrical Engineering, Czech Technical University in Prague, Prague, Czech Republic
{cuchy,stolba,jakob}@agents.fel.cvut.cz

**Abstract.** Over the last two decades, route planning algorithms have revolutionized the way we organize car travel. The advent of electric vehicles (EVs), however, bring new challenges for travel planning. Because of electric vehicle limited range and long charging times, it is beneficial to plan routes, charging, and activities jointly and in the context of the whole day—rather than for single, isolate journeys as done by standard route planning approaches. In this work, we therefore present a novel approach to solving such a whole day mobility problem. Our method works by first preprocessing an energy-constrained route planning problem and subsequently planning the temporally and spatially constrained activities. We propose both an optimal algorithm for the day mobility planning problem and a set of sub-optimal speedup heuristics. We evaluate the proposed algorithm on a set of benchmarks based on real-world data and show that it is significantly faster than the previous state-of-the-art approach. Moreover, the speedups provide dramatic memory and time improvements with a negligible loss in solution quality.

**Keywords:** Electromobility · Route planning
Day mobility planning · Charging allocation

## 1 Introduction

One of the most prominent hurdles in the wider adoption of electric vehicles (EVs) is their limited driving range, long times necessary for charging, and limited availability of charging resources. If EV users could organize their EV-based travel in such a way that the necessary EV charging, implied by their mobility needs, could happen at times and locations where charging can be collocated with other activities, the use of EVs would be more convenient.

Planning mobility in such a way is, however, no easy task. This is because travel -- and even more so charging -- is a derived demand, stemming from the primary need to carry out activities constrained in space and time. Given the huge number of ways activities and trips between them can be arranged into *mobility plans*, making (near) optimum decisions about these plans is a complex


J. van den Herik and A. P. Rocha (Eds.): ICAART 2018, LNAI 11352, pp. 274–289, 2019.
https://doi.org/10.1007/978-3-030-05453-3_13

problem beyond usual human capabilities. That is why we have been developing an artificial intelligence system that would help EV users to organize their travel and, consequently, charging in a way that best meets their mobility needs while respecting the supply constraints of the electrical grid, such as maximum available power at the given location.

In this work, we propose a novel approach based on preprocessing and query phases, as is common in many routing applications. Nevertheless, such approach was previously not used in the context of day mobility planning with EVs. To do so, we utilize the inherent hierarchy of the discussed problem and propose a preprocessing phase which solves the energy-constrained routing sub-problem and a query phase which tackles the combinatorially hard traveling salesman problem with spatial, temporal, and energy constraints. The previous state-of-the-art solution was able to plan only toy-sized problems. In contrast, our integrated solver is able to solve real-world-scale problems with a reasonable preprocessing time, practical query time, and near-optimal solutions.

### 1.1 Example

Here we present a simple example scenario (Fig. 1), originally described in [1]. The user starts and ends in the home location A, may charge the EV at B and D and shop at B. The user's goal is to spend 8 h at the workplace and to shop for 30 min. The initial (and maximal) capacity of the EV battery is 30 kWh and charging to full takes 60 min. In the naive plan shown in Fig. 1(a), the user first decides the order of activities, that is, first go to work and then do the shopping. Also the charging is postponed until necessary. By this approach, the user first goes to the location C (the EV has enough charge to do that) and works for 8 h. Next, the user wants to go home and make a stop for shopping, but the charge of the EV is not high enough to do so and thus the user must first go to a nearby charging station at location C. Then the user can get to the location B and do the shopping, while also charging the EV. Finally the user gets home, with the overhead of time caused by charging of 45 min (we do not count the charging time while shopping).

By optimizing for the whole day formulation of the problem, the user can obtain the optimized plan shown in Fig. 1(b), where the shopping is scheduled before work. In that case, the user first arrives at B, does the shopping while recharging the battery to full and continues to work. At the way back, the EV does not have enough charge for the whole trip and thus a short (10 min.) charging stop is scheduled. Overall, the user arrives 30 min earlier than in the naive case and spends only 10 min on charging overhead. Notice also, that the total energy consumed from the charging stations is 10 kWh less which might also save money. Obviously, this simple problem is easy to optimize, but the problem gets too complicated for a human when the number of locations and activities increase and the temporal constraints are more complicated.

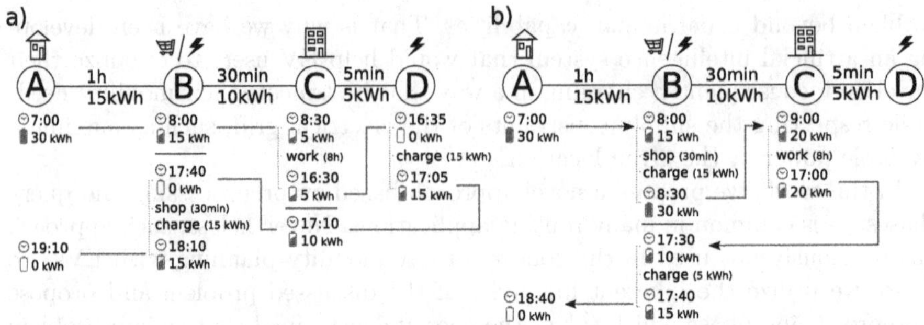


**Fig. 1.** Example scenario: A - home location, C - work location, B, D - chargers, B - shop. Activities are 8 h work, 30 min shop. Maximal state of charge (SOC) - 30 kWh, charging to full takes 60 min. (a) Naive approach: The user first decides the order of activities (work, shop). Charging postponed until necessary. (b) Whole day formulation: Optimize the order of activities and charging (shop,work). (Published in [1]).

## 2 Problem Definition

The Whole Day Mobility Planning with Electric Vehicles (WDMEV) problem was first proposed in [1]. Here we rephrase and extend the problem and consider its relation to other existing problems. Informally, the problem consists of finding a day schedule of activities, where each activity has associated locations where it can be performed and a time window when it can be performed. The activities may have a partial ordering defined over them. Moreover, a route between each two consecutive activities needs to be determined taking into account the battery state of charge (SOC) constraints and possible charging stops. Charging can take place at designated charging stations which may differ in their charging rate. In the real world, the time spent charging may also differ depending on the time of the day, as in peak hours the vehicle may have to wait until other vehicles are charged. To account for such delays we extend the WDMEV problem with time-dependent charging times.

In [1] the authors propose a solution based on a label-setting algorithm which is able to solve only unrealistically small instances. In the contrary, we aim for a more scalable solution. We define the problem as a road graph structure together with the properties of the electric vehicle (EV), and we define a query as the particular day activities to be performed including the temporal, spatial, and precedence constraints.

**The WDMEV Problem.** Formally, we define the WDMEV problem as a tuple

$$W = \langle G, V_{\mathsf{POI}}, C, B, B_C, T \rangle$$

where $G = \langle V, E, \tau, \epsilon \rangle$ is the underlying road network represented by an oriented graph with $V$ being the set of graph nodes and $E$ the set of graph edges. The graph $G$ has a time cost $\tau(e)$ and an energy cost $\epsilon(e)$ associated with each oriented edge $e \in E$. The set $V_{\mathsf{POI}} \subseteq V$ defines all possible points of interest (POI), that is, shops, workplaces, leisure activities, and charging station locations, denoted as POI nodes. The set $B$ defines the discretized levels of state of charge (SOC) of the electric vehicle (e.g., Watthours) where $\beta_{\min} = \min B, \beta_{\max} = \max B$ define the minimal and maximal SOC respectively and the set $B_C \subseteq B$ defines a subset of SOC levels to which the electric vehicle can be charged at the charging stations. The set $T$ defines discretized time points (e.g., seconds).

Each charging station $c$ in the set of charging stations $C$ is defined as a tuple $c = \langle v_c, \tau_c \rangle$ where $v_c \in V_{\mathsf{POI}}$ is a POI node where the charging station is located, $V_C = \bigcup_{c \in C} \{v_c\}$ is the set of all CS locations. The function $\tau_c : B_C \times T \times B \mapsto \mathbb{N}$ defines the time required to charge given amount depending on the current time and current SOC. The only constraint we place on the function $\tau_c$ is that it adheres to the FIFO property, that is, $\tau_1 + \tau_c(\beta_2, \tau_1, \beta_1) \leq \tau_2 + \tau_c(\beta_2, \tau_2, \beta_1)$ for any $\tau_1, \tau_2 \in T$ such that $\tau_1 \leq \tau_2$.

**The WDMEV Query.** Each WDMEV query is defined as a tuple $Q = \langle A, v_{\mathsf{home}}, \beta_{\mathsf{init}}, \tau_{\mathsf{init}} \rangle$ where $A$ is the set of activities to be performed, $v_{\mathsf{home}} \in V_{\mathsf{POI}}$ is a POI node where the vehicle initially starts and also must end, and $\beta_{\mathsf{init}} \in B$ and $\tau_{\mathsf{init}} \in T$ define the initial SOC of the electric vehicle and initial time respectively.

Each activity $a$ in the set of activities $A$ is defined as a tuple $a = \langle V_a, \mathsf{est}_a, \mathsf{let}_a, \mathsf{d}_a, \mathsf{pre}_a \rangle$ where $V_a \subseteq V_{\mathsf{POI}}$ is the subset of graph nodes where the activity $a$ can be performed ($V_A = \bigcup_{a \in A} V_a$ is the set of all activity locations), the interval between the earliest start time $\mathsf{est}_a$ and latest end time $\mathsf{let}_a$ defines the time window when the activity can be performed and the duration of the activity is defined by $\mathsf{d}_a$. The latest start time can be derived as $\mathsf{lst}_a = \mathsf{let}_a - \mathsf{d}_a$. Moreover, the set $\mathsf{pre}_a \subseteq A$ defines the subset of activities that have to precede $a$.

**The WDMEV Solution.** A solution of the WDMEV query $Q = \langle A, v_{\mathsf{home}}, \beta_{\mathsf{init}}, \tau_{\mathsf{init}} \rangle$ on the WDMEV problem $W = \langle G, V_{\mathsf{POI}}, C, B, B_C, T \rangle$ is a sequence $\mathsf{sol} = (s_0, ..., s_k)$ of tuples $s_i = \left\langle v_i, e_i, a_i, \tau_i^{\mathsf{arr}}, \tau_i^{\mathsf{dep}}, \beta_i^{\mathsf{arr}}, \beta_i^{\mathsf{dep}} \right\rangle$ where $v_i \in V$ is the respective visited graph node, $e_i \in E \cup \{\emptyset\}$ is the edge by which the vehicle arrives at $v_i$ (may be empty if $v_{i-1} = v_i$), $a_i = \langle V_{a_i}, \mathsf{est}_{a_i}, \mathsf{let}_{a_i}, \mathsf{d}_{a_i}, \mathsf{pre}_{a_i} \rangle \in A \cup \{\emptyset\}$ is the activity performed at $v_i$ (may be empty), $\tau_i^{\mathsf{arr}}, \tau_i^{\mathsf{dep}}$ is the time when the vehicle arrives at $v_i$ and departs from $v_i$ respectively, and $\beta_i^{\mathsf{arr}}, \beta_i^{\mathsf{dep}}$ is the SOC of the vehicle when arriving and departing $v_i$ respectively.

In order for the solution $\mathsf{sol}$ to be valid, for the initial state holds $\tau_0^{\mathsf{arr}} = \tau_0^{\mathsf{dep}} = \tau_{\mathsf{init}}$, $v_0 = v_{\mathsf{home}}$ and $v_k = v_{\mathsf{home}}$. For each $s_i \in \mathsf{sol}$ holds $e_i$ is an edge in $G$ starting in node $v_{i-1}$ and ending in $v_i$ or $e_i = \emptyset$ and $v_{i-1} = v_i$ or $i = 0$. Also $\tau_i^{\mathsf{arr}} = \tau_{i-1}^{\mathsf{dep}} + \tau(e_i)$ and $\beta_i^{\mathsf{arr}} = \beta_{i-1}^{\mathsf{dep}} + \epsilon(e_i)$.

If there is an activity performed in $s_i$, i.e., $a_i \neq \emptyset$, then $v_i \in V_{a_i}$, $\tau_i^{\mathsf{arr}} \leq \mathsf{lst}_{a_i}$, $\tau_i^{\mathsf{arr}} + \mathsf{d}_{a_i} \leq \tau_i^{\mathsf{dep}}$, and for each $a' \in \mathsf{pre}_{a_i}$ there must be some $s_j \in \mathsf{sol}$ such that

$j < i$ and $a' = a_j$. If charging is performed in $s_i$, i.e., $\beta_i^{\mathsf{dep}} - \beta_i^{\mathsf{arr}} > 0$, then $\beta_i^{\mathsf{dep}} \in B_C$ and there must be a charging station $c_i = \langle v_{c_i}, \tau_{c_i} \rangle \in C$ such that $v_{c_i} = v_i$ and $\tau_i^{\mathsf{arr}} + \tau_{c_i}(\beta_i^{\mathsf{dep}}, \tau_i^{\mathsf{arr}}, \beta_i^{\mathsf{arr}}) \leq \tau_i^{\mathsf{dep}}$.

The cost of the solution $\mathsf{sol}$ is defined as $\tau(\mathsf{sol}) = \tau_k^{\mathsf{arr}}$.

## 2.1 Relation to Other Problems

Let us now have a closer look on the particular components of the WDMEV problem and their relation to well known problems. The most important property of WDMEV is that it combines both temporal and resource constraints. Let us first focus on the resource constraints, where the most fundamental problem is.

**Constrained Shortest Path Problem (CSPP).** There is a number of variants of CSPP [2] which differ from the classical shortest path problem by additional constraints which have to be satisfied by the solution. In general, CSPP is NP-hard. In the case of the WDMEV problem, both the time and SOC can be seen as resource constraints [3]. The time resource is monotonically increasing by $\tau(e)$ for each traversed edge. Such problem with monotonic resources and constraints can be solved in pseudo-polynomial time [4], but the SOC resource in WDMEV is updated either by discharging on edges, recuperation on edges or charging at nodes and therefore it is not monotonic. Also, $\beta_v \leq \beta_{\max}$ is not a hard constraint but rather a limit of the maximum charged or recuperated energy. Edge which would result in higher SOC is still valid, but results only in $\beta_{\max}$. Shortest path problem with energy constraints (but no temporal constraints) has been studied in [5] in a framework based on the A* search [6].

**Traveling Salesman Problem (TSP).** TSP (or even more general Vehicle Routing Problem) is a classical NP-hard problem, in our case, the more relevant variant is the Steiner TSP [7] where only some of the nodes of a graph are required do be visited by the solution walk. Moreover, the edges and nodes may repeat as in our case. The WDMEV problem subsumes a combination of three extensions to the classical (or Steiner) TSP.

The first is Generalized TSP [8], where each city to be visited is represented as a subset of the graph nodes and it is sufficient to visit one node from each subset. The second variant is TSP with Time Windows where the cities have to be visited in a given time window (in our case, the lower bound constraint is soft). This is related to TSP with Deadlines where there is no lower bound on the visit time and for which no constant approximation ratio can ever be achieved [9]. The main difference of WDMEV is that the activities have durations on their own which has to be spent at the location. The last related variant of TSP is the Resource-Constrained TSP [10] where a resource $r$ is consumed when traversing an edge and the solution path cannot consume more than $R_{\max}$ of the resource. The WDMEV differs in that the resource in question (SOC) can be also replenished on some edges due to recuperation and at the charging stations (at an additional time cost).

The most relevant related problem is the Electric TSP with Time Windows (E-TSPTW) [11] which considers both the temporal and energy constraints but still exhibits a number of differences from WDMEV. Similarily to TSPTW, the time window $[\mathsf{est}_v, \mathsf{lst}_v]$ of node $v$ can be visited before $\mathsf{est}_v$ and wait, but in WDMEV the activity $a$ can be started at any time between $[\mathsf{est}_a, \mathsf{lst}_a]$ but the vehicle has to stay at the respective node for the whole duration $\mathsf{d}_a$. The discharging and charging models in WDMEV differ significantly from E-TSPTW. In E-TSPTW, all charging stations have the same charging rate and both the discharged energy and charged energy depend linearly on the traveled distance or charging time respectively. The WDMEV is more realistic in that we place no assumptions on the energy cost $\epsilon(e)$ ( e.g., it can depend on the elevation profile of edge $e$ and can even be negative for recuperation on downhill edges) and on the charging time function $\tau_c$ which depends on the amount of energy, charging rate, on the time when the charging is initiated, and on the current SOC.

**Single-Machine Job Scheduling (SMJS).** SMJS [12] is the problem of scheduling a set of jobs with durations and time windows (due date and deadline) and precedence constraints on a single machine (resource). Although such problem when minimizing the solution makespan is polynomial [13] and the SMJS problem corresponds to the high-level scheduling sub-problem of WDMEV, the spatial (TSP) and energy constraints induce complexities as discussed above.

**Baseline Solution.** In [1] we have proposed a simplified version of the WDMEV problem, where the possibility of time-dependent charging times was not considered. The proposed algorithm is a straightforward extension of the A* algorithm [6] to include labels with SOC and other state-dependent properties. The main proposed modification is that instead of a single label per state, the algorithm maintains a Pareto set of non-dominated labels. The algorithm was evaluated on a rather restricted set of benchmarks with only 8 charging stations, 18 POIs, and up to 5 activities.

## 3 Optimal Solution

Our solution approach involves a preprocessing phase and a query phase (see Fig. 2). The preprocessing phase considers only traveling between the Points of Interest (POIs) and Charging stations (CSs) while the query phase uses the result of the preprocessing to find the actual activity schedule and charging stops respecting given constraints. Unlike the techniques in most of the related literature, our approach to the query phase is based on a systematic label-setting heuristic search which allows us to solve problems with nonlinear constraints (e.g., the energy cost function ) and time-dependent costs and constraints (e.g., the speed of charging depends on the time of the day).

As proposed in [1], the WDMEV problem can be solved using a single-phase heuristic search but with a significant limit on scalability. In such a unified approach, many search states are expanded only to find the shortest paths between

POIs and CSs. In this work we present a technique that significantly improves scalability by preprocessing the shortest path computations and using the heuristic search only to solve the combinatorially hard activity and charging planning master problem. Let us first focus on the preprocessing phase.

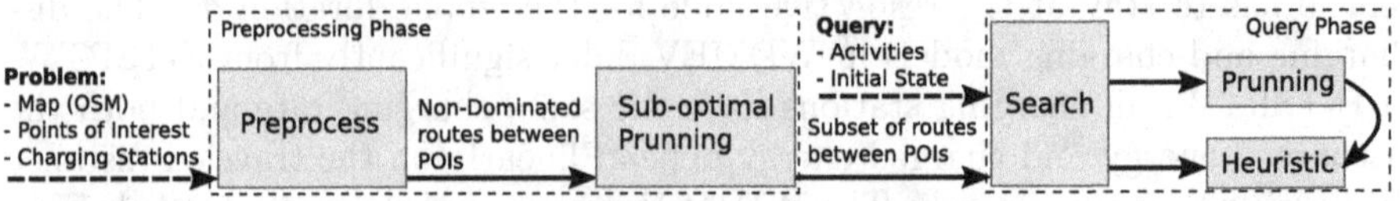


**Fig. 2.** Overview of the preprocessing and query phase of the planning system.

## 3.1 Preprocessing Phase

The preprocessing phase considers the WDMEV problem $W = \langle G, V_{\mathsf{POI}}, C, B, B_C, T\rangle$. The preprocessing phase consists of computing and storing the shortest paths between all pairs of high-level nodes $v \in V_{\mathsf{POI}}$, denoted as routes. We use the multi-criteria Dijkstra's algorithm [14] to find the routes.

**Definition 1.** *Let $G = \langle V, E, \tau, \epsilon\rangle$ be a directed graph with the associated time and energy costs and let $V_{\mathsf{POI}} \subseteq V$ be the set of POI nodes. We say that a path $r = (v_1, e_1, ..., e_{n-1}, v_n)$ in $G$ is a $v_1, v_n$-*route *iff $v_1, v_n \in V_{\mathsf{POI}}$.*

**Definition 2.** *We define the time cost of $r$ as $\tau(r) = \sum_{i=1}^{n-1} \tau(e_i)$. The energy cost is defined by a recursive equation. Let $r_i = (v_1, e_1, ..., e_{i-1}, v_i)$ denote a subroute of $r$ ending at $v_i$, then $\epsilon(r_i) = \min(\epsilon(r_{i-1})+\epsilon(e_{i-1}), \beta_{\max})$ and $\epsilon(r) = \epsilon(r_n)$.*

We can use the route definition to provide a more high-level definition of the WDMEV problem

$$\bar{W} = \langle R, V_{\mathsf{POI}}, C, B, B_C, T\rangle$$

where $R$ is the set of all $v_1, v_n$-routes. An important observation is that even if optimizing for a single criterion (e.g., the time cost), it is not enough to find a single shortest $u, v$-route for each two POI nodes $u, v$ as the resulting SOC or time might not be enough to find a solution (or an optimal solution) to a given WDMEV query. In order to find an optimal solution the whole set of non-dominated routes has to be kept and considered in the planning phase. We define the dominance of routes as follows.

**Definition 3.** *Let $r_1, r_2$ be two $v_1, v_n$- routes for some POI nodes $v_1, v_n \in V_{\mathsf{POI}}$. We say that $r_1$ dominates $r_2$ iff $\tau(r_1) \leq \tau(r_2) \wedge \epsilon(r_1) \leq \epsilon(r_2)$.*

**Proposition 1.** *Let $\bar{W} = \langle R, V_{\mathsf{POI}}, C, B, B_C, T\rangle$ be a high-level WDMEV problem and let $\mathsf{sol} = (s_0, ..., s_k)$ be an optimal solution of the original problem $W$ for the query $Q = \langle A, v_{\mathsf{home}}, \beta_{\mathsf{init}}, \tau_{\mathsf{init}}\rangle$. Let $r_1, r_2 \in R$ be two $v_1, v_n$-routes such that $r_1$ dominates $r_2$. Let $\mathsf{sol}' = (s'_0, ..., s'_k)$ be an optimal solution of the WDMEV problems $\bar{W}' = \langle R \setminus \{r_2\}, V_{\mathsf{POI}}, C, B, B_C, T\rangle$ for the query $Q$. Then $\tau(\mathsf{sol}) = \tau(\mathsf{sol}')$.*

*Proof.* It is easy to see that by removing $r_2$ no optimal solution can be removed as $r_1$ dominates $r_2$ and thus $r_2$ cannot be part of any optimal solution.

Based on Proposition 1 the dominated paths are removed in the preprocessing step without the loss of optimality. More aggressive pruning techniques which do not preserve optimality are described in Sect. 4.

### 3.2 Query Phase

The task of the query phase is to find a solution $\mathsf{sol} = (s_0, ..., s_k)$ to a query $Q = \langle A, v_{\mathsf{home}}, \beta_{\mathsf{init}}, \tau_{\mathsf{init}} \rangle$ given a high-level WDMEV problem $\bar{W} = \langle R, V_{\mathsf{POI}}, C, B, B_C, T \rangle$. To do so we propose a heuristic search which associates sets of labels to the POI nodes from $V_{\mathsf{POI}}$. The label for a node $v \in V_{\mathsf{POI}}$ is defined by the following tuple

$$l_v = \langle v, A_{\mathsf{DONE}}, \tau_v, \beta_v, h_v, l'_v \rangle$$

where $v \in V_{\mathsf{POI}}$ is the associated high-level graph node, $A_{\mathsf{DONE}} \subseteq A$ is the set of finished activities, $\tau_v$ is the aggregate time cost of the partial solution represented by $l_v$, $\beta_v$ is the current SOC at node $v$, $h_v$ is the heuristic value of respective partial solution, and $l'_v$ is the parent label from which $l_v$ was extended and which is used to reconstruct the solution.

Similarly to the preprocessing phase, in order to maintain optimality, the search has to keep all labels for each node, except for the dominated ones, formally.

**Definition 4.** *Let $l_v, l'_v$ be two labels of a single POI node $v \in V_{\mathsf{POI}}$. We say that $l_v$ dominates $l'_v$ (denoted as $l_v \succ l'_v$) iff all the following conditions are satisfied:*

$$\begin{aligned} A_{\mathsf{DONE}} &\supseteq A'_{\mathsf{DONE}} \\ \tau_v &\leq \tau'_v \\ \beta_v &\geq \beta'_v \end{aligned} \tag{1}$$

The heuristic search algorithm is a modified Multi-Objective A* [15] which differs in that the proposed algorithm is not searching for the set of Pareto-optimal solutions as it optimizes only for time, but it needs to consider the Pareto sets during the search because of the temporal and energy constraints.

In each iteration, the best label according to the heuristic estimate is extracted from the priority queue and extended using one of the following operations. Let $l_v = \langle v, A_{\mathsf{DONE}}, \tau_v, \beta_v, h_v, l'_v \rangle$ be the extracted label, then

**(i) move.** For each $u \in (V_C \cup V_A) \setminus \{v\}$, let $R_{v,u}$ be the Pareto set of $v, u$-routes between the POI nodes $v$ and $u$. For each $r \in R_{v,u}$ a new label

$$l_{u,r} = \langle u, A_{\mathsf{DONE}}, \tau_v + \tau(r), \min(\beta_v - \epsilon(r), \beta_{\max}), h_u, l_v \rangle$$

is added to the queue with a newly computed heuristic value $h_u$ (The heuristic is computed only once per node $u$). The labels with state of charge bellow $\beta_{\min}$ are discarded.

**(ii) activity.** For each activity $a = \langle V_a, \mathsf{est}_a, \mathsf{let}_a, \mathsf{d}_a, \mathsf{pre}_a \rangle$ such that $a \notin A_{\mathsf{DONE}}$, $v \in V_a$, $\tau_v \leq \mathsf{let}_a - \mathsf{d}_a$, and $\mathsf{pre}_a \subseteq A_{\mathsf{DONE}}$ a new label

$$l_a = \langle v, A_{\mathsf{DONE}} \cup \{a\}, \max(\tau_v + \mathsf{d}_a, \mathsf{est}_a + \mathsf{d}_a), \beta_v, h_a, l_v \rangle$$

is added to the queue with a new heuristic value $h_a$.

**(iii) charging.** For each charging station $c = \langle v_c, \tau_c \rangle$ such that $v_c = v$, for each charging level $b \in B_C$ such that $b > \beta_v$ a new label

$$l_{c,b} = \langle v, A_{\mathsf{DONE}}, \tau_v + \tau_c(b - \beta_v, \tau_v, \beta_v), b, h_c, l_v \rangle$$

is added to the queue with a new heuristic value $h_c$.

**(iv) activity and charging.** If $v \in V_a$ for some activity satisfying the conditions in (ii) and there is a charging station $c$ s.t. $v = v_c$ the combination of parallel activity and charging has to be considered. For each such activity $a$, charging station $c$, and each charging level $b \in B_C$ such that $b > \beta_v$ a new label

$$l_{a,c,b,d} = \langle v, A_{\mathsf{DONE}} \cup \{a\}, \tau'_v, b, h_a, l_v \rangle$$

is added to the queue with a newly computed heuristic value $h_a$ and a new time $\tau'_v$. The new time $\tau'_v$ is calculated as maximum of the times computed in the cases (ii) and (iii).

**Admissible Heuristic.** The search is guided by a heuristic function which relaxes the SOC constraints and takes maximum of the estimates for single activities. Let $l_v = \langle v, A_{\mathsf{DONE}}, \tau_v, \beta_v, h_v, l'_v \rangle$ be the currently extracted label. For each activity $a \in A \setminus A_{\mathsf{DONE}}$ which was not finished yet we define its estimated time to finish as

$$\tau_a = \min_{u \in V_a} (\tau_v + \tau(r_{v,u}) + \tau(r_{u,v_{\mathsf{home}}})) \tag{2}$$

where $r_{v,u} \in R$ is the shortest-time $v,u$-route and $r_{u,v_{\mathsf{home}}} \in R$ is the shortest $u, v_{\mathsf{home}}$-route leading to the initial and goal POI node. Intuitively, $\tau_a$ denotes the time spent on the shortest trip from the node $v$ to a node $u$ where the activity can be performed and then to the initial node $v_{\mathsf{home}}$ excluding the time spent on the activity itself.

The heuristic itself can be expressed as

$$h(v, \tau_v, A_{\mathsf{DONE}}) = \max_{a \in A \setminus A_{\mathsf{DONE}}} \tau_a + \sum_{a \in A \setminus A_{\mathsf{DONE}}} \mathsf{d}_a \tag{3}$$

that is, we take the worst time of a trip to an activity and to the goal node and add the sum of the durations of activities that still need to be achieved.

**Lemma 1.** *Let* $\bar{W} = \langle R, V_{\mathsf{POI}}, C, B, B_C, T \rangle$ *be a high-level WDMEV problem. For any nodes* $v_1, v_2, v_3 \in V_{\mathsf{POI}}$ *the respective shortest-time routes* $r_{1,3}, r_{1,2}, r_{2,3} \in R$ *satisfy triangle inequality with respect to the time cost.*

*Proof.* For a contradiction, let us assume that $\tau(r_{1,3}) > \tau(r_{1,2}) + \tau(r_{2,3})$. That means that in the graph $G = \langle V, E, \tau, \epsilon \rangle$ there exists a $v_1, v_3$-route $r'$ such that $\tau(r') < \tau(r_{1,3})$ which, based on Definition 1, is a contradiction with $r_{1,3}$ being a shortest-time route.

**Proposition 2.** *Let* $\bar{W} = \langle R, V_{\mathsf{POI}}, C, B_C, \beta_{\min}, \beta_{\max} \rangle$ *be a high-level WDMEV problem and* $Q = \langle A, v_{\mathsf{home}}, \beta_{\mathsf{init}}, \tau_{\mathsf{init}} \rangle$ *a query. Let* $l_v = \langle v, A_{\mathsf{DONE}}, \tau_v, \beta_v, h_v, l'_v \rangle$ *be a label assigned to some* $v \in V_{\mathsf{POI}}$. *Then* $h(v, \tau_v, A_{\mathsf{DONE}})$ *defined by Eq. 3 is an admissible heuristic estimate of the time cost of a query* $Q' = \langle A \setminus A_{\mathsf{DONE}}, v, \beta_v, \tau_v \rangle$.

*Proof.* Let $h^*$ denote the cost of optimal solution to $Q' = \langle A \setminus A_{\mathsf{DONE}}, v, \beta_v, \tau_v \rangle$. Clearly, such solution must achieve all $a \in A \setminus A_{\mathsf{DONE}}$. We will now show that for any $a \in A \setminus A_{\mathsf{DONE}}$ holds $\tau_a \leq h^*$ where $\tau_a$ is defined in Eq. 2. Because of Lemma 1, the shortest-time possibility how to get from $v$ to any $u \in V_a$ is the shortest-time $v, u$-route $r_{v,u} \in R$. The activity cannot be started earlier than when the vehicle arrives to $u$, i.e., $\tau_v + \tau(r_{v,u})$. Due to Lemma 1, the shortest time to get from $u$ to the goal node $v_{\mathsf{home}}$ is the shortest $u, v_{\mathsf{home}}$-route $r_{u,v_{\mathsf{home}}} \in R$. As $\tau_a$ takes the minimum over all $u \in V_a$, $\tau_a \leq h^*$ as the vehicle has to get to $u$ to achieve the activity and subsequently to $v_{\mathsf{home}}$. All $a \in A \setminus A_{\mathsf{DONE}}$ have fixed durations not dependent on time and all of them have to be achieved. The inequality $h^* \leq h(v, \tau_v, A_{\mathsf{DONE}})$ follows directly.

## 4 Sub-optimal Speedups

As many of the sub-problems of WDMEV are NP-hard, it is clear that finding an optimal solution in a real-world scale scenario is not tractable. Here we present a two speedups which allow us to compute such solutions at the price of loosing optimality, completeness, or both. In Sect. 6 we evaluate the trade-off.

**Route Reduction.** One of the main factor in complexity of the search algorithm is the size of the set $R$ of all routes (formally shown in Sect. 5). One possible technique to reduce the number of routes is to select a subset of $k$ $u, v$-routes between each two nodes $u, v \in V_{\mathsf{POI}}$. Here we describe how we select such subset of size $k$. We propose a heuristic selection technique as in the worst case it is not possible to select the proper subset without solving the entire WDMEV problem. It is not possible to ensure optimality, but also completeness might be jeopardized by discarding a non-dominated route. The proposed solution proceeds as follows.

Let $R_{u,v} \subseteq R$ be the set of all non-dominated $u, v$-routes. We proceed by clustering the routes in $R_{u,v}$ by each of the constraints (time, energy) and then by selecting the best route in each cluster based on the other one. For clustering we use the well known k-means algorithm [16].

1. Find $k/2$ clusters in $R_{u,v}$ based on $\tau(r)$.
2. For each cluster select the route $r$ with the highest $\epsilon(r)$.

The same is done for $\epsilon(r)$ and $\tau(r)$ respectively (we take the lowest $\tau(r)$). The result is a set of $k$ routes which are a representative sample w.r.t. one constraint and the best w.r.t. the other constraint.

**Dominance Relaxation.** The authors in [1] use $\epsilon$-relaxation of the dominance rule (Eq. 1) to speed-up the search. We can use the same technique to speed-up the preprocessing phase by using $\epsilon$-relaxed dominance criterion in the multi-criteria Dijkstra's algorithm used to find the $u, v$-routes. This also results in smaller set $R$ of all such routes.

**Limit of Charging Stops.** The third speed-up technique is based on an observation of the real-world properties of the WDMEV problem. Similarly to public-transport planning where it is common to let the user give an upper bound on the number of transfers, we can realistically assume, that the EV user is willing to allow at most $q$ charging stops between each two activities. By assuming such bound we can significantly limit the number of label extensions as follows.

Let $l_v$ be a label of a POI node. We extend the label $l_v$ by a field $q_v$ which equals the length of a sequence of parent labels of $l_v$ such that the EV was charged at the respective POI nodes. We add the following rule to the move extension (i) from Sect. 3.2:

- If $q_v < q$ use $V_{\mathsf{POI}}$ as the set of possible move destinations.
- If $q_v \geq q$ use $V_{\mathsf{POI}} \setminus V_C$ as the set of possible move destinations where $V_C$ is the set of all charging station locations.

In Sect. 6 we evaluate the speed-up technique with $q = 1$ where the extension of the labels is not even necessary as the above rule can be based only on the last stop. Charging stops can be extended only by moves to activity locations and vice versa. It also is reasonable to assume that the user is not willing to make more than one charging stop between two activities. It is also possible to determine $q$ based on the distance (or energy cost) between the two consecutive activity locations.

## 5 Complexity Analysis

Here we present a complexity analysis of the preprocessing and query phases and compare it with complexity analysis of the solution provided in [1]. Let $\mathsf{Dij}(n, m)$ denote time complexity of multi-criteria Dijkstra algorithm [14] where $n, m$ is the number of nodes and edges respectively. The preprocessing consists of running such multi-criteria Dijkstra algorithm from each POI node to all other POI nodes in the problem. Thus the time complexity of the preprocessing phase is

$$O(|V_{\mathsf{POI}}|\mathsf{Dij}(|V|, |E|))$$

and the memory complexity is dominated by the need to store all non-dominated routes, that is, $O(|R|)$. If we limit the number of stored routes per each two nodes to a constant $k$ (as in Sect. 4), we can express the space complexity as $O(k|V_{\mathsf{POI}}|^2)$.

To understand the worst-case time complexity of the WDMEV query we assume the heuristic to give no guidance and thus the complexity is equal to $O(\mathsf{Dij}(n,m))$ where the number of search states is limited by the number of all possible labels

$$n \leq |V_A \cup V_C| \cdot |S| \tag{4}$$

where $V_A \cup V_C$ is the set of all activity and CS locations and $S = 2^{|A|} \times T \times B$ represents all possible combinations of subsets of activities $2^{|A|}$, time-steps $T$, and SOC levels $B$. The number of all possible label extensions from Sect. 3.2 is

$$m \leq (|R_{A,C}| + |V_A| + |V_C| \cdot |B_C| + |V_C \cap V_A| \cdot |B_C|) \cdot |S| \tag{5}$$

where $|R_{A,C}|$ is the number of all possible move extensions (i) by routes between the subset $V_A \cup V_C$ of POI nodes, $|V_A|$ is the number of all possible activity extensions (ii), $|V_C| \cdot |B_C|$ is the number of all possible charging extensions (iii), and $|V_C \cap V_A| \cdot |B_C|$ is the number of possible combined activity and charging extensions (iv), all for all possible combinations of finished activities, time-steps, and SOC levels.

Let us compare the above complexity to the algorithm presented in [1]. To do so, we can again assume the worst case where the algorithm is equal to $O(\mathsf{Dij}(n,m))$ as well. The difference is that in this case are the search nodes and label extensions computed over the whole graph $G = \langle V, E \rangle$. This means that in Eq. 4 we need to replace $|V_A \cup V_C|$ with $|V|$ and in Eq. 5 we need to replace $|R_{A,C}|$ with $|E|$, everything else keeping as it is. Importantly, $V_{\mathsf{POI}}$ is by orders of magnitude smaller than $V$ and $V_A \cup V_C$ can be by orders of magnitude smaller than $V_{\mathsf{POI}}$ (depending on the size of $V_a$ of the activities). Nevertheless, in the worst case, $R_{A,C}$ contains all possible routes in $G$ between each two $u, v \in V_{\mathsf{POI}}$. Similarly to the preprocessing phase, if we limit the number of stored routes to $k$ per each two $u, v \in V_{\mathsf{POI}}$ we obtain $|R_{A,C}| \leq k|V_A \cup V_C|^2$.

## 6 Evaluation

In this section we provide an evaluation of the presented approach. We mainly present two results. First is the comparison of the optimal solution and the solution utilizing the speed-ups where we focus on the trade-off between speed and memory improvement and quality degradation. Second is the comparison of our novel approach and the state of the art published in [1] which does not use any preprocessing phase.

We base our evaluation on a set of benchmarks based on a real-world data set. Similarly to [1] we use the road network of Germany bounded by Munich, Regensburg and Passau extracted from OSM[1] with the exception of residential edges, leading to a graph with 75k nodes and 160k edges. We select 500–5000

[1] https://download.geofabrik.de/europe/germany/bayern.html.

random locations acting as possible POIs for the activities and add 324 real-world charging station locations[2] (CSs which appear on the same graph node are considered a single CS). Each charging station is randomly assigned one of three charging rates (11 kW, 30 kW, and 50 kW) and randomly parametrized waiting time which models morning and evening peak hours. Each benchmark problem is generated based on the temporal schema of 4–8 activities by randomly selecting particular sets of locations for the activities as shown in Table 1.

**Table 1.** Temporal schema of activities.

| #Act. | Activity $a$ | Time window | Dur. | $\lvert V_a \rvert$ |
|---|---|---|---|---|
| 1 | Work 1 | [7:00,19:00] | 4 h | 1 |
| 2 | Work 2 | [7:00,19:00] | 4 h | 1 |
| 3 | Shopping | [7:00,21:00] | 0.5 h | 50–200 |
| 4 | Other | [16:00,22:00] | 1 h | 10 |
| 5–8 | ... | ... | ... | ... |

### 6.1 Evaluation of the Preprocessing Phase

In this experiment we evaluate the scalability of the preprocessing phase. Table 2 shows the relation of memory (in GB) and speed (in seconds) requirements with respect to $\lvert V_{\mathsf{POI}} \rvert$ for various preprocessing techniques where full is the full preprocessed set of all non-dominated routes, $\epsilon = 0.99$ uses the $\epsilon$-pruning with given value of $\epsilon$, and $k$ uses the route reduction with given $k$ . The results show, that the memory consumption grows approximately quadratically which corresponds to the theoretical results in Sect. 5. The lowest memory footprint gives the route reduction with $k = 6$ (see Sect. 4). The $\epsilon$-relaxation has a slightly larger memory footprint than $k = 6$, but smaller than $k = 10$ which suggests that the average number of $u, v$-routes for each $u, v$ resulting from the $\epsilon$-relaxation pruning technique lies between 6 and 10.

Regarding the speed of computation of the set $R$ we compare only the full set of routes and the $\epsilon$-relaxation as for route limit $k$ the time is dominated by the computation of the routes and the subset selection is trivial w.r.t. time. The results in Table 2 show that the speedup of $\epsilon$-relaxation is more than 10× which is very significant.

### 6.2 Evaluation of the Query Phase

In this section, we evaluate the speed and quality of the WDMEV query solution depending on a number of factors. Let us first have a look on the effect of the

[2] The charging station locations are based on http://ev-charging.com.

**Table 2.** Time and memory consumption of the preprocessing phase depending on $|V_{\mathsf{POI}}|$ and on speedup used.

| $\|V_{\mathsf{POI}}\|$ | Memory (MB) | | | | | Time (min.) | |
|---|---|---|---|---|---|---|---|
| | full | Route limit $k$ | | | $\epsilon$-rel. | full | $\epsilon$-rel. |
| | | 20 | 10 | 6 | 0.99 | | 0.99 |
| 824 | 620 | 255 | 149 | 95 | 107 | 70 | 5.3 |
| 1324 | 1640 | 666 | 388 | 247 | 282 | 119 | 8.6 |
| 1824 | 3190 | 1290 | 749 | 477 | 546 | 168 | 11.8 |
| 2324 | 5200 | 2098 | 1219 | 776 | 885 | 215 | 15.2 |
| 5324 | - | - | - | - | 4700 | - | 36.6 |

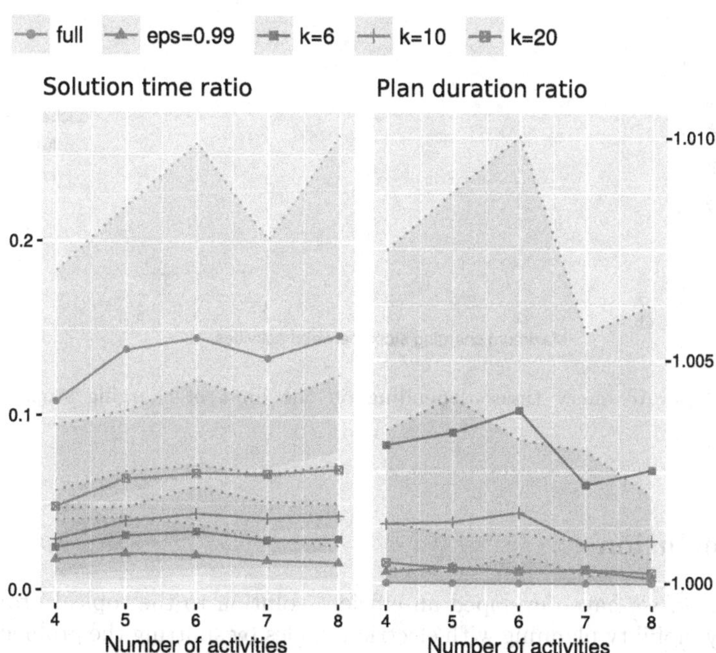


**Fig. 3.** Comparison of the effect of preprocessing speedups on the solution time (left) and quality (right). Values are average for 500 instances on 324 charging stations and 1000 POIs, the colored area corresponds to the region between the 1st and 9th quantile.

preprocessing speedups. Figure 3 (left) shows the average ratio $t_{\mathsf{pre}}/t_{\mathsf{SOTA}}$ of the time needed to find a solution where $t_{\mathsf{pre}}$ is the solution time using a preprocessing technique (as in Sect. 6.1) and $t_{\mathsf{SOTA}}$ is the solution using a single multi-criteria A* as in [1]. All solutions (including SOTA) use the charging limit $q = 1$ (see Sect. 4). The figure shows that the best solution time improvement comes from the $\epsilon$-relaxation with less than 5% of solution time needed. Even the optimal variant with full set of routes provides more than 5× speedup on average.

Figure 3 (right) shows the average ratio $\tau(\mathsf{sol})_{\mathsf{pre}}/\tau(\mathsf{sol})_{\mathsf{SOTA}}$ of solution quality. Apart from the optimal full set of routes, the best quality solutions are provided by the $\epsilon$-relaxation technique with solutions less than 0.1% worse than optimum which for a 12 hour day corresponds to less than a minute.

Figure 4 shows the average and 1st to 9th quantile region of the query phase running times. The figure shows the respective values only for the full set of routes (full) and the set of routes found using $\epsilon$-relaxation with $\epsilon = 0.99$ (eps). Moreover, the values are provided for a number of settings of the charging limit $q$ (see Sect. 4) which is set to 1–5. The results clearly show that the query times of the $\epsilon$-relaxation variant are below 5 s, which is a reasonable time. The full route set requires slightly longer running times but provides optimal solutions.

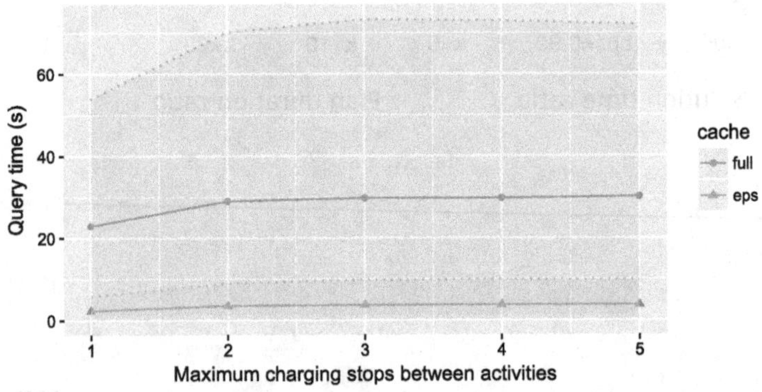


**Fig. 4.** Absolute query times depending on the limit of charging stops between activities.

## 7 Conclusion

In this work, we have developed an efficient solution to the topical problem of whole day mobility planning with electric vehicles by splitting the problem into a preprocessing and query phase. The proposed $\epsilon$-relaxation of dominance speedup used in the preprocessing phase proved to be the best approach with respect to the speed and memory footprint of preprocessing, and speed and quality of the solutions. The proposed technique was able to solve real-world problems from the region of Bavaria.

The proposed algorithms are well suited to prospectively consider also other optimization criteria and constraints such as the cost of charging or ecological footprint of the electricity used.

**Acknowledgments.** This research was funded by the European Union Horizon 2020 research and innovation programme under the grant agreement $N°713864$ and by the Grant Agency of the Czech Technical University in Prague, grant No. SGS16/235/OHK3/3T/13.

## References


1. Cuchý, M., Štolba, M., Jakob, M.: Whole day mobility planning with electric vehicles. In: ICAART (2018)
2. Aneja, Y.P., Nair, K.P.K.: The constrained shortest path problem. Nav. Res. Logist. Q. **25**, 549–555 (1978)
3. Desaulniers, G.: Shortest path problems with resource constraints. Column Gener. **5**, 33 (2006)
4. Desrochers, M., Soumis, F.: A column generation approach to the urban transit crew scheduling problem. Transp. Sci. **23**, 1–13 (1989)
5. Sachenbacher, M., Leucker, M., Artmeier, A., Haselmayr, J.: Efficient energy-optimal routing for electric vehicles. In: AAAI (2011)
6. Hart, P.E., Nilsson, N.J., Raphael, B.: A formal basis for the heuristic determination of minimum cost paths. IEEE Trans. Syst. Sci. Cybern. **4**, 100–107 (1968)
7. Cornuéjols, G., Fonlupt, J., Naddef, D.: The traveling salesman problem on a graph and some related integer polyhedra. Math. Program. **33**, 1–27 (1985)
8. Rice, M.N., Tsotras, V.J.: Parameterized algorithms for generalized traveling salesman problems in road networks. In: Proceedings of the 21st ACM SIGSPATIAL International Conference on Advances in Geographic Information Systems, SIGSPATIAL 2013, New York, NY, USA, pp. 114–123. ACM (2013)
9. Bockenhauer, H.J., Hromkovic, J., Kneis, J., Kupke, J.: The parameterized approximability of TSP with deadlines. Theory Comput. Syst. **41**, 431–444 (2007)
10. Pekny, J.F., Miller, D.L.: An exact parallel algorithm for the resource constrained traveling salesman problem with application to scheduling with an aggregate deadline. In: Proceedings of the 1990 ACM Annual Conference on Cooperation, pp. 208–214. ACM (1990)
11. Roberti, R., Wen, M.: The electric traveling salesman problem with time windows. Transp. Res. Part E: Logist. Transp. Rev. **89**, 32–52 (2016)
12. Davari, M., Demeulemeester, E., Leus, R., Talla Nobibon, F.: Exact algorithms for single-machine scheduling with time windows and precedence constraints. J. Sched. **19**, 309–334 (2016)
13. Lawler, E.L., Lenstra, J.K., Kan, A.H.R., Shmoys, D.B.: Sequencing and scheduling: algorithms and complexity. In: Logistics of Production and Inventory, Handbooks in Operations Research and Management Science, vol. 4, pp. 445–522. Elsevier (1993)
14. Loui, R.P.: Optimal paths in graphs with stochastic or multidimensional weights. Commun. ACM **26**, 670–676 (1983)
15. Mandow, L., De la Cruz, J.P., et al.: A new approach to multiobjective a* search. In: IJCAI, vol. 8 (2005)
16. Hartigan, J.A., Wong, M.A.: Algorithm AS 136: a k-means clustering algorithm. J. Roy. Stat. Soc. Ser. C (Appl. Stat.) **28**, 100–108 (1979)

# Scalable Collaborative Filtering Based on Splitting-Merging Clustering Algorithm

Nabil Belacel(✉), Guillaume Durand, Serge Leger, and Cajetan Bouchard

National Research Council, Digital Technologies Research Center, Ottawa, ON, Canada
nabil.belacel@nrc-cnrc.gc.ca

**Abstract.** Recommender systems apply information filtering technologies to identify a set of items that could be of interest to a user. Collaborative filtering (CF) is one of the most well-known successful filtering techniques in recommender systems and has been widely applied. However the usual CF techniques face issues that limit their application, especially in dealing with highly sparse and large-scale data. For instance, CF algorithms using the $k$-Nearest Neighbor approach are very efficient in filtering interesting items to users but in the same time they require a very expensive computation and grow non-linearly with the number of users and items in a database. To address this scalability issues, some researchers propose to use clustering methods. $K$-means is among the well-known clustering algorithms but has the shortcomings of dependency on the number of the clusters and on the initial centroids, which lead to inaccurate recommendations and increase computation time. In this paper, we will show by comparing with $K$-means based approaches how a clustering algorithm called $K$-means+ that considers the statistical nature of data can improve the performances of recommendation with reasonable computation time. The results presented that predictions of substantially better quality are obtained with the proposed $K$-means+ method. These results also provide significant evidences that the proposed Splitting-Merging clustering based CF is more scalable than the conventional one.

**Keywords:** Recommender systems · Collaborative filtering
Information filtering · Clustering · Splitting-merging clustering

## 1 Introduction

In todays digital world it is difficult to make a good decision with the inundation of choices and options offered to us every day: What movie should we see this week-end? Which digital camera do I need to buy? Which agency funding my company can apply? Which courses do I need to take? What tweet should I tweet about? etc. Personalized recommendation systems have been regarded


J. van den Herik and A. P. Rocha (Eds.): ICAART 2018, LNAI 11352, pp. 290–311, 2019.
https://doi.org/10.1007/978-3-030-05453-3_14

as an important mechanism to cope with these challenges. Personalized Recommendation systems use information filtering to overcome the difficulty of information overload. Thanks to the success of this technology, they have become an important research area for both academia and industry. Based on the historical records of users, the recommendation system initially recommends the information to them for choosing according to their preferences [1]. The preferences of active users are calculated either by predicting ratings of unrated items or by building a top-N list of unrated items ordered by predicted rating [2,3]. In general, recommendation systems use mainly three types of filtering techniques: content based filtering, collaborative filtering and hybrid filtering (the combination of content based filtering and collaborative filtering) [4]. The content based filtering recommendation technique recommends specific items that are similar to those have been already positively rated in the past by the active user. Content based filtering uses only the content of the items in order to make a recommendation [5]. The collaborative filtering (CF) recommendation technique recommends items that were preferred in the past by similar users to the active user. CF techniques make the assumption that the active users will be interested in items that users similar to them have rated highly [6]. The hybrid based filtering techniques recommend items by combining CF and content-based filtering [4]. CF is one of the most popular filtering techniques in recommendation systems [2,7–9]. CF is, for instance, widely used in the fields of e-commerce [10–12], e-learning [13], e-government [14], movies and TV programs [15,16], music [17], books [18], web pages [19] and in twitter [20]. Methods in CF can be either memory-based or model-based. Memory-based algorithms operate on the whole user-item rating matrix and make recommendations by identifying the neighborhood of the target user to whom the recommendations will be made, based on his preferences [21]. The memory based filtering algorithms are easy to implement and to understand and they are working very well in many real world applications. While, memory based CF are widely applied [6,11,20], however they face important problems limiting their applications in large scale problems. Most prominent problems are the data sparsity and the low scalability. Data sparsity refers to the difficulty that most users rate only a small number of items and hence a very sparse user-item matrix is available [7]. On the scalability side, the memory based filtering algorithms do not scale satisfactory when the users and items in ratings database increase [6,7,22]. As a result, one of the main challenges faced by CF is to improve the scalability of the memory based filtering algorithms. As an alternative, model-based techniques were proposed. Model based techniques use machine learning algorithms on users-rating training data to learn a model and to make predictions on the users-rating test data or on real data [23]. Several algorithms have been used for model based CF. Among them, let's list Bayesian networks [24], matrix factorization [25,26], probabilistic latent space models [27], neural networks [28,29] and clustering methods [30,31]. Clustering methods using the $K$-means algorithm have been widely used to model based CF because of its simplicity and low complexity. However, the usability of $K$-means is limited by the fact that the clustering results are heavily dependent on the user defined variants, i.e., the selection of the initial centroids seeds and the number of clusters. In practice, these shortcomings lead to inaccurate recommendations and dramatic computation time increases. To avoid the shortcomings of the k-means algorithms and at the same time to solve scalability and sparsity in CF, this paper proposes an automatic clustering approach based on $K$-means+, known also as $y$-means. $K$-means+ can automatically determine a pseudo-optimal number of clusters according to the statistical nature of data so that the initial centroids seeds are not critical to the clustering [32,33]. This paper proposes a recommendation method that alleviates the scalability difficulty of CF and improves the $K$-means CF-based recommendation approaches proposed in literature by performing extensive experiments using three different data sets classified as small, medium and large from MovieLens [34]. The rest of the article is organized as follows: Sect. 2 presents related works on traditional CF as well as different algorithms including the clustering methods used. Section 3 describes the proposed approach to automatic clustering for CF. Section 4 provides experimental results and Sect. 5 outlines conclusions and future work.

## 2 Related Work

CF is a popular personalized recommendation technique that relies on past users items ratings. It predicts user preferences on items that have not been seen yet based on the historical preference judgments (rating values) from a community of users. The preference judgments are presented as a user-item rating matrix. Note that user rating can be either implicit or explicit [35]. CF approach uses only the past users' behaviors and does not require any user profile [36,37]. It has the advantage of not requiring any external data such as demographic information hence reducing the time consumed by the recommendation process [7]. Techniques used in CF can be either memory based or model based [2,7].

### 2.1 Memory Based Filtering

Memory based filtering uses the entire user-item data to generate a prediction. Based on some similarities, the algorithms find a set of users with similar tastes or preferences, called neighbors, to target user. These neighbors have a history of agreeing with the target user. They rate different items similarly. Once neighbors of users are found, the algorithms predict the preferences on new items for the target user. These algorithms are known as nearest-neighbor or user-based CF.

**General Approach of $k$-NN Based Collaborative Filtering.** The most prevalent algorithm used in collaborative filtering is the neighborhood based method also known as $k$-nearest neighbor CF. It was the first automated CF system introduced by GroupLens [36]. The $k$-nearest neighbor for collaborative filtering follows three phases to generate a recommendation:

1. Compute the similarities between the active user and all other users in database;

2. Determine the $k$ nearest neighbors to the active user;
3. Compute the prediction from the weighted combination of the selected neighbors ratings. The highest predicted items ratings are recommended to the active users.

**Similarity Weighting.** Even though there are several algorithms for CF, all of them use similarity measurement between users to recommend items. The similarity is usually based on a neighborhood based filtering algorithm [2]. The first step in K-NN based CF is to weight all users with respect to similarity. The similarity reflects the correlation, distance or weight among users. Various approaches have been proposed to compute the similarity $sim(u, v)$ between users $u$ and $v$ based on ratings of items that both users have rated [38]. Different similarity measures have been proposed and evaluated in the literature. Among these measures we can list: Cosine vector [2], Pearson correlation [36,39], Spearman Rank correlation [40], mean squared difference [41] and these are few similarity measures used in CF among others [42,43]. Popular approaches for similarity weighting in CF are Pearson correlation and cosine vector. As a result, we used both Pearson correlation and cosine vector in the proposed modeled based filtering algorithm. In many research works, the Pearson correlation tends to lead to better results [2,21,22,44]. The Pearson correlation between the active user $a$ and $v$ is given as follows:

$$w(a,v) = \frac{\sum_{i\in I}(r_{a,i} - \bar{r_a})(r_{v,i} - \bar{r_v})}{\sqrt{\sum_{i\in I}(r_{a,i} - \bar{r_a})^2 \sum_{i\in I}(r_{v,i} - \bar{r_v})^2}} \tag{1}$$

where $I$ is the set of co-rated items by the two users $a$ and $v$. $r_{a,i}$ and $r_{v,i}$ refer to the rating of the target item $i$ by the user $a$ and $v$ respectively. $\bar{r_a}$ and $\bar{r_v}$ are the average rating of the co-rated items of the users $u$ and $v$ respectively. Pearson correlation can be problematic when computing similarities between users who have rated only few items. To alleviate this difficulty some researchers have proposed an improved Pearson correlation calculation by adding a significance weighting factor that would devalue similarity weights based on a small number of co-rated items [21,40]. Some experiments have shown a threshold value of 50 to be useful in improving prediction accuracy. The threshold can be applied by multiplying the similarity function by $\min\{|I_u \bigcap I_u|/50, 1\}$ [21,40,44]. In our work we were able to confirm that the threshold of 50 is indeed the best choice. Shardanand and Maes [41] proposed a constrained Pearson correlation for their Ringo music recommender. They claimed that they get better performances by computing their constrained Pearson correlation similarity weights. The other well known similarity measure used for collaborative filtering is vector cosine based similarity. In this measure the users are presented as vectors of items in $|I| - dimensional$ and similarity is measured by the dot product of two rating vectors. Hence the cosine similarity between two users $a$ and $v$ is:

$$sim(a,v) = \frac{r_a.r_v}{\|r_a\|_2 \, \|r_v\|_2} = \frac{\sum_{i\in I} r_{a,i}.r_{v,i}}{\sqrt{\sum_{i\in I} r_{a,i}^2}\sqrt{\sum_{i\in I} r_{v,i}^2}} \tag{2}$$

In cosine similarity the unknown items are considered to be zero, which will drop them out from the numerator. If we consider in cosine similarity only the co-rated items, it will be the same as a Pearson correlation. The cosine similarity function is naturally self-damping, based on $\frac{|I_a \cap I_v|}{|I_a||I_v|}$, the ratio of co-rated items to user item set sizes. The authors in [44] show in their offline experiments that the dynamic self-damping in cosine vector similarity was more effective than significance weighting. Using cosine adds also the benefit of not depending on the fairly arbitrary cutoff of 50 as in [44,45].

**Neighborhoods Selection.** Once the similarity between the active user and all other users are calculated, CF selects a subset of users that will be used for items prediction [20]. As mentioned in [41], it is more efficient to use a subset of users that are the most similar to the active user, known as neighbors, than to use the whole user data set. The challenging question is how many neighbors should be selected though? In the original collaborative filtering GroupLens system, all users are considered as neighbors [36], which is obviously not practical for very large data sets. In their empirical study, [40] shows how the mean absolute error of prediction increases as the neighborhood size is increased. Therefore, the system has to choose the best neighbors to the active user, discarding the remaining users [21]. Two main techniques were suggested in CF literature: the correlation or similarity threshold and the $n$-best neighbors with $n$ being the best $k$ users most similar to the active user who have rated the target item $i$. The similarity threshold technique chooses as best neighbors only the users with similarity to the active user greater than a given threshold [2]. In the empirical studies done by Shardanand and Maes [21,41], setting a high threshold limits the correlate neighborhood resulting in small neighborhoods that can not provide prediction coverage for many items. However, setting a lower correlation threshold results in a large number of lower correlates, which is like using all the available users in the data set. The best $n$ selection technique is the one that can provide high performances with no loss in coverage [21,40,44]. The author in [21] found that the similarity threshold technique performed best with a high threshold but all concluded that it yielded a lower coverage prediction. Another technique to select the best $n$ correlates for a given $n$ was proposed by [44]. As the particular number of neighbors to be selected is domain and system specific, an analysis of relevant data set can help to choose the best neighborhood size [44]. The analysis of MovieLens data found that $n = 20$ was a good size for neighbors [21]. As shown in different analysis, a number of $n$ neighbors between 20 and 50 is usually a reasonable starting point in CF.

**Prediction.** After that the similarities are computed between the active user with other users and the $n$ neighbors are selected, the CF system combines the items rating from those $n$ users to predict the user's preferences for an item. The formula used to generate prediction is the weighted average of deviation from the neighbor's mean, using the similarity calculated in Eqs. (1) and (2):

$$p_{a,i} = \bar{r_a} + \frac{\sum_{v=1}^{n}(r_{v,i} - \bar{r_a}) * sim(a,v)}{\sum_{v=1}^{n}|sim(a,v)|} \tag{3}$$

where $p_{a,i}$ represents the prediction for the active user $a$ for the target item $i$. $n$ is the selected number of neighbors and $sim(a,u)$ is the weighted similarity calculated by Eqs. (1) and (2). In order to take into account the differences in spread between users' rating distributions, the authors in [21] proposed an extension of the Eq. (3) by converting ratings to z-score and to compute the weighted average of the z-score by the following formula:

$$p_{a,i} = \bar{r_a} + \sigma_a * \frac{\sum_{v=1}^{n}\frac{(r_{v,i} - \bar{r_a})}{\sigma_a} * sim(a,v)}{\sum_{v=1}^{n}|sim(a,v)|} \tag{4}$$

Herlocker et al. [21] found that the weighted average deviation of neighbor's rating from that neighbor's mean rating performs significantly better than the non-normalized ratings approach and there is no significant difference with average weighted of z-scores. In our experiment we chose to use Eq. (3).

**Challenges of Memory Based Collaborative Filtering.** Memory based CF have been very successful due to their simplicity and their good performances. However, and as previously mentioned, they suffer limitations such as scalability and data sparsity. In practice recommender systems are used for large numbers of user and items. Hence, memory based CF has difficulty scaling for systems such as amazon.com or e-bay e-commerce. These systems contain millions of users and items. In this paper we propose an approach that can deal with the scalability issue, and test it on millions of users and items. In addition, most recommender systems dealing with millions of items have active users rating only a small number of them, resulting in a poor recommendation accuracy. Another illustration of sparsity is when a new user or item occurs, making difficult to find similar neighbors as there is no information available on them. More details on memory based collaborative filtering challenges can be found in [6,7,38]. To overcome these difficulties researchers have proposed model based filtering approaches.

### 2.2 Model Based Filtering

Model based filtering first builds a model on the training set to predict the items for the active users on the independent sets or on the new users. Since the model is built offline, the system uses less memory and the prediction time decreases [23, 46]. The model based CF provides more accurate predictions for sparse data and addresses scalability problems as shown in [47–49]. Several popular model based filtering approaches are based on probabilistic latent semantic CF and clustering techniques [7]. The goal of the latent semantic analysis is to discover latent features that explain observed ratings [50]. Techniques of latent semantic analysis count probabilistic latent space models [27], neural network [51], latent Dirichlet allocation or based on topic modeling [52], and Markov decision process based models [53,54]. The clustering CF techniques are extensively used to address the scalability and sparsity problems. Researchers including [28,47–49] show in their experiments that clustering CF provide more accurate predictions for sparse data than memory based filtering and addressing the scalability issue as well as the items cold start problems. In the next section, we give an overview of clustering methods for CF.

**Clustering Based CF.** Clustering is an unsupervised process through which a large number of data are classified into homogeneous groups, based on some observable features. Clustering methods can unlock precious information that can help experts make critical decisions, especially when there is no or little prior information. The clustering methods consist in assembling patterns or entities in restricted classes so that all patterns of the same class are less dispersed than in the whole sample [55]. Clustering can be used as an exploratory tool for analyzing large datasets. As such, it has been applied extensively in a wide range of disciplines ranging from pattern recognition, cybersecurity, biometrics, bioinformatics, psychology, image segmentation, information retrieval and filtering and many other real world applications [33,56–59]. In CF, the clustering techniques can be used to group either the items into clusters that have same users' preferences or users into clusters with similar items ratings. In users' CF, users who have same items' preferences are grouped in restricted clusters. Therefore, when a new user is identified as similar to a given cluster, items liked by those users' cluster are recommended to this new user [60,61]. In their clustering methods, Ungar and Foster [31] clustered users and rated items separately using variations of $K$-means with Expectation Maximization (EM) and Gibbs sampling [62]. Their experiments showed that the results of EM clustering based CF on real data were not very promising but when they used the repeated $K$-means with Gibbs sampling their results get better. Moreover, their model could be easily extended to much complex models and it may handle clustering with multiple attributes. However, Gibbs sampling is computationally expensive [31]. Kohrs *et al.* [63] applied hierarchy clustering using the top down approach for CF with sparse rating matrix. Their approach was more efficient than other traditional CF when applied to few users and provided high prediction values even for users who rated only a limited number of items. Hierarchical clustering is particularly efficient in providing recommendations for new users who rated only few items. Xue *et al.* [64] applied the $K$-means algorithm to cluster users before analyzing clusters obtained and choosing an adequate cluster for the active user. They applied the smoothing strategies to the unseen items using the same idea used in natural language processing [65] where the cluster is used as topic in order to alleviate the sparsity difficulty. They showed that their approach outperformed other CF approaches on small data sets. Sarwar *et al.* [61] addressed the scalability issues by users clustering and used the user's cluster as the neighborhood. The author in [66] showed the efficiency of their newly proposed clustering based CF in rating predictions with addressing the data sparsity and cold start problems. Hu *et al.* [67] proposed a clustering method for CF. Their approach was divided into two phases: clustering and then CF. The clustering method was based on $K$-means and used as pre-processing for CF. By using clustering technique, the data size was reduced so that the computation time of CF algorithm decreased significantly. The results of their approach depend strongly on the number of clusters and unfortunately this number of clusters is initially unknown. Dakhal and Mahdavi [68] proposed a filtering algorithm based on user $K$-means clustering and voting. They used their approach on the small data base 100k MovieLens users and they show that the proposed method provides high prediction with less computation time than traditional CF. A generalization of $K$-means known as fuzzy $c$-means method has also been applied to CF. Fuzzy $c$-means assigns objects to a given number of clusters such that each of them belongs to more than one cluster with different degrees of membership. Wu and Li applied fuzzy $c$-means to CF on NETFLIX data set. The limitation of fuzzy $c$-means is that they do not perform well in high dimensional space and are unreliable in a noisy environment [22]. Other works considered both clustering users and items to address the cold start problems [69]. Zahra et al. [22] studied the impact of the initial centroids on the clustering based CF performances and computational time. They proposed twenty algorithms for centroids selection and they analyzed their impact on $K$-means, fuzzy $c$-means and EM clustering based CF. This recent studies point out that a better clustering algorithm can further improve the performance of the recommendation. This motivated us to develop clustering algorithms for CF presented in the next section.

## 3 General Approach of Clustering Based CF

The main contribution of this paper is to propose a recommendation method that alleviates the scalability and sparsity difficulties of CF by introducing the splitting and merging clustering based on $K$-means+ algorithm and by performing extensive experiments using three different data sets classified as small, medium and large from MovieLens data sets [34]. Predictions in clustering based CF approach are performed in following steps:

- step 1: Cluster users $u \in U$ in $K$ clusters using any clustering algorithm
- step 2: Evaluate the distance between active user and centroids
- step 3: Choose the closest cluster for the active user
- step 4: Select the $n$ nearest neighbor from the chosen active user's cluster
- Step 5: predict items' active user preferences.

The $K$-means is the most well known and commonly used clustering algorithm for CF as detailed in the following subsection.

### 3.1 $K$-means Clustering Algorithm for CF

Many researchers show that $K$-means is very efficient for model based CF [64,68]. Algorithm 1 presents the different steps of $K$-means clustering method.

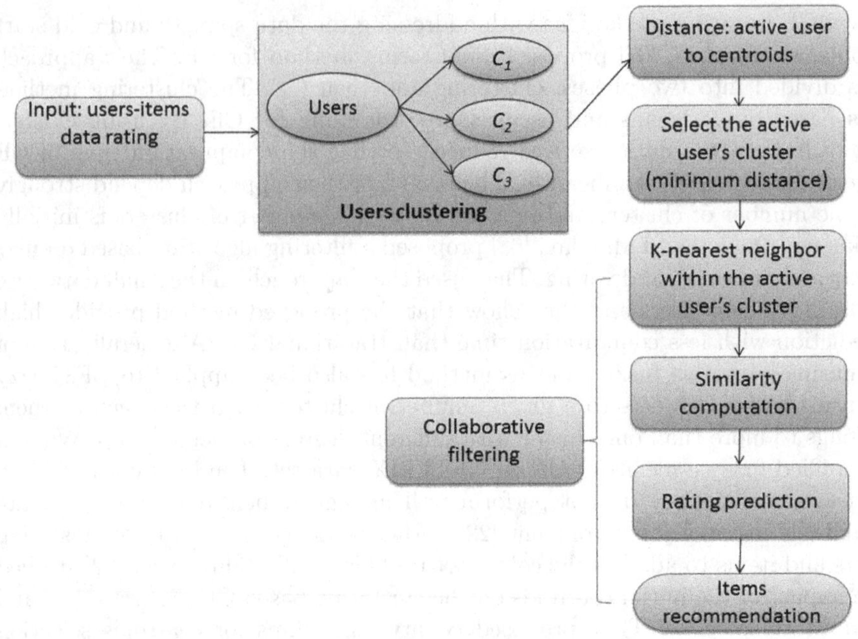


**Fig. 1.** General approach of clustering based collaborative filtering.

$K$-means is relatively scalable and efficient when processing large data sets as its time complexity is $O(|U| \times K \times t)$, where $t$ is the number of iterations, $|U|$ is the total number of users and $K$ is the number of clusters. It can also converge to local optimum in a relatively small number of iterations. However, the usability of $K$-means is limited since clustering results are heavily dependent on the user defined variants, i.e., the selection of the initial centroids seeds and the number of clusters. Consequently, these shortcomings lead to inaccurate recommendation and increase the computation time of collaborative filtering. To overcome the $K$-means algorithm issue and in the same time to solve both problems scalability and sparsity in CF, we applied $K$-means+ [32,33]. $K$-means+ can automatically determine a pseudo optimal number of clusters according to the statistical nature of the data. The initial centroid seeds are not critical to the $K$-means+ clustering [32,33,70]. $K$-means is sensitive to outliers and noise in data since a small number of such data can substantially influence the mean value. The resulting cluster centroids may not be excellent representatives of their cluster. However, $K$-means+ can handle noise and outliers in the data. The clusters with outliers in $K$-means+ can be split depending on the data distribution of the cluster. In a sparse matrix as in the case of CF, data contains outliers that are not appropriate for clustering algorithms like $K$-means. In such situation, $K$-means can end with several empty clusters to which no data points are allocated during the assignment step. Two approaches are proposed to handle empty clusters: deleting the empty clusters or replacing the empty cluster with newly created

**Algorithm 1.** $K$-Means algorithm.

**Input**:$U$: training users; $K$: the number of clusters
**Output**: $K$ users' clusters with $K$ centroids, $\{C_1, C_2, ..., C_K\}$
Step 1: **Initialization**: Randomly select $K$ users uniformly at random from $U$, as initial starting points. Calculate centroids as the means value of the users for each cluster.
**Alternate steps**
**repeat**
Step 2: assign each user to the cluster with nearest centroid;
Step 3: update the centroid clusters, i.e., calculate the mean value of the users for each cluster
**until** (no user changes its cluster membership or any other stopping condition is satisfied)

non-empty clusters. The second approach chooses the point that is farthest away from its current centroid, replaces it as the centroid of the empty cluster, and then perform the re-clustering. This strategy as proposed by [71] eliminates the farthest point that contributes most to the total sum of squared errors. In our experiments, in case of empty clusters situation, $K$-means+ follows the first approach by removing the empty clusters using a splitting and merging strategy. The second approach was deemed more complicated and expensive.

### 3.2 Proposed Splitting Merging Clustering Approach for Collaborative Filtering

The main contribution of this paper is to propose a recommendation method that alleviates the scalability and sparsity difficulties of CF by introducing $K$-means+ and by performing extensive experiments using three different data sets classified as small, medium and large from MovieLens [34]. Our proposed splitting and merging clustering based CF is presented in the Algorithms 2 and 3. Algorithm 2 presents a general steps of the clustering method $K$-means+ [32,33]. During the splitting phase, the data points that are far beyond the threshold $d = 5\sigma$ are considered as outliers and they are removed from each cluster. Meanwhile, the adjacent clusters whose overlap is over the threshold $d = 1.414(\sigma_1 + \sigma_2)$ are merged. Therefore the clustering results are not sensitive to the initial partitions and to the number of clusters. The effect of outliers in $K$-means+ is well handled. As shown in Fig. 1, our proposed clustering based CF method proceeds into two phases. The first phase is done on the historical users-items ratings data. In this phase users are clustered in different groups such that users with similar preferences are grouped in the same cluster. Algorithm 3 presents the different steps of the prediction phase on the testing data. The prediction of the items' ratings for the active user is done by following two steps. The first step aims at choosing the closest cluster for the active user by calculating the distance between the active user and the centroid of the classes. Therefore, the cluster of the active user is determined by the closest distance between the active user and the centroid of the corresponding cluster. The second step of this phase

**Algorithm 2.** Splitting and merging $K$-Means+ algorithm for CF.

```
Input: U: training users; K: the initial number of clusters
Output: K' centroids, C_1, C_2, ..., C_K'; K' is the adjusted number of clusters;
Step 1: Initialization: arbitrarily choose K users uniformly at random from U, as
initial starting points. Calculate centroids as the means value of the users for each
cluster.
Apply K-means;
Search for an empty Cluster
if (there are empty clusters ) then
    delete the empty clusters
end if
hasOutlier ← true
/*Splitting Steps*/
while (hasOutlier) do
    search all the clusters
    if (there is an outlier) then
        hasOutlier ← true
        remove the first found outlier
        Create a new cluster with this deleted outlier
        Apply K-means with centroids of new clusters as initial solution
        Search for an empty Cluster
        if (there are empty clusters ) then
            delete the empty clusters
        end if
    else
        hasOutlier ← false
    end if
end while
/*merging steps*/
for i = 1 to K' − 1 do
    for j = i + 1 to K' do
        if (cluster_i and cluster_j can be merged) then
            group cluster_i and cluster_j
        end if
    end for
end for
```

applies the $k$-nearest neighbor based CF as presented in Sect. 2.1 on active user's cluster only (do not include all users data) as in the classical CF technique. Consequently, the execution time on the testing set is reduced as well as the sparsity difficulty. Our model based collaborative filtering is based on $K$-means+ that is characterized by exploiting the statistical nature of the data to adjust autonomously the number of clusters $K$ [32,33]. It partitions the data into an appropriate number of clusters rather than an adhoc fixed number of clusters with an initial clustering state that is not critical to the final clustering results. $K$-means+ considers the statistical nature of data distribution. By splitting and merging clusters, it self-adjusts the number of clusters $K$. If the initial value of

**Algorithm 3.** Clustering based recommendation: Generate recommendation from users' cluster.

**Input:** The $K\prime$ clusters $\{C_1, C_2, ..., C_{K\prime}\}$ with the corresponding $K\prime$ centroids obtained by applying $K$-means+
**Output:** Target items' predictions
**Predict the rating for target items**
**Phase 1:** Calculate the distance between the active user and $K\prime$ centroids;
Find the closest centroid to the active user with the corresponding cluster;
**Phase 2:** Use the ratings from those like-minded users within the active user's cluster found in step 1 to calculate items' prediction for the active user; then top-N items can be presented to the active user.

$K$ is too small, the splitting strategy is used to increase the number of clusters; likewise the merging strategy reduces the number of clusters in case it is too large.

# 4 Experiment

## 4.1 Datasets

In the experimentation we considered three data sets from the movie rating application MovieLens. More details on the different MovieLens data sets can be found in [34]. The first data set used is MovieLens 100,000 ratings, we called it **SML**. It contains 100,000 ratings provided by 943 users for 1682 movies. Movies are rated on an integer scale going from 1 (bad) to 5 (excellent) with 0 for not rated movies. The second data set called **MML** in the paper is a medium size MovieLens data set. MML contains slightly more than 1 million ratings and 209 ratings rated by 6040 users on 3900 movies using the same integer scale as SML. The third data set called **LML** is large MovieLens data set. LML contains 10 millions and 5 ratings applied to 10681 movies by 71567 users of the online movie recommender service MovieLens http://files.grouplens.org/datasets/movielens/ml-10m-README.html. The ratings of LML data set is different from SML and MML. Rates in LML are made on a 5-stars scale and with half-star increments. As a result there is 10 rates possibilities ranged from 0.5 to 5 and 0 standing as a not rated item.

## 4.2 Metrics

In order to evaluate the quality of CF algorithms, several metrics have been proposed in the literature. The authors in [72] classified the metrics into two categories the error metrics and the classification accuracy metrics. Accuracy metric are more suitable for CF recommender systems with binary ratings. To use this category of metrics, it is necessary to consider a binary rating scheme. Recall&precision and Receiver Operating Characteristic (ROC) metrics have been proposed for evaluating binary rating CF and measure how well a CF algorithm recommends the relevant items to the active users [61,73]. In this paper we considered the error metrics because they were suitable for non binary data sets such as Movielens. This metric evaluates how good the prediction rating of the test items are close to the true numerical rating given by the active user. Thus, these metrics can be applied only for the items that have been rated. The Mean Squared Error (MSE) and the Root Means Squared Error (RMSE) are an example of error metrics used for CF [72]. These metrics are very easy to implement but also sensitive to outliers. However, the Mean Absolute Error (MAE) metric is less sensitive to outliers and it is also very easy to implement while giving a direct and simple interpretation [72]. Even though some authors critic the use of MAE in finding good items and for ranking the $N$ best items to be proposed to the active user [72,74]), we have used the *Mean Absolute Error* (*MAE*) because of its versatility in CF literature [22,74]. The MAE calculates the average absolute deviation between predicted rating provided by CF algorithm and true rating assigned by user in the testing data test. It is defined as:

$$MAE = \frac{1}{n}\sum_{i=1}^{n} |p_i - r_i| \tag{5}$$

where $n$ is the total of ratings provided by the test set, $p_i$ is the predicted rating provided by the CF algorithm and $r_i$ is the actual rating assigned by user to item $i$. The lower the MAE, the more accurately the recommendation engine predicts user ratings.

### 4.3 Evaluation Methodology

In this study, we used a ten fold cross validation technique to evaluate the developed algorithms for collaborative filtering on SML, MML and LML data sets; 20% of the users were randomly selected to be test set and the 80% remaining were used for training. From each user in the test set, ratings for 20% of items were withheld, and rating predictions were computed for those withheld items. Finally, the average results on the ten folds including the *MAE* cluster numbers and the execution time were reported. In the paper [75] we used the cross validation only for SML and for MML. For LML we divided the users into two folds: one fold was used for training and the other one was used for testing.

## 5 Results and Discussion

To compare the performance of different algorithms in terms of scalability, we calculated the predictive accuracy using MAE and measured the execution time to get a prediction on the test data set. We tested on this way three algorithms including the nearest neighbor based CF, the $K$-means and $K$-means+ clustering based CF. In this comparative study, different numbers of clusters ranging from 3 to 150 have been used as initial condition for clustering methods.

### 5.1 Comparing with Traditional and $K$-means CF in Terms of MAE

The results over SML dataset in Fig. 2 show that the CF based on splitting and merging as presented in Algorithm 2 $K$-means+ clearly outperforms the CF based $K$-means algorithm when the number of clusters is greater than 20 and slightly better with a smaller number of clusters. As shown in Fig. 2, the performances obtained by the classical CF is slightly better than our proposed clustering based CF and much better than $K$-means based CF specifically when the number of clusters is greater than 20. The classical collaborative filtering is designated in the graph as $k$-nn CF with number of clusters is one and it is presented by the green color. The results over MML dataset in Fig. 3 show that $K$-means+ outperforms $K$-means while slightly not being as good as classical CF. However, it is two times faster than the classical collaborative filtering when the initial number of clusters is 150 as presented in Fig. 4. As we mentioned in related work, the CF algorithms suffer from the scalability problem. Our $K$-means+ based CF is less time consuming than traditional CF method. As seen in Figs. 2, 3 and 4 our proposed $K$-means+ based CF outperforms $K$-means based CF and has almost the same prediction time on MML data sets and less time consuming than both classical CF and $K$-means based CF methods. Our proposed method with $K$-means+ takes about one fifth of the traditional CF average prediction running time. As shown in Fig. 5, on average, the final number of clusters obtained by $K$-means+ is decreased. For example, for the initial number of cluster $K = 150$, on average the final number of clusters is about $K = 7$. This is why the performances of CF based $K$-means+ is better than CF based on $K$-means. However, the CPU time for online prediction will increase a little bit because the closest cluster to target user will have more users than in case with $K$-means.

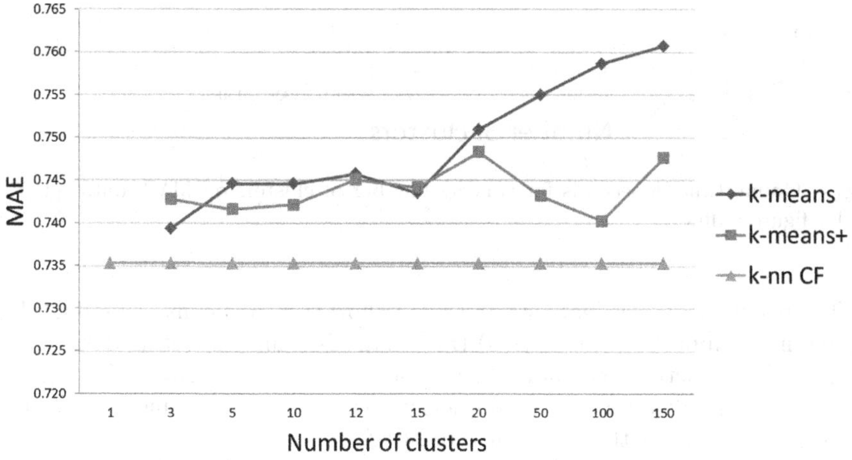


**Fig. 2.** MAE for varying number of clusters on SML data [75]. (Color figure online)

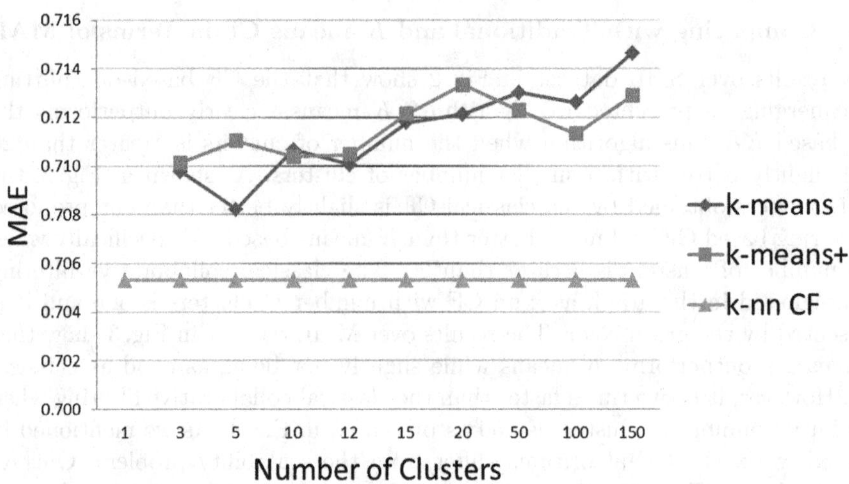


**Fig. 3.** MAE for varying number of clusters on MML data [75]. (Color figure online)

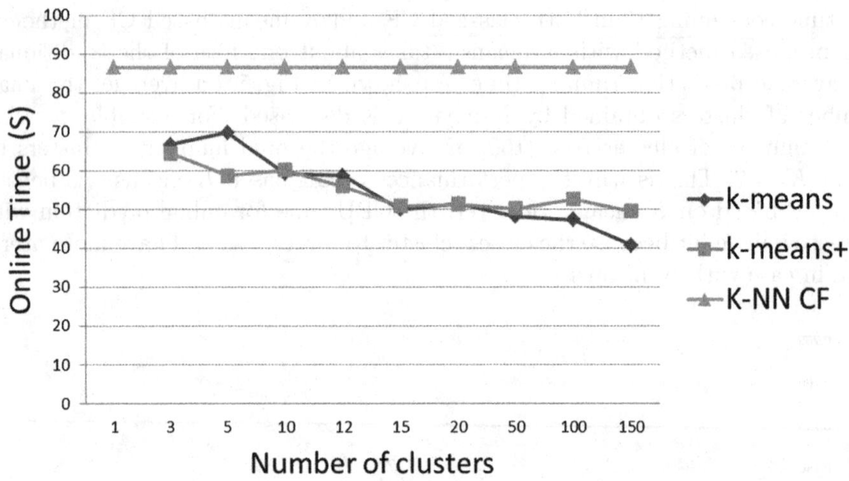


**Fig. 4.** Online time in seconds for varying number of clusters on MML data set [75]. (Color figure online)

The results over LML data set in Table 1 show that $K$-means+ based CF has less online computation (prediction) time than $K$-means on testing data with a comparable prediction accuracy. We can note from the last row of Table 1 the average item prediction time of $K$-means+ is almost three times faster than $K$-means with almost the same value of MAE.

To the best of our knowledge this is the first time the LML data set are tested using clustering based CF.

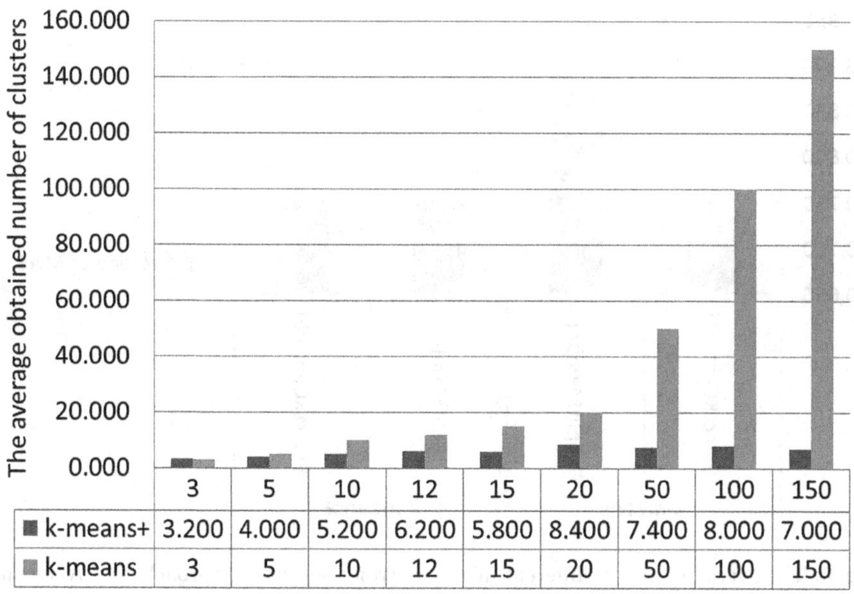


**Fig. 5.** The average number of clusters obtained by $K$-means+ on training set (SML data).

**Table 1.** The comparative results between $K$-means and $K$-means+ in terms of MAE and prediction time per item in nanoseconds.

| Clusters $K$ | K-means+ | | K-means | |
|---|---|---|---|---|
| | MAE | Prediction time (ns) | MAE | Prediction time (ns) |
| 5 | 0.6682 | 93543.78 | 0.656971 | 682253.4 |
| 10 | 0.668694 | 93682.28 | 0.655701 | 379354.4 |
| 12 | 0.666 | 95831.71 | 0.655802 | 322917.2 |
| 15 | 0.667372 | 96263.53 | 0.65572 | 276949.8 |
| 20 | 0.668505 | 92198.23 | 0.656269 | 221514.6 |
| 50 | 0.666655 | 96794.09 | 0.660763 | 127763.2 |
| 100 | 0.670033 | 74658.26 | 0.667641 | 74809.03 |
| 150 | 0.674332 | 71529.03 | 0.673229 | 68923.54 |
| Average | 0.668724 | 89312.61 | 0.660262 | 269310.6 |

### 5.2 Impact of the Initial Centroids Seeds for Clustering Based CF

Figure 6 summarizes our results using different initial centroids approaches. In this experiments we have tested only two approaches, the first one selects $K$ users from training set uniformly at random and the second one, splits the users in $K$ subsets and then calculates centroids as the means value of the users for each subset. As shown in Fig. 6, our CF based $K$-means+ algorithm provides almost

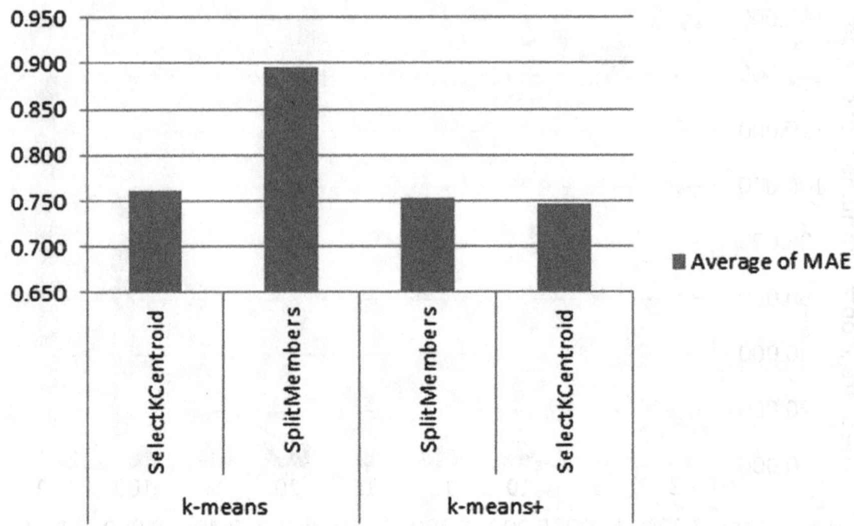


**Fig. 6.** The average MAE of different initial centroids selection approaches on $K$-means and $K$-means+ over the SML test sets with $K = 150$[75].

same predictions with different initial centroid seeds approaches. As a result, CF based $K$-means+ approach seems more robust and stable to the initial centroid seeds than in CF based $K$-means algorithm.

### 5.3 Selecting the Neighborhoods

The average prediction evaluated by MAE for different number of neighborhood is given in Fig. 7. In this figure we present only two variations of neighborhoods

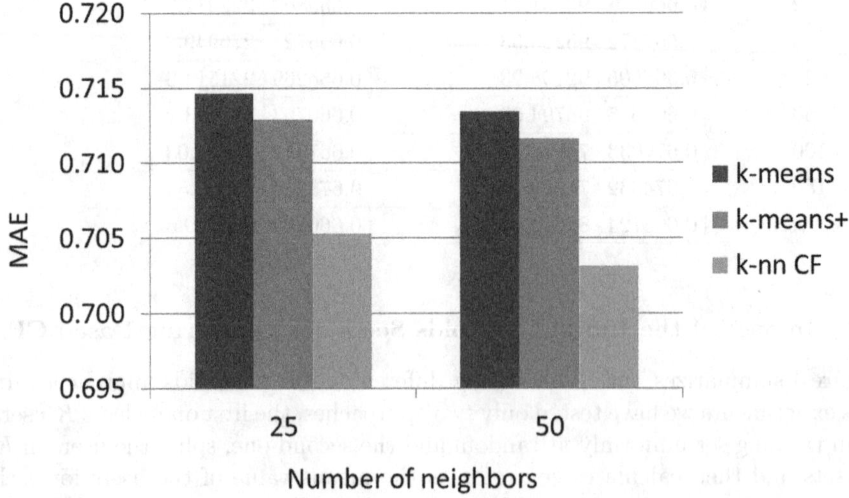


**Fig. 7.** MAE for varying number of neighbors on MML with the number of clusters 150.

$n = 25$ and $n = 50$. This empirical study shows that the three CF algorithms perform better when increasing the number of neighborhoods.

## 6 Conclusions

Recommender systems have become an essential functionality for many E-commerce Web applications. Many systems using $k$ nearest neighbor based CF are very efficient in filtering interesting items to users. However, these CF algorithms see their computation time growing non-linearly with the number of users and items in the database. To address this scalability issue, we investigated the application of a clustering method based on a splitting and merging heuristic for model based collaborative filtering. We considered an aspect that is usually ignored in CF, the statistical nature of the data. The experimental results obtained show that the recommendation method based on splitting and merging heuristic is a viable approach for scalable collaborative filtering. The comparative results have shown that splitting-merging clustering algorithm has a lower prediction error (MAE) comparing to $K$-means clustering methods especially for a large amount of data with a high dimensional space. Moreover, the experimental results on Movielens data illustrate the robustness of $K$-means+ clustering algorithm and the fact that initial centroid seeds are not critical to the clustering results. In this study we have considered only user collaborative filtering and it would be interesting to investigate the application of k-means+ clustering method to item based collaborative filtering and compare the results with user based collaborative filtering. More precisely, we could apply our proposed clustering method $K$-means+ to the item based filtering method. Once the items are clustered and the closest cluster to the new item is determined, the item based CF would be applied to produce the recommendation to the target user. To improve the performances of the splitting and merging heuristic for CF, we will investigate the application of different meta-heuristic techniques such as variable neighborhood search to $K$-means+ heuristic as presented in [76].

## References


1. Bobadilla, J., Ortega, F., Hernando, A., GutiéRrez, A.: Recommender systems survey. Knowl.-Based Syst. **46**, 109–132 (2013)
2. Breese, J.S., Heckerman, D., Kadie, C.: Empirical analysis of predictive algorithms for collaborative filtering. In: Proceedings of the Fourteenth Conference on Uncertainty in Artificial Intelligence, pp. 43–52 (1998)
3. Deshpande, M., Karypis, G.: Item-based top-N recommendation algorithms. ACM Trans. Inf. Syst. (TOIS) **22**, 143–177 (2004)
4. Burke, R.: Hybrid recommender systems: survey and experiments. User Model. User-Adapt. Interact. **12**, 331–370 (2002)
5. Pazzani, M.J., Billsus, D.: Content-based recommendation systems. In: Brusilovsky, P., Kobsa, A., Nejdl, W. (eds.) The Adaptive Web. LNCS, vol. 4321, pp. 325–341. Springer, Heidelberg (2007). https://doi.org/10.1007/978-3-540-72079-9_10

6. Lu, J., Wu, D., Mao, M., Wang, W., Zhang, G.: Recommender system application developments: a survey. Decis. Support. Syst. **74**, 12–32 (2015)
7. Su, X., Khoshgoftaar, T.M.: A survey of collaborative filtering techniques. Adv. Artif. Intell. **2009**, 4 (2009)
8. Shi, Y., Larson, M., Hanjalic, A.: Collaborative filtering beyond the user-item matrix: a survey of the state of the art and future challenges. ACM Comput. Surv. (CSUR) **47**, 1–45 (2014)
9. Polatidis, N., Georgiadis, C.K.: A multi-level collaborative filtering method that improves recommendations. Expert Syst. Appl. **48**, 100–110 (2016)
10. Linden, G., Smith, B., York, J.: Amazon.com recommendations: Item-to-item collaborative filtering. IEEE Internet Comput. **7**, 76–80 (2003)
11. Zhang, W.: Research on application of collaborative filtering in electronic commerce recommender systems. In: Lin, S., Huang, X. (eds.) CSEE 2011. CCIS, vol. 215, pp. 539–544. Springer, Heidelberg (2011). https://doi.org/10.1007/978-3-642-23324-1_87
12. Huang, Z., Zeng, D., Chen, H.: A comparative study of recommendation algorithms in e-commerce applications. EEE Intell. Syst. **22**(5), 68–78 (2007)
13. Bobadilla, J., Serradilla, F., Hernando, A.: Collaborative filtering adapted to recommender systems of e-learning. Knowl.-Based Syst. **22**, 261–265 (2009)
14. Shambour, Q., Lu, J.: A hybrid trust-enhanced collaborative filtering recommendation approach for personalized government-to-business e-services. Int. J. Intell. Syst. **26**, 814–843 (2011)
15. Zhang, Y., Chen, W., Yin, Z.: Collaborative filtering with social regularization for TV program recommendation. Knowl.-Based Syst. **54**, 310–317 (2013)
16. Winoto, P., Tang, T.Y.: The role of user mood in movie recommendations. Expert Syst. Appl. **37**, 6086–6092 (2010)
17. Cohen, W.W., Fan, W.: Web-collaborative filtering: recommending music by crawling the web. Comput. Netw. **33**, 685–698 (2000)
18. Benkoussas, C., Hamdan, H., Albitar, S., Ollagnier, A., Bellot, P.: Collaborative filtering for book recommandation. In: Working Notes for CLEF 2014 Conference, Sheeld, UK, 15–18 September 2014, pp. 501–507 (2014)
19. Singh, A., Sharma, A., Dey, N., Ashour, A.S.: Web recommendation techniques: status, issues and challenges. J. Netw. Commun. Emerg. Technol. **5**, 57–65 (2015)
20. Chen, K., Chen, T., Zheng, G., Jin, O., Yao, E., Yu, Y.: Collaborative personalized tweet recommendation. In: Proceedings of the 35th International ACM SIGIR Conference on Research and Development in Information Retrieval, pp. 661–670. ACM (2012)
21. Herlocker, J.L., Konstan, J.A., Borchers, A., Riedj, J.: An algorithmic framework for performing collaborative filtering. In: Proceedings of the 22nd Annual International ACM SIGIR Conference on Research and Development in Information Retrieval, SIGIR 1999, pp. 230–237. ACM, New York (1999)
22. Zahra, S., Ghazanfar, M.A., Khalid, A., Azam, M.A., Naeem, U., Prugel-Bennett, A.: Novel centroid selection approaches for KMeans-clustering based recommender systems. Inf. Sci. **320**, 156–189 (2015)
23. Gong, S., Ye, H., Tan, H.: Combining memory-based and model-based collaborative filtering in recommender system. In: Pacific-Asia Conference on Circuits, Communications and Systems, PACCS 2009, pp. 690–693. IEEE (2009)
24. Su, X., Khoshgoftaar, T.M.: Collaborative filtering for multi-class data using belief nets algorithms. In: 18th IEEE International Conference on Tools with Artificial Intelligence, ICTAI 2006, pp. 497–504. IEEE (2006)

25. Bokde, D., Girase, S., Mukhopadhyay, D.: Matrix factorization model in collaborative filtering algorithms: a survey. Procedia Comput. Sci. **49**, 136–146 (2015). Proceedings of 4th International Conference on Advances in Computing, Communication and Control (ICAC3 2015)
26. Zhang, Z., Liu, H.: Application and research of improved probability matrix factorization techniques in collaborative filtering. Int. J. Control Autom. **7**, 79–92 (2014)
27. Hofmann, T., Puzicha, J.: Latent class models for collaborative filtering. In: IJCAI, vol. 99, pp. 688–693 (1999)
28. Roh, T.H., Oh, K.J., Han, I.: The collaborative filtering recommendation based on SOM cluster-indexing CBR. Expert Syst. Appl. **25**, 413–423 (2003)
29. Feng, Z., Huiyou, C.: Employing BP neural networks to alleviate the sparsity issue in collaborative filtering recommendation algorithms. J. Comput. Res. Dev. **4**, 014 (2006)
30. Salah, A., Rogovschi, N., Nadif, M.: A dynamic collaborative filtering system via a weighted clustering approach. Neurocomputing **175**, 206–215 (2016)
31. Ungar, L.H., Foster, D.P.: Clustering methods for collaborative filtering. In: AAAI Workshop on Recommendation Systems, vol. 1, pp. 114–129 (1998)
32. Guan, Y., Ghorbani, A.A., Belacel, N.: Y-means: a clustering method for intrusion detection. In: Canadian Conference on Electrical and Computer Engineering, IEEE CCECE 2003, vol. 2, pp. 1083–1086. IEEE (2003)
33. Guan, Y., Ghorbani, A.A., Belacel, N.: Y-means: a clustering method for intrusion detection. In: Canadian Conference on Electrical and Computer Engineering, IEEE CCECE 2003, vol. 2, pp. 1083–1086. IEEE (2003)
34. Harper, F.M., Konstan, J.A.: The movielens datasets: history and context. ACM Trans. Interact. Intell. Syst. **5**, 19:1–19:19 (2015)
35. Jawaheer, G., Szomszor, M., Kostkova, P.: Comparison of implicit and explicit feedback from an online music recommendation service. In: Proceedings of the 1st International Workshop on Information Heterogeneity and Fusion in Recommender Systems, pp. 47–51. ACM (2010)
36. Resnick, P., Iacovou, N., Suchak, M., Bergstrom, P., Riedl, J.: GroupLens: an open architecture for collaborative filtering of netnews. In: Proceedings of the 1994 ACM Conference on Computer Supported Cooperative Work, pp. 175-186. ACM (1994)
37. Konstan, J., Miller, B., Maltz, D., Herlocker, J., Gordon, L., Riedl, J.: GroupLens: applying collaborative filtering to usenet news. Commun. ACM **40**, 77–87 (1997)
38. Adomavicius, G., Tuzhilin, A.: Toward the next generation of recommender systems: a survey of the state-of-the-art and possible extensions. IEEE Trans. Knowl. Data Eng. **17**, 734–749 (2005)
39. Hill, W., Stead, L., Rosenstein, M., Furnas, G.: Recommending and evaluating choices in a virtual community of use. In: Proceedings of the SIGCHI Conference on Human Factors in Computing Systems, pp. 194–201. ACM Press/Addison-Wesley Publishing Co. (1995)
40. Herlocker, J., Konstan, J.A., Riedl, J.: An empirical analysis of design choices in neighborhood-based collaborative filtering algorithms. Inf. Retr. **5**, 287–310 (2002)
41. Shardanand, U., Maes, P.: Social information filtering: algorithms for automating word of mouth. In: Proceedings of the SIGCHI Conference on Human Factors in Computing Systems, pp. 210–217. ACM Press/Addison-Wesley Publishing Co. (1995)
42. Al-Shamri, M.Y.H.: Power coefficient as a similarity measure for memory-based collaborative recommender systems. Expert Syst. Appl. **41**, 5680–5688 (2014)

43. Liu, H., Hu, Z., Mian, A., Tian, H., Zhu, X.: A new user similarity model to improve the accuracy of collaborative filtering. Knowl.-Based Syst. **56**, 156–166 (2014)
44. Ekstrand, M.D., Riedl, J.T., Konstan, J.A.: Collaborative filtering recommender systems. Found. Trends Hum.-Comput. Interact. **4**, 81–173 (2011)
45. Ekstrand, M.D., Ludwig, M., Konstan, J.A., Riedl, J.T.: Rethinking the recommender research ecosystem: reproducibility, openness, and lenskit. In: Proceedings of the fifth ACM Conference on Recommender systems, pp. 133–140. ACM (2011)
46. Darvishi-Mirshekarlou, F., Akbarpour, S., Feizi-Derakhshi, M., et al.: Reviewing cluster based collaborative filtering approaches. Int. J. Comput. Appl. Technol. Res. **2**, 650–659 (2013)
47. Huang, C., Yin, J.: Effective association clusters filtering to cold-start recommendations. In: 2010 Seventh International Conference on Fuzzy Systems and Knowledge Discovery (FSKD), vol. 5, pp. 2461–2464. IEEE (2010)
48. Birtolo, C., Ronca, D., Armenise, R., Ascione, M.: Personalized suggestions by means of collaborative filtering: a comparison of two different model-based techniques. In: 2011 Third World Congress on Nature and Biologically Inspired Computing (NaBIC), pp. 444–450 (2011)
49. Birtolo, C., Ronca, D.: Advances in clustering collaborative filtering by means of fuzzy c-means and trust. Expert Syst. Appl. **40**, 6997–7009 (2013)
50. Koren, Y.: Factor in the neighbors: scalable and accurate collaborative filtering. ACM Trans. Knowl. Discov. Data **4**, 1–24 (2010)
51. Salakhutdinov, R., Mnih, A., Hinton, G.: Restricted Boltzmann machines for collaborative filtering. In: Proceedings of the 24th International Conference on Machine Learning, ICML 2007, pp. 791–798. ACM, New York (2007)
52. Wilson, J., Chaudhury, S., Lall, B.: Improving collaborative filtering based recommenders using topic modelling. In: Proceedings of the 2014 IEEE/WIC/ACM International Joint Conferences on Web Intelligence (WI) and Intelligent Agent Technologies (IAT)-Volume 01, pp. 340–346. IEEE Computer Society (2014)
53. Sahoo, N., Singh, P.V., Mukhopadhyay, T.: A hidden Markov model for collaborative filtering. MIS Q. **36**, 1329–1356 (2012)
54. Durand, G., Laplante, F., Kop, R.: A learning design recommendation system based on Markov decision processes. In: ACM SIG KDD 2011 Workshop: Knowledge Discovery in Educational Data (2011)
55. Belacel, N., Hansen, P., Mladenovic, N.: Fuzzy J-means: a new heuristic for fuzzy clustering. Pattern Recognit. **35**, 2193–2200 (2002)
56. Belacel, N., Wang, C., Cupelovic-Culf, M.: Clustering: Unsupervised Learning in Large Biological Data, pp. 89–127. Wiley, Hoboken (2010)
57. LaPlante, F., Kardouchi, M., Belacel, N.: Image categorization using a heuristic automatic clustering method based on hierarchical clustering. In: Kamel, M., Campilho, A. (eds.) ICIAR 2015. LNCS, vol. 9164, pp. 150–158. Springer, Cham (2015). https://doi.org/10.1007/978-3-319-20801-5_16
58. Wu, W., Xiong, H., Shekhar, S.: Clustering and Information Retrieval, vol. 11. Springer, Heidelberg (2013). https://doi.org/10.1007/978-1-4613-0227-8
59. Zhang, C.X., Zhang, Z.K., Yu, L., Liu, C., Liu, H., Yan, X.Y.: Information filtering via collaborative user clustering modeling. Phys. A: Stat. Mech. Appl. **396**, 195–203 (2014)
60. Tsai, C.F., Hung, C.: Cluster ensembles in collaborative filtering recommendation. Appl. Soft Comput. **12**, 1417–1425 (2012)

61. Sarwar, B.M., Karypis, G., Konstan, J., Riedl, J.: Recommender systems for large-scale e-commerce: Scalable neighborhood formation using clustering. In: Proceedings of the fifth international conference on computer and information technology, vol. 1, pp. 1–5 (2002)
62. Geman, S., Geman, D.: Stochastic relaxation, Gibbs distributions, and the Bayesian restoration of images. IEEE Trans. Pattern Anal. Mach. Intell. PAMI **6**, 721–741 (1984)
63. Kohrs, A., Merialdo, B.: Clustering for collaborative filtering applications. Intell. Image Process. Data Anal. Inf. Retr. **3**, 199–205 (1999)
64. Xue, G.R., et al.: Scalable collaborative filtering using cluster-based smoothing. In: Proceedings of the 28th Annual International ACM SIGIR Conference on Research and Development in Information Retrieval, SIGIR 2005, pp. 114–121. ACM, New York (2005)
65. Brown, P.F., deSouza, P.V., Mercer, R.L., Pietra, V.J.D., Lai, J.C.: Class-based n-gram models of natural language. Comput. Linguist. **18**, 467–479 (1992)
66. Ma, X., Lu, H., Gan, Z., Zhao, Q.: An exploration of improving prediction accuracy by constructing a multi-type clustering based recommendation framework. Neurocomputing **191**, 388–397 (2016)
67. Hu, R., Dou, W., Liu, J.: Clustering-based collaborative filtering approach for mashups recommendation over big data. In: 2013 IEEE 16th International Conference on Computational Science and Engineering (CSE), pp. 810–817 (2013)
68. Dakhel, G., Mahdavi, M.: A new collaborative filtering algorithm using k-means clustering and neighbors' voting. In: 2011 11th International Conference on Hybrid Intelligent Systems (HIS), pp. 179–184 (2011)
69. Pereira, A.L.V., Hruschka, E.R.: Simultaneous co-clustering and learning to address the cold start problem in recommender systems. Knowl.-Based Syst. **82**, 11–19 (2015)
70. Huang, H., et al.: K-means+ method for improving gene selection for classification of microarray data. In: Computational Systems Bioinformatics Conference, pp. 110–111. IEEE (2005)
71. Hansen, P., Mladenovic, N.: J-means: a new local search heuristic for minimum sum of squares clustering. Pattern Recognit. **34**, 405–413 (2001)
72. Cremonesi, P., Turrin, R., Lentini, E., Matteucci, M.: An evaluation methodology for collaborative recommender systems. In: International Conference on Automated solutions for Cross Media Content and Multi-channel Distribution, AXMEDIS 2008, pp. 224–231 (2008)
73. Sarwar, B.M., Karypis, G., Konstan, J.A., Riedl, J.T.: Application of dimensionality reduction in recommender system-a case study. In: ACM WEBKDD Workshop, pp. 1–12 (2000)
74. Herlocker, J.L., Konstan, J.A., Terveen, L.G., Riedl, J.T.: Evaluating collaborative filtering recommender systems. ACM Trans. Inf. Syst. (TOIS) **22**, 5–53 (2004)
75. Belacel, N., Durand, G., Leger, S., Bouchard, C.: Splitting-merging clustering algorithm for collaborative filtering recommendation system. In: Proceedings of the 10th International Conference on Agents and Artificial Intelligence - Volume 2: ICAART, INSTICC, pp. 165–174. SciTePress (2018)
76. Wang, C., Belacel, N.: VNSOptClust: a variable neighborhood search based approach for unsupervised anomaly detection. In: Le Thi, H.A., Bouvry, P., Pham Dinh, T. (eds.) MCO 2008. CCIS, vol. 14, pp. 607–616. Springer, Heidelberg (2008). https://doi.org/10.1007/978-3-540-87477-5_64

# Foundations of Inconsistency-Tolerant Model Checking: Logics, Translations, and Examples

Norihiro Kamide[1(✉)] and Kazuki Endo[2]

[1] Faculty of Science and Engineering, Department of Information and Electronic Engineering, Teikyo University, Toyosatodai 1-1, Utsunomiya, Tochigi 320-8551, Japan
drnkamide08@kpd.biglobe.ne.jp

[2] Faculty of Science and Engineering, Department of Human Information Systems, Teikyo University, Toyosatodai 1-1, Utsunomiya-shi, Tochigi 320-8551, Japan
1462059u@stu.teikyo-u.ac.jp

**Abstract.** We develop logics and translations for inconsistency-tolerant model checking that can be used to verify systems having inconsistencies. Paraconsistent linear-time temporal logic (pLTL), paraconsistent computation tree logic (pCTL), and paraconsistent full computation tree logic (pCTL*) are introduced. These are extensions of standard linear-time temporal logic (LTL), standard computation tree logic (CTL), and standard full computation tree logic (CTL*), respectively. These novel logics can be applied when handling inconsistency-tolerant temporal reasoning. They are also regarded as four-valued temporal logics that extend Belnap and Dunn's four-valued logic. Translations from pLTL into LTL, pCTL into CTL, and pCTL* into CTL*, are defined, and these are used to prove the theorems for embedding pLTL into LTL, pCTL into CTL, and pCTL* into CTL*. These embedding theorems allow the standard LTL-, CTL-, and CTL*-based model checking algorithms to be used for verifying inconsistent systems that are modeled and specified by pLTL, pCTL, and pCTL*. Some illustrative examples for inconsistency-tolerant model checking are presented based on the proposed logics and translations.

## 1 Introduction

The goal of this study is to develop simple logics and translations for *inconsistency-tolerant model checking* (or *paraconsistent model checking*) that

---

A preliminary short version of the results of this paper was published in the Proceedings of the 10th International Conference on Agents and Artificial Intelligence (ICAART 2018) [20]. The results of Sect. 4 in the present paper are not included in [20] (i.e., these are new results presented in this paper). The results of Sect. 5 in the present paper include some new results which were not presented in [20]. The results of the other sections in the present paper are slight extensions (with some detailed proofs and explanations) of the results presented in [20].


J. van den Herik and A. P. Rocha (Eds.): ICAART 2018, LNAI 11352, pp. 312–342, 2019.
https://doi.org/10.1007/978-3-030-05453-3_15

can be used to verify systems having inconsistencies. Inconsistencies are frequent and inevitable when specifying and verifying large, complex, and open systems. *Model checking* is a formal and automated technique for verifying concurrent systems [6,7,16]. We develop three novel and simple versions of paraconsistent four-valued temporal logics, namely, *paraconsistent linear-time temporal logic* (pLTL), *paraconsistent computation tree logic* (pCTL), and *paraconsistent full computation tree logic* (pCTL*). These are extensions of the standard temporal logics, namely, *linear-time temporal logic* (LTL) [29], *computation-tree logic* (CTL) [6], and *full computation-tree logic* (CTL*) [12,13] that are typically used in model checking. The proposed logics pLTL, pCTL, and pCTL* may be applied when handling inconsistency-tolerant temporal reasoning and may also provide the base logics for inconsistency-tolerant model checking. These proposed four-valued temporal logics are also regarded as extensions of *Belnap and Dunn's four-valued logic* [3,4,10]. In this study, we define the translations of pLTL into LTL, pCTL into CTL, and pCTL* into CTL*. These translations are used to prove the theorems for embedding pLTL into LTL, pCTL into CTL, and pCTL* into CTL*. These embedding theorems also allow us to repurpose the standard LTL-, CTL-, and CTL*-based model checking algorithms for verifying inconsistent systems that are modeled and specified by pLTL, pCTL, and pCTL*.

LTL [29] is one of the most useful temporal logics for model checking based on the *linear-time paradigm*, which uses linear order to represent the passage of time. CTL [6] is another form of temporal logic that is widely used for model checking and is based on the *branching-time paradigm* that uses computation trees to represent the passage of time. CTL* [12,13] is known to be more expressive than both LTL and CTL and is based on the branching-time paradigm with *path quantifiers* to represent the passage of time. Because these standard temporal logics lack *paraconsistency*, they are unsuitable for specifying and verifying inconsistent systems. The satisfaction relation $\models$ of a logic is considered to be paraconsistent with respect to a negation connective $\sim$ if the following condition holds: $\exists\alpha, \beta\ (M, x) \not\models (\alpha \wedge {\sim}\alpha){\rightarrow}\beta$, where $x$ is a state or position in a semantic structure $M$ of the underlying logic. This condition reflects that formulas of the form $(\alpha \wedge {\sim}\alpha){\rightarrow}\beta$ are not valid in the underlying logics.

Compared to other non-classical logics, *paraconsistent logics* such as pLTL, pCTL, and pCTL* can be appropriately used in inconsistency-tolerant reasoning [8,30,33]. For example, the following scenario is undesirable: $(s(x) \wedge {\sim}s(x)){\rightarrow}d(x)$ is valid for any symptom $s$ and disease $d$, where ${\sim}s(x)$ implies that "a person $x$ does not have a symptom $s$" and $d(x)$ implies that "a person $x$ suffers from a disease $d$." The inconsistent scenario written as $melancholia(john) \wedge {\sim}melancholia(john)$ will inevitably arise from the uncertain definition of melancholia; the statement "John has melancholia" may be judged true or false based on the perception of different pathologists. In this case, the formula $(melancholia(john) \wedge {\sim}melancholia(john)) \rightarrow cancer(john)$ is valid in classical logic (as an inconsistency that has an undesirable consequence), but invalid in paraconsistent logics (as these logics are inconsistency-tolerant). Typical examples of non-temporal paraconsistent logics are Belnap and Dunn's four-valued logic [3,4,10] and *Nelson's paraconsistent four-valued logic* [1,27]. The proposed logics pLTL, pCTL, and pCTL* are based on these typical paraconsistent four-valued logics.

The idea of introducing paraconsistent versions of LTL, CTL, and CTL* is not new. *Multi-valued computation tree logic* ($\chi$CTL) was introduced by Easterbrook and Chechik [11] as the base logic for *multi-valued model checking* and is considered to be the first framework for inconsistency-tolerant model checking. *Quasi-classical temporal logic* (QCTL) was introduced by Chen and Wu [5] to verify inconsistent concurrent systems using inconsistency-tolerant model checking. *Paraconsistent full computation tree logic* (4CTL*) proposed by Kamide [17] applied bisimulations to inconsistency-tolerant model checking. Another paraconsistent linear-time temporal logic (PLTL) was introduced by Kamide and Wansing [24] to obtain a cut-free and complete Gentzen-type sequent calculus. Another paraconsistent computation tree logic (PCTL) was proposed by Kamide and Kaneiwa [21,26] that offered an alternative inconsistency-tolerant model checking framework. Kamide [18] also introduced *sequence-indexed paraconsistent computation tree logic* (SPCTL), which extended CTL by adding a paraconsistent negation connective and a sequence modal operator. SPCTL was used to represent and verify medical reasoning with hierarchical and inconsistent information. *Paraconsistent probabilistic computation tree logic* (PpCTL) was introduced by Kamide and Koizumi [22] for verifying randomized and stochastic inconsistent systems.

In this study, we developed pLTL, pCTL, and pCTL* as novel versions of paraconsistent temporal logics by extending LTL, CTL, and CTL*, respectively. Although PLTL [24], PCTL [21,26], 4CTL* [17], SPCTL [18], and PpCTL [22] have two types of dual-satisfaction relations $\models^+$ (verification or justification) and $\models^-$ (refutation or falsification), pLTL and pCTL are simpler; they have a single-satisfaction relation $\models^*$ that is highly compatible with the standard single-satisfaction relations of LTL, CTL, and CTL*. These single-satisfaction relations provide simple proofs for the embedding theorems of pLTL, pCTL, and pCTL*, and the paraconsistent negation connective $\sim$ used in pLTL, pCTL, and pCTL* can be simply formalized and uniformly handled. pLTL is also more expressive than PLTL because it lacks the standard Until and Release temporal operators found in LTL. Furthermore, pLTL, pCTL, and pCTL* employ novel sets of axiom schemes for combining the paraconsistent negation connective $\sim$, classical negation connective $\neg$, and implication connective $\rightarrow$. The negated implication and negation axioms used in pLTL, pCTL, and pCTL* are $\sim(\alpha{\rightarrow}\beta) \leftrightarrow \neg{\sim}\alpha \wedge {\sim}\beta$ and ${\sim}\neg\alpha \leftrightarrow \neg{\sim}\alpha$. These recently introduced axiom schemes by De and Omori are natural and plausible from the point of view of many-valued semantics [9]. The logic BD+ [9] of these axiom schemes was observed to be essentially equivalent to *Béziau's four-valued modal logic* (PM4N) [2] and *Zaitsev's paraconsistent logic* (FDEP) [35].

The remainder of this paper is organized as follows.

Section 2 discusses the linear-time case based on LTL and pLTL. The new formulation pLTL is introduced based on the single-satisfaction relation $\models^*$. The function that translates pLTL into LTL is defined, which is a simplification of the translation functions used in [18,21,22,24,26]. The proposed translation function is then used to prove the theorem for embedding pLTL into LTL. The present and previous versions of these translation functions are regarded as modifications or extensions of those used by Gurevich [15], Rautenberg [31] and Vorob'ev [32] to embed Nelson's constructive logic [1,27] into intuitionistic logic. Similar translations have recently been used [19,23] to embed some of the paraconsistent logics into classical logic.

Section 3 discusses the branching-time case based on CTL and pCTL. Similar to the linear-time case, pCTL is introduced based on the single-satisfaction relation $\models^*$. In addition, a function translating pCTL into CTL is defined and the theorem for embedding pCTL into CTL is proved. The translation function is constructed in a similar manner to that of pLTL.

Section 4 discusses the full branching-time case based on CTL* and pCTL*. Similar to the linear- and branching-time cases, pCTL* is introduced based on the single-satisfaction relation $\models^*$. In addition, a function translating pCTL* into CTL* is defined and the theorem for embedding pCTL* into CTL* is proved. The translation function is constructed in a similar manner to those of pLTL and pCTL.

Section 5 presents some illustrative examples for inconsistency-tolerant model checking based on the proposed logics and translations.

Section 6 concludes our study. It is noted that three further alternative logics, namely, oLTL, oCTL, and oCTL*, can be obtained from pLTL, pCTL, and pCTL*, respectively, by replacing the axiom schemes ${\sim}(\alpha \rightarrow \beta) \leftrightarrow \neg{\sim}\alpha \wedge {\sim}\beta$ and ${\sim}\neg\alpha \leftrightarrow \neg{\sim}\alpha$ with ${\sim}(\alpha \rightarrow \beta) \leftrightarrow \alpha \wedge {\sim}\beta$ and ${\sim}\neg\alpha \leftrightarrow \alpha$ by Odintsov [28]. It is further noted that by appropriate modification of the translation functions for pLTL, pCTL, and pCTL*, the embedding theorems for oLTL into LTL, oCTL into CTL, and oCTL* into CTL* can also be obtained.

## 2 Linear-Time Case

### 2.1 LTL and pLTL

*Formulas* of *linear-time temporal logic* (LTL) are constructed from countably many propositional variables, $\rightarrow$ (implication), $\wedge$ (conjunction), $\vee$ (disjunction), $\neg$ (classical negation), X (next), G (globally), F (eventually), U (until) and R (release). An expression $\alpha \leftrightarrow \beta$ is used to denote $(\alpha{\rightarrow}\beta) \wedge (\beta{\rightarrow}\alpha)$. Lower-case letters $p, q, \ldots$ are used to denote propositional variables, and Greek lower-case letters $\alpha, \beta, \ldots$ are used to denote formulas. The symbol $\omega$ is used to represent the set of natural numbers. Lower-case letters $i, j$ and $k$ are used to denote any natural numbers. The symbol $\geq$ or $\leq$ is used to represent the linear order on $\omega$. An expression $A \equiv B$ is used to indicate the syntactical identity between $A$ and $B$.

**Definition 2.1.** *Formulas of* LTL *are defined by the following grammar, assuming p represents propositional variables:*

$$\alpha ::= p \mid \alpha \wedge \alpha \mid \alpha \vee \alpha \mid \alpha \rightarrow \alpha \mid \neg\alpha \mid \mathrm{X}\alpha \mid \mathrm{G}\alpha \mid \mathrm{F}\alpha \mid \alpha\mathrm{U}\alpha \mid \alpha\mathrm{R}\alpha.$$

**Definition 2.2 (LTL).** *Let $S$ be a non-empty set of states, and $\Phi$ be the set of propositional variables.*

*A structure $M := (\sigma, I)$ is a* model *iff*

1. *$\sigma$ is an infinite sequence $s_0, s_1, s_2, \ldots$ of states in $S$,*
2. *$I$ is a mapping from $\Phi$ to the power set of $S$.*

*A satisfaction relation $(M, i) \models \alpha$ for any formula $\alpha$, where $M$ is a model $(\sigma, I)$ and $i$ ($\in \omega$) represents some position within $\sigma$, is defined inductively by:*

1. *for any $p \in \Phi$, $(M,i) \models p$ iff $s_i \in I(p)$,*
2. *$(M,i) \models \alpha \wedge \beta$ iff $(M,i) \models \alpha$ and $(M,i) \models \beta$,*
3. *$(M,i) \models \alpha \vee \beta$ iff $(M,i) \models \alpha$ or $(M,i) \models \beta$,*
4. *$(M,i) \models \alpha \rightarrow \beta$ iff $(M,i) \models \alpha$ implies $(M,i) \models \beta$,*
5. *$(M,i) \models \neg\alpha$ iff $(M,i) \not\models \alpha$,*
6. *$(M,i) \models \mathrm{X}\alpha$ iff $(M,i+1) \models \alpha$,*
7. *$(M,i) \models \mathrm{G}\alpha$ iff $\forall j \geq i\ [(M,j) \models \alpha]$,*
8. *$(M,i) \models \mathrm{F}\alpha$ iff $\exists j \geq i\ [(M,j) \models \alpha]$,*
9. *$(M,i) \models \alpha\mathrm{U}\beta$ iff $\exists j \geq i\ [(M,j) \models \beta$ and $\forall i \leq k < j\ (M,k) \models \alpha]$,*
10. *$(M,i) \models \alpha\mathrm{R}\beta$ iff $\forall j \geq i\ [(M,j) \models \beta$ or $\exists i \leq k < j\ (M,k) \models \alpha]$.*

*A formula $\alpha$ is* valid *in* LTL *iff $(M,0) \models \alpha$ for any model $M := (\sigma, I)$.*

The language of *paraconsistent linear-time temporal logic* (pLTL) is obtained from that of LTL by adding $\sim$ (paraconsistent negation).

**Definition 2.3.** *Formulas of* pLTL *are defined by the following grammar, assuming $p$ represents propositional variables:*

$$\alpha ::= p \mid \alpha \wedge \alpha \mid \alpha \vee \alpha \mid \alpha \rightarrow \alpha \mid \neg\alpha \mid \mathrm{X}\alpha \mid \mathrm{G}\alpha \mid \mathrm{F}\alpha \mid \alpha\mathrm{U}\alpha \mid \alpha\mathrm{R}\alpha \mid {\sim}\alpha.$$

**Definition 2.4 (pLTL).** *Let $S$ be a non-empty set of states, $\Phi$ be the set of propositional variables and $\Phi^{\sim}$ be the set $\{{\sim}p \mid p \in \Phi\}$ of negated propositional variables.*

*A structure $M := (\sigma, I^*)$ is a* paraconsistent model *iff*

1. *$\sigma$ is an infinite sequence $s_0, s_1, s_2, \ldots$ of states in $S$,*
2. *$I^*$ is a mapping from $\Phi \cup \Phi^{\sim}$ to the power set of $S$.*

*A paraconsistent satisfaction relation $(M,i) \models^* \alpha$ for any formula $\alpha$, where $M$ is a paraconsistent model $(\sigma, I^*)$ and $i$ ($\in \omega$) represents some position within $\sigma$, is defined inductively by:*

1. *for any $p \in \Phi$, $(M,i) \models^* p$ iff $s_i \in I^*(p)$,*
2. *for any ${\sim}p \in \Phi^{\sim}$, $(M,i) \models^* {\sim}p$ iff $s_i \in I^*({\sim}p)$,*
3. *$(M,i) \models^* \alpha \wedge \beta$ iff $(M,i) \models^* \alpha$ and $(M,i) \models^* \beta$,*
4. *$(M,i) \models^* \alpha \vee \beta$ iff $(M,i) \models^* \alpha$ or $(M,i) \models^* \beta$,*
5. *$(M,i) \models^* \alpha \rightarrow \beta$ iff $(M,i) \models^* \alpha$ implies $(M,i) \models^* \beta$,*

6. $(M, i) \models^* \neg\alpha$ *iff* $(M, i) \not\models^* \alpha$,
7. $(M, i) \models^* \mathrm{X}\alpha$ *iff* $(M, i+1) \models^* \alpha$,
8. $(M, i) \models^* \mathrm{G}\alpha$ *iff* $\forall j \geq i\ [(M, j) \models^* \alpha]$,
9. $(M, i) \models^* \mathrm{F}\alpha$ *iff* $\exists j \geq i\ [(M, j) \models^* \alpha]$,
10. $(M, i) \models^* \alpha \mathrm{U} \beta$ *iff* $\exists j \geq i\ [(M, j) \models^* \beta$ *and* $\forall i \leq k < j\ (M, k) \models^* \alpha]$,
11. $(M, i) \models^* \alpha \mathrm{R} \beta$ *iff* $\forall j \geq i\ [(M, j) \models^* \beta$ *or* $\exists i \leq k < j\ (M, k) \models^* \alpha]$,
12. $(M, i) \models^* {\sim}{\sim}\alpha$ *iff* $(M, i) \models^* \alpha$,
13. $(M, i) \models^* {\sim}(\alpha \wedge \beta)$ *iff* $(M, i) \models^* {\sim}\alpha$ *or* $(M, i) \models^* {\sim}\beta$,
14. $(M, i) \models^* {\sim}(\alpha \vee \beta)$ *iff* $(M, i) \models^* {\sim}\alpha$ *and* $(M, i) \models^* {\sim}\beta$,
15. $(M, i) \models^* {\sim}(\alpha \rightarrow \beta)$ *iff* $(M, i) \not\models^* {\sim}\alpha$ *and* $(M, i) \models^* {\sim}\beta$,
16. $(M, i) \models^* {\sim}\neg\alpha$ *iff* $(M, i) \not\models^* {\sim}\alpha$,
17. $(M, i) \models^* {\sim}\mathrm{X}\alpha$ *iff* $(M, i+1) \models^* {\sim}\alpha$,
18. $(M, i) \models^* {\sim}\mathrm{G}\alpha$ *iff* $\exists j \geq i\ [(M, j) \models^* {\sim}\alpha]$,
19. $(M, i) \models^* {\sim}\mathrm{F}\alpha$ *iff* $\forall j \geq i\ [(M, j) \models^* {\sim}\alpha]$,
20. $(M, i) \models^* {\sim}(\alpha \mathrm{U} \beta)$ *iff* $\forall j \geq i\ [(M, j) \models^* {\sim}\beta$ *or* $\exists i \leq k < j\ (M, k) \models^* {\sim}\alpha]$,
21. $(M, i) \models^* {\sim}(\alpha \mathrm{R} \beta)$ *iff* $\exists j \geq i\ [(M, j) \models^* {\sim}\beta$ *and* $\forall i \leq k < j\ (M, k) \models^* {\sim}\alpha]$.

*A formula* $\alpha$ *is* valid *in* pLTL *iff* $(M, 0) \models^* \alpha$ *for any paraconsistent model* $M := (\sigma, I^*)$.

**Remark 2.5.** *We make the following remarks.*

1. *The following formulas are valid in* pLTL*: For any formulas* $\alpha$, $\beta$,
   (a) ${\sim}{\sim}\alpha \leftrightarrow \alpha$,
   (b) ${\sim}(\alpha \wedge \beta) \leftrightarrow {\sim}\alpha \vee {\sim}\beta$,
   (c) ${\sim}(\alpha \vee \beta) \leftrightarrow {\sim}\alpha \wedge {\sim}\beta$,
   (d) ${\sim}(\alpha \rightarrow \beta) \leftrightarrow \neg{\sim}\alpha \wedge {\sim}\beta$,
   (e) ${\sim}\neg\alpha \leftrightarrow \neg{\sim}\alpha$,
   (f) ${\sim}\mathrm{X}\alpha \leftrightarrow \mathrm{X}{\sim}\alpha$,
   (g) ${\sim}\mathrm{F}\alpha \leftrightarrow \mathrm{G}{\sim}\alpha$,
   (h) ${\sim}\mathrm{G}\alpha \leftrightarrow \mathrm{F}{\sim}\alpha$,
   (i) ${\sim}(\alpha \mathrm{U} \beta) \leftrightarrow ({\sim}\alpha)\mathrm{R}({\sim}\beta)$,
   (j) ${\sim}(\alpha \mathrm{R} \beta) \leftrightarrow ({\sim}\alpha)\mathrm{U}({\sim}\beta)$.
2. *As presented above, the temporal operators* F *and* G *are duals of each other not only with respect to* $\neg$ *but also with respect to* $\sim$*, and* X *is a self dual not only with respect to* $\neg$ *but also with respect to* $\sim$*. The negation connectives* $\neg$ *and* $\sim$ *are self-duals with respect to* $\sim$ *and* $\neg$*, respectively.*
3. pLTL *is* paraconsistent *with respect to* $\sim$*. The reason is explained as follows. Assume a paraconsistent model* $M := (\sigma, I^*)$ *such that* $s_i \in I^*(p)$, $s_i \in I^*({\sim}p)$ *and* $s_i \notin I^*(q)$ *for a pair of distinct propositional variables* $p$ *and* $q$*. Then,* $(M, i) \models^* (p \wedge {\sim}p) \rightarrow q$ *does not hold.*
4. pLTL *is regarded as a four-valued logic. The reason is explained as follows. For each* $i \in \sigma$ *and each formula* $\alpha$*, we can take one of the following four cases:*
   (a) $\alpha$ *is verified at* $i$*, i.e.,* $(M, i) \models^* \alpha$,
   (b) $\alpha$ *is falsified at* $i$*, i.e.,* $(M, i) \models^* {\sim}\alpha$,
   (c) $\alpha$ *is both verified and falsified at* $i$,
   (d) $\alpha$ *is neither verified nor falsified at* $i$.

## 2.2 Translation from pLTL into LTL

**Definition 2.6.** *Let $\Phi$ be a non-empty set of propositional variables, and $\Phi'$ be the set $\{p' \mid p \in \Phi\}$ of propositional variables. The language $\mathcal{L}^{\rm p}$ (the set of formulas) of* pLTL *is defined using $\Phi$, $\wedge, \vee, \rightarrow, \neg$, X, G, F, U, R and $\sim$. The language $\mathcal{L}$ of* LTL *is obtained from $\mathcal{L}^{\rm p}$ by adding $\Phi'$ and deleting $\sim$.*

*A mapping $f$ from $\mathcal{L}^{\rm p}$ to $\mathcal{L}$ is defined inductively by:*

1. *for any $p \in \Phi$, $f(p) := p$ and $f(\sim p) := p' \in \Phi'$,*
2. *$f(\alpha \sharp \beta) := f(\alpha) \sharp f(\beta)$ where $\sharp \in \{\wedge, \vee, \rightarrow, {\rm U}, {\rm R}\}$,*
3. *$f(\sharp\alpha) := \sharp f(\alpha)$ where $\sharp \in \{\neg, {\rm X}, {\rm F}, {\rm G}\}$,*
4. *$f(\sim\sim\alpha) := f(\alpha)$,*
5. *$f(\sim(\alpha \wedge \beta)) := f(\sim\alpha) \vee f(\sim\beta)$,*
6. *$f(\sim(\alpha \vee \beta)) := f(\sim\alpha) \wedge f(\sim\beta)$,*
7. *$f(\sim(\alpha \rightarrow \beta)) := \neg f(\sim\alpha) \wedge f(\sim\beta)$,*
8. *$f(\sim\sharp\alpha) := \sharp f(\sim\alpha)$ where $\sharp \in \{\neg, {\rm X}\}$,*
9. *$f(\sim{\rm F}\alpha) := {\rm G}f(\sim\alpha)$,*
10. *$f(\sim{\rm G}\alpha) := {\rm F}f(\sim\alpha)$,*
11. *$f(\sim(\alpha{\rm U}\beta)) := f(\sim\alpha){\rm R}f(\sim\beta)$,*
12. *$f(\sim(\alpha{\rm R}\beta)) := f(\sim\alpha){\rm U}f(\sim\beta)$.*

**Lemma 2.7.** *Let $f$ be the mapping defined in Definition 2.6, and $S$ be a non-empty set of states. For any paraconsistent model $M := (\sigma, I^*)$ of* pLTL*, any paraconsistent satisfaction relation $\models^*$ on $M$, and any state $s_i$ in $\sigma$, we can construct a model $N := (\sigma, I)$ of* LTL *and a satisfaction relation $\models$ on $N$ such that for any formula $\alpha$ in $\mathcal{L}^{\rm p}$,*

$$(M, i) \models^* \alpha \text{ iff } (N, i) \models f(\alpha).$$

**Proof.** Let $\Phi$ be a non-empty set of propositional variables, $\Phi^{\sim}$ be $\{\sim p \mid p \in \Phi\}$, and $\Phi'$ be $\{p' \mid p \in \Phi\}$. Suppose that $M$ is a paraconsisitent model $(\sigma, I^*)$ where

$I^*$ is a mapping from $\Phi \cup \Phi^{\sim}$ to the power set of $S$.

We then define a model $N := (\sigma, I)$ such that

1. $I$ is a mapping from $\Phi \cup \Phi'$ to the power set of $S$,
2. for any $s_i$ in $\sigma$,
   (a) $s_i \in I^*(p)$ iff $s_i \in I(p)$,
   (b) $s_i \in I^*(\sim p)$ iff $s_i \in I(p')$,

Then, this lemma is proved by induction on the complexity of $\alpha$.

- Base step:
  1. Case $\alpha \equiv p \in \Phi$: We obtain: $(M, i) \models^* p$ iff $s_i \in I^*(p)$ iff $s_i \in I(p)$ iff $(N, i) \models p$ iff $(N, i) \models f(p)$ (by the definition of $f$).
  2. Case $\alpha \equiv \sim p \in \Phi^{\sim}$: We obtain: $(M, i) \models^* \sim p$ iff $s_i \in I^*(\sim p)$ iff $s_i \in I(p')$ iff $(N, i) \models p'$ iff $(N, i) \models f(\sim p)$ (by the definition of $f$).
- Induction step: We show some cases.

1. Case $\alpha \equiv \beta \wedge \gamma$: We obtain: $(M,i) \models^* \beta \wedge \gamma$ iff $(M,i) \models^* \beta$ and $(M,i) \models^* \gamma$ iff $(N,i) \models f(\beta)$ and $(N,i) \models f(\gamma)$ (by induction hypothesis) iff $(N,i) \models f(\beta) \wedge f(\gamma)$ iff $(N,i) \models f(\beta \wedge \gamma)$ (by the definition of $f$).
2. Case $\alpha \equiv \beta \rightarrow \gamma$: We obtain: $(M,i) \models^* \beta \rightarrow \gamma$ iff $(M,i) \models^* \beta$ implies $(M,i) \models^* \gamma$ iff $(N,i) \models f(\beta)$ implies $(N,i) \models f(\gamma)$ (by induction hypothesis) iff $(N,i) \models f(\beta) \rightarrow f(\gamma)$ iff $(N,i) \models f(\beta \rightarrow \gamma)$ (by the definition of $f$).
3. Case $\alpha \equiv \neg\beta$: We obtain: $(M,i) \models^* \neg\beta$ iff $(M,i) \not\models^* \beta$ iff $(N,i) \not\models f(\beta)$ (by induction hypothesis) iff $(N,i) \models \neg f(\beta)$ iff $(N,i) \models f(\neg\beta)$ (by the definition of $f$).
4. Case $\alpha \equiv \mathrm{X}\beta$: We obtain: $(M,i) \models^* \mathrm{X}\beta$ iff $(M,i+1) \models^* \beta$ iff $(N,i+1) \models f(\beta)$ (by induction hypothesis) iff $(N,i) \models \mathrm{X}f(\beta)$ iff $(N,i) \models f(\mathrm{X}\beta)$ (by the definition of $f$).
5. Case $\alpha \equiv \mathrm{G}\beta$: We obtain: $(M,i) \models^* \mathrm{G}\beta$ iff $\forall j \geq i\ [(M,j) \models^* \beta]$ iff $\forall j \geq i\ [(N,j) \models f(\beta)]$ (by induction hypothesis) iff $(N,i) \models \mathrm{G}f(\beta)$ iff $(N,i) \models f(\mathrm{G}\beta)$ (by the definition of $f$).
6. Case $\alpha \equiv \beta\mathrm{U}\gamma$: We obtain:
   $(M,i) \models^* \beta\mathrm{U}\gamma$
   iff $\exists j \geq i\ [(M,j) \models^* \gamma$ and $\forall i \leq k < j\ (M,k) \models^* \beta]$
   iff $\exists j \geq i\ [(N,j) \models f(\gamma)$ and $\forall i \leq k < j\ (N,k) \models f(\beta)]$ (by induction hypothesis)
   iff $(N,i) \models f(\beta)\mathrm{U}f(\gamma)$
   iff $(N,i) \models f(\beta\mathrm{U}\gamma)$ (by the definition of $f$).
7. Case $\alpha \equiv {\sim}(\beta \wedge \gamma)$: We obtain: $(M,i) \models^* {\sim}(\beta \wedge \gamma)$ iff $(M,i) \models^* {\sim}\beta$ or $(M,i) \models^* {\sim}\gamma$ iff $(N,i) \models f({\sim}\beta)$ or $(N,i) \models f({\sim}\gamma)$ (by induction hypothesis) iff $(N,i) \models f({\sim}\beta) \vee f({\sim}\gamma)$ iff $(N,i) \models f({\sim}(\beta \wedge \gamma))$ (by the definition of $f$).
8. Case $\alpha \equiv {\sim}(\beta{\rightarrow}\gamma)$: We obtain: $(M,i) \models^* {\sim}(\beta{\rightarrow}\gamma)$ iff $(M,i) \not\models^* {\sim}\beta$ and $(M,i) \models^* {\sim}\gamma$ iff $(N,i) \not\models f({\sim}\beta)$ and $(N,i) \models f({\sim}\gamma)$ (by induction hypothesis) iff $(N,i) \models \neg f({\sim}\beta) \wedge f({\sim}\gamma)$ iff $(N,i) \models f({\sim}(\beta{\rightarrow}\gamma))$ (by the definition of $f$).
9. Case $\alpha \equiv {\sim}\neg\beta$: We obtain: $(M,i) \models^* {\sim}\neg\beta$ iff $(M,i) \not\models^* {\sim}\beta$ iff $(N,i) \not\models f({\sim}\beta)$ (by induction hypothesis) iff $(N,i) \models \neg f({\sim}\beta)$ iff $(N,i) \models f({\sim}\neg\beta)$ (by the definition of $f$).
10. Case $\alpha \equiv {\sim}{\sim}\beta$: We obtain: $(M,i) \models^* {\sim}{\sim}\beta$ iff $(M,i) \models^* \beta$ iff $(N,i) \models f(\beta)$ (by induction hypothesis) iff $(N,i) \models f({\sim}{\sim}\beta)$ (by the definition of $f$).
11. Case $\alpha \equiv {\sim}\mathrm{X}\beta$: We obtain: $(M,i) \models^* {\sim}\mathrm{X}\beta$ iff $(M,i+1) \models^* {\sim}\beta$ iff $(N,i+1) \models f({\sim}\beta)$ (by induction hypothesis) iff $(N,i) \models \mathrm{X}f({\sim}\beta)$ iff $(N,i) \models f({\sim}\mathrm{X}\beta)$ (by the definition of $f$).
12. Case $\alpha \equiv {\sim}\mathrm{G}\beta$: We obtain: $(M,i) \models^* {\sim}\mathrm{G}\beta$ iff $\exists j \geq i\ [(M,j) \models^* {\sim}\beta]$ iff $\exists j \geq i\ [(N,j) \models f({\sim}\beta)]$ (by induction hypothesis) iff $(N,i) \models \mathrm{F}f({\sim}\beta)$ iff $(N,i) \models f({\sim}\mathrm{G}\beta)$ (by the definition of $f$).
13. Case $\alpha \equiv {\sim}(\beta\mathrm{U}\gamma)$: We obtain:
    $(M,i) \models^* {\sim}(\beta\mathrm{U}\gamma)$
    iff $\forall j \geq i\ [(M,j) \models^* {\sim}\gamma$ or $\exists i \leq k < j\ (M,k) \models^* {\sim}\beta]$

iff $\forall j \geq i$ [$(N,j) \models f(\sim\gamma)$ or $\exists i \leq k < j$ $(N,k) \models f(\sim\beta)$] (by induction hypothesis)
iff $(N,i) \models f(\sim\beta)\mathrm{R}f(\sim\gamma)$
iff $(N,i) \models f(\sim(\beta\mathrm{U}\gamma))$ (by the definition of $f$).

14. Case $\alpha \equiv \sim(\beta\mathrm{R}\gamma)$: We obtain:
$(M,i) \models^* \sim(\beta\mathrm{R}\gamma)$
iff $\exists j \geq i$ [$(M,j) \models^* \sim\gamma$ and $\forall i \leq k < j$ $(M,k) \models^* \sim\beta$]
iff $\exists j \geq i$ [$(N,j) \models f(\sim\gamma)$ and $\forall i \leq k < j$ $(N,k) \models f(\sim\beta)$] (by induction hypothesis)
iff $(N,i) \models f(\sim\beta)\mathrm{U}f(\sim\gamma)$
iff $(N,i) \models f(\sim(\beta\mathrm{R}\gamma))$ (by the definition of $f$). ∎

**Lemma 2.8.** *Let $f$ be the mapping defined in Definition 2.6, and $S$ be a non-empty set of states. For any model $N := (\sigma, I)$ of* LTL*, any satisfaction relation $\models$ on $N$, and any state $s_i$ in $\sigma$, we can construct a paraconsistent model $M := (\sigma, I^*)$ of* pLTL *and a satisfaction relation $\models^*$ on $M$ such that for any formula $\alpha$ in $\mathcal{L}^p$,*

$$(N,i) \models f(\alpha) \text{ iff } (M,i) \models^* \alpha.$$

**Proof.** Similar to the proof of Lemma 2.7. ∎

**Theorem 2.9 (Embedding from pLTL into LTL).** *Let $f$ be the mapping defined in Definition 2.6. For any formula $\alpha$,*

*$\alpha$ is valid in* pLTL *iff $f(\alpha)$ is valid in* LTL.

**Proof.** By Lemmas 2.7 and 2.8. ∎

By using Theorem 2.9 and Lemmas 2.7 and 2.8, we can obtain the following theorem.

**Theorem 2.10 (Decidability of pLTL).** *The validity, satisfiability, and model checking problems of* pLTL *are decidable.*

**Proof.** In the following, we show only the proof of the validity problem of pLTL. By decidability of LTL, for each $\alpha$, it is possible to decide if $f(\alpha)$ is valid in pLTL. Then, by Theorem 2.9, pLTL is decidable. ∎

**Remark 2.11.** *We remark that the complexities of the decision procedures for the validity, satisfiability, and model checking problems of* pLTL *are the same as those of* LTL*, since the translation function $f$ defined in Definition 2.6 is a polynomial time reduction.*

## 3 Branching-Time Case

### 3.1 CTL and pCTL

*Formulas* of *computation tree logic* (CTL) are constructed from countably many propositional variables, $\rightarrow$, $\wedge$, $\vee$, $\neg$, X, G, F, U, R, A (all computation paths), and E (some computation path). The same notions and notations as those in the previous sections are also used in the following.

**Definition 3.1.** *Formulas of* CTL *are defined by the following grammar, assuming* $p$ *represents propositional variables:*

$$\alpha ::= p \mid \alpha \wedge \alpha \mid \alpha \vee \alpha \mid \alpha {\rightarrow} \alpha \mid \neg\alpha \mid \mathrm{AX}\alpha \mid \mathrm{EX}\alpha \mid \mathrm{AG}\alpha \mid \mathrm{EG}\alpha \mid \mathrm{AF}\alpha \mid \mathrm{EF}\alpha \mid \mathrm{A}(\alpha\mathrm{U}\alpha) \mid \mathrm{E}(\alpha\mathrm{U}\alpha) \mid \mathrm{A}(\alpha\mathrm{R}\alpha) \mid \mathrm{E}(\alpha\mathrm{R}\alpha).$$

**Remark 3.2.** *Note that pairs of symbols like* AX *and* EU *are indivisible, and that the symbols* X, G, F, U, *and* R *cannot occur without being preceded by an* A *or an* E. *Similarly, every* A *or* E *must have one of* X, G, F, U, *and* R *to accompany it.*

**Definition 3.3 (CTL).** *A structure* $(S, S_0, R, L)$ *is a* model *iff*

1. $S$ *is the set of states,*
2. $S_0$ *is a set of initial states and* $S_0 \subseteq S$,
3. $R$ *is a binary relation on* $S$ *which satisfies the condition:*
   $\forall s \in S\ \exists s' \in S\ [(s, s') \in R]$,
4. $L$ *is a mapping from* $S$ *to the power set of a nonempty set* $\Phi$ *of propositional variables.*

*A* path *in a model is an infinite sequence of states,* $\pi = s_0, s_1, s_2, \ldots$ *such that* $\forall i \geq 0\ [(s_i, s_{i+1}) \in R]$.

*A* satisfaction relation $(M, s) \models \alpha$ *for any formula* $\alpha$, *where* $M$ *is a model* $(S, S_0, R, L)$ *and* $s$ *represents a state in* $S$, *is defined inductively by:*

1. *for any* $p \in \Phi$, $(M, s) \models p$ *iff* $p \in L(s)$,
2. $(M, s) \models \alpha \wedge \beta$ *iff* $(M, s) \models \alpha$ *and* $(M, s) \models \beta$,
3. $(M, s) \models \alpha \vee \beta$ *iff* $(M, s) \models \alpha$ *or* $(M, s) \models \beta$,
4. $(M, s) \models \alpha {\rightarrow} \beta$ *iff* $(M, s) \models \alpha$ *implies* $(M, s) \models \beta$,
5. $(M, s) \models \neg\alpha$ *iff* $(M, s) \not\models \alpha$,
6. $(M, s) \models \mathrm{AX}\alpha$ *iff* $\forall s_1 \in S\ [(s, s_1) \in R$ *implies* $(M, s_1) \models \alpha]$,
7. $(M, s) \models \mathrm{EX}\alpha$ *iff* $\exists s_1 \in S\ [(s, s_1) \in R$ *and* $(M, s_1) \models \alpha]$,
8. $(M, s) \models \mathrm{AG}\alpha$ *iff for all paths* $\pi \equiv s_0, s_1, s_2, \ldots$, *where* $s \equiv s_0$, *and all states* $s_i$ *along* $\pi$, *we have* $(M, s_i) \models \alpha$,
9. $(M, s) \models \mathrm{EG}\alpha$ *iff there is a path* $\pi \equiv s_0, s_1, s_2, \ldots$, *where* $s \equiv s_0$, *and for all states* $s_i$ *along* $\pi$, *we have* $(M, s_i) \models \alpha$,
10. $(M, s) \models \mathrm{AF}\alpha$ *iff for all paths* $\pi \equiv s_0, s_1, s_2, \ldots$, *where* $s \equiv s_0$, *there is a state* $s_i$ *along* $\pi$ *such that* $(M, s_i) \models \alpha$,
11. $(M, s) \models \mathrm{EF}\alpha$ *iff there is a path* $\pi \equiv s_0, s_1, s_2, \ldots$, *where* $s \equiv s_0$, *and for some state* $s_i$ *along* $\pi$, *we have* $(M, s_i) \models \alpha$,
12. $(M, s) \models \mathrm{A}(\alpha\mathrm{U}\beta)$ *iff for all paths* $\pi \equiv s_0, s_1, s_2, \ldots$, *where* $s \equiv s_0$, *there is a state* $s_j$ *along* $\pi$ *such that* $(M, s_j) \models \beta$ *and* $\forall 0 \leq k < j\ (M, s_k) \models \alpha$,
13. $(M, s) \models \mathrm{E}(\alpha\mathrm{U}\beta)$ *iff there is a path* $\pi \equiv s_0, s_1, s_2, \ldots$, *where* $s \equiv s_0$, *and for some state* $s_j$ *along* $\pi$, *we have* $(M, s_j) \models \beta$ *and* $\forall 0 \leq k < j\ (M, s_k) \models \alpha$,
14. $(M, s) \models \mathrm{A}(\alpha\mathrm{R}\beta)$ *iff for all paths* $\pi \equiv s_0, s_1, s_2, \ldots$, *where* $s \equiv s_0$, *and all states* $s_j$ *along* $\pi$, *we have* $(M, s_j) \models \beta$ *or* $\exists 0 \leq k < j\ (M, s_k) \models \alpha$,
15. $(M, s) \models \mathrm{E}(\alpha\mathrm{R}\beta)$ *iff there is a path* $\pi \equiv s_0, s_1, s_2, \ldots$, *where* $s \equiv s_0$, *and for all states* $s_j$ *along* $\pi$, *we have* $(M, s_j) \models \beta$ *or* $\exists 0 \leq k < j\ (M, s_k) \models \alpha$.

*A formula* $\alpha$ *is* valid *in* CTL *iff* $(M, s) \models \alpha$ *holds for any model* $M := (S, S_0, R, L)$, *any* $s \in S$, *and any satisfaction relation* $\models$ *on* $M$.

The language of *paraconsistent computation tree logic* (pCTL) is obtained from that of CTL by adding $\sim$.

**Definition 3.4.** *Formulas of* pCTL *are defined by the following grammar, assuming* $p$ *represents propositional variables:*

$$\alpha ::= p \mid \alpha \wedge \alpha \mid \alpha \vee \alpha \mid \alpha \rightarrow \alpha \mid \neg\alpha \mid \mathrm{AX}\alpha \mid \mathrm{EX}\alpha \mid \mathrm{AG}\alpha \mid \mathrm{EG}\alpha \mid \mathrm{AF}\alpha \mid \mathrm{EF}\alpha \mid \mathrm{A}(\alpha \mathrm{U} \alpha) \mid \mathrm{E}(\alpha \mathrm{U} \alpha) \mid \mathrm{A}(\alpha \mathrm{R} \alpha) \mid \mathrm{E}(\alpha \mathrm{R} \alpha) \mid {\sim}\alpha.$$

**Definition 3.5 (pCTL).** *Let* $\Phi$ *be a non-empty set of propositional variables, and* $\Phi^{\sim}$ *be the set* $\{{\sim}p \mid p \in \Phi\}$ *of negated propositional variables.*

*A structure* $(S, S_0, R, L^*)$ *is a* paraconsistent model *iff*

1. $S$ *is the set of states,*
2. $S_0$ *is a set of initial states and* $S_0 \subseteq S$,
3. $R$ *is a binary relation on* $S$ *which satisfies the condition:* $\forall s \in S\ \exists s' \in S\ [(s, s') \in R]$,
4. $L^*$ *is a mapping from* $S$ *to the power set of* $\Phi \cup \Phi^{\sim}$.

*A* path *in a paraconsistent model is an infinite sequence of states,* $\pi = s_0, s_1, s_2, \ldots$ *such that* $\forall i \geq 0\ [(s_i, s_{i+1}) \in R]$.

*A* paraconsistent satisfaction relation $(M, s) \models^* \alpha$ *for any formula* $\alpha$, *where* $M$ *is a paraconsistent model* $(S, S_0, R, L^*)$ *and* $s$ *represents a state in* $S$, *is defined inductively by:*

1. *for any* $p \in \Phi$, $(M, s) \models^* p$ *iff* $p \in L^*(s)$,
2. *for any* ${\sim}p \in \Phi^{\sim}$, $(M, s) \models^* {\sim}p$ *iff* ${\sim}p \in L^*(s)$,
3. $(M, s) \models^* \alpha \wedge \beta$ *iff* $(M, s) \models^* \alpha$ *and* $(M, s) \models^* \beta$,
4. $(M, s) \models^* \alpha \vee \beta$ *iff* $(M, s) \models^* \alpha$ *or* $(M, s) \models^* \beta$,
5. $(M, s) \models^* \alpha \rightarrow \beta$ *iff* $(M, s) \models^* \alpha$ *implies* $(M, s) \models^* \beta$,
6. $(M, s) \models^* \neg\alpha$ *iff* $(M, s) \not\models^* \alpha$,
7. $(M, s) \models^* \mathrm{AX}\alpha$ *iff* $\forall s_1 \in S\ [(s, s_1) \in R$ *implies* $(M, s_1) \models^* \alpha]$,
8. $(M, s) \models^* \mathrm{EX}\alpha$ *iff* $\exists s_1 \in S\ [(s, s_1) \in R$ *and* $(M, s_1) \models^* \alpha]$,
9. $(M, s) \models^* \mathrm{AG}\alpha$ *iff for all paths* $\pi \equiv s_0, s_1, s_2, \ldots$, *where* $s \equiv s_0$, *and all states* $s_i$ *along* $\pi$, *we have* $(M, s_i) \models^* \alpha$,
10. $(M, s) \models^* \mathrm{EG}\alpha$ *iff there is a path* $\pi \equiv s_0, s_1, s_2, \ldots$, *where* $s \equiv s_0$, *and for all states* $s_i$ *along* $\pi$, *we have* $(M, s_i) \models^* \alpha$,
11. $(M, s) \models^* \mathrm{AF}\alpha$ *iff for all paths* $\pi \equiv s_0, s_1, s_2, \ldots$, *where* $s \equiv s_0$, *there is a state* $s_i$ *along* $\pi$ *such that* $(M, s_i) \models^* \alpha$,
12. $(M, s) \models^* \mathrm{EF}\alpha$ *iff there is a path* $\pi \equiv s_0, s_1, s_2, \ldots$, *where* $s \equiv s_0$, *and for some state* $s_i$ *along* $\pi$, *we have* $(M, s_i) \models^* \alpha$,
13. $(M, s) \models^* \mathrm{A}(\alpha \mathrm{U} \beta)$ *iff for all paths* $\pi \equiv s_0, s_1, s_2, \ldots$, *where* $s \equiv s_0$, *there is a state* $s_j$ *along* $\pi$ *such that* $(M, s_j) \models^* \beta$ *and* $\forall 0 \leq k < j\ (M, s_k) \models^* \alpha$,
14. $(M, s) \models^* \mathrm{E}(\alpha \mathrm{U} \beta)$ *iff there is a path* $\pi \equiv s_0, s_1, s_2, \ldots$, *where* $s \equiv s_0$, *and for some state* $s_j$ *along* $\pi$, *we have* $(M, s_j) \models^* \beta$ *and* $\forall 0 \leq k < j\ (M, s_k) \models^* \alpha$,

15. $(M,s) \models^* \mathrm{A}(\alpha\mathrm{R}\beta)$ *iff for all paths* $\pi \equiv s_0, s_1, s_2, \ldots$, *where* $s \equiv s_0$, *and all states* $s_j$ *along* $\pi$, *we have* $(M,s_j) \models^* \beta$ *or* $\exists 0 \le k < j\ (M,s_k) \models^* \alpha$,
16. $(M,s) \models^* \mathrm{E}(\alpha\mathrm{R}\beta)$ *iff there is a path* $\pi \equiv s_0, s_1, s_2, \ldots$, *where* $s \equiv s_0$, *and for all states* $s_j$ *along* $\pi$, *we have* $(M,s_j) \models^* \beta$ *or* $\exists 0 \le k < j\ (M,s_k) \models^* \alpha$,
17. $(M,s) \models^* {\sim}{\sim}\alpha$ *iff* $(M,s) \models^* \alpha$,
18. $(M,s) \models^* {\sim}(\alpha \wedge \beta)$ *iff* $(M,s) \models^* {\sim}\alpha$ *or* $(M,s) \models^* {\sim}\beta$,
19. $(M,s) \models^* {\sim}(\alpha \vee \beta)$ *iff* $(M,s) \models^* {\sim}\alpha$ *and* $(M,s) \models^* {\sim}\beta$,
20. $(M,s) \models^* {\sim}(\alpha{\rightarrow}\beta)$ *iff* $(M,s) \not\models^* {\sim}\alpha$ *and* $(M,s) \models^* {\sim}\beta$,
21. $(M,s) \models^* {\sim}\neg\alpha$ *iff* $(M,s) \not\models^* {\sim}\alpha$,
22. $(M,s) \models^* {\sim}\mathrm{AX}\alpha$ *iff* $\exists s_1 \in S\ [(s,s_1) \in R$ *and* $(M,s_1) \models^* {\sim}\alpha]$,
23. $(M,s) \models^* {\sim}\mathrm{EX}\alpha$ *iff* $\forall s_1 \in S\ [(s,s_1) \in R$ *implies* $(M,s_1) \models^* {\sim}\alpha]$,
24. $(M,s) \models^* {\sim}\mathrm{AG}\alpha$ *iff there is a path* $\pi \equiv s_0, s_1, s_2, \ldots$, *where* $s \equiv s_0$, *and for some state* $s_i$ *along* $\pi$, *we have* $(M,s_i) \models^* {\sim}\alpha$,
25. $(M,s) \models^* {\sim}\mathrm{EG}\alpha$ *iff for all paths* $\pi \equiv s_0, s_1, s_2, \ldots$, *where* $s \equiv s_0$, *there is a state* $s_i$ *along* $\pi$ *such that* $(M,s_i) \models^* {\sim}\alpha$,
26. $(M,s) \models^* {\sim}\mathrm{AF}\alpha$ *iff there is a path* $\pi \equiv s_0, s_1, s_2, \ldots$, *where* $s \equiv s_0$, *and for all states* $s_i$ *along* $\pi$, *we have* $(M,s_i) \models^* {\sim}\alpha$,
27. $(M,s) \models^* {\sim}\mathrm{EF}\alpha$ *iff for all paths* $\pi \equiv s_0, s_1, s_2, \ldots$, *where* $s \equiv s_0$, *and all states* $s_i$ *along* $\pi$, *we have* $(M,s_i) \models^* {\sim}\alpha$,
28. $(M,s) \models^* {\sim}\mathrm{A}(\alpha\mathrm{U}\beta)$ *iff there is a path* $\pi \equiv s_0, s_1, s_2, \ldots$, *where* $s \equiv s_0$, *and for all states* $s_j$ *along* $\pi$, *we have* $(M,s_j) \models^* {\sim}\beta$ *or* $\exists 0 \le k < j\ (M,s_k) \models^* {\sim}\alpha$,
29. $(M,s) \models^* {\sim}\mathrm{E}(\alpha\mathrm{U}\beta)$ *iff for all paths* $\pi \equiv s_0, s_1, s_2, \ldots$, *where* $s \equiv s_0$, *and all states* $s_j$ *along* $\pi$, *we have* $(M,s_j) \models^* {\sim}\beta$ *or* $\exists 0 \le k < j\ (M,s_k) \models^* {\sim}\alpha$,
30. $(M,s) \models^* {\sim}\mathrm{A}(\alpha\mathrm{R}\beta)$ *iff there is a path* $\pi \equiv s_0, s_1, s_2, \ldots$, *where* $s \equiv s_0$, *and for some state* $s_j$ *along* $\pi$, *we have* $(M,s_j) \models^* {\sim}\beta$ *and* $\forall 0 \le k < j\ (M,s_k) \models^* {\sim}\alpha$,
31. $(M,s) \models^* {\sim}\mathrm{E}(\alpha\mathrm{R}\beta)$ *iff for all paths* $\pi \equiv s_0, s_1, s_2, \ldots$, *where* $s \equiv s_0$, *there is a state* $s_j$ *along* $\pi$ *such that* $(M,s_j) \models^* {\sim}\beta$ *and* $\forall 0 \le k < j\ (M,s_k) \models^* {\sim}\alpha$.

*A formula* $\alpha$ *is* valid *in* pCTL *iff* $(M,s) \models^* \alpha$ *holds for any paraconsistent model* $M := (S, S_0, R, L^*)$, *any* $s \in S$, *and any paraconsistent satisfaction relation* $\models^*$ *on* $M$.

**Remark 3.6.** *We make the following remarks.*

1. *The following formulas are valid in* pCTL*: For any formulas* $\alpha$ *and* $\beta$,
   (a) ${\sim}{\sim}\alpha \leftrightarrow \alpha$,
   (b) ${\sim}(\alpha \wedge \beta) \leftrightarrow {\sim}\alpha \vee {\sim}\beta$,
   (c) ${\sim}(\alpha \vee \beta) \leftrightarrow {\sim}\alpha \wedge {\sim}\beta$,
   (d) ${\sim}(\alpha{\rightarrow}\beta) \leftrightarrow \neg{\sim}\alpha \wedge {\sim}\beta$,
   (e) ${\sim}\neg\alpha \leftrightarrow \neg{\sim}\alpha$,
   (f) ${\sim}\mathrm{AX}\alpha \leftrightarrow \mathrm{EX}{\sim}\alpha$,
   (g) ${\sim}\mathrm{EX}\alpha \leftrightarrow \mathrm{AX}{\sim}\alpha$,
   (h) ${\sim}\mathrm{AG}\alpha \leftrightarrow \mathrm{EF}{\sim}\alpha$,
   (i) ${\sim}\mathrm{EG}\alpha \leftrightarrow \mathrm{AF}{\sim}\alpha$,
   (j) ${\sim}\mathrm{AF}\alpha \leftrightarrow \mathrm{EG}{\sim}\alpha$,

(k) $\sim\mathrm{EF}\alpha \leftrightarrow \mathrm{AG}{\sim}\alpha$,
(l) $\sim\mathrm{A}(\alpha\mathrm{U}\beta) \leftrightarrow \mathrm{E}((\sim\alpha)\mathrm{R}(\sim\beta))$,
(m) $\sim\mathrm{E}(\alpha\mathrm{U}\beta) \leftrightarrow \mathrm{A}((\sim\alpha)\mathrm{R}(\sim\beta))$,
(n) $\sim\mathrm{A}(\alpha\mathrm{R}\beta) \leftrightarrow \mathrm{E}((\sim\alpha)\mathrm{U}(\sim\beta))$,
(o) $\sim\mathrm{E}(\alpha\mathrm{R}\beta) \leftrightarrow \mathrm{A}((\sim\alpha)\mathrm{U}(\sim\beta))$.

2. pCTL *is paraconsistent with respect to* $\sim$. *The reason is explained as follows. Assume a paraconsistent model* $M = (S, S_0, R, L^*)$ *such that* $p \in L^*(s)$, $\sim p \in L^*(s)$ *and* $q \notin L^*(s)$ *for a pair of distinct propositional variables* $p$ *and* $q$. *Then,* $(M, s) \models^* (p \wedge \sim p) \rightarrow q$ *does not hold.*
3. pCTL *is regarded as a four-valued logic. The reason is explained as follows. For each* $s \in S$ *and each formula* $\alpha$, *we can take one of the following four cases:*
   (a) $\alpha$ *is verified at* $s$, *i.e.,* $(M, s) \models^* \alpha$,
   (b) $\alpha$ *is falsified at* $s$, *i.e.,* $(M, s) \models^* \sim\alpha$,
   (c) $\alpha$ *is both verified and falsified at* $s$,
   (d) $\alpha$ *is neither verified nor falsified at* $s$.

### 3.2 Translation from pCTL into CTL

**Definition 3.7.** *Let* $\Phi$ *be a non-empty set of propositional variables, and* $\Phi'$ *be the set* $\{p' \mid p \in \Phi\}$ *of propositional variables. The language* $\mathcal{L}^p$ *(the set of formulas) of* pCTL *is defined using* $\Phi$, $\wedge, \vee, \rightarrow, \neg$, X, F, G, U, R, A, E *and* $\sim$. *The language* $\mathcal{L}$ *of* CTL *is obtained from* $\mathcal{L}^p$ *by adding* $\Phi'$ *and deleting* $\sim$.

*A mapping* $f$ *from* $\mathcal{L}^p$ *to* $\mathcal{L}$ *is defined inductively by:*

1. *for any* $p \in \Phi$, $f(p) := p$ *and* $f(\sim p) := p' \in \Phi'$,
2. $f(\alpha \sharp \beta) := f(\alpha) \sharp f(\beta)$ *where* $\sharp \in \{\wedge, \vee, \rightarrow\}$,
3. $f(\sharp\alpha) := \sharp f(\alpha)$ *where* $\sharp \in \{\neg, \mathrm{AX}, \mathrm{EX}, \mathrm{AG}, \mathrm{EG}, \mathrm{AF}, \mathrm{EF}\}$,
4. $f(\mathrm{A}(\alpha\mathrm{U}\beta))) := \mathrm{A}(f(\alpha)\mathrm{U}f(\beta))$,
5. $f(\mathrm{E}(\alpha\mathrm{U}\beta))) := \mathrm{E}(f(\alpha)\mathrm{U}f(\beta))$,
6. $f(\mathrm{A}(\alpha\mathrm{R}\beta))) := \mathrm{A}(f(\alpha)\mathrm{R}f(\beta))$,
7. $f(\mathrm{E}(\alpha\mathrm{R}\beta))) := \mathrm{E}(f(\alpha)\mathrm{R}f(\beta))$,
8. $f(\sim\sim\alpha) := f(\alpha)$,
9. $f(\sim(\alpha \wedge \beta)) := f(\sim\alpha) \vee f(\sim\beta)$,
10. $f(\sim(\alpha \vee \beta)) := f(\sim\alpha) \wedge f(\sim\beta)$,
11. $f(\sim(\alpha\rightarrow\beta)) := \neg f(\sim\alpha) \wedge f(\sim\beta)$,
12. $f(\sim\neg\alpha) := \neg f(\sim\alpha)$,
13. $f(\sim\mathrm{AX}\alpha) := \mathrm{EX}f(\sim\alpha)$,
14. $f(\sim\mathrm{EX}\alpha) := \mathrm{AX}f(\sim\alpha)$,
15. $f(\sim\mathrm{AG}\alpha) := \mathrm{EF}f(\sim\alpha)$,
16. $f(\sim\mathrm{EG}\alpha) := \mathrm{AF}f(\sim\alpha)$,
17. $f(\sim\mathrm{AF}\alpha) := \mathrm{EG}f(\sim\alpha)$,
18. $f(\sim\mathrm{EF}\alpha) := \mathrm{AG}f(\sim\alpha)$,
19. $f(\sim(\mathrm{A}(\alpha\mathrm{U}\beta))) := \mathrm{E}(f(\sim\alpha)\mathrm{R}f(\sim\beta))$,
20. $f(\sim(\mathrm{E}(\alpha\mathrm{U}\beta))) := \mathrm{A}(f(\sim\alpha)\mathrm{R}f(\sim\beta))$,
21. $f(\sim(\mathrm{A}(\alpha\mathrm{R}\beta))) := \mathrm{E}(f(\sim\alpha)\mathrm{U}f(\sim\beta))$,
22. $f(\sim(\mathrm{E}(\alpha\mathrm{R}\beta))) := \mathrm{A}(f(\sim\alpha)\mathrm{U}f(\sim\beta))$.

**Lemma 3.8.** *Let $f$ be the mapping defined in Definition 3.7. For any paraconsistent model $M := (S, S_0, R, L^*)$ of* pCTL, *and any paraconsistent satisfaction relation $\models^*$ on $M$, we can construct a model $N := (S, S_0, R, L)$ of* CTL *and a satisfaction relation $\models$ on $N$ such that for any formula $\alpha$ in $\mathcal{L}^p$ and any state $s$ in $S$,*

$(M, s) \models^* \alpha$ *iff* $(N, s) \models f(\alpha)$.

**Proof.** Let $\Phi$ be a nonempty set of propositional variables, $\Phi^{\sim}$ be $\{{\sim}p \mid p \in \Phi\}$, and $\Phi'$ be $\{p' \mid p \in \Phi\}$. Suppose that $M$ is a paraconsistent model $(S, S_0, R, L^*)$ such that

$L^*$ is a mapping from $S$ to the power set of $\Phi \cup \Phi^{\sim}$.

We then define a model $N := (S, S_0, R, L)$ such that

1. $L$ is a mapping from $S$ to the power set of $\Phi \cup \Phi'$,
2. for any $s \in S$ and any $p \in \Phi$,
   (a) $p \in L^*(s)$ iff $p \in L(s)$,
   (b) ${\sim}p \in L^*(s)$ iff $p' \in L(s)$.

Then, this lemma is proved by induction on the complexity of $\alpha$.

- Base step:
  1. Case $\alpha \equiv p \in \Phi$: We obtain: $(M, s) \models^* p$ iff $p \in L^*(s)$ iff $p \in L(s)$ iff $(N, s) \models p$ iff $(N, s) \models f(p)$ (by the definition of $f$).
  2. We obtain: $(M, s) \models^* {\sim}p$ iff ${\sim}p \in L^*(s)$ iff $p' \in L(s)$ iff $(N, s) \models p'$ iff $(N, s) \models f({\sim}p)$ (by the definition of $f$).
- Induction step: We show some cases.
  1. Case $\alpha \equiv \beta \wedge \gamma$: We obtain: $(M, s) \models^* \beta \wedge \gamma$ iff $(M, s) \models^* \beta$ and $(M, s) \models^* \gamma$ iff $(N, s) \models f(\beta)$ and $(N, s) \models f(\gamma)$ (by induction hypothesis) iff $(N, s) \models f(\beta) \wedge f(\gamma)$ iff $(N, s) \models f(\beta \wedge \gamma)$ (by the definition of $f$).
  2. Case $\alpha \equiv \beta \rightarrow \gamma$: We obtain: $(M, s) \models^* \beta \rightarrow \gamma$ iff $(M, s) \models^* \beta$ implies $(M, s) \models^* \gamma$ iff $(N, s) \models f(\beta)$ implies $(N, s) \models f(\gamma)$ (by induction hypothesis) iff $(N, s) \models f(\beta) \rightarrow f(\gamma)$ iff $(N, s) \models f(\beta \rightarrow \gamma)$ (by the definition of $f$).
  3. Case $\alpha \equiv \neg\beta$: We obtain: $(M, s) \models^* \neg\beta$ iff $(M, s) \not\models^* \beta$ iff $(N, s) \not\models f(\beta)$ (by induction hypothesis) iff $(N, s) \models \neg f(\beta)$ iff $(N, s) \models f(\neg\beta)$ (by the definition of $f$).
  4. Case $\alpha \equiv \mathrm{AX}\beta$: We obtain: $(M, s) \models^* \mathrm{AX}\beta$ iff $\forall s_1 \in S$ $[(s, s_1) \in R$ implies $(M, s_1) \models^* \beta]$ iff $\forall s_1 \in S$ $[(s, s_1) \in R$ implies $(N, s_1) \models f(\beta)]$ (by induction hypothesis) iff $(N, s) \models \mathrm{AX}f(\beta)$ iff $(N, s) \models f(\mathrm{AX}\beta)$ (by the definition of $f$).
  5. Case $\alpha \equiv \mathrm{AG}\beta$: We obtain:
     $(M, s) \models^* \mathrm{AG}\beta$
     iff for all paths $\pi \equiv s_0, s_1, s_2, \ldots$, where $s \equiv s_0$, and all states $s_i$ along $\pi$, we have $(M, s_i) \models^* \beta$

iff for all paths $\pi \equiv s_0, s_1, s_2, \ldots$, where $s \equiv s_0$, and all states $s_i$ along $\pi$, we have $(N, s_i) \models f(\beta)$ (by induction hypothesis)
iff $(N, s) \models \mathrm{AG}f(\beta)$
iff $(N, s) \models f(\mathrm{AG}\beta)$ (by the definition of $f$).

6. Case $\alpha \equiv \mathrm{A}(\beta\mathrm{U}\gamma)$: We obtain:
$(M, s) \models^* \mathrm{A}(\beta\mathrm{U}\gamma)$
iff for all paths $\pi \equiv s_0, s_1, s_2, \ldots$, where $s \equiv s_0$, there is a state $s_j$ along $\pi$ such that $(M, s_j) \models^* \gamma$ and $\forall 0 \leq k < j\ (M, s_k) \models^* \beta$
iff for all paths $\pi \equiv s_0, s_1, s_2, \ldots$, where $s \equiv s_0$, there is a state $s_j$ along $\pi$ such that $(N, s_j) \models f(\gamma)$ and $\forall 0 \leq k < j\ (N, s_k) \models f(\beta)$ (by induction hypothesis)
iff $(N, s) \models \mathrm{A}(f(\beta)\mathrm{U}f(\gamma))$
iff $(N, s) \models f(\mathrm{A}(\beta\mathrm{U}\gamma))$ (by the definition of $f$).

7. Case $\alpha \equiv {\sim}{\sim}\beta$: We obtain: $(M, s) \models^* {\sim}{\sim}\beta$ iff $(M, s) \models^* \beta$ iff $(N, s) \models f(\beta)$ (by induction hypothesis) $(N, s) \models f({\sim}{\sim}\beta)$ (by the definition of $f$).

8. Case $\alpha \equiv {\sim}(\beta \wedge \gamma)$: We obtain: $(M, s) \models^* {\sim}(\beta \wedge \gamma)$ iff $(M, s) \models^* {\sim}\beta$ or $(M, s) \models^* {\sim}\gamma$ iff $(N, s) \models f({\sim}\beta)$ or $(N, s) \models f({\sim}\gamma)$ (by induction hypothesis) iff $(N, s) \models f({\sim}\beta) \vee f({\sim}\gamma)$ iff $(N, s) \models f({\sim}(\beta \wedge \gamma))$ (by the definition of $f$).

9. Case $\alpha \equiv {\sim}(\beta{\rightarrow}\gamma)$: We obtain: $(M, s) \models^* {\sim}(\beta{\rightarrow}\gamma)$ iff $(M, s) \not\models^* {\sim}\beta$ and $(M, s) \models^* {\sim}\gamma$ iff $(N, s) \not\models f({\sim}\beta)$ and $(N, s) \models f({\sim}\gamma)$ (by induction hypothesis) iff $(N, s) \models \neg f({\sim}\beta) \wedge f({\sim}\gamma)$ iff $(N, s) \models f({\sim}(\beta{\rightarrow}\gamma))$ (by the definition of $f$).

10. Case $\alpha \equiv {\sim}\neg\beta$: We obtain: $(M, s) \models^* {\sim}\neg\beta$ iff $(M, s) \not\models^* {\sim}\beta$ iff $(N, s) \not\models f({\sim}\beta)$ (by induction hypothesis) iff $(N, s) \models \neg f({\sim}\beta)$ iff $(N, s) \models f({\sim}\neg\beta)$ (by the definition of $f$).

11. Case $\alpha \equiv {\sim}\mathrm{AX}\beta$: We obtain: $(M, s) \models^* {\sim}\mathrm{AX}\beta$ iff $\exists s_1 \in S\ [(s, s_1) \in R$ and $(M, s_1) \models^* {\sim}\beta]$ iff $\exists s_1 \in S\ [(s, s_1) \in R$ and $(N, s_1) \models f({\sim}\beta)]$ (by induction hypothesis) iff $(N, s) \models \mathrm{EX}f({\sim}\beta)$ iff $(N, s) \models f({\sim}\mathrm{AX}\beta)$ (by the definition of $f$).

12. Case $\alpha \equiv {\sim}\mathrm{AG}\beta$: We obtain:
$(M, s) \models^* {\sim}\mathrm{AG}\beta$
iff there is a path $\pi \equiv s_0, s_1, s_2, \ldots$, where $s \equiv s_0$, for some state $s_i$ along $\pi$, we have $(M, s_i) \models^* {\sim}\beta$
iff there is a path $\pi \equiv s_0, s_1, s_2, \ldots$, where $s \equiv s_0$, for some state $s_i$ along $\pi$, we have $(N, s_i) \models f({\sim}\beta)$ (by induction hypothesis)
iff $(N, s) \models \mathrm{EF}f({\sim}\beta)$
iff $(N, s) \models f({\sim}\mathrm{AG}\beta))$ (by the definition of $f$).

13. Case $\alpha \equiv {\sim}\mathrm{A}(\beta\mathrm{U}\gamma)$: We obtain:
$(M, s) \models^* {\sim}\mathrm{A}(\beta\mathrm{U}\gamma)$
iff there is a path $\pi \equiv s_0, s_1, s_2, \ldots$, where $s \equiv s_0$, and for all states $s_j$ along $\pi$, we have $(M, s_j) \models^* {\sim}\gamma$ or $\exists 0 \leq k < j\ (M, s_k) \models^* {\sim}\beta$
iff there is a path $\pi \equiv s_0, s_1, s_2, \ldots$, where $s \equiv s_0$, and for all states $s_j$ along $\pi$, we have $(N, s_j) \models f({\sim}\gamma)$ or $\exists 0 \leq k < j\ (N, s_k) \models f({\sim}\beta)$ (by induction hypothesis)
iff $(N, s) \models \mathrm{E}(f({\sim}\beta)\mathrm{R}f({\sim}\gamma))$

iff $(N, s) \models f({\sim}\mathrm{A}(\beta \mathrm{U} \gamma))$ (by the definition of $f$).

14. Case $\alpha \equiv {\sim}\mathrm{A}(\beta \mathrm{R} \gamma)$: We obtain:
$(M, s) \models^* {\sim}\mathrm{A}(\beta \mathrm{R} \gamma)$
iff there is a path $\pi \equiv s_0, s_1, s_2, \ldots$, where $s \equiv s_0$, and for some state $s_j$ along $\pi$, we have $(M, s_j) \models^* {\sim}\gamma$ and $\forall 0 \leq k < j\ (M, s_k) \models^* {\sim}\beta$
iff there is a path $\pi \equiv s_0, s_1, s_2, \ldots$, where $s \equiv s_0$, and for some state $s_j$ along $\pi$, we have $(N, s_j) \models f({\sim}\gamma)$ or $\forall 0 \leq k < j\ (N, s_k) \models f({\sim}\beta)$ (by induction hypothesis)
iff $(N, s) \models \mathrm{E}(f({\sim}\beta) \mathrm{U} f({\sim}\gamma))$
iff $(N, s) \models f({\sim}\mathrm{A}(\beta \mathrm{R} \gamma))$ (by the definition of $f$). ∎

**Lemma 3.9.** *Let $f$ be the mapping defined in Definition 3.7. For any model $N := (S, S_0, R, L)$ of* CTL*, and any satisfaction relation $\models$ on $N$, we can construct a paraconsistent model $M := (S, S_0, R, L^*)$ of* pCTL *and a paraconsistent satisfaction relation $\models^*$ on $M$ such that for any formula $\alpha$ in $\mathcal{L}^p$ and any state $s$ in $S$,*

$(N, s) \models f(\alpha)$ *iff* $(M, s) \models^* \alpha$,

**Proof.** Similar to the proof of Lemma 3.8. ∎

**Theorem 3.10 (Embedding from pCTL into CTL).** *Let $f$ be the mapping defined in Definition 3.7. For any formula $\alpha$,*

*$\alpha$ is valid in* pCTL *iff $f(\alpha)$ is valid in* CTL.

**Proof.** By Lemmas 3.8 and 3.9. ∎

**Theorem 3.11 (Decidability of pCTL).** *The validity, satisfiability, and model checking problems of* pCTL *are decidable.*

**Proof.** Similar to the proof of Theorem 2.10. ∎

**Remark 3.12.** *We remark that the complexities of the decision procedures for the validity, satisfiability, and model checking problems of* pCTL *are the same as those of* CTL*, since the translation function $f$ defined in Definition 3.7 is a polynomial time reduction.*

## 4 Full Branching-Time Case

### 4.1 CTL* and pCTL*

*Formulas* of *full computation tree logic* (CTL*) are defined by combining two types of formulas: *state formulas* and *path formulas*. These formulas are constructed from countably many propositional variables, $\rightarrow$, $\wedge$, $\vee$, $\neg$, X, G, F, U, R, A and E. The symbol "path" is used to denote an auxiliary function from the set of state formulas to the set of path formulas, i.e., path($\gamma$) means that a state formula $\gamma$ is a path formula. The same notions and notations as those in the previous sections are also used in the following.

**Definition 4.1.** *State formulas* $\alpha$ *and path formulas* $\beta$ *of* CTL* *are defined by the following grammar, assuming* $p$ *represents propositional variables:*

$$\alpha ::= p \mid \alpha \wedge \alpha \mid \alpha \vee \alpha \mid \alpha {\to} \alpha \mid \neg\alpha \mid \mathrm{A}\beta \mid \mathrm{E}\beta$$
$$\beta ::= \mathrm{path}(\alpha) \mid \beta \wedge \beta \mid \beta \vee \beta \mid \beta {\to} \beta \mid \neg\beta \mid \mathrm{X}\beta \mid \mathrm{G}\beta \mid \mathrm{F}\beta \mid \beta\mathrm{U}\beta \mid \beta\mathrm{R}\beta.$$

*State formulas and path formulas of* CTL* *are formulas of* CTL*.

The operators E and A are called the *path quantifiers*, and the operators X, G, F, U and R are called the *temporal operators*.

**Definition 4.2 (CTL*).** *A structure* $(S, S_0, R, L)$ *is a* model *iff*

1. *$S$ is the set of states,*
2. *$S_0$ is a set of initial states and $S_0 \subseteq S$,*
3. *$R$ is a binary relation on $S$ which satisfies the condition:*
   $\forall s \in S\ \exists s' \in S\ [(s, s') \in R]$,
4. *$L$ is a mapping from $S$ to the power set of a nonempty set $\Phi$ of propositional variables.*

A path *in a model is an infinite sequence of states,* $\pi = s_0, s_1, s_2, \ldots$ *such that* $\forall i \geq 0\ [(s_i, s_{i+1}) \in R]$. *An expression* $\pi^i$ *means the suffix of* $\pi$ *starting at* $s_1$.

A satisfaction relation $(M, x) \models \alpha$ *for any formula* $\alpha$, *where* $M$ *is a model* $(S, S_0, R, L)$ *and* $x$ *is a state* $s$ *in* $S$ *or a path* $\pi$ *constructed from* $S$, *is defined inductively by:*

1. *for any* $p \in \Phi$, $(M, s) \models p$ *iff* $p \in L(s)$,
2. $(M, s) \models \alpha \wedge \beta$ *iff* $(M, s) \models \alpha$ *and* $(M, s) \models \beta$,
3. $(M, s) \models \alpha \vee \beta$ *iff* $(M, s) \models \alpha$ *or* $(M, s) \models \beta$,
4. $(M, s) \models \alpha {\to} \beta$ *iff* $(M, s) \models \alpha$ *implies* $(M, s) \models \beta$,
5. $(M, s) \models \neg\alpha$ *iff* $(M, s) \not\models \alpha$,
6. $(M, s) \models \mathrm{E}\beta$ *iff for some path* $\pi$ *starting from* $s$, $(M, \pi) \models \beta$,
7. $(M, s) \models \mathrm{A}\beta$ *iff for any path* $\pi$ *starting from* $s$, $(M, \pi) \models \beta$,
8. $(M, \pi) \models \mathrm{path}(\alpha)$ *iff* $s$ *is the first state of* $\pi$ *and* $(M, s) \models \alpha$,
9. $(M, \pi) \models \alpha \wedge \beta$ *iff* $(M, \pi) \models \alpha$ *and* $(M, \pi) \models \beta$,
10. $(M, \pi) \models \alpha \vee \beta$ *iff* $(M, \pi) \models \alpha$ *or* $(M, \pi) \models \beta$,
11. $(M, \pi) \models \alpha {\to} \beta$ *iff* $(M, \pi) \models \alpha$ *implies* $(M, \pi) \models \beta$,
12. $(M, \pi) \models \neg\alpha$ *iff* $(M, \pi) \not\models \alpha$,
13. $(M, \pi) \models \mathrm{X}\alpha$ *iff* $(M, \pi^1) \models \alpha$,
14. $(M, \pi) \models \mathrm{G}\alpha$ *iff* $\forall j \geq 0\ [(M, \pi^j) \models \alpha]$,
15. $(M, \pi) \models \mathrm{F}\alpha$ *iff* $\exists j \geq 0\ [(M, \pi^j) \models \alpha]$,
16. $(M, \pi) \models \alpha\mathrm{U}\beta$ *iff* $\exists j \geq 0\ [(M, \pi^j) \models \beta$ *and* $\forall 0 \leq k < j\ (M, \pi^k) \models \alpha]$,
17. $(M, \pi) \models \alpha\mathrm{R}\beta$ *iff* $\forall j \geq 0\ [(M, \pi^j) \models \beta$ *or* $\exists 0 \leq k < j\ (M, \pi^k) \models \alpha]$.

*A state formula* $\alpha$ *is* valid under branching-time interpretation *in* CTL* *(denoted* $\models_B \alpha$*) iff* $(M, s) \models \alpha$ *holds for any model* $M := (S, S_0, R, L)$, *any* $s \in S$, *and any satisfaction relation* $\models$ *on* $M$. *A path formula* $\beta$ *is* valid under linear-time interpretation *in* CTL* *(denoted* $\models_L \alpha$*) iff* $(M, \pi) \models \alpha$ *holds for any model* $M := (S, S_0, R, L)$, *any path* $\pi$ *starting from* $s \in S$, *and any satisfaction relation* $\models$ *on* $M$. *A formula* $\alpha$ *is* valid *in* CTL* *(denoted* $\models \alpha$*) iff* $\models_B \alpha$ *or* $\models_L \alpha$.

The language of *paraconsistent full computation tree logic* (pCTL*) is obtained from that of CTL* by adding $\sim$ (paraconsistent negation).

**Definition 4.3** *State formulas $\alpha$ and path formulas $\beta$ of* pCTL* *are defined by the following grammar, assuming p represents propositional variables:*

$$\alpha ::= p \mid \alpha \wedge \alpha \mid \alpha \vee \alpha \mid \alpha {\rightarrow} \alpha \mid \neg\alpha \mid {\sim}\alpha \mid \mathrm{A}\beta \mid \mathrm{E}\beta$$
$$\beta ::= \mathrm{path}(\alpha) \mid \beta \wedge \beta \mid \beta \vee \beta \mid \beta {\rightarrow} \beta \mid \neg\beta \mid {\sim}\beta \mid \mathrm{X}\beta \mid \mathrm{G}\beta \mid \mathrm{F}\beta \mid \beta\mathrm{U}\beta \mid \beta\mathrm{R}\beta.$$

*State formulas and path formulas of* pCTL* *are formulas of* pCTL*.

**Definition 4.4 (pCTL*).** *Let $\Phi$ be a non-empty set of propositional variables, and $\Phi^{\sim}$ be the set $\{{\sim}p \mid p \in \Phi\}$ of negated propositional variables.*

*A structure $(S, S_0, R, L^*)$ is a* paraconsistent model *iff*

1. *$S$ is the set of states,*
2. *$S_0$ is a set of initial states and $S_0 \subseteq S$,*
3. *$R$ is a binary relation on $S$ which satisfies the condition:* $\forall s \in S\ \exists s' \in S\ [(s, s') \in R]$,
4. *$L^*$ is a mapping from $S$ to the power set of $\Phi \cup \Phi^{\sim}$.*

*A* path *in a paraconsistent model is an infinite sequence of states, $\pi = s_0, s_1, s_2, \ldots$ such that $\forall i \geq 0\ [(s_i, s_{i+1}) \in R]$. An expression $\pi^i$ means the suffix of $\pi$ starting at $s_1$.*

*A* paraconsistent satisfaction relation $(M, x) \models^* \alpha$ *for any formula $\alpha$, where $M$ is a paraconsistent model $(S, S_0, R, L^*)$ and $x$ is a state $s$ in $S$ or a path $\pi$ constructed from $S$, is defined inductively by:*

1. *for any $p \in \Phi$, $(M, s) \models^* p$ iff $p \in L^*(s)$,*
2. *for any ${\sim}p \in \Phi^{\sim}$, $(M, s) \models^* {\sim}p$ iff ${\sim}p \in L^*(s)$,*
3. *$(M, s) \models^* \alpha \wedge \beta$ iff $(M, s) \models^* \alpha$ and $(M, s) \models^* \beta$,*
4. *$(M, s) \models^* \alpha \vee \beta$ iff $(M, s) \models^* \alpha$ or $(M, s) \models^* \beta$,*
5. *$(M, s) \models^* \alpha {\rightarrow} \beta$ iff $(M, s) \models^* \alpha$ implies $(M, s) \models^* \beta$,*
6. *$(M, s) \models^* \neg\alpha$ iff $(M, s) \not\models^* \alpha$,*
7. *$(M, s) \models^* \mathrm{E}\beta$ iff for some path $\pi$ starting from $s$, $(M, \pi) \models^* \beta$,*
8. *$(M, s) \models^* \mathrm{A}\beta$ iff for any path $\pi$ starting from $s$, $(M, \pi) \models^* \beta$,*
9. *$(M, \pi) \models^* \mathrm{path}(\alpha)$ iff $s$ is the first state of $\pi$ and $(M, s) \models^* \alpha$,*
10. *$(M, \pi) \models^* \alpha \wedge \beta$ iff $(M, \pi) \models^* \alpha$ and $(M, \pi) \models^* \beta$,*
11. *$(M, \pi) \models^* \alpha \vee \beta$ iff $(M, \pi) \models^* \alpha$ or $(M, \pi) \models^* \beta$,*
12. *$(M, \pi) \models^* \alpha {\rightarrow} \beta$ iff $(M, \pi) \models^* \alpha$ implies $(M, \pi) \models^* \beta$,*
13. *$(M, \pi) \models^* \neg\alpha$ iff $(M, \pi) \not\models^* \alpha$,*
14. *$(M, \pi) \models^* \mathrm{X}\alpha$ iff $(M, \pi^1) \models^* \alpha$,*
15. *$(M, \pi) \models^* \mathrm{G}\alpha$ iff $\forall j \geq 0\ [(M, \pi^j) \models^* \alpha]$,*
16. *$(M, \pi) \models^* \mathrm{F}\alpha$ iff $\exists j \geq 0\ [(M, \pi^j) \models^* \alpha]$,*
17. *$(M, \pi) \models^* \alpha\mathrm{U}\beta$ iff $\exists j \geq 0\ [(M, \pi^j) \models^* \beta$ and $\forall 0 \leq k < j\ (M, \pi^k) \models^* \alpha]$,*
18. *$(M, \pi) \models^* \alpha\mathrm{R}\beta$ iff $\forall j \geq 0\ [(M, \pi^j) \models^* \beta$ or $\exists 0 \leq k < j\ (M, \pi^k) \models^* \alpha]$,*
19. *$(M, s) \models^* {\sim}{\sim}\alpha$ iff $(M, s) \models^* \alpha$,*
20. *$(M, s) \models^* {\sim}(\alpha \wedge \beta)$ iff $(M, s) \models^* {\sim}\alpha$ or $(M, s) \models^* {\sim}\beta$,*

21. $(M, s) \models^* \sim(\alpha \vee \beta)$ *iff* $(M, s) \models^* \sim\alpha$ *and* $(M, s) \models^* \sim\beta$,
22. $(M, s) \models^* \sim(\alpha \to \beta)$ *iff* $(M, s) \not\models^* \sim\alpha$ *and* $(M, s) \models^* \sim\beta$,
23. $(M, s) \models^* \sim\neg\alpha$ *iff* $(M, s) \not\models^* \sim\alpha$,
24. $(M, s) \models^* \sim\mathrm{E}\beta$ *iff for any path* $\pi$ *starting from* $s$, $(M, \pi) \models^* \sim\beta$,
25. $(M, s) \models^* \sim\mathrm{A}\beta$ *iff for some path* $\pi$ *starting from* $s$, $(M, \pi) \models^* \sim\beta$,
26. $(M, \pi) \models^* \sim\mathrm{path}(\alpha)$ *iff* $s$ *is the first state of* $\pi$ *and* $(M, s) \models^* \sim\alpha$,
27. $(M, \pi) \models^* \sim\sim\alpha$ *iff* $(M, \pi) \models^* \alpha$,
28. $(M, \pi) \models^* \sim(\alpha \wedge \beta)$ *iff* $(M, \pi) \models^* \sim\alpha$ *or* $(M, \pi) \models^* \sim\beta$,
29. $(M, \pi) \models^* \sim(\alpha \vee \beta)$ *iff* $(M, \pi) \models^* \sim\alpha$ *and* $(M, \pi) \models^* \sim\beta$,
30. $(M, \pi) \models^* \sim(\alpha \to \beta)$ *iff* $(M, \pi) \not\models^* \sim\alpha$ *and* $(M, \pi) \models^* \sim\beta$,
31. $(M, \pi) \models^* \sim\neg\alpha$ *iff* $(M, \pi) \not\models^* \sim\alpha$,
32. $(M, \pi) \models^* \sim\mathrm{X}\alpha$ *iff* $(M, \pi^1) \models^* \sim\alpha$,
33. $(M, \pi) \models^* \sim\mathrm{G}\alpha$ *iff* $\exists j \geq 0\ [(M, \pi^j) \models^* \sim\alpha]$,
34. $(M, \pi) \models^* \sim\mathrm{F}\alpha$ *iff* $\forall j \geq 0\ [(M, \pi^j) \models^* \sim\alpha]$,
35. $(M, \pi) \models^* \sim(\alpha \mathrm{U} \beta)$ *iff* $\forall j \geq 0\ [(M, \pi^j) \models^* \sim\beta$ *or* $\exists 0 \leq k < j\ (M, \pi^k) \models^* \sim\alpha]$,
36. $(M, \pi) \models^* \sim(\alpha \mathrm{R} \beta)$ *iff* $\exists j \geq 0\ [(M, \pi^j) \models^* \sim\beta$ *and* $\forall 0 \leq k < j\ (M, \pi^k) \models^* \sim\alpha]$.

*A state formula* $\alpha$ *is* valid under branching-time interpretation *in* pCTL$^*$ *(denoted* $\models^*_B \alpha$*) iff* $(M, s) \models^* \alpha$ *holds for any paraconsistent model* $M := (S, S_0, R, L^*)$*, any* $s \in S$*, and any paraconsistent satisfaction relation* $\models^*$ *on* $M$*. A path formula* $\beta$ *is* valid under linear-time interpretation *in* pCTL$^*$ *(denoted* $\models^*_L \alpha$*) iff* $(M, \pi) \models^* \alpha$ *holds for any paraconsistent model* $M := (S, S_0, R, L^*)$*, any path* $\pi$ *starting from* $s \in S$*, and any paraconsistent satisfaction relation* $\models^*$ *on* $M$*. A formula* $\alpha$ *is* valid *in* pCTL$^*$ *(denoted* $\models^* \alpha$*) iff* $\models^*_B \alpha$ *or* $\models^*_L \alpha$*.*

**Remark 4.5.** *We make the following remarks.*

1. *The following formulas are valid in* pCTL$^*$*: For any formulas* $\alpha$, $\beta$,
   (a) $\sim\sim\alpha \leftrightarrow \alpha$,
   (b) $\sim(\alpha \wedge \beta) \leftrightarrow \sim\alpha \vee \sim\beta$,
   (c) $\sim(\alpha \vee \beta) \leftrightarrow \sim\alpha \wedge \sim\beta$,
   (d) $\sim(\alpha \to \beta) \leftrightarrow \neg\sim\alpha \wedge \sim\beta$,
   (e) $\sim\neg\alpha \leftrightarrow \neg\sim\alpha$,
   (f) $\sim\mathrm{X}\alpha \leftrightarrow \mathrm{X}\sim\alpha$,
   (g) $\sim\mathrm{F}\alpha \leftrightarrow \mathrm{G}\sim\alpha$,
   (h) $\sim\mathrm{G}\alpha \leftrightarrow \mathrm{F}\sim\alpha$,
   (i) $\sim(\alpha \mathrm{U} \beta) \leftrightarrow (\sim\alpha)\mathrm{R}(\sim\beta)$,
   (j) $\sim(\alpha \mathrm{R} \beta) \leftrightarrow (\sim\alpha)\mathrm{U}(\sim\beta)$,
   (k) $\sim\mathrm{path}(\alpha) \leftrightarrow \mathrm{path}(\sim\alpha)$,
   (l) $\sim\mathrm{A}\alpha \leftrightarrow \mathrm{E}\sim\alpha$,
   (m) $\sim\mathrm{E}\alpha \leftrightarrow \mathrm{A}\sim\alpha$.
2. pCTL$^*$ *is paraconsistent with respect to* $\sim$*. The reason is explained as follows. Assume a paraconsistent model* $M = (S, S_0, R, L^*)$ *such that* $p \in L^*(s)$, $\sim p \in L^*(s)$ *and* $q \notin L^*(s)$ *for a pair of distinct propositional variables* $p$ *and* $q$*. Then,* $(M, s) \models^* (p \wedge \sim p) \to q$ *does not hold.*

*3.* pCTL* *is regarded as a four-valued logic. The reason is explained as follows. For each* $s \in S$ *and each formula* $\alpha$*, we can take one of the following four cases:*
*(a)* $\alpha$ *is verified at* $s$*, i.e.,* $(M, x) \models^* \alpha$,
*(b)* $\alpha$ *is falsified at* $s$*, i.e.,* $(M, x) \models^* {\sim}\alpha$,
*(c)* $\alpha$ *is both verified and falsified at* $x$,
*(d)* $\alpha$ *is neither verified nor falsified at* $x$.

### 4.2 Translation from pCTL* into CTL*

**Definition 4.6.** *Let* $\Phi$ *be a non-empty set of propositional variables, and* $\Phi'$ *be the set* $\{p' \mid p \in \Phi\}$ *of propositional variables. The language* $\mathcal{L}^p$ *(the set of formulas) of* pCTL* *is defined using* $\Phi$, $\wedge, \vee, \rightarrow, \neg$, X, G, F, U, R, A, E, path *and* $\sim$*. The language* $\mathcal{L}$ *of* CTL* *is obtained from* $\mathcal{L}^p$ *by adding* $\Phi'$ *and deleting* $\sim$.
*A mapping* $f$ *from* $\mathcal{L}^p$ *to* $\mathcal{L}$ *is defined inductively by:*

1. *for any* $p \in \Phi$, $f(p) := p$ *and* $f({\sim}p) := p' \in \Phi'$,
2. $f(\alpha \sharp \beta) := f(\alpha) \sharp f(\beta)$ *where* $\sharp \in \{\wedge, \vee, \rightarrow, \mathrm{U}, \mathrm{R}\}$,
3. $f(\sharp\alpha) := \sharp f(\alpha)$ *where* $\sharp \in \{\neg, \mathrm{X}, \mathrm{F}, \mathrm{G}, \mathrm{A}, \mathrm{E}\}$,
4. $f(\mathrm{path}(\alpha)) := \mathrm{path}(f(\alpha))$,
5. $f({\sim}{\sim}\alpha) := f(\alpha)$,
6. $f({\sim}(\alpha \wedge \beta)) := f({\sim}\alpha) \vee f({\sim}\beta)$,
7. $f({\sim}(\alpha \vee \beta)) := f({\sim}\alpha) \wedge f({\sim}\beta)$,
8. $f({\sim}(\alpha \rightarrow \beta)) := \neg f({\sim}\alpha) \wedge f({\sim}\beta)$,
9. $f({\sim}\sharp\alpha) := \sharp f({\sim}\alpha)$ *where* $\sharp \in \{\neg, \mathrm{X}\}$,
10. $f({\sim}\mathrm{G}\alpha) := \mathrm{F}f({\sim}\alpha)$,
11. $f({\sim}\mathrm{F}\alpha) := \mathrm{G}f({\sim}\alpha)$,
12. $f({\sim}(\alpha \mathrm{U} \beta)) := f({\sim}\alpha)\mathrm{R}f({\sim}\beta)$,
13. $f({\sim}(\alpha \mathrm{R} \beta)) := f({\sim}\alpha)\mathrm{U}f({\sim}\beta)$,
14. $f({\sim}\mathrm{A}\alpha) := \mathrm{E}f({\sim}\alpha)$,
15. $f({\sim}\mathrm{E}\alpha) := \mathrm{A}f({\sim}\alpha)$,
16. $f({\sim}\mathrm{path}(\alpha)) := \mathrm{path}(f({\sim}\alpha))$.

**Lemma 4.7.** *Let* $f$ *be the mapping defined in Definition 4.6. For any paraconsistent model* $M := (S, S_0, R, L^*)$ *of* pCTL**, and any paraconsistent satisfaction relation* $\models^*$ *on* $M$*, we can construct a model* $N := (S, S_0, R, L)$ *of* CTL* *and a satisfaction relation* $\models$ *on* $N$ *such that for any formula* $\alpha$ *in* $\mathcal{L}^p$ *and any state or path* $x$ *in* $S$*, i.e.,* $x$ *is a state in* $S$ *or a path constructed from* $S$*,*

$(M, x) \models^* \alpha$ *iff* $(N, x) \models f(\alpha)$.

**Proof.** Let $\Phi$ be a nonempty set of propositional variables, $\Phi^{\sim}$ be $\{{\sim}p \mid p \in \Phi\}$, and $\Phi'$ be $\{p' \mid p \in \Phi\}$. Suppose that $M$ is a paraconsistent model $(S, S_0, R, L^*)$ such that

$L^*$ is a mapping from $S$ to the power set of $\Phi \cup \Phi^{\sim}$.

We then define a model $N := (S, S_0, R, L)$ such that

1. $L$ is a mapping from $S$ to the power set of $\Phi \cup \Phi'$,
2. for any $s \in S$ and any $p \in \Phi$,
   (a) $p \in L^*(s)$ iff $p \in L(s)$,
   (b) $\sim\!p \in L^*(s)$ iff $p' \in L(s)$.

Then, this lemma is proved by induction on the complexity of $\alpha$.

- Base step:
  1. Case $\alpha \equiv p \in \Phi$: We obtain: $(M, s) \models^* p$ iff $p \in L^*(s)$ iff $p \in L(s)$ iff $(N, s) \models p$ iff $(N, s) \models f(p)$ (by the definition of $f$).
  2. We obtain: $(M, s) \models^* \sim\!p$ iff $\sim\!p \in L^*(s)$ iff $p' \in L(s)$ iff $(N, s) \models p'$ iff $(N, s) \models f(\sim\!p)$ (by the definition of $f$).
- Induction step: We show some cases.
  1. Case $\alpha \equiv \beta \wedge \gamma$: We obtain: $(M, x) \models^* \beta \wedge \gamma$ iff $(M, x) \models^* \beta$ and $(M, x) \models^* \gamma$ iff $(N, x) \models f(\beta)$ and $(N, x) \models f(\gamma)$ (by induction hypothesis) iff $(N, x) \models f(\beta) \wedge f(\gamma)$ iff $(N, x) \models f(\beta \wedge \gamma)$ (by the definition of $f$).
  2. Case $\alpha \equiv \beta \rightarrow \gamma$: We obtain: $(M, x) \models^* \beta \rightarrow \gamma$ iff $(M, x) \models^* \beta$ implies $(M, x) \models^* \gamma$ iff $(N, x) \models f(\beta)$ implies $(N, x) \models f(\gamma)$ (by induction hypothesis) iff $(N, x) \models f(\beta) \rightarrow f(\gamma)$ iff $(N, x) \models f(\beta \rightarrow \gamma)$ (by the definition of $f$).
  3. Case $\alpha \equiv \neg\beta$: We obtain: $(M, x) \models^* \neg\beta$ iff $(M, x) \not\models^* \beta$ iff $(N, x) \not\models f(\beta)$ (by induction hypothesis) iff $(N, x) \models \neg f(\beta)$ iff $(N, x) \models f(\neg\beta)$ (by the definition of $f$).
  4. Case $\alpha \equiv \sim\sim\!\beta$: We obtain: $(M, x) \models^* \sim\sim\!\beta$ iff $(M, x) \models^* \beta$ iff $(N, x) \models f(\beta)$ (by induction hypothesis) $(N, x) \models f(\sim\sim\!\beta)$ (by the definition of $f$).
  5. Case $\alpha \equiv \sim\!(\beta \wedge \gamma)$: We obtain: $(M, x) \models^* \sim\!(\beta \wedge \gamma)$ iff $(M, x) \models^* \sim\!\beta$ or $(M, x) \models^* \sim\!\gamma$ iff $(N, x) \models f(\sim\!\beta)$ or $(N, x) \models f(\sim\!\gamma)$ (by induction hypothesis) iff $(N, x) \models f(\sim\!\beta) \vee f(\sim\!\gamma)$ iff $(N, x) \models f(\sim\!(\beta \wedge \gamma))$ (by the definition of $f$).
  6. Case $\alpha \equiv \sim\!(\beta \rightarrow \gamma)$: We obtain: $(M, x) \models^* \sim\!(\beta \rightarrow \gamma)$ iff $(M, x) \not\models^* \sim\!\beta$ and $(M, s) \models^* \sim\!\gamma$ iff $(N, x) \not\models f(\sim\!\beta)$ and $(N, s) \models f(\sim\!\gamma)$ (by induction hypothesis) iff $(N, x) \models \neg f(\sim\!\beta) \wedge f(\sim\!\gamma)$ iff $(N, x) \models f(\sim\!(\beta \rightarrow \gamma))$ (by the definition of $f$).
  7. Case $\alpha \equiv \sim\neg\beta$: We obtain: $(M, x) \models^* \sim\neg\beta$ iff $(M, x) \not\models^* \sim\!\beta$ iff $(N, x) \not\models f(\sim\!\beta)$ (by induction hypothesis) iff $(N, x) \models \neg f(\sim\!\beta)$ iff $(N, x) \models f(\sim\neg\beta)$ (by the definition of $f$).
  8. Case $\alpha \equiv \mathrm{X}\beta$: We obtain: $(M, \pi) \models^* \mathrm{X}\beta$ iff $(M, \pi^1) \models^* \beta$ iff $(N, \pi^1) \models f(\beta)$ (by induction hypothesis) iff $(N, \pi) \models \mathrm{X}f(\beta)$ iff $(N, \pi) \models f(\mathrm{X}\beta)$ (by the definition of $f$).
  9. Case $\alpha \equiv \mathrm{G}\beta$: We obtain: $(M, \pi) \models^* \mathrm{G}\beta$ iff $\forall j \geq 0$ $[(M, \pi^j) \models^* \beta]$ iff $\forall j \geq 0$ $[(N, \pi^j) \models f(\beta)]$ (by induction hypothesis) iff $(N, \pi) \models \mathrm{G}f(\beta)$ iff $(N, \pi) \models f(\mathrm{G}\beta)$ (by the definition of $f$).
  10. Case $\alpha \equiv \beta\mathrm{U}\gamma$: We obtain:
      $(M, \pi) \models^* \beta\mathrm{U}\gamma$
      iff $\exists j \geq 0$ $[(M, \pi^j) \models^* \gamma$ and $\forall 0 \leq k < j$ $(M, \pi^k) \models^* \beta]$

iff $\exists j \geq 0$ [$(N, \pi^j) \models f(\gamma)$ and $\forall 0 \leq k < j$ $(N, \pi^k) \models f(\beta)$] (by induction hypothesis)
iff $(N, \pi) \models f(\beta)\mathrm{U}f(\gamma)$
iff $(N, \pi) \models f(\beta\mathrm{U}\gamma)$ (by the definition of $f$).

11. Case $\alpha \equiv {\sim}\mathrm{X}\beta$: We obtain: $(M, \pi) \models^* {\sim}\mathrm{X}\beta$ iff $(M, \pi^1) \models^* {\sim}\beta$ iff $(N, \pi^1) \models f({\sim}\beta)$ (by induction hypothesis) iff $(N, \pi) \models \mathrm{X}f({\sim}\beta)$ iff $(N, \pi) \models f({\sim}\mathrm{X}\beta)$ (by the definition of $f$).
12. Case $\alpha \equiv {\sim}\mathrm{G}\beta$: We obtain: $(M, \pi) \models^* {\sim}\mathrm{G}\beta$ iff $\exists j \geq 0$ [$(M, \pi^j) \models^* {\sim}\beta$] iff $\exists j \geq 0$ [$(N, \pi^j) \models f({\sim}\beta)$] (by induction hypothesis) iff $(N, \pi) \models \mathrm{F}f({\sim}\beta)$ iff $(N, \pi) \models f({\sim}\mathrm{G}\beta)$ (by the definition of $f$).
13. Case $\alpha \equiv {\sim}(\beta\mathrm{U}\gamma)$: We obtain:
    $(M, \pi) \models^* {\sim}(\beta\mathrm{U}\gamma)$
    iff $\forall j \geq 0$ [$(M, \pi^j) \models^* {\sim}\gamma$ or $\exists 0 \leq k < j$ $(M, \pi^k) \models^* {\sim}\beta$]
    iff $\forall j \geq 0$ [$(N, \pi^j) \models f({\sim}\gamma)$ or $\exists 0 \leq k < j$ $(N, \pi^k) \models f({\sim}\beta)$] (by induction hypothesis)
    iff $(N, \pi) \models f({\sim}\beta)\mathrm{R}f({\sim}\gamma)$
    iff $(N, \pi) \models f({\sim}(\beta\mathrm{U}\gamma))$ (by the definition of $f$).
14. Case $\alpha \equiv {\sim}(\beta\mathrm{R}\gamma)$: We obtain:
    $(M, \pi) \models^* {\sim}(\beta\mathrm{R}\gamma)$
    iff $\exists j \geq 0$ [$(M, \pi^j) \models^* {\sim}\gamma$ and $\forall 0 \leq k < j$ $(M, \pi^k) \models^* {\sim}\beta$]
    iff $\exists j \geq 0$ [$(N, \pi^j) \models f({\sim}\gamma)$ and $\forall 0 \leq k < j$ $(N, \pi^k) \models f({\sim}\beta)$] (by induction hypothesis)
    iff $(N, \pi) \models f({\sim}\beta)\mathrm{U}f({\sim}\gamma)$
    iff $(N, \pi) \models f({\sim}(\beta\mathrm{R}\gamma))$ (by the definition of $f$).
15. Case $\alpha \equiv {\sim}\mathrm{E}\beta$: We obtain:
    $(M, s) \models^* {\sim}\mathrm{E}\beta$
    iff for any path $\pi$ starting from $s$, $(M, \pi) \models^* {\sim}\beta$
    iff for any path $\pi$ starting from $s$, $(N, \pi) \models f({\sim}\beta)$ (by induction hypothesis)
    iff $(N, s) \models \mathrm{A}f({\sim}\beta)$
    iff $(N, s) \models f({\sim}\mathrm{E}\beta)$ (by the definition of $f$).
16. Case $\alpha \equiv {\sim}\mathrm{path}(\beta)$: We obtain:
    $(M, \pi) \models^* {\sim}\mathrm{path}(\beta)$
    iff $s$ is the first state of $\pi$, $(M, s) \models^* {\sim}\beta$
    iff $s$ is the first state of $\pi$, $(N, s) \models f({\sim}\beta)$ (by induction hypothesis)
    iff $(N, \pi) \models \mathrm{path}(f({\sim}\beta))$
    iff $(N, \pi) \models f({\sim}\mathrm{path}(\beta))$ (by the definition of $f$). ∎

**Lemma 4.8.** *Let $f$ be the mapping defined in Definition 4.6. For any model $N := (S, S_0, R, L)$ of* CTL*, *and any satisfaction relation $\models$ on $N$, we can construct a paraconsistent model $M := (S, S_0, R, L^*)$ of* pCTL* *and a paraconsistent satisfaction relation $\models^*$ on $M$ such that for any formula $\alpha$ in $\mathcal{L}^p$ and any state or path $x$ in $S$, i.e., $x$ is a state in $S$ or a path constructed from $S$,*

$$(N, x) \models f(\alpha) \textit{ iff } (M, x) \models^* \alpha.$$

**Proof.** Similar to the proof of Lemma 4.7. ∎

**Theorem 4.9 (Embedding from pCTL* into CTL*).** *Let $f$ be the mapping defined in Definition 4.6. For any formula $\alpha$,*

$\alpha$ *is valid in* pCTL* *iff* $f(\alpha)$ *is valid in* CTL*.

**Proof.** By Lemmas 4.7 and 4.8. ■

**Theorem 4.10 (Decidability of pCTL*).** *The validity, satisfiability, and model checking problems of* pCTL* *are decidable.*

**Proof.** Similar to the proof of Theorems 2.10 and 3.11. ■

**Remark 4.11.** *We remark that the complexities of the decision procedures for the validity, satisfiability, and model checking problems of* pCTL* *are the same as those of* CTL*, *since the translation function $f$ defined in Definition 4.6 is a polynomial time reduction.*

## 5 Illustrative Examples

### 5.1 First Example

We present a new illustrative example for inconsistency-tolerant model checking, as shown in Fig. 1 for representing the health of a person who has a tumor. The proposed example is regarded as a modification of the example presented in [21,26]. A NuSMV-based implementation of this example was presented by Endo in [14].

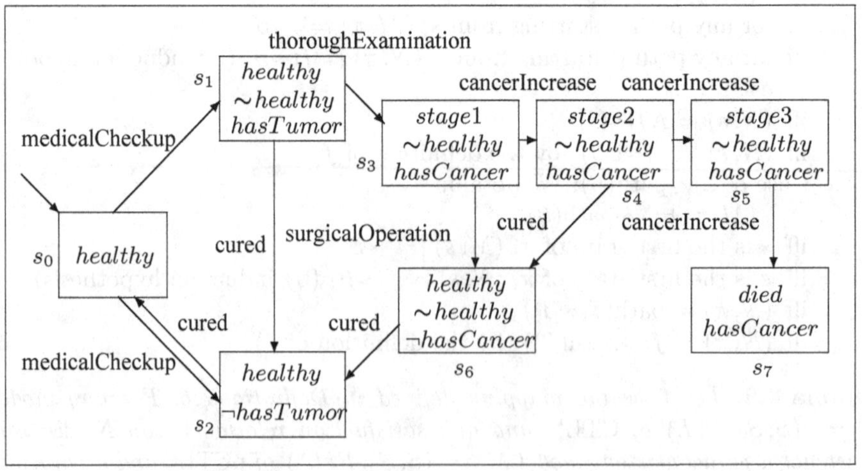


**Fig. 1.** A clinical reasoning process model for cancer.

In this example, a paraconsistent negation connective $\sim$ is used to express the negation of ambiguous concepts. If we cannot determine whether someone is healthy, then the ambiguous concept *healthy* can be represented by asserting the inconsistent formula $healthy \wedge {\sim}healthy$. This is well-formalized because $(healthy \wedge {\sim}healthy) \rightarrow \bot$ is not valid in pLTL, pCTL, and pCTL*. On the other hand, we can decide whether someone has a tumor. The decision is represented by $hasTumor$ or $\neg hasTumor$, where $(hasTumor \wedge \neg hasToumor) \rightarrow \bot$ is valid in pLTL, pCTL, and pCTL*.

In the model of Fig. 1, the initial state implies that a person is healthy. When a person undergoes a medical checkup, his or her state changes to one of the two states. If a tumor is detected in a person by the medical checkup, he or she is both healthy and not healthy (i.e., both *healthy* and ${\sim}healthy$ are true), because it is unknown if the tumor is malignant (i.e., cancer) or not. If cancer is detected in a person (i.e., the tumor is diagnosed with cancer), then ${\sim}healthy$ is true. This means that the person is not healthy, but he or she may return to good health if the cancer is completely removed by surgical operation. Moreover, when the cancer increases, the diagnosis reveals worse cancer. If the cancer is cured, the person will be healthy. Otherwise, if the cancer is not controlled, the person will die.

In what follows, we focus only on the pCTL verification. We can define a paraconsistent model (w.r.t. pCTL) for the model presented in Fig. 1 as follows:

$$M = \langle S, S_0, R, L^* \rangle$$

such that

1. $S = \{s_0, s_1, s_2, s_3, s_4, s_5, s_6, s_7\}$,
2. $S_0 = \{s_0\}$,
3. $R = \{(s_0, s_1), (s_0, s_2), (s_2, s_0), (s_1, s_2), (s_1, s_3), (s_3, s_4), (s_3, s_6), (s_4, s_5), (s_4, s_6), (s_5, s_7), (s_6, s_2), (s_5, s_7)\}$,
4. $L^*(s_0) = \{healthy\}$,
5. $L^*(s_1) = \{healthy, {\sim}healthy, hasTumor\}$,
6. $L^*(s_2) = \{healthy\}$,
7. $L^*(s_3) = \{stage1, {\sim}healthy, hasCancer\}$,
8. $L^*(s_4) = \{stage4, {\sim}healthy, hasCancer\}$,
9. $L^*(s_5) = \{stage3, {\sim}healthy, hasCancer\}$,
10. $L^*(s_6) = \{healthy, {\sim}healthy\}$,
11. $L^*(s_7) = \{died, hasCancer\}$.

Then, based on the embedding theorem of pCTL into CTL, we can construct the model (w.r.t. CTL) which just correspond to the paraconsistent model (w.r.t. pCTL) as follows:

$$N = \langle S, S_0, R, L \rangle$$

such that

1. $S = \{s_0, s_1, s_2, s_3, s_4, s_5, s_6, s_7\}$,
2. $S_0 = \{s_0\}$,
3. $R = \{(s_0, s_1), (s_0, s_2), (s_2, s_0), (s_1, s_2), (s_1, s_3), (s_3, s_4), (s_3, s_6), (s_4, s_5), (s_4, s_6), (s_5, s_7), (s_6, s_2), (s_5, s_7)\}$,

4. $L(s_0) = \{healthy\}$,
5. $L(s_1) = \{healthy, healthy', hasTumor\}$,
6. $L(s_2) = \{healthy\}$,
7. $L(s_3) = \{stage1, healthy', hasCancer\}$,
8. $L(s_4) = \{stage4, healthy', hasCancer\}$,
9. $L(s_5) = \{stage3, healthy', hasCancer\}$,
10. $L(s_6) = \{healthy, healthy'\}$,
11. $L(s_7) = \{died, hasCancer\}$.

By using the translation function of pCTL into CTL, any pCTL-formulas can be transformed into the corresponding CTL-formulas. We present a translation example for pCTL-formula. The pCTL-formula:

$$\sim\mathrm{AG}(\neg{\sim}healthy \rightarrow \mathrm{EF}healthy)$$

is transformed into the CTL-formula:

$$\mathrm{EF}(\neg\neg healthy \wedge \mathrm{AG}healthy')$$

as follows:

$$\begin{aligned} & f(\sim\mathrm{AG}(\neg{\sim}healthy \rightarrow \mathrm{EF}healthy)) \\ &= \mathrm{EF}f(\sim(\neg{\sim}healthy \rightarrow \mathrm{EF}healthy)) \\ &= \mathrm{EF}(\neg f(\sim\neg{\sim}healthy) \wedge f(\sim\mathrm{EF}healthy)) \\ &= \mathrm{EF}(\neg\neg f(\sim{\sim}healthy) \wedge f(\sim\mathrm{EF}healthy)) \\ &= \mathrm{EF}(\neg\neg f(healthy) \wedge f(\sim\mathrm{EF}healthy)) \\ &= \mathrm{EF}(\neg\neg healthy \wedge f(\sim\mathrm{EF}healthy)) \\ &= \mathrm{EF}(\neg\neg healthy \wedge \mathrm{AG}f(\sim healthy)) \\ &= \mathrm{EF}(\neg\neg healthy \wedge \mathrm{AG}healthy'). \end{aligned}$$

We now consider some verification examples. We can verify the statement

"Is there a state in which a person is both healthy and not healthy?"

This statement is true and expressed as:

$$\mathrm{EF}(healthy \wedge \sim healthy).$$

We can verify the statement

"Is there a state in which a dead person will not be alive again?"

This statement is true and expressed as:

$$\mathrm{EF}(died \wedge \neg\mathrm{EF}\neg died).$$

We can also verify the following statements:

1. "If a person is in the third stage of worse cancer, then he or she will die."
2. "If a person is in the second stage of worse cancer, then he or she will die."

The first statement is true, but the second statement is not true, and these statements are expressed as:

1. AG($\sim$*healthy* ∧ *hasCanser* ∧ *stage3*→EF*died*),
2. AG($\sim$*healthy* ∧ *hasCanser* ∧ *stage2*→EF*died*).

As already pointed out in [21,26], two negative expressions can be differently interpreted as

1. ¬*healthy* (definitely unhealthy),
2. $\sim$*healthy* (not healthy).

The first statement indicates that a person is definitely unhealthy that is inconsistent with his or her health. The second statement means that we can say that a person is not healthy but he or she may be healthy. The interpretation of the two negations leads to some useful verification examples. For example, the statement

"Is there a state in which a person is not definitely unhealthy?"

can be expressed as

EF¬¬*healthy*.

Moreover, the statement

"Is there a state in which it is not true that a person is not healthy?"

can be expressed as:

EF¬$\sim$*healthy*.

### 5.2 Second Example

We present another new illustrative example for inconsistency-tolerant model checking, as shown in Fig. 2 for representing the health of a person who is a drinker. In this example, an alcoholic will die in hospital after the second stage of *alcoholism*, also known as *alcohol use disorder* (AUD). This example is regarded as a modification of the example presented in [25] for hierarchical model checking. A NuSMV-based implementation of a similar example was presented by Yano in [34].

In what follows, we focus only on the pCTL verification. We can define a paraconsistent model (w.r.t. pCTL) for the reasoning process model presented in Fig. 2 as follows:

$$M = \langle S, S_0, R, L^* \rangle$$

such that

1. $S = \{s_0, s_1, s_2, s_3, s_4, s_5, s_6, s_7, s_8, s_9, s_{10}\}$,
2. $S_0 = \{s_0\}$,
3. $R = \{(s_0, s_1), (s_1, s_2), (s_1, s_3), (s_2, s_3), (s_2, s_4), (s_3, s_5), (s_4, s_6), (s_5, s_7), (s_6, s_8), (s_5, s_7), (s_6, s_8), (s_7, s_9), (s_8, s_{10}), (s_9, s_{10})\}$,
4. $L^*(s_0) = \{born\}$,

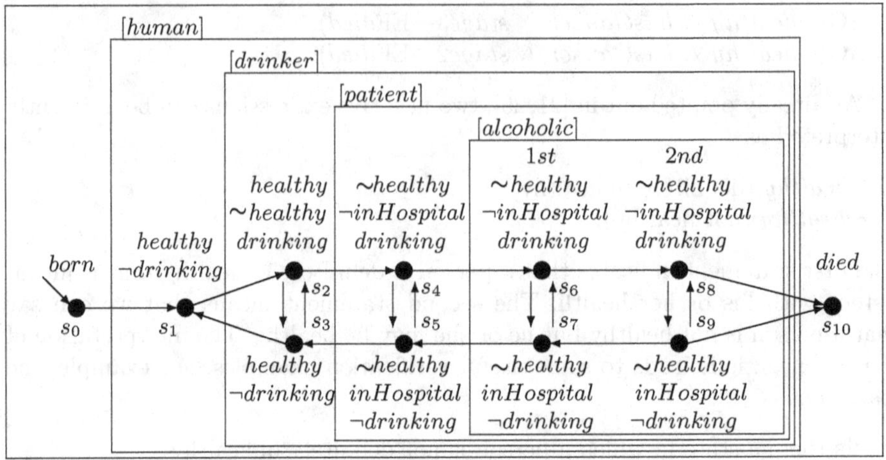


**Fig. 2.** A clinical reasoning process model for alcoholic.

5. $L^*(s_1) = \{human, healthy, {\sim}healthy\}$,
6. $L^*(s_2) = \{human, drinker, healthy, {\sim}healthy, drinking\}$,
7. $L^*(s_3) = \{human, drinker, healthy\}$,
8. $L^*(s_4) = \{human, drinker, patient, drinking\}$,
9. $L^*(s_5) = \{human, drinker, patient, {\sim}healthy, inHospital\}$,
10. $L^*(s_6) = \{human, drinker, patient, alcoholic, 1st, {\sim}healthy, drinking\}$,
11. $L^*(s_7) = \{human, drinker, patient, alcoholic, 1st, {\sim}healthy, inHospital\}$,
12. $L^*(s_8) = \{human, drinker, patient, alcoholic, 2nd, {\sim}healthy, drinking\}$,
13. $L^*(s_9) = \{human, drinker, patient, alcoholic, 2nd, {\sim}healthy, inHospital\}$,
14. $L^*(s_{10}) = \{died\}$.

Then, based on the embedding theorem of pCTL into CTL, we can construct the model (w.r.t. CTL) which just correspond to the paraconsistent model (w.r.t. pCTL) as follows:

$$N = \langle S, S_0, R, L\rangle$$

such that

1. $S = \{s_0, s_1, s_2, s_3, s_4, s_5, s_6, s_7, s_8, s_9, s_{10}\}$,
2. $S_0 = \{s_0\}$,
3. $R = \{(s_0, s_1), (s_1, s_2), (s_1, s_3), (s_2, s_3), (s_2, s_4), (s_3, s_5), (s_4, s_6), (s_5, s_7), (s_6, s_8), (s_5, s_7), (s_6, s_8), (s_7, s_9), (s_8, s_{10}), (s_9, s_{10})\}$,
4. $L(s_0) = \{born\}$,
5. $L(s_1) = \{human, healthy, healthy'\}$,
6. $L(s_2) = \{human, drinker, healthy, healthy', drinking\}$,
7. $L(s_3) = \{human, drinker, healthy\}$,
8. $L(s_4) = \{human, drinker, patient, drinking\}$,
9. $L(s_5) = \{human, drinker, patient, healthy', inHospital\}$,

10. $L(s_6) = \{human, drinker, patient, alcoholic, 1st, healthy', drinking\}$,
11. $L(s_7) = \{human, drinker, patient, alcoholic, 1st, healthy', inHospital\}$,
12. $L(s_8) = \{human, drinker, patient, alcoholic, 2nd, healthy', drinking\}$,
13. $L(s_9) = \{human, drinker, patient, alcoholic, 2nd, healthy', inHospital\}$,
14. $L(s_{10}) = \{died\}$.

By using a pCTL formula, we can represent a temporal property for the concept *alcoholic* as follows:

$$\mathrm{AF}(alcoholic \wedge {\sim}healthy \wedge \neg died \wedge \mathrm{AF}died) \wedge \mathrm{A}(\neg died\mathrm{U}(\mathrm{AG}died))).$$

This formula implies that every alcoholic is alive until they die.

By using a pCTL formula, we can also verify:

"Is there an alcoholic out of the hospital who is drinking in the second stage of the AUD?"

This statement is true and is expressed as follows:

$$\mathrm{EF}(alcoholic \wedge {\sim}healthy \wedge \neg inHospital \wedge drinking \wedge 2nd).$$

In addition, by using a pCTL formula, we can verify:

"Is there drinker who is both healthy and not healthy?"

This statement is true and is expressed as:

$$\mathrm{EF}(drinker \wedge drinking \wedge healthy \wedge {\sim}healty).$$

Moreover, we can verify:

"Is there a human drinker who will die?"

This statement is not true and is expressed by the following pCTL formula:

$$\mathrm{AG}(human \wedge drinker {\rightarrow} \mathrm{EF}died).$$

A counter example of this statement is as follows:

$$\cdots \rightarrow s_2 \rightarrow s_3 \rightarrow s_2 \rightarrow s_3 \rightarrow s_3 \rightarrow s_2 \rightarrow s_3 \rightarrow \cdots$$

which means that there are an infinite loop in between two states on the stage of drinker, i.e., a human drinker will not proceed to the next stage to die. This shows that the underlying reasoning process model is not appropriate for modeling the fact that every human will die.

## 6 Concluding Remarks

In this study, we proposed pLTL, pCTL, and pCTL* as novel versions of paraconsistent temporal logics. These provided a logical basis for inconsistency-tolerant model checking and were developed by extending the standard temporal logics LTL, CTL, and CTL*. These are also regarded as extensions of Belnap and Dunn's four-valued logics. The translations from pLTL into LTL, pCTL into CTL, and pCTL* into CTL* were defined and used to prove the theorems for embedding pLTL into LTL, pCTL into CTL, and pCTL* into CTL*. It was thus demonstrated that the standard LTL-, CTL-, and CTL*-based model checking algorithms can be repurposed for verifying inconsistent systems that are modeled and specified using pLTL, pCTL, and pCTL*. Some illustrative examples for verifying clinical reasoning process were presented based on the proposed logics and translations.

Finally, we note that the proposed framework can be applied to other new variants oLTL, oCTL, and oCTL* of pLTL, pCTL, and pCTL*, respectively. The proposed logics pLTL, pCTL, and pCTL* have the axiom schemes $\sim(\alpha \rightarrow \beta) \leftrightarrow \neg\sim\alpha \wedge \sim\beta$ and $\sim\neg\alpha \leftrightarrow \neg\neg\sim\alpha$ by De and Omori [9], using the paraconsistent negation connective $\sim$ and the classical negation connective $\neg$. These axiom schemes are known to be plausible candidates for combining $\sim$ and $\neg$ within a logic [9]. Our framework is equally applicable to the logics oLTL, oCTL, and oCTL*, which are obtained from pLTL, pCTL, and pCTL* by replacing the following clauses for $x \in \{i, s\}$:

1. $(M, x) \models^* \sim(\alpha{\rightarrow}\beta)$ iff $(M, x) \not\models^* \sim\alpha$ and $(M, x) \models^* \sim\beta$,
2. $(M, x) \models^* \sim\neg\alpha$ iff $(M, x) \not\models^* \sim\alpha$,

with the following clauses for $x \in \{i, s\}$, which correspond to the axiom schemes $\sim(\alpha{\rightarrow}\beta) \leftrightarrow \alpha \wedge \sim\beta$ and $\sim\neg\alpha \leftrightarrow \alpha$ by Odintsov [28]:

1. $(M, x) \models^* \sim(\alpha{\rightarrow}\beta)$ iff $(M, x) \models^* \alpha$ and $(M, x) \models^* \sim\beta$,
2. $(M, x) \models^* \sim\neg\alpha$ iff $(M, x) \models^* \alpha$.

By applying appropriate modifications to the translation functions of pLTL, pCTL, and pCTL*, we obtain the embedding theorems of oLTL into LTL, oCTL into CTL, and oCTL* into CTL*, in the same manner as with pLTL, pCTL and pCTL*.

**Acknowledgments.** This research was supported by JSPS KAKENHI Grant Numbers JP16KK0007 and JP18K11171. This research has been supported by the Kayamori Foundation of Informational Science Advancement and JSPS Core-to-Core Program (A. Advanced Research Networks).

## References

1. Almukdad, A., Nelson, D.: Constructible falsity and inexact predicates. J. Symbol. Log. **49**, 231–233 (1984)
2. Béziau, J.-Y.: A new four-valued approach to modal logic. Logique et Analyse **54**(213), 109–121 (2011)
3. Belnap, N.D.: A useful four-valued logic. In: Epstein, G., Dunn, J.M. (eds.) Modern Uses of Multiple-Valued Logic, pp. 5–37. Reidel, Dordrecht (1977)
4. Belnap, N.D.: How a computer should think. In: Ryle, G. (ed.) Contemporary Aspects of Philosophy, pp. 30–56. Oriel Press, Stocksfield (1977)
5. Chen, D., Wu, J.: Reasoning about inconsistent concurrent systems: a non-classical temporal logic. In: Wiedermann, J., Tel, G., Pokorný, J., Bieliková, M., Štuller, J. (eds.) SOFSEM 2006. LNCS, vol. 3831, pp. 207–217. Springer, Heidelberg (2006). https://doi.org/10.1007/11611257_18
6. Clarke, E.M., Emerson, E.A.: Design and synthesis of synchronization skeletons using branching time temporal logic. In: Kozen, D. (ed.) Logic of Programs 1981. LNCS, vol. 131, pp. 52–71. Springer, Heidelberg (1982). https://doi.org/10.1007/BFb0025774
7. Clarke, E.M., Grumberg, O., Peled, D.A.: Model Checking. The MIT Press, Cambridge (1999)
8. da Costa, N.C.A., Béziau, J., Bueno, O.A.: Aspects of paraconsistent logic. Bull. IGPL **3**(4), 597–614 (1995)
9. De, M., Omori, H.: Classical negation and expansions of Belnap-Dunn logic. Studia Logica **103**(4), 825–851 (2015)
10. Dunn, J.M.: Intuitive semantics for first-degree entailment and 'coupled trees'. Philos. Stud. **29**(3), 149–168 (1976)
11. Easterbrook, S., Chechik, M.: A framework for multi-valued reasoning over inconsistent viewpoints. In: Proceedings of the 23rd International Conference on Software Engineering (ICSE 2001), pp. 411–420 (2001)
12. Emerson, E.A., Halpern, J.Y.: "Sometimes" and "not never" revisited: on branching versus linear time temporal logic. J. ACM **33**(1), 151–178 (1986)
13. Emerson, E.A., Sistla, P.: Deciding full branching time logic. Inf. Control **61**, 175–201 (1984)
14. Endo, K.: Applications of inconsistency-tolerant model checking to clinical reasoning verification. Bachelor thesis, Faculty of Science and Engineering, Department of Human Information Systems, Teikyo University, 59 p. (2018). (in Japanese)
15. Gurevich, Y.: Intuitionistic logic with strong negation. Studia Logica **36**, 49–59 (1977)
16. Holzmann, G.J.: The SPIN Model Checker: Primer and Reference Manual. Addison-Wesley, Boston (2006)
17. Kamide, N.: Extended full computation-tree logics for paraconsistent model checking. Log. Log. Philos. **15**(3), 251–276 (2006)
18. Kamide, N.: Inconsistency-tolerant temporal reasoning with hierarchical information. Inf. Sci. **320**, 140–155 (2015)
19. Kamide, N.: Paraconsistent double negation that can simulate classical negation. In: Proceedings of the 46th IEEE International Symposium on Multiple-Valued Logic (ISMVL 2016), pp. 131–136 (2016)
20. Kamide, N., Endo, K.: Logics and translations for inconsistency-tolerant model checking. In: Proceedings of the 10th International Conference on Agents and Artificial Intelligence (ICAART 2018), vol. 2, pp. 191–200 (2018)

21. Kamide, N., Kaneiwa, K.: Paraconsistent negation and classical negation in computation tree logic. In: Proceedings of the 2nd International Conference on Agents and Artificial Intelligence (ICAART 2010), vol. 1, pp. 464–469. INSTICC Press (2010)
22. Kamide, N., Koizumi, D.: Method for combining paraconsistency and probability in temporal reasoning. J. Adv. Comput. Intell. Intell. Inform. **20**, 813–827 (2016)
23. Kamide, N., Shramko, Y.: Embedding from multilattice logic into classical logic and vice versa. J. Log. Comput. **27**(5), 1549–1575 (2017)
24. Kamide, N., Wansing, H.: A paraconsistent linear-time temporal logic. Fundamenta Informaticae **106**(1), 1–23 (2011)
25. Kamide, N., Yano, R.: Logics and translations for hierarchical model checking. In: Proceedings of the 21st International Conference on Knowledge-Based and Intelligent Information & Engineering Systems, vol. 112, pp. 31–40 (2017). (Procedia Comput. Sci.)
26. Kaneiwa, K., Kamide, N.: Paraconsistent computation tree logic. New Gener. Comput. **29**(4), 391–408 (2011)
27. Nelson, D.: Constructible falsity. J. Symbol. Log. **14**, 16–26 (1949)
28. Odintsov, S.P.: The class of extensions of Nelson paraconsistent logic. Studia Logica **80**, 291–320 (2005)
29. Pnueli, A.: The temporal logic of programs. In: Proceedings of the 18th IEEE Symposium on Foundations of Computer Science, pp. 46–57 (1977)
30. Priest, G.: Paraconsistent logic. In: Gabbay, D., Guenthner, F. (eds.) Handbook of Philosophical Logic, vol. 6, 2nd edn. Kluwer Academic Publishers, Dordrecht (2002)
31. Rautenberg, W.: Klassische und nicht-klassische Aussagenlogik. Vieweg, Braunschweig (1979)
32. Vorob'ev, N.: A constructive propositional logic with strong negation. Doklady Akademii Nauk SSSR **85**, 465–468 (1952). (in Russian)
33. Wansing, H.: The Logic of Information Structures. LNAI, vol. 681, pp. 1–163. Springer, Heidelberg (1993). https://doi.org/10.1007/3-540-56734-8
34. Yano, R.: Applications of hierarchical model checking to hierarchical reasoning process verification. Bachelor thesis, Faculty of Science and Engineering, Department of Human Information Systems, Teikyo University, 52 p. (2018). (in Japanese)
35. Zaitsev, D.: Generalized relevant logic and models of reasoning. Moscow State Lomonosov University doctoral dissertation (2012)

# Inherited Properties of $\mathcal{FL}_0$ Concept Similarity Measure Under Preference Profile

Teeradaj Racharak[1,2(✉)] and Satoshi Tojo[2]

[1] School of Information, Computer, and Communication Technology, Sirindhorn International Institute of Technology, Thammasat University, Pathum Thani, Thailand
r.teeradaj@gmail.com, racharak@jaist.ac.jp
[2] School of Information Science, Japan Advanced Institute of Science and Technology, Ishikawa, Japan
tojo@jaist.ac.jp

**Abstract.** Measuring concept similarity in ontologies is central to the functioning of many techniques such as ontology matching, ontology learning, and many related applications in the bio-medical domain. Generally, it can be seen as a generalization of concept equivalence problem in Description Logics. That is, any two concepts are equivalent if and only if their similarity degree is one. The recently introduced measures can be used to identify such kind of similarity degree between $\mathcal{FL}_0$ concept descriptions not only w.r.t. the objective factors (*e.g.* the structure of concept descriptions) but also w.r.t. the subjective factors called *preference profile* (*e.g.* the agent's preferences). In this paper, we provide proofs of theorems about their inherited properties including their relationship to the classical reasoning problem of concept equivalence.

**Keywords:** Concept similarity measure · Semantic web ontology Preference profile · Description Logics

## 1 Introduction

Description Logics (DLs) are a family of logic-based knowledge representation formalisms that are tailored for representing the knowledge of an application domain in a structured and formally well-understood way [1]. Most of DLs are decidable fragments of first-order logic (FOL) with clearly defined computational properties. DLs have been used as the logical underpinnings of the standard ontology languages for the semantic web *viz.* OWL and OWL 2. This close connection gives an advantage that the extensive DLs literature and implementation experiences can be directly exploited by OWL tools. The availability of a formal and unambiguous semantics of DLs, which is based on Tarski-style semantics of FOL, enables to formalize and design algorithms for a number of reasoning


J. van den Herik and A. P. Rocha (Eds.): ICAART 2018, LNAI 11352, pp. 343–360, 2019.
https://doi.org/10.1007/978-3-030-05453-3_16

services. These make the development of ontology applications to become prominent. For instance, the subsumption service determines subconcept-superconcept relationships of concepts in an ontology *i.e.* concept $C$ is subsumed by concept $D$ iff all instances of $C$ are instances of $D$ (*cf.* Definition 1 for its formal definition). The concept equivalence service can be defined as bi-directional subsumption between two concepts and can be seen as an operation for comparing concepts. For instance, comparing $\mathsf{Man}$ and $\mathsf{Person}$ with their natural definitions, it is not hard to be convinced that both concepts are not equivalent because $\mathsf{Man}$ is a subconcept of $\mathsf{Person}$ but not vice versa. Unfortunately, these traditional services merely give two-valued responses *i.e.* inferring two concepts are equivalent or not. Consequently, a considerable amount of research effort has been devoted to develop an elastic notion of concept equivalence called *concept similarity measure* for identifying the degree of commonalities between concepts.

Intuitively, concept similarity refers to human judgment of a degree to which a pair of concepts in question is similar. This notion has been employed in various kinds of applications. For example, it was employed in bio-medical ontology-based applications to discover functional similarities of gene such as [2], it is often used by ontology alignment algorithms such as [3], it can be employed in approximate reasoning such as [4,5] and in analogical reasoning such as [6,7]. Computational approaches for concept similarity are known as concept similarity measure and can be defined in several means (*cf.* Sect. 5 for related work). Our approach (*cf.* Sects. 3 and 4) generalizes from the concept equivalence in DLs, which means that it can identify the degree of concept equivalence when two concepts are not in this relation. Furthermore, when concept similarity is employed by a cognitive agent, the degree of similarity may vary w.r.t. his/her need and preferences. Example 1 illustrates such a case in which concept similarity measured not only w.r.t. objective factors (but also w.r.t. subjective factors) can give more intuitive results.

*Example 1.* An agent A is searching for a hotel room during his vacation. At that moment, he prefers to stay in a Japanese-style room or something similar. In the following, his desired room may be expressed as the concept $\mathsf{DesiredRoom}$. Suppose $\mathsf{RoomA}$ and $\mathsf{RoomB}$ are concepts in a room ontology as follows:

$$\begin{aligned} \mathsf{DesiredRoom} &\sqsubseteq \mathsf{Room} \sqcap \forall \mathsf{floor}.\mathsf{Tatami} \\ \mathsf{RoomA} &\sqsubseteq \mathsf{Room} \sqcap \forall \mathsf{floor}.\mathsf{Bamboo} \\ \mathsf{RoomB} &\sqsubseteq \mathsf{Room} \sqcap \forall \mathsf{floor}.\mathsf{Marble} \end{aligned}$$

Without considering his preference, it may be understood that both $\mathsf{RoomA}$ and $\mathsf{RoomB}$ are equally similar to $\mathsf{DesiredRoom}$. However, taking into account his preference, $\mathsf{RoomA}$ may appear more suitable (assuming that tatami and bamboo invoke similar feeling). In other words, he will not be happy if an intelligent system happens to choose $\mathsf{RoomB}$ for him.

Other cognitive examples can be found in [8] where intended behaviors (or desirable properties) of similarity measures were investigated. For example, the author of [8] claimed that people usually speak "the portrait resembles the person" rather than "the person resembles the portrait". Also, people usually say that "the son resembles the father" rather than "the father resembles the son". These examples clearly point out that cognitive agents make similarity judgment under some subjective factors. Unfortunately, existing measures do not usually take into account subjective factors during computational procedures, though some may consider such as [9,10].

In order to develop similarity measures which can be performed under subjective factors, [11] has introduced a general notion called *concept similarity measure under preference profile* (and later extended in [12]). Instead of implicitly including preferential elements in the computational representation, [12] clearly separated those preferential elements from the computational procedures. Hence, the general notion makes an investigation of concept similarity measure under subjective factors more easily and provides more natural understanding when concept similarity measures are used under subjective factors.

The main part of this new paper is to study proofs of theorems about the intricate properties of measures defined in [13]. In order to study this, we had to rely on the earlier publication from which we adapted the introduction. We also added [24–26] in the related literature. Our contributions are summarized as follows. Firstly, since our proposed measures are generalized from the procedures for proving concept subsumption (indeed, concept equivalence), we show the relationships between our approaches and these two classical procedures *i.e.* our approaches can be considered as the elastic versions of them. Secondly, we also study the relationship between measuring concept similarity without regard to the agent's preferences and the one with regard to the agent's preferences. Finally, we show that the approaches can be used to decide whether two arbitrary concept names are similar to each other under the agent's preferences or not. We note that this work concentrates on the DL $\mathcal{FL}_0$, which offers the constructors conjunction ($\sqcap$), value restriction ($\forall r.C$), and the top concept ($\top$). Preliminaries and the conclusion are discussed in Sects. 2 and 6, respectively.

## 2 Preliminaries

In this section, we review the basics of Description Logic $\mathcal{FL}_0$ in Subsect. 2.1, particularly its syntax, semantics, and normal form which is used by concept similarity measures for $\mathcal{FL}_0$ in Sects. 3 and 4. Then, we review the notion of preference profile in Subsect. 2.2.

### 2.1 Description Logic $\mathcal{FL}_0$

We assume finite sets $\mathsf{CN}$ of concept names and $\mathsf{RN}$ of role names that are fixed and disjoint. The set of concept descriptions, or simply concepts, for a specific DL $\mathcal{L}$ is denoted by $\mathsf{Con}(\mathcal{L})$. The set $\mathsf{Con}(\mathcal{FL}_0)$ of all $\mathcal{FL}_0$ concepts can be inductively defined by the following grammar:

$$\mathsf{Con}(\mathcal{FL}_0) ::= A \mid \top \mid C \sqcap D \mid \forall r.C$$

where $\top$ denotes the *top concept*, $A \in \mathsf{CN}$, $r \in \mathsf{RN}$, and $C, D \in \mathsf{Con}(\mathcal{FL}_0)$. Conventionally, concept names are denoted by $A$ and $B$, concept descriptions are denoted by $C$ and $D$, and role names are denoted by $r$ and $s$, all possibly with subscripts.

*Terminology* or *TBox* $\mathcal{T}$ is a finite set of primitive concept definitions and full concept definitions, whose syntax is an expression of the form $A \sqsubseteq D$ and $A \equiv D$, respectively. A TBox is called *unfoldable* if it contains at most one concept definition for each concept name in $\mathsf{CN}$ and does not contain cyclic dependencies. Concept names occurring on the left-hand side of concept definitions are called *defined concept names* (denoted by $\mathsf{CN}^{\mathsf{def}}$), all other concept names are *primitive concept names* (denoted by $\mathsf{CN}^{\mathsf{pri}}$). A primitive definition $A \sqsubseteq D$ can easily be transformed into a semantically equivalent full definition $A \equiv X \sqcap D$ where $X$ is a fresh concept name. When TBox $\mathcal{T}$ is unfoldable, concept names can be expanded by exhaustively replacing all defined concept names by their definitions until only primitive concept names remain. Such concept names are called *fully expanded concept names.*[1]

Interpretation $\mathcal{I}$ is a pair $\mathcal{I} = \langle \Delta^{\mathcal{I}}, \cdot^{\mathcal{I}} \rangle$, where $\Delta^{\mathcal{I}}$ is a non-empty set representing the domain of the interpretation and $\cdot^{\mathcal{I}}$ is an interpretation function which assigns to every concept name $A$ a set $A^{\mathcal{I}} \subseteq \Delta^{\mathcal{I}}$, and to every role name $r$ a binary relation $r^{\mathcal{I}} \subseteq \Delta^{\mathcal{I}} \times \Delta^{\mathcal{I}}$. The interpretation function $\cdot^{\mathcal{I}}$ is inductively extended to $\mathcal{FL}_0$ concepts in the usual manner:

$$\top^{\mathcal{I}} = \Delta^{\mathcal{I}}; \qquad (C \sqcap D)^{\mathcal{I}} = C^{\mathcal{I}} \cap D^{\mathcal{I}};$$
$$(\forall r.C)^{\mathcal{I}} = \{a \in \Delta^{\mathcal{I}} \mid \forall b \in \Delta^{\mathcal{I}} : (a, b) \in r^{\mathcal{I}} \rightarrow b \in C^{\mathcal{I}}\},$$

Interpretation $\mathcal{I}$ is said to be a *model* of TBox $\mathcal{T}$ (in symbols, $\mathcal{I} \models \mathcal{T}$) if it satisfies all axioms in $\mathcal{T}$. $\mathcal{I}$ satisfies axioms $A \sqsubseteq C$ and $A \equiv C$, respectively, if $A^{\mathcal{I}} \subseteq C^{\mathcal{I}}$ and $A^{\mathcal{I}} = C^{\mathcal{I}}$. The main inference problem in $\mathcal{FL}_0$ is the concept subsumption problem.

**Definition 1 (Concept Subsumption).** *Given $C, D \in \mathsf{Con}(\mathcal{FL}_0)$ and TBox $\mathcal{T}$, $C$ is* subsumed *by $D$ w.r.t. $\mathcal{T}$ (denoted by $C \sqsubseteq_{\mathcal{T}} D$) if $C^{\mathcal{I}} \subseteq D^{\mathcal{I}}$ for every model $\mathcal{I}$ of $\mathcal{T}$. Moreover, $C$ and $D$ are* equivalent *w.r.t. $\mathcal{T}$ (denoted by $C \equiv_{\mathcal{T}} D$) if $C \sqsubseteq_{\mathcal{T}} D$ and $D \sqsubseteq_{\mathcal{T}} C$.*

When TBox $\mathcal{T}$ is clear from the context, we simply drop $\mathcal{T}$, *i.e.* $C \sqsubseteq D$ or $C \equiv D$.

Using the rewrite rule $\forall r.(C \sqcap D) \longrightarrow \forall r.C \sqcap \forall r.D$ together with the associativity, the commutativity, and the idempotence of $\sqcap$, any $\mathcal{FL}_0$ concepts can be transformed into an equivalent one of the form $\forall r_1 \ldots \forall r_n.A$ where $\{r_1, \ldots, r_n\} \subseteq \mathsf{RN}$ and $A \in \mathsf{CN}$. Such concepts can be abbreviated as $\forall r_1 \ldots r_n.A$ where $r_1 \ldots r_n$ is viewed as a word $w$ over the alphabet of all role names. We note that when $n = 0$, *i.e.* the empty word $\epsilon$, $\forall \epsilon.A$ corresponds to $A$. Furthermore, a conjunction of the form $\forall w_1.A \sqcap \cdots \sqcap \forall w_m.A$ can be abbreviated as

[1] In this work, we assume that concept names are fully expanded and the TBox can be omitted.

$\forall L.A$ where $L := \{w_1, \ldots, w_m\}$ is a finite set of words over the alphabet. We also note that $\forall\emptyset.A$ corresponds to $\top$. Using these abbreviations, any concepts $C, D \in \mathsf{Con}(\mathcal{FL}_0)$ can be rewritten as:

$$C \equiv \forall U_1.A_1 \sqcap \cdots \sqcap \forall U_k.A_k \tag{1}$$

$$D \equiv \forall V_1.A_1 \sqcap \cdots \sqcap \forall V_k.A_k \tag{2}$$

where $\{A_1, \ldots, A_k\} \subseteq \mathsf{CN}$ and $U_i, V_i$ are finite sets of words over the alphabet of role names. This normal form provides us the following characterization of subsumption in $\mathcal{FL}_0$ [14]:

$$C \sqsubseteq D \Longleftrightarrow U_i \supseteq V_i \text{ for all } i, 1 \leq i \leq k \tag{3}$$

**Theorem 1** ([15]). *Concept subsumption and concept equivalence without TBox (i.e. when the TBox is empty) in $\mathcal{FL}_0$ can be decided in polynomial time.*

*Example 2* (Continuation of Example 1). After unfolding and transforming into normal forms, each concept is represented as:[2]

$$\begin{aligned}
\mathsf{DesiredRoom} &\equiv \forall\{\epsilon\}.X \sqcap \forall\emptyset.Y \sqcap \forall\emptyset.Z \sqcap \forall\{\epsilon\}.\mathsf{R} \\
&\quad \sqcap \forall\{\mathsf{f}\}.\mathsf{T} \sqcap \forall\emptyset.\mathsf{B} \sqcap \forall\emptyset.\mathsf{M} \\
\mathsf{RoomA} &\equiv \forall\emptyset.X \sqcap \forall\{\epsilon\}.Y \sqcap \forall\emptyset.Z \sqcap \forall\{\epsilon\}.\mathsf{R} \\
&\quad \sqcap \forall\{\mathsf{f}\}.\mathsf{B} \sqcap \forall\emptyset.\mathsf{T} \sqcap \forall\emptyset.\mathsf{M} \\
\mathsf{RoomB} &\equiv \forall\emptyset.X \sqcap \forall\emptyset.Y \sqcap \forall\{\epsilon\}.Z \sqcap \forall\{\epsilon\}.\mathsf{R} \\
&\quad \sqcap \forall\{\mathsf{f}\}.\mathsf{M} \sqcap \forall\emptyset.\mathsf{T} \sqcap \forall\emptyset.\mathsf{B}
\end{aligned}$$

where $X, Y$, and $Z$ are fresh concept names. Using Eq. 3, it yields that $\mathsf{DesiredRoom} \not\sqsubseteq_\emptyset \mathsf{RoomA}$ and $\mathsf{DesiredRoom} \not\sqsubseteq_\emptyset \mathsf{RoomB}$.

### 2.2 Preference Profile

*Preference profile* was first introduced in [16] as a collection of preferential elements in which any developments of concept similarity measure should consider (later, it was improved in [12]). Its first intuition is to model different forms of preferences (of an agent) based on concept names and role names. Measures adopted this notion are flexible to be tuned by an agent and can determine the degree of similarity conformable to that agent's perception. We give its formal definition of each preferential aspect in the following definition.

**Definition 2 (Preference Profile** [12]**).** *Let* $\mathsf{CN}^{\mathsf{pri}}(\mathcal{T})$, $\mathsf{RN}^{\mathsf{pri}}(\mathcal{T})$, *and* $\mathsf{RN}(\mathcal{T})$ *be a set of primitive concept names occurring in* $\mathcal{T}$, *a set of primitive role names occurring in* $\mathcal{T}$, *and a set of role names occurring in* $\mathcal{T}$, *respectively. A* preference profile *(denoted by* $\pi$*) is a quintuple* $\langle \mathfrak{i}^{\mathtt{c}}, \mathfrak{i}^{\mathtt{r}}, \mathfrak{s}^{\mathtt{c}}, \mathfrak{s}^{\mathtt{r}}, \mathfrak{d} \rangle$ *where* $\mathfrak{i}^{\mathtt{c}}, \mathfrak{i}^{\mathtt{r}}, \mathfrak{s}^{\mathtt{c}}, \mathfrak{s}^{\mathtt{r}}$, *and* $\mathfrak{d}$ *are "partial" functions such that:*

- $\mathfrak{i}^{\mathtt{c}} : \mathsf{CN}^{\mathsf{pri}}(\mathcal{T}) \to [0, 2]$ *is called a* primitive concept importance;

[2] Obvious abbreviations are used for succinctness.

- $\mathfrak{i}^{\mathfrak{r}} : \mathsf{RN}(\mathcal{T}) \to [0,2]$ *is called a* role importance;
- $\mathfrak{s}^{\mathfrak{c}} : \mathsf{CN}^{\mathsf{pri}}(\mathcal{T}) \times \mathsf{CN}^{\mathsf{pri}}(\mathcal{T}) \to [0,1]$ *is called a* primitive concepts similarity;
- $\mathfrak{s}^{\mathfrak{r}} : \mathsf{RN}^{\mathsf{pri}}(\mathcal{T}) \times \mathsf{RN}^{\mathsf{pri}}(\mathcal{T}) \to [0,1]$ *is called a* primitive roles similarity; *and*
- $\mathfrak{d} : \mathsf{RN}(\mathcal{T}) \to [0,1]$ *is called a* role discount factor.

We discuss the interpretation of each above function in order. Firstly, for any $A \in \mathsf{CN}^{\mathsf{pri}}(\mathcal{T})$, $\mathfrak{i}^{\mathfrak{c}}(A) = 1$ captures an expression of normal importance on $A$, $\mathfrak{i}^{\mathfrak{c}}(A) > 1$ and $\mathfrak{i}^{\mathfrak{c}}(A) < 1$ indicate that A has higher and lower importance, respectively, and $\mathfrak{i}^{\mathfrak{c}}(A) = 0$ indicates that $A$ has no importance to the agent. Secondly, we define the interpretation of $\mathfrak{i}^{\mathfrak{r}}$ in the similar fashion as $\mathfrak{i}^{\mathfrak{c}}$ for any $r \in \mathsf{RN}(\mathcal{T})$. Thirdly, for any $A, B \in \mathsf{CN}^{\mathsf{pri}}(\mathcal{T})$, $\mathfrak{s}^{\mathfrak{c}}(A, B) = 1$ captures an expression of total similarity between $A$ and $B$ and $\mathfrak{s}^{\mathfrak{c}}(A, B) = 0$ captures an expression of total dissimilarity between $A$ and $B$. Fourthly, the interpretation of $\mathfrak{s}^{\mathfrak{r}}$ is defined in the similar fashion as $\mathfrak{s}^{\mathfrak{c}}$ for any $r, s \in \mathsf{RN}^{\mathsf{pri}}(\mathcal{T})$. Lastly, for any $r \in \mathsf{RN}(\mathcal{T})$, $\mathfrak{d}(r) = 1$ captures an expression of total importance on a role (over a corresponding nested concept) and $\mathfrak{d}(r) = 0$ captures an expression of total importance on a nested concept (over a corresponding role), *e.g.* let $\mathfrak{d}(r_1) = 0.3$, then the degree of similarity under this preference between $\forall r_1.A$ and $\forall r_1.B$ can be understood as 0.3 degree because the identical occurrence of $r_1$ contributes 0.3 importance.

It is worth noticing that role names appearing in $\mathcal{FL}_0$ are always primitive. This suggests that both $\mathsf{RN}^{\mathsf{pri}}(\mathcal{T})$ and $\mathsf{RN}(\mathcal{T})$ can be considered identically in Definition 2. Furthermore, due to the employed characterization, $\mathfrak{i}^{\mathfrak{r}}$, $\mathfrak{s}^{\mathfrak{r}}$, and $\mathfrak{d}$ are not used in this paper.

## 3 Properties of Subsumption Degree Under Preference Profile in Description Logic $\mathcal{FL}_0$

The idea of computing subsumption degree under preference profile between $\mathcal{FL}_0$ concepts was proposed in [13] in which the computational approaches were derived from the characterization of language inclusion. Their methodologies are outlined as follows:

1. Generalize the notion of concept subsumption to the notion of subsumption degree, which contributes to a "concrete" concept similarity measure as its immediate outcome;
2. Generalize the notion of subsumption degree to the notion of subsumption degree under the agent's preferences; and
3. Generalize the logical conjunction (*i.e.* "and") for aggregating two numerical values to result in a unit interval.

Their actual definitions are immediately included in the following for the purposes of showing their inherited properties. Definitions 3 and 4 are the immediate results of step 1 mentioned above. Definition 6 is also the immediate result of step 2 mentioned above.

**Definition 3 (Skeptical $\mathcal{FL}_0$ Subsumption Degree).** *Let $C, D \in \mathsf{Con}(\mathcal{FL}_0)$ be in their normal forms and $\mathsf{W}(E, A)$ be a set of words w.r.t. the concept $E$ and the primitive $A$. Then, a* skeptical $\mathcal{FL}_0$ degree *from $C$ to $D$ (denoted by $C \rightsquigarrow^s D$) is defined as follows:*

$$C \rightsquigarrow^s D = \frac{|\{P \in \mathsf{CN}^{\mathsf{pri}} \mid \mathsf{W}(D,P) \subseteq \mathsf{W}(C,P)\}|}{|\mathsf{CN}^{\mathsf{pri}}|}, \tag{4}$$

*where $|\cdot|$ denotes the set cardinality.*

**Definition 4 (Credulous $\mathcal{FL}_0$ Subsumption Degree).** *Let $C, D \in \mathsf{Con}(\mathcal{FL}_0)$ be in their normal forms and $\mathsf{W}(E, A)$ be a set of words w.r.t. the concept $E$ and the primitive $A$. Then, a* credulous $\mathcal{FL}_0$ subsumption degree *from $C$ to $D$ (denoted by $C \rightsquigarrow^c D$) is defined as follows:*

$$C \rightsquigarrow^c D = \frac{\sum_{P \in \mathsf{CN}^{\mathsf{pri}}} \mu(D,C,P)}{|\mathsf{CN}^{\mathsf{pri}}|}, \tag{5}$$

*where $|\cdot|$ denotes the set cardinality and*

$$\mu(D,C,P) = \begin{cases} 1 & \text{if } \mathsf{W}(D,P) = \emptyset \\ \frac{|\mathsf{W}(D,P) \cap \mathsf{W}(C,P)|}{|\mathsf{W}(D,P)|} & \text{otherwise} \end{cases} \tag{6}$$

It is worth observing that if $(|\mathsf{W}(D,P) \cap \mathsf{W}(C,P)|)/(|\mathsf{W}(D,P)|) = 1$, then $\mathsf{W}(D,P) \subseteq \mathsf{W}(C,P)$ holds (and vice versa). Using this observation, we can show the following property.

**Proposition 1.** *For any $C, D \in \mathsf{Con}(\mathcal{FL}_0)$, it follows that $C \rightsquigarrow^s D \leq C \rightsquigarrow^c D$.*

**Proof.** *Fix any $C, D \in \mathsf{Con}(\mathcal{FL}_0)$. We show the following inequality:*

$$|\{P \in \mathsf{CN}^{\mathsf{pri}} \mid \mathsf{W}(D,P) \subseteq \mathsf{W}(C,P)\}| \leq \sum_{P \in \mathsf{CN}^{\mathsf{pri}}} \frac{|\mathsf{W}(D,P) \cap \mathsf{W}(C,P)|}{|\mathsf{W}(D,P)|}$$

*Fix any $P \in \mathsf{CN}^{\mathsf{pri}}$. We show inequality of the following three cases.*

*Case 1 (both $\mathsf{W}(D,P)$ and $\mathsf{W}(C,P)$ are identical): Let $\mathsf{W}(D,P) = \{r_1, \ldots, r_n\}$ and $\mathsf{W}(C,P) = \{r_1, \ldots, r_n\}$. Then, we show $(\mathsf{W}(D,P) \subseteq \mathsf{W}(C,P)) \leq (|\mathsf{W}(D,P) \cap \mathsf{W}(C,P)|)/(|\mathsf{W}(D,P)|) \iff 1 \leq 1$.*

*Case 2 (both $\mathsf{W}(D,P)$ and $\mathsf{W}(C,P)$ share some commonalities): Let $\mathsf{W}(D,P) = \{r_1, \ldots, r_n, s_1, \ldots, s_m\}$ and $\mathsf{W}(C,P) = \{r_1, \ldots, r_n, t_1, \ldots, t_o\}$. Then, we show $(\mathsf{W}(D,P) \subseteq \mathsf{W}(C,P)) \leq (|\mathsf{W}(D,P) \cap \mathsf{W}(C,P)|)/(|\mathsf{W}(D,P)|) \iff 0 \leq (n)/(n+m)$.*

*Case 3 (both $\mathsf{W}(D,P)$ and $\mathsf{W}(C,P)$ do not share any commonalities): Let $\mathsf{W}(D,P) = \{s_1, \ldots, s_m\}$ and $\mathsf{W}(C,P) = \{t_1, \ldots, t_o\}$. Then, we show $(\mathsf{W}(D,P) \subseteq \mathsf{W}(C,P)) \leq (|\mathsf{W}(D,P) \cap \mathsf{W}(C,P)|)/(|\mathsf{W}(D,P)|) \iff 0 \leq (0/m)$.* □

**Definition 5 (Ordering of Functions).** *Let $\alpha$ and $\beta$ be different functions. Then, $\alpha$ is* more skeptical than or equal to *$\beta$ (denoted by $\alpha \preceq \beta$) if $(C\ \alpha\ D) \leq (C\ \beta\ D)$ for all concepts $C, D \in \mathsf{Con}(\mathcal{L})$.*

**Proposition 2.** *Let $C, D \in \mathsf{Con}(\mathcal{FL}_0)$. Then, the following ordering holds:*

$$\sqsubseteq \preceq \rightsquigarrow^s \preceq \rightsquigarrow^c$$

**Proof.** *Let us view $\sqsubseteq$ as a function which returns 1 if $C \sqsubseteq D$ holds for any $C, D$ or 0 otherwise. If $C \sqsubseteq D$ holds, then $C \rightsquigarrow^s D = C \rightsquigarrow^c D = 1$. Otherwise, it immediately follows from Proposition 1 that $C \sqsubseteq D \leq C \rightsquigarrow^s D \leq C \rightsquigarrow^c D$ together with considering $C \not\sqsubseteq D$ as the value 0.* □

**Theorem 2.** *Let $C, D \in \mathsf{Con}(\mathcal{FL}_0)$. Then, the following are equivalent:*

1. *$C \sqsubseteq D$;*
2. *$C \rightsquigarrow^s D = 1$; and*
3. *$C \rightsquigarrow^c D = 1$.*

**Proof.** *Let $C := \forall L_1.A_1 \sqcap \cdots \sqcap \forall L_n.A_n$ and $D := \forall M_1.A_1 \sqcap \cdots \sqcap \forall M_n.A_n$. We need to show $C \sqsubseteq D \iff C \rightsquigarrow^s D = 1$ and $C \rightsquigarrow^s D = 1 \iff C \rightsquigarrow^c D = 1$.*

*($1 \implies 2$) Assume $C \sqsubseteq D$ i.e. $M_i \subseteq L_i$ for $i = 1, \ldots, n$. Then, we have $C \rightsquigarrow^s D = 1$.*

*($2 \implies 1$) Assume $C \rightsquigarrow^s D = 1$. This implies that $M_i \subseteq L_i$ for $i = 1, \ldots, n$. Thus, we conclude $C \sqsubseteq D$.*

*($2 \implies 3$) Assume $C \rightsquigarrow^s D = 1$. We have $C \rightsquigarrow^c D = 1$ (by Proposition 1).*

*($3 \implies 2$) Assume $C \rightsquigarrow^c D = 1$. This implies that $M_i \subseteq L_i$ for $i = 1, \ldots, n$. Thus, we conclude $C \rightsquigarrow^s D = 1$.* □

We also provide a proof that both $\rightsquigarrow^s$ and $\rightsquigarrow^c$ can be computed in polynomial time. We note that, in [13], a sketch proof was provided.

**Theorem 3.** *Let $L, M$ be sets of words over the alphabet of role names corresponding to concepts $C, D$, respectively. The computational complexity of both $\rightsquigarrow^s$ and $\rightsquigarrow^c$ is $\mathcal{O}(n|M||L|)$, where $n$ is the size of concepts $C, D$.*

**Proof.** *Let $C := \forall L_1.A_1 \sqcap \cdots \sqcap \forall L_n.A_n$ and $D := \forall M_1.A_1 \sqcap \cdots \sqcap \forall M_n.A_n$, where $L_i, M_i$ ($1 \leq i \leq n$) are sets of words over the alphabet of role names. Checking the inclusion of finite languages (cf. Definition 3) and the proportion of finite languages (cf. Definition 4) can be done in polynomial time, i.e. in the worst case we have to check for all words $w \in M_i$ and $v \in L_i$ whether $w = v$. Each equality checking can be done in $\min(|w|, |v|)$ and such tests have to be done for $|M_i| \cdot |L_i|$. Assume in the worst case that each $M_i$ and $L_i$ are identical i.e. $|M_i| = |M|$ and $|L_i| = |L|$ for every $i$. Therefore, we have shown that both measures are bound by $\mathcal{O}(n|M||L|)$.* □

**Definition 6 (Skeptical $\mathcal{FL}_0$ Subsumption Degree under $\pi$).** *Let $C, D \in \mathsf{Con}(\mathcal{FL}_0)$ be in their normal forms and $\mathsf{W}(E, A)$ be a set of words w.r.t. the concept $E$ and the primitive $A$. Then, a* skeptical $\mathcal{FL}_0$ subsumption degree under $\pi$ *from $C$ to $D$ (denoted by $C \overset{\pi}{\rightsquigarrow} s\ D$) is defined as follows:*

$$C \overset{\pi}{\rightsquigarrow} s\ D = \frac{\sum_{P \in \mathsf{CN}^{\mathsf{pri}}} \hat{\imath}(P) \cdot \max_{Q \in \mathsf{CN}^{\mathsf{pri}}} \{\hat{\mathfrak{s}}(P, Q) | \mathsf{W}(D, P) \subseteq \mathsf{W}(C, Q)\}}{\sum_{P \in \mathsf{CN}^{\mathsf{pri}}} \hat{\imath}(P)} \tag{7}$$

*where* $\hat{\mathfrak{i}} : \mathsf{CN}^{\mathsf{pri}} \to [0,2]$ *is defined as:*

$$\hat{\mathfrak{i}}(x) = \begin{cases} \mathfrak{i}^{\mathfrak{c}}(x) & \text{if } x \in \mathsf{CN}^{\mathsf{pri}} \text{ and } \mathfrak{i}^{\mathfrak{c}} \text{ is defined on } x \\ 1 & \text{otherwise;} \end{cases} \tag{8}$$

*and* $\hat{\mathfrak{s}} : \mathsf{CN}^{\mathsf{pri}} \times \mathsf{CN}^{\mathsf{pri}} \to [0,1]$ *is defined as:*

$$\hat{\mathfrak{s}}(x,y) = \begin{cases} 1 & \text{if } x = y \\ \mathfrak{s}^{\mathfrak{c}}(x,y) & \text{if } (x,y) \in \mathsf{CN}^{\mathsf{pri}} \times \mathsf{CN}^{\mathsf{pri}} \\ & \text{and } \mathfrak{s}^{\mathfrak{c}} \text{ is defined on } (x,y) \\ 0 & \text{otherwise} \end{cases} \tag{9}$$

Under a special setting of preference profile, the function $\overset{\pi}{\leadsto}s$ can be reduced backward to $\leadsto^s$. This means that $\overset{\pi}{\leadsto}s$ can be also used for a situation when preferences are not given. Following the convention introduced in [12,16], let us call this special setting the *default preference profile* (denoted by $\pi_0$). We give its formal definition as follows:

**Definition 7 (Default Preference Profile).** *Let* $\mathsf{CN}^{\mathsf{pri}}(\mathcal{T})$ *be a set of primitive concept names occurring in* $\mathcal{T}$*. The* default preference profile, *in symbol* $\pi_0$, *is the pair* $\langle \mathfrak{i}^{\mathfrak{c}}_0, \mathfrak{s}^{\mathfrak{c}}_0 \rangle$ *where*

$$\mathfrak{i}^{\mathfrak{c}}_0(A) = 1 \text{ for all } A \in \mathsf{CN}^{\mathsf{pri}}(\mathcal{T}) \text{ and}$$
$$\mathfrak{s}^{\mathfrak{c}}_0(A,B) = 0 \text{ for all } (A,B) \in \mathsf{CN}^{\mathsf{pri}}(\mathcal{T}) \times \mathsf{CN}^{\mathsf{pri}}(\mathcal{T})$$

As for its syntactic sugar, let us denote a setting on $\overset{\pi}{\leadsto}s$ by replacing the setting with $\pi$. For instance, we may write the setting with $\pi_0$ as $\overset{\pi_0}{\leadsto}s$. In the following, we show a more detailed proof from [13] that, under this special setting on $\overset{\pi}{\leadsto}s$, the computation produces the same outcome as $\leadsto^s$.

**Proposition 3.** *For any* $C, D \in \mathsf{Con}(\mathcal{FL}_0)$, $C \overset{\pi_0}{\leadsto}s\ D = C \leadsto^s D$.

**Proof.** *Recall by Definition 7 that default preference profile* $\pi_0$ *is the pair* $\langle \mathfrak{i}^{\mathfrak{c}}_0, \mathfrak{s}^{\mathfrak{c}}_0 \rangle$. *Fix any* $C, D \in \mathsf{Con}(\mathcal{FL}_0)$, *we show that, under this special setting,* $C \overset{\pi_0}{\leadsto}s\ D = C \leadsto^s D$ *as follows:*

$$C \overset{\pi_0}{\leadsto}s\ D = \frac{\sum_{P \in \mathsf{CN}^{\mathsf{pri}}} 1 \cdot \max_{Q \in \mathsf{CN}^{\mathsf{pri}}} \{\hat{\mathfrak{s}}(P,Q) | \mathsf{W}(D,P) \subseteq \mathsf{W}(C,Q)\}}{\sum_{P \in \mathsf{CN}^{\mathsf{pri}}} 1}$$
$$= \frac{1 \cdot \sum_{P \in \mathsf{CN}^{\mathsf{pri}}} \max_{Q \in \mathsf{CN}^{\mathsf{pri}}} \{\hat{\mathfrak{s}}(P,Q) | \mathsf{W}(D,P) \subseteq \mathsf{W}(C,Q)\}}{|\mathsf{CN}^{\mathsf{pri}}|}$$

*Since* $\mathfrak{s}^{\mathfrak{c}}_0$ *maps identity to 1 and else to 0,* $\sum_{P \in \mathsf{CN}^{\mathsf{pri}}} \max_{Q \in \mathsf{CN}^{\mathsf{pri}}} \{\hat{\mathfrak{s}}(P,Q) | \mathsf{W}(D,P) \subseteq \mathsf{W}(C,Q)\} = |\{P \in \mathsf{CN}^{\mathsf{pri}} \mid \mathsf{W}(D,P) \subseteq \mathsf{W}(C,P)\}|$. *We have shown that* $C \overset{\pi_0}{\leadsto}s\ D = C \leadsto^s D$. □

## 4 Properties of Concept Similarity Under Preference Profile in Description Logic $\mathcal{FL}_0$

We recall from the step 3 discussed in the previous section that the degree of concept similarity with (and without) regards to the agent's preferences can be determined from the two directional subsumption degree of each corresponding direction. Mathematically, such aggregation can be defined as any binary operators accepting the unit interval *e.g.* the average, the multiplication, and the root mean square. In the following, we include their actual definitions which are the average-based definitions as given in [13]. As mentioned in step 1 discussed in Sect. 3, Definitions 8 and 9 are the immediate results from the notion of subsumption degree. Also, Definition 10 is the result from the notion of subsumption degree under the agent's preferences.

**Definition 8 (Skeptical $\mathcal{FL}_0$ Similarity Degree).** *Let $C, D \in \mathsf{Con}(\mathcal{FL}_0)$. The* skeptical $\mathcal{FL}_0$ similarity degree *between $C$ and $D$ (denoted by $C \sim^s D$), is defined as follows:*

$$C \sim^s D = \frac{(C \rightsquigarrow^s D) + (D \rightsquigarrow^s C)}{2} \tag{10}$$

**Definition 9 (Credulous $\mathcal{FL}_0$ Similarity Degree).** *Let $C, D \in \mathsf{Con}(\mathcal{FL}_0)$. The* credulous $\mathcal{FL}_0$ similarity degree *between $C$ and $D$ (denoted by $C \sim^c D$), is defined as follows:*

$$C \sim^c D = \frac{(C \rightsquigarrow^c D) + (D \rightsquigarrow^c C)}{2} \tag{11}$$

As aforementioned, other choices of the operator may be used. However, redefining the aggregation operator may produce a different behavior. Relevant discussions can be found in [12,13] in which some extreme cases were tested with other binary operators accepting the unit interval.

The following propositions discuss about some inherited properties of the two measures for $\mathcal{FL}_0$ concepts. That is, they are symmetric measures and preserve ordering in the viewpoint of skepticism between relations.

**Proposition 4 (Symmetry).** *Let $C, D \in \mathsf{Con}(\mathcal{FL}_0)$. The following holds:*

*1. $C \sim^s D = D \sim^s C$, and*
*2. $C \sim^c D = D \sim^c C$.*

**Proof.** *These are obvious by the average.* □

**Proposition 5.** *Let $C, D \in \mathsf{Con}(\mathcal{FL}_0)$. Then, the following ordering holds*[3]

$$\equiv \;\preceq\; \sim^s \;\preceq\; \sim^c$$

[3] See Definition 5 for the meaning of $\preceq$.

**Proof.** *By average, it suffices to show* $\sqsubseteq \preceq \rightsquigarrow^s \preceq \rightsquigarrow^c$. *This has already been proven by Proposition 2.* □

Intuitively, the above property spells out that, for any $C, D \in \mathsf{Con}(\mathcal{FL}_0)$, we have $(C \equiv D) \leq (C \sim^s D) \leq (C \sim^c D)$. In particular, if $C \equiv D$, then $(C \sim^s D) = (C \sim^c D) = 1$. It also tells us that both $\sim^s$ and $\sim^c$ can be used to identify the equivalent degree between concepts when the equivalent relation between them does not hold. In other words, they can be regarded as the elastic versions of the concept equivalence.

**Theorem 4.** *Let $L, M$ be sets of words over the alphabet of role names corresponding to concepts $C, D$, respectively. The computational complexity of both $\sim^s$ and $\sim^c$ is $\mathcal{O}(n|M||L|)$, where $n$ is the size of concepts $C, D$.*

**Proof.** *This is immediately followed from Theorem 3 and the average.* □

We can also show that both $\sim^s$ and $\sim^c$ are decision procedures. That is, they are sound *i.e.* the positive answers are correct. They are complete *i.e.* the negative answers are correct. Furthermore, they are terminating *i.e.* they always provide an answer in finite time.

**Lemma 1 (Soundness).** *For any $\mathcal{FL}_0$ concepts $C, D$, it follows that:*

- *if $C \sim^s D \in (0, 1]$, then both $C$ and $D$ are similar to each other; and*
- *if $C \sim^c D \in (0, 1]$, then both $C$ and $D$ are similar to each other.*

**Proof.** *Fix any $\mathcal{FL}_0$ concepts $C, D$. By the average, it suffices to show:*

- *if $C \rightsquigarrow^s D \in (0, 1]$, then $C$ is "partially subsumed" by $D$; and*
- *if $C \rightsquigarrow^c D \in (0, 1]$, then $C$ is "partially subsumed" by $D$.*

*To show the first point, we assume that $C \sim^s D \in (0, 1]$. By assumption and Proposition 2, we know that $C$ is partially subsumed by $D$ (based on the characterization of language inclusion).*

*We can also show the second point with an analogous manner.* □

**Lemma 2 (Completeness).** *For any $\mathcal{FL}_0$ concepts $C, D$, it follows that:*

- *if both $C$ and $D$ are similar to each other, then $C \sim^s D \in (0, 1]$; and*
- *if both $C$ and $D$ are similar to each other, then $C \sim^c D \in (0, 1]$.*

**Proof.** *Fix any $\mathcal{FL}_0$ concepts $C, D$. We show their contraposition i.e.*

- *if $C \sim^s D = 0$, then both $C$ and $D$ are totally dissimilar to each other; and*
- *if $C \sim^c D = 0$, then both $C$ and $D$ are totally dissimilar to each other.*

*To show the first point, we assume that $C \sim^s D = 0$. By assumption and the average, we know that $C \rightsquigarrow^s D = 0$ and $D \rightsquigarrow^s C = 0$. This means that both $C$ and $D$ do not share any commonalities with each other. Hence, both $C$ and $D$ are totally dissimilar to each other.*

*We can also show the second point with an analogous manner.* □

**Theorem 5.** *Both $\sim^s$ and $\sim^c$ are decision procedures.*

**Proof.** *We need to show that $\sim^s$ and $\sim^c$ are sound, complete, and terminating. These are obvious by Lemmas 1, 2, and Theorem 4, respectively.* □

**Definition 10.** *Let $C, D \in \mathsf{Con}(\mathcal{FL}_0)$ be in their normal forms and $\pi = \langle \mathfrak{i}^c, \mathfrak{i}^r, \mathfrak{s}^c, \mathfrak{s}^r, \mathfrak{d} \rangle$ be a preference profile. Then, the* skeptical $\mathcal{FL}_0$ similarity measure under preference profile $\pi$ *between $C$ and $D$ (denoted by $C \overset{\pi}{\sim}_s D$) is defined as follows:*

$$C \overset{\pi}{\sim}_s D = \frac{C \overset{\pi}{\rightsquigarrow}_s D + D \overset{\pi}{\rightsquigarrow}_s C}{2} \tag{12}$$

Similar to Definitions 8 and 9, other choices of the aggregation operator may be considered. However, it may produce a different behavior. Relevant discussions can be also found in [12,13] in which some extreme cases were tested with other binary operators accepting the unit interval.

The measure $\overset{\pi}{\sim}_s$ can be also used in the case that a preference profile is not given by the agent. In such a case, we tune the profile setting to $\pi_0$. That is, computing $\overset{\pi_0}{\sim}_s$ yields the degree of concept similarity measure merely w.r.t. the structure of concept descriptions in question.

**Theorem 6.** *Let $C, D \in \mathsf{Con}(\mathcal{FL}_0)$, $C \overset{\pi_0}{\sim}_s D = C \sim^s D$.*

**Proof.** *It immediately follows from Proposition 3, Definitions 8, and 10.* □

Theorem 6 tells us that $\overset{\pi}{\sim}_s$ is backward compatible in the sense that using $\sim^s$ with $\pi = \pi_0$, *i.e.* $\overset{\pi_0}{\sim}_s$, coincides with $\sim^s$. Technically speaking, $\overset{\pi_0}{\sim}_s$ can be used to handle the case of similar concepts regardless of the agent's preferences.

In [12], four desirable properties of concept similarity measure under preference profile were introduced. Symmetric property was one of them. The following theorem shows that $\overset{\pi}{\sim}_s$ is a symmetric measure.

**Theorem 7 (Symmetry).** *For any $C, D \in \mathsf{Con}(\mathcal{FL}_0)$, $C \overset{\pi}{\sim}_s D = D \overset{\pi}{\sim}_s C$.*

**Proof.** *Let $\Pi$ be a countably infinite set of preference profile. Fix any $\pi \in \Pi$ and $C, D \in \mathsf{Con}(\mathcal{FL}_0)$, we have $C \overset{\pi}{\sim}_s D = D \overset{\pi}{\sim}_s C$ by the average.* □

**Theorem 8.** *Assume that a value from any preference functions is retrieved in $\mathcal{O}(1)$. Let $L, M$ be sets of words over the alphabet of role names corresponding to $C, D$, respectively. Then, $C \overset{\pi}{\sim}_s D \in \mathcal{O}(|\mathsf{CN}^{\mathsf{pri}}|^2 |L||M|)$.*

**Proof.** *Let $C, D \in \mathsf{Con}(\mathcal{FL}_0)$, $\pi$ be any preference profile; and, let $L, M$ be sets of words over the alphabet of role names corresponding to $C, D$, respectively. By Definition 10, we need to show that $C \overset{\pi}{\rightsquigarrow}_s D \in \mathcal{O}(|\mathsf{CN}^{\mathsf{pri}}|^2 |L||M|)$ and $D \overset{\pi}{\rightsquigarrow}_s C \in \mathcal{O}(|\mathsf{CN}^{\mathsf{pri}}|^2 |L||M|)$. By the average, it suffices to show $C \overset{\pi}{\rightsquigarrow}_s D \in \mathcal{O}(|\mathsf{CN}^{\mathsf{pri}}|^2 |L||M|)$ as follows.*

*Checking the inclusion of finite similar languages can be done in polynomial time i.e. to decide $\sum_{P \in \mathsf{CN}^{\mathsf{pri}}} \hat{\mathfrak{i}}(P) \cdot \max_{Q \in \mathsf{CN}^{\mathsf{pri}}} \{\hat{\mathfrak{s}}(P, Q) \mid \mathsf{W}(D, P) \subseteq \mathsf{W}(C, Q)\}$, in the* *worst case we have to check for all possible pairs* $P \in \mathsf{CN}^{\mathsf{pri}}$ *and* $Q \in \mathsf{CN}^{\mathsf{pri}}$. *Such test can be done in time* $|\mathsf{CN}^{\mathsf{pri}}||\mathsf{CN}^{\mathsf{pri}}|$. *To decide* $\mathsf{W}(D,P) \subseteq \mathsf{W}(C,Q)$ *in the inner loop, another polynomial time operation is also required i.e. we have to check whether, for all words* $w \in \mathsf{W}(D,P)$, $w \in \mathsf{W}(C,Q)$ *for checking the set inclusion. This requires* $|L||M|$ *numbers of the operation. The summation (cf. the denominator of Definition 6) requires linear time i.e. in the size of* $\mathsf{CN}^{\mathsf{pri}}$. □

In the following, we show $\overset{\pi}{\sim}s$ is also a decision procedure, *i.e.* sound, complete, and terminating, for deciding whether two given $\mathcal{FL}_0$ concepts are similar with a particular degree under a given preference profile or not.

**Lemma 3 (Soundness).** *Let* $\pi' = \langle \mathfrak{i}^{\mathfrak{c}}, \mathfrak{i}^{\mathfrak{r}}, \mathfrak{s}^{\mathfrak{c}}, \mathfrak{s}^{\mathfrak{r}}, \mathfrak{d} \rangle$ *be any preference profile. For any* $\mathcal{FL}_0$ *concepts* $C, D$,

$$if\ C \overset{\pi'}{\sim} s\ D \in (0,1],\ then\ both\ C\ and\ D\ are\ similar\ under\ \pi'\ to\ each\ other,$$

**Proof.** *Let* $C, D \in \mathsf{Con}(\mathcal{FL}_0)$ *and* $\pi'$ *be any preference profile. By the average, it suffices to show that if* $C \overset{\pi'}{\rightsquigarrow} s\ D \in (0,1]$, *then* $C$ *is "partially subsumed" under* $\pi'$ *by* $D$.

*Assume* $C \overset{\pi'}{\rightsquigarrow} s\ D \in (0,1]$. *By assumption, we know that (cf. Definition 6), for some* $P \in \mathsf{CN}^{\mathsf{pri}}$, *for some* $Q \in \mathsf{CN}^{\mathsf{pri}}$, *it holds that* $\hat{\mathfrak{i}}(P) > 0$, $\hat{\mathfrak{s}}(P,Q) > 0$, *and* $\mathsf{W}(D,P) \subseteq \mathsf{W}(C,Q)$. *This shows that* $C$ *is partially subsumed under* $\pi'$ *by* $D$ *based on the characterization of language inclusion.* □

**Lemma 4 (Completeness).** *Let* $\pi' = \langle \mathfrak{i}^{\mathfrak{c}}, \mathfrak{i}^{\mathfrak{r}}, \mathfrak{s}^{\mathfrak{c}}, \mathfrak{s}^{\mathfrak{r}}, \mathfrak{d} \rangle$ *be any preference profile. For any* $\mathcal{FL}_0$ *concepts* $C, D$,

$$if\ both\ C\ and\ D\ are\ similar\ under\ \pi'\ to\ each\ other,\ then\ C \overset{\pi'}{\sim} s\ D \in (0,1],$$

**Proof.** *Let* $C, D \in \mathsf{Con}(\mathcal{FL}_0)$ *and* $\pi'$ *be any preference profile. We show its contraposition i.e. if* $C \overset{\pi'}{\sim} s\ D = 0$, *then both* $C$ *and* $D$ *are totally dissimilar under* $\pi'$ *to each other.*

*Assume* $C \overset{\pi'}{\sim} s\ D = 0$. *By assumption and the average, we know that* $C \overset{\pi'}{\rightsquigarrow} s\ D = 0$ *and* $D \overset{\pi'}{\rightsquigarrow} s\ C = 0$. *This means that (cf. Definition 6), for any* $P \in \mathsf{CN}^{\mathsf{pri}}$, *for any* $Q \in \mathsf{CN}^{\mathsf{pri}}$, *it does not hold that* $\hat{\mathfrak{i}}(P) > 0$, $\hat{\mathfrak{s}}(P,Q) > 0$, *and* $\mathsf{W}(D,P) \subseteq \mathsf{W}(C,Q)$. *Also, for any* $P \in \mathsf{CN}^{\mathsf{pri}}$, *for any* $Q \in \mathsf{CN}^{\mathsf{pri}}$, *it does not hold that* $\hat{\mathfrak{i}}(P) > 0$, $\hat{\mathfrak{s}}(P,Q) > 0$, *and* $\mathsf{W}(C,P) \subseteq \mathsf{W}(D,Q)$. *This means that both* $C$ *and* $D$ *do not share any commonalities under* $\pi'$ *with each other. Hence, both* $C$ *and* $D$ *are totally dissimilar under* $\pi'$ *to each other.* □

**Theorem 9.** $\overset{\pi}{\sim}s$ *is a decision procedure.*

**Proof.** *We need to show that* $\overset{\pi}{\sim}s$ *is sound, complete, and terminating. These are obvious by Lemmas 3, 4, and Theorem 8, respectively.* □

## 5 Related Work

Concept similarity has been widely studied in various fields, *e.g.* psychological science, computer science, artificial intelligence, and linguistic literature. Roughly, they can be classified into five ways, *viz.* path finding, information content, context vector, structure similarity, and semantic similarity. We review each way as follows.

The path finding approach requires to firstly construct the concept hierarchy. That is, the more general concepts they are, the more they are closer to the root of the hierarchy. Also, the more specific they are, the more they are closer to the leaves of the hierarchy. Once the hierarchy is constructed, the degree of concept similarity is computed from paths between concepts. Indeed, there are various ways for determining the degree. For instance, [17] used a path length between concepts according to successively either more specific concepts or less specific concepts. A similar approach was introduced in [18] where the degree was computed based on the shortest path between concepts. Ones may also assign different weights to the role depth as in [19]. Unfortunately, this approach fully relies on the concept hierarchy and ignores constraints defined in the ontology.

The information content approach augments each concept with a corpus-based statistics. Generally, the information content of each concept in a hierarchy is calculated based on the frequency of occurrence of that concept in a corpus. The more specific concepts they are, the higher information content values of them will be. For instance, [20] defined the degree of similarity between concepts as the information content of the least common subsumer of them. Intuitively, this measure was defined to calculate the degree of the shared information between concepts. However, this approach requires a set of world descriptions such as a text corpus; and also, may be not sufficient since many concept pairs may share the same least common subsumer.

On the one hand, the first two approaches may utilize the concept hierarchy to compute the degree of concept similarity. On the other hand, the context vector totally relies on the vector representation. Roughly speaking, each concept is represented by a context vector and the cosine of the angle between vectors is used to determine the degree of similarity between related concepts. Work which employs this approach includes [21–23].

Similarity can be measured based on the structure or the form tied to particular concepts. This approach has been shown to be useful for many natural language processing tasks, in which sentences or words are represented by particular structures (*e.g.* strings, trees, *etc.*) and structure-based techniques are developed to measure their similarity. For example, string edit distance is a way of quantifying the degree of dissimilarity from one string to another by counting the minimum number of operations required to transform one string to the other. Work which employs this approach includes [24,25]. Another analogous method is called *tree edit distance* [26], which considers the minimum number of node edit operations for transforming one tree to another.

The semantic similarity approach basically uses the syntax and semantics of DLs for the development of measures. A simple approach was proposed in [27] for the basic DL $\mathcal{L}_0$ (*i.e.* no use of roles). Later, the idea was extended in [9] for the DL $\mathcal{ELH}$. The extended work suggested a new framework that satisfied several properties for similarity measure. The framework was defined in general; thus, functions and operators were parameterized and were left to be specified. A different approach for the same $\mathcal{ELH}$ was proposed in [10] in which the measure was developed based on the structural subsumption characterization of tree homomorphism. Indeed, this approach had its root in the study of similarity measure for the DL $\mathcal{EL}$ [28]. Later, it was extended to the DL $\mathcal{ALEH}$ in [29]. Furthermore, [30] suggested two measures for the DL $\mathcal{FL}_0$ based on the structural subsumption characterization of language inclusion. It is worth observing that these measures calculated the degree of concept similarity according to the structure of concept descriptions in question.

Instead of using the structure of concept descriptions, ones may try to compute the degree based on an interpretation of concepts for semantic similarity. These measures often employ the canonical interpretation and the set cardinality such as work in [31,32]. Unfortunately, these measures strictly require an ABox.

Another approach for semantic similarity was proposed in [33]. This work introduced a family of similarity measures in which a classical subsumption reasoner was used to determine features for calculating the degree based on the feature model.

While many similarity measures exist, a few of them utilize the agent's preferences for calculating the degree of concept similarity. In addition, existing approaches may implicitly use the agent's preferences in their computational procedures; thus, it is not easy to investigate intended behaviors of similarity measures if they are used under the agent's preferences. An experiment in [34] also suggests that measures should be made personalized to the target application (*e.g.* the agent). To help such investigation, a general notion called concept similarity measure under preference profile was introduced in [11] with the developed measure $\mathsf{sim}^{\pi}$ for the DL $\mathcal{ELH}$. This work was continuously studied in [12]. With an analogous development, [13] investigated the development of the measure $\overset{\pi}{\sim}_s$ for the DL $\mathcal{FL}_0$.

## 6 Discussion and Future Research

In [13], a measure was developed based on the calculation of subsumption degree under preferences w.r.t. the two corresponding directions. Its underlying mechanism was generalized from the approach of identifying the subsumption degree between $\mathcal{FL}_0$ concepts based on the recently introduced notion called preference profile. Therefore, the measure could be regarded as an instance of concept similarity measure under preference profile *i.e.* a binary function assigning a unit interval under a given preference profile. This paper is an extended study of [13], in which proofs of theorems about the inherited properties are studied in detail. More specifically, we show the relationship between (1) concept subsumption and subsumption degree functions, (2) a subsumption degree function and a subsumption degree under preference profile function; and also, (3) we show that the developed measures are decision procedures *i.e.* they solve similarity problems with "yes" or "no" answers. They say "yes" if the similarity degree between two concepts are greater than 0 and say "no" otherwise.

In [11,12], the measure $\mathsf{sim}^\pi$ was introduced as a concrete measure of concept similarity measure under preference profile for the DL $\mathcal{ELH}$[4]. On the one hand, $\mathsf{sim}^\pi$ allowed to fully define preferential expressions over all types of preference profile. On the other hand, ones might still want to understand how concrete measures of $\overset{\pi}{\sim}$ for other DLs should be developed. To answer this question, [13] concentrated on another sub-Boolean DL, *i.e.* $\mathcal{FL}_0$. We recall that $\mathcal{FL}_0$ offers the constructors conjunction ($\sqcap$), value restriction ($\forall r.C$), and the top concept ($\top$) (*cf.* Subsect. 2.1). The approach presented in [13] also differs to [12] on the adopted characterization, *i.e.* the language inclusion. As an extended study of [13], several of theorems on the results in the proceeding paper are investigated. These tell us that the approaches developed in [13] (*i.e.* $\overset{\pi}{\sim}s$) can be used to identify a subsumption degree (thus, an equivalent degree) between $\mathcal{FL}_0$ concepts, develop recommendation systems based on the agent's preferences with $\mathcal{FL}_0$ DL knowledge base, and solve various problems in knowledge engineering and analogical reasoning in which their ontologies can be represented in $\mathcal{FL}_0$.

There are several possible directions for its future work. Firstly, we may try to conduct an experiment on an appropriate ontology of real-world domains. Similar experiments as conducted in [12] can be carried out. Secondly, we still remain to show certain desirable properties (of concept similarity measure under preference profile) introduced in [12] for the measure $\overset{\pi}{\sim}s$ *viz. equivalence invariance*, *structural dependence*, and *preference invariance w.r.t. equivalence*. This work only shows that $\overset{\pi}{\sim}s$ is symmetric. Thirdly, we are also interested to explore similarity measures for more expressive DLs. Lastly, as reported in [34] about the need of having multiple measures, it would be interesting to investigate the possible classes of similarity measures w.r.t. their potential use cases and applications.

**Acknowledgments.** This work is supported by the Japan Society for the Promotion of Science (JSPS kaken no. 17H02258) and is part of the JAIST-NECTEC-SIIT dual doctoral degree program. The authors would also like to thank the editors for the comments.

## References

1. Baader, F., Calvanese, D., McGuinness, D.L., Nardi, D., Patel-Schneider, P.F.: The Description Logic Handbook: Theory, Implementation and Applications, 2nd edn. Cambridge University Press, New York (2010)
2. Ashburner, M., et al.: Gene ontology: tool for the unification of biology. Nat. Genet. **25**(1), 25–29 (2000)

[4] We recall that $\mathcal{ELH}$ offers the constructors conjunction ($\sqcap$), full existential quantification ($\exists r.C$), and the top concept ($\top$); also, the TBox can contain (possibly primitive) concept definitions and role hierarchy axioms.

3. Euzenat, J., Valtchev, P.: Similarity-based ontology alignment in OWL-lite. In: de Mántaras, R.L., Saitta, L. (eds.) Proceedings of the 16th European Conference on Artificial Intelligence (ECAI 2004), pp. 333–337. IOS Press (2004)
4. Raha, S., Hossain, A., Ghosh, S.: Similarity based approximate reasoning: fuzzy control. J. Appl. Log. **6**(1), 47–71 (2008)
5. Sessa, M.I.: Approximate reasoning by similarity-based SLD resolution. Theor. Comput. Sci. **275**(1–2), 389–426 (2002)
6. Racharak, T., Tojo, S., Hung, N.D., Boonkwan, P.: Argument-based logic programming for analogical reasoning. In: Kurahashi, S., Ohta, Y., Arai, S., Satoh, K., Bekki, D. (eds.) JSAI-isAI 2016. LNCS (LNAI), vol. 10247, pp. 253–269. Springer, Cham (2017). https://doi.org/10.1007/978-3-319-61572-1_17
7. Racharak, T., Tojo, S., Hung, N.D., Boonkwan, P.: Combining answer set programming with description logics for analogical reasoning under an agent's preferences. In: Benferhat, S., Tabia, K., Ali, M. (eds.) IEA/AIE 2017. LNCS (LNAI), vol. 10351, pp. 306–316. Springer, Cham (2017). https://doi.org/10.1007/978-3-319-60045-1_33
8. Tversky, A.: Features of similarity. Psychol. Rev. **84**(4), 327–352 (1977)
9. Lehmann, K., Turhan, A.-Y.: A Framework for semantic-based similarity measures for $\mathcal{ELH}$-concepts. In: del Cerro, L.F., Herzig, A., Mengin, J. (eds.) JELIA 2012. LNCS (LNAI), vol. 7519, pp. 307–319. Springer, Heidelberg (2012). https://doi.org/10.1007/978-3-642-33353-8_24
10. Tongphu, S., Suntisrivaraporn, B.: Algorithms for measuring similarity between $\mathcal{ELH}$ concept descriptions: a case study on SNOMED CT. J. Comput. Inform. **36**, 733–764 (2017)
11. Racharak, T., Suntisrivaraporn, B., Tojo, S.: $\mathsf{sim}^{\pi}$: a concept similarity measure under an agent's preferences in description logic $\mathcal{ELH}$. In: Proceedings of the 8th International Conference on Agents and Artificial Intelligence, pp. 480–487 (2016)
12. Racharak, T., Suntisrivaraporn, B., Tojo, S.: Personalizing a concept similarity measure in the description logic $\mathcal{ELH}$ with preference profile. J. Comput. Inform. **37**, 581–613 (2018)
13. Racharak, T., Tojo, S.: Concept similarity under the agent's preferences for the description logic $\mathcal{FL}_0$ with unfoldable TBox. In: Proceedings of the 10th International Conference on Agents and Artificial Intelligence, pp. 201–210 (2018)
14. Baader, F., Narendran, P.: Unification of concept terms in description logics. J. Symb. Comput. **31**(3), 277–305 (2001)
15. Brachman, R.J., Levesque, H.J.: The tractability of subsumption in frame-based description languages. In: AAAI, vol. 84, pp. 34–37 (1984)
16. Racharak, T., Suntisrivaraporn, B., Tojo, S.: Identifying an agent's preferences toward similarity measures in description logics. In: Qi, G., Kozaki, K., Pan, J.Z., Yu, S. (eds.) JIST 2015. LNCS, vol. 9544, pp. 201–208. Springer, Cham (2016). https://doi.org/10.1007/978-3-319-31676-5_14
17. Rada, R., Mili, H., Bicknell, E., Blettner, M.: Development and application of a metric on semantic nets. IEEE Trans. Syst., Man, Cybern. **19**(1), 17–30 (1989)
18. Caviedes, J.E., Cimino, J.J.: Towards the development of a conceptual distance metric for the UMLS. J. Biomed. Inform. **37**(2), 77–85 (2004)
19. Ge, J., Qiu, Y.: Concept similarity matching based on semantic distance. In: Proceedings of the 4th International Conference on Semantics, Knowledge and Grid, pp. 380–383, December 2008

20. Resnik, P.: Using information content to evaluate semantic similarity in a taxonomy. In: Proceedings of the 14th International Joint Conference on Artificial Intelligence, IJCAI 1995, vol. 1, pp. 448–453. Morgan Kaufmann Publishers Inc., San Francisco (1995)
21. Pedersen, T., Pakhomov, S.V., Patwardhan, S., Chute, C.G.: Measures of semantic similarity and relatedness in the biomedical domain. J. Biomed. Inform. **40**(3), 288–299 (2007)
22. Patwardhan, S.: Using WordNet-based context vectors to estimate the semantic relatedness of concepts. In: Proceedings of the EACL 2006 Workshop Making Sense of Sense-bringing Computational Linguistics and Psycholinguistics Together, vol. 1501, pp. 1–8 (2006)
23. Schütze, H.: Automatic word sense discrimination. Comput. Linguist. **24**(1), 97–123 (1998)
24. Lai, K.H., Topaz, M., Goss, F.R., Zhou, L.: Automated misspelling detection and correction in clinical free-text records. J. Biomed. Inform. **55**, 188–195 (2015)
25. Gabrys, R., Yaakobi, E., Milenkovic, O.: Codes in the Damerau distance for DNA storage. In: 2016 IEEE International Symposium on Information Theory (ISIT), pp. 2644–2648. IEEE (2016)
26. Bille, P.: A survey on tree edit distance and related problems. Theor. Comput. Sci. **337**(1–3), 217–239 (2005)
27. Jaccard, P.: Étude comparative de la distribution florale dans une portion des alpeset des jura. Bull. de la Societe Vaudoise des Sci. Nat. **37**, 547–579 (1901)
28. Suntisrivaraporn, B.: A similarity measure for the description logic EL with unfoldable terminologies, pp. 408–413 (2013)
29. Suntisrivaraporn, B., Tongphu, S.: A structural subsumption based similarity measure for the description logic $\mathcal{ALEH}$. In: Proceedings of the 8th International Conference on Agents and Artificial Intelligence, ICAART 2016, pp. 204–212. SCITEPRESS - Science and Technology Publications, Lda (2016)
30. Racharak, T., Suntisrivaraporn, B.: Similarity measures for $\mathcal{FL}_0$ concept descriptions from an automata-theoretic point of view. In: Proceedings of the 6th International Conference of Information and Communication Technology for Embedded Systems (IC-ICTES), pp. 1–6, March 2015
31. D'Amato, C., Fanizzi, N., Esposito, F.: A semantic similarity measure for expressive description logics. CoRR abs/0911.5043 (2009)
32. d'Amato, C., Staab, S., Fanizzi, N.: On the influence of description logics ontologies on conceptual similarity. In: Gangemi, A., Euzenat, J. (eds.) EKAW 2008. LNCS (LNAI), vol. 5268, pp. 48–63. Springer, Heidelberg (2008). https://doi.org/10.1007/978-3-540-87696-0_7
33. Alsubait, T., Parsia, B., Sattler, U.: Measuring conceptual similarity in ontologies: how bad is a cheap measure? In: Informal Proceedings of the 27th International Workshop on Description Logics, Vienna, Austria, 17–20 July 2014, pp. 365–377 (2014)
34. Bernstein, A., Kaufmann, E., Bürki, C., Klein, M.: How similar is it? Towards personalized similarity measures in ontologies. In: Ferstl, O.K., Sinz, E.J., Eckert, S., Isselhorst, T. (eds.) Wirtschaftsinformatik 2005: eEconomy, eGovernment, eSociety, pp. 1347–1366. Physica-Verlag HD, Heidelberg (2005). https://doi.org/10.1007/3-7908-1624-8_71

# SEMTec: Social Emotion Mining Techniques for Analysis and Prediction of Facebook Post Reactions

Tobias Moers, Florian Krebs, and Gerasimos Spanakis(✉)

Department of Data Science and Knowledge Engineering, Maastricht University, 6200 MD Maastricht, The Netherlands
{tobias.moers,florian.krebs}@student.maastrichtuniversity.nl, jerry.spanakis@maastrichtuniversity.nl

**Abstract.** Nowadays social media are utilized by many people in order to review products and services. Subsequently, companies can use this feedback in order to improve customer experience. Facebook provided its users with the ability to express their experienced emotions by using five so-called 'reactions'. Since this launch happened in 2016, this paper is one of the first approaches to provide a complete framework for evaluating different techniques for predicting reactions to user posts on public pages. For this purpose, we used the FacebookR dataset that contains Facebook posts (along with their comments and reactions) of the biggest international supermarket chains. In order to build a robust and accurate prediction pipeline state-of-the-art neural network architectures (convolutional and recurrent neural networks) were tested using pretrained word embeddings. The models are further improved by introducing a bootstrapping approach for sentiment and emotion mining on the comments for each post and a data augmentation technique to obtain an even more robust predictor. The final proposed pipeline is a combination of a neural network and a baseline emotion miner and is able to predict the reaction distribution on Facebook posts with a mean squared error (or misclassification rate) of 0.1326.

**Keywords:** Emotion mining · Social media · Deep learning
Natural language processing

## 1 Introduction

The ubiquitous use of social media has raised the need to improve techniques of analyzing short text messages' content and improve performance on tasks like topic modeling, topic classification, sentiment analysis, etc. Social media pages related to (and managed by) firms/companies are drowned in content posted every day by users who share their customer experience. These large amounts of

T. Moers and F. Krebs—Equal contribution.


J. van den Herik and A. P. Rocha (Eds.): ICAART 2018, LNAI 11352, pp. 361–382, 2019.
https://doi.org/10.1007/978-3-030-05453-3_17

data can be further analyzed and grasp the feelings, emotions and sentiments of the users which has yielded many research works with applications in political science, social sciences, business, education, etc. [1–3].

Customer experience (CX) represents a holistic perspective on customer interactions with a firm's products and/or services. If managers have enough information about customer experiences with product and service offerings, then it is possible to quantify these and through standardized measurements to improve future actions and decisions. The rise of social media analytics [4] offers managers a tool to manage this process since customer data (in terms of reviews and content sharing) are widely available in social media.

This paper is building on authors' previous work [5] on identifying the sentiment and emotion of Facebook posts and trying to predict user reactions and to our knowledge it was the first research work on working with Facebook posts reactions. Analyzing Facebook posts can help firm managers to better manage posts by allowing customer care teams to reply faster to unsatisfied customers or maybe even delegate posts to employees based on their expertise. Also, it would be possible to estimate how the reply on a post affects the reaction from other customers.

The main goals and contributions of this paper are the following: (a) highlight the use of an (augmented) dataset which can be used for predicting reactions on Facebook posts, useful for both machine learners and marketing experts and (b) perform improved sentiment analysis and emotion mining to Facebook posts and comments of several supermarket chains by predicting the distribution of the user reactions. Firstly, sentiment analysis and emotion mining baseline techniques are utilized in order to analyze the sentiment/emotion of a post and its comments. Afterwards, neural networks with pretrained word embeddings are used in order to accurately predict the distribution of reactions to a post. Combination of the two approaches gives a working final ensemble which leaves promising directions for future research.

The remainder of the paper is organized as follows. Section 2 presents related work about sentiment and emotion analysis on short informal text like from Facebook and Twitter. The dataset along with any pre-processing and augmentation steps are described in Sect. 3, followed by the model (pipeline) description in Sect. 4. Section 5 presents the detailed experimental results and finally, Sect. 6 concludes the paper and presents future research directions.

## 2 Related Work

Deep learning based approaches have recently become more popular for sentiment classification since they automatically extract features based on word embeddings. Convolutional Neural Networks (CNN), originally proposed in [6] for document recognition, have been extensively used for short sentence sentiment classification. [7] uses a CNN and achieves state-of-the art results in sentiment classification. They also highlight that one CNN layer in the model's architecture is sufficient to perform well on sentiment classification tasks. Recurrent

Neural Networks (RNN) and more specifically their variants Long Short Term Memory (LSTM) networks [8] and Gated Recurrent Units (GRU) networks [9] have also been extensively used for sentiment classification since they are able to capture long term relationships between words in a sentence while avoiding vanishing and exploding gradient problems of normal recurrent network architectures [10]. [11] proves that combining different architectures, such as CNN and GRU, in an ensemble learner improves the performance of individual base learners for sentiment classification, which makes it relevant for this research work as well.

Most of the work on short text sentiment classification concentrates around Twitter and different machine learning techniques [12–15]. These are some examples of the extensive research already done on Twitter sentiment analysis. Not many approaches for Facebook posts exist, partly because it is difficult to get a labeled dataset for such a purpose.

Emotion lexicons like EmoLex [16] can be used in order to annotate a corpus, however, results are not satisfactory and this is the reason that bootstrapping techniques have been attempted in the past. For example, [17] propose such a technique which enhances EmoLex with synonyms and then combines word vectors [18] in order to annotate more examples based on sentence similarity measures.

Recently, [19] presented some first results which associate Facebook reactions with emojis but their analysis stopped there. [20] utilized the actual reactions on posts in a distant supervised fashion to train a support vector machine classifier for emotion detection but they are not attempting at actually predicting the distribution of reactions.

Moreover, analysis of customer feedback is an area which gains interest for many companies over the years. Given the amount of text feedback available, there are many approaches around this topic, however none of them are handling the increasing amounts of information available through Facebook posts. For the sake of completeness, we highlight here some these approaches. Sentiment classification [21–23] deals only with the sentiment analysis (usually mapping sentiments to positive, negative and neutral (or other 5-scale classification)) and similarly emotion classification [24,25] only considers emotions. Some work exists on Twitter data [26] but does not take into account the reactions of Facebook. Moreover, work has been conducted towards customer review analysis [27–29] but none of them are dealing with the specific nature of Facebook (or social media in general).

Due to the lack of enough labeled data, data augmentation is necessary to extend the dataset for systems like neural networks. Typically, data augmentation for images is done by adding noise, or transforming the image like rotating or scaling [30]. Also, for time-series data of signals like sensory data, one is able to add a certain amount of noise to augment the dataset. Recent approaches like [31–34] augment image data by using Generative Adversarial Networks (GANs) to generate new data that is based on the given data distribution. However, augmenting text is still a weakly researched area as it is a complex problem. There is no Gaussian noise, no rotation or translation that can be made to augment the text. Instead, [35] use a thesaurus to enhance the dataset by replacing words of the training text with synonyms. They report that they receive the best results when using the thesaurus data augmentation.

In this work, we show how we can create a big enough dataset using standard NLP tools and augmentation techniques. Then we demonstrate how the combination of traditional sentiment and emotion mining techniques with modern neural network architectures can help accurately predicting the distribution of reactions on Facebook posts.

## 3 Dataset Construction

Our dataset consists out of Facebook posts on the customer service page of 12 US/UK big supermarket/retail chains, namely Tesco, Sainsbury, Walmart, Aldi UK, The Home Depot, Target, Walgreens, Amazon, Best Buy, Safeway, Macys and publix. The vast majority of these posts are initiated by customers of these supermarkets. In addition to the written text of the posts, we also fetch the Facebook's reaction matrix[1] as well as the comments attached to this post made by other users. Such reactions only belong to the initial post, and not to replies to the post since the feature to post a reaction on a reply has only been introduced very recently (May 2017) and would result in either a very small dataset or an incomplete dataset. These reactions include *like*, *love*, *wow*, *haha*, *sad*, *angry* as shown in Fig. 1. This form of communication was introduced by Facebook on February 24th, 2016 and allows users to express an 'emotion' towards the posted content.

**Fig. 1.** The Facebook reaction icons that users are able to select for an original post [5].

In total, there were more than 70,000 posts without any reaction. Apart from this problem, people are using the 'like' reaction not only to show that they like what they see/read but also to simply tell others that they have seen this post or to show sympathy. This results in a way too often used 'like'-reaction which is why likes could be ignored in the constructed dataset. So, instead of using all crawled data, the developed models will be trained on posts that have at least one other reaction than likes. After applying this threshold the size of the training

[1] http://newsroom.fb.com/news/2016/02/reactions-now-available-globally/.

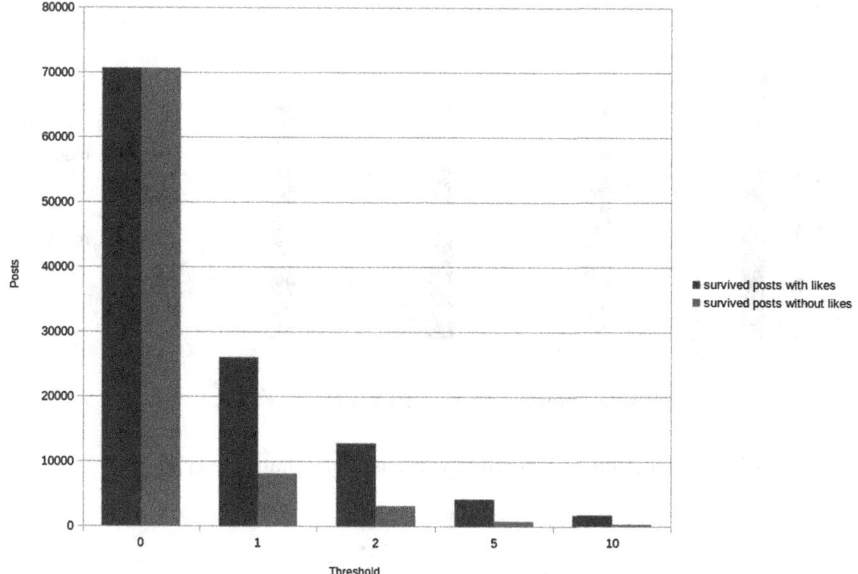


**Fig. 2.** Amount of survived posts for different thresholds including/excluding likes [5].

set reduced from 70,649 to 25,969. The threshold of 1 is still not optimal since it leaves much space for noise in the data (e.g. miss-clicked reactions) but using a higher threshold will lead to extreme loss of data. Statistics on the dataset and on how many posts 'survive' by using different thresholds can be seen in Fig. 2.

Exploratory analysis on the dataset shows that people tend to agree in the reactions they have to Facebook posts (which is consistent for building a prediction system), i.e. whenever there are more than one types of reactions they seem to be the same in a great degree (over 80%) as can be seen in Fig. 3. In addition, Fig. 4 shows that even by excluding the *like* reaction, which seems to dominate all posts, the distribution of the reactions remains the same, even if the threshold of minimum reactions increases. Using all previous insights and the fact that there are 25,969 posts with at least one reaction and since the *like* reaction dominates the posts, we chose to include posts with at least one reaction which is not a *like*, leading to finally 8,103 posts. Full dataset is available[2].

### 3.1 Pre-processing

Pre-processing on the dataset is carried out using the Stanford CoreNLP parser [36] and includes the following steps:

- Convert everything to lower case
- Replace URLs with "__URL__" as a generic token
- Replace user/profile links with "__AT_USER__" as a generic token

[2] https://github.com/jerryspan/FacebookR.

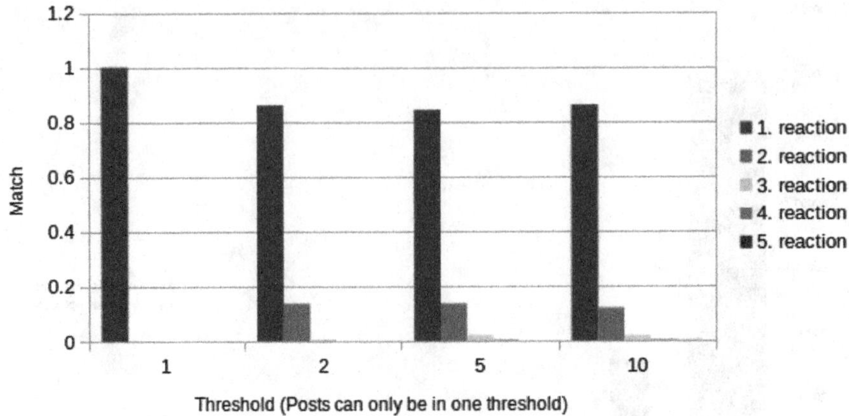


**Fig. 3.** Reaction match when there is more than one type [5].

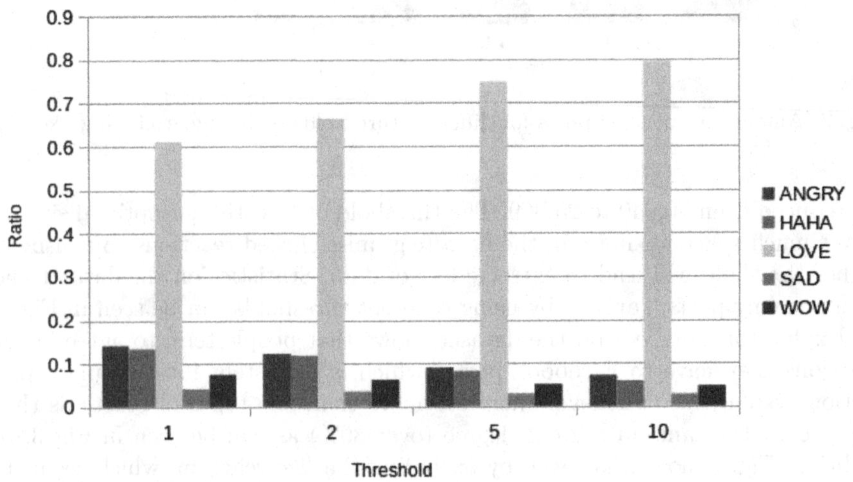


**Fig. 4.** Distribution of reactions with different minimum thresholds [5].

- Remove the hash from a hashtag reference (e.g. #hashtag becomes "hashtag")
- Replace three or more occurrences of one character in a row with the character itself (e.g. "looooove" becomes "love")
- Remove sequences containing numbers (e.g. "gr34t").

Afterwards, each post is split using a tokenizer based on spaces and after some stop-word filtering the final list of different tokens is derived. Since pre-processing on short text has attracted much attention recently [37], we also demonstrate the effect of it on the developed models in the Experiments section.

### 3.2 Data Augmentation

As mentioned in the previous subsection, our final dataset consists of 8,103 relevant posts. However, this is a relatively small amount of data which might lead to unsatisfying results or to overfitting depending on the network architecture. We noticed that the networks are overfitting after several epochs when using such a small dataset and this raised the need for performing data augmentation. We used the same approach like [35], namely a thesaurus data augmentation. Similar to image data augmentation, thesaurus data augmentation tries to change the form but not the underlying features of textual sentences. This is achieved by replacing words that have the same meaning (synonyms). Therefore, the underlying feature, namely the semantics, is not changed. The augmentation pipeline is as follows:

1. Collect all posts that at least have one reaction except 'likes'.
2. Annotate each word within each post with a Part-of-Speech (POS) tag and split sentences using the CoreNLP Server.
3. Use NLTK [38] with WordNet [39] to request the closest synonym of each noun, adjective and verb.
4. Build new posts by replacing original words with their closest synonyms.
5. Finally, save the new posts with the same reactions as the original post in the database.

The data augmentation process increased the number of relevant posts from 8,103 to 486,471, which of course is a massive increase of the volume. We are aware of the fact, that there might be some error cases (due to e.g. language properties or when the closest synonym does not make sense). In Sect. 5, we evaluate the difference between training with original data and with augmented data and how it affects the results.

## 4 Reaction Distribution Prediction System Pipeline

In this Section, the complete prediction system is described. There are three core components: emotion mining applied to Facebook comments, artificial neural networks that predict the distribution of the reactions for a Facebook post and a combination of the two in the final prediction of the distribution of reactions.

### 4.1 Emotion Mining

The overall pipeline of the emotion miner can be found in Fig. 5. The first step is to split posts into sentences and pre-process the sentences by using CoreNLP. The processed sentences are then tokenized to be fit into a word-based emotion classifier, that allows one to annotate an emotion set to each word and therefore, to each sentence. However, the word-based classifier will not be able to annotate all words. The last step is a Support Vector Machine that predicts the emotions of the left non-annotated sentences. In the end, we are annotated the complete data set by processing through the emotion pipeline.

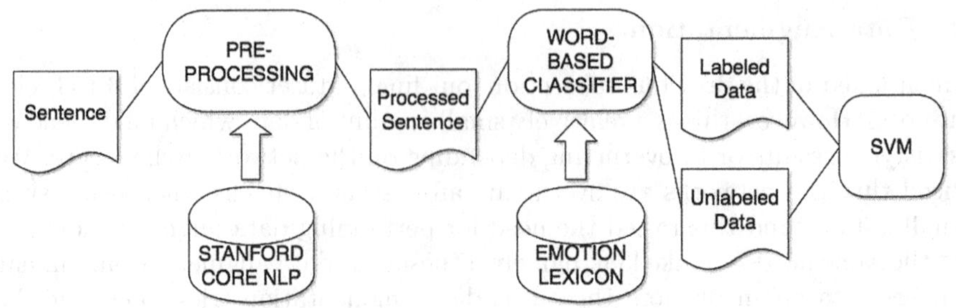


**Fig. 5.** Emotion miner pipeline [5].

The emotion lexicon that we utilize is created by [16] and is called NRC Emotion Lexicon (EmoLex). This lexicon consists of 14,181 words with eight basic emotions (anger, fear, anticipation, trust, surprise, sadness, joy, and disgust) associated with each word in the lexicon. It is possible that a single word is associated with more than one emotion. An example can be seen in Table 1. Annotations were manually performed by crowd-sourcing.

**Table 1.** Examples from EmoLex showing the emotion association to the words 'abuse' and 'shopping' [5].

| | Anger | Anticipation | Disgust | Fear | Joy | Sadness | Surprise | Trust |
|---|---|---|---|---|---|---|---|---|
| abuse | **1** | 0 | **1** | **1** | 0 | **1** | 0 | 0 |
| shopping | 0 | **1** | 0 | 0 | **1** | 0 | **1** | **1** |

Inspired by the approach of [17], EmoLex is extended by using WordNet [39]: for every synonym found, new entries are introduced in EmoLex having the same emotion vector as the original words. By applying this technique the original database has increased in size from 14,181 to 31,485 words that are related to an emotion vector. The lexicon can then be used to determine the emotion of the comments to a Facebook post. For each sentence in a comment, the emotion is determined by looking up all words in the emotion database and the found emotion vectors are added to the sentence emotion vector. By merging and normalizing all emotion vectors, the final emotion distribution for a particular Facebook post, based on the equivalent comments, can be computed. However, this naive approach yielded poor results, thus several enhancements were considered, implemented and described in Subsect. 4.1.

**Negation Handling.** The first technique that was used to improve the quality of the mined emotions is negation handling. By detecting negations in a sentence, the ability to 'turn' this sentiment or emotion is provided. In this paper, only basic negation handling is applied since the majority of the dataset contains only small sentences and this is sufficient for our goal. The following list of negations and pre- and suffixes are used for detection (based on work of [40]) (Table 2):

**Table 2.** Negation patterns [5] that we use for the negation handling. Those are standard negations, prefixes and suffixes used in the normal life.

| | |
|---|---|
| Negations | no, not, rather, wont, never, none, nobody, nothing, neither, nor, nowhere, cannot, without, n't |
| Prefixes | a, de, dis, il, im, in, ir, mis, non, un |
| Suffixes | less |

The following two rules are applied:

1. The first rule is used when a negation word is instantly followed by an emotion-word (which is present in our emotion database).
2. The second rule tries to handle adverbs and past particle verbs (POS tags: RB, VBN). If a negation word is followed by one or more of these POS-tags and a following emotion-word, the emotion-word's value will be negated. For example this rule would apply to 'not very happy'.

There are two ways to obtain the emotions of a negated word:

1. Look up all combinations of negation pre- and suffixes together with the word in our emotion lexicon.
2. If there is no match in the lexicon a manually created mapping is used between the emotions and their negations. This mapping is shown in Table 3.

**Table 3.** Mapping between emotion and negated emotions [5].

| | Anger | Anticipation | Disgust | Fear | Joy | Sadness | Surprise | Trust |
|---|---|---|---|---|---|---|---|---|
| Anger | 0 | 0 | 0 | 0 | **1** | 0 | 0 | 0 |
| Anticipation | 0 | 0 | 0 | 0 | **1** | 0 | **1** | 0 |
| Disgust | 0 | 0 | 0 | 0 | **1** | 0 | 0 | **1** |
| Fear | 0 | 0 | 0 | 0 | **1** | 0 | 0 | **1** |
| Joy | **1** | 0 | **1** | **1** | 0 | **1** | 0 | 0 |
| Sadness | 0 | 0 | 0 | **1** | 0 | 0 | 0 | 0 |
| Surprise | 0 | **1** | 0 | 0 | 0 | 0 | 0 | **1** |
| Trust | 0 | 0 | **1** | 0 | 0 | 0 | **1** | 0 |

**Sentence Similarity Measures.** [17]'s approach is using word vectors [18] in order to calculate similarities between sentences and further annotate sentences. In the context of this paper, a more recent approach was attempted [41], together with an averaging word vector approach for comparison. [41] creates a

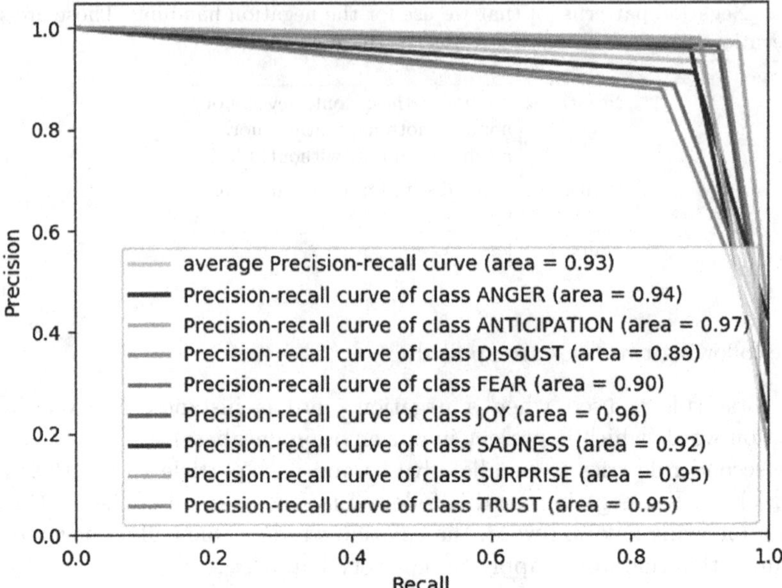


**Fig. 6.** Precision-Recall (ROC) curve using a linear SVM in an one-versus-all classifier [5]. The average precision recall has an area of about 0.93. The best precision-recall is achieved by the anticipation class as it has the most significant samples in the training set. The worst score is surprisingly reached by the disgust class. One would think that the disgust class has striking word representations and patterns.

representation for a whole sentence instead of only for one word as word2vec. The average word vector approach is summing up the word vector of each word and then taking the mean of this sum. To find a similarity between two sentences, one then uses the cosine similarity. Surprisingly, both approaches return comparable similarity scores. One main problem which occurred here is that two sentences with different emotions but with the same structure are measured as 'similar'. This problem is exemplified with an example:

```
Sentence 1: "I really love your car."
Sentence 2: "I really hate your car."
Sentence2Vec similarity: 0.9278
Avg vector similarity: 0.9269
```

This high similarity is problematic since the emotions of the two sentences are completely different. Also, one can see that the two models output almost the same result and that there is no advantage by using the approach of [41] over the simple average word vector approach. Hence, the sentence similarity measure method to annotate more sentences is not suited for this emotion mining task because one would annotate positive emotions to a negative sentence. Therefore, sentence similarity measurement is not used for our pipeline.

**Classification of Not Annotated Sentences.** If after executing these enhancement steps any non-emotion-annotated sentences remain, then a Support Vector Machine (SVM) is used to estimate the emotions of these sentences based on the existing annotations. The SVM is trained as a one-versus-all classifier with a linear kernel (8 models are trained, one for each emotion of EmoLex) and the TF-IDF model [42] is used for providing the input features. The input consists of a single sentence as data (transformed using the TF-IDF model) and an array of 8 values representing the emotions as a label. With a training/test-split of 80%/20%, the average precision-recall is about 0.93. Full results of the SVM training can be seen in Fig. 6 together with the precision-recall curve for all emotions. The result in this case was judged to be sufficient in order to utilize it for the next step, which is the reaction prediction and is used as presented here.

### 4.2 Reaction Distribution Predictor

In order to predict the distribution of the post reactions, neural networks are built and trained using TensorFlow [43]. Two networks were tested, based on literature research: a Convolutional Neural Network (CNN) and a Recurrent Neural Network (RNN) that uses LSTMs.

Both networks start with a word embedding layer. Since the analyzed posts were written in English, the GloVe [44] pre-trained embeddings (with 50 as a vector dimension) were used. Moreover, posts are short texts and informal language is expected, thus we opted for using embeddings previously trained on Twitter data instead of the Wikipedia versions.

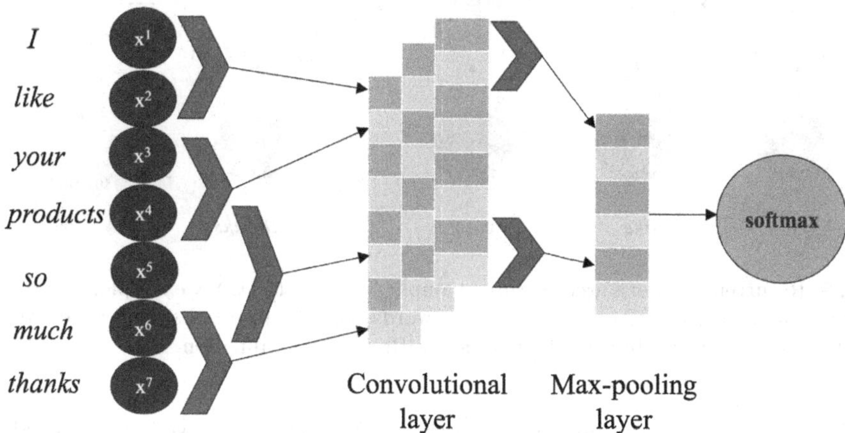


**Fig. 7.** A convolutional network architecture example [5]. The text input is vectorized with a pre-trained word embedding and then fed into the network. The convolutions extract meaningful features and the softmax activation forces the output to be a distribution output. (Color figure online)

**CNN.** The CNN model is based on existing successful architectures (see [7]) but is adapted to give a distribution of reactions as an output. An overview of the used architecture is provided in Fig. 7.

First issue to be handled with CNNs is that since they deal with variable length input sentences, padding is needed so as to ensure that all posts have the same length. In our case, we padded all posts to the maximum post length which also allows efficient batching of the data. In the example of Fig. 7 the length of the sentence is seven and each word $x_i$ is represented by the equivalent word vector (of dimension 50).

The convolutional layer is the core building block of a CNN. Common patterns in the training data are extracted by applying the convolution operation which in our case is limited into 1 dimension: we adjust the height of the filter, i.e. the number of adjacent rows (words) that are considered together (see also red arrows in Fig. 7). These patterns are then fed to a pooling layer. The primary role of the pooling layer is to reduce the spatial dimensions of the learned representations (that's why this layer is also known to perform down sampling). This is beneficial, since it controls for over-fitting but also allows for faster computations. Finally, the output of the pooling layer is fed to a fully-connected layer (with dropout) which has a softmax as output and each node corresponds to each predicted reaction (thus we have six nodes initially). However, due to discarding *like* reaction later on in the research stage, the effective number of output nodes was decreased to five (see Experiments). The softmax classifier computes a probability distribution over all possible reactions, thus provides a probabilistic and intuitive interpretation.

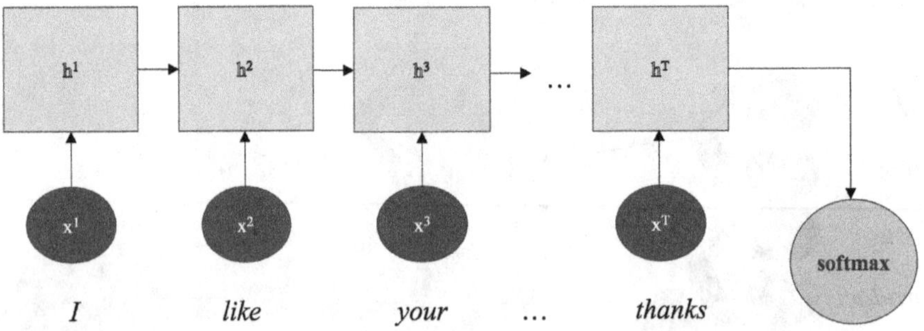


**Fig. 8.** Recurrent network architecture example [5]. As in the CNN example, the input text is converted to word embeddings. The words are then inserted step per step until the last layer that outputs the distribution with a softmax function.

**RNN.** Long short-term memory networks (LSTM) were proposed by [8] in order to address the issue of learning long-term dependencies. The LSTM maintains a separate memory cell inside it that updates and exposes its content only when deemed necessary, thus making it possible to capture content as needed. The implementation used here is inspired by [45] and an overview is provided in Fig. 8.

An LSTM unit (at each time step $t$) is defined as a collection of vectors: the input gate ($i_t$), the forget gate ($f_t$), the output gate ($o_t$), a memory cell ($c_t$) and a hidden state ($h_t$). Input is provided sequentially in terms of word vectors ($x_t$) and for each time step $t$ the previous time step information is used as input. Intuitively, the forget gate controls the amount of which each unit of the memory cell is replaced by new info, the input gate controls how much each unit is updated, and the output gate controls the exposure of the internal memory state.

In our case, the RNN model utilizes one recurrent layer (which has 50 LSTM cells) and the rest of the parameters are chosen based on current default working architectures. The output then comes from a weighted fully connected 5-class softmax layer. Figure 8 explains the idea of recurrent architecture based on an input sequence of words.

### 4.3 Prediction Ensemble

The final reaction ratio prediction is carried out by a combination of the neural networks and the mined emotions on the post/comments. For a given post, both networks provide an estimation of the distributions, which are then averaged and normalized. Next, emotions from the post and the comments are extracted following the process described in Sect. 4.1. The ratio of estimations and emotions are combined into a single vector which is then computed through a simple regression model, which re-estimates the predicted reaction ratios. The whole pipeline combining the emotion miner and the neural networks can be seen in Fig. 9 and experimental results are presented in the next Section.

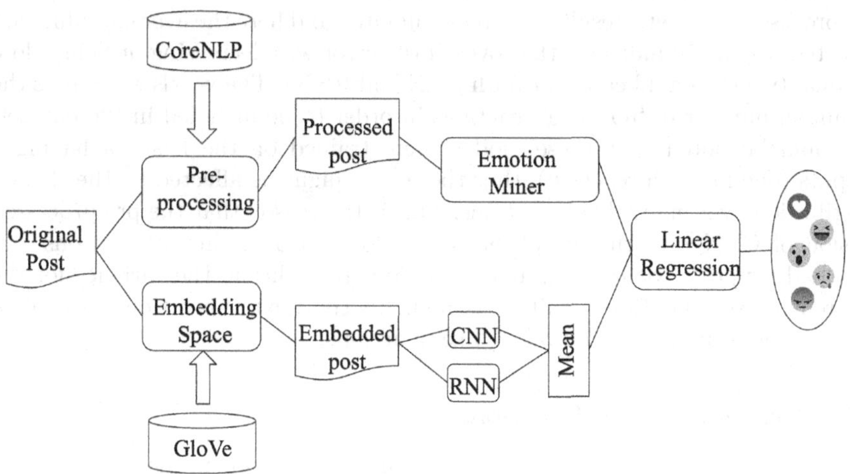


**Fig. 9.** Complete pipeline for the final prediction of the reaction distributions [5].

# 5 Experiments

Several experiments were conducted in order to assess different effects on the reaction distribution prediction. Firstly, the effect of pre-processing on posts is examined in Subsect. 5.1. Since Facebook reactions were not introduced too long ago, a lot of posts in the dataset still contain primarily *like* reactions. This might lead to uninteresting results as described in the Dataset Section and in Subsect. 5.2. Finally, Subsect. 5.3 discusses the training with respect to the mean squared error (MSE) for CNN and RNN models, as well as the effect of the combined approach.

As mentioned before, both networks utilized the GloVe pre-trained embeddings (with size 50). Batch size was set to 16 for the CNN and 100 for the RNN/LSTM.

CNN used 40 filters for the convolution (with varying height sizes from 3 to 5), stride was set to 1 and padding to the maximum post length was used. Rectified Linear Unit (ReLU) [46] activation function was used.

Learning rate was set to 0.001 and dropout was applied to both networks and performance was measured by the cross entropy loss with scores and labels with L2-regularization [47]. Mean Squared Error (MSE) is used in order to assess successful classifications (which effectively means that every squared error will be a 0) and in the end MSE is just the misclassification rate of predictions.

## 5.1 Raw Vs Pre-processed Input

In order to assess the effect of pre-processing on the quality of the trained models, two versions for each neural network were trained. One instance was trained without pre-processing the dataset and the other instance was trained with the pre-processed dataset. Results are cross-validated and here the average values are reported. Figure 10 indicates that overall the error was decreasing or being close to equal (which is applicable for both CNN and RNN). The x-axis represents the minimum number of 'non-like' reactions in order to be included in the dataset. It should be noted that these models were trained on the basis of having 6 outputs (one for each reaction), thus the result might be affected by the skewed distribution over many 'like' reactions. This is the reason that the pre-processed version of CNN performs very well for posts with 5 minimum reactions and very bad for posts with 10 minimum reactions In addition, the variance for the different cross-validation results was high. In the next subsection we explore what happens after the removal of 'like' reactions.

## 5.2 Exclusion of Like Reactions

Early results showed that including the original *like* reaction in the models would lead to meaningless results. The huge imbalanced dataset led to predicting a 100% ratio for the *like* reaction. In order to tackle this issue, the *like* reactions are not fed into the models during the training phase (moreover the *love* reaction can be used for equivalent purposes, since they express similar emotions). Figure 11

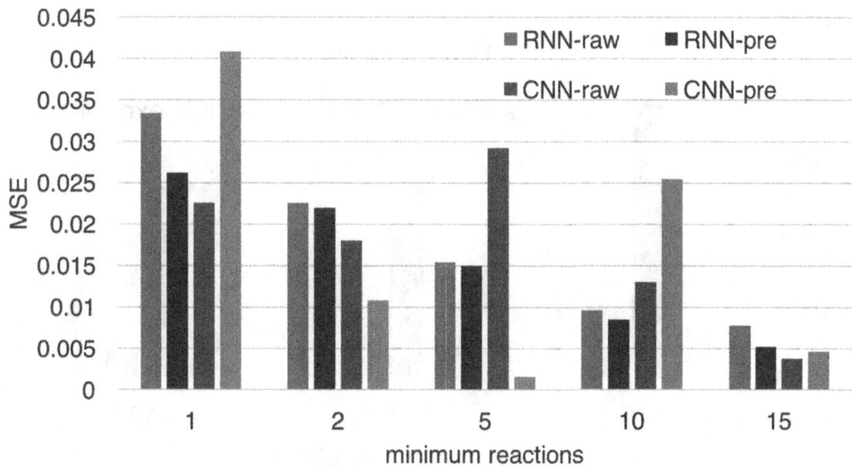


**Fig. 10.** Effect of pre-processing on different models [5].

shows an increase of the error when the likes are ignored. The explanation for this increase is related to heavily unbalanced distribution of *like* reactions: Although there is an increase in the error, predictions now are more meaningful than always predicting a like ratio close to 100%. After all, it is the relative reaction distribution that we are interested in predicting.

### 5.3 Ensemble Performance

Table 4 summarizes the testing error for the CNN and RNN with respect to the same split dataset and by also taking the validation error into account. One can see that RNN performs better than CNN, although it requires additional training time. Results are cross-validated on 10 different runs and variances are presented in the Table as well.

**Table 4.** RNN and CNN comparison after cross-validation [5].

| | MSE | # Epochs |
|---|---|---|
| CNN | 0.186 (+- 0.023) | 81 |
| RNN | 0.159 (+- 0.017) | 111 |

Combined results for either of the networks and the emotion miner can be seen in Fig. 12. The networks themselves have the worst results but an average combination of both is able to achieve a better result. Optimal result is achieved by the emotions + cnn combination, although this difference is not significantly better than other combinations. These results can be boosted by optimizing the

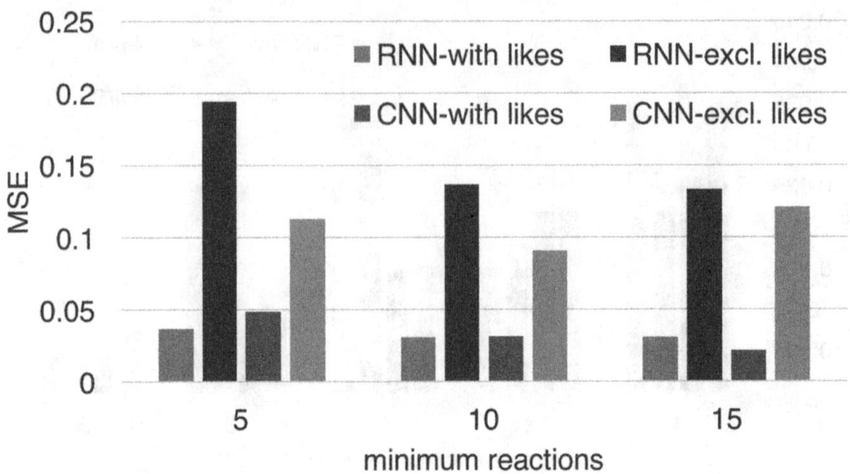


**Fig. 11.** Effect of inclusion/exclusion of likes on different models [5].

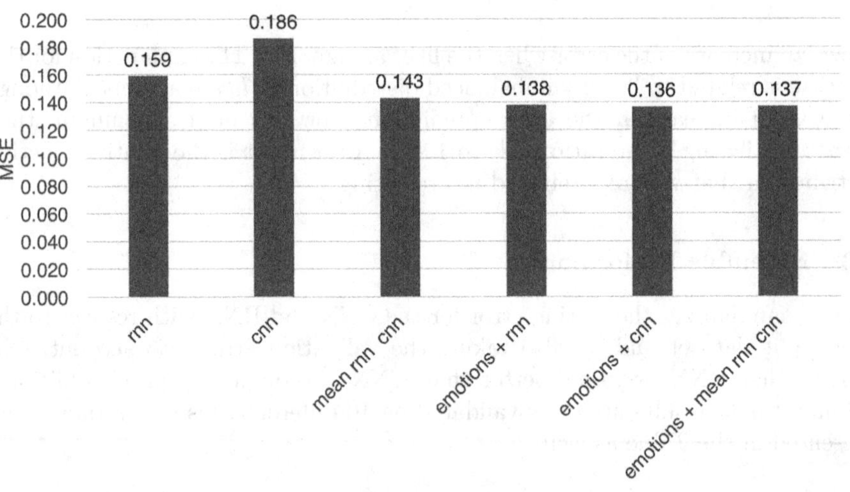


**Fig. 12.** Performance results for different combinations of the neural networks and emotions [5].

hyperparameters of the networks and also by varying different amount of posts. As a conclusion one can say that using emotions to combine them with neural network output improves the results of prediction.

### 5.4 Initial Data Vs Augmented Data

In this section we compare the initial dataset with the augmented dataset. The augmentation method is described in Sect. 3.2.

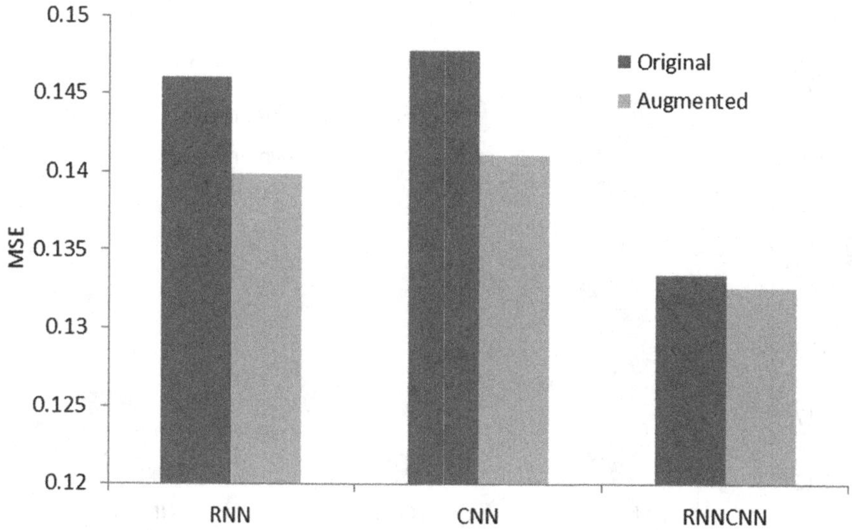


**Fig. 13.** Mean squared error of the three different models with and without augmented data.

Figure 13 shows that using augmented data improves the result of all three networks. But even the CNN, on which the data augmentation had the highest impact, could decrease its error by only 4.5% while the RNN changed by 4.2%. The combined network, which was the best performing model already, barely changed at all (0.6%). Even though the data augmentation improved our results the changes were not as significant as we hoped them to be. The reason could be that even though we achieved much more training data most of the posts still have very few reactions and hence are weak against noise. Those noisy posts are even multiplied due to data augmentation and leads to a higher error. Another reason might be that each original post has been augmented multiple times. In each of these copies we replaced a single word with the best matching synonym and copied reactions and emotions of the original post. This leads to a high number of similar posts that each have the exact same label. This could be reduced by adding some small Gaussian noise to the labels of each augmented copy. Since using both, the neural network's predictions and mined emotions, proofed to be a successful combination earlier (see Fig. 12) we also tried to do that but it seems that the emotion miner does not work well on the augmented dataset. The results were much worse and especially the mean squared error of the RNN increased drastically as shown in Fig. 14.

### 5.5 Visualization

Finally, we present a simple, yet effective visualization environment which highlights the results of the current paper, that can be found in Fig. 15. In this figure, one can see at the input field of the Facebook post on the top and then four

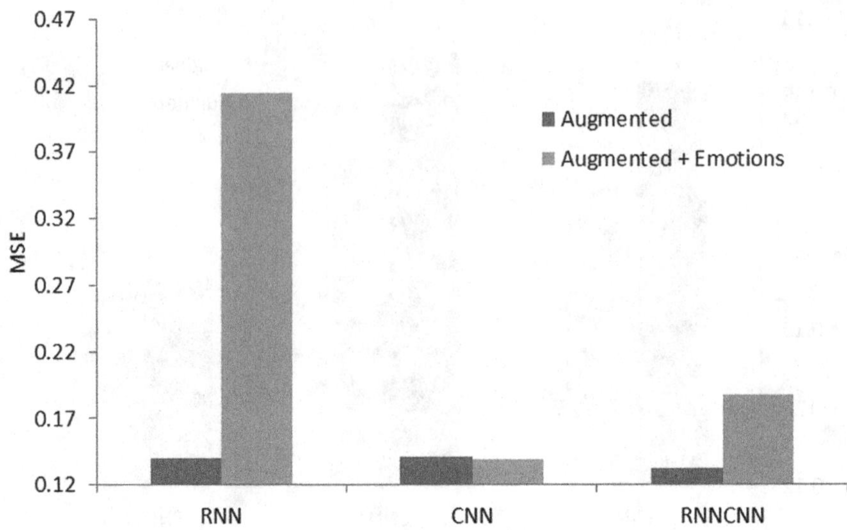


**Fig. 14.** Mean squared error of the three different models using the augmented dataset and the mined emotions.

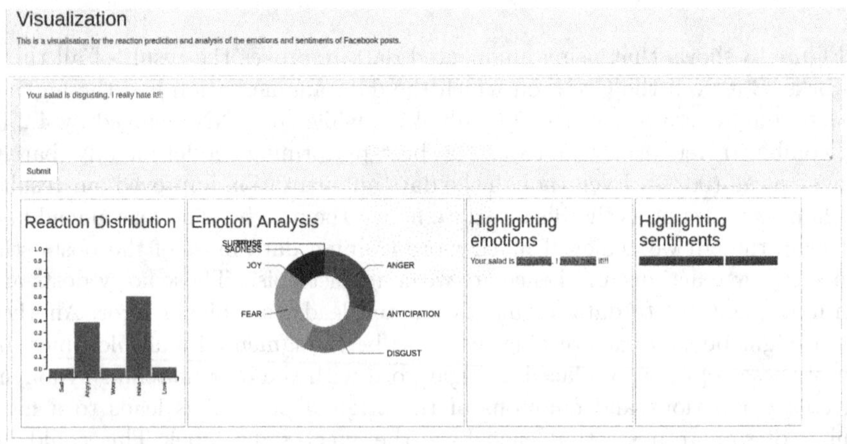


**Fig. 15.** Example visualization containing all components of SEMTec [5]. The user is able to write a post and to see the predicted reactions, an emotions pie diagram and an emotion and sentiment word highlighting of the input.

different result panels: the first one shows the reaction distribution, the second panel shows the proportions of the eight emotions, the third panel highlights the emotions (and by hovering, one can see the total shows the overall distribution (vector of eight)) and the fourth panel shows the highlighting of the sentiments. The visualization enabled us to analyze the network in a more interactive way and to point out where it fails and where it works. Also, it gives a good overview of the different components that this paper uses.

## 6 Conclusion

In this paper we presented and shared a dataset containing Facebook posts (with their reactions and comments) taken from public pages of several big supermarket chains. A framework for predicting the post reaction distribution was described and the effect of using the initial (small) dataset with an augmented (large) dataset was presented. We were able to show that data augmentation improved the quality of our neural networks by reducing the overall error for all three models. Our experiments demonstrate that combining a traditional emotion/sentiment mining technique with the output of modern neural network architectures can effectively predict the Facebook reactions. Furthermore, since most research works focus on sentiment analysis, our paper also contributes towards putting emotion analysis to the spotlight (especially in a social media context). Finally, the scrapped dataset developed during this work is available for other researchers and can be also used as a baseline for performing further experiments. It is in our future goals to further curate the dataset and more accurately evaluate the emotion mining part by using the MPQA corpus [48].

Despite recent distrust towards social media, it is clear that a transparent system which utilizes Facebook reaction predictions can enhance customer experience analytics. Identifying the emotion/reaction prediction of a post in almost real-time can be used to provide effective and useful feedback to customers and improve their experience. As long as page owners provide accurate recommendations and answers to complaints that are transparent and clear to the users, such a machine learning system remains extremely useful.

For future work, we plan to incorporate information that is currently not used in the dataset. That includes the reaction of the page owner and could contain useful information on how the post was addressed (or could be addressed). Another direction would be to combine the images that users attach to their posts with the actual text content. This synergy can reveal more about the sentiment/emotion of the user and can potentially highlight new directions in the language/vision domain. Since we are dealing with the social media domain, using external parameters (e.g. popularity of the post/poster, inclusion of other media external links, etc.), would also be a promising direction.

Finally, once there are enough posts (with potential comments) and resolutions from the page owner, we could build an automated reply system that based on the content of the post and the subsequent emotion/sentiment would be able to provide feedback to the customers in a minimal amount of time with minimal human intervention.

## References

1. Ortigosa, A., Martín, J.M., Carro, R.M.: Sentiment analysis in Facebook and its application to e-learning. Comput. Hum. Behav. **31**, 527–541 (2014)
2. Feldman, R.: Techniques and applications for sentiment analysis. Commun. ACM **56**, 82–89 (2013)

3. Troussas, C., Virvou, M., Espinosa, K.J., Llaguno, K., Caro, J.: Sentiment analysis of Facebook statuses using Naive Bayes classifier for language learning. In: 2013 Fourth International Conference on Information, Intelligence, Systems and Applications (IISA), pp. 1–6. IEEE (2013)
4. Fan, W., Gordon, M.D.: The power of social media analytics. Commun. ACM **57**, 74–81 (2014)
5. Krebs, F., Lubascher, B., Moers, T., Schaap, P., Spanakis, G.: Social emotion mining techniques for Facebook posts reaction prediction. In: Proceedings of the 10th International Conference on Agents and Artificial Intelligence, pp. 211–220 (2018)
6. LeCun, Y., Bottou, L., Bengio, Y., Haffner, P.: Gradient-based learning applied to document recognition. Proc. IEEE **86**, 2278–2324 (1998)
7. Kim, Y.: Convolutional neural networks for sentence classification. CoRR abs/1408.5882 (2014)
8. Hochreiter, S., Schmidhuber, J.: Long short-term memory. Neural Comput. **9**, 1735–1780 (1997)
9. Chung, J., Gulcehre, C., Cho, K., Bengio, Y.: Empirical evaluation of gated recurrent neural networks on sequence modeling. arXiv preprint arXiv:1412.3555 (2014)
10. Hochreiter, S.: The vanishing gradient problem during learning recurrent neural nets and problem solutions. Int. J. Uncertainty Fuzziness Knowl.-Based Syst. **6**, 107–116 (1998)
11. Wang, G., Sun, J., Ma, J., Xu, K., Gu, J.: Sentiment classification: the contribution of ensemble learning. Decis. Support Syst. **57**, 77–93 (2014)
12. Wang, X., Wei, F., Liu, X., Zhou, M., Zhang, M.: Topic sentiment analysis in Twitter: a graph-based hashtag sentiment classification approach. In: Proceedings of the 20th ACM International Conference on Information and Knowledge Management, pp. 1031–1040. ACM (2011)
13. Kouloumpis, E., Wilson, T., Moore, J.D.: Twitter sentiment analysis: the good the bad and the omg!. Icwsm **11**, 164 (2011)
14. Saif, H., He, Y., Alani, H.: Semantic sentiment analysis of Twitter. In: Cudré-Mauroux, P., et al. (eds.) ISWC 2012. LNCS, vol. 7649, pp. 508–524. Springer, Heidelberg (2012). https://doi.org/10.1007/978-3-642-35176-1_32
15. Sarlan, A., Nadam, C., Basri, S.: Twitter sentiment analysis. In: 2014 International Conference on Information Technology and Multimedia (ICIMU), pp. 212–216. IEEE (2014)
16. Mohammad, S.M., Turney, P.D.: Crowdsourcing a word-emotion association lexicon. Comput. Intell. **29**, 436–465 (2013)
17. Canales, L., Strapparava, C., Boldrini, E., Martínez-Barco, P.: Exploiting a bootstrapping approach for automatic annotation of emotions in texts. In: 2016 IEEE International Conference on Data Science and Advanced Analytics (DSAA), pp. 726–734 (2016)
18. Mikolov, T., Chen, K., Corrado, G., Dean, J.: Efficient estimation of word representations in vector space. arXiv preprint arXiv:1301.3781 (2013)
19. Tian, Y., Galery, T., Dulcinati, G., Molimpakis, E., Sun, C.: Facebook sentiment: Reactions and emojis. In: SocialNLP 2017, p. 11 (2017)
20. Pool, C., Nissim, M.: Distant supervision for emotion detection using Facebook reactions. arXiv preprint arXiv:1611.02988 (2016)
21. Pang, B., Lee, L., Vaithyanathan, S.: Thumbs up?: sentiment classification using machine learning techniques. In: Proceedings of the ACL-02 Conference on Empirical Methods in Natural Language Processing, vol. 10, pp. 79–86. Association for Computational Linguistics (2002)

22. Glorot, X., Bordes, A., Bengio, Y.: Domain adaptation for large-scale sentiment classification: a deep learning approach. In: Proceedings of the 28th International Conference on Machine Learning (ICML 2011), pp. 513–520 (2011)
23. Socher, R., et al.: Recursive deep models for semantic compositionality over a sentiment treebank. In: Proceedings of the 2013 Conference on Empirical Methods in Natural Language Processing, pp. 1631–1642 (2013)
24. Yang, C., Lin, K.H.Y., Chen, H.H.: Emotion classification using web blog corpora. In: IEEE/WIC/ACM International Conference on Web Intelligence, pp. 275–278. IEEE (2007)
25. Wen, S., Wan, X.: Emotion classification in microblog texts using class sequential rules. In: AAAI, pp. 187–193 (2014)
26. Pak, A., Paroubek, P.: Twitter as a corpus for sentiment analysis and opinion mining. In: LREc, vol. 10 (2010)
27. Yang, Z., Fang, X.: Online service quality dimensions and their relationships with satisfaction: a content analysis of customer reviews of securities brokerage services. Int. J. Serv. Indus. Manag. **15**, 302–326 (2004)
28. Hu, M., Liu, B.: Mining and summarizing customer reviews. In: Proceedings of the Tenth ACM SIGKDD International Conference on Knowledge Discovery and Data Mining, pp. 168–177. ACM (2004)
29. Cambria, E., Schuller, B., Xia, Y., Havasi, C.: New avenues in opinion mining and sentiment analysis. IEEE Intell. Syst. **28**, 15–21 (2013)
30. Perez, L., Wang, J.: The effectiveness of data augmentation in image classification using deep learning (2017)
31. Mariani, G., Scheidegger, F., Istrate, R., Bekas, C., Malossi, C.: BAGAN: Data Augmentation with Balancing GAN. ArXiv e-prints (2018)
32. Antoniou, A., Storkey, A., Edwards, H.: Data Augmentation Generative Adversarial Networks. ArXiv e-prints (2017)
33. Frid-Adar, M., Klang, E., Amitai, M., Goldberger, J., Greenspan, H.: Synthetic data augmentation using GAN for improved liver lesion classification. CoRR abs/1801.02385 (2018)
34. Frid-Adar, M., Diamant, I., Klang, E., Amitai, M., Goldberger, J., Greenspan, H.: GAN-based Synthetic Medical Image Augmentation for increased CNN Performance in Liver Lesion Classification. ArXiv e-prints (2018)
35. Zhang, X., LeCun, Y.: Text understanding from scratch (2015) cite arxiv:1502.01710 Comment: This technical report is superseded by a paper entitled "Character-level Convolutional Networks for Text Classification", arXiv:1509.01626. It has considerably more experimental results and a rewritten introduction
36. Manning, C.D., Surdeanu, M., Bauer, J., Finkel, J., Bethard, S.J., McClosky, D.: The stanford CoreNLP natural language processing toolkit. In: Association for Computational Linguistics (ACL) System Demonstrations, pp. 55–60 (2014)
37. Singh, T., Kumari, M.: Role of text pre-processing in Twitter sentiment analysis. Procedia Comput. Sci. **89**, 549–554 (2016)
38. Bird, S., Klein, E., Loper, E.: Natural Language Processing with Python, 1st edn. O'Reilly Media, Inc., Sebastopol (2009)
39. Fellbaum, C.: WordNet: An Electronic Lexical Database. Bradford Books (1998)
40. Farooq, U., Nongaillard, A., Ouzrout, Y., Qadir, M.A.: Negation handling in sentiment analysis at sentence level. In: International Conference on Information Management, London, United Kingdom (2016)
41. Arora, S., Yingyu Liang, T.M.: A simple but tough-to-beat baseline for sentence embeddings (2017)

42. Salton, G., Buckley, C.: Term-weighting approaches in automatic text retrieval. Inf. Process. Manag. **24**, 513–523 (1988)
43. Abadi, M., et al.: Tensorflow: large-scale machine learning on heterogeneous distributed systems. arXiv preprint arXiv:1603.04467 (2016)
44. Pennington, J., Socher, R., Manning, C.D.: Glove: global vectors for word representation. In: Empirical Methods in Natural Language Processing (EMNLP), pp. 1532–1543 (2014)
45. Graves, A.: Generating sequences with recurrent neural networks. arXiv preprint arXiv:1308.0850 (2013)
46. Glorot, X., Bordes, A., Bengio, Y.: Deep sparse rectifier neural networks. In: Proceedings of the Fourteenth International Conference on Artificial Intelligence and Statistics, pp. 315–323 (2011)
47. Masnadi-Shirazi, H., Vasconcelos, N.: On the design of loss functions for classification: theory, robustness to outliers, and savageboost. In: Advances in Neural Information Processing Systems, pp. 1049–1056 (2009)
48. Deng, L., Wiebe, J.: MPQA 3.0: an entity/event-level sentiment corpus. In: Mihalcea, R., Chai, J.Y., Sarkar, A. (eds.) HLT-NAACL, The Association for Computational Linguistics, pp. 1323–1328 (2015)

# Gamma-Star Canonical Forms in the Type-Theory of Acyclic Algorithms

Roussanka Loukanova(✉)

Stockholm University, Stockholm, Sweden
rloukanova@gmail.com

**Abstract.** This work elaborates on the theoretical results of the gamma-star reduction calculus and its potentials for applications in AI and other intelligent technologies. We strengthen the computational properties of the extended gamma-star calculus, by employing a stricter gamma-star rule and adding a formal, recursive definition of the gamma-star canonical forms. A term in a gamma-star normal form provides the algorithm for computing its denotation, without unnecessary calculations that can be required by the initial terms. The extended gamma-star reduction calculus redices every term to its gamma-star normal form.

**Keywords:** Recursion · Types · Semantics · Algorithmic semantics Denotation · Canonical computations

## 1 Introduction

In a sequence of papers, Moschovakis [25–27], introduced a new approach to the mathematical notion of algorithm, by the concept of recursion and mutually recursive computations. The approach, as a class of Theories of Moschovakis Recursion, uses formal languages of recursion with semantic distinctions between denotations of formal terms and algorithms for computing the denotations. That is, a major feature of these theories is that their formal languages have two semantic layers: denotational and algorithmic semantics. The initial work on untyped theory of algorithms is the basis of type-theory of recursion, as formalisation of the concepts of algorithmic computations in typed models of functional spaces. Moschovakis [28] introduced the initial, standard higher-order theory $L^{\lambda}_{ar}$ of acyclic algorithms, by demonstrating its potentials for applications to algorithmic semantics of human language. Such applications are analogous to semantics of programming languages, where a given denotation can be computed by different algorithms.

Our ongoing work is on extending the expressiveness of $L^{\lambda}_{ar}$ by development of a class of formal languages and theories of typed, acyclic recursion, for covering various computational aspects of the mathematical concept of algorithm. We target development of formal systems and calculi, for applications to contemporary intelligent systems. In particular, we develop a class of type-theories of


J. van den Herik and A. P. Rocha (Eds.): ICAART 2018, LNAI 11352, pp. 383–407, 2019.
https://doi.org/10.1007/978-3-030-05453-3_18

algorithms, which have more adequate computational applications in Artificial Intelligence (AI), by covering context dependent algorithms that depend on AI agents and other contextual parameters. For instance, such work was initiated in Loukanova [6,12,20].

Collectively, we call the classes of Moschovakis typed theories of acyclic and full recursion, respectfully, *typed theory of acyclic recursion* (TTofAR) and *typed theory of (full) recursion* (TTofR).

TTofAR has potentials for applications to algorithmic semantics of formal and natural languages. Among the formal languages, we consider applications to semantics of programming languages, formalisation of compilers, languages used in database systems, data science, and many areas of AI, including robotics. For instance, the untyped theory of recursion, introduced in Moschovakis [25,27], is applied in Hurkens et al. [2] to model reasoning. The potentials of typed, acyclic recursion have been used in various applications, in particular, to computational semantics of human language, starting with the introduction of $L^{\lambda}_{ar}$, see Moschovakis [28]. Application of $L^{\lambda}_{ar}$ to logic programming in linguistics and cognitive science is given in Van Lambalgen and Hamm [1].

We have initiated extending the original $L^{\lambda}_{ar}$, to provide more powerful expressiveness of $L^{\lambda}_{ar}$ for applications to AI and intelligent systems. For example, see Loukanova [3–14,24], for applications of $L^{\lambda}_{ar}$ to computational semantics and computational syntax-semantics interface of human language. For broader applications to computational neuroscience and AI, see Loukanova [17–20]. By adding polymorphism, the work in [18] offers potentials for varieties of applications with polymorphic, or otherwise parametric, types. The work in Loukanova [15–17,22] provides a formal technique for applications of $L^{\lambda}_{ar}$ and its extended versions to data science, for representation of factual and situated content of underspecified and partial information. The work Loukanova [19,21] extends $L^{\lambda}_{ar}$ and provides a basis for applications to computational neuroscience for mathematical modeling of neural structures and connections.

In this paper, at first, we present the standard reduction calculus of the type-theory $L^{\lambda}_{ar}$ of acyclic recursion, which effectively reduces terms to their canonical forms. By this, we extend mildly the original reduction calculus Moschovakis [28] by extending the congruence relation between terms to accommodate terms with empty sequences of recursion assignments. This does not affect the theoretical results of $L^{\lambda}_{ar}$, while extending original reduction calculus to handle such special expressions as $L^{\lambda}_{ar}$-terms, instead of abbreviations. The standard reduction calculus of $L^{\lambda}_{ar}$, originally and also by including these special terms, determines a strong algorithmic equivalence between $L^{\lambda}_{ar}$-terms. In the rest of the paper, we present our contribution. We extend the reduction calculus of $L^{\lambda}_{ar}$ to a strict *$\gamma^*$-reduction calculus*, denoted also, in words, by *gamma-star reduction calculus*. The $\gamma^*$-reduction calculus is very useful for simplifying terms, by eliminating sub-terms having superfluous sequences of $\lambda$-abstraction and corresponding spurious functional applications. We give motivation by using abstract examples, because the theory has broader applications, not only for semantics of human language, but also in other intelligent technologies. For better understanding, we give supplementary examples that render expressions of human language to $L_{ar}^{\lambda}$-terms. The theory has direct potentials for applications to computerised processing of human language, including, in large-scale, computational grammars of human language, and various approaches to Natural Language Processing (NLP) in AI.

This paper is an extended work based on Loukanova [23], where we briefly presented a simpler version of the $\gamma^*$-reduction calculus and concentrated more on its applications, by providing examples, which are instances of typical patterns for computations, with detailed reductions in them. Here, we overview major points by relevant parts of some of the sequences of reductions. Section 2.6 gives Example 1, which is a typical abstract pattern, by containing parameters for mathematical functions. It presents the idea of formalisation of abstract, parametric algorithms. Section 5 presents Example 2 from the areas of applications of the type-theory $L_{ar}^{\lambda}$ of algorithms and its $\gamma^*$-reduction to language processing, including NLP, which is important across the fields of AI.

The focus of this work is on the theoretical presentation of the type-theory $L_{ar}^{\lambda}$ of acyclic recursion and extending its reduction calculus to $\gamma^*$-reduction calculus. In addition, we introduce a strict version of the $\gamma^*$-rule subjected to a stricter condition for its applicability, than in Loukanova [23]. We provide detailed definitions of the notions of canonical forms in both reduction systems, and major theoretical results about them. For example, the theorem Reducibility to $\gamma^*$-Canonical Form provides the computational relation between $\gamma^*$-reduction calculus and $\gamma^*$-canonical forms. The $\gamma^*$-canonical form of a term $A$ determines the $\gamma^*$-algorithm for computing the denotation $\mathsf{den}(A)$ of $A$. The $\gamma^*$-algorithm can be significantly simpler then the one determined by the standard canonical form of $A$, by using lesser algorithmic steps.

## 2 Type-Theory of Acyclic Recursion

### 2.1 Syntax of $L_{ar}^{\lambda}$

**Basic Types:** $\mathsf{BTypes} = \{\mathsf{e}, \mathsf{t}, \mathsf{s}\}$ The basic type $\mathsf{e}$ is the type of the entities in the semantic domains and the expressions denoting entities; $\mathsf{t}$ of the truth values and corresponding expressions, $\mathsf{s}$ of the states.

**Types:** the set $\mathsf{Types}$ (i.e., the set of type terms) is the smallest set defined recursively, by using notation in the style[1] of Backus-Naur Form (BNF-style) as follows:

$$\theta :\equiv \mathsf{e} \mid \mathsf{t} \mid \mathsf{s} \mid \sigma \mid (\tau \to \sigma) \tag{1}$$

The type terms $(\tau \to \sigma)$ are the types of functions from objects of type $\tau$ to objects of type $\sigma$, and of expressions denoting such functions.

[1] Note that recursive rules in BNF-style are not per se BNF rules, by using different meta-variables in the rules instead of nonterminals for syntactic categories.

**Notation 1.** *The types in* (2a)–(2d) *are, respectively, of state-dependent individuals, state-dependent truth values (i.e., type representing propositions), and for state-dependent objects, of type* $\widetilde{\tau}$, $\tau \in \mathsf{Types}$, *with the notation introduced by Moschovakis* [28].

$$(\mathsf{e} \to \mathsf{t}) \equiv \mathsf{e} \to \mathsf{t}, \quad \text{of characteristic functions of sets of entities} \tag{2a}$$
$$\widetilde{\mathsf{e}} \equiv (\mathsf{s} \to \mathsf{e}), \quad \text{of state dependent entities} \tag{2b}$$
$$\widetilde{\mathsf{t}} \equiv (\mathsf{s} \to \mathsf{t}), \quad \text{of state dependent truths} \tag{2c}$$
$$\widetilde{\tau} \equiv (\mathsf{s} \to \tau), \quad \text{of state dependent objects of type } \tau \tag{2d}$$

The vocabulary of $\mathrm{L}^{\lambda}_{\mathrm{ar}}$ consists of pairwise disjoint sets:

**Constants:**
$K = \bigcup_{\tau \in \mathsf{Types}} K_{\tau}$,
where, for each $\tau \in \mathsf{Types}$, $K_{\tau} = \{\mathsf{c}_0{}^{\tau}, \ldots, \mathsf{c}_k^{\tau}, \ldots\}$
**Pure variables:**
$\mathsf{PureVars} = \bigcup_{\tau \in \mathsf{Types}} \mathsf{PureVars}_{\tau}$,
where, for $\tau \in \mathsf{Types}$, $\mathsf{PureVars}_{\tau} = \{\mathsf{v}_0, \mathsf{v}_1, \ldots\}$
**Recursion variables (locations):**
$\mathsf{RecVars} = \bigcup_{\tau \in \mathsf{Types}} \mathsf{RecVars}_{\tau}$,
where, for each $\tau \in \mathsf{Types}$, $\mathsf{RecVars}_{\tau} = \{\mathsf{r}_0, \mathsf{r}_1, \ldots\}$

**Definition 1** *(Terms of* $\mathrm{L}^{\lambda}_{\mathrm{ar}}$*). The set* Terms *is defined by recursion expressed by using a typed variant of BNF-style, with the type assignments given either as superscripts or with column sign:*

$$A :\equiv \mathsf{c}^{\tau} \mid x^{\tau} \mid \tag{3a}$$
$$\left[B^{(\sigma\to\tau)}(C^{\sigma})\right]^{\tau} \mid \tag{3b}$$
$$\left[\lambda(v^{\sigma})\,(B^{\tau})\right]^{(\sigma\to\tau)} \mid \tag{3c}$$
$$\left[A_0^{\sigma_0} \text{ where } \{\, p_1^{\sigma_1} := A_1^{\sigma_1}, \ldots, p_n^{\sigma_n} := A_n^{\sigma_n} \,\}\right]^{\sigma_0} \tag{3d}$$

*where the meta-variables in the BNF-style definition* (3a)–(3d) *are as follows: for* $n, m \geq 0$, $\mathsf{c}^{\tau} \in K_{\tau}$ *is a constant;* $x^{\tau} \in \mathsf{PureVars}_{\tau} \cup \mathsf{RecVars}_{\tau}$ *is a pure or recursion variable;* $v^{\sigma} \in \mathsf{PureVars}_{\sigma}$ *is a pure variable;* $A, B, A_i^{\sigma_i} \in \mathsf{Terms}$ $(i = 0, \ldots, n)$ *are terms of the respective types;* $p_i \in \mathsf{RecVars}_{\sigma_i}$ $(i = 1, \ldots, n)$ *are pairwise different recursion variables; and, in the expressions of the form* (3d), *the subexpression* $\{p_1^{\sigma_1} := A_1^{\sigma_1}, \ldots, p_n^{\sigma_n} := A_n^{\sigma_n}\}$ *is a sequence of assignments that satisfies the* acyclicity constraint*:*

***Acyclicity Constraint AC.*** *For any given terms* $A_1 : \sigma_1, \ldots, A_n : \sigma_n$, *and recursion variables* $p_1 : \sigma_1, \ldots, p_n : \sigma_n$, *(with* $n \geq 0$, *and* $p_i \neq p_j$ *for all* $i, j$ *such that* $i \neq j$ *and* $1 \leq i, j \leq n$*), the sequence* $\{p_1 := A_1, \ldots, p_n := A_n\}$ *is an* acyclic system of assignments *iff there is a ranking function* $\mathsf{rank} : \{p_1, \ldots, p_n\} \longrightarrow \mathbb{N}$ *such that, for all* $p_i, p_j \in \{p_1, \ldots, p_n\}$,

$$\text{if } p_j \text{ occurs freely in } A_i \text{ then } \mathsf{rank}(p_j) < \mathsf{rank}(p_i) \tag{4}$$

*(1) The terms of the form* (3d) *are called* recursion terms, *or alternatively* where-terms *(2) a term* $A \in \mathsf{Terms}$ *is called* explicit, *if the constant* where *does not occur in* $A$ *(3)* $A \in \mathsf{Terms}$ *is called a* $\lambda$*-calculus term, if no recursion variable occurs in* $A$.

**Definition 2.** *The sets of the free and bound variables of the terms are defined by induction on the structure of the terms:*

- *for every* $\mathsf{c}^\tau \in K_\tau$: $\mathsf{FreeV}(\mathsf{c}) = \varnothing$, $\mathsf{BoundV}(\mathsf{c}) = \varnothing$.
- *for every* $x^\tau \in \mathit{PureVars}_\tau \cup \mathit{RecVars}_\tau$: $\mathsf{FreeV}(x) = \{ x \}$, $\mathsf{BoundV}(x) = \varnothing$
- *for every* $A, B \in \mathsf{Terms}$:

$$\mathsf{FreeV}(A(B)) = \mathsf{FreeV}(A) \cup \mathsf{FreeV}(B) \tag{5a}$$

$$\mathsf{BoundV}(A(B)) = \mathsf{BoundV}(A) \cup \mathsf{BoundV}(B) \tag{5b}$$

- *for every* $v \in \mathit{PureVars}$, $A \in \mathsf{Terms}$:

$$\mathsf{FreeV}(\lambda v\,(B)) = \mathsf{FreeV}(B) - \{v\} \tag{6a}$$

$$\mathsf{BoundV}(\lambda v\,(B)) = \mathsf{BoundV}(B) \cup \{v\} \tag{6b}$$

- *for every* $A_i^{\sigma_i} \in \mathsf{Terms}$ $(i = 0, \ldots, n)$, $p_i \in \mathit{RecVars}_{\sigma_i}$ $(i = 1, \ldots, n)$:

$$\mathsf{FreeV}(A_0 \text{ where } \{ p_1 := A_1, \ldots, p_n := A_n \}) = \bigcup_{i=0}^{i=n} \mathsf{FreeV}(A_i) - \{p_i \mid i = 1, \ldots, n\} \tag{7a}$$

$$\mathsf{BoundV}(A_0 \text{ where } \{ p_1 := A_1, \ldots, p_n := A_n \}) = \bigcup_{i=0}^{i=n} \mathsf{BoundV}(A_i) \cup \{p_i \mid i = 1, \ldots, n\} \tag{7b}$$

**Notation 2.** *Usually, the type assignments in the term expressions are skipped, as in* (8b). *Parentheses can be skippes if that does not cause misunderstanding, and for better visualisation, extra and sized parentheses can be added. We also abbreviate sequences of assignments, as in* (8c)*:*

$$[A_0^\sigma \text{ where } \{p_1^{\sigma_1} := A_1^{\sigma_1}, \ldots, p_n^{\sigma_n} := A_n^{\sigma_n}\}]^{\sigma_0} \tag{8a}$$

$$\equiv A_0 \text{ where } \{ p_1 := A_1, \ldots, p_n := A_n \} \tag{8b}$$

$$\equiv A_0 \text{ where } \{ \overrightarrow{p} := \overrightarrow{A} \} \tag{8c}$$

**For sequences of** $\lambda$**-abstractions, we use the following notations,** (9a)–(9b)**:**

$$(\overrightarrow{\vartheta} \to \tau) \equiv (\vartheta_1 \to (\vartheta_2 \to \ldots (\vartheta_n \to \tau))) \tag{9a}$$

$$\lambda(\overrightarrow{u}^{\overrightarrow{\vartheta}})(P^\tau) \equiv \lambda(u_1^{\vartheta_1})(\lambda(u_2^{\vartheta_2}) \ldots (\lambda(u_n^{\vartheta_n})(P^\tau))) : (\overrightarrow{\vartheta} \to \tau) \tag{9b}$$

$$\lambda(\overrightarrow{u}^{\overrightarrow{\vartheta}})\,\lambda(u^\vartheta)(P^\tau) \equiv \lambda(u_1^{\vartheta_1})(\lambda(u_2^{\vartheta_2}) \ldots (\lambda(u_n^{\vartheta_n})\,\lambda(u^\vartheta)(P^\tau))) : (\overrightarrow{\vartheta} \to (\vartheta \to \tau)) \tag{9c}$$

**for** $i = 1, \ldots, n$ $(n \geq 0)$, $\tau, \vartheta, \vartheta_i \in \mathsf{Types}$, $u, u_i \in \mathbf{PureVars}$, $u : \vartheta$, $u_i : \vartheta_i$, $P \in \mathsf{Terms}$, $P : \tau$.

### 2.2 Semantics of $L^{\lambda}_{ar}$

*Denotational Semantics of* $L^{\lambda}_{ar}$: An $L^{\lambda}_{ar}$ *semantic structure*, also called *model*, is a tuple $\mathfrak{A} = \langle \mathbb{T}, \mathcal{I} \rangle$, satisfying the following conditions (S1)–(S4):

**(S1)** $\mathbb{T}$ is a set, called a *frame*, of sets

$$\mathbb{T} = \cup \{ \mathbb{T}_\sigma \mid \sigma \in \mathit{Types} \} \tag{10}$$

where $\mathbb{T}_e \neq \varnothing$ is a nonempty set of entities, $\mathbb{T}_t = \{0, 1, er\} \subseteq \mathbb{T}_e$ is the set of the *truth values*, $\mathbb{T}_s \neq \varnothing$ is a nonempty set of objects called *states*
**(S2)** $\mathbb{T}_{(\tau_1 \to \tau_2)} = \{ p \mid p \colon \mathbb{T}_{\tau_1} \longrightarrow \mathbb{T}_{\tau_2} \}$
**(S3)** $\mathcal{I}$ is a function $\mathcal{I} \colon K \longrightarrow \mathbb{T}$, called the *interpretation function* of $\mathfrak{A}$, such that for every $\mathsf{c} \in K_\tau$, $\mathcal{I}(\mathsf{c}) = c$ for some $c \in \mathbb{T}_\tau$
**(S4)** The set $G$ of the variable assignments for the semantic structure $\mathfrak{A}$ is: $G = \{ g \mid g \colon \mathit{PureVars} \cup \mathit{RecVars} \longrightarrow \mathbb{T} \text{ and } g(x) \in \mathbb{T}_\sigma, \text{ for every } x \colon \sigma \}$.

**Definition 3 (Denotation Function).** *The* denotation function den, *when it exists, of the semantics structure* $\mathfrak{A}$, *is a function:*

$$\mathsf{den} \colon \mathit{Terms} \longrightarrow \{ f \mid f \colon G \longrightarrow \mathbb{T} \} \tag{11}$$

*which is defined, for each* $g \in G$, *by induction on the structure of the terms, as follows:*

**(D1)** $\mathsf{den}(x)(g) = g(x)$; $\mathsf{den}(\mathsf{c})(g) = \mathcal{I}(\mathsf{c})$
**(D2)** *for application terms:*

$$\mathsf{den}([B^{(\sigma \to \tau)}(C^\sigma)]^\tau)(g) = \mathsf{den}(B)(g)(\mathsf{den}(C)(g)) \tag{12}$$

**(D3)** *for* $\lambda$*-terms:*
$\mathsf{den}([\lambda\, v^\sigma\, (B^\tau)]^{(\sigma \to \tau)})(g) : \mathbb{T}_\tau \longrightarrow \mathbb{T}_\sigma$,
*where* $x : \tau$ *and* $B : \sigma$, *is the function such that, for every* $t \in \mathbb{T}_\tau$*:*

$$[\mathsf{den}([\lambda\, v^\sigma\, (B^\tau)]^{(\sigma \to \tau)})(g)](t) \tag{13a}$$
$$= \mathsf{den}(B)(g\{x := t\}) \tag{13b}$$

**(D4)** *for recursion terms:*

$$\mathsf{den}([A_0^{\sigma_0} \text{ where } \{ p_1^{\sigma_1} := A_1^{\sigma_1}, \ldots, p_n^{\sigma_n} := A_n^{\sigma_n} \}]^{\sigma_0}) \tag{14a}$$
$$= \mathsf{den}(A_0)(g\{p_1 := \overline{p}_1, \ldots, p_n := \overline{p}_n\}) \tag{14b}$$

*where for all* $i \in \{1, \ldots, n\}$, $\overline{p}_i \in \mathbb{T}_{\tau_i}$ *are defined by recursion on* $\mathsf{rank}(p_i)$, *so that:*

$$\overline{p_i} = \mathsf{den}(A_i)(g\{p_{k_1} := \overline{p}_{k_1}, \ldots, p_{k_m} := \overline{p}_{k_m}\}) \tag{15}$$

*where* $p_{k_1}, \ldots, p_{k_m}$ *are all the recursion variables* $p_j \in \{p_1, \ldots, p_n\}$ *such that* $\mathsf{rank}(p_j) < \mathsf{rank}(p_i)$

Intuitively, a system $\{p_1 := A_1, \ldots, p_n := A_n\}$ defines recursive computations of the values to be assigned to the recursion variables (locations) $p_1, \ldots, p_n$. When $p_j$ occurs freely in $A_i$, the denotational value of $A_i$, which is assigned to $p_i$, may depend on the values of the variable $p_j$, as well as on the values of the variables $p_k$ having lower rank than $p_j$. Requiring a ranking function rank, such that $\mathsf{rank}(p_j) < \mathsf{rank}(p_i)$, i.e., an acyclic system guarantees that computations end after finite number of steps. Omitting the acyclicity condition gives an extended type system $\mathrm{L}_{\mathrm{r}}^{\lambda}$, which admits full recursion. This is not in the subject of this paper.

*Algorithmic Semantics:* The notion of algorithmic meaning (algorithmic semantics) in the languages of recursion covers the most essential, computational aspect of the concept of meaning. The *algorithmic meaning*, $\mathsf{Int}(A)$, of a meaningful term $A$ is the tuple of functions, a recursor, that is defined by the denotations $\mathsf{den}(A_i)$ ($i \in \{0, \ldots n\}$) of the parts (i.e., the head sub-term $A_0$ and of the terms $A_1, \ldots,$ $A_n$ in the system of assignments of its canonical form (see the next sections) $\mathsf{cf}(A) \equiv A_0$ where $\{p_1 := A_1, \ldots, p_n := A_n\}$. Intuitively, for each meaningful term $A$, the algorithmic meaning $\mathsf{Int}(A)$ of $A$, is the mathematical *algorithm* for computing the denotation $\mathsf{den}(A)$.

Two meaningful expressions $A$ and $B$ are algorithmically equivalent, $A \approx B$ i.e., algorithmically synonymous iff their recursors $\mathsf{Int}(A)$ and $\mathsf{Int}(B)$ are naturally isomorphic, i.e., they are the same algorithms. Thus, the formal languages of recursion offer a formalisation of central computational aspects: denotation, with at least two semantic "levels": *algorithmic meanings* and *denotations.* The terms in canonical form represent the algorithmic steps for computing semantic denotations.

### 2.3 Standard Reduction Calculus of $\mathbf{L}_{\mathbf{ar}}^{\lambda}$

**Definition 4 (Congruence Relation).** *For any terms $A, B \in$ Terms, $A$ and $B$ are congruent, $A \equiv_c B$, if and only if*

*(1) one of them can be obtained from the other by renaming bound variables or reordering assignments in recursion terms, or one of the following holds:*
*(2) $A \equiv B$ or $A \equiv B$ where $\{\ \}$ or $B \equiv A$ where $\{\ \}$*

*I.e., the congruence relation $\equiv_c$ is the smallest equivalence relation between terms, which is closed under renaming bound variables, reordering recursion assignments, adding or removing empty sequences of assignments.*

### 2.4 Reduction Rules

**Congruence:** If $A \equiv_c B$, then $A \Rightarrow B$ (cong)
**Transitivity:**
If $A \Rightarrow B$ and $B \Rightarrow C$, then $A \Rightarrow C$ (trans)

**Compositionality:**

$$\text{If } A \Rightarrow A' \text{ and } B \Rightarrow B', \text{ then } \quad A(B) \Rightarrow A'(B') \tag{c-ap}$$

$$\text{If } A \Rightarrow B, \text{ then } \quad \lambda(u)(A) \Rightarrow \lambda(u)(B) \tag{c-$\lambda$}$$

$$\text{If } A_i \Rightarrow B_i, \text{ for } i = 0, \ldots, n, \text{ then}$$

$$\begin{aligned} &A_0 \text{ where } \{ p_1 := A_1, \ldots, p_n := A_n \} \\ \Rightarrow\ &B_0 \text{ where } \{ p_1 := B_1, \ldots, p_n := B_n \} \end{aligned} \tag{c-rec}$$

**Head Rule:** given that no $p_i$ occurs freely in any $B_j$, for $i = 1, \ldots, n$, and $j = 1, \ldots, m$ $(n, m \geq 0)$

$$\begin{aligned} &(A_0 \text{ where } \{\overrightarrow{p} := \overrightarrow{A}\}) \text{ where } \{\overrightarrow{q} := \overrightarrow{B}\} \\ \Rightarrow\ &A_0 \text{ where } \{\overrightarrow{p} := \overrightarrow{A},\ \overrightarrow{q} := \overrightarrow{B}\} \end{aligned} \tag{head}$$

**Bekič-Scott Rule:** given that no $q_i$ occurs free in any $A_j$, for $i = 1, \ldots, n$, and $j = 0, \ldots, m$ $(n, m \geq 0)$

$$\begin{aligned} &A_0 \text{ where } \{ p := (B_0 \text{ where } \{\overrightarrow{q} := \overrightarrow{B}\}), \\ &\qquad\qquad \overrightarrow{p} := \overrightarrow{A} \} \\ \Rightarrow\ &A_0 \text{ where } \{ p := B_0, \overrightarrow{q} := \overrightarrow{B}, \\ &\qquad\qquad \overrightarrow{p} := \overrightarrow{A}\} \end{aligned} \tag{B-S}$$

**Recursion-application Rule:** given that no $p_i$ occurs free in $B$, for $i = 1, \ldots, n$ $(n \geq 0)$

$$\begin{aligned} &(A_0 \text{ where } \{ \overrightarrow{p} := \overrightarrow{A} \})(B) \\ \Rightarrow\ &A_0(B) \text{ where } \{ \overrightarrow{p} := \overrightarrow{A} \} \end{aligned} \tag{recap}$$

**Application Rule:** given that $B$ is a proper term and $p$ is a fresh recursion variable (location)

$$A(B) \Rightarrow A(p) \text{ where } \{p := B\}$$

**$\lambda$-rule:**

$$\begin{aligned} &\lambda(u)(A_0 \text{ where } \{ p_1 := A_1, \ldots, p_n := A_n \}) \\ \Rightarrow\ &\lambda(u)A'_0 \text{ where } \{ p'_1 := \lambda(u)A'_1, \ldots, p'_n := \lambda(u)A'_n \} \end{aligned} \tag{$\lambda$}$$

where, for all $i = 1, \ldots, n$ $(n \geq 0)$, $p'_i$ is a fresh recursion variable (location), and $A'_i$ is the result of the replacement of the free occurrences of $p_1, \ldots, p_n$ in $A_i$ with $p'_1(u), \ldots, p'_n(u)$, respectively, i.e.:

$$\begin{aligned} A'_i \equiv\ & A_i\{p_1 :\equiv p'_1(u), \ldots, p_n :\equiv p'_n(u)\} \\ & \text{for all } i \in \{ 1, \ldots, n\}\ (n \geq 0) \end{aligned} \tag{20}$$

**Definition 5.** *The* reduction relation *is the smallest relation between terms that is closed under the reduction rules.*

*The reduction relation is denoted by $\Rightarrow$. That is, for any two terms $A$ and $B$, $A$ reduces to $B$, denoted by $A \Rightarrow B$, iff $B$ can be obtained from $A$ by finite number of applications of reduction rules.*

**Definition 6 (Term Irreducibility).** *We say that a term $A \in \mathsf{Terms}$ is* irreducible *if and only if*

$$\begin{aligned} &\textit{for all } B \in \mathsf{Terms}, \\ &\quad \textit{if } A \Rightarrow B \textit{ then } A \equiv_c B \end{aligned} \tag{21}$$

**Theorem 1 (Criteria for Irreducibility).** *See Moschovakis* [28].

1. *If $A \in \mathit{Const} \cup \mathit{Vars}$, then $A$ is irreducible.*
2. *An application term $A(B)$ is irreducible if and only if $A$ is explicit and irreducible, and $B$ is immediate.*
3. *A $\lambda$-term $\lambda(x)A$ is irreducible if and only if $A$ is explicit and irreducible.*
4. *A recursion term $A \equiv A_0$ where $\{p_1 := A_1, \ldots, p_n := A_n\}$ $(n \geq 0)$ is irreducible if and only if all of its parts $A_0, \ldots, A_n$ are explicit and irreducible.*

*Proof.* By structural induction on terms using the rules of the reduction calculus.

### 2.5 Canonical Forms

For each term $A \in \mathsf{Terms}$, we define a term, called a *canonical form of $A$* and denoted by $\mathsf{cf}(A)$, by recursion on the term structure of $A$.

In each clause of Definition 7, we assume that the bound recursion variables are distinct, and distinct from the free recursion variables.

**Definition 7 (Canonical Forms)**

**(CF1)** *For every $\mathsf{c} \in K_\tau$, $\mathsf{cf}(\mathsf{c}) :\equiv \mathsf{c}$;*
*for every $x \in \mathit{PureVars}_\tau \cup \mathit{RecVars}_\tau$, $\mathsf{cf}(x) :\equiv x$*

**(CF2)** *Given that $A \in \mathsf{Terms}$, and*
$\mathsf{cf}(A) \equiv A_0$ where $\{p_1 := A_1, \ldots, p_n := A_n\} \equiv A_0$ where $\{\overrightarrow{p} := \overrightarrow{A}\}$ $(n \geq 0)$, *then:*

**(CF2a)** *if $X$ is an immediate term, then*

$$\begin{aligned} \mathsf{cf}(A(X)) &:\equiv A_0(X) \text{ where } \{p_1 := A_1, \ldots, p_n := A_n\} \\ &\equiv A_0(X) \text{ where } \{\overrightarrow{p} := \overrightarrow{A}\} \end{aligned} \tag{22}$$

**(CF2b)** *if $B$ is a proper term and*
$\mathsf{cf}(B) \equiv B_0$ where $\{q_1 := B_1, \ldots, q_m := B_m\} \equiv B_0$ where $\{\overrightarrow{q} := \overrightarrow{B}\}$ *$(m \geq 0)$, then*

$$\begin{aligned} \mathsf{cf}(A(B)) &:\equiv A_0(q_o) \text{ where } \{p_1 := A_1, \ldots, p_n := A_n, \\ &\qquad\qquad q_0 := B_0, q_1 := B_1, \ldots, q_m := B_m\} \\ &\equiv A_0(q_0) \text{ where } \{\overrightarrow{p} := \overrightarrow{A}, q_0 := B_0, \overrightarrow{q} := \overrightarrow{B}\} \end{aligned} \tag{23}$$

**(CF3)** *Given that* $A \in \mathsf{Terms}$, *and*
$\mathsf{cf}(A) \equiv A_0 \text{ where } \{p_1 := A_1, \ldots, p_n := A_n\} \equiv A_0 \text{ where } \{\overrightarrow{p} := \overrightarrow{A}\}$ $(n \geq 0)$, *then, for every* $u \in \mathit{PureVars}_\tau$:

$$\begin{aligned} \mathsf{cf}(\lambda(u)A) &:\equiv \lambda(u)A'_0 \text{ where } \{p'_1 := \lambda(u)A'_1, \ldots, p'_n := \lambda(u)A'_n\} \\ &\equiv \lambda(u)A'_0 \text{ where } \{\overrightarrow{p'} := \overrightarrow{\lambda(u)A'}\} \end{aligned} \tag{24}$$

*where for every* $i = 1, \ldots, n$ $(n \geq 0)$, *the recursion variable* $p'_i$ *is fresh and* $A'_i$ *is the result of the replacement of all the free occurrences of* $p_1, \ldots, p_n$ *in* $A_i$ *with* $p'_1(u), \ldots, p'_n(u)$, *respectively, i.e.:*

$$\begin{aligned} A'_i &\equiv A_i\{p_1 :\equiv p'_1(u), \ldots, p_n :\equiv p'_n(u)\} \\ &\equiv A_i\{\overrightarrow{p} :\equiv \overrightarrow{p'(u)}\} \end{aligned} \tag{25}$$

**(CF4)** *Given* (26a)–(26b)

$$A \equiv A_0 \text{ where } \{p_1 := A_1, \ldots, p_n := A_n\}, (n \geq 0) \tag{26a}$$

$$\begin{aligned} \mathsf{cf}(A_i) &\equiv A_{i,0} \text{ where } \{p_{i,1} := A_{i,1}, \ldots, p_{i,k_i} := A_{i,k_i}\} \\ &\equiv A_{i,0} \text{ where } \{\overrightarrow{p_i} := \overrightarrow{A_i}\} \ (k_i \geq 0), \textit{for } i = 0, \ldots, n \end{aligned} \tag{26b}$$

*then:*

$$\begin{aligned} \mathsf{cf}(A) :\equiv A_{0,0} \text{ where } \{ \quad & p_{0,1} := A_{0,1}, \ldots, p_{0,k_0} := A_{0,k_0}, \\ p_1 := A_{1,0}, \ & p_{1,1} := A_{1,1}, \ldots, p_{1,k_1} := A_{1,k_1}, \\ & \vdots \\ p_n := A_{n,0}, \ & p_{n,1} := A_{n,1}, \ldots, p_{n,k_n} := A_{n,k_n} \} \end{aligned} \tag{27a}$$

$$\begin{aligned} \equiv A_{0,0} \text{ where } \{ \quad & \overrightarrow{p_0} := \overrightarrow{A_0}, \\ p_1 := A_{1,0}, \ & \overrightarrow{p_1} := \overrightarrow{A_1}, \\ & \vdots \\ p_n := A_{n,0}, \ & \overrightarrow{p_n} := \overrightarrow{A_n} \} \end{aligned} \tag{27b}$$

The following theorems are major results that are essential for algorithmic semantics.

**Theorem 2 (Canonical Form Theorem: Existence and Uniqueness of the Canonical Forms).** *See Moschovakis* [28], *but here we give a more detailed statement of the theorem.*

*For each term A, there is a unique up to congruence, irreducible term C,* $C \equiv \mathsf{cf}(A)$, *such that:*

*(1) (existence of a canonical form of A) there exist explicit, irreducible terms* $A_0, \ldots, A_n \in \mathsf{Terms}$ $(n \geq 0)$, *such that* (28) *holds, and, thus, the term* $\mathsf{cf}(A)$ *is irreducible:*

$$\mathsf{cf}(A) \equiv A_0 \text{ where } \{p_1 := A_1, \ldots, p_n := A_n\} \tag{28}$$

*(2) A constant or a variable* $\xi \in K \cup \mathsf{RecVars} \cup \mathsf{PureVars}$ *occurs freely in* $\mathsf{cf}(A)$ *if and only if it occurs freely in* $A$

*(3)* $A \Rightarrow \mathsf{cf}(A)$

*(4) if* $A$ *is irreducible, then* $A \equiv \mathsf{cf}(A)$

*(5) if* $A \Rightarrow B$, *then* $\mathsf{cf}(A) \equiv_c \mathsf{cf}(B)$

*(6) (Uniqueness of the Canonical Form) if* $A \Rightarrow B$ *and* $B$ *is irreducible, then* $B \equiv_c \mathsf{cf}(A)$, *i.e.,* $\mathsf{cf}(A)$ *is the unique, up to congruence, irreducible term to which* $A$ *can be reduced.*

*Proof.* (1) is proved by induction on the term structure of $A$ and using Definition 7. (3) is by induction on the term structure of $A$ and the reduction rules. (4) is by criteria for irreducibility, i.e., Theorem 1. (5) is proved by induction on the definition of the reduction relation $\Rightarrow$ (with long calculations). (6) follows from (5).

**Notation 3.** $A \Rightarrow_{\mathsf{cf}} B \iff B \equiv_c \mathsf{cf}(A)$.

**Theorem 3 (Referential Synonymy Theorem).** *See Moschovakis [28].*

*Two terms* $A, B$ *are algorithmically equivalent, i.e., synonymous,* $A \approx B$, *if and only if both are immediate or both are pure, and there are explicit, irreducible terms of corresponding types,* $A_0 : \sigma_0, \ldots, A_n : \sigma_n, B_0 : \sigma_0, \ldots, B_n : \sigma_n$ $(n \geq 0)$, *such that:*

$$A^{\sigma_0} \Rightarrow_{\mathsf{cf}} A_0^{\sigma_0} \text{ where } \{ p_1 := A_1^{\sigma_1}, \ldots, p_n := A_n^{\sigma_n} \} \tag{29a}$$

$$B^{\sigma_0} \Rightarrow_{\mathsf{cf}} B_0^{\sigma_0} \text{ where } \{ p_1 := B_1^{\sigma_1}, \ldots, p_n := B_n^{\sigma_n} \} \tag{29b}$$

*and for all* $i = 0, \ldots, n$,

$$\mathsf{den}(A_i) = \mathsf{den}(B_i), \text{ i.e.: } \mathsf{den}(A_i)(g) = \mathsf{den}(B_i)(g), \quad \text{for all } g \in G \tag{30}$$

## 2.6 Algorithmic Patterns and λ-Reductions

In this section, we give an example for an underspecified, parametric algorithm, represented by the term $P_1$ in (31a)–(31b), with parametric $C, q$, with underspecified, i.e., free recursion variable $C \in \mathsf{RecVars}$ and a specification of $q$ in (31b). For a little bit more explanation of the underspecified nature of such terms, see Loukanova [23].

*Example 1.* Here we use this example to motivate the need of the $\gamma^*$-reduction. By using the reduction calculus given in Sect. 2.3, $P_1$ can be reduced to the term (31h)–(31o).

$$P_1 \equiv \lambda(x_1)\,\lambda(x_2)\,\lambda(x_3)\big[C(q)(W(h))(J) \text{ where } \{ \tag{31a}$$

$$q := (G_1(x_1) + G_2(x_2)) \}\big] \tag{31b}$$

$$\Rightarrow \ldots \Rightarrow \lambda(x_1)\,\lambda(x_2)\,\lambda(x_3)\big[C(q)(w)(j) \text{ where } \{ \tag{31c}$$

$$q := (q_1 + q_2), \tag{31d}$$

$$j := J, \tag{31e}$$
$$w := W(h), \tag{31f}$$
$$q_1 := G_1(x_1),\, q_2 := G_2(x_2)\,\}] \tag{31g}$$
$$\Rightarrow \ldots \Rightarrow_{\mathsf{cf}} \lambda(x_1)\,\lambda(x_2)\,\lambda(x_3)\Big[ \tag{31h}$$
$$\big[C(q'(x_1)(x_2)(x_3))\big]\,\big[w'(x_1)(x_2)(x_3)\big] \tag{31i}$$
$$\big[j'(x_1)(x_2)(x_3)\big]\Big] \text{ where } \{ \tag{31j}$$
$$q' := \lambda(x_1)\,\lambda(x_2)\,\lambda(x_3)\Big[q_1'(x_1)(x_2)(x_3)+ q_2'(x_1)(x_2)(x_3)\Big], \tag{31k}$$
$$j' := \lambda(x_1)\,\lambda(x_2)\,\lambda(x_3)[J], \tag{31l}$$
$$w' := \lambda(x_1)\,\lambda(x_2)\,\lambda(x_3)[W(h)], \tag{31m}$$
$$q_1' := \lambda(x_1)\,\lambda(x_2)\,\lambda(x_3)\big[G_1(x_1)\big], \tag{31n}$$
$$q_2' := \lambda(x_1)\,\lambda(x_2)\,\lambda(x_3)\big[G_2(x_2)\big]\,\} \tag{31o}$$

The term (31h)–(31o) has vacuous $\lambda$-abstractions, e.g., (31l), (31m), (31n), (31o), which denote constant functions, and corresponding applications, e.g., in (31h), that give these constant values. The $\gamma^*$-reduction, introduced in this paper, reduces such spurious sub-terms.

The above Examples 1 and 2 from Sect. 5 are discussed in more details in Loukanova [23]. Here, they provide brief motivation of the $\gamma^*$-reduction and the corresponding $\gamma^*$-canonical forms of terms, which are presented in the following sections.

# 3 Gamma-Star Reduction of $\mathbf{L}^{\lambda}_{\mathbf{ar}}$

## 3.1 The ($\gamma^*$)-Rule

In the following sections, we give the definition of the ($\gamma^*$)-rule, see Table 1, and its major properties. Expanding the reduction calculus of $\mathrm{L}^{\lambda}_{\mathrm{ar}}$ with the ($\gamma^*$)-rule simplifies some terms, by reducing sub-terms with vacuous $\lambda$-abstractions, while maintaining closely the original algorithmic structure. By using the ($\gamma^*$)-rule, the reduced terms determine more efficient versions of algorithms, by maintaining the essential computational steps.

**Definition 8 (Strict $\gamma^*$-Condition).** *Assume that, for* $i = 1, \ldots, n$ $(n \geq 0)$, $\tau, \vartheta, \vartheta_i \in \mathsf{Types}$, $u, u_i \in \mathit{PureVars}$, $p \in \mathit{RecVars}$, $P \in \mathsf{Terms}$, *are such that* $u : \vartheta$, $u_i : \vartheta_i$, $p : (\overrightarrow{\vartheta} \to (\vartheta \to \tau))$, $P : \tau$, *and thus,* $\lambda(\overrightarrow{u}^{\,\overrightarrow{\vartheta}})\,\lambda(v^{\vartheta})(P^{\tau}) : (\overrightarrow{\vartheta} \to (\vartheta \to \tau))$.

*A recursion term* $A \in \mathsf{Terms}$ *satisfies the strict* $\gamma^*$*-condition for an assignment* $p := \lambda(\overrightarrow{u}^{\,\overrightarrow{\vartheta}})\,\lambda(v^{\vartheta})(P^{\tau}) : (\overrightarrow{\vartheta} \to (\vartheta \to \tau))$, *with respect to* $\lambda(v)$, *if and only if* $A$ *is of the form:* (32a)–(32c)*:*

$$A \equiv A_0 \text{ where } \{\, \overrightarrow{a} := \overrightarrow{A}, \tag{32a}$$

$$p := \lambda(\overrightarrow{u})\,\lambda(v)P, \tag{32b}$$
$$\overrightarrow{b} := \overrightarrow{B}\,\} \tag{32c}$$

*such that the following holds:*

1. *$P \in \mathsf{Terms}_\tau$ does not have any free occurrences of $v$ in it, i.e., $v \notin \mathsf{FreeV}(P)$*
2. *All occurrences of $p$ in $A_0$, $\overrightarrow{A}$, and $\overrightarrow{B}$ are occurrences in sub-terms $p(\overrightarrow{u})(v)$ that are in the scope of $\lambda(\overrightarrow{u})\,\lambda(v)$, modulo renaming the variables $\overrightarrow{u}, v$*

In Loukanova [23], we used a version of the $\gamma^*$-condition which does not require $p(\overrightarrow{u})(v)$ have to be in the scope of $\lambda\,\overrightarrow{u})\,\lambda(v)$, see Note 1. This allows the $\Rightarrow_{(\gamma^*)}$-rule to remove innessential free variables.

**Table 1.** ($\gamma^*$)-Rule.

($\gamma^*$)

$$A \equiv A_0 \text{ where } \{\,\overrightarrow{a} := \overrightarrow{A}, \tag{33a}$$
$$p := \lambda(\overrightarrow{u})\,\lambda(v)P, \tag{33b}$$
$$\overrightarrow{b} := \overrightarrow{B}\,\} \tag{33c}$$
$$\Rightarrow_{(\gamma^*)} A'_0 \text{ where } \{\,\overrightarrow{a} := \overrightarrow{A}', \tag{33d}$$
$$p' := \lambda(\overrightarrow{u})P, \tag{33e}$$
$$\overrightarrow{b} := \overrightarrow{B'}\,\} \tag{33f}$$
$$\equiv A_0\{\,p(\overrightarrow{u})(v) :\equiv p'(\overrightarrow{u})\,\} \text{ where } \{ \tag{33g}$$
$$\overrightarrow{a} := \overrightarrow{A}\{\,p(\overrightarrow{u})(v) :\equiv p'(\overrightarrow{u})\,\} \tag{33h}$$
$$p' := \lambda(\overrightarrow{u})P, \tag{33i}$$
$$\overrightarrow{b} := \overrightarrow{B}\{\,p(\overrightarrow{u})(v) :\equiv p'(\overrightarrow{u})\,\}\,\} \tag{33j}$$

where

- the term $A \in$ Terms satisfies the strict $\gamma^*$-condition (given in Definition 8) for the assignment $p := \lambda(\overrightarrow{u})\,\lambda(v)P : (\overrightarrow{\vartheta} \to (\vartheta \to \tau))$
- $p' \in \mathsf{RecVars}_{(\overrightarrow{\vartheta} \to \tau)}$ is a fresh recursion variable
- for each part $X_i$ of $X$ in (33d)–(33f), and thus in (33g)–(33j) (i.e., for each $X_i \equiv A_i$ in $X \equiv A$, and each $X_i \equiv B_i$ in $X \equiv B$), $X'_i$ is the result of the replacements $X'_i \equiv X_i\{\,p(\overrightarrow{u})(v) :\equiv p'(\overrightarrow{u})\,\}$ of all occurrences of $p(\overrightarrow{u})(v)$ by $p'(\overrightarrow{u})$, modulo renaming the variables $\overrightarrow{u}, v$, for $i \in \{0, \ldots, n_X\}$, i.e.:

$$\overrightarrow{X'} \equiv \overrightarrow{X}\{\,p(\overrightarrow{u})(v) :\equiv p'(\overrightarrow{u})\,\} \tag{34}$$

Adding the $\Rightarrow_{(\gamma^*)}$ to the standard set of reduction rules of $\mathrm{L}^\lambda_{\mathrm{ar}}$ determines the extended reduction relation $\Rightarrow^*_{\gamma^*}$ between $\mathrm{L}^\lambda_{\mathrm{ar}}$-terms $A, B$, i.e., $A \Rightarrow^*_{\gamma^*} B$, by Definition 9.

**Definition 9 ($\gamma^*$-Reduction).** *The set of the* $\gamma^*$-reduction rules *is obtained by adding the ($\gamma^*$)-rule from Table 1 to the standart ones given in Sect. 2.4.*

*The* $\gamma^*$-reduction *relation* $\Rightarrow^*_{\gamma^*}$ *is the smallest relation* $\Rightarrow^*_{\gamma^*} \subseteq \mathsf{Terms} \times \mathsf{Terms}$ *(also denoted by* $\Rightarrow_{\gamma^*}$*) between terms, which is closed under the* $\gamma^*$*-reduction rules.*

**Notation 4.** *In addition to the notations* $\Rightarrow^*_{\gamma^*}$ *and* $\Rightarrow_{\gamma^*}$ *for the* $\gamma^*$*-reduction relation, we also use the usual notations for the reflexive and transitive closure of a relation, given in* (35a)–(35c)*. To specify that the ($\gamma^*$)-rule has been applied certain number of times, including zero times, possibly intervened by applications of some of the other reduction rules, we use the notation* (35b)–(35c).

$$A \Rightarrow^n_{\gamma^*} B \iff A \Rightarrow^*_{\gamma^*} B \iff A \Rightarrow_{\gamma^*} B, \textbf{for } n \geq 0$$
$$\textbf{by } n \textbf{ applications of } \gamma^*\textbf{-reduction rules,} \tag{35a}$$
$$\textbf{possibly, including the } (\gamma^*)\textbf{-rule}$$

$$A \Rightarrow^*_{\gamma^*} B \iff A \Rightarrow_{(\gamma^*)^n} B, \textbf{for } n \geq 0$$
$$\textbf{by using (possibly zero) } \gamma^*\textbf{-reduction rules,} \tag{35b}$$
$$\textbf{including } n \textbf{ applications of the } (\gamma^*)\textbf{-rule}$$

$$A \Rightarrow^+_{\gamma^*} B \iff A \Rightarrow^+_{(\gamma^*)^n} B, \textbf{ for } n \geq 0$$
$$\textbf{by using at least one of the } \gamma^*\textbf{-reduction rules,}$$
$$\textbf{including } n \textbf{ applications of the } (\gamma^*)\textbf{-rule} \tag{35c}$$

**Definition 10 ($\gamma^*$-Irreducible Terms).** *We say that a term* $A \in \mathsf{Terms}$ *is* $\gamma^*$-irreducible *if and only if* (36) *holds:*

$$\begin{aligned} &\textit{for all } B \in \mathsf{Terms}, \\ &A \Rightarrow^*_{\gamma^*} B \implies A \equiv_c B \end{aligned} \tag{36}$$

**Lemma 1 ($\gamma^*$-Irreducible Recursion Terms for Specific Assignments).** *Let the term* $A \in \mathsf{Terms}$ *be of the form* (37)*:*

$$A \equiv A_0 \text{ where } \{ \overrightarrow{a} := \overrightarrow{A},\ b := \lambda(\overrightarrow{u})\, \lambda(v)B,\ \overrightarrow{c} := \overrightarrow{C} \} \tag{37}$$

*Then,* $A$ *is* $\gamma^*$-irreducible *for the assignment* $b := \lambda(\overrightarrow{u})\, \lambda(v)B$ *in it, with respect to* $\lambda(v)$*, if and only if one of the following (1)–(2) holds (i.e., the* $\gamma^*$*-condition given in Definition 8 is not satisfied for it):*

*(1)* $v \in \mathsf{FreeV}(B)$*, or*
*(2)* $v \notin \mathsf{FreeV}(B)$ *and it is not the case that every occurrence of* $b$ *in* $A_0$, $\overrightarrow{A}$, $\overrightarrow{C}$ *is an occurrence in a sub-term* $b(\overrightarrow{u})(v)$ *that is in the scope of* $\lambda(\overrightarrow{u})\, \lambda(v)$*, modulo congruence by renaming the variables* $\overrightarrow{u}, v \in \mathit{PureVars}$.

**Lemma 2 ($\gamma^*$-Reducing Multiple, Innessential $\lambda$-Abstractions in an Assignment).** *Assume that* $A \in \mathsf{Terms}$ *is of the form* (38a)–(38c)*:*

$$A \equiv A_0 \text{ where } \{ \overrightarrow{a} := \overrightarrow{A}, \tag{38a}$$

$$b := \lambda(\overrightarrow{u_1})\,\lambda(v_1)\ldots\lambda(\overrightarrow{u_k})\,\lambda(v_k)\,\lambda(\overrightarrow{u_{k+1}})B, \tag{38b}$$

$$\overrightarrow{c} := \overrightarrow{C}\,\} \tag{38c}$$

*such that $A$ satisfies the $\gamma^*$-condition (given in Definition 8) for the assignment in* (38b)*, with respect to all $\lambda$-abstractions $\lambda(v_j)$, for $1 \leq j \leq k$, $k \in \mathbb{N}$, i.e.:*

*Then, the following reduction* (39a)–(39c) *can be done:*

$$A \Rightarrow^*_{\gamma^*} A_0^k \text{ where } \{\, \overrightarrow{a} := \overrightarrow{A^k}, \tag{39a}$$

$$b^k := \lambda(\overrightarrow{u_1})\ldots\lambda(\overrightarrow{u_k})\,\lambda(\overrightarrow{u_{k+1}})B, \tag{39b}$$

$$\overrightarrow{c} := \overrightarrow{C^k}\,\} \tag{39c}$$

*where for each part $X_i$ of $X$ in* (38a)–(38c) *(i.e., for $X_i \equiv A_i$ in $X \equiv A$ or $X_i \equiv C_i$ in $X \equiv C$) $X_i^k$ in $X^k$ is the result of the replacements* (40a)–(40b)*, modulo renaming the bound variables $\overrightarrow{u_l}, v_j$, for $i \in \{0, \ldots, n_X\}$:*

$$X_i^k \equiv X_i\{\, b(\overrightarrow{u_1})(v_1)\ldots(\overrightarrow{u_k})(v_k)(\overrightarrow{u_{k+1}}) :\equiv b^k(\overrightarrow{u_1})\ldots(\overrightarrow{u_k})(\overrightarrow{u_{k+1}})\,\} \quad \text{for } i \in \{0, \ldots, n_X\} \tag{40a}$$

$$\overrightarrow{X^k} \equiv \overrightarrow{X^k}\{b(\overrightarrow{u_1})(v_1)\ldots(\overrightarrow{u_k})(v_k)(\overrightarrow{u_{k+1}}) :\equiv b^k(\overrightarrow{u_1})\ldots(\overrightarrow{u_k})(\overrightarrow{u_{k+1}})\,\} \tag{40b}$$

*Proof.* The proof is by induction on $k \in \mathbb{N}$, and we do not provide it here, because it is long.

We note that the sequences $\lambda(\overrightarrow{u_l})$ of $\lambda$-abstractions can be empty, and in this lemma, we do not consider whether the $\gamma^*$-condition is satisfied with respect to them.

The inductive proof uses Definition 8, by which it follows that

(1) $v_j \notin \mathsf{FreeV}(B)$, for $1 \leq j \leq k$

I.e., the value of the function denoted by the term in the assignment (38b), $b := \lambda(\overrightarrow{u_1})\,\lambda(v_1)\ldots\lambda(\overrightarrow{u_k})\,\lambda(v_k)\,\lambda(\overrightarrow{u_{k+1}})B$, doesn't depend on the values of the arguments corresponding to $\lambda(v_1), \ldots, \lambda(v_k)$.

(2) All occurrences of $b$ in $A_0$, $\overrightarrow{A}$, $\overrightarrow{C}$ are occurrences in sub-terms of $A$, $b(\overrightarrow{u_1})(v_1)\ldots(\overrightarrow{u_k})(v_k)(\overrightarrow{u_{k+1}})$, that are in the scope of the $\lambda$-abstractions over these variables, $\lambda(\overrightarrow{u_1})\,\lambda(v_1)\ldots\lambda(\overrightarrow{u_k})\,\lambda(v_k)\,\lambda(\overrightarrow{u_{k+1}})$, modulo corresponding renaming of these bound variables $u_l, v_j$. □

**Lemma 3** **($\gamma^*$-Reduction of the Assignments of a Recursion Term).** *For every recursion term $P \equiv P_0$ where $\{\, \overrightarrow{p} := \overrightarrow{P}\,\}$,* (41a)*, there is a term $Q$, of the form in* (41b)*, such that $Q$ does not satisfy the $\gamma^*$-condition, for any of its assignments $q_i := Q_i$ $(i = 1, \ldots, n)$ in* (41b)*, and $P \Rightarrow^*_{\gamma^*} Q$.*

$$P \equiv P_0 \text{ where } \{\, p_1 := P_1, \ldots, p_n := P_n \,\} \tag{41a}$$

$$\Rightarrow^*_{\gamma^*} Q \equiv Q_0 \text{ where } \{\, q_1 := Q_1, \ldots, q_n := Q_n \,\} \tag{41b}$$

*Proof.* The proof is by induction on the $\mathsf{rank}(p_i)$ for the assignments in (41a), that satisfy the $\gamma^*$-condition given in Definition 8. The induction step is done by applying Lemma 2 to all the assignments with the least $\mathsf{rank}(p_i)$.

*Inductiin Assumption:* Assume that $P$ is of the form (42a)–(42d), modulo congruence:

$$P \equiv_{\mathsf{c}} A_0 \text{ where } \{\, \overrightarrow{a} := \overrightarrow{A}, \tag{42a}$$
$$b_1 := \lambda(\overrightarrow{u_{1,1}})\,\lambda(v_{1,1}) \ldots \lambda(\overrightarrow{u_{1,k_1}})\,\lambda(v_{1,k_1})\,\lambda(\overrightarrow{u_{1,k_1+1}})B_1, \tag{42b}$$
$$\ldots$$
$$b_m := \lambda(\overrightarrow{u_{m,1}})\,\lambda(v_{m,1}) \ldots \lambda(\overrightarrow{u_{m,k_m}})\,\lambda(v_{m,k_m})\,\lambda(\overrightarrow{u_{m,k_m+1}})B_m, \tag{42c}$$
$$\overrightarrow{c} := \overrightarrow{C}\,\} \tag{42d}$$

where, for all $j = 1, \ldots, m$:

(1) $b_j$ are all recursion variables in the recursion assignments of $P$, with the least $\mathsf{rank}(b_j) \geq 0$, such that (42b)–(42c) satisfy the $\gamma^*$-condition
(2) $v_{j,1}, \ldots, v_{j,k_j}$ are all the variables for $b_j$, for which $\gamma^*$-rule can be applied, i.e.:
$\lambda(\overrightarrow{u_{j,1}})\,\lambda(v_{j,1}) \ldots \lambda(\overrightarrow{u_{j,k_j}})\,\lambda(v_{j,k_j})\,\lambda(\overrightarrow{u_{j,j_{k+1}}})$ is the longest $\lambda$-prefix of the corresponding term assigned to $b_j$ in (42b)–(42c);
$v_{j,i} \notin \mathsf{FreeV}(B_j)$, for $i = 1, \ldots, k_j$; and, $u_{j,i} \in \mathsf{FreeV}(B_j)$, for $i = 1, \ldots, k_j + 1$
(3) (42d) are all assignments, with $\mathsf{rank}(c_l) < \mathsf{rank}(b_j)$, and therefore no $b_j$ occurs in any $C_l$.

By applying Lemma 2 to each of the assignments (42b)–(42c), we reduce $P$ to the term (43a)–(43d):

$$P \Rightarrow^*_{\gamma^*} A'_0 \text{ where } \{\, \overrightarrow{a} := \overrightarrow{A'}, \tag{43a}$$
$$b'_1 := \lambda(\overrightarrow{u_{1,1}}) \ldots \lambda(\overrightarrow{u_{1,k_1}})\,\lambda(\overrightarrow{u_{1,k_1+1}})B_1, \tag{43b}$$
$$\ldots$$
$$b'_m := \lambda(\overrightarrow{u_{m,1}}) \ldots \lambda(\overrightarrow{u_{m,k_m}})\,\lambda(\overrightarrow{u_{m,k_m+1}})B_m, \tag{43c}$$
$$\overrightarrow{c} := \overrightarrow{C}\,\} \tag{43d}$$

From (1)–(3) of the induction assumption, it follows that $B_j$ doesn't begin with $\lambda$, and the $\gamma^*$-condition is not satisfied with respect to any of the $\lambda$-abstractions in the sequences $\lambda(\overrightarrow{u_{j,i}})$, for $j = 1, \ldots, m$ and $i = 1, \ldots, k_j$. Therefore, the $\gamma^*$-condition is not applicable to (43b)–(43b). And, by the induction assumption, it is not applicable to (43d).

Thus, in case that $\gamma^*$-condition is satisfied, that is for some of the assignments $a_i := A_i$ from (43a), for which the $\gamma^*$-rule can be applied. Since $b_j$ are all the recursion variables with the least $\mathsf{rank}(b_j)$, in (42a)–(42d), satisfying $\gamma^*$-condition, then $\mathsf{rank}(a_i) > \mathsf{rank}(b_j)$. Inductively,

$$P' \Rightarrow^*_{\gamma^*} Q \equiv Q_0 \text{ where } \{\, q_1 := Q_1, \ldots, q_n := Q_n \,\} \tag{44}$$

where $Q$ doesn't satisfy the $\gamma^*$-condition for any of its assignments $q_i := Q_i$.

**Theorem 4 (Criteria for $\gamma^*$-Irreducibility).** *By structural induction:*

1. *If $A \in \mathsf{Const} \cup \mathsf{Vars}$, then $A$ is $\gamma^*$-irreducible.*
2. *A term $A(B)$ is $\gamma^*$-irreducible iff $A$ is explicit and $\gamma^*$-irreducible, and $B$ is immediate.*
3. *A $\lambda$-term $\lambda(x)A$ is $\gamma^*$-irreducible iff $A$ is explicit and $\gamma^*$-irreducible.*
4. *A recursion term $A \equiv [A_0 \text{ where } \{p_1 := A_1, \ldots, p_n := A_n\}]$ $(n \geq 0)$ is $\gamma^*$-irreducible if and only if*
   (a) *all of the parts $A_0, \ldots, A_n$ are explicit and $\gamma^*$-irreducible, and*
   (b) *the term $A$ does not satisfy the $\gamma^*$-condition, for any of the assignments in $\{p_1 := A_1, \ldots, p_n := A_n\}$.*

*Proof.* By structural induction on terms and the $\gamma^*$-reduction rules.

## 4 Gamma-Star Canonical Forms

By recursion on the term structure, for each term $A \in \mathsf{Terms}$, we define a term, denoted by $\mathsf{cf}_{\gamma^*}(A)$ and called a *$\gamma^*$-canonical form of $A$* or *gamma-star canonical form of $A$*.

In each clause of Definition 11, we assume that the bound recursion variables are distinct, and distinct from the free recursion variables.

**Definition 11** **($\gamma^*$-Canonical Forms)**

**(GSCF1)** *For every $\mathsf{c} \in K_\tau$, $\mathsf{cf}_{\gamma^*}(\mathsf{c}) :\equiv \mathsf{c}$;*
*for every $x \in \mathsf{PureVars}_\tau \cup \mathsf{RecVars}_\tau$, $\mathsf{cf}_{\gamma^*}(x) :\equiv x$*

**(GSCF2)** *Assume that $A \in \mathsf{Terms}$, and*
$\mathsf{cf}_{\gamma^*}(A) \equiv A_0 \text{ where } \{p_1 := A_1, \ldots, p_n := A_n\} \equiv A_0 \text{ where } \{\overrightarrow{p} := \overrightarrow{A}\}$ *$(n \geq 0)$, then*

**(GSCF2a).** *if $X$ is an immediate term, then*

$$\begin{aligned}\mathsf{cf}_{\gamma^*}(A(X)) &:\equiv A_0(X) \text{ where } \{p_1 := A_1, \ldots, p_n := A_n\} \\ &\equiv A_0(X) \text{ where } \{\overrightarrow{p} := \overrightarrow{A}\}\end{aligned} \tag{45}$$

**(GSCF2b)** *if $B$ is a proper term and*
$\mathsf{cf}_{\gamma^*}(B) \equiv B_0 \text{ where } \{q_1 := B_1, \ldots, q_m := B_m\} \equiv B_0 \text{ where } \{\overrightarrow{q} := \overrightarrow{B}\}$ *$(m \geq 0)$, then*

$$\begin{aligned}\mathsf{cf}_{\gamma^*}(A(B)) :\equiv\ & A_0(q_o) \text{ where } \{p_1 := A_1, \ldots, p_n := A_n, \\ & \qquad q_0 := B_0, q_1 := B_1, \ldots, q_m := B_m\} \\ \equiv\ & A_0(q_0) \text{ where } \{\overrightarrow{p} := \overrightarrow{A}, q_0 := B_0, \overrightarrow{q} := \overrightarrow{B}\}\end{aligned} \tag{46}$$

**(GSCF3).** *Assume that $A \in \mathsf{Terms}$, and*
$\mathsf{cf}_{\gamma^*}(A) \equiv A_0 \text{ where } \{p_1 := A_1, \ldots, p_n := A_n\} \equiv A_0 \text{ where } \{\overrightarrow{p} := \overrightarrow{A}\}$ *$(n \geq 0)$.*

*Then, for every $u \in \mathit{PureVars}_\tau$, the term $\mathsf{cf}_{\gamma^*}(\lambda(u)A)$ is any $\gamma^*$-irreducible term, such that* (47a)–(47c)*:*

$$\lambda(u)\big(\mathsf{cf}_{\gamma^*}(A)\big) \tag{47a}$$

$$\Rightarrow_{(\lambda)} \lambda(u)A'_0 \text{ where } \{\, p'_1 := \lambda(u)A'_1, \ldots, p'_n := \lambda(u)A'_n \,\}$$

$$\equiv \lambda(u)A'_0 \text{ where } \{\, \overrightarrow{p'} := \overrightarrow{\lambda(u)A'} \,\} \tag{47b}$$

$$\Rightarrow^{k}_{(\gamma^*)} \mathsf{cf}_{\gamma^*}(\lambda(u)A), \qquad \textit{by } k \textit{ applications of } (\gamma^*)\textit{-rule, } k \geq 0 \tag{47c}$$

*where for every $i = 1, \ldots, n$, the recursion variable $p'_i$ is fresh and $A'_i$ is the result of the replacement of all the free occurrences of $p_1, \ldots, p_n$ in $A_i$ with $p'_1(u), \ldots, p'_n(u)$, respectively, i.e.:*

$$\begin{aligned} A'_i &\equiv A_i\{p_1 :\equiv p'_1(u), \ldots, p_n :\equiv p'_n(u)\} \\ &\equiv A_i\{\overrightarrow{p} :\equiv \overrightarrow{p'(u)}\} \end{aligned} \tag{48}$$

**(GSCF4).** *Assume that $A \equiv A_0$ where $\{p_1 := A_1, \ldots, p_n := A_n\}$, $n \geq 0$, and, for every $i = 0, \ldots, n$:*

$$\mathsf{cf}_{\gamma^*}(A_i) \equiv A_{i,0} \text{ where } \{p_{i,1} := A_{i,1}, \ldots, p_{i,k_i} := A_{i,k_i}\} \tag{49a}$$

$$\equiv A_{i,0} \text{ where } \{\, \overrightarrow{p_i} := \overrightarrow{A_i} \,\} \qquad (k_i \geq 0) \tag{49b}$$

*Then, the term $\mathsf{cf}_{\gamma^*}(A)$ is any $\gamma^*$-irreducible term, such that the reduction (50a)–(50c) can be done by $k$ applications of $(\gamma^*)$-rule, $k \geq 0$:*

$$\begin{aligned} C \equiv A_{0,0} \text{ where } \{ \quad & p_{0,1} := A_{0,1}, \ldots, p_{0,k_0} := A_{0,k_0}, \\ & p_1 := A_{1,0},\ p_{1,1} := A_{1,1}, \ldots, p_{1,k_1} := A_{1,k_1}, \\ & \vdots \\ & p_n := A_{n,0},\ p_{n,1} := A_{n,1}, \ldots, p_{n,k_n} := A_{n,k_n} \,\} \end{aligned} \tag{50a}$$

$$\begin{aligned} \equiv A_{0,0} \text{ where } \{ \quad & \overrightarrow{p_0} := \overrightarrow{A_0}, \\ & p_1 := A_{1,0},\ \overrightarrow{p_1} := \overrightarrow{A_1}, \\ & \vdots \\ & p_n := A_{n,0},\ \overrightarrow{p_n} := \overrightarrow{A_n} \,\} \end{aligned} \tag{50b}$$

$$\Rightarrow^{k}_{(\gamma^*)} \mathsf{cf}_{\gamma^*}(A) \tag{50c}$$

Notice that, while $\mathsf{cf}_{\gamma^*}(A_i) \equiv A_{i,0}$ where $\{p_{i,1} := A_{i,1}, \ldots, p_{i,k_i} := A_{i,k_i}\}$ can be $\gamma^*$-irreducible, for some $i \geq 1$, the head term $A_{i,0}$ can be such that the term $C$ satisfies the $\gamma^*$-condition for the assignment $p_i := A_{i,0}$. E.g., if $A_{i,0} \equiv \lambda(\overrightarrow{x})\,\lambda(x)B$, $x \notin \mathsf{FreeV}(B)$, and all occurrences of $p_i$ in $A_{j,l}$ are occurrences of $p_i(\overrightarrow{x})(x)$ in the scope of $\lambda(\overrightarrow{x})\,\lambda(x)$ 6.

### 4.1 Canonical Forms and $\gamma^*$-Reduction

**Theorem 5 (Reducibility to $\gamma^*$-Canonical Form)** *For every term $A \in$ Terms, there is a unique, up to congruence, $\gamma^*$-irreducible term $C$, which is the $\gamma^*$-canonical form of $A$, $C \equiv \mathsf{cf}_{\gamma^*}(A)$, such that:*

1. *(Existence of a $\gamma^*$-canonical form of $A$) There exist explicit, $\gamma^*$-irreducible $A_0, \ldots, A_n \in$ Terms $(n \geq 0)$, such that* (51) *holds and, thus, the term $\mathsf{cf}_{\gamma^*}(A)$ is $\gamma^*$-irreducible:*

$$\mathsf{cf}_{\gamma^*}(A) \equiv A_0 \text{ where } \{ p_1 := A_1, \ldots, p_n := A_n \} \tag{51}$$

2. *A constant or a variable $\xi \in K \cup \mathit{RecVars} \cup \mathit{PureVars}$ occurs freely in $\mathsf{cf}_{\gamma^*}(A)$ if and only if it occurs freely in $A$*
3. *$A \Rightarrow^*_{\gamma^*} \mathsf{cf}_{\gamma^*}(A)$*
4. *If $A$ is $\gamma^*$-irreducible, then $A \equiv_c \mathsf{cf}_{\gamma^*}(A)$*
5. *If $A \Rightarrow^*_{\gamma^*} B$, then $\mathsf{cf}_{\gamma^*}(A) \equiv_c \mathsf{cf}_{\gamma^*}(B)$*
6. *(Uniqueness of $\mathsf{cf}_{\gamma^*}(A)$ wrt congruence) If $A \Rightarrow^*_{\gamma^*} B$ and $B$ is $\gamma^*$-irreducible, then $B \equiv_c \mathsf{cf}_{\gamma^*}(A)$, i.e., $\mathsf{cf}_{\gamma^*}(A)$ is unique, up to congruence, $\gamma^*$-irreducible term.*

*Proof.* The statement (1) is proved by induction on term structure, using Definition 11 of the $\mathsf{cf}_{\gamma^*}(A)$, and Lemmas 2–3.

The statements (2) and (3) are proved by induction on term structure, using the criteria for $\gamma^*$-irreducibility 4.

(4) is proved by induction on the definition of the $\gamma^*$-reduction relation. (5) follows from (3) and (4).

**Notation 5.** *Often, we use the following notations:*

$$A \Rightarrow_{\mathsf{gscf}} B \iff B \equiv_c \mathsf{cf}_{\gamma^*}(A) \tag{52a}$$

$$A \Rightarrow_{\mathsf{gscf}} \mathsf{cf}_{\gamma^*}(A) \tag{52b}$$

**Definition 12 ($\gamma^*$-Equivalence Relation $\approx_{\gamma^*}$).** *For all terms $A, B \in$ Terms:*

$$A \approx_{\gamma^*} B \iff \mathsf{cf}_{\gamma^*}(A) \approx \mathsf{cf}_{\gamma^*}(B) \tag{53}$$

*When $A \approx_{\gamma^*} B$, we say that $A$ and $B$ are $\gamma^*$-equivalent, alternatively, that $A$ and $B$ are $\gamma^*$-synonymous.*

*Note 1.* We have added an additional restriction in the $\gamma^*$-condition, given in Definition 8, of the ($\gamma^*$)-rule that all the occurrences of the sub-terms $p(\overrightarrow{u})(v)$ have to be in the scope of $\lambda \overrightarrow{u}) \lambda(v)$ (modulo renaming congruence). By this, the $\Rightarrow_{(\gamma^*)}$-rule preserves all the free variables of $A$ in $\mathsf{cf}_{\gamma^*}(A)$, including the free pure variables, not only the free recursion variables, so that $\mathsf{FreeV}(\mathsf{cf}_{\gamma^*}(A)) = \mathsf{FreeV}(A)$ (see the $\gamma^*$-Canonical Form Theorem 5). Thus, the strict $\gamma^*$-reduction, respects this extra restriction, to maintain all occurrences of free variables, even when denotations do not depend on the values of these free variables provided by the variable assignments. This additional restriction for removing only bound pure variables, which are inessential, is not included in Loukanova [23].

### 4.2 Properties of the $\gamma^*$-Equivalence

**Theorem 6 ($\gamma^*$-Equivalence Theorem).** *Two terms $A, B$ are algorithmically $\gamma^*$-synonymous, $A \approx_{\gamma^*} B$, if and only if both are immediate or both are prure, and there are explicit, irreducible terms of corresponding types, $A_i : \sigma_i$, $B_i : \sigma_i$ $(i = 0, \ldots, n)$, $(n \geq 0)$, such that:*

$$\begin{aligned} A &\Rightarrow_{\mathsf{gscf}} A_0 \text{ where } \{ p_1 := A_1, \ldots, p_n := A_n \} \\ &\equiv \mathsf{cf}_{\gamma^*}(A) \qquad (\textit{i.e., } \gamma^*\textit{-irreducible}) \end{aligned} \tag{54a}$$

$$\begin{aligned} B &\Rightarrow_{\mathsf{gscf}} B_0 \text{ where } \{ p_1 := B_1, \ldots, p_n := B_n \} \\ &\equiv \mathsf{cf}_{\gamma^*}(B) \qquad (\textit{i.e., } \gamma^*\textit{-irreducible}) \end{aligned} \tag{54b}$$

*and for all $i = 0, \ldots, n$,*

$$\mathsf{den}(A_i)(g) = \mathsf{den}(B_i)(g), \quad \textit{for all } g \in G \tag{55}$$

*Proof.* The theorem follows from Definition 12 of $\gamma^*$-equivalence and Theorem 3.

**Definition 13 (Syntactic Equivalence, i.e. Synonymy, Relation $\approx_s$).** *For any $A, B \in$ Terms,*

$$A \approx_s B \iff \mathsf{cf}(A) \equiv_c \mathsf{cf}(B) \tag{56}$$

For more details about syntactic synonymy, see Moschovakis [28]. The difference between syntactic and algorithmic synonymies is that syntactic synonymy does not apply to denotationally equivalent constants and syntactic constructs such as $\lambda$-terms. For instance, assuming that *dog* and *canine* are constants, such that $\mathsf{den}(dog) = \mathsf{den}(canine)$, it follows by the Referential Synonymy Theorem 3 that $dog \approx canine$. Both terms are in canonical forms, with the same denotations, i.e., they denote the same function the values of which are computed by the same algorithm, provided by the interpretation function $I$ of the semantics structure $\mathfrak{A} = \langle \mathbb{T}, \mathcal{I} \rangle$. On the other hand, $dog \not\approx_s canine$, since $dog \not\equiv_c canine$. Also, $\mathsf{den}(dog) = \mathsf{den}(\lambda(x) dog(x))$ (by Definition 3 of the denotation function). Therefore, $dog \approx \lambda(x) dog(x)$ (by the Referential Synonymy Theorem 3), because both terms are in canonical forms. These terms are syntactically different, $dog \not\approx_s \lambda(x) dog(x)$, because $dog \not\equiv_c \lambda(x) dog(x)$.

**Theorem 7.** *For any $A, B \in$ Terms,*

$$\begin{aligned} A \Rightarrow B &\Longrightarrow A \approx_s B && (57a) \\ &\Longrightarrow A \approx B && (57b) \\ &\Longrightarrow A \approx_{\gamma^*} B \Longrightarrow A \models\!\mid B && (57c) \end{aligned}$$

*Proof.* By using the definitions.

**Theorem 8.** *For any $A, B \in$ Terms,*

$$\mathsf{cf}(A) \approx_{\gamma^*} \mathsf{cf}(B) \iff$$

$$\mathsf{cf}(A) \Rightarrow^*_{\gamma^*} A',\ \mathsf{cf}(B) \Rightarrow^*_{\gamma^*} B',\ \textit{and}\ A' \approx_{\gamma^*} B',\ \textit{for some}\ A', B' \in \mathsf{Terms} \tag{58a}$$

$$\mathsf{cf}(A) \approx_{\gamma^*} \mathsf{cf}(B) \iff A \approx_{\gamma^*} B \tag{58b}$$

*Proof.* The directions $\Longleftarrow$ are proved by using Definition 12, Referential Synonymy Theorem 3, and Extended $\gamma^*$-Canonical Form Theorem 5.

**Corollary 1.** *For all* $A, B, C \in \mathsf{Terms}$,

$$A \Rightarrow B \Rightarrow^*_{\gamma^*} C \implies A \approx B \quad \implies \quad A \approx_{\gamma^*} B \approx_{\gamma^*} C \tag{59}$$

*while there exist (many) terms* $A, B, C \in \mathsf{Terms}$ *such that*

$$A \Rightarrow B \Rightarrow^*_{\gamma^*} C,\quad C \not\approx B,\quad \textit{and}\quad C \not\approx A \tag{60}$$

*Proof.* (59) follows from Definition 12, the Canonical Form Theorem 2, and the Theorem 5 of Reducibility to $\gamma^*$-Canonical Form. The terms in Sect. 5 contribute to the proof of (60).

By Definition 12 of $\gamma^*$-equivalence between two terms $A, B$ as algorithmic synonymy between their $\gamma^*$-canonical forms, various properties of algorithmic synonymy are inherited by $\gamma^*$-equivalence, reflected, e.g., by the $\gamma^*$-Equivalence Theorem 6 and the compositionality of $\gamma^*$-equivalence, with the very restricted form of $\beta$-reduction.

Assume that the $(\gamma*)$-rule, see Table 1, is applied to a term $A$ in canonical form, i.e., $A \equiv_{\mathsf{c}} \mathsf{cf}(A)$. By application of the $(\gamma*)$-rule until we obtain the $\gamma^*$ canonical form $\mathsf{cf}_{\gamma^*}(A)$ of $A$. The corresponding parts in the assignments (33b)–(33e) are not denotationally equivalent, since they are not of the same type. By the $\gamma^*$-Equivalence Theorem 6, $A \approx \mathsf{cf}(A) \not\approx \mathsf{cf}_{\gamma^*}(A)$.

The $\gamma^*$-reduction calculus does not preserve per se the algorithmic synonymy between terms. That is, in general, it is possible that $A \approx B$, while $A \not\approx_{\gamma^*} B$.

Nevertheless, the $\gamma^*$-reduction relation $\Rightarrow^*_{\gamma^*}$ between terms is very useful. For any terms $A$ and $B$, a $\gamma^*$-reduction $A \Rightarrow_{(\gamma^*)} \mathsf{cf}_{\gamma^*}(A)$ preserves the most essential algorithmic components of the canonical form $\mathsf{cf}(A)$ in $\mathsf{cf}_{\gamma^*}(A)$. It reduces vacuous $\lambda$-abstractions, which denote constant functions, and corresponding applications that give the constant values.

## 5 Applications of the $\gamma^*$-Reduction

In this section, we give pattern examples for possible renderings of expressions in human language to $\mathrm{L}^{\lambda}_{\mathrm{ar}}$-terms that can represent their algorithmic semantics. A definition of a rendering relation between human language expressions and their semantic representations by $\mathrm{L}^{\lambda}_{\mathrm{ar}}$-terms is not in the subject of this paper. Rendering can be defined in a computational mode, via syntax-semantics interfaces, within a computational grammar, e.g., see Loukanova [8, 22]. Typically, $\mathrm{L}^{\lambda}_{\mathrm{ar}}$ offers alternative terms for representing algorithmic semantics of human language expressions. The choice would depend on applications.

Developments of new, hybrid machine learning techniques and statistical approaches for extraction of semantic information from text can provide more possibilities for rendering human language expressions to $\mathrm{L}^{\lambda}_{\mathrm{ar}}$-terms.

*Example 2.* Assume that the sentence (61) is either directly rendered to a $\mathrm{L}^{\lambda}_{\mathrm{ar}}$-term $B_1$, which is given in (62a)–(62h), or alternatively, depending on specific applications, to a term that is reduced to the term $B_1$.

$$\begin{aligned}
&[\text{Jim}]_j \text{ sent Mia the article about} && (61)\\
&\text{the [discovery of Protein353 by } [\text{him}]_j] &&\\
&\xrightarrow{\text{render}} B \Rightarrow B_1 &&
\end{aligned}$$

where

$$\begin{aligned}
&B \Rightarrow B_1 \equiv && (62a)\\
&\lambda(z)\Big[\lambda(x)\big[\mathit{send}(m^1)(a^1)(z) \text{ where} && (62b)\\
&\{a^1 := \mathit{the}(r^1), && (62c)\\
&\;\; r^1 := \mathit{article\text{-}about}(b^1), && (62d)\\
&\;\; b^1 := \mathit{the}(d^1), && (62e)\\
&\;\; d^1 := \mathit{discovery\text{-}of\text{-}by}(p^1)(z), && (62f)\\
&\;\; p^1 := \mathit{protein353}, && (62g)\\
&\;\; m^1 := \mathit{mia}\}\big]\Big](\mathit{jim}) && (62h)
\end{aligned}$$

Further, the term $B_1$ can be reduced to its canonical form $\mathsf{cf}(B_1)$ in the standard reduction calculus of $\mathrm{L}^{\lambda}_{\mathrm{ar}}$. Due to the presence of multiple $\lambda$-abstractions and recursive assignments, the term $\mathsf{cf}(B_1)$ contains redundant abstractions over variables that occur only in some parts of $\mathsf{cf}(B_1)$, with corresponding vacuous applications.

In (63a), the term $B_1$ is reduced to $\mathsf{cf}_{\gamma^*}(B_1)$

$$\begin{aligned}
&B_1 \Rightarrow^*_{\gamma^*} \mathsf{cf}_{\gamma^*}(B_1) \equiv && (63a)\\
&\Big[\lambda(z)\,\lambda(x)\mathit{send}(m)(a(z))(z)\Big](j) && (63b)\\
&\text{where} &&\\
&\{\, a := \lambda(z)\mathit{the}(r(z)), && (63c)\\
&\;\; r := \lambda(z)\mathit{article\text{-}about}(b(z)), && (63d)\\
&\;\; b := \lambda(z)\mathit{the}(d(z)), && (63e)\\
&\;\; d := \lambda(z)\mathit{discovery\text{-}of\text{-}by}(p)(z), && (63f)\\
&\;\; p := \mathit{protein353}, && (63g)\\
&\;\; m := \mathit{mia},\, j := \mathit{jim}\,\} && (63h)
\end{aligned}$$

## 6 Future Work

The $(\gamma^*)$-rule, and the extended $(\gamma^*)$-reduction calculus of $L^{\lambda}_{ar}$, provide significant simplifications and reduction of the complexity of algorithmic calculations. This is important in theoretical foundations and applications in contemporary technologies, especially for computational semantics of natural and formal languages in NLP and other AI technologies.

We work on theoretic development and applications of the type-theory of acyclic algorithms. We have promising results for applications to language processing of formal and natural languages. Specific theoretical results are directed to applications of $L^{\lambda}_{ar}$ to computational semantics and computational syntax-semantics interfaces.

A new direction of applications is to computational neuroscience, by algorithmic modelling of procedural, factual, and declarative memory, and dependencies between those, by mutual recursion.

The results in this paper are part of our long-term work on development of dependent-type theory of situated information.

## References


1. Hamm, F., van Lambalgen, M.: Moschovakis' notion of meaning as applied to linguistics. In: Logic Colloqium, vol. 1 (2004)
2. Hurkens, A.J.C., McArthur, M., Moschovakis, Y.N., Moss, L.S., Whitney, G.T.: The logic of recursive equations. J. Symbol. Log. **63**(2), 451–478 (1998). http://projecteuclid.org/euclid.jsl/1183745513
3. Loukanova, R.: Constraint based syntax of modifiers. In: 2011 IEEE/WIC/ACM International Conferences on Web Intelligence and Intelligent Agent Technology, vol. 3, pp. 167–170 (2011). http://doi.ieeecomputersociety.org/10.1109/WI-IAT.2011.229
4. Loukanova, R.: From Montague's rules of quantification to minimal recursion semantics and the language of acyclic recursion. In: Bel-Enguix, G., Dahl, V., Jiménez-López, M.D. (eds.) Biology, Computation and Linguistics – New Interdisciplinary Paradigms. Frontiers in Artificial Intelligence and Applications, vol. 228, pp. 200–214. IOS Press, Amsterdam (2011). http://ebooks.iospress.nl/volumearticle/6486
5. Loukanova, R.: Minimal recursion semantics and the language of acyclic recursion. In: Bel-Enguix, G., Dahl, V., Puente, A.O.D.L. (eds.) AI Methods for Interdisciplinary Research in Language and Biology, pp. 88–97. SciTePress – Science and Technology Publications, Rome, January 2011. https://doi.org/10.5220/0003309800880097
6. Loukanova, R.: Modeling context information for computational semantics with the language of acyclic recursion. In: Pérez, J.B., et al. (eds.) Highlights in Practical Applications of Agents and Multiagent Systems. AISC, vol. 89, pp. 265–274. Springer, Heidelberg (2011). https://doi.org/10.1007/978-3-642-19917-2_32
7. Loukanova, R.: Reference, co-reference and antecedent-anaphora in the type theory of acyclic recursion. In: Bel-Enguix, G., Jiménez-López, M.D. (eds.) Bio-Inspired Models for Natural and Formal Languages, pp. 81–102. Cambridge Scholars Publishing, Cambridge (2011). http://www.cambridgescholars.com/bio-inspired-models-for-natural-and-formal-languages-16

8. Loukanova, R.: Semantics with the language of acyclic recursion in constraint-based grammar. In: Bel-Enguix, G., Jiménez-López, M.D. (eds.) Bio-inspired Models for Natural and Formal Languages, pp. 103–134. Cambridge Scholars Publishing, Cambridge (2011). http://www.cambridgescholars.com/bio-inspired-models-for-natural-and-formal-languages-16
9. Loukanova, R.: Syntax-semantics interface for lexical inflection with the language of acyclic recursion. In: Bel-Enguix, G., Dahl, V., Jiménez-López, M.D. (eds.) Biology, Computation and Linguistics – New Interdisciplinary Paradigms, Frontiers in Artificial Intelligence and Applications, vol. 228, pp. 215–236. IOS Press, Amsterdam (2011). http://ebooks.iospress.nl/volumearticle/6487
10. Loukanova, R.: Algorithmic semantics of ambiguous modifiers by the type theory of acyclic recursion. In: IEEE/WIC/ACM International Conference on Web Intelligence and Intelligent Agent Technology, vol. 3, pp. 117–121 (2012). https://doi.org/10.1109/WI-IAT.2012.246
11. Loukanova, R.: Semantic information with type theory of acyclic recursion. In: Huang, R., Ghorbani, A.A., Pasi, G., Yamaguchi, T., Yen, N.Y., Jin, B. (eds.) AMT 2012. LNCS, vol. 7669, pp. 387–398. Springer, Heidelberg (2012). https://doi.org/10.1007/978-3-642-35236-2_39
12. Loukanova, R.: Algorithmic granularity with constraints. In: Imamura, K., Usui, S., Shirao, T., Kasamatsu, T., Schwabe, L., Zhong, N. (eds.) BHI 2013. LNCS (LNAI), vol. 8211, pp. 399–408. Springer, Cham (2013). https://doi.org/10.1007/978-3-319-02753-1_40
13. Loukanova, R.: Algorithmic semantics for processing pronominal verbal phrases. In: Larsen, H.L., Martin-Bautista, M.J., Vila, M.A., Andreasen, T., Christiansen, H. (eds.) FQAS 2013. LNCS (LNAI), vol. 8132, pp. 164–175. Springer, Heidelberg (2013). https://doi.org/10.1007/978-3-642-40769-7_15
14. Loukanova, R.: A predicative operator and underspecification by the type theory of acyclic recursion. In: Duchier, D., Parmentier, Y. (eds.) CSLP 2012. LNCS, vol. 8114, pp. 108–132. Springer, Heidelberg (2013). https://doi.org/10.1007/978-3-642-41578-4_7
15. Loukanova, R.: Situation theory, situated information, and situated agents. In: Nguyen, N.T., Kowalczyk, R., Fred, A., Joaquim, F. (eds.) Transactions on Computational Collective Intelligence XVII. LNCS, vol. 8790, pp. 145–170. Springer, Heidelberg (2014). https://doi.org/10.1007/978-3-662-44994-3_8
16. Loukanova, R.: Representing parametric concepts with situation theory. In: Ganzha, M., Maciaszek, L., Paprzycki, M. (ed.) Proceedings of the 2015 Federated Conference on Computer Science and Information Systems, vol. 5, pp. 89–100. IEEE (2015). (Ann. Comput. Sci. Inf. Syst.). https://doi.org/10.15439/2015F409
17. Loukanova, R.: Underspecified relations with a formal language of situation theory. In: Loiseau, S., Filipe, J., Duval, B., van den Herik, J. (eds.) Proceedings of the 7th International Conference on Agents and Artificial Intelligence, vol. 1, pp. 298–309. SCITEPRESS – Science and Technology Publications, Lda. (2015). https://doi.org/10.5220/0005353402980309
18. Loukanova, R.: Acyclic recursion with polymorphic types and underspecification. In: van den Herik, J., Filipe, J. (eds.) Proceedings of the 8th International Conference on Agents and Artificial Intelligence, vol. 2, pp. 392–399. SCITEPRESS – Science and Technology Publications, Lda. (2016). https://doi.org/10.5220/0005749003920399
19. Loukanova, R.: Relationships between specified and underspecified quantification by the theory of acyclic recursion. ADCAIJ: Adv. Distrib. Comput. Artif. Intell.

J. **5**(4), 19–42 (2016). http://campus.usal.es/~revistas_trabajo/index.php/2255-2863/article/view/ADCAIJ2016541942
20. Loukanova, R.: Specification of underspecified quantifiers via question-answering by the theory of acyclic recursion. In: Andreasen, T., et al. (eds.) Flexible Query Answering Systems 2015. AISC, vol. 400, pp. 57–69. Springer, Cham (2016). https://doi.org/10.1007/978-3-319-26154-6_5
21. Loukanova, R.: Binding operators in type-theory of algorithms for algorithmic binding of functional neuro-receptors. In: 2017 Federated Conference on Computer Science and Information Systems (FedCSIS), vol. 11, pp. 57–66. IEEE (2017). https://doi.org/10.15439/2017F465
22. Loukanova, R.: Typed theory of situated information and its application to syntax-semantics of human language. In: Christiansen, H., Jiménez-López, M.D., Loukanova, R., Moss, L.S. (eds.) Partiality and Underspecification in Information, Languages, and Knowledge, pp. 151–188. Cambridge Scholars Publishing,Cambridge (2017). http://www.cambridgescholars.com/partiality-and-underspecification-in-information-languages-and-knowledge
23. Loukanova, R.: Gamma-star reduction in the type-theory of acyclic algorithms. In: Rocha, A.P., van den Herik, J. (eds.) Proceedings of the 10th International Conference on Agents and Artificial Intelligence (ICAART 2018), vol. 2, pp. 231–242. INSTICC, SciTePress – Science and Technology Publications, Lda. (2018). https://dx.doi.org/10.5220/0006662802310242
24. Loukanova, R., Jiménez-López, M.D.: On the syntax-semantics interface of argument marking prepositional phrases. In: Pérez, J.B., et al. (eds.) Highlights on Practical Applications of Agents and Multi-Agent Systems. Advances in Intelligent and Soft Computing, vol. 156, pp. 53–60. Springer, Heidelberg (2012). https://doi.org/10.1007/978-3-642-28762-6_7
25. Moschovakis, Y.N.: The formal language of recursion. J. Symbol. Log. **54**(04), 1216–1252 (1989)
26. Moschovakis, Y.N.: Sense and denotation as algorithm and value. In: Oikkonen, J., Vaananen, J. (eds.) Logic Colloquium'90. LNL, vol. 2, pp. 210–249. Springer, Heidelberg (1994)
27. Moschovakis, Y.N.: The logic of functional recursion. In: Dalla Chiara, M.L., Doets, K., Mundici, D., van Benthem, J. (eds.) Logic and Scientific Methods, vol. 259, pp. 179–207. Springer, Dordrecht (1997). https://doi.org/10.1007/978-94-017-0487-8_10
28. Moschovakis, Y.N.: A logical calculus of meaning and synonymy. Linguist. Philos. **29**(1), 27–89 (2006). https://doi.org/10.1007/s10988-005-6920-7

# The Application of Keirsey's Temperament Model to Twitter Data in Portuguese

Cristina Fátima Claro(✉), Ana Carolina E. S. Lima(✉), and Leandro N. de Castro(✉)

Mackenzie Presbyterian University, Rua da Consolação-930, São Paulo, Brazil
cristinafatclaro@gmail.com, aceslima@gmail.com, lnunes@mackenzie.br

**Abstract.** Temperament is a set of innate tendencies of the mind related with the processes of perception, analysis and decision making. The purpose of this paper is to predict Twitter users temperament based on Portuguese tweets and following Keirsey's model, which classifies the temperament into artisan, guardian, idealist and rational. The proposed methodology uses a Portuguese version of LIWC, which is a dictionary of words, to analyze the context of words, and supervised learning using the KNN, SVM and Random Forests for training the classifiers. The resultant average accuracy obtained was 88.37% for the artisan temperament, 86.92% for the guardian, 55.61% for the idealist, and 69.09% for the rational. For classification using TF-IDF the SVM algorithm obtained the best performance to the artisan temperament with average accuracy of 88.28%.

**Keywords:** Machine learning · Social media · Keirsey temperament model

## 1 Introduction

A set of characteristics is defined according to the personality and describe the individual behavior, temperament and emotion [1]. Personality represents a mix of characteristics and qualities that build the character of an individual. Thus, personality prediction is of interest in the areas of health, psychology, human resources and also has many commercial applications. Several researches investigate the link between human behavior in social media, personality types and psychological illnesses, such as depression and post-traumatic stress [2–4].

Social media are composed of different types of social sites, including traditional media, such as newspaper, radio and television, as well as non-traditional media, such as Facebook, Twitter and others [5]. Social media mining is the process that allows the analysis and extraction of patterns from social media data [6].

Through the behavior of the user in social media it is possible to predict psychological characteristics, such as temperament, that is, the way one perceives and interacts with the world [7]. This can be useful to the user himself and help in self-knowledge. From a corporate perspective, the temperament can be used by companies in recruitment and selection.


J. van den Herik and A. P. Rocha (Eds.): ICAART 2018, LNAI 11352, pp. 408–421, 2019.
https://doi.org/10.1007/978-3-030-05453-3_19

In this context, this paper develops a system to predict the temperament of Twitter users, using tweets in the Portuguese language. The temperament model used was introduced by David Keirsey, and divides the temperament into four categories: artisan; guardian; idealist; and rational. In order to do so, we will use the TECLA framework adapted to work with Portuguese texts [3]. In addition, it will be shown an analysis of the context of words by temperament using the dictionary of words Linguistic Inquiry and Word Count (LIWC) [4, 8].

This paper is structured as follows. Section 2 presents the David Keirsey temperament model used in TECLA, and Sect. 3 describes the TECLA framework. Section 4 presents the methodology and the results achieved and, finally, Sect. 5 concludes and discusses future perspectives.

## 2 Keirsey's Temperament Model

Temperament is a set of innate tendencies of the mind that relates to the processes of perceiving, analyzing, and decision making [7]. People seek success, happiness, love, pleasure, etc., in different ways and with distinct intensities and, therefore, there are different types of temperament [4, 9].

The temperament has its history marked in the proposal of the four humors described by Hippocrates, which gave origin to the theory of the four humors to interpret the state of health and illness of a person [9]. From this theory, Galen (190 AD) created the model of the first temperament typology [4, 10].

David Keirsey, an American psychologist, directed his studies to temperament in action, paying attention to choices, behavior patterns, congruencies, and consistencies. The temperament model proposed by David Keirsey divide the psychological types in artisan, guardian, idealist and rational. For Keirsey, the temperaments are driven by aspirations and interests, which motivate us to live, act, move, and play a role in society [3, 4, 7, 11].

The artisans are usually impulsive, they speak what comes to their minds and tend to do what works; whereas the guardians speak mainly of their duties and responsibilities, and how well they obey the laws. Idealists normally act from a good conscience and the rationals are pragmatic, act efficiently to reach their objectives, sometimes ignoring the rules and conventions if necessary [4, 12, 13].

Keirsey's temperament can be obtained by mapping the result of the MBTI test (Myers-Briggs Type Indicator), which uses four dimensions to classify users, totaling 16 psychological types [2, 7, 11]. Psychological types are acronyms formed by letters that begin with E and I (extraversion and introversion), which are attitudes; S and N indicate sensation and intuition, which is the process of perception; the letters T and F indicate thinking and feeling, and usually use logical reasoning, think first and feel later; and letters J and P indicate judgment and perception, which are attitudes and reflect the individuals' style in the external world [4, 9].

The mapping of the MBTI into Keirsey's model occurs by means of the classification of the acronyms defined by Myers-Briggs, as shown in Table 1 [11].

**Table 1.** Keirsey temperament model classification from the MBTI [4].

| Keirsey | Myers-Briggs | | | |
|---|---|---|---|---|
| Artisan | ESTP | ISTP | ESFP | ISFP |
| Guardian | ESTJ | ISTJ | ESFJ | ISFJ |
| Idealist | ENFJ | INFJ | ENFP | INFP |
| Rational | ENTJ | INTJ | ENTP | INTP |

## 3 The Tecla Framework

The Temperament Classification Framework TECLA was developed by Lima & de Castro [3, 13] with the objective of offering a modular tool for the classification of temperaments based on the Keirsey and Myers-Briggs models [13]. It is structured in a modular form, giving greater independence for each stage of the process and making it possible to couple and test different techniques in each module [4, 13]. Figure 1 shows the TECLA's modules, which are detailed in the following.

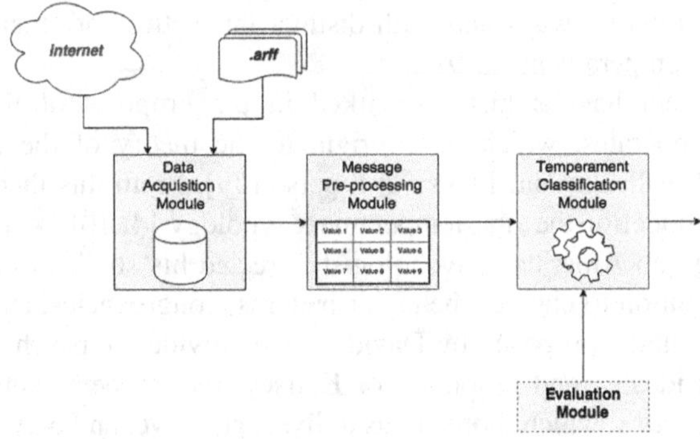


**Fig. 1.** The TECLA framework structure [4].

- **Data Acquisition Module:** Receives information from the user to be classified, including the number of tweets, the number of followers and followed, and a set of messages (tweets) from the user;
- **Message Pre-preprocessing Module:** Processes the data by creating an object matrix (meta-base) represented by meta-attributes. The information in the TECLA are divided in two categories: grammatical and behavioral. The behavior category uses information from Twitter, such as number of tweets, number of followed, followers, favorites, and number of times the user has been favorited. The grammar category uses information from LIWC, MRC, Taggers, or oNLP [3];
- **Temperament Classification Module:** Responsible for identifying the temperament of social media users. It performs the classification in the Keirsey model by using a set of classifiers;
- **Evaluation Module:** Used to quantify the framework performance [3].

In the version proposed in this paper, the TECLA will be adapted to work with texts written in Portuguese and will use the information provided by LIWC [8].

## 4 Metodology and Results

The description to be presented in this section will follow the modular structure of the TECLA framework. First, we will explain how we implemented each module of the framework and then the computational results.

### 4.1 Data Acquisition

To validate this work we used a database from the literature, called Twisty, available in a JSON file named TwiSty-PT.json, which has tweets in Portuguese and is provided by the Computational Linguists & Psycholinguistics Research Center (CLiPS) [14]. The dataset is composed of: user id; tweet id; other tweets id; confirmed tweets id; Myers-Briggs Type Indicators (MBTI) result; and gender. The tweets were captured by using the Twitter API [15], and we captured the number of tweets, number of followers, number of favorites, and total number of friends [16] of each user.

The original database consists of 4,090 user ids. From this universe it was not possible to collect 222 user ids due to denied access, leaving 3,868 valid user ids. Table 2 shows the descriptive analysis of the database according to David Keirsey's model, where Tweets_Statuses_Count refers to the number of tweets from the opening of the user account, and Tweets_base refers to the number of tweets collected.

**Table 2.** Temperament and Twitter data of the users (A = artisan, G = guardian, I = idealist, R = rational) [4].

| | A | G | I | R | Total |
|---|---|---|---|---|---|
| Users | **450** | **506** | **1.717** | **1.195** | **3.868** |
| Tweets_Statuses_Count | 12.343.807 | 15.648.860 | 65.593.286 | 45.198.150 | **138.784.103** |
| Tweets_Base | 674.211 | 738.755 | 2.570.646 | 1.751.624 | **5.735.236** |
| Followers | 292.413 | 423.549 | 1.497.093 | 1.799.686 | **4.012.741** |
| Friends | 168.893 | 225.371 | 825.969 | 640.529 | **1.860.762** |
| Favorites | 1.768.903 | 2.371.924 | 10.006.749 | 6.683.984 | **20.831.560** |

Figure 2 shows the temperament distribution of the users. It is noted that the idealist temperament is the predominant one, totaling 44% of the database.

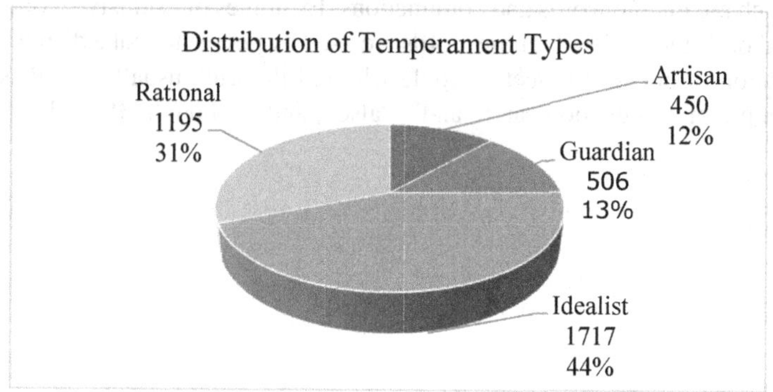


**Fig. 2.** Distribution of the users by temperament [4].

### 4.2 Pre-processing and Category Analysis

At this stage the texts are prepared for the application of the classification algorithms, which consists of the removal of special characters, blank spaces, numbers, symbols, URLs, tokenization, and stopwords removal [17, 18]. After that, a bag-of-words technique was applied to specify the importance of each attribute (token) by assigning a weight to each token based on its TF-IDF [4, 19].

Another way to structure documents is through the use of dictionaries, such as the Linguistic Inquiry and Word Count (LIWC), which allows the grouping of words into psychologically meaningful categories. The LIWC was created by Dr. James Pennebaker to examine relationships between language and personality [20, 21]. It is a textual analysis tool that structures documents into categories by assigning each word to the corresponding category [4, 8].

By using the Portuguese LIWC dictionary it was calculated the frequency of words by temperament. The messages were read by temperament and the counting was performed of words in the respective categories. The results found are presented in Table 3, which contains the average frequency of the words by temperament. The calculation of the average frequency of the words is given by the number of words in the category divided by the number of messages of the respective temperament.

The average frequencies of the words by category presented in Table 3 are very similar in most cases. This is because the same word may be present in more than one category, distorting the average frequency of words, returning values very close to each other. Thus, it is very difficult to say in which category a particular temperament has more prominence in writing. However, the categories presented in Table 3 can be grouped into the following three macro-categories: Language Dimensions; Other Grammar; and Psychological Processes.

To determine the relevance of the categories within the macro-categories the total number of words in each category was divided by the total number of words of the macro-category and the results were presented in Table 4. Then, within the category Psychological Processes it is possible to observe the prominence of the categories present, cogmech (cognitive processes), social, incl (inclusive), and relativ (relativity).

The most relevant category is cogmech, which corresponds to cognitive processes associated with components of reasoning. The processes are represented by two categories, which are unique words and conjunctions. Examples of exclusive words include: "but", "without" and "delete". These words are used by people to make distinc-tions in a given situation or between objects. People who tell the truth usually use these words. Some example of conjunctions are: "and", "also", and "although" [8, 22].

**Table 3.** Average frequency of the words in each LIWC category by temperament [4].

| Category | Artisan | Guardian | Idealist | Rational | Category | Artisan | Guardian | Idealist | Rational |
|---|---|---|---|---|---|---|---|---|---|
| **Funct** | 5,2641 | 5,3476 | 5,3397 | 5,4318 | **cogmech** | 4,0733 | 4,1533 | 4,1322 | 4,1950 |
| **Pronoun** | 1,8610 | 1,8672 | 1,9123 | 1,9354 | **insight** | 0,7209 | 0,7283 | 0,7402 | 0,7520 |
| **Ppron** | 1,2148 | 1,2236 | 1,2497 | 1,2637 | **cause** | 0,4820 | 0,4974 | 0,4925 | 0,5050 |
| **I** | 0,3874 | 0,3610 | 0,4185 | 0,4068 | **discrep** | 0,6802 | 0,6774 | 0,6907 | 0,6995 |
| **We** | 0,0361 | 0,0393 | 0,0363 | 0,0340 | **tentat** | 0,9828 | 0,9961 | 1,0050 | 1,0229 |
| **You** | 0,6654 | 0,6999 | 0,6646 | 0,6874 | **certain** | 0,3770 | 0,3945 | 0,3904 | 0,3930 |
| **Shehe** | 0,6436 | 0,6697 | 0,6474 | 0,6752 | **inhib** | 0,5352 | 0,5511 | 0,5386 | 0,5497 |
| **They** | 0,1234 | 0,1304 | 0,1263 | 0,1304 | **incl** | 1,3993 | 1,4232 | 1,4022 | 1,4143 |
| **Ipron** | 1,2253 | 1,2500 | 1,2437 | 1,2788 | **excl** | 0,7987 | 0,8009 | 0,8111 | 0,8311 |
| **Article** | 0,7698 | 0,8075 | 0,7837 | 0,8143 | **percept** | 0,7834 | 0,7899 | 0,7998 | 0,7966 |
| **Verb** | 1,8885 | 1,9006 | 1,9039 | 1,9359 | **see** | 0,2561 | 0,2591 | 0,2630 | 0,2609 |
| **Auxverb** | 0,6880 | 0,7072 | 0,6976 | 0,7217 | **hear** | 0,1803 | 0,1738 | 0,1854 | 0,1856 |
| **Past** | 0,4239 | 0,4271 | 0,4306 | 0,4336 | **feel** | 0,3069 | 0,3210 | 0,3121 | 0,3130 |
| **Presente** | 1,1402 | 1,1528 | 1,1444 | 1,1673 | **bio** | 0,7105 | 0,6924 | 0,7154 | 0,7243 |
| **Future** | 0,0828 | 0,0818 | 0,0841 | 0,0841 | **body** | 0,3162 | 0,3063 | 0,3156 | 0,3254 |
| **Adverb.** | 0,4854 | 0,5001 | 0,5019 | 0,5050 | **health** | 0,1277 | 0,1277 | 0,1278 | 0,1257 |
| **Preps** | 1,4831 | 1,5268 | 1,4636 | 1,4987 | **sexual** | 0,2114 | 0,1975 | 0,2138 | 0,2127 |
| **Conj** | 0,9127 | 0,9066 | 0,9230 | 0,9317 | **ingest** | 1,0826 | 1,1002 | 1,0586 | 1,0634 |
| **Negate** | 0,2489 | 0,2545 | 0,2530 | 0,2614 | **relativ** | 2,3242 | 2,3847 | 2,3072 | 2,3392 |
| **Quant** | 0,5927 | 0,6064 | 0,6155 | 0,6259 | **motion** | 0,7575 | 0,7632 | 0,7410 | 0,7578 |
| **Number** | 0,1385 | 0,1433 | 0,1475 | 0,1530 | **space** | 0,9843 | 1,0173 | 0,9749 | 0,9925 |
| **Swear** | 0,7151 | 0,7086 | 0,7245 | 0,7288 | **time** | 0,9860 | 1,0282 | 0,9607 | 0,9687 |
| **Social** | 2,1694 | 2,1791 | 2,2166 | 2,2422 | **work** | 0,2332 | 0,2510 | 0,2343 | 0,2417 |
| **Family** | 0,0412 | 0,0399 | 0,0414 | 0,0409 | **achieve** | 0,4628 | 0,4894 | 0,4647 | 0,4728 |
| **Friend** | 0,1065 | 0,1004 | 0,1009 | 0,0937 | **leisure** | 0,3137 | 0,3162 | 0,3094 | 0,3108 |
| **Humans** | 1,1086 | 1,1109 | 1,1570 | 1,1438 | **home** | 0,0605 | 0,0598 | 0,0565 | 0,0547 |
| **Affect** | 1,0763 | 1,0988 | 1,0931 | 1,0864 | **money** | 0,2899 | 0,2980 | 0,2901 | 0,3091 |
| **Posemo** | 0,6992 | 0,7222 | 0,7089 | 0,6907 | **relig** | 0,0812 | 0,0896 | 0,0855 | 0,0830 |
| **Negemo** | 0,3487 | 0,3438 | 0,3559 | 0,3654 | **death** | 0,0595 | 0,0610 | 0,0605 | 0,0618 |
| **Anx** | 0,0508 | 0,0525 | 0,0530 | 0,0540 | **assente** | 0,1250 | 0,1270 | 0,1258 | 0,1265 |
| **Anger** | 0,1352 | 0,1316 | 0,1377 | 0,1463 | **nonfl** | 0,2620 | 0,2762 | 0,2652 | 0,2695 |
| **Sad** | 0,1665 | 0,1655 | 0,1709 | 0,1723 | **Filler** | 0,0297 | 0,0273 | 0,0322 | 0,0323 |

It is observed that in this category people speak words that are denominated causal, such as "why", "effect", "consequently", and words that are denominated vision, such as "think", "know", and "consider". In the studies carried out with this category it was noticed that the causal words are more frequently used when someone has to justify a situation or to organize a thought.

In these categories relevant to the macro-category Psychological Processes is remarkable the highlight for the idealistic temperament. In the Dimensions of Language category, the emphasis was on funct (functional words), pronoum, ppron (personal pronouns), I (first person singular), and we (first person plural). The highest values presented are for idealist and rational temperaments in the funct category, which

**Table 4.** Frequency of words in each main category by temperament. PP: Psychological Processes; LD: Language Dimensions; AG: Another Grammar.

| Category | Artisan | Guardian | Idealist | Rational | Category | Artisan | Guardian | Idealist | Rational |
|---|---|---|---|---|---|---|---|---|---|
| **PP** | | | | | | | | | |
| **humans** | 0,44% | 0,48% | 1,75% | 1,18% | **time** | 0,39% | 0,45% | 1,45% | 1,00% |
| **past** | 0,17% | 0,19% | 0,65% | 0,45% | **work** | 0,09% | 0,11% | 0,35% | 0,25% |
| **present** | 0,45% | 0,50% | 1,73% | 1,20% | **achieve** | 0,18% | 0,21% | 0,70% | 0,49% |
| **future** | 0,03% | 0,04% | 0,13% | 0,09% | **leisure** | 0,12% | 0,14% | 0,47% | 0,32% |
| **affect** | 0,43% | 0,48% | 1,65% | 1,12% | **home** | 0,02% | 0,03% | 0,09% | 0,06% |
| **posemo** | 0,28% | 0,31% | 1,07% | 0,71% | **money** | 0,12% | 0,13% | 0,44% | 0,32% |
| **negemo** | 0,14% | 0,15% | 0,54% | 0,38% | **relig** | 0,03% | 0,04% | 0,13% | 0,09% |
| **anx** | 0,02% | 0,02% | 0,08% | 0,06% | **death** | 0,02% | 0,03% | 0,09% | 0,06% |
| **anger** | 0,05% | 0,06% | 0,21% | 0,15% | **assent** | 0,05% | 0,06% | 0,19% | 0,13% |
| **sad** | 0,07% | 0,07% | 0,26% | 0,18% | **nonfl** | 0,10% | 0,12% | 0,40% | 0,28% |
| **cogmech** | 1,62% | 1,81% | 6,26% | 4,33% | **filler** | 0,01% | 0,01% | 0,05% | 0,03% |
| **insight** | 0,29% | 0,32% | 1,12% | 0,78% | **Total** | 11,62% | 12,92% | 44,69% | 30,78% |
| **swear** | 0,28% | 0,31% | 1,10% | 0,75% | **Category** | **Artisan** | **Guardian** | **Idealist** | **Rational** |
| **social** | 0,86% | 0,95% | 3,36% | 2,31% | **LD** | | | | |
| **family** | 0,02% | 0,02% | 0,06% | 0,04% | **funct** | 4,02% | 4,48% | 15,55% | 10,78% |
| **friend** | 0,04% | 0,04% | 0,15% | 0,10% | **pronoun** | 1,42% | 1,56% | 5,57% | 3,84% |
| **cause** | 0,19% | 0,22% | 0,75% | 0,52% | **ppron** | 0,93% | 1,02% | 3,64% | 2,51% |
| **discrep** | 0,27% | 0,29% | 1,05% | 0,72% | **i** | 0,30% | 0,30% | 1,22% | 0,81% |
| **tentat** | 0,39% | 0,43% | 1,52% | 1,06% | **we** | 0,03% | 0,03% | 0,11% | 0,07% |
| **certain** | 0,15% | 0,17% | 0,59% | 0,41% | **you** | 0,51% | 0,59% | 1,94% | 1,36% |
| **inhib** | 0,21% | 0,24% | 0,82% | 0,57% | **shehe** | 0,49% | 0,56% | 1,89% | 1,34% |
| **incl** | 0,56% | 0,62% | 2,12% | 1,46% | **they** | 0,09% | 0,11% | 0,37% | 0,26% |
| **excl** | 0,32% | 0,35% | 1,23% | 0,86% | **ipron** | 0,94% | 1,05% | 3,62% | 2,54% |
| **percept** | 0,31% | 0,34% | 1,21% | 0,82% | **article** | 0,59% | 0,68% | 2,28% | 1,62% |
| **see** | 0,10% | 0,11% | 0,40% | 0,27% | **auxverb** | 0,53% | 0,59% | 2,03% | 1,43% |
| **hear** | 0,07% | 0,08% | 0,28% | 0,19% | **adverb** | 0,37% | 0,42% | 1,46% | 1,00% |
| **feel** | 0,12% | 0,14% | 0,47% | 0,32% | **conj** | 0,70% | 0,76% | 4,26% | 1,85% |
| **bio** | 0,28% | 0,30% | 1,08% | 0,75% | **negate** | 0,19% | 0,21% | 2,69% | 0,52% |
| **body** | 0,13% | 0,13% | 0,48% | 0,34% | **Total** | 11,10% | 12,36% | 46,62% | 29,92% |
| **health** | 0,05% | 0,06% | 0,19% | 0,13% | **Category** | **Artisan** | **Guardian** | **Idealist** | **Rational** |
| **sexual** | 0,08% | 0,09% | 0,32% | 0,22% | **AG** | | | | |
| **ingest** | 0,43% | 0,48% | 1,60% | 1,10% | **verb** | 8,30% | 9,16% | 31,92% | 22,11% |
| **relativ** | 0,92% | 1,04% | 3,49% | 2,41% | **quant** | 2,61% | 2,92% | 10,32% | 7,15% |
| **motion** | 0,30% | 0,33% | 1,12% | 0,78% | **number** | 0,61% | 0,69% | 2,47% | 1,75% |
| **space** | 0,39% | 0,44% | 1,48% | 1,02% | **Total** | 11,52% | 12,77% | 44,70% | 31,01% |

contains functional words composed of pronouns, prepositions, articles, conjunctions, auxiliary verbs, and some other categories, such as: "this", "him", "for", "no", "was", "and". These words reflect the way people communicate and are associated with the psychological and social world of people.

In Other Grammar the highlight occurs in the verb category with higher values for the idealist and rational temperaments. Verbs are used to identify a focus, an intention, display a priority and processing [8, 22].

With the values obtained in Tables 3 and 4, it is not possible to precise in which category a particular temperament has highlight. However, in Table 4 it is remarkable the relevance of a category within a macro-category, although it is not possible to state in what category a temperament appears more.

The next analysis to be presented refers to the context study of words by TF-IDF. The tweets of each temperament were read and then a tokenization was performed, followed by the removal of stopwords and morphological affixes of the words (stemming). After this pre-processing, the TF-IDF was applied. As a word selection criterion by temperament it were chosen 10 words that have higher frequency in tweets. Table 5 shows 10 words by temperament according to what is commonly written in each temperament.

**Table 5.** Relevant words by temperament using TF-IDF.

| TF-IDF (Artisan, Guardian, Idealist, Rational) | | | |
|---|---|---|---|
| Artisan | Guardian | Idealist | Rational |
| renovação | porqu | Brasil | Brasil |
| fenomen | impeach | leia | sempr |
| cachorro | antagonista | perplexo | medio |
| ilustrações | niterói | paí | casa |
| otima | governo | petista | film |
| bolsa | década | obrigado | vida |
| divulgar | agora | estadão | unicamp |
| taubaté | brasil | palestrar | galera |
| ipad | malvadeza | inovação | agora |
| petição | pt | pt | montevidéu |

The artisan temperament is impulsive and more daring, likes novelties, new experiences. They have the sensory function and prefer things that cause them pleasure [7]. Note that the relevant words of this temperament denote a writing referring to arts, technology and disclosure.

People of the guardian temperament are focused on goals, are proud of themselves because they are efficient in acting. They like to belong to a family or social group, are patriotic and philanthropic [7]. The words presented by the guardians are mainly related to politics and patriotism.

Idealists have natural talents, such as diplomats, who make use of interpersonal and linguistic intelligence. This temperament prefers the world of abstraction, believes in a better future, is geared toward activities that involve people and tend to be good leaders [7]. The most relevant words of the idealist temperament have a connection with politics, as in the guardian temperament.

The rational temperament does not present a very clear context, being able to be connected to education and media. This temperament often involves excellent military and business strategists, thinkers, inventors, and engineers.

Table 6 presents the 40 most relevant words found by the TF-IDF method with all the temperaments. It is possible to observe some words in common with Table 5 (highlighted), particularly referring to the artisan temperament.

**Table 6.** 40 most relevant words considering all temperaments.

| TF-IDF (Artisan, Guardian, Idealist, Rational) | | | |
|---|---|---|---|
| trade | bondosa | mercado | taubaté |
| cãozinho | batalhão | indulto | bombeiro |
| sedentário | pobr | ações | cachorro |
| arquiteta | appl | assin | sorteando |
| assinem | bovespa | drugstor | divulgar |
| arrancado | ajuda | renovaçao | ilustrações |
| fabricar | capit | salva | otima |
| exam | batom | carreira | fenomen |
| ambientai | severa | bolsa | petição |
| support | aguardarei | chapéu | ipad |

In another analysis of the context of words, the user messages were submitted to the LDA algorithm. A total of 3,868 files were read, each containing an average of 2,000 messages. The goal is to extract from the tweets the main words of each topic.

Therefore, it was decided to select ten words by temperament to perform the analysis. The analysis in topics contributes to the evaluation of a text, dividing it into topics and assigning a weight to each text of each topic. Thus, it is possible to know which subject is more frequent in the text, discover the category of a product and, in the case of temperament, what is being talked about in each profile.

Table 7 presents the most frequent words by temperament. The first insight in visualizing the words of the artisan temperament is that they may present a conversation writing in the future or a writing pertaining to rest. The guardian temperament has words like work, home and will, which can denote interest in work, pleasure in work or a context concerning home and love.

In the idealistic temperament it seems that the context is related to news, because there is the presence of the words world, someone, week, middle, night. The rational

**Table 7.** Words identified by the LDA algorithm.

| Tópico 1 | | | |
|---|---|---|---|
| Artisan | Guardian | Idealist | Rational |
| casa | casa | mundo | mundo |
| ficar | ano | ficar | ano |
| dar | amor | alguém | alguém |
| amanhã | sabe | noite | fica |
| quer | vem | semana | tanto |
| facebook | quer | quer | noite |
| dias | trabalho | nova | feliz |
| vontade | vontade | meio | gostei |
| falando | vezes | falando | quase |
| lindo | dizer | vontade | facebook |

temperament includes the words world, someone, night, happy and enjoyed, that can demonstrate a moment of happiness, a pleasant moment, a writing referring to a good situation.

It were defined 4 topics and 10 words for each topic in the LDA algorithm and Table 8 presents the words with the highest frequency in each topic.

**Table 8.** Relevant words by topic by LDA algorithm.

| LDA (Artisan, Guardian, Idealist, Rational) | | | |
|---|---|---|---|
| Tópic 0 | Tópic 1 | Tópic 2 | Tópic 3 |
| gostei | facebook | amanha | casa |
| tens | publiquei | indo | deus |
| official | noite | segue | amor |
| têm | amor | noite | tanto |
| portugal | quer | sabado | falando |
| estás | menos | ate | feliz |
| demasiado | pouco | sonhar | fico |
| bocado | verdade | facul | noite |
| telemóvel | dar | música | semana |
| teste | dizer | pc | amiga |

The goal of generating the topics in the LDA is to identify which subject is being addressed in the messages. A possible interpretation of the messages in Topic 0 would be as referring to Portugal, since the word mobile phone refers to cellular and this form of writing and speaking occurs in Portugal, but not in Brazil. Topic 1 may denote the publication of a message due to the occurrence of the words Facebook, published, night and say. The words in Topic 2 may be referring to study, because of the presence of the word facul and pc. Topic 3 presents the words house, love, happy and friendly, which can be interpreted as a context of friendship or a writing of great affection.

## 4.3 Classification

In this experiment, the whole dataset was processed. The processing was performed in the Intel 64 architecture, which improves performance by allowing systems to address more than 4 GB of both virtual and physical memory [23]. The experiments used a workstation composed of one Intel® Core™ i5-3210 M @ 3.10 GHz, 3 MB smart cache, quad-core on hyper-threading, 6 GB RAM memory, 904 GB HD @ 5400 RPM, Windows 8.1 operation system.

To perform the temperament classification, the following classifiers available in the Scikit-learn [24] were used: KNN; SVM; and Random Forest [1, 3]. Each temperament was divided into a binary problem, as proposed by Lima and de Castro [3]. To estimate the generalization performance, a cross-validation with 6 folders was used, and the *accuracy*, *precision*, *recall*, and *F-measure* were calculated. For the KNN classifier, which uses the object classification according to the K-nearest neighbors, K = 1 and K = 3 and the cosine similarity was used for determining the neighbors. The tests were separated into LIWC word dictionary [8] and TF-IDF [19].

Table 9 shows the results achieved by the TECLA for a validation with 6 folders executed 10 times. The values in bold are the best average accuracy and F-measure results obtained by the classifiers for each temperament.

**Table 9.** Accuracy (Acc), Precision (Pre), Recall (Rec) and F-measure (M-F) for the four temperaments using 6 folders and 10 iterations.

| | LIWC | 1NN | 3NN | Random Forest | SVM |
|---|---|---|---|---|---|
| Artisan | Acc | 80.44% ± 0.71% | 87.62% ± 0.37% | 87.95% ± 0.16% | **88.37% ± 0.00%** |
| | Pre | 88.79% ± 0.14% | 88.47% ± 0.07% | 88.41% ± 0.06% | 88.37% ± 0.00% |
| | Rec | 89.10% ± 0.87% | 98.86% ± 0.44% | 99.39% ± 0.15% | 100.00% ± 0.00% |
| | M-F | 88.91% ± 0.47% | 93.37% ± 0.23% | 93.58% ± 0.09% | **93.82% ± 0.00%** |
| Guardian | Acc | 78.36% ± 0.62% | 85.74% ± 0.10% | 86.32% ± 0.11% | **86.92% ± 0.01%** |
| | Pre | 87.05% ± 0.07% | 86.94% ± 0.04% | 87.03% ± 0.06% | 86.92% ± 0.00% |
| | Rec | 88.22% ± 0.76% | 98.36% ± 0.09% | 99.02% ± 0.11% | 100.00% ± 0.01% |
| | M-F | 87.61% ± 0.43% | 92.30% ± 0.06% | 92.63% ± 0.06% | **93.00% ± 0.01%** |
| Idealist | Acc | 54.97% ± 0.46% | 52.57% ± 0.61% | 54.27% ± 0.40% | **55.61% ± 0.01%** |
| | Pre | 56.80% ± 0.27% | 57.88% ± 0.57% | 56.67% ± 0.26% | 55.61% ± 0.01% |
| | Rec | 79.44% ± 0.80% | 54.18% ± 0.97% | 75.65% ± 1.04% | 100.00% ± 0.00% |
| | M-F | 66.19% ± 0.33% | 55.86% ± 0.67% | 64.76% ± 0.49% | **71.46% ± 0.02%** |
| Rational | Acc | 59.12% ± 0.58% | **87.62% ± 0.37%** | 66.62% ± 0.26% | 69.09% ± 0.03% |
| | Pre | 69.72% ± 0.21% | 88.47% ± 0.07% | 69.74% ± 0.14% | 69.10% ± 0.01% |
| | Rec | 72.17% ± 1.20% | 98.86% ± 0.44% | 91.38% ± 0.40% | 99.97% ± 0.04% |
| | M-F | 70.85% ± 0.65% | 74.78% ± 0.27% | 79.09% ± 0.19% | **81.71% ± 0.03%** |

For the artisan temperament, the KNN algorithm with K = 1 obtained an average accuracy of 80.44% and an F-measure of 88.91%. With a better performance, that is, a greater number of correctly labeled objects, it was the SVM algorithm with an average accuracy of 88.37%, followed by the Random Forest with an average accuracy of 87.95%. The SVM presented a higher average accuracy and a 100% recall, whilst the Random Forest presented a better precision than SVM.

In relation to the guardian temperament, the most assertive prediction was by the SVM algorithm, with an average accuracy of 86.92% and F-measure of 93%, followed by the Random Forest with an average accuracy of 86.32%. The lowest average accuracy (78.36%) was for the KNN with K = 1. The SVM also performed better for the idealist and rational temperaments. In general, the SVM obtained better accuracy for all temperaments, but for the artisan and guardian temperaments the Random Forests presented very close average accuracies to the SVM. For the classification of temperaments using TF-IDF tests were also performed using a cross-validation with 6 folders, and the accuracy, precision, recall and F-measures were calculated. Table 10 presents the results achieved for a validation with 6 folders executed 10 times. The best performance was obtained by the SVM algorithm with average accuracy of 88.28% ± 0.01% for the artisan temperament. The guardian temperament obtained for the Random Forest an average accuracy of 86.63% ± 0.05%, very close to the SVM performance, which was 86.62% ± 0.03%. SVM was superior for the idealist and rational temperaments with a small margin in relation to the random forest algorithm.

**Table 10.** Accuracy (Acc), Precision (Pre), Recall (Rec) e measure-F (M-F) for temperaments using 6 folders and 10 iterations.

| 6-Folders | TFIDF | 1NN | 3NN | RandomForest | SVM |
|---|---|---|---|---|---|
| Artisan | Acc | 76.79% ± 0.37% | 85.58% ± 0.25% | 88.15% ± 0.07% | **88.28% ± 0.01%** |
| | Prec | 88.80% ± 0.11% | 86.64% ± 0.05% | 88.27% ± 0.01% | 88.28% ± 0.00% |
| | Rev | 84.37% ± 0.42% | 98.57% ± 0.29% | 99.84% ± 0.07% | 100.0% ± 0.01% |
| | M-F | 86.49% ± 0.23% | 92.21% ± 0.14% | 93.69% ± 0.03% | 93.77% ± 0.01% |
| Guardian | Acc | 81.87% ± 0.21% | 85.58% ± 0.25% | **86.63% ± 0.05%** | **86.62% ± 0.03%** |
| | Prec | 86.67% ± 0.06% | 86.64% ± 0.05% | 86.69% ± 0.02% | 86.67% ± 0.00% |
| | Rev | 93.46% ± 0.27% | 98.57% ± 0.29% | 99.92% ± 0.05% | 99.93% ± 0.04% |
| | M-F | 89.93% ± 0.13% | 92.21% ± 0.14% | **92.83% ± 0.03%** | **92.83% ± 0.02%** |
| Idealist | Acc | 50.86% ± 0.39% | 50.22% ± 0.39% | 52.66% ± 0.71% | **52.92% ± 0.42%** |
| | Prec | 55.77% ± 0.34% | 55.27% ± 0.31% | 55.44% ± 0.47% | 56.14% ± 0.30% |
| | Rev | 56.57% ± 0.40% | 55.66% ± 0.60% | 76.29% ± 0.85% | 70.54% ± 0.55% |
| | M-F | 56.06% ± 0.32% | 55.30% ± 0.44% | 64.17% ± 0.57% | 62.47% ± 0.37% |
| Rational | Acc | 56.53% ± 0.55% | 61.88% ± 0.46% | 67.27% ± 0.34% | **68.23% ± 0.21%** |
| | Prec | 69.59% ± 0.40% | 69.81% ± 0.29% | 69.28% ± 0.16% | 69.50% ± 0.10% |
| | Rev | 66.42% ± 0.60% | 79.45% ± 0.44% | 94.98% ± 0.38% | 96.66% ± 0.24% |
| | M-F | 67.85% ± 0.45% | 74.29% ± 0.33% | 80.10% ± 0.22% | **80.84% ± 0.13%** |

## 5 Conclusion and Future Work

Temperament influences the way we perceive and react to the world. Understanding temperament is of crucial importance to our lives and to position ourselves properly in the market. Normally, one's temperament can be known by filling in tests, such as the MBTI (Myers-Briggs Type Indicator). The hypothesis of this research is that it is possible to identify the temperament of a person in a passive way, only by using data obtained from the social media of the person. For this, a database of tweets containing the MBTI result of Twitter users was employed. These data were used to generate predictive models of temperament.

The documents (Tweets) were structured with the Portuguese dictionary LIWC that groups words into categories. The calculation of the frequency of words was carried out to show which category is most talked about by artisan, guardian, idealist and rational temperaments. In this analysis it is possible to identify the writing style of the user associated with the subject that is most identified, perception among others.

The tweets were structured using LIWC and TF-IDF. When the TF-IDF was applied to the context analysis of the words the objective was to identify the writing of each temperament and what they have in common. It was observed that all temperaments cite proper names.

For classification the tweets were structured with LIWC and TF-IDF. Via LIWC, the best accuracy results were obtained for the artisan and guardian temperaments trained with SVM, followed by the Random Forest algorithm, which presented average accuracy close to the SVM accuracy. For the binary classification the highest average values were for the temperaments artisan and guardian, also for the SVM algorithm. The lowest average accuracy was presented for the idealist temperament.

As a future work, we intend to carry out a case study using the TECLA framework with a database composed of a set of volunteer users who will answer the MBTI test form and share their social profiles so that we can use their data to train the TECLA framework and classify their temperament. Another improvement to be made is the study of the content of the documents to investigate why the classifiers have low accuracy and how much the unbalanced classes interferes with this result.

**Acknowledgements.** The authors thank CAPES, CNPq, Fapesp, and MackPesquisa for the financial support. The authors also acknowledge the support of Intel for the Natural Computing and Machine Learning Laboratory as an Intel Center of Excellence in Artificial Intelligence.

## References

1. Nor Rahayu, N., Zainol, Z., Yoong, T.L.C.: A comparative study of different classifiers for automatic personality prediction. In: 2016 6th IEEE International Conference on Control System, Computing and Engineering (ICCSCE), pp. 435–440. IEEE (2016)
2. Plank, B., Dirk, H.: Personality traits on Twitter-or-How to Get 1, 500 personality tests in a week. In: Proceedings of the 6th Workshop on Computational Approaches to Subjectivity, Sentiment and Social Media Analysis (WASSA 2015), pp. 92–98 (2015)

3. Lima, A.C.E.S, de Castro, L.N.: Predicting temperament from Twitter data. In: 2016 5th IIAI International Congress on Advanced Applied Informatics (IIAI-AAI). IEEE (2016)
4. Claro, C.F., Lima, A.C.E.S., de Castro, L.N.: Predicting temperament using Keirsey's model for Portuguese Twitter data. In Proceedings of the 10th International Conference on Agents and Artificial Intelligence, pp. 250–256 (2018)
5. Gundecha, P., Liu, H.: Mining social media: a brief introduction. In: New Directions in Informatics, Optimization, Logistics, and Production. Informs, pp. 1–17 (2012)
6. Tang, J., Chang, Y., Liu, H.: Mining social media with social theories: a survey. ACM SIGKDD Explor. Newsl. **15**(2), 20–29 (2014)
7. Calegari, M.d.L., Gemignani, O.H.: Temperamento e Carreira. Summus Editorial, São Paulo (2006)
8. Pennebaker, J.W., Boyd, R.L., Jordan, K., Blackburn, K.: The Development and Psychometric Properties of LIWC2015 (2015)
9. Hall, C.S., Lindzey, G., Campbell, J.B.: Teorias da Personalidade. Artmed, Porto Alegre (2000)
10. Ito, P.d.C.P., Guzzo, R.S.L.: Diferenças individuais: temperamento e personalidade; importância da teoria. In: Estudos de Psicologia, pp. 91–100 (2002)
11. Keirsey, D.: Please Undestand Me II: Temperament, Character, Intelligence. Prometheus Nemesis Book Company (1998)
12. Keirsey, D.M.: Keirsey.com, Corporate Offices (1996). http://www.keirsey.com/4temps/overview_temperaments.asp. Accessed 12 Oct 2017
13. Lima, A.C.E.S.: Mineração de Mídias Sociais como Ferramenta para a Análise da Tríade da Persona Virtual. São Paulo (2016)
14. Verhoeven, B., Daelemans, W., Plank, B.: Twisty: a multilingual twitter stylometry corpus for gender and personality profiling. In: Proceedings of the 10th International Conference on Language Resources and Evaluation (2016)
15. Xavier, O.C., Carvalho, C.L.D.: Desenvolvimento de Aplicações Sociais A Partir de APIs em Redes Sociais Online. UFG, Goiânia (2011)
16. Kwak, H., Lee, C., Park, H., Moon, S.: What is Twitter, a social network or a news media? In: Proceedings of the 19th International Conference on World Wide Web, pp. 591–600. ACM (2010)
17. Haddi, E., Liu, X., Shi, Y.: The role of text pre-processing in sentiment analysis. Procedia Comput. Sci. **17**, 26–32 (2013)
18. Spencer, J., Uchyigit, G.: Sentimentor: sentiment analysis of Twitter data. In: Proceedings of European Conference on Machine Learning and Principles and Practice of Knowledge Discovery in Databases (2012)
19. Feldman, R., Sanger, J.: The Text Mining Handbook: Advanced approaches in Analyzing Unstructured Data. Cambridge University Press, New York (2007)
20. Komisin, M.C., Guinn, C.I.: Identifying personality types using document classification methods. In: FLAIRS Conference (2012)
21. Pennebaker, W., King, L.A.: Linguistic styles: language use as an individual difference. J. Pers. Soc. Psychol. **77**(6), 1296 (1999)
22. Tausczik, Y.R., Pennebaker, J.W.: The psychological meaning of words: LIWC and computerized text analysis methods. J. Lang. Soc. Psychol. **29**(1), 24–54 (2010)
23. I. Corporation, Intel, Intel Corporation. https://www.intel.com.br/content/www/br/pt/architecture-and-technology/microarchitecture/intel-64-architecture-general.html. Accessed 15 Apr 2018
24. Pedregosa, F., et al.: Scikit-learn: machine learning in Python. J. Mach. Learn. Res. **12**, 2825–2830 (2011)

# A Constraint Solving Web Service for a Handwritten Japanese Historical Kana Reprint Support System

Kazuki Sando, Tetsuya Suzuki(✉), and Akira Aiba

Shibaura Institute of Technology, Saitama, Japan
{mf17032,tetsuya,aiba}@shibaura-it.ac.jp

**Abstract.** Reading Japanese historical manuscripts is one of the first steps for researching Japanese classical literature. It is, however, difficult and time-consuming even for Japanese people to read such manuscripts since they are handwritten in cursive style and may contain different characters from those currently used. We formulated the human process for reading Japanese historical manuscripts as a constraint satisfaction problem, and proposed a framework to assist the process. In this paper, we present a constraint solving Web service as a part of a system based on the framework. To realize the Web service, we added a Web service layer to our constraint solver previously implemented in Ruby as a UNIX command. Thanks to the loose coupling realized by the Web service, any programming language can be used for implementation of other parts of the whole system. We experimentally confirmed the solver as a Web service is faster than that as a UNIX command if both the solver and a client are connected to a same local area network. We finally summarized technical issues concerning the system based on the framework.

**Keywords:** Natural language processing · Morphological analysis
Constraint solving · Web service · Reprint · Historical document

## 1 Introduction

In Japan, before printing technology had spread in the 17th century, all of the documents were handwritten. Because they were transcribed by hand, the contents of the documents were sometimes altered intentionally, or by the error. As a result, there are multiple versions of the same text at present. For example, Kokin Waka Shu which is the first anthology edited in 905 A.D. by the instruction of the Emperor has more than 10 different versions.

The first step of Japanese classical literature study is comparing those different texts to create a standard text. One has to read them to compare various handwritten texts, but it is time consuming and requires training for several reasons. First, they have different shapes of characters among texts because they are handwritten. Second, characters used in them are different from those currently


J. van den Herik and A. P. Rocha (Eds.): ICAART 2018, LNAI 11352, pp. 422–442, 2019.
https://doi.org/10.1007/978-3-030-05453-3_20

used. This is the reason why current automatic character recognition systems cannot be used to read those historical texts.

To assist the human process for reading Japanese historical manuscripts, we proposed a framework which consists of an image recognizer and a constraint solver [1]. The image recognizer analyzes a given document image and outputs a constraint satisfaction problem (CSP) which specifies allowable combinations of character segmentation results, reading order among the segmented characters and character recognition results. Then the constraint solver solves the CSP. Thanks to constraint solving, we can find maximally better solutions from all combinations of them. We experimentally implemented a backtrack-based constraint solver for reading Japanese historical manuscripts using one kind of Japanese characters called hiragana. The solver is a part of the whole system based on the framework. Because of the insufficient pruning in search, the backtrack-based constraint solver can not suppress combinatorial explosion. We then proposed a minimum-cost-based constraint solver as a successor of the backtrack-based solver [2], which successfully suppresses combinatorial explosion by the $A^*$ algorithm.

In this paper, we present a constraint solving Web service. We added a Web service layer to the minimum-cost-based constraint solver because the constraint solver was implemented in Ruby as a UNIX command and there was a demand for loose coupling between the constraint solver and the other subsystems in the framework. Thanks to the loose coupling, suitable programming languages can be used to implement other parts of the whole system. In addition, the constraint solving Web service can be available to other researchers concerning reprinting of Japanese historical text through the Internet.

The organization of this paper is as follows. We introduce hiragana in Sect. 2, and summarize existing researches in Sect. 3. We define the constraint satisfaction problem for reading Japanese historical manuscripts in Sect. 4, and briefly explain the constraint solving process of the minimum-cost-based constraint solver in Sect. 5. In Sect. 6, we present a constraint solving Web service. We summarize experimental results in Sect. 7. Section 8 states concluding remarks. In this paper, we use the word "kana" as well as "hiragana" for the sake of convenience though hiragana is a part of kana in general.

This paper is an extended version of our paper presented at the 10th International Conference on Agents and Artificial Intelligence [3]. We especially enriched Sects. 4 and 8.

## 2 Reading Historical Japanese Characters

### 2.1 Hiragana Used in Japanese Classic Texts

A set of Chinese characters called kanji was brought to Japan from China in the 4th or 5th century, and eventually in the 8th century, ways of writing Japanese texts using kanji were thought out. This is called Man'yo-gana. There were a couple of ways to write Japanese texts in Man'yo-gana, for example, abandoning the meaning of kanji and expressing Japanese phonology using its pronunciation. In fact, more than 900 Chinese characters were used to write Japanese.

From the 8th century to the 9th century, a new method of writing Japanese was invented. It was a way to use hiragana made by further breaking the cursive form of Chinese characters, and it was mainly used by court women in the 9th century to write Japanese short poem called Waka. Waka is also essential for companionship of men and women, so men who wrote official documents in Chinese writing also needed to write hiragana [4].

**Fig. 1.** A fragment of a classic Japanese text which reads (mu)-(ka)-(si)-(o)-(to)-(ko) (adopted from [5]).

### 2.2 Reading Hiragana in Classic Texts

Hiragana used in Japanese classic documents, we will call "historical hiragana" hereafter, had a big difference from what is used today as listed below:

1. Historical hiragana contains many hiragana which are not used today, and there were several hiragana to represent one syllable.
2. A special symbol called odori-ji was used to represent the same syllable as just above.
3. In some cases, a method called Ren-men that connects multiple hiragana characters was used.
4. In particular, in the case of handwritten documents, even though they were the same letters, their shapes greatly differed depending on the authors.

Because of these characteristics, reading Japanese classic texts is difficult even for Japanese people. In fact, hiragana which is not currently used has not been taught in elementary schools in Japan since the decision of the Japanese government in 1900.

Figure 1 shows a part of "Tales of Ise" [5], which is a famous Japanese classic literature, copied in 1547 A.D. All these six characters are hiragana, the first, third, fifth and sixth letters are still in use. They are (mu), (si), (to), and (ko). However, the second and fourth letters are not currently used.

For example, the second character might be (tu), (ka), or (he). So, how does the trained person read the hiragana which is difficult to distinguish like this? By focusing at the second hiragana, the first three hiraganas are (mu)-(?)-(si). A Japanese word (mu)-(ka)-(si) exist, but (mu)-(tu)-(si) and (mu)-(he)-(si) do not exist as Japanese words. Therefore, these three characters are determined as (mu)-(ka)-(si), that is "the past" in Japanese. Likewise, a trained person can read the fourth hiragana as (o), and these three hiragana here are (o)-(to)-(ko), that is "a man" in Japanese. By observing this small example, it is clear that knowledge on the shape of hiragana is not sufficient and knowledge on classic Japanese words is necessary, to read Japanese classic texts.

## 3 Related Work

We introduce existing researches regarding recognition of Japanese historical kana including our former work.

Yamamoto and Osawa proposed an optical character recognition (OCR) method for kana and kanji characters in cursive style [6]. Manually segmented characters are recognized by a word spotting technique [7]. Word spotting is an indexing technique, which was initially proposed in [8] according to [9]. In this method, readings are assigned to prepared character images in advance, and distances between the segmented character images and prepared character images are measured by the word spotting method [7] based on continuous dynamic programming [10] to find prepared characters similar to the segmented ones. According to the result of their experiment, the accuracy of pattern recognition is more than 80%.

Hayasaka et al. applied a convolutional neural network (CNN) to recognition of Japanese historical kana [11]. The accuracy of pattern recognition is more than 91% in their experiment. They also confirmed that it takes about 0.4 s for recognition of a character on a computer without a graphical processing unit. They demonstrate their method as a Web application on a website [12], which accepts a Japanese historical kana image and returns recognition results using the CNN.

Yamada et al. combined OCR and character $n$-gram for reprinting characters in debt deeds in Edo-era (1603 A.D. – 1867 A.D.) [13]. Because the debt deeds are official documents, they are written in a style of handwriting, take fixed format and have many fixed form representations. Given unreadable characters, OCR outputs the results. These results are associated with prepared $n$-gram information to output candidates of recognition. Even though $n$-gram is used, $n$ is at most 3.

Though characters are recognized one-by-one or at most three characters are recognized at once in the existing researches described above, we think that using information on a sequence of characters is useful for getting a generality of recognition.

We proposed a framework for assisting the human process for reading Japanese historical manuscripts by employing constraint solving [1]. The overall structure of the framework is shown in Fig. 2. There are two major subsystems in the framework, which are an image recognizer and a constraint solver. The image recognizer segments an input document image into characters, enumerates hiragana candidates for the segmented characters, and determines reading order among the segmented characters to construct a CSP called a Reprint-CSP. Thanks to constraints, the overall sequence of characters is at least constrained to form a sequence of words in a dictionary for historical Japanese. Then the constraint solver solves the CSP by assigning possible reading using a word dictionary. The solutions of the CSP are returned to the image recognizer to revise recognition. This feed-back is repeated if necessary. The system finally outputs the assigned reading.

Technical issues of the proposal are the method of document layout analysis including text line segmentation [14] and character segmentation [15], the character recognition method, the modeling method of reprinting as a Reprint-CSP, and the efficient constraint solving method.

We focused on the constraint solving issue and experimentally implemented a backtrack-based constraint solver for Reprint-CSPs [1]. It targets to Japanese historical manuscripts using hiragana, and finds maximally better solutions according to a solution comparator. It fails to suppress combinatorial explosion because of an insufficient branch-and-bound pruning in search.

We then implemented a minimum-cost-based solver as a successor of the backtrack-based solver [2]. Given a Reprint-CSP, a word dictionary and an positive integer $n$, it finds $n$-best solutions according to solution cost, which are based on both occurrence cost for words and connection cost between adjacent words, and extracts maximally better solutions according to the solution comparator from the $n$-best solutions. The solver avoids combinatorial explosion using the $A^*$ algorithm when it finds $n$-best solutions.

Both the backtrack-based solver and the minimum-cost-based solver are implemented in Ruby as UNIX commands.

## 4 Reprint Constraint Satisfaction Problem

### 4.1 Overview

A CSP for reading historical kana text, which we call a Reprint-CSP, consists of finite number of variables, their domains, a dictionary, a directed acyclic graph (DAG) which represents reading order, and constraints.

Each variable corresponds to a two-dimensional region on a historical document image which contains one character. Because of complex shapes of historical kana characters, the image recognizer may not be able to uniquely determine if a two-dimensional region includes just one character or more characters. In such

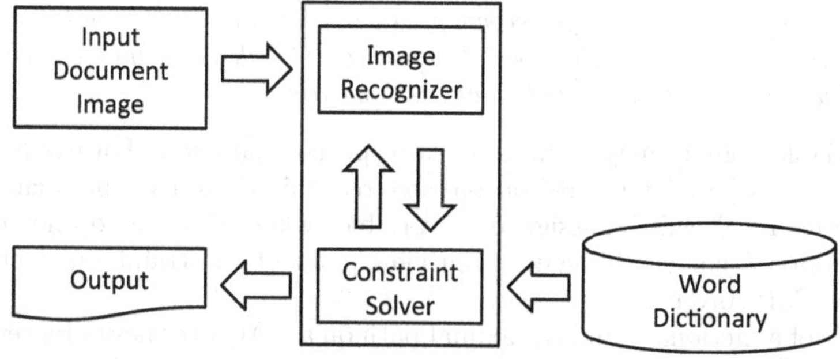


**Fig. 2.** System configuration (amended from Fig. 2 in [3]).

a case, the image recognizer enumerates possible cases. As a result, the two-dimensional region of a variable may overlap the regions of different variables.

The domain of each variable is a finite set of currently used characters for the two-dimensional region. Because it is difficult to determine a unique character for a segmented character in a historical document image as described in the Sect. 2.2, the image recognizer adds possible character recognition results for the segmented character to the variable's domain.

A constraint is a relation over the domains. Constraints are labeled with priority levels to deal with over-constrained problems. If there do not exist any solutions which satisfy all given constraints, we abandon constraints with weak priority levels. In a Reprint-CSP, a constraint that a sequence of characters forms a sequence of words in a dictionary is given by a pair of a DAG over nodes representing variables and a dictionary of words. The DAG determines reading order of variables and the dictionary constrains local character sequences. A maximal path over the DAG determines a solution of a Reprint-CSP. Other constraints are, for example, used to declare constraints of odori-ji. Satisfaction level of constrains is boolean: satisfied or not satisfied.

Solutions are compared according to their costs and the priority levels of constraints.

### 4.2 Definition of Reprint-CSP

A constraint relevant to the variables $x_1, \ldots, x_n$, which is described as $C_{x_1,\ldots,x_n}$, is defined as follows.

**Definition 1.** *For variables and their domains $x_1 \in D_1 \ldots, x_n \in D_n$, a constraint relevant to the variables $x_1, \ldots, x_n$ is a subset of the product of their domains $D_1 \times \cdots \times D_n$.*

The following alphabet $\Sigma$ is the universal set of variable domains.

**Definition 2.** *The alphabet $\Sigma$ is a union of a set of all current hiraganas and a set of two special characters "?" and "!". The special character "?" denotes that* *a region on a document image recognized as one character does not correspond to any current hiragana. The special character "!" denotes that a recognition result of a region on a document image is incorrect.*

Each variable domain may include the two special characters. For example, the character "?" is used for a region on text recognized as a Chinese character. The character "!" will be assigned to variables whose domains do not include any appropriate current hiragana from view point of constraint satisfaction by a Reprint-CSP solver.

A pair of a dictionary and a maximal path on a DAG over nodes representing variables determines a constraint such that a sequence of characters assigned to variables on the maximal path forms a sequence of words in the dictionary.

**Definition 3.** *A dictionary is a finite subset of strings over the alphabet $\Sigma$, that is, a finite subset of $\bigcup_{i=1}^{\infty} \Sigma^i$.*

To deal with over-constrained situations, we use constraint hierarchies [16].

**Definition 4.** *A strength of a constraint is a priority level of the constraint. The priority levels are integers 0 ... m. The smaller a priority level is, the priorer constraints with the level are. Constraints labeled with priority level 0 are required constraints which have to be satisfied. Constraints labeled with priority level 1 ... m are preferred constraints which only have to be satisfied as well as possible.*

**Definition 5.** *A set of constraints with strengths forms a constraint hierarchy $H = (H_0, H_1, \ldots, H_m)$ where $H_i$ is a set of constraints labeled with priority level $i$.*

We define CSPs for reading historical kana text, which we call Reprint-CSPs, as follows.

**Definition 6.** *A Reprint-CSP consists of the following five components.*

- *a finite set of variables $V = \{x_1, \ldots, x_n\}$*
- *finite domains $D_1, \ldots, D_n$ where $x_1 \in D_1, \ldots, x_n \in D_n$*
- *a dictionary $R$ which is a finite set of words*
- *a directed acyclic graph $G = (V, E)$ where $E \subset V \times V$*
- *explicitly-given constraints relevant to a subset of $V$*

*For each maximal path over $G$, a constraint is implicitly given. Let $p$ be a $k$-length maximal path $(x_{j_1}, \ldots, x_{j_k})$ over $G$. Then the implicitly-given constraint relevant to $k$-variables $x_{j_1}, \ldots, x_{j_k}$ is defined as follows.*

$$C_{x_{j_1},\ldots,x_{j_k}} = \{(s_1, \ldots, s_k) \in D_{j_1} \times \cdots \times D_{j_k} | s_1 \ldots s_k \in R^+\} \quad (1)$$

*where $R^+ = \bigcup_{i=1}^{\infty} R^i$.*

*All implicitly-given constraints are required constraints while all explicitly-given constraints are preferred constraints.*

We use equality constraints and non-equality constraints as explicitly-given constraints. The equality constraints of the form $x_i = x_j$ are used to declare constraints of odori-ji or constraints among characters with similar shapes. The non-equality constraints of the form $x_i \neq x_j$ are used to declare that each variable does not take the special character "!" as its value.

In the following, we define solutions of Reprint-CSPs. If there exist two variables whose regions on text overlap each other, we need not read both of them at the same time. In other words, if we have a solution which assigns a value to one of such variables, we need not any value to another. For this reason, we introduce a special value $\perp$ to denote that we do not read a variable with the special value, and regard constraints relevant to a variable with the special value as satisfied constraints.

**Definition 7.** *A solution of a Reprint-CSP with a set of variables* $V = \{x_1, \ldots, x_n\}$ *is an n-tuple* $(d_1, \ldots, d_n) \in (D_1 \cup \{\perp\}) \times \ldots \times (D_n \cup \{\perp\})$ *which denotes a map* $\{x_1 \to d_1, \ldots, x_n \to d_n\}$. *For a variable* $x$ *of a Reprint-CSP and a solution* $\theta$ *relevant to* $x$, $x\theta$ *denotes the value which the solution* $\theta$ *assigns to* $x$. *A valuation* $x_i \to \perp$ *denotes the segmented character corresponding to the variable* $x_i$ *is not read. If a solution assigns a value except* $\perp$ *to a variable* $x$, *we say that the solution is relevant to the variable* $x$.

*For a solution* $\theta$ *and a constraint* $C_{x_{j_1},\ldots,x_{j_k}}$, $C_{x_{j_1},\ldots,x_{j_k}}\ \theta$ *denotes the boolean result of applying the solution to the constraint such that:*

- $(x_{j_1}\theta, \ldots, x_{j_k}\theta) \in C_{x_{j_1},\ldots,x_{j_k}}$ *if the solution* $\theta$ *is relevant to all of the variables* $x_{j_1}, \ldots, x_{j_k}$
- *true otherwise*

*A solution* $\theta$ *satisfies a constraint* $C_{x_{j_1},\ldots,x_{j_k}}$ *if* $C_{x_{j_1},\ldots,x_{j_k}}\ \theta$ *is true.*

Though a solution which assigns $\perp$ to all variables satisfies any constraint according to the definition above, it is not what we expect. We want to extract better solutions from admissible solutions defined below.

**Definition 8.** *Let* $G$ *be the directed acyclic graph of a Reprint-CSP, which can be divided into disjoint subgraphs* $G_1, \ldots, G_m$ *where a union of* $G_1, \ldots, G_m$ *is equal to* $G$ *and the undirected graph of* $G_i$ *is connected for* $1 \leq i \leq m$. *A promising path of the Reprint-CSP is a path over* $G$ *of the form* $(p_1, \ldots, p_m)$ *where* $p_i$ *is a maximal path over* $G_i$ *for* $1 \leq i \leq m$.

**Definition 9.** *A promising solution of a Reprint-CSP is a solution of the CSP which is relevant only to all variables in a promising path of the CSP.*

**Definition 10.** *A admissible solution of a Reprint-CSP is a promising solution of the CSP which satisfies all required constraints of the CSP.*

Better admissible solutions can be selected from two different viewpoints: solution cost and priority levels of constraints.

An admissible solution $\theta$ is better than an admissible solution $\sigma$ from a viewpoint of cost if the cost of $\theta$ is smaller than that of $\sigma$. For example, the minimum-cost-based solver described in Sect. 5 uses the following cost function.

$$cost(\theta, p) = \min_{\substack{w_1,\ldots,w_m \in R \\ w_1\ldots w_m = x_{i_1}\theta\ldots x_{i_k}\theta}} \sum_{i=1}^{m} f_w(w_i) + \sum_{i=1}^{m-1} f_c(w_i, w_{i+1}) + \sum_{j=1}^{k} f_r(x_{i_j}, x_{i_j}\theta) \quad (2)$$

- $\theta$ is a solution of a Reprint-CSP
- $p$ is a maximal path $(x_{i_1}, \ldots\ x_{i_k})$ over the DAG of the Reprint-CSP.
- A function $f_w$ assigns an occurrence cost to a word: $R \to \mathcal{R}$.
- A function $f_c$ assigns a connection cost to two words: $R \times R \to \mathcal{R}$.
- A function $f_r$ assigns a rank of a character in the recognition result of a segmented character corresponding to a variable to the character: $\Sigma \to \mathcal{N}$

The better admissible solutions, which satisfy preferred constraints as well as possible, can be selected using solution comparators which determine partial orders over admissible solutions. Some solution comparators are introduced in [16]. The minimum-cost-based solver described in Sect. 5 uses one of the comparators called locally-predicate-better defined below.

**Definition 11.** *For two admissible solutions $\theta$, $\sigma$ and a constraint hierarchy $H = (H_0, H_1, \ldots, H_m)$, a comparator locally-predicate-better($\theta$, $\sigma$, $H$) is defined as follows.*

$$\begin{aligned} &\textit{locally-predicate-better}(\theta, \sigma, H) \\ &= \exists k > 0 \textit{ such that } \forall i \in \{1 \ldots k-1\}\ \forall p \in H_i\ e(p\theta) = e(p\sigma) \\ &\quad \wedge\ \exists q \in H_k\ e(q\theta) < e(q\sigma) \wedge\ \forall r \in H_k\ e(r\theta) \le e(r\sigma) \end{aligned}$$

*The function e is an error function. For a constraint p and a solution $\theta$, the function e is defined as follows.*

- $e(p\theta) = 0$ *if the solution $\theta$ satisfies the constraint p.*
- $e(p\theta) = 1$ *otherwise.*

### 4.3 Example

Figure 3 shows an image of a Japanese classic text consisting of five characters taken from "Tales of Ise" [5], and a Reprint-CSP constructed from the text. The DAG of Fig. 3 represents reading order among segmented characters. A variable $x_1$ is assigned to the first character. Similarly, variables $x_2$, $x_5$, $x_6$ and $x_7$ are assigned to the 2nd, the 3rd, the 4th, and the 5th character respectively. Because the segmented character corresponding to the variable $x_2$ can be recognized as a combination of two characters, it is divided into two characters corresponding to two variables $x_3$ and $x_4$. As this example, segmented characters corresponding to variables may overlap with each other on the document image.

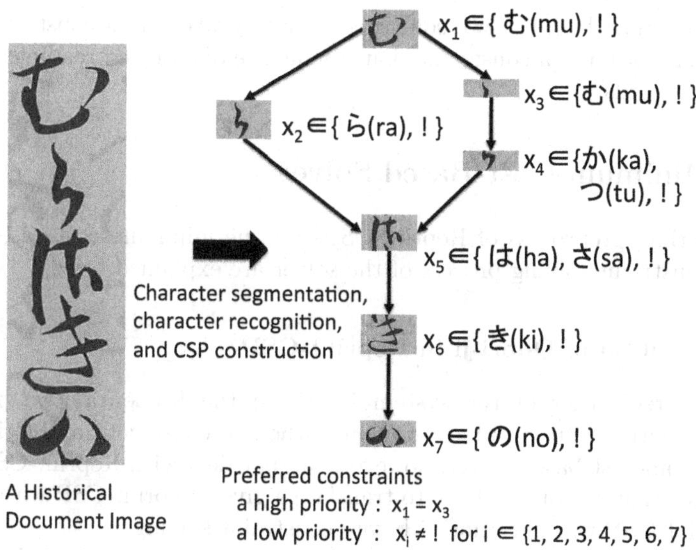


**Fig. 3.** A fragment of a classic Japanese text which reads (mu)-(ra)-(sa)-(ki)-(no) and a constraint satisfaction problem constructed from the fragment (This figure is amended from Fig. 3 in [3], and the document images in this figure are adopted from [5]).

The domain of the variable $x_4$ includes two elements (ka) and (tu) in Fig. 3 because the segmented character corresponding to $x_4$ can be read as (ka) or (tu). All variables' domains in Fig. 3 include an element "!". We use the symbol as a special character meaning an unreadable character. Because the segmented character corresponding to $x_3$ can be read as an odori-ji, the domain of $x_1$, which is immediately prior to $x_3$ in the reading order, is added to the domain of $x_3$ so that the value of $x_3$ can be equal to that of $x_1$.

In Fig. 3, constraints $x_i \neq$ "!" for $i \in \{1, 2, 3, 4, 5, 6, 7\}$ are imposed not to assign the unreadable character "!" to the variables. A constraint $x_1 = x_3$ is a constraint for the odori-ji. An equality constraint $x_i = x_j$ can be also used if their characters have similar shapes.

In Fig. 3, there are two maximal paths $p_1$ and $p_2$ as follows.

$$p_1 \equiv (x_1, x_2, x_5, x_6, x_7)$$
$$p_2 \equiv (x_1, x_3, x_4, x_5, x_6, x_7)$$

The following functions $\theta_1$ and $\theta_2$ are admissible solutions on the maximal path $p_1$.

$$\theta_1 \equiv \{x_1 \to (mu), x_2 \to (ra), x_5 \to (sa), x_6 \to (ki), x_7 \to (no)\}$$
$$\theta_2 \equiv \{x_1 \to (mu), x_2 \to (ra), x_5 \to (ha), x_6 \to (ki), x_7 \to (no)\}$$

For example, the solution $\theta_1$ can be obtained by a word sequence (a noun (mu)-(ra)-(sa)-(ki), a particle (no)), a word sequence (a noun (mu)-(ra), a noun (sa)-(ki), a particle (no)) and so on. Because the two solutions $\theta_1$ and $\theta_2$ do not give any value to $x_3$ and $x_4$, the two solutions $\theta_1$ and $\theta_2$ satisfy four constraints $x_1 = x_3$, $x_3 \neq !$, $x_4 \neq !$ and a constraint that a sequence of assigned readings forms a sequence of words.

## 5 A Minimum-Cost-Based Solver

In this section, preprocess of Reprint-CSPs for the minimum-cost-based solver and the constraint solving process of the solver are explained briefly.

### 5.1 Resolution of Odori-ji in Reprint-CSP

The image recognizer of the system based on the framework we proposed may add odori-ji into variables' domains when it constructs a Reprint-CSP. The minimum-cost-based solver, however, can not deal with Reprint-CSPs with odori-ji. For that reason, we have to translate a given Reprint-CSP with odori-ji to a Reprint-CSP without odori-ji before constraint solving.

Let a Reprint-CSP have a set of variables $\{x_1, \ldots, x_n\}$ and a DAG $G$. For each variable $x_i$ whose domain includes odori-ji in the topological order for $G$, we apply the following procedure.

1. We introduce new two variables $x_{\mathrm{rest}}$ and $x_{\mathrm{odori-ji}}$. The domain $D_{\mathrm{rest}}$ is equal to $D_i$ except odori-ji. The domain $D_{\mathrm{odori-ji}}$ is equal to $\cup_{(x_j,x_i)\in E} D_j$ if there exists an incoming edge to $x_i$. Otherwise, the domain $D_{\mathrm{odori-ji}}$ is equal to the alphabet $\Sigma$.
2. For each directed edge $(x_j, x_i)$, which is an incoming edge to $x_i$, we replace the edge $(x_j, x_i)$ with two edges $(x_j, x_{\mathrm{rest}})$ and $(x_j, x_{\mathrm{odori-ji}})$, and introduce a constraint $x_j = x_{\mathrm{odori-ji}}$.
3. For each directed edge $(x_i, x_k)$, which is an outgoing edge from $x_i$, we replace the edge $(x_i, x_k)$ with two edges $(x_{\mathrm{rest}}, x_k)$ and $(x_{\mathrm{odori-ji}}, x_k)$.
4. We remove the variable $x_i$.

Figures 4 and 5 show the resolving process. Figure 4(1) shows a part of a DAG where a variable $x_i$ does not have any incoming edge and its domain $D_i$ includes an odori-ji, and Fig. 4(2) shows a result of resolving the odori-ji. Figure 5(1) shows a part of a DAG where a variable $x_i$ has incoming edges and its domain $D_i$ includes an odori-ji, Fig. 4(2) shows a result of resolving the odori-ji.

### 5.2 Constraint Solving

The minimum-cost-based solver takes a Reprint-CSP, a dictionary of words and a positive integer $n$ as its input, and works as follows.

1. The solver constructs a reading assignment graph with costs from a given Reprint-CSP. It is a directed acyclic graph with a most upstream node and a most downstream node. Each node is labeled with a sequence of variables, a reading (a word in the dictionary) assigned to the variable sequence, a part of

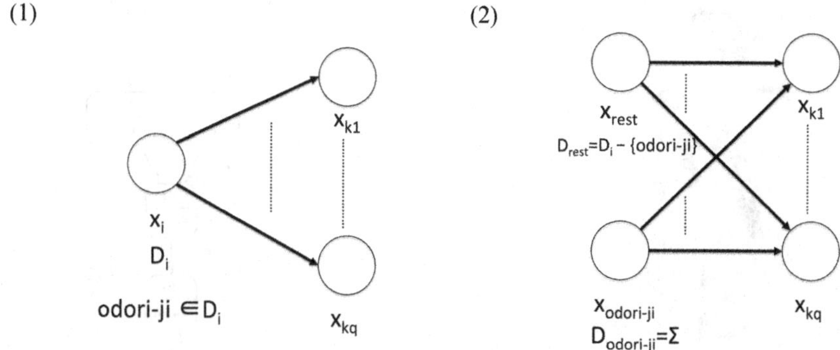


**Fig. 4.** A resolution of an odori-ji in the domain of a variable without any incoming edge

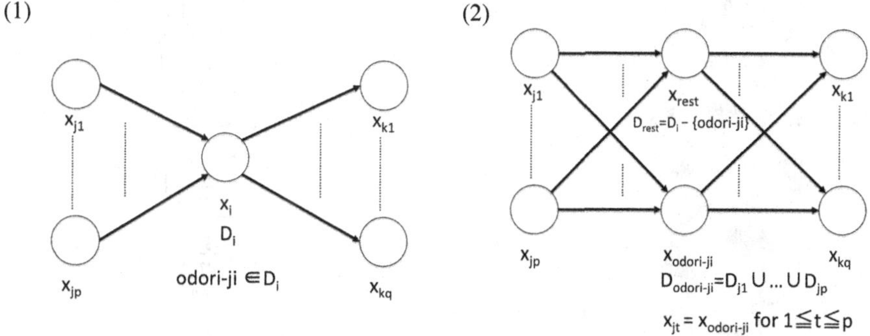


**Fig. 5.** A resolution of an odori-ji in the domain of a variable with incoming edges.

speech of the word, and two costs. The two costs are an occurrence cost of the word and the minimum cost from the most upstream node to the node. Each directed edge represents a reading order between two nodes, and is labeled with a connection cost.

2. The solver enumerates $n$-best admissible solutions over the reading assignment graph with costs from a view point of costs, and extracts locally-predicate-better solutions from the $n$-best admissible solutions.

In the following, an example of the constraint solving process is shown using Figs. 6, 7, 8 and 9.

Figure 6 shows a fragment of a classic Japanese text [5] which reads (si)-(no)-(hu)-(su)-(ri)-(no)-(ka)-(ri)-(ki)-(nu)-(wo).

Figure 7 shows a directed acyclic graph over variables of a Reprint-CSP for the text of Fig. 6. Each node is labeled with a variable in the upper part and its domain in the lower part. Each directed edge between two nodes represents a reading order between the two variables.

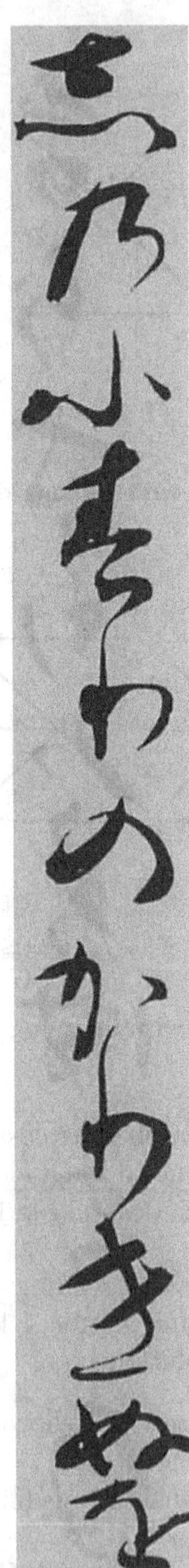

Fig. 6. A classic Japanese text which reads (si)-(no)-(hu)-(su)-(ri)-(no)-(ka)-(ri)-(ki)-(nu)-(wo) (adopted from [5]).

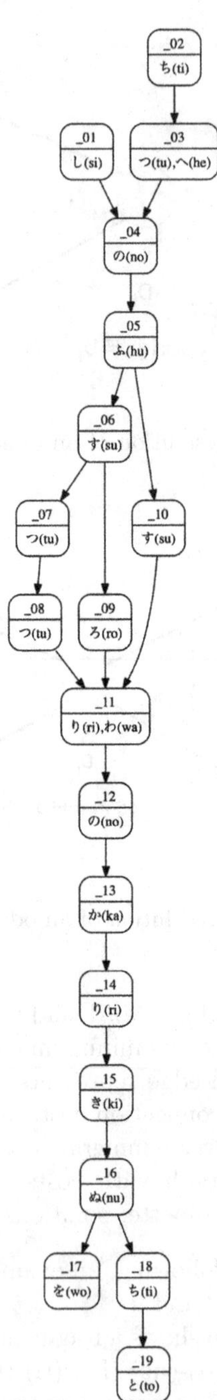


Fig. 7. A directed acyclic graph over variables of a Reprint-CSP for the text in Fig. 6.

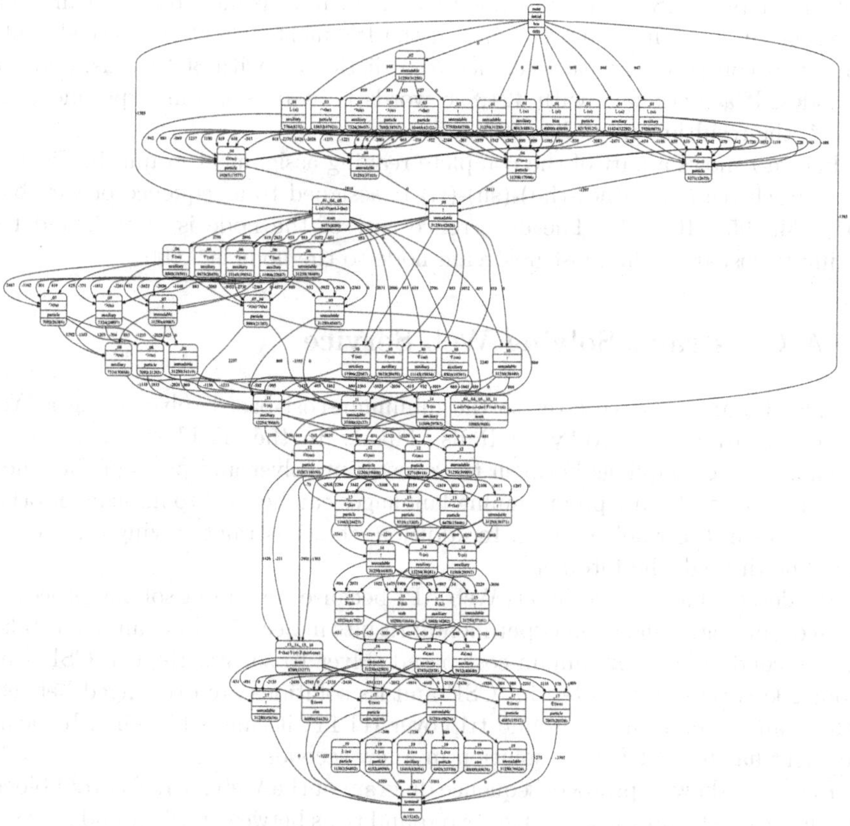

Fig. 8. A complete reading assignment graph with costs.

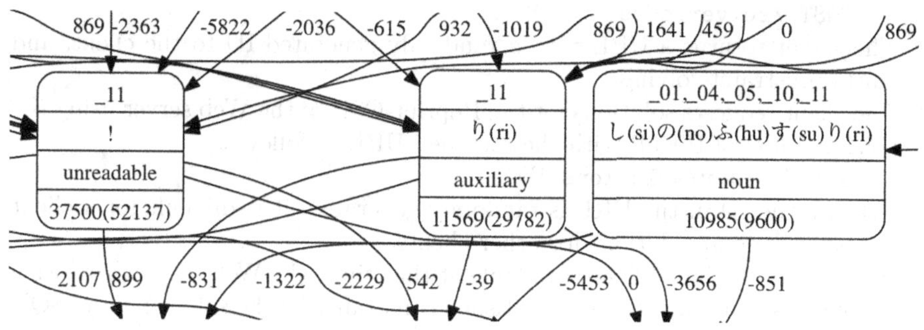


Fig. 9. A part of the reading assignment graph with costs in Fig. 8.

Figure 8 shows a complete reading assignment graph with costs constructed from the Reprint-CSP. The most upstream node and the most downstream node represent the beginning and the end of the fragment of text respectively. The graph was constructed with reference to a dictionary with 363 words, and has 74 nodes. If a dictionary with 421,896 words is used as in our experiments in Sect. 7, the resulting graph has 507 nodes.

Figure 9 shows a part of the complete reading assignment graph. In Fig. 9, a noun which reads (si)-(no)-(hu)-(su)-(ri) is assigned to a sequence of variables (_01, _04, _05, _10, _11). The occurrence cost of the node is 10,985, and the minimum cost from the most upstream node to the node is 9,600.

## 6 A Constraint Solving Web Service

We added a Web service layer to the minimum-cost-based solver using a Web application framework Ruby on Rails. Thanks to the HTTP-based protocol, it realizes loose couplings between the constraint solver and parts of the whole system. As a result, any programming languages can be used to implement other subsystems in the whole system. In addition, the constraint solving service can be public through the Internet.

We designed an asynchronous Web API because constraint solving process is time-consuming as shown in experimental results in Sect. 7. For example, it takes a few seconds for the minimum-cost-based solver to solve a Reprint-CSP with about 200 variables. If a Reprint-CSP and its solutions are exchanged between a client and a server in one round trip over HTTP, it causes blocking. It means the client has to wait for the solution in a few seconds.

Figure 10 shows a protocol sequence diagram of the Web API. To avoid blocking, the Web API protocol involves two round trips between a client and a server. The following is a brief explanation of the protocol.

1. A client sends a Reprint-CSP, a dictionary name, and a positive integer $n$ in a JSON format [17] using the POST method of HTTP to a Web server as follows.
   `POST /solver/csps`
2. The server returns a URL with a randomly generated ID to the client, and starts constraint solving.
3. The client requests solutions for the Reprint-CSP to the Web server using the GET method of HTTP with the returned URL as follows.
   `GET /solver/solutions/ID`
   Because the ID in the URL is randomly generated, it is difficult for a client to steal a look at solutions for other clients.
4. If solutions for the URL are available at that time, the Web server provides a set of pairs of a solution and unsatisfied constraints in the solution in a JSON format. If they are not available, the Web server provides an error message in a JSON format. Unsatisfied constraints sent from the Web server will be hints to revise the original Reprint-CSP.

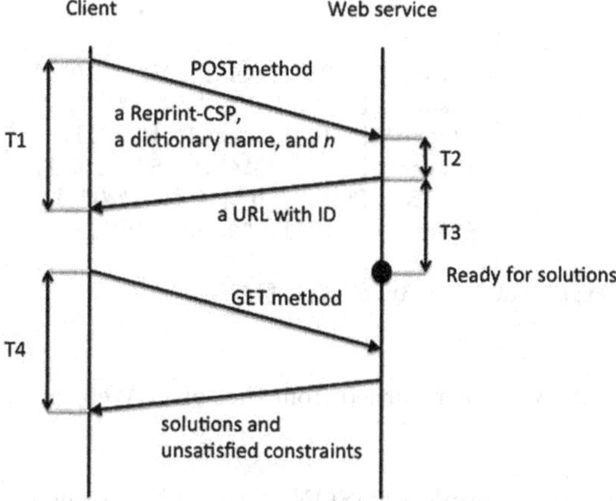


**Fig. 10.** A protocol sequence diagram of the Web service (adopted from [3]).

```
{
  "ConstraintSatisfactionProblem":{
    "vars":{"_01":["し"], "_02":["ち"], "_03":["つ","へ"], "_04":["の"],
            "_05":["ふ"], "_06":["す"], "_07":["つ"], "_08":["つ"],
            "_09":["ろ"], "_10":["す"], "_11":["り", "わ"], "_12":["の"],
            "_13":["か"], "_14":["り"], "_15":["き"], "_16":["ぬ"],
            "_17":["を"], "_18":["ち"], "_19":["と"]},
    "connectivity":[["_01", "_04"], ["_03", "_04"], ["_04", "_05"],
                    ["_05", "_06"], ["_05", "_10"], ["_08", "_11"],
                    ["_09", "_11"], ["_10", "_11"], ["_11", "_12"],
                    ["_12", "_13"], ["_13", "_14"], ["_14", "_15"],
                    ["_15", "_16"], ["_16", "_17"], ["_16", "_18"],
                    ["_02", "_03"], ["_06", "_07"], ["_06", "_09"],
                    ["_07", "_08"], ["_18", "_19"]],
    "constraints":[[],
                   [["ne", "_01", "!"], ["ne", "_02", "!"],
                    ["ne", "_03", "!"], ["ne", "_04", "!"],
                    ["ne", "_05", "!"], ["ne", "_06", "!"],
                    ["ne", "_07", "!"], ["ne", "_08", "!"],
                    ["ne", "_09", "!"], ["ne", "_10", "!"],
                    ["ne", "_11", "!"], ["ne", "_12", "!"],
                    ["ne", "_13", "!"], ["ne", "_14", "!"],
                    ["ne", "_15", "!"], ["ne", "_16", "!"],
                    ["ne", "_17", "!"], ["ne", "_18", "!"],
                    ["ne", "_19", "!"]]],
    "odoriji":{}},
  "dictionary":"cyukowabunUnidic",
  "n_best":"1"
}
```

**Fig. 11.** A request to the solver Web service.

```
{
  "solutions":[
               [{"vars":["_01","_04","_05","_10","_11"],
                 "word":["し", "の", "ふ", "す", "り"]},
                {"vars":["_12"], "word":["の"]},
                {"vars":["_13","_14","_15","_16"],
                 "word":["か", "り", "き", "ぬ"]},
                {"vars":["_17"], "word":["を"]}]
              ],
  "unsatisfiedConstraints":[[],[]]
}
```


**Fig. 12.** A result returned from the solver Web service.

Figure 11 shows an example of JSON data which a client sends to a Web server to request constraint solving. It has a key-value structure as follows.

- The value of the key "`ConstraintSatisfactionProblem`" represents a Reprint-CSP by a key-value structure as follows.
  - The value of the key "`vars`" represents pairs of a variable and its domain. The special character "`!`" is automatically added to each domain by the solver. The order of characters in a domain represents ranks of the character in the result of character recognition. The first character has the first rank 0, the second has the second rank 1 and so on.
  - The value of the key "`connectivity`" represents a DAG over the variables.
  - The value of the key "`constraints`" represents a constraint hierarchy. Each constraint is described in prefix notation. An array `["ne", "_01", "!"]` in the example represents a constraint $\_01 \neq !$ which avoids assigning the special character "`!`" to a variable _01.
  - The value of the key "`odoriji` represents pairs of a variable corresponding to an odori-ji and its rank. In the example, it is empty because any odori-ji is not used.
- The value of the key "`dictionary`" represents a dictionary name.
- The value of the key "`n_best`" represents a positive integer.

Figure 12 shows an example of JSON data which a Web server returns to a client as a result of constraint solving. It has a key-value structure as follows.

- The value of the key "`solutions`" represents solutions.
- The value of the key "`unsatisfiedConstraints` represents a constraint hierarchy consisting of unsatisfied constraints.

## 7 Experimental Results

In this section, we experimentally compare the minimum-cost-based solver implemented as a UNIX command and the solver implemented as a Web service. In

**Table 1.** Reprint-CSPs for experiments (adopted from [3]).

| | # of variables | Average size of variables' domains | # of constraints |
|---|---|---|---|
| Reprint-CSP 1 | 211 | 1.22 | 220 |
| Reprint-CSP 2 | 214 | 2.00 | 215 |
| Reprint-CSP 3 | 303 | 1.23 | 318 |

**Table 2.** Average execution time (adopted from [3]).

| | UNIX command (sec) | Web service | | | | |
|---|---|---|---|---|---|---|
| | | T1 (sec) | T2 (sec) | T3 (sec) | T4 (sec) | T1+T3+T4 (sec) |
| Reprint-CSP 1 | 5.538 | 1.258 | 0.044 | 2.576 | 0.002 | 3.836 |
| Reprint-CSP 2 | 12.358 | 1.286 | 0.041 | 8.961 | 0.002 | 10.249 |
| Reprint-CSP 3 | 7.146 | 1.260 | 0.047 | 3.913 | 0.002 | 5.176 |

addition, we evaluates the design of Web API according to the experimental results.

We built a Linux environment on a virtual machine on OS X El Capitan, and run our Web service on the environment on a Mac mini with 2.3 GHz Intel Core i7 CPU and 16GB memory. We used a Mac mini with same specification in a same local area network for a Web client (a UNIX command `curl`) and the solver implemented as a UNIX command.

The two solvers use a same dictionary called UniDic for Early Middle Japanese [18], which includes 421,896 words. Every time we invoke the solver as a UNIX command, the command reads the dictionary, stores it as a trie tree and use the trie tree for a constraint solving. After finishing the constraint solving, the trie tree is lost. On the other hand, when we start the solver as a Web service, the Web service reads the dictionary, stores it as a trie tree, and keep the trie tree for constraint solving as long as the Web service is running.

We used a classic Japanese manuscript "Tales of Ise" [5] to create three Reprint-CSPs shown in Table 1. Reprint-CSP 1 and Reprint-CSP 2 are CSPs for a page, and Reprint-CSP 3 is a CSP for two pages.

We gave each of the three Reprint-CSPs to the two solvers five times, and measured their average execution time. For the solver as a Web service, we measured four durations T1, T2, T3, and T4 in Fig. 10.

- T1 is a waiting time of a client between sending a Reprint-CSP and receiving a URL.
- T2 is an execution time in a Web service between receiving a Reprint-CSP and sending a URL.
- T3 is an execution time for constraint solving in a Web service.
- T4 is a waiting time of a client between requesting solutions and receiving the solutions.

Because T1 and T3 may overlap, a waiting time of a client between sending a Reprint-CSP and receiving solutions is at most T1+T3+T4.

Table 2 shows the results. In the three cases, the solver as a Web service is faster than the solver as a UNIX command by about 2 s. The execution time of a Web service (T1+T3+T4) ranges between 69% and 84% of that of the solver as a UNIX command. The reason is that the solver as a Web service is ready to solve when it receives a Reprint-CSP while the solver as a UNIX command has to read the dictionary before solving when it receives a Reprint-CSP.

In addition, $T_3$ ranges between about 2.6 s and about 9.0 s in Table 2. It supports the asynchronous Web API which avoids blocking.

## 8 Conclusion

We added a Web service layer to our constraint solver implemented as a UNIX command for reprinting Japanese historical text. Thanks to the Web service layer, we can use suitable programming languages to implement other parts of the whole reprint support system based on a framework proposed by us. In addition, we will also be able to publish our constraint solver on a Web site as a Web service so that other researchers concerning reprinting of Japanese historical text can use it. We conducted experiments and confirmed the solver as a Web service is faster than the original solver as a UNIX command by about two seconds if we use both a client and the Web server in a same local area network. It is because the solver as a Web service can reuse a setup done at startup of the Web service while the solver as a UNIX command has to do setup every time it is invoked. We also confirmed the asynchronous protocol is suitable for this application because the constraint solving is time-consuming.

Our future works involve various issues as follows. If a constraint satisfaction problem (CSP) for the solver includes a Japanese repetition mark called odori-ji, we have to resolve the repetition mark in the CSP before we pass the CSP to the solver, and also have to translate obtained solutions for the preprocessed CSP into solutions for the original CSP. We have to implement both the preprocess and the postprocess to do them automatically. It is also one of our future works to publish our Web service on a Web site. We are developing a graphical user interface (GUI) application for the reprint support system. We are using C# for the implementation because C# is suitable for building GUIs. The GUI application successfully communicates with the constraint solving Web service. We, however, have to create a CSP manually in the GUI application from scratch because other subsystems in the reprint support system have not been implemented yet. We plan to implement them as a set of Web services, which are systems for text line segmentation, character segmentation and character recognition. The GUI application will work as a glue among the Web services after we implement them, and it will be able to create CSPs semi-automatically. A graph layout problem is one of issues in the GUI application because it displays a CSP as a graph for editing.

**Acknowledgements.** This work was supported by JSPS KAKENHI Grant Number JP16K00463.

## References


1. Arai, Y., Suzuki, T., Aiba, A.: Recognizing historical KANA texts using constraints. In: Nishizaki, S., Numao, M., Caro, J., Suarez, M.T. (eds.) WCTP 2012. PICT, vol. 7, pp. 151–164. Springer, Tokyo (2013). https://doi.org/10.1007/978-4-431-54436-4_12
2. Watanabe, S., Suzuki, T., Aiba, A.: Reducing of the number of solutions using adjacency relation of words in recognizing historical KANA texts. IPSJ J. **56**(3), 951–959 (2015)
3. Sando, K., Suzuki, T., Aiba, A.: A constraint solving web service for recognizing historical Japanese KANA texts. In: Rocha, A.P., van den Herik, J. (eds.) Proceedings of the 10th International Conference on Agents and Artificial Intelligence, ICAART 2018, vol. 2, Funchal, Madeira, Portugal, 16–18 January 2018, pp. 257–265. SciTePress (2018)
4. Frellesvig, B.: A History of the Japanese Language. Cambridge University Press, Cambridge (2010)
5. Reizei, T.: Tales of Ise (photocopy). Kasama Shoin (1994)
6. Yamamoto, S., Osawa, T.: Labor saving for reprinting Japanese rare classical books. J. Inf. Process. Manag. **58**(11), 819–827 (2016)
7. Terasawa, K., Kawashima, T.: Word spotting online. In: Proceedings of the Computers and the Humanities Symposium, vol. 2011, pp. 329–334 (2011)
8. Manmatha, R., Han, C., Riseman, E.M., Croft, W.B.: Indexing handwriting using wordmatching. In: Proceedings of the First ACM International Conference on Digital Libraries, DL 1996, pp. 151–159. ACM, New York (1996)
9. Rath, T.M., Manmatha, R.: Word spotting for historical documents. Int. J. Doc. Anal. Recogn. **9**(2–4), 139–152 (2007)
10. Oka, R.: Spotting method for classification of real world data. Comput. J. **41**(8), 559–565 (1998)
11. Hayasaka, T., Ohno, W., Kato, Y., Yamamoto, K.: Trial production of application software for machine transcription of Hentaigana by deep learning. In: Proceedings of the 31st Annual Conference of the Japanese Society for Artificial Intelligence (2017)
12. Hayasaka, T., Ohno, W., Kato, Y., Yamamoto, K.: Recognition of kuzushiji (hentaigana and cursive script) by deep learning (ver.0.5.1) (2017). http://vpac.toyota-ct.ac.jp/kuzushiji/
13. Yamada, S., Shibayama, M.: An estimation method of unreadable historical character for manuscripts in fixed forms using n-gram and OCR. IPSJ SIG Notes 2003(59), pp. 17–24, May 2003
14. Likforman-Sulem, L., Zahour, A., Taconet, B.: Text line segmentation of historical documents: a survey. Int. J. Doc. Anal. Recogn. (IJDAR) **9**(2), 123–138 (2007)
15. Casey, R.G., Lecolinet, E.: A survey of methods and strategies in character segmentation. IEEE Trans. Pattern Anal. Mach. Intell. **18**(7), 690–706 (1996)
16. Borning, A., Feldman-Benson, B., Wilson, M.: Constraint hierarchies. Lisp Symbolic Comput. **5**, 48–60 (1992)

17. Bray, T.: The JavaScript object notation (JSON) data interchange format. RFC 7159 (2014)
18. Ogiso, T., Komachi, M., Den, Y., Matsumoto, Y.: UniDic for early middle Japanese: a dictionary for morphological analysis of classical Japanese. In: Calzolari, N., et al. (eds.) Proceedings of the Eight International Conference on Language Resources and Evaluation (LREC 2012), Istanbul, Turkey. European Language Resources Association (ELRA), May 2012

# Parameterized Mapping Distances for Semi-Structured Data

Kilho Shin[1(✉)] and Taro Niiyama[2]

[1] Graduate School of Applied Informatics, University of Hyogo, Kobe, Japan
yshin@ai.u-hyogo.ac.jp
[2] NTT DoCoMo, Tokyo, Japan
niiyamat@nttdocomo.com
http://www.ai.u-hyogo.ac.jp

**Abstract.** The edit distances have been widely used as an effective method to analyze similarity of semi-structured data such as strings, trees and graphs. For example, the Levenshtein distance for strings is known to be effective to analyze DNA and proteins, and the Taï distance and its variations are attracting wide attention of researchers who study tree-type data such as glycan, HTML-DOM-trees, parse trees of natural language processing and so on. The problem that we recognize here is that the way of engineering new edit distances was ad-hoc and lacked a unified view. To solve the problem, we introduce the concept of the mapping distance and a hyper-parameter that controls costs of label mismatch. One of the most important advantages of our parameterized mapping distances consists in the fact that the distances can be defined for arbitrary finite sets in a consistent manner and some important properties such as satisfaction of the axioms of metrics can be discussed abstractly regardless of the structures of data. The second important advantage is that mapping distances themselves can be parameterized, and therefore, we can identify the best distance to a particular application by parameter search. The mapping distance framework can provide a unified view over various distance measures for semi-structured data focusing on partial one-to-one mappings between data. These partial one-to-one mappings are a generalization of what are known as mappings of edit paths in the legacy study of edit distances. This is a clear contrast to the legacy edit distance framework, which defines distances through edit operations and edit paths. Our framework enables us to design new distance measures in a consistent manner, and also, various distance measures can be described using a small number of parameters. In fact, in this paper, we take ordered rooted trees as an example and introduce three independent dimensions to parameterize mapping distance measures. Through intensive experiments using ten datasets, we identify two important mapping distances that can exhibit good classification performance when used with the $k$-NN classifier. These mapping distances are novel and have not been discussed in the literature.

**Keywords:** Edit distance · Kernel · Mapping · Tree


J. van den Herik and A. P. Rocha (Eds.): ICAART 2018, LNAI 11352, pp. 443–466, 2019.
https://doi.org/10.1007/978-3-030-05453-3_21

## 1 Introduction

Machine learning algorithms perform their functions totally relying on analysis of similarity of data. On the other hand, many datasets that can be targets of data analysis include data instances serialized in the form of vectors of feature values. To evaluate similarity of vectors, distance measures have been a common tool, because vectors can be naturally understood as points in Euclidean spaces, and we have multiple distance measures defined over Euclidean spaces including as Euclidean distance, Manhattan distance, $L_p$-norm and Mahalanobis' distance. We should notice that inner products (dot products) and cosine similarities of vectors, which are the foundation of the kernel method and the multivariable analysis, can be also derived from their Euclidean distances by the cosine formula.

On the other hand, it is also a fact that there are a variety of data that are not represented as vectors. For example, DNA's include crucial information to determine physiology and diseases of the human being and are represented as strings of letters A, C, G and T, which indicates four nucleosides, namely, adenine, cytosine, guanine and thymine. Glycans (sugar chains) are also important chemical compounds intensively studied in biochemistry, also known as the third bio-polymer following DNA and proteins. A glycan consists of monosaccharides (single sugars) connected in the form of tree by glycosidic bonds. Web pages are written using Hyper Text Mark-up Language (HTML), which can represent nesting structure of document components using tags, and DOM trees that associate with Web pages represent the nesting structure of document components.

To denote a datum that consists of one or components that are related with one another by some means, we use the term *semi-structures data*. It is evident that we cannot use the conventional distance measures for points in Euclidean spaces in a straightforward manner. To solve the issue, a set of *edit distances* have been proposed as distance measures for semi-structured data in the literature and have proven to be effective. The Levenshtein distance for strings [10] is a well-known example of edit distance measures. Taï extended the Levenshtein distance to trees [19]. Since computing Taï distances is heavy, a number of variations have been proposed in the literature including the *constrained* distance [22], the *less-constrained* distance [11] and the *degree-two* distances [24]. Their definitions are all stemmed from the Taï distance, and they have succeeded in reducing computational complexity of Taï distance. On the other hand, Wang and Zhang [20] introduced the *alignment* distance to extend the concept of string alignments to trees. In fact, the alignment distance has turned out to be identical to the less constrained distance [9]. For graphs, a definition of edit distances is given in [13].

The common fundamental idea of edit distances is to determine a set of primitive edit operations that transforms a datum into another datum and to determine a distance between two data by the smallest number of edit operations necessary to transform one into the other. Hence, with a different set of primitive edit operations, a different distance will be obtained even for the same pair of data.

In fact, many different definitions of edit distances for trees have been introduced in the literature, but the ways to introduce them appears *ad-hoc* rather than being amenable to discipline. Therefore, we cannot deny the possibility that we have missed instances of the edit distance measure that can have good performance in accuracy or time-efficiency or both.

The first of the two important contributions of this paper is to introduce the notion of the *mapping distance*, which generalizes the legacy edit distance with a consistent view. We initially introduced the idea of the mapping distance in [18], and in this paper, we introduce a hyper-parameter that controls the likelihood that mismatch of elements can occur. The second important contribution is to engineer new distance measures for trees, which can be reasonably parameterized by two additional hyper-parameters, and therefore, we can identify the best distances for specific applications through parameter search. Through intensive experiments with ten datasets of trees, we have added one important mapping distance to the mapping distance identified to be important in [18]. The newly identified distance is novel and has not been discussed in the literature.

The sections that follow this introductory section are organized as follows. In Sect. 2, we give a review over some well-known edit distance measures, including Levenshtein distance for strings and Taö edit distance for trees. In Sect. 3, we first describe the notion of the mapping distance initially initialized in [18]. Some important properties of mapping distances are newly given with mathematical proofs. Secondly, we introduce a hyper-parameter that controls the cost when mismatch occurs in mappings. In Sect. 4, we develop our discussion focusing on application to trees. In fact, we introduce multiple instances of mapping distance measures for trees, three of which are well-known in the literature. In addition, we report the results of experiments that we run to compare these mapping distance measures.

## 2 Examples of Legacy Edit Distances for Strings and Trees

### 2.1 Levenshtein Distance for Strings [10]

Levenshtein distance [10] is well-known and widely used to evaluate similarity between strings. Levenshtein distance determines three primitive edit operations: *substitution*, *deletion* and *insertion*. For example, from a string `ACGT`, we obtain `AGGT` by substituting `G` for `C`, `AGT` by deleting `C`, and `ACAGT` by inserting `A` immediately after `C`.

Given an alphabet $\Sigma$, $\Sigma+$ denotes the entire set of non-empty strings. Letting $\Sigma^+$ be a vertex set a graph, we can determine an infinite undirected graph $G_\Sigma = (\Sigma^+, E)$. An edge of $G_\Sigma$ connects two strings that can be mutually transformed by means of a singe primitive edit operation. For example, the vertex `ACGT` has edges to the vertices of `AGGT`, `AGT` and `ACAGT`, and then, the distance between two vertices (strings) is defined by the length of the shortest path between the two vertices in $G_\Sigma$.

When an edge between two strings $s$ and $t$ is defined due to replacement of a letter $a$ in $s$ with a letter $b$ in $t$, we label it with $(a, b)$. On the other hand, if it is associated with deletion of a letter $a$ from $s$ or insertion of a letter $b$ into $t$, we label it with $(a, \perp)$ or $(\perp, b)$.

For $\{s, t\} \in \Sigma^+$, a path from $s$ to $t$ is called an *edit path* and represented by a sequence of edge labels. For example, there is a path from ACGT to GCTA that is represented by $(\mathtt{A}, \mathtt{G})(\mathtt{G}, \perp)(\perp\, \mathtt{T})$. In fact, this turns out to be the shortest path between the strings, and hence, their distance is three.

Moreover, the *mapping* of the path is determined as $\{(\mathtt{A}, \mathtt{G}), (\mathtt{C}, \mathtt{C}), (\mathtt{G}, \mathtt{G})\}$. In general, the mapping of an edit path determines a one-to-one partial mapping between the letters consisting of ACGT and the letters consisting of GCTA that are not deleted or inserted in the edit path. For mappings of Levenshtein distance, we have

**Theorem 1.** *The mapping of an edit path of Levenshtein distance preserves the order of letters in the original strings.*

### 2.2 Taï Distance for Trees [19]

In this paper, we mean *rooted trees* simply by "trees". Therefore, a tree always has a *root* vertex, which is a unique common ancestor of all of the other vertices. We first define Taï distance for *unordered* trees, and then extend the definition to *ordered* trees.

In graph theories, an unordered tree is defined as a connected acyclic undirected graph. Between arbitrary two distinct vertices, there exists a unique path from one to the other. An unordered tree can be viewed as a rooted tree by specifying an arbitrary vertex as a root.

In addition, we can introduce an order among vertices into an unordered rooted tree so that it becomes a partially ordered set (poset): for distinct vertices $v$ and $w$ of a rooted tree with a root $r$, we denote $v > w$, if, and only if, the unique path from $r$ to $v$ includes the unique path from $r$ to $w$. This order $>$ is called a *generation order*, and we say that $w$ is an ancestor of $v$, if $v > w$.

It is worth noting that we can define an unordered rooted tree as a poset as well: A poset $(V, >)$ is an unordered rooted tree, if, and only if, the following two conditions are met:

1. There is a minimum element $r$ such that $r < v$ holds for any $v \in V \setminus \{r\}$;
2. For $A_v = \{w \in V \mid w < v\}$, the poset $(A_v, <)$ is totally ordered: that is, any two distinct vertices $u$ and $w$ in $A_v$, either $u > w$ or $u < w$ holds.

Taï distance is a straightforward extension of Levenshtein distance to trees, and the difference from Levenshtein distance is twofold.

- Although Taï distance determines the same three types of primitive edit operations of substitution, deletion and insertion as Levenshtein distance does, the targets of these edit operations are vertices of trees instead of letters.

- The substitution and deletion edit operations of Taï distance are defined in the same way as Levenshtein distance. On the other hand, to define insertion of $v$ immediately below $w$, we first specify a subset of children of $w$, add $v$ as a child of $w$, and then redefine the specified children of $w$ as the entire children of $v$.

In the same way as we saw for Levenshtein distance, we can determine a graph $G_U = (U_V, E)$ that represents the entire space of unordered rooted trees. We let $V$ be a set of vertices of trees and $U$ be the entire set of unordered rooted trees. Each tree has elements of $V$ as vertices. An edge $(X, Y) \in E$ indicates a primitive edit operation that converts $X$ into $Y$. We call a path in $G_U$ by an edit path. Then, the Taï distance between two trees is determined by the length of the shortest edit path that connects the trees.

Figure 1 exemplifies an edit path for the Taï distance. The path is from the leftmost tree, denoted by $X = X_1$, to the rightmost tree, denoted by $Y$. We first substitute the vertex $v_f$, identified by the symbol $f$, for the vertex $v_e$, identified by the symbol e, to convert $X$ into $X_2$. Secondly, the vertex $v_b$ of $X_2$ is deleted to obtain $X_3$. Lastly, we insert the vertex $v_g$ below the vertex $v_a$ of $X_2$. To perform the insertion, we identify the set $\{v_d, v_f\}$ and then place $v_g$ so that $v_g$ is a child of $v_a$ and a common parent of $v_d$ and $v_f$. Thus, $(v_e, v_f)(v_b \perp)(\perp, v_g)$ represents the edit path. Furthermore, this edit path is the shortest of the edit paths that connect $X$ and $Y$ in $G_U$, and hence, the Taï distance between $X$ and $Y$ is three.

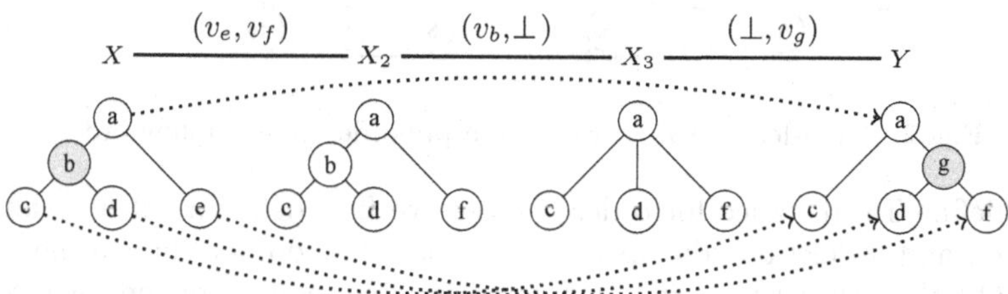


**Fig. 1.** An edit path and a mapping (dotted arrows) of Taï distance for unordered rooted trees.

The mapping of an edit path is also defined in the same way as Levenshtein distance: given an edit path from an unordered rooted tree $X$ to another unordered rooted tree $Y$, the mapping of the edit path is the canonical correspondence from the vertices of $X$ that are not deleted to the vertices of $Y$ that are not inserted. In Fig. 1, the mapping of the edit path $(v_e, v_f)(v_b \perp)(\perp, v_g)$ is depicted by dotted arrows. The vertex $v_b$ is deleted in $X$, and the vertex $v_g$ is an inserted vertex in $Y$. The mapping determines the one-to-one partial mapping $\{(v_a, v_a), (v_c, v_c), (v_d, v_d), (v_e, v_f)\}$.

Taï proved an important property to mappings of edit paths.

**Theorem 2** ([19]). *A partial one-to-one mapping between vertices of two unorderd rooted trees is a mapping of an edit path, if, and only if, the partial mapping preserves generation order.*

For example, the mapping shown in Fig. 1 determines a partial mapping between vertices of $X$ and $Y$. It is a partial mapping, because $v_b$ in $X$ is not included in the domain of the correspondence. As Theorem 2 asserts, the mapping preserves the generation order: $v_c > v_a$, $v_d > v_a$ and $v_e > v_a$ hold in the tree $X$, and $\mu(v_c) > \mu(v_a)$, $\mu(v_d) > \mu(v_a)$ and $\mu(v_e) > \mu(v_a)$ hold in the tree $X$, when $\mu$ denotes the mapping.

An ordered rooted tree, on the other hand, is equipped with a *pre-order* in addition to a generation order. To denote a pre-order, we use the symbol $\prec$. A pre-order is a total order that meets the following conditions: (1) either $v \prec w$ or $w \prec v$ for arbitrary distinct vertices $v$ and $w$; (2) if $v < w$, then $v \prec w$; and (3) if $u > v$, $v \prec w$ and $v \not< w$, then $u \prec w$. A pre-order determines an order among vertices that share the same parent vertex, and we call the order a *sibling order*. In reverse, if a sibling order is given for every parent vertex of the tree, it can be uniquely extended to a pre-order. To denote a sibling order, we use the same symbol $\prec$ as a pre-order. Figure 2 depicts a pre-order and the derived sibling order: The numbers assigned to vertices represent the pre-order, and the solid arrows do the sibling order derived from the pre-order.

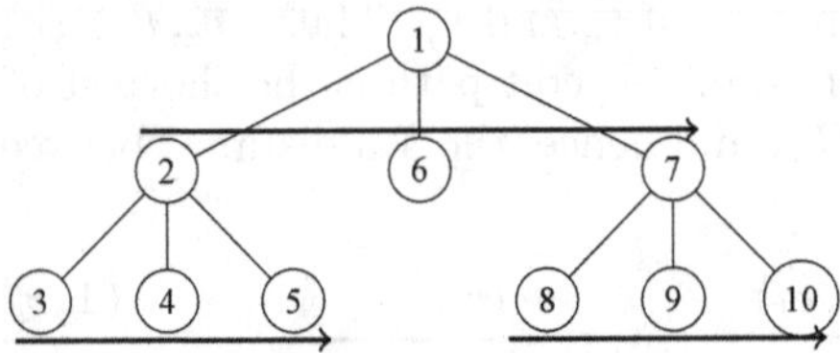

**Fig. 2.** An ordered rooted tree with a pre-order and a sibling order.

To define Taï distance for ordered trees, we first define a substitution edit operation and a deletion edit operation so that they do not change the sibling order. On the other hand, we need some modification to define an insertion edit operation. When we insert a new vertex $v$ as a child of a vertex $w$ with children $w_1, w_2, \ldots, w_k$ in the sibling order, we first specify a set of children of $w$ so that the specified set becomes an interval. That is to say, we choose two integer $a$ and $b$ such that $1 \leq a \leq b \leq k$ and specify the set $W = \{w_i \mid$

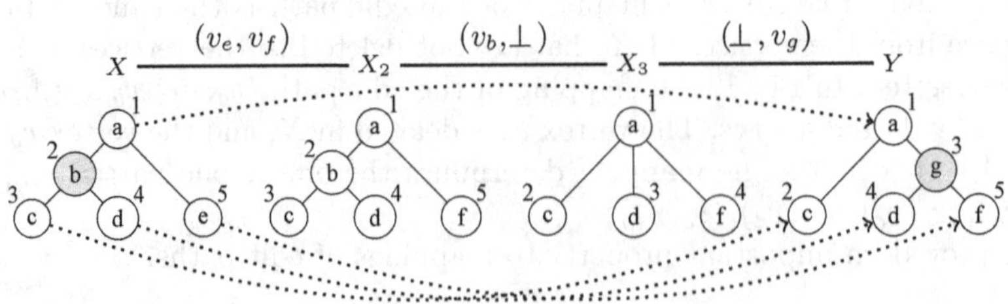


**Fig. 3.** An edit path and a mapping (dotted arrows) of Taï distance for ordered rooted trees.

$a \leq i \leq b\}$. Then, we replace $W$ with $v$ and update the sibling order under $w$ to be $w_1, \ldots, w_{a-1}, v, w_{b+1}, \ldots, w_k$. Finally, we let $W$ be the children of $v$ and determine a sibling order so that $w_i \prec w_j$ for any $a \leq i < j \leq b$.

Figure 3 depicts an example of an edit path of Taï distance for ordered rooted trees. $(v_e, v_f)(v_b \perp)(\perp, v_g)$ represents the edit path depicted. The numbers attached to vertex circles represents a pre-order of each tree. For the transformation from $X$ to $X_2$, the vertex $v_e$ of $X$ is replaced with $v_f$, and the same pre-order is assigned to $v_f$ as $v_e$. For the transformation from $X_2$ to $X_3$, the vertex $v_b$ of $X_2$ is deleted, and the pre-order of the remaining vertices remains the same. For the last transformation from $X_3$ to $Y$, the vertex $v_g$ is inserted, and $v_d$ and $v_f$ are redefined as children of $v_g$. The sibling order between $v_d$ and $v_f$ is the same between before and after the transformation.

Theorem 2 for ordered rooted trees is stated as follows.

**Theorem 3.** *A partial one-to-one mapping between vertices of two ordered rooted trees is a mapping of an edit path, if, and only if, the partial mapping preserves the generation order and the pre-order.*

### 2.3 Variations of Taï Distance

The most serious problem of Taï distance is its heavy computational complexity. Computing Taï distances for unordered rooted trees is known NP-hard. Although its computational complexity for ordered rooted trees is polynomial-time, the known algorithm required too much computation in practice. Hence, much effort has been made to develop efficient algorithms to compute Taï distances. Zhang and Shasha [23] proposed an algorithm of $O(|X||Y| \min(w(X), h(X)) \min(w(Y), h(Y)))$-time, where $|X|$, $w(x)$ and $h(x)$ denote the size (the number of vertices), the width (the number of leaves) and the height (the length of the longest path from the root to a leaf) of a tree $X$. According to shapes of trees, this varies between $O(|X||Y|)$ and $O(|X|^2|Y|^2)$. Klein [8] improved the efficiency to $O(|X|^2|Y| \log |y|)$-time by taking advantage of decomposition strategies [5]. Demaine et al. [4] further optimized this technique and presented an algorithm of $O(|X|^3)$-time. When we only look at the asymptotic evaluations, Demaine's algorithm looks the fastest, but it easily lapses into the worst case. Therefore, the algorithm of Zhang and Shasha in fact outperforms Demaine's algorithm in many practical cases. In this regard, *RTED*, an algorithm that Pawlik and Augsten [14] have developed, not only has the same asymptotic complexity as Demaine's algorithm but also almost always outperforms the competitors in practice. Furthermore, the space complexity of Zhang's algorithm, Demaine's algorithm and RTED is $O(|X||Y|)$, which is practically small.

Although the aforementioned improvement in efficiency was remarkable, the asymptotic time complexity of $O(|X|^3)$ is still too heavy for some practical applications. In the literature, several new distances have been proposed to take over Taï distance.

The degree-two distance [24] is one of the typical examples and imposes the following constraint on the primitive edit operations of substitution, deletion and insertion: roots must not be deleted or inserted; only vertices with degree one and two can be deleted and inserted. The degree of a vertex is the number of edges that the vertex has, and the degree-two distance is the minimum length of edit paths under this constraint. The time and space complexity of the degree-two distance is $O(|X||Y|)$.

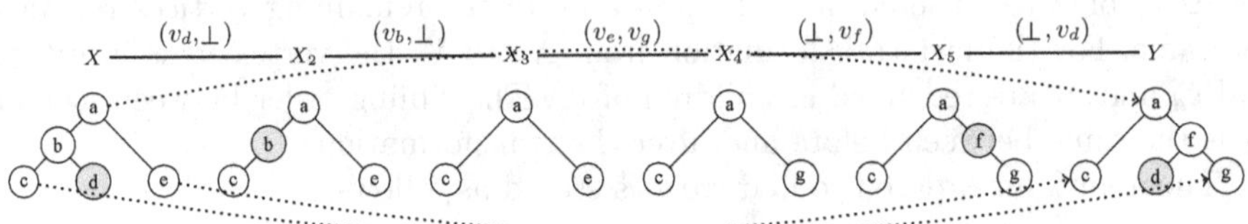


**Fig. 4.** An edit path of the degree-two distance: $(v_d, \bot)(v_b, \bot)(v_e, v_g)(\bot, v_f)(\bot, v_d)$.

Figure 4 exemplifies an edit path of the degree-two distance. $(v_d, \bot)(v_b, \bot)$ $(v_e, v_g)(\bot, v_f)(\bot, v_d)$ represents the edit path. In $X$, the vertex $v_d$ is of degree one, and hence, we can delete it under the constraint of the degree-two distance. By deleting $v_d$, the degree of $v_b$ has changed from three to two in $X_2$, and hence, we are allowed to delete it. Also, we can insert $v_f$ between $v_a$ and $v_g$, because the resulting degree of $v_f$ in $X_5$ is two. For the same reason, we can insert $v_d$ below $v_f$. The length of this edit path is five, and furthermore, this is the shortest edit path. Hence, the degree-two distance between $X$ and $Y$ turns out to be five.

To show an important property of the degree-two distance, we introduce the *nearest common ancestor* (NCA) of a set of vertices in a rooted tree.

**Definition 1.** *For $S$ a set of vertices of a rooted tree, the nearest common ancestor $S^{\smile}$ is the maximum element of $\{v \mid w \in S, v \leq w\}$ with respect to the generation order.*

We let $v \smile w$ denote $\{v, w\}^{\smile}$ for simplicity of description. For a mapping $\mu$ of an edit path of the degree-two distance, we denote the domain of $\mu$ by $\mathrm{Dom}(\mu)$.

**Theorem 4.** *Let $\mu$ be a mapping of an edit path of the degree-two distance. For any $\{v, w\} \in \mathrm{Dom}(\mu)$, $v \smile w \in \mathrm{Dom}(\mu)$ and $\mu(v \smile w) = \mu(v) \smile \mu(w)$ hold.*

*Proof.* We assume that $v$ and $w$ are in $\mathrm{Dom}(\mu)$ and $v \smile w$ is not a root. Then, in the course of an edit path, $v \smile w$ always has at least three edges, one to $v$, one to $w$ and the other to the root, and hence, the degree of $v \smile w$ is always no smaller than three. $\square$

The *constrained* distance, which Zhang [22] has introduced, is also important in practice. The constrained distance is defined by imposing the certain constraint described below on mappings of Taï distance. Zhang has also presented an efficient algorithm to compute constrained distances, whose time and space complexity is $O(|X||Y|)$. Although Richter [16] independently introduced the *structure-respecting* distance tailoring Taï distance to particular applications, Bille [2] has shown the identity between the constrained and structure-respecting distances.

To describe the constraint of the constrained distance, we have to introduce the concept of separable vertex sets.

**Definition 2.** *Two subsets $S$ and $T$ of vertices of a tree are* separable, *if, and only if, neither $S^{\smile} < T^{\smile}$ nor $S^{\smile} < T^{\smile}$ holds.*

**Definition 3.** *A one-to-one partial mapping $\mu$ from vertices of a tree $X$ to vertices of a tree $Y$ is said to be* separable, *when $S \subseteq \mathrm{Dom}(\tau)$ and $T \subseteq \mathrm{Dom}(\tau)$ are separable in $X$, if, and only if, $\mu(S)$ and $\mu(T)$ are separable in $Y$.*

The partial mapping depicted by Fig. 5, which was also given in Fig. 1, is not separable. In fact, when we let $S = \{v_c, v_d\}$ and $T = \{v_e\}$, $S$ and $T$ are separable. However, $\mu(S)$ and $\mu(T)$ are not separable, because $\mu(v_c) \smile \mu(v_d)$ is the root of $Y$.

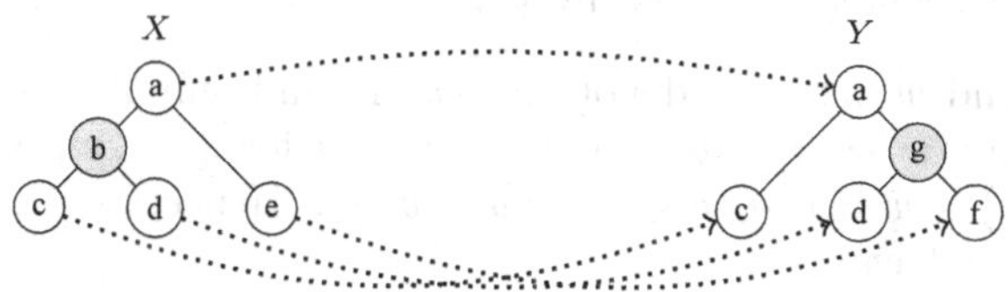


**Fig. 5.** An example of non-separable mappings.

**Definition 4.** *An edit path of Taï distance is said to be separable, if, and only if, the associated mapping is separable.*

The constrained distance between two trees is defined as the length of the shortest edit path that is separable.

## 3 Parameterized Mapping Distances

As seen in Sect. 2, the legacy edit distances are defined through primitive edit operations and edit paths. The definitions of primitive edit operations are dependent on the structures of data, and it is not always straightforward to understand the meanings of the definitions. By contrast, as shown below, mappings of edit operations can be characterized more clearly. Furthermore, the edit distances can be generalized to arbitrary finite data in a consistent manner by defining distances through mappings instead of edit operations.

### 3.1 Canonical Characterization of Mappings of Edit Distances

**Levenshtein Distance.** A string can be viewed as a totally ordered set of letters. Theorem 1 implies that the mappings of edit paths of Levenshtein distance are identical to the partial mappings between totally ordered sets that preserve the order.

**Taï Distance.** As seen in Sect. 2.2, unordered rooted trees are viewed as posets. Theorem 2 implies that mappings of edit paths of Taï distance are nothing other than partial mappings between posets that preserve the generation order.

Also, two orders, that is, a generation order and a pre-order, are given to ordered rooted trees, and Theorem 3 asserts that the set of mappings of edit paths of Taï distance is identical to the set of partial mapping that preserves the two orders.

**The Degree-Two Distance.** We can also define an unordered rooted tree as an algebraic structure. Let $V$ be a set of vertices and $\smile$ be a binary operation such that $(V, \smile)$ is a commutative semigroup: for any $\{u, v, w\} \subseteq V$, $v \smile w = w \smile v$ and $(u \smile v) \smile w = u \smile (v \smile w)$ hold. The operation $\smile$ will be the NCA operation when $V$ is organized as a tree. We further assume that the semigroup $(V, \smile)$ meets the following conditions:

1. $v \smile v = v$ for any $v \in V$;
2. $|\{u \smile v, v \smile w, w \smile u\}| \leq 2$ for any $\{u, v, w\} \subseteq V$.

For distinct $v$ and $w$ in $V$, we denote $v < w$, if, and only if, $v \smile w = v$ holds. When we assume $u \smile v = u$ and $v \smile w = v$ for $\{u, v, w\} \subseteq V$, we have $u \smile w = (u \smile v) \smile w = u \smile (v \smile w) = u \smile v = u$. Hence, we see that $(V, <)$ is a poset. Then, we have

**Theorem 5.** *The poset* $(V, <)$ *is an unordered rooted tree with a generation order* $<$.

*Proof.* By the commutative and associative properties of $(V, <)$, $V^{\smile}$ uniquely determines an element of $V$. Since $(V^{\smile}) \smile v = ((V \setminus \{v\})^{\smile}) \smile v \smile v = V^{\smile}$, $V^{\smile} < v$ always holds. Thus, $V^{\smile}$ is the minimum element of $(V, <)$, and we can determine it as a root. Secondly, we assume $u \smile v = v$ and $u \smile w = w$ for $\{u, v, w\} \subseteq V$. Since the order of the set $S = \{v, w, v \smile w\} = \{u \smile v, u \smile w, v \smile w\}$ is no greater than two, and since $u \smile v = v$ and $u \smile w = w$ are distinct, $v \smile w$ is identical to either $v$ or $w$ Hence, it turns out that either $v < w$ or $w < v$ holds. □

When we view unordered rooted trees as algebraic structures in the manner as stated above, Theorem 4 indicates that mappings of edit paths are homomorphisms with respect to the operation $\smile$: if $\mu$ is a mapping of an edit path from $(X, \smile)$ to $(Y, \smile)$, $\mathrm{Dom}(\mu)$ is a sub-semigroup of $(X, \smile)$, and $\mu(v \smile w) = \mu(v) \smile \mu(w)$ holds for any $\{v, w\} \subseteq \mathrm{Dom}(\mu)$.

**The Constrained Distance.** As seen in Sect. 2.3, a mapping of an edit path of the constrained distance is defined as a separable partial mapping of vertices that preserves the generation order.

### 3.2 Mapping Distance

Shin and Niiyama [18] have introduced the concept of *mapping distances*, which is a generalization of the legacy edit distance in the sense that a distance can be defined for arbitrary pair of finite sets not depending on the structures incorporated into them.

**Definition 5 (Length of Mapping).** *For a one-to-one partial mapping $\mu$ from a finite set $X$ and a finite set $Y$, its length $\ell(\mu)$ is determined by*

$$\ell(\mu) = |X \setminus \mathrm{Dom}(\mu)| + |Y \setminus \mu(\mathrm{Dom}(\mu))| + |\{x \in \mathrm{Dom}(\mu) \mid x \neq \mu(x)\}|. \quad (1)$$

We assume that a set $M_{X,y}$ of one-to-one partial mappings between $X$ and $Y$ is given. Then, the *mapping distance* is defined by

**Definition 6 (Mapping Distance).** *Given $M_{X,Y}$, the distance from $X$ to $Y$ derived from $M_{X,Y}$ is determined by $d_M(X,Y) = \min\{\ell(\mu) \mid \mu \in M_{X,Y}\}$.*

When $\mu$ is a mapping of an edit path of any of the legacy edit distances that we saw in Sect. 2, , $\ell(\mu)$ is identical to the length of the edit path, and hence, the resulting $d_M(X,Y)$ is identical to the edit distance between $X$ and $Y$.

Different from the legacy definition of edit distances, the definition of mapping distances does not use information of structures in $X$ and $Y$ (for example, strings, trees) and only assume that $X$ and $Y$ are finite sets.

### 3.3 Exact Match Mapping Distance

Shin and Niiyama [18] also introduces a class of mapping distances that requires that a mapping $\mu$ meets the condition of $\mu(x) = x$ for any $x \in \mathrm{Dom}(\mu)$. We call such mapping distances *exact match mapping distance.*

In [17], a method to convert edit distance problems into pattern extraction problems is shown. In particular, the author of the paper has derived *Mostly Adjusted Agreement Sub-Tree* (*MAAST*) problem from the degree-two distance, which relaxes the constraint of exact match of labels of the well-known MAST problem [7].

In the following, we briefly review the MAST and MAAST problems. We take two unordered rooted trees $X$ and $Y$ and consider *agreement subtrees* between them. In Fig. 6, $Z$ is an agreement subtree with embeddings $\epsilon_X : Z \to X$ and $\epsilon_Y : Z \to Y$. The embeddings are required to preserve the generation order, the NCA relation and vertex labels. The MAST problem is a problem to find the largest agreement subtree in size. In other words, the objective function of optimization is the size $|Y|$.

On the other hand, Fig. 7 depicts the mapping $\mu$ of the edit path depicted in Fig. 4. $\epsilon_2 \circ \epsilon_1^{-1}$ is comparable with $\tau$, and the only difference is that $\mu$ does not necessarily preserve labels of vertices, while $\epsilon_2 \circ \epsilon_1^{-1}$ preserves them. Hence, the MAAST problem defined from the degree-two distance by the conversion method relaxes the requirement of label preserving of the MAST problem. As a

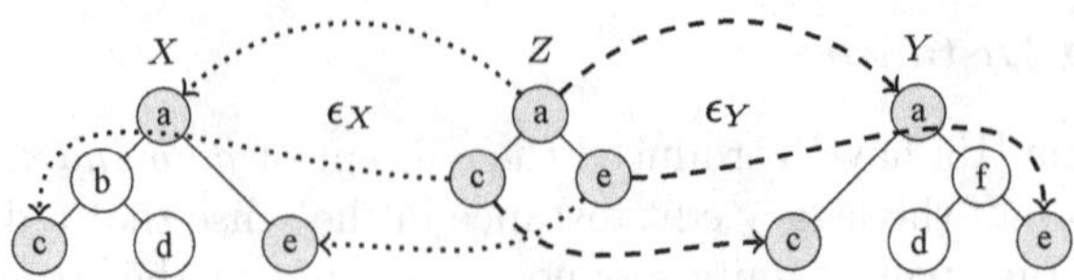


**Fig. 6.** An agreement.

result, the objective function of the MAAST problem cannot be the simple size function of agreement subtrees but must incorporate penalties by mismatch of labels in an appropriate manner into evaluation. To be precise, for an appropriate penalty function $p(\mu)$, the objective function is defined by $|\mathrm{Dom}(\mu)| - p(\mu)$. For more details, see [17].

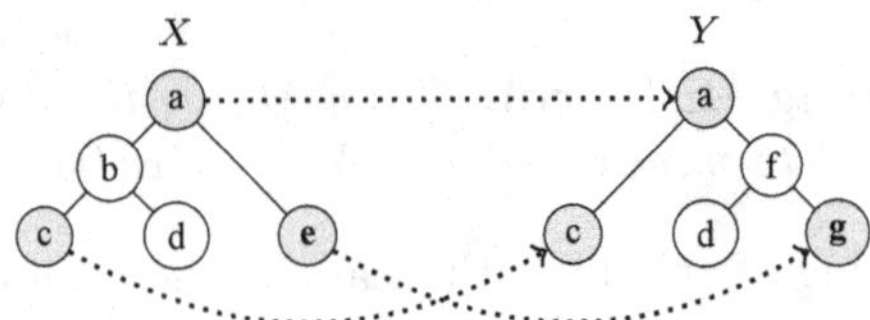


**Fig. 7.** A mapping of an edit path of the degree-two distance.

This conversion method is invertible, and hence, we can obtain a definition of a novel mapping distance from the MAST problem. For convenience, we call the mapping distance the *MAST* distance. The set of mappings for the MAST distance is a subset of the set of mappings for the degree-two distance, and mappings for the MAST distance are required to preserve labels of vertices. Therefore, for a mapping $\mu$ of the MAST distance, we have

$$\ell(\mu) = |X \setminus \mathrm{Dom}(\mu)| + |Y \setminus \mu(\mathrm{Dom}(\mu))| + |\mathrm{Dom}(\mu)| = |X| + |Y| - |\mathrm{Dom}(\mu)|,$$

and it turns out that computing the MAST distance between $X$ and $Y$ is equivalent to solving the MAST problem for the same $X$ and $Y$.

This way of introducing the MAST distance can be generalized. When any mapping in $M_{X,Y}$ is required to preserve labels, the resulting mapping distance is called a *exact match mapping distance*. Conversely, if exact label match is not required, we use the term *flexible match mapping distance* to refer to the resulting distance.

### 3.4 Satisfaction of Axioms of Metrics

In mathematics, a distance or a metric must satisfy the following conditions:

**Non-separability:** $d(X,Y) \geq 0$;
**Identity of Indiscernibles:** $d(X,Y) = 0 \Leftrightarrow X = Y$;
**Symmetry:** $d(X,Y) = d(Y,X)$;
**Triangle Inequality:** $d(X,Z) \leq d(X,Y) + d(Y,Z)$.

Interestingly, the known edit distances do not necessarily satisfy all of these conditions. For example, the less-constrained distance for trees [11] and the alignment distance for tree [20] do not support the triangle inequality.

For mapping distances, on the other hand, we have an explicit sufficient condition for a mapping distance to satisfy the axioms of metrics. To clarify, we let $\Omega$ denote the entire space over which a mapping distance $d_M$ is defined.

**Proposition 1.** *If the identity $id_X$ is a member of $M_{X,X}$ for any $X \in \Omega$, the associated mapping distance $d_M$ supports identity of indiscernibles.*

*Proof.* By Eq. (2), $\ell\mu = 0$ holds, if, and only if, $|X \backslash \mathrm{Dom}(\mu)| = |Y \backslash \mu(\mathrm{Dom}(\mu))| = |\{x \in \mathrm{Dom}(\mu) \mid x \neq \mu(x)\}| = 0$. This indicates that $\mu$ is bijective, and $\mu(v) = v$ holds for every $c \in X$. Such a $\mu$ is nothing other than the identity. □

**Proposition 2.** *If $M_{Y,X} = \{\mu^{-1} \mid \mu \in M_{X,Y}\}$ holds for any $\{X, Y\} \subseteq \Omega$, the associated mapping distance $d_M$ supports symmetry.*

*Proof.* The assertion follows from $\ell(\mu) = \ell(\mu^{-1})$. □

To investigate whether the triangle inequality holds for $d_M$, we need to define transitivity of a mapping set.

**Definition 7.** *A mapping system $\{M_{X,Y} \mid \{X, Y\} \subseteq \Omega\}$ is said to be* transitive, *if, and only if, $\nu \circ \mu \in M_{X,Z}$ holds for any $\mu \in M_{X,Y}$ and any $\nu \in M_{Y,Z}$.*

Then, we have

**Proposition 3.** *If a mapping system $\{M_{X,Y} \mid \{X, Y\} \subseteq \Omega\}$ is transitive, the triangle inequality holds for the associated mapping distance $d_M$.*

*Proof.* It is easy to see that $\ell(\nu \circ \mu) \leq \ell(\mu) + \ell(\nu)$ holds. The assertion follows. □

Hence, in the remainder of this paper, whenever we define a mapping distance, we require that the following conditions are met:

1. $id_X \in M_{X,X}$;
2. $\mu \in M_{X,Y} \Rightarrow \mu^{-1} \in M_{Y,X}$;
3. $\mu \in M_{X,Y}, \nu \in M_{Y,Z} \Rightarrow \nu \circ \mu \in M_{X,Z}$.

As a result, the resulting mapping distance satisfies all of the axioms of metrics.

### 3.5 Introduction of Substitution Cost Parameter

A mapping distance between data represents the similarity of the data and can be used for the purposes of classification and clustering, for example. For example, the $k$-nearest-neighborhood classification algorithm and the hierarchical agglomerative clustering algorithm take matrices of distances of data as input and perform their function.

To obtain better performance of classification and clustering, introduction of adjustable hyper parameters can be effective in general. In this paper, we introduce a hyper parameter $\gamma$ that controls occurrence of substitution of vertices. The range of $\gamma$ is determined to be $[0, \infty]$, and we determine the $\gamma$-length of mappings by

$$\ell_\gamma(\mu) = |X \setminus \mathrm{Dom}(\mu)| + |Y \setminus \mu(\mathrm{Dom}(\mu))| + \gamma \cdot |\{x \in \mathrm{Dom}(\mu) \mid x \neq \mu(x)\}|. \quad (2)$$

As stated, $\gamma$ controls occurrence of substitution of vertices. In fact, if $\gamma$ is small, substitution is likely to occur in the optimal solutions that yield the minimum length. On the other hand, as $\gamma$ increases, occurrence of substitution is suppressed more severely. In the extreme case where $\gamma = \infty$, the mapping of an optimal solution always preserves labels, and hence, the distance obtained is identical the exact match distance computed when only label preserving mappings are evaluated.

In the next section (Sect. 4), we take mapping distances for ordered rooted trees as an example, and examine effectiveness of mapping distances.

## 4 Comprehensive Study of Mapping Distances for Ordered Rooted Trees

### 4.1 Parameters that Describe Mapping Distances

The framework of the mapping distance also suits parameterizing mapping distances. In this section, we introduce two parameters that describe a certain class of mapping distances for trees. Once such parameters are given, by testing all of the combinations of parameter values, we can find the distance that fits to the relevant application the best.

For the mapping distances that we investigate in this section, we assume the following.

- We focus on mapping distances for ordered rooted trees. This constraint is imposed because computing mapping distances for unordered rooted trees can be easily NP-hard in most of cases.
- The partial mappings to investigate are supposed to preserve the generation order and the pre-order of ordered rooted trees.
- The partial mappings to investigate meet the three conditions described in Sect. 3.4 for the resulting mapping distances to satisfy the axioms of metrics.

The parameters that we will introduce control the shape type of domains of mappings and whether domains of mappings can include inter-vertex gaps.

**Shape Type of Domain of Mappings.** This parameter is to determine domains and ranges of partial mappings, and we determine the parameter can take the values of `Forest`, `Tree`, `Agreement`, `Path` and `Separable`. These values require a partial mapping $\mu$ in $M_{X,Y}$ to meet the conditions described below.

**Forest:** This value specifies that Dom($\mu$) can be arbitrary subsets of $X$. Hence, Dom($\mu$) turns out to be a sub-forest, that is, a sequence of ordered rooted subtrees of $X$.

**Tree:** This value specifies that Dom($\mu$) includes the maximum vertex in it with respect to the generation order. Hence, Dom($\mu$) becomes an ordered rooted subtree of $X$.

**Agreement:** This value specifies that Dom($\tau$) is a sub-semigroup with respect to the NCA operation. Also, we require that $\mu$ is a homomorphism of semigroups with respect to the NCA operator.

**Path:** This value specifies that Dom($\tau$) is a totally ordered sets with respect to the generation order.

**Separable:** This value specifies that Dom($\mu$) can be arbitrary subsets of $X$, but $\mu$ is a separable partial mapping.

**Inter-vertex Gap.** The parse-tree kernel [3] counts the number of so-called *co-rooted subtrees* shared between two trees. The basic idea of the kernel is that, the more co-rooted subtrees trees share, the more similar are the trees. What we should note here is that a co-rooted subtree does not allow gaps between their vertices: if two vertices are in the relation of parent and child in a co-rooted subtree, they are also a parent and a child in the original tree.

By contrast, all of the edit distances for trees that we saw in Sect. 2 allow gaps.

Figure 8 depicts a subtree that does not include any gap (left) and a subtree that includes gaps (right). The vertices displayed in gray indicates subtrees.

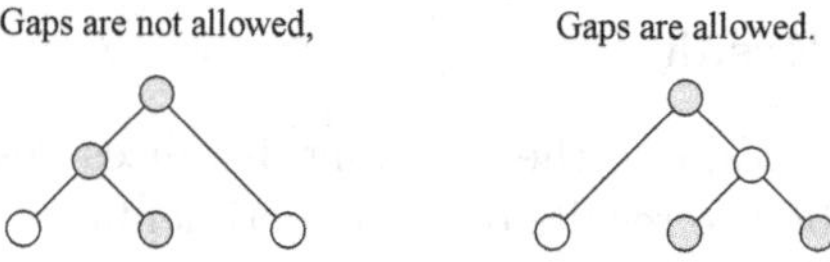
Gaps are not allowed,
Gaps are allowed.

**Fig. 8.** Inter-vertex gaps: the vertices in gray indicate subtrees.

The parameter *inter-vertex gap* determines whether Dom($\mu$) can include gaps between their adjacent vertices. If the value is `true`, Dom($\mu$) as a substructure of $X$ can include gaps.

### 4.2 Combinations of Parameters

In this section, we investigate the mapping distances that are described by the three parameters of SHAPE_TYPE, INTER_VERTEX_GAP and LABEL_MISMATCH_COST. The parameter of LABEL_MISMATCH_COST is the hyper-parameter $\gamma$ introduced in Sect. 3.5, and we examine the six values of $\gamma = 2^{-1.0}, 2^{-0.5}, 2^{0}, 2^{0.5}, 2^{1.0}$ and $\infty$.

Table 1 shows the combinations of parameter values that we investigate in Sect. 4.3 For convenience of expression, values for the parameters of SHAPE_TYPE and INTER_VERTEX_GAP are displayed simply by their capitals. `ff1.41`, for example, represents the combination of SHAPE_TYPE = `forest`, INTER_VERTEX_GAP = `false` and $\gamma = 2^{0.5} = 1.41$.

When $\gamma = 1.0$, three of the distances in Table 1 are known in the literature: `ft1.0` indicates Taï distance [19]; `st1.0` indicates the constrained distance [22]; `at1.0` indicates the degree-two distance [24].

In addition, for any value of $\gamma$, the mapping distances of type `tf` are identical to the mapping distances of type `af`.

**Table 1.** The combinations of parameter values to investigate. In the SHAPE column: `f` = Forest; `t` = Tree; `s` = Separable; `a` = Agreement; `p` = Path; In the GAP column: `t` = True; `f` = False.

| SHAPE | GAP | $\gamma$ | DESCRIPTION |
|---|---|---|---|
| f | t | $0.5, 0.71, 1.0, 1.41, 2.0, \infty$ | When $\gamma = 1$, the mapping distance is identical to Taï edit distance [20]. |
| f | f | $0.5, 0.71, 1.0, 1.41, 2.0, \infty$ | |
| t | t | $0.5, 0.71, 1.0, 1.41, 2.0, \infty$ | |
| t | t | $0.5, 0.71, 1.0, 1.41, 2.0, \infty$ | For any $\gamma$, the mapping distances are identical to those of type A−F. |
| s | t | $0.5, 0.71, 1.0, 1.41, 2.0, \infty$ | When $\gamma = 1$, the mapping distance is identical to the constrained distance[24]. |
| s | f | $0.5, 0.71, 1.0, 1.41, 2.0, \infty$ | |
| a | t | $0.5, 0.71, 1.0, 1.41, 2.0, \infty$ | When $\gamma = 1$, the mapping distance is identical to the degree-two distance[26]. |
| a | f | $0.5, 0.71, 1.0, 1.41, 2.0, \infty$ | For any $\gamma$, the mapping distances are identical to those of type T−F. |
| p | t | $0.5, 0.71, 1.0, 1.41, 2.0, \infty$ | |
| p | f | $0.5, 0.71, 1.0, 1.41, 2.0, \infty$ | |

### 4.3 Experimental Results

We ran experiments to evaluate the mapping distances described in Table 1. In this section, we describe the results of the experiments.

**Datasets.** In the experiments, we use ten datasets, which cover three different areas of applications: bioinformatics (three), natural language processing (six) and web access analysis (one). Three (COLON, CYSTIC and LEUKEMIA) are retrieved from the KEGG/ GLYCAN database ([6]) and contain glycan structures annotated relating to colon cancer, cystic fibrosis and leukemia cells. One (SYNTACTIC) is the dataset PropBank provided in [12]. This dataset includes parse trees labeled with two syntactic role classes for modeling the syntactic/semantic relation between a predicate and the semantic roles of its arguments in a sentence. Five (AIMED, BIOINFER, HPRD50 IEPA and LLL) are the corpora that include parse trees obtained by analyzing documents regarding protein-protein interaction (PPI) extraction ([15]). PPI is a problem of the BioNLP field that is intensively studied. The remaining one (WEB), used in [21], consists of trees representing web-page accesses by users, and the annotation is based on whether the user is from a .edu site or not. Table 2 describes the basic features of these datasets. The datasets of AIMED, BIOINFER and WEB are reduced in number of instances included from the original datasets, because the run-time was impractically large when we used the original datasets.

**Table 2.** Datasets: Number of examples, averaged sizes and averaged heights of trees.

| Dataset | AIMED | BIOINFER | COLON | CYSTIC | HPRD50 | IEPA | LEUKEMIA | LLL | SYNTACTIC | WEB |
|---|---|---|---|---|---|---|---|---|---|---|
| Examples | 200 | 200 | 134 | 160 | 433 | 817 | 479 | 330 | 225 | 500 |
| Positive | 42 | 54 | 87 | 89 | 163 | 335 | 177 | 164 | 112 | 113 |
| Negative | 158 | 146 | 47 | 71 | 270 | 482 | 302 | 166 | 113 | 387 |
| Size | 94.4 | 116.4 | 8.4 | 8.3 | 84.4 | 105.2 | 13.5 | 106.4 | 19.7 | 12.0 |
| Height | 13.5 | 14.1 | 5.6 | 5.0 | 12.7 | 13.6 | 7.4 | 14.3 | 6.5 | 4.3 |

**Method of Comparison.** We compare the mapping distances determined by Table 1 with respect to the classification performance when they are used with with the $k$-nearest-neighborhood ($k$-NN) classification. To be specific, we ran a $k$-NN classifier in a ten-fold cross validation setting, and computed confusion matrices increasing the value of $k$ from one to 20 by one. The accuracy performance is measured by the accuracy score, which is defined by $\frac{\text{TP+TN}}{\text{TP+FP+FN+TN}}$, and the F-measure, which is defined by $\frac{2\text{TP}}{2\text{TP+FP+FN}}$: TP stands for *True Positive* and indicates the number of positive examples rightly predicted to be positive by a classifier; FP stands for *False Positive* and indicates the number of negative examples wrongly predicted to be positive; FN stands for *False Negative* and indicates the number of positive examples wrongly predicted to be negative; TN stands for *True Negative* and indicates the number of negative examples rightly predicted to be negative.

**Comparison Between Exact Match and Flexible Match Mapping Distances.** The ten charts of Fig. 9 exhibit the accuracy scores of the 16 mapping distances whose $\gamma$ values are 1 and $\infty$. Figure 10 compares the same distances with respect to the F-measure scores.

Table 3 shows the mapping distances that have shown the best scores for accuracy and F-measure for the datasets described in Table 2. We should notice the following from the table.

1. The best tree mapping distance with respect to accuracy scores is always identical to the best with respect to F-measure.
2. All of the best distances require the exact match of vertex labels, that is, $\gamma = \infty$.
3. The values of $k$ that have yielded the best scores are mostly one. In fact, 16 of the 24 values of $k$ shown in Table 3 are one.

On the other hand, the best shape types vary across the sparse subpath (`pt`), the agreement subtree (`at`), the sparse subforest (`ft`), the separable forest (`st`)

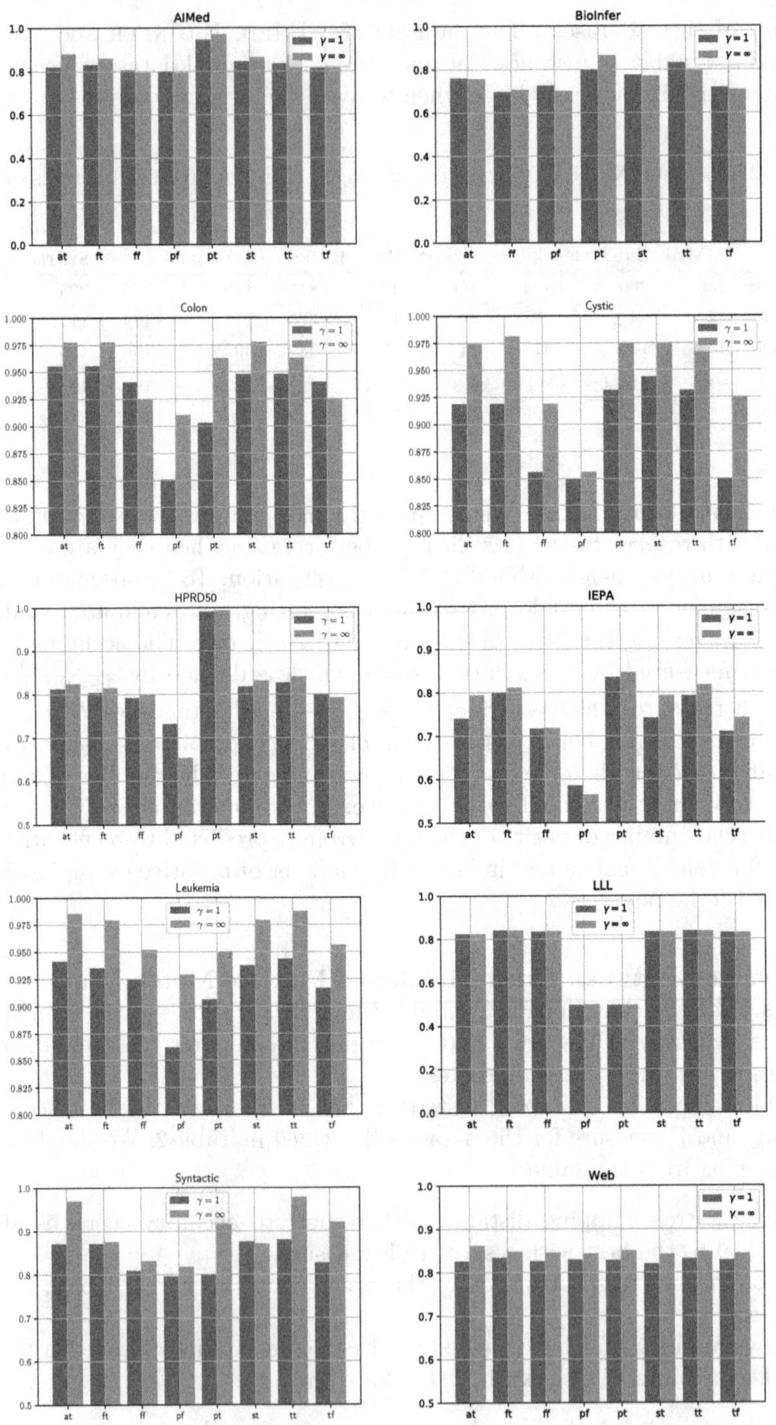


**Fig. 9.** Best accuracy scores across $1 \leq k \leq 20$: comparison between $\gamma = 1$ and $\gamma = \infty$.

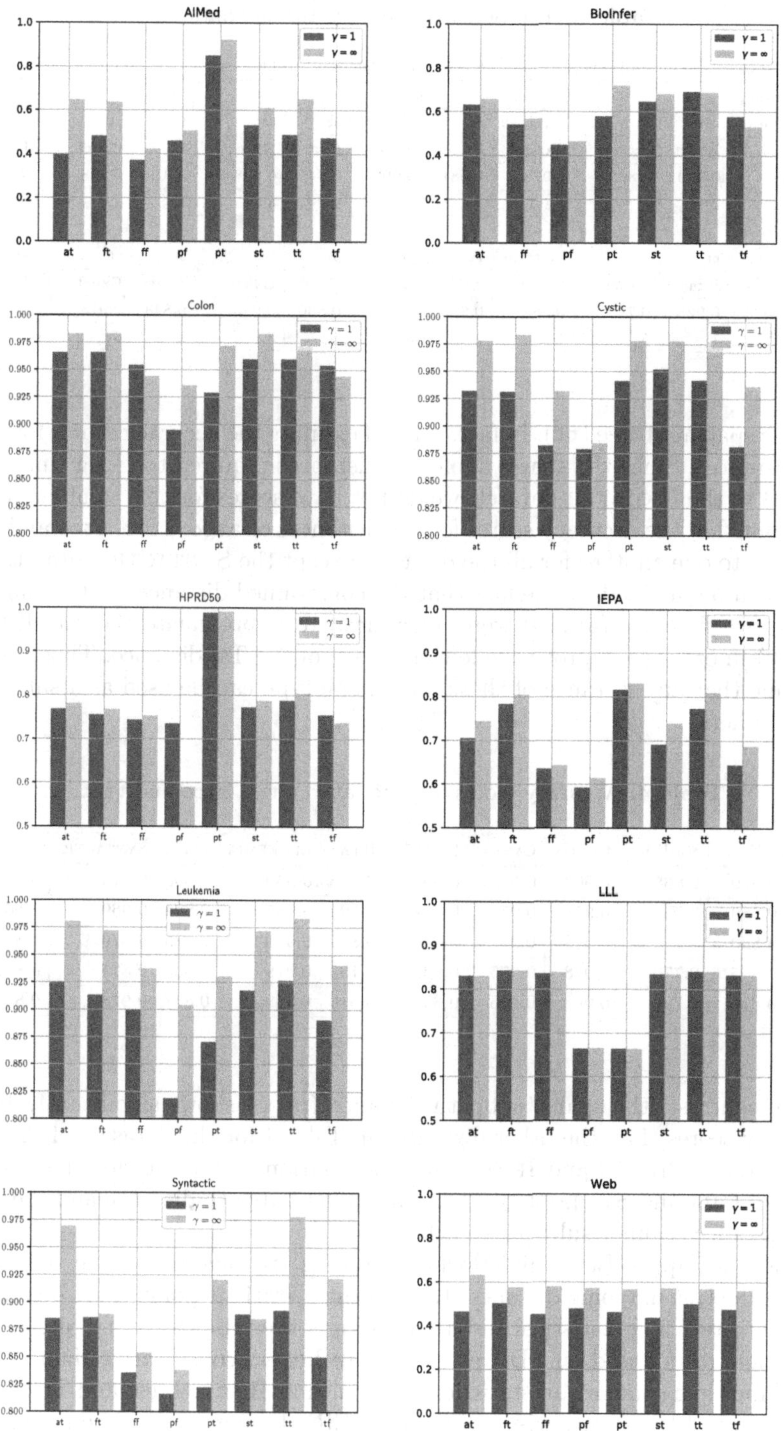


**Fig. 10.** Best F-measure scores across $1 \leq k \leq 20$: comparison between $\gamma = 1$ and $\gamma = \infty$.

**Table 3.** The best distances for the ten datasets.

| Distance | AIMED | BIOINFER | COLON | CYSTIC | HPRD50 | IEPA | LEUKEMIA | LLL | SYNTACTIC | WEB |
|---|---|---|---|---|---|---|---|---|---|---|
| *Accuracy* | | | | | | | | | | |
| Shape | pt | pt | at,ft,st | ft | pt | pt | tt | ft | tt | at |
| Match | Exact | Exact | Exact | Exact | Exact | Exact | Exact | Exact | Exact | Exact |
| Score | 0.970 | 0.865 | 0.978 | 0.981 | 0.993 | 0.846 | 0.988 | 0.839 | 0.978 | 0.862 |
| $k =$ | 1 | 1 | 1,1,1 | 1 | 3 | 1 | 3 | 1 | 3 | 5 |
| *F-Measure* | | | | | | | | | | |
| Shape | pt | pt | at,ft,st | ft | pt | pt | tt | at | tt | at |
| Match | Exact | Exact | Exact | Exact | Exact | Exact | Exact | Exact | Exact | Exact |
| Score | 0.923 | 0.718 | 0.983 | 0.983 | 0.991 | 0.830 | 0.983 | 0.843 | 0.978 | 0.633 |
| $k =$ | 1 | 5 | 1,1,1 | 1 | 3 | 1 | 3 | 1 | 3 | 1 |

and the sparse subtree (`tt`). In fact, Table 4 exhibits the accuracy scores for these five distances. Since the sparse subforest distances required too long time when applied to the BIOINFER dataset, we do not have scores for this combination. It turns out that the accuracy scores for the distances of at∞, ft∞, st∞ and tt∞ are close to one another for all the datasets except the SYNTACTIC dataset. This result can be justified by the fact that the constrained distance (`st1.0`) and the degree-two distance (`at1.0`) were introduced to approximate the Taï distance (`ft1.0`) in order to improve the low efficiency of the Taï distance. Thus, we can presume that any distance of these four shape type can be used as a substitute of the others.

**Table 4.** Accuracy scores of pt∞, at∞, ft∞, st∞ and tt∞.

| | AIMED | BioInfer | COLON | CYSTIC | HPRD50 | IEPA | LEUKEMIA | LLL | SYNTACTIC | WEB |
|---|---|---|---|---|---|---|---|---|---|---|
| pt∞ | 0.970 | 0.865 | 0.963 | 0.975 | 0.993 | 0.846 | 0.950 | 0.500 | 0.916 | 0.850 |
| at∞ | 0.880 | 0.755 | 0.978 | 0.975 | 0.824 | 0.794 | 0.985 | 0.824 | 0.969 | 0.862 |
| ft∞ | 0.860 | – | 0.978 | 0.981 | 0.815 | 0.812 | 0.979 | 0.839 | 0.876 | 0.848 |
| st∞ | 0.865 | 0.770 | 0.978 | 0.975 | 0.831 | 0.793 | 0.979 | 0.833 | 0.871 | 0.842 |
| tt∞ | 0.875 | 0.795 | 0.963 | 0.975 | 0.841 | 0.818 | 0.988 | 0.837 | 0.978 | 0.848 |

By contrast, the sparse subpath distance (pt∞) shows significantly better accuracy scores than the other distances in Table 4 for the datasets of AIMED, BIOINFER, HPRD50 and IEPA, while the relation is opposite for the datasets of LEUKEMIA and SYNTACTIC. Thus, the sparse subpath distance and the other four distances cannot substitute each other.

Also, we apply Benjamini-Hochberg test [1] to investigate the differences among the tree mapping distances tested from a statistic point view. Benjamini-Hochberg test is a statistical test that controls the false discovery rate (FDR). Statistical tests based on FDR are known to be less conservative than conventional multiple comparison statistical tests such as Hommel test and Tukey test, which control the family-wise error rate (FER). Benjamini-Hochberg test computes certain probability-like values called $q$-values from $p$-values of more than two null hypothesis. In the same way as multiple comparison tests, the test rejects the null hypotheses whose $q$-values are smaller than a given significance level.

In our experiments, we calculate averaged ranks and $p$-values of the tree mapping distances tested by Wilcoxon's signed rank test, and define 15 null hypotheses, each of which claims that the classification performance of one of the distances tested is identical to that of the distance whose averaged rank is the best. Table 5 shows the averaged ranks of the 16 distances, and the sparse subtree exact match distance (tt∞) turns out to be the best. Then, we determine the tt∞ distance as a control and compute the $q$-values of Benjamini-Hochberg test computed based on $p$-values of Wilcoxon test. With a significance level of 0.01, we can reject the ten null hypotheses for all the distances that are displayed to the right of the st∞ distance. Consequently, Benjamini-Hochberg test conclude that the tt∞ distance statistically significantly outperforms the distances of tt1.0, ft1.0, ff∞, st1.0, tf∞, at1.0, tf1.0, ff1.0, pf∞ and pf1.0.

**Table 5.** Results of Benjamini-Hochberg test.

| | tt∞ | pt∞ | at∞ | ft∞ | pt1.0 | st∞ | tt1.0 | ft1.0 | ff∞ | st1.0 | tf∞ | at1.0 | tf1.0 | ff1.0 | pf∞ | pf1.0 |
|---|---|---|---|---|---|---|---|---|---|---|---|---|---|---|---|---|
| Rank | 3.1 | 4.3 | 4.1 | 4.0 | 9.6 | 5.4 | 7.1 | 8.0 | 9.9 | 8.6 | 8.7 | 10.3 | 12.3 | 12.4 | 13.3 | 14.8 |
| $q$-val. | CTRL | 1.0 | 0.53 | 0.34 | 0.34 | 0.10 | 0.01 | 0.01 | 0.01 | 0.008 | 0.008 | 0.008 | 0.008 | 0.008 | 0.008 | 0.008 |

The result of the statistical test supports the aforementioned observation. In fact, The test does not deny the possibility that the tt∞, at∞, ft∞ and st∞ distances are mutually replaceable. On the other hand, although the pt1.0 distance was not discussed in the previous observation, the $p$-value of Wilcoxon test between the pt∞ and pt1.0 distances is as large as 0.496, and hence, the pt1.0 distance can also substitute for the pt∞ distance.

In summary, we can draw the conclusion that, if we have to focus on a small number of tree mapping distances, and if we want to obtain good classification results at least when using a $k$-nearest-neighborhood classifier, we should try the sparse subtree exact match distance (tt∞) and the sparse subpath exact match distance (pt∞) first. Since the time complexity of the fastest algorithm to compute tt∞ is a cubic function of the size of input trees, to our best knowledge, and also since that for at∞ is quadratic, it could be a good idea to try at∞ instead of tt∞.

**Effect of $\gamma$.** As we saw in Table 3, all the tree mapping distances that have shown the best scores with respect to the accuracy measure and the F-measure require exact match of vertex labels, that is, $\gamma = \infty$. This tendency holds generally. In fact, we can see in Fig. 9 that an exact match distance outperforms the associated flexible match distance for 56 combinations of dataset and distance, while a flexible distance outperforms the associated rigid distance for only 13 combinations. The $p$-value of the $\chi^2$ test turns out to be $6.8 \times 10^{-7}$, and we can

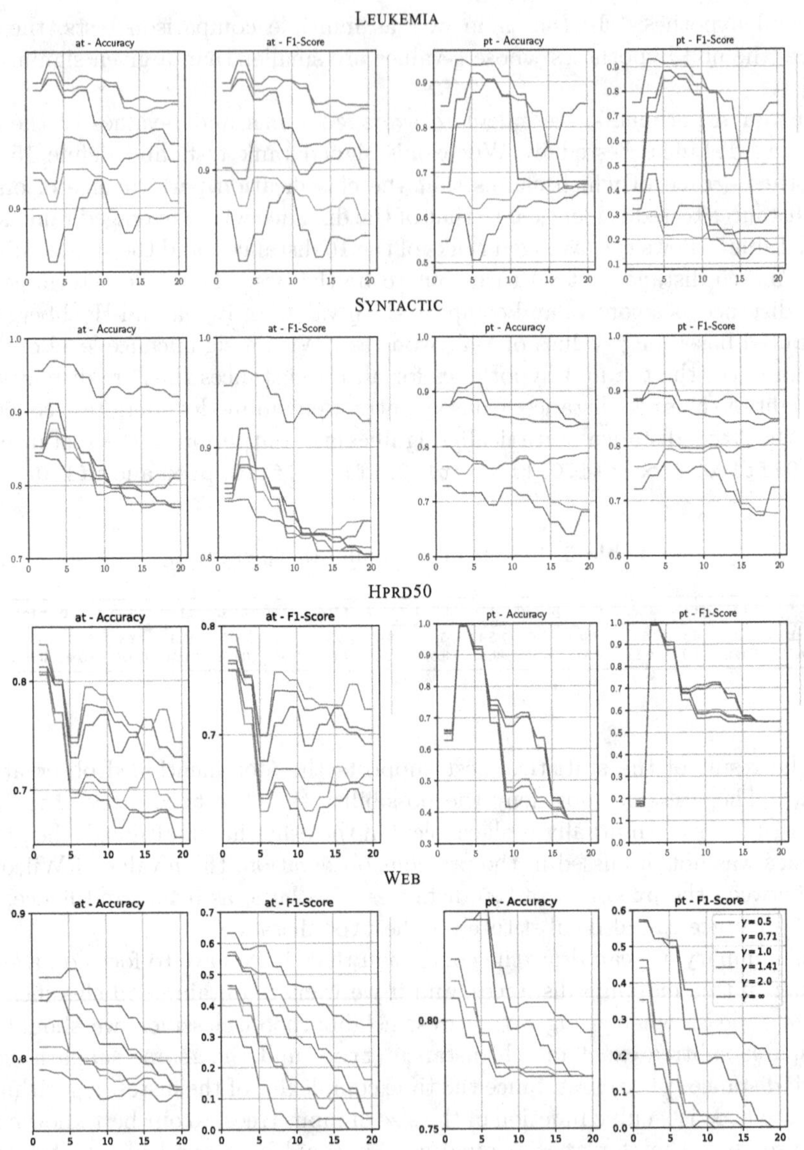


**Fig. 11.** Accuracy and F-measure scores for $\gamma = 2^{-1}$ (blue), $\gamma = 2^{-0.5}$ (yellow), $\gamma = 2^{0.0}$ (green), $\gamma = 2^{0.5}$ (red), $\gamma = 2^{1.0}$ (purple) and $\gamma = \infty$ (brown). The $x$ axis represents $k$ of a $k$-NN classifier. (Color figure online)

conclude that this difference is statistically significant. With respect to comparison in the F-measure scores, the number of combinations where exact match distances outperform flexible match distances increases to 47 as seen in Fig. 10.

Figure 11 shows how accuracy and F-measure scores change as the value of $\gamma$ increases for four typical datasets of LEUKEMIA, SYNTACTIC, HPRD50 and WEB. For the value of $\gamma$, we tested $\gamma = 2^{-1.0} = 0.5, 2^{-0.5} = 0.71, 2^{0.0} = 1.0, 2^{0.5} = 1.41, 2^{1.0} = 2.0$ and $\infty$. We note that $\gamma = \infty$ means the exact match of vertex labels.

Except for the combination of HPRD50 and the sparse subpath shape type, we see that the scores increase as the value of $\gamma$ increases, and the scores for the exact match of vertex labels, that is, when $\gamma = \infty$ are the highest. For the combination of HPRD50 and `at`, the best accuracy and F-measure score are obtained when $\gamma = 2.0$, and the scores for $\gamma = \infty$ follow.

## 5 Conclusion

We have extended the notion of the mapping distance initially introduced in [18] and have incorporated a hyper-parameter that controls the likelihood of occurrence of mismatch of components. The most important advantage of the mapping distance consists in the fact that mapping distances can be defined for arbitrary finite sets and can be engineered within a consistent framework regardless of structures of data. Moreover, by adding a certain hyper-parameter, we can have a method to improve the performance of classification and clustering when used with distance-based classification and clustering algorithms. To verify the effectiveness of the mapping distance, we take an application to ordered rooted trees as an example and have designed two parameters that consistently describe tree mapping distances. Through more intensive experiments than conducted in [18], we have identified two important mapping distances that exhibited excellent classification accuracy in our experiments when it is used with a $k$-nearest-neighborhood algorithm. These distances are novel and have not been discussed in the literature before.

**Acknowledgement.** This work was supported by JSPS KAKENHI Grant Number JP17H007623 and JP16K12491.

## References

1. Benjamini, Y., Hochberg, Y.: Controlling the false discovery rate: a practical and powerful approach to multiple testing. J. Roy. Stat. Soc. B **57**(1), 289–300 (1995)
2. Bille, P.: A survey on tree edit distance and related problems. Theoret. Comput. Sci. **337**(1–3), 217–239 (2005)
3. Collins, M., Duffy, N.: Convolution kernels for natural language. In: Advances in Neural Information Processing Systems 14 [Neural Information Processing Systems: Natural and Synthetic NIPS, vol. 2001], pp. 625–632. MIT Press, Boca Raton (2001)
4. Demaine, E.D., Mozes, S., Rossman, B., Weimann, O.: An optimal decomposition algorithm for tree edit distance. ACM Trans. Algo. **6**, 2 (2006)
5. Dulucq, S., Touzet, H.: Analysis of tree edit distance algorithms. In: The 14th Annual Symposium on Combinatorial Pattern Matching (CPM), pp. 83–95 (2003)

6. Hashimoto, K., Goto, S., Kawano, S., Aoki-Kinoshita, K.F., Ueda, N.: KEGG as a glycome informatics resource. Glycobiology **16**, 63R–70R (2006)
7. Kao, M.Y., Lam, T.W., Sung, W.K., Ting, H.F.: An even faster and more unifying algorithm for comparing trees via unbalanced bipartite matchings, July 2007
8. Klein, P.N.: Computing the edit-distance between unrooted ordered trees. In: Bilardi, G., Italiano, G.F., Pietracaprina, A., Pucci, G. (eds.) ESA 1998. LNCS, vol. 1461, pp. 91–102. Springer, Heidelberg (1998). https://doi.org/10.1007/3-540-68530-8_8
9. Kuboyama, T., Shin, K., Miyahara, T., Yasuda, H.: A theoretical analysis of alignment and edit problems for trees. In: Coppo, M., Lodi, E., Pinna, G.M. (eds.) ICTCS 2005. LNCS, vol. 3701, pp. 323–337. Springer, Heidelberg (2005). https://doi.org/10.1007/11560586_26
10. Levenshtein, V.I.: Binary codes capable of correcting deletions, insertions, and reversals. Sov. Phys. Dokl. **10**(8), 707–710 (1966)
11. Lu, C.L., Su, Z.-Y., Tang, C.Y.: A new measure of edit distance between labeled trees. In: Wang, J. (ed.) COCOON 2001. LNCS, vol. 2108, pp. 338–348. Springer, Heidelberg (2001). https://doi.org/10.1007/3-540-44679-6_37
12. Moschitti, A.: Example data for tree kernels in SVM-light. http://disi.unitn.it/moschitti/Tree-Kernel.htm
13. Neuhaus, M., Bunke, H.: Bridging the gap between graph edit distance and kernel machines. World Scientific (2007)
14. Pawlik, M., Augsten, N.: Rted: a robust algorithm for the tree edit distance. Proc. VLDB Endowment. **5**, 334–345 (2011)
15. Pyysalo, S., Airola, A., Heimonen, J., Bjorne, J., Ginter, F., Salakoski, T.: Comparative analysis of five protein-protein interaction corpora. BMC Bioinform. **9**(S–3), S6 (2008)
16. Richter, T.: A new measure of the distance between ordered trees and its applications. Tech. Rep. 85166-CS, Dept. of Computer Science, Univ. of Bonn (1997). http://citeseer.ist.psu.edu/richter97new.html
17. Shin, K.: Tree edit distance and maximum agreement subtree. Inf. Process. Lett. **115**(1), 69–73 (2015). https://doi.org/10.1016/j.ipl.2014.09.002
18. Shin, K., Niiyama, T.: The mapping distance - a generalization of the edit distance - and its application to trees. In: Proceedings of the 10th International Conference on Agent and Artificial Intelligence ICAART 2018, vol. 2, pp. 266–275. SciTePress (2018)
19. Taï, K.C.: The tree-to-tree correction problem. J. ACM **26**(3), 422–433 (1979)
20. Wang, J.T.L., Zhang, K.: Finding similar consensus between trees: an algorithm and a distance hierarchy. Pattern Recognit. **34**, 127–137 (2001)
21. Zaki, M.J., Aggarwal, C.C.: XRules: an effective algorithm for structural classification of XML data. Mach. Learn. **62**, 137–170 (2006)
22. Zhang, K.: Algorithms for the constrained editing distance between ordered labeled trees and related problems. Pattern Recognit. **28**(3), 463–474 (1995)
23. Zhang, K., Shasha, D.: Simple fast algorithms for the editing distance between trees and related problems. SIAM J. Comput. **18**(6), 1245–1262 (1989)
24. Zhang, K., Wang, J.T.L., Shasha, D.: On the editing distance between undirected acyclic graphs. Int. J. Found. Comput. Sci. **7**(1), 43–58 (1996). http://citeseer.ist.psu.edu/article/zhang95editing.html

# Aspectual Classifications: Use of Raters' Associations and Co-occurrences of Verbs for Aspectual Classification in German

Michael Richter[1(✉)], Jürgen Hermes[2], and Claes Neuefeind[2]

[1] Department of Automatic Language Processing, Leipzig University, Augustusplatz 10, Leipzig, Germany
richter@informatik.uni-leipzig.de
[2] Institute for Digital Humanities, Cologne University, Albertus-Magnus-Platz, Cologne, Germany
{jhermes,c.neuefeind}@uni-koeln.de
http://www.dh.uni-koeln.de

**Abstract.** The present study examines the results of experiments on the automatic classification of German verbs into five aspectual classes [1]: An experiment within an unsupervised framework based on associations of raters [1] and a couple of experiments within a distributional framework, i.e. in window-based and in a subcategorization-frame-based approach [2]. We compare the predictive power of raters' associations against two types of verbal cooccurrences: i. pure, unstructured co-occurrences and ii. linguistically motivated, well defined co-occurrences which we denote as *informed distributional framework*. We observed substantial (unsupervised) and excellent (supervised) agreements with a Gold Standard classification.

**Keywords:** Machine learning · Classification
Aspectual verb classes · Unsupervised learning · Supervised learning

## 1 Introduction

This paper presents a comparison between aspectual classifications based on raters' associations [1] that is, user based data, and from corpus-based data in a distributional framework ([3], see also [4–8]), i.e. usage based data. Linguistic and philosophical point of departure is the Vendlerian quadripartition [9]. The distributional study is reported in [2].

The primary motivation for undertaking this research is the (almost complete) lack of studies on the automatic aspectual classification in typological research on German. The motivation for utilizing raters' associations for classification tasks are the studies of [10,11] and [12], which demonstrated the use of raters' associations for discriminating, albeit not aspectual, verb classes. Our research question is thus whether human associations can be utilized in order to


J. van den Herik and A. P. Rocha (Eds.): ICAART 2018, LNAI 11352, pp. 467–491, 2019.
https://doi.org/10.1007/978-3-030-05453-3_22

enclose aspectual classes of verbs and whether they support the results in [2], which provide strong evidence that aspectual verb classes can be inferred from linguistic data.

By comparing classifications both from an unsupervised and a supervised approach, i.e. cluster analysis of raters' associations and classification of the distributional data by a Support Vector Machine classifier [13], we aim to assess the strengths and weaknesses of the approaches and hope to get additional evidence for the aspectual verb classes in [1].

The distributional approach [2] is twofold, consisting of an aspectual verb classification within a framework which utilizes subcategorization frames of verbs (henceforth *informed distributional* framework), extracting classified nouns in the argument positions of verbs [14,15] accompained by an aspectual verb classification in a *purely* distributional framework considering co-occurrences of all types.

In [2] we posed the question of whether a classification in a linguistically well grounded (or *informed*) distributional framework would yield better classification results than a classification in a purely distributional framework and we compared these results to a classification which is based on raters' associations. The purely distributional approach employs verb vectors of very high dimensionality consisting of a considerably higher amount of linguistic material than the vectors used within the *informed* distributional setup or when utilizing human associations. At a first glance, this could be a point in favor of the *purely* distributional framework. On the other hand, the studies of [14] and [15] with sets of 35 and 95 German verbs, respectively, achieved promising classification results within an *informed* distributional framework. A classification inspired by Vendler was used as Gold Standard. This classification is the extension of the Vendlerian typology through the addition of one class (henceforth 'Vendler + 1'): The additional aspectual class *accomplishments with an affected subject*. The studies mentioned above (see also [1]) provide evidence for this class. The *accomplishments with an affected subject* class differs from the classical *accomplishments* in the semantic role of the subject. Instead of exclusively assigning the agent role to the subject, the subject in the *accomplishments with an affected subject* class is assigned both a patient role and an agent role. Consider verbs such as *drink*, where an agent subject also has the semantic properties of a patient since the drinker-agent is affected and undergoes a change of state (temporarily puts on weight, gets drunk etc.)[1].

In the present study, we exclusively focus on lexical aspect that is, aspectual properties of bare verbs (or *the fundamental aspectual category* in the terminology of [17]). Thus, aspectual properties of sentences and VPs as results of aspectual coercion or aspectual shift, respectively, are not subject of this study.

[1] [16] refers to these semantic roles as *volitional undergoers*.

It is rather our aim to predict the aspectual classes of verbs from their contexts.[2] The aspectual classification of verb classes from contexts might give indications how language learners manage to build up aspectual verb classes in their mental lexicon. From that perspective, research on verb classes is vital due to their relevance for the processing of natural language by human beings and, in addition, for the theory of natural language acquisition (see [20–26]). Research on aspectual classes is of particular relevance because it models the temporal and causal structures of events (see [9,27–31]). Theory-driven work by [32] and experimental studies by [33] and [17] highlight the potential of aspect for classifying linguistic units such as verbs and documents.

## 2 Related Work

There are hardly any studies which address automatic classifications of the complete Vendlerian typology, let alone comparing different types of distributional approaches. By focusing on tense, [34] determined gradual state-properties of verbs. [33] and [17] classified verbs into states and events using temporal and modal indicators from contexts such as temporal adverbs, tense forms and manner and evaluation adverbs. [35] presented an automatic classification of the four Vendlerian aspect classes in Italian utilizing, amongst others, syntactic and semantic features of the arguments of the target verbs and verb tense. The authors, however, aimed at modelling aspectual shift and consequently focus on aspectual properties of sentences, decomposing the components of sentential event types. [36] presented an automatic classification of aspectual verb classes in English using contextual features including tense forms, albeit only distinguishing between stative, dynamic and mixed type verbs.

Studies on the automatic assignment of non-aspectual verb classes within a distributional framework from [37–42] and [43] for German verbs provide corpus based evidence that argument frames, syntactic subcategorization information and, in addition, aspect [39] are reliable predictors. In addition, studies by [10, 11] and [12] brought to light that plausible subcategorization frames of verbs could be derived from the associations and, in addition that associations can help to uncover semantic concepts and detect semantic, sometimes non-classical relations between verbs. The conclusion is that associations of humans to verbs provide a base for a classification of verbs.

[2] As an example of aspectual coercion, consider an atelic verb such as *walk*, which can be combined with a PP denoting a destination as in *he walks to the store* and expressing a telic event. The sentence *walks to the store* is no longer an activity, instead, it is an accomplishment. Aspectual coercion can also be triggered by quantification [18]. A prototypical accomplishment verb such as *kill* can occur in a sentence expressing an activity, as in *he is killing carpet moths* (note the present progressive form of the verb) which stands classical tests of activities, e.g. *he is killing carpet moths for an hour, permanently/forever*. The direct object is a bare plural, expressing cumulative objects [19] which combine well with atelic verbs. With a quantized direct object [18] however, the sentence is clearly telic: *he kills two carpet moths in one hour/*for hours*.

## 3 Vendler's Aspectual Verb Classes

[9] defines four aspectual classes[3]: *States*, *activities*, *achievements* and *accomplishments*, based on the time schemata of verbs and verb phrases. He gives the following illustrative examples [9, 149]: Activities such as *A was running at time t* are true if the instantiation of t is "on a time stretch throughout A was running". An accomplishment such as *A was drawing the circle at t* is true if "t is on the time stretch in which A drew that circle". An achievement such as *A won the race between $t_1$ and $t_2$* means that the time at which A won that race is between $t_1$ and $t_2$; and a statement such as *A loves somebody from $t_1$ and $t_2$* means that "at any instant between $t_1$ and $t_2$ A loved that person".

In (1) below we give [46]'s description of the four Vendler classes and in addition a description of the additional class *accomplishments with an affected subject* which extends the description of the accomplishment class with a subject variable. In line with [9,47], and [27,46] distinguished the event types *process*, *state* and *transition* (see also [48,49] and [50]). The latter is a function from any event type to its opposite. For instance, *x closes the door* expresses a transition from an event type $e_1$, the open door, to an event type $e_2$, the closed door, by acting of agent x and $e_2$ is the opposite of $e_1$ ($\neg e1$). The combinatorial variations within the three event types *process*, *state* and *transition* allows for the formal description of the complete Vendlerian typology.

The abbreviation 'LCS' in (1) means the *lexical conceptual structure* which gives a decomposition of predicates ([28,46,51,52]). Hence, LCS is the minimal decomposed event structure of verbs.

(1) **Accomplishments**

$ES:\ \ process \xrightarrow{transition} state$
$LCS':[act(x,y)\&\neg Q(y)] \quad [Q(y)]$
$LCS: cause([act(x,y)], become(Q(y)))$

**Achievements**

$ES:\ \ process \xrightarrow{transition} state$
$LCS':[\neg P(y)] \quad [P(y)]$
$LCS: become(P(y))$

**Activities**

$ES:\ \ process$
$LCS':[act(x)]$
$LCS: act(x)$

[3] The Vendlerian quadripartition has been modified and extended: [27] added *degree achievements*, [44] added *semelfactices*, [45] in contrast defined a tripartition consisting of *states*, *processes* and *events*.

**States**
$ES:\quad state$
$LCS': [Q(x)]$
$LCS: Q(x)$

**Accomplishments with an affected subject**
$ES:\quad process \xrightarrow{transition} state$
$LCS': [act(x,y) \& \neg P(x) \& \neg Q(y)] \quad [P(x) \& Q(y)]$
$LCS: cause([act(x,y)], become(P(x), become(Q(y))))$

The classes *Accomplishments* and *accomplishments with an affected subject* can be interpreted as a combination of *activities* and *achievements*. The latter express a result, the former a result preceded by an activity. [53] gives a slightly different description of the *achievements* class: he formulates a transition from the event type *point* instead of *process* to *state* where *point* is an atomic event whose internal temporal structure (if it may have any) is ignored.[4]

# 4 Methodology

## 4.1 Raters' Associations

Our first approach of an automatic aspectual verb classification utilizes associations of raters [1]. The question was whether the "typical", i.e. most frequent associations are typical for the classes of the stimulus verbs.

35 undergraduates of German language studies at Münster University (Germany) participated in an association test. The participants performed an online test on 35 German verbs [1] implemented with the open source software *OrVis* [54]. On the screen a verb was shown in its infinitive form and the participants were asked to associate five verbs to the stimulus. It was possible to type in a 'x' in case a participant could not find an association. Six stimulus verbs were presented to each participant. There was no time limit. 1100 ratings and 107 non-associations were given in total. About 71% of the associations were idiosyncratic that is, they occurred just once, and associations were given for 30 verbs in total. Since the lowest number of associations assigned to a verb was 4, we took the four most frequent associations of each stimulus verb. In case of ties, i.e. multiple associations with equal frequencies, we considered all of them. Each association was manually assigned to a verb class from the classes *states*, *accomplishments*, *accomplishments with an affected subject*, *achievements* and *activities*. i.e. Vendler + 1. The manual assignment of verbs to aspect classes was not a hard task since the associated verbs predominantly had the typical distinguishing properties of the five aspectual verb classes. In Fig. 1 an example from the test with the accomplishment stimulus verb *herstellen* 'produce' is given.

[4] Consider the achievement verb *find*. According to [53] the event of finding has a resultant state, the finding itself however is an atomic event, ignoring a possible complex event structure consisting for instance of discovering something on the ground, taking a decision to pick it up, bending down etc.

| A | B |
|---|---|
| **Zeilenbeschriftungen** | **Anzahl von Probanden ID** |
| **herstellen** | **35** |
| anfertigen | 1 |
| bauen | 2 |
| erbauen | 1 |
| errichten | 1 |
| erzeugen | 1 |
| fabrizieren | 2 |
| hämmern | 1 |
| machen | 8 |
| produzieren | 14 |
| reüssieren | 1 |
| stricken | 1 |
| x | 2 |

**Fig. 1.** The associations of the accomplishment stimulus verb *herstellen* 'to produce'. The most frequently associated verbs (*produzieren* 'to produce', *machen* 'to make', *fabrizieren* 'to produce' and *bauen* 'to build') clearly exhibit properties of accomplishment verbs.

All associations clearly belong to the same semantic area like *herstellen* 'produce' and can therefore unambiguously be classified as accomplishments.

The verbs' vectors are constituted by the weighted values of the associations using the TF-IDF measure [55], given in (1):

$$w_{i,j} = t_i f_j \times log\frac{N}{n_i} \tag{1}$$

When applied to the data in the association study, $t_f$ is the frequency of judges of an associated verb to a stimulus verb, $N$ is the total number of verbs and $n$ is the number of verbs co-occurring with the associated verb. Each verb is represented as a 35-dimensional vector providing seven positions for each of the aspectual classes (Vendler + 1).

As a second example, Fig. 2 shows the associations for the stimulus verb *existieren* 'to exist'. The most frequent associations are *sein* 'to be', $TF\text{-}IDFvalue$ : .89; *leben* 'to live', $TF - IDFvalue$ : .42; *bestehen* 'to exist', $TF - IDFvalue$ : .11, *da sein/dasein* 'to be there', $TF - IDFvalue$ : .11; *vorhanden sein* 'to be available', $TF - IDFvalue$ : .11.

### 4.2 Corpus Data

In [2] we addressed the question of whether informed distributional methods perform better with regards to the prediction of aspectual verb classes than

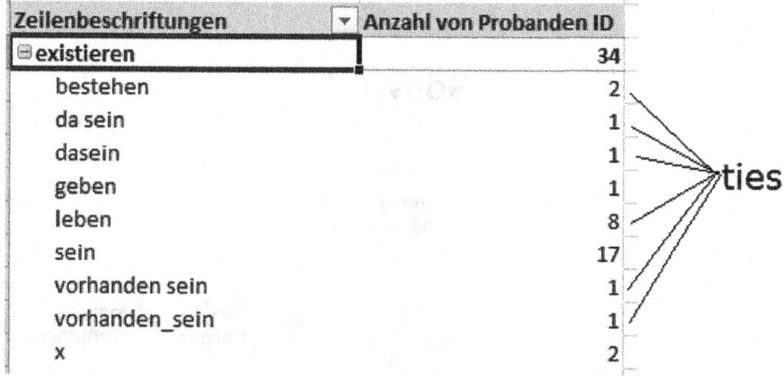


**Fig. 2.** The associations of the accomplishment stimulus verb *existieren* 'to exist' with ties. The most frequently associated verbs (*sein* 'to be', *leben* 'to live', *da sein/dasein* 'to be there' and *vorhanden sein* 'to be available') clearly exhibit properties of accomplishment verbs.

distributional methods on shallow input. In that study, we tested different workflows to classify a selection of 95 common German verbs taken from [56]. Schumacher defines seven lexical semantic macrofields: *Verben der allgemeinen Existenz* ('verbs of general existence'), *Verben der speziellen Existenz* ('verbs of special existence'), *Verben des sprachlichen Ausdrucks* ('verbs of linguistic expression'), *Verben der Differenz* ('verbs of difference'), *Verben der Relation und des geistigen Handelns* ('verbs of relation and mental processing'), *Verben des Handlungsspielraums* ('verbs of freedom of action') and *Verben der vitalen Bedürfnisse* ('verbs of vital needs'). The macrofields are split into 30 subfields. We chose the verbs randomly from the thirty subfields, the only criterion being the inclusion of every subfield in order to cover the complete semantic range of Schumacher's typology.

Figure 3 (taken from [2]) shows the different analysis workflows of our analyses, starting with raw sentence data taken from the SdeWaC corpus [57] at the top, to sets of classified verbs at the bottom. The different methods are applied in four experiments, each employing an individual process chain combining a different set of components. The four experiments are depicted as varying paths in Fig. 3, all starting at the top (SdeWaC) but ending with four different sets of verb classes at the bottom.

An overview showing which method combination is unique in each experiment is given in Table 1 (taken from [2]).

**Table 1.** Combination of workflow elements.

| Combination | – N Cluster | + N Cluster |
|---|---|---|
| – Parsed input | 1 | 2 |
| + Parsed input | 3 | 4 |

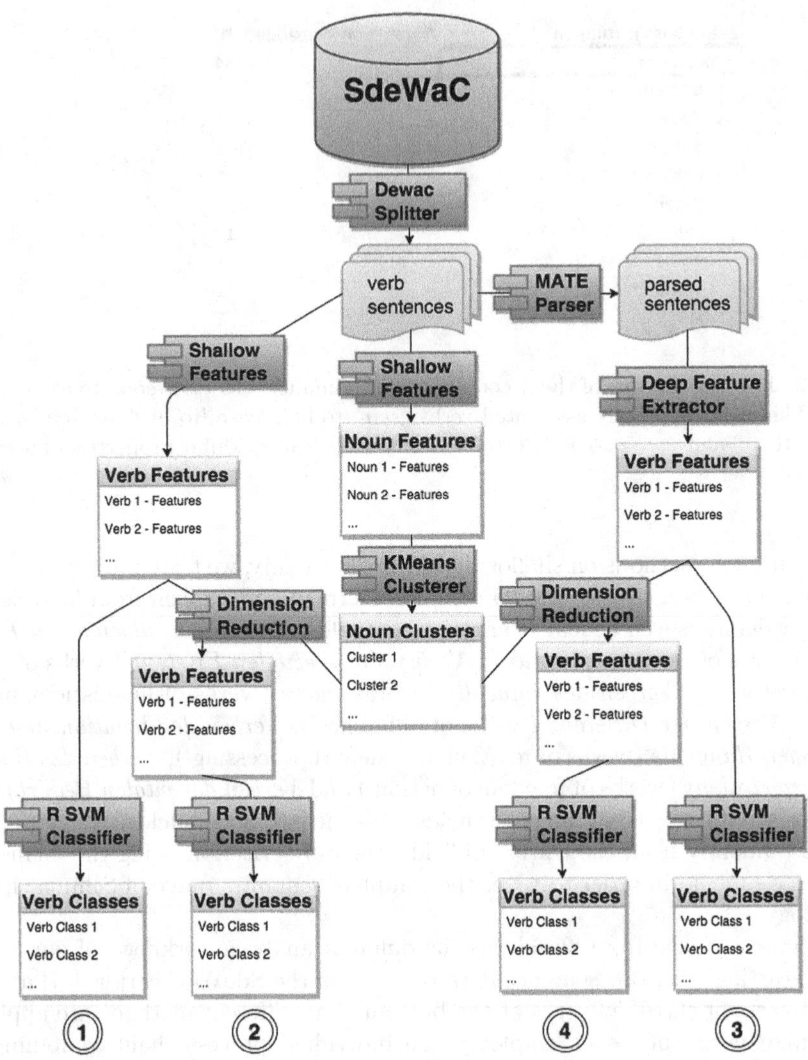


**Fig. 3.** Overview of the complete workflow of all experiments performed in [2]. The experiments were implemented via 4 process chains which can be identified by the numbers at the bottom of the figure. Each process chain uses a different combination of components (see also Table 1 for an overview).

We implemented each process chain on the basis of combined and configurable components within the workflow management tool Tesla[5] so that every experiment performed can be reproduced by other researchers.

[5] Tesla (*T*ext *E*ngineering *S*oftware *LA*boratory), see http://tesla.spinfo.uni-koeln.de is an open source virtual research environment, integrating both a visual editor for conducting text-engineering experiments and a Java IDE for developing software components [58].

For the classification of the 95 verbs, we used a Support Vector Machine classifier [13] with a polynomial kernel. For 35 verbs, we adapted the aspectual classification as the gold standard which was validated in [1], i.e. Vendler + 1, and we assigned 60 verbs to aspectual classes applying the criteria in [1]. We trained the SVM using this aspectual classification as training data and tested it with a 10-fold cross-validation: The data was randomly split into a training and a test set (proportion: 90% training, 10% test set). The classifier was both trained and tested on each of the 10 combinations of training and test set. Thus, in total we obtained 10 sets of class predictions and took the mean accuracy as final result. We used a SVM classifier with a polynomial kernel (which turned out to outperform other kernel types) and a multiclass classifier (instead of training a single classifier per class, we employed just one classifier for the complete set of our aspectual classes.

In the following list we give some examples of the verb classes of the aspectual gold standard classification below; the complete list of all 95 pre-classified verbs used in this study can be found in the appendix.

1. **accomplishments:** *aufbauen* auf ('build on/be based on'), *herstellen* ('produce'), *schneiden* ('cut'), *zersägen* ('saw into pieces'), *verlängern* ('extend'), *mitteilen* ('tell/inform'), *übermitteln* ('communicate/forward'), *verhindern* ('prevent'), *abgrenzen* ('mark off /define'), *verändern* ('change')
2. **accomplishments with affected subject:** *untersuchen* ('examine'), *bedenken* ('consider'), *erörtern* ('debate'), *nachprüfen* ('ascertain/check'), *aufessen* ('eat up'), *essen* ('eat'), *beachten* ('note'), *kaufen* ('buy')
3. **activities:** *laufen* ('walk/run'), *eingehen auf* ('respond to so./sth.'), *hämmern* ('hammer'), *sich orientieren an* ('be geared to') *ansteigen* ('increase'), *fallen* ('fall'), *richten auf* ('direct towards/focus'), *denken* ('think'), *stattfinden* ('take place'), *wachsen* ('grow')
4. **achievements:** *einschlafen* ('fall asleep'), *vergehen* ('go (by)/pass/ diasappear'), *übersehen* ('overlook'), *verlieren* ('lose'), *anfangen* ('begin'), *abweichen* ('deviate')
5. **states:** *existieren* ('exist'), *fehlen* ('lack'), *müssen* ('must'), *halten für* ('take so./sth. for so./sth.'), *folgen aus* ('follow from'), *angehören* ('belong to'), *übereinstimmen* ('agree'), *betreffen* ('concern'), *sein* ('be'), *vorherrschen* ('predominate')

### 4.3 Classification of Verbs Using Co-Occurrence Vectors

The first experiment (marked with 1, left side of Fig. 3) is taken as a benchmark for purely distributional methods: We extracted 2000 sentences for each verb from the SdeWaC corpus and collected the most frequent co-occurrences using the frequency-based heuristics described in [59], simply taking the $k$ most frequent types of our corpus as vector features.[6] The vectors were computed in three different configurations. As a baseline, we first took the 200 most frequently occurring elements (mostly closed class function words such as *und* 'and', *zu* 'to', *weil* 'because/since', etc.), and a context window of size 1 (henceforth 1–200), accepting only the direct neighbors as co-occurrences. In the second configuration, co-occurrences were computed against the 2000 most frequently occurring elements within a fixed context window of 5 items to both sides (henceforth 5–2k). In addition, we employed a positional weighting scheme using the HAL model (*Hyperspace Analogue to Language*, [60]). In a third configuration, we took the 10.000 most frequently occurring words and a window size of 10 words (henceforth 10–10k), again using the HAL-weighting scheme. While the restriction to function words within a narrow window mainly reflects grammar-related distributional properties, the consideration of content words in combination with a broader window and position weighting emphasizes the more semantically oriented aspects of their distribution. The resulting verb vectors were normalized and weighted with the TF-IDF measure before they were passed to the final classification step.

### 4.4 Classification of Verbs Using Co-Occurrence Vectors with Reduced Dimensionality

As a first step towards more informed methods, we restricted the vector features to nominal co-occuurrences (tagged as NN and NE in the *SdeWaC* corpus). In order to reduce the feature space and to increase the allocation density of the vectors, we clustered all of these nominal co-occurrences. At this stage we set foot on path 2 in Fig. 3. Here, we computed co-occurrence vectors based on the same subset of the *SdeWaC* corpus that we used to determine the verb features, again using frequency-based feature selection. The resulting vectors (10–10k) were again weighted by the TF-IDF measure and passed to the cluster analysis.

For cluster analysis we used three different implementations from the *ELKI Data Mining API*[7], namely KmeansLloyd with cluster sizes of $k = 10$.

[6] We decided for the heuristics because of economy considerations (Ockham's razor), giving preference to the simpler method that performs on a par with more complex ones: As [59] show in their paper, performance in tasks like synonym detection is comparable to more sophisticated methods of feature selection, such as taking the most variant elements (see [60]), the most 'reliable' (see [61], or to perform a dimensionality reduction (e.g. by singular value decomposition as done in the LSA model, see [6]).

[7] The open source framework ELKI (Environment for DeveLoping KDD-Applications Supported by Index-Structures) was developed at the LMU Munich, see http://elki.dbs.ifi.lmu.de.

### 4.5 Classification of Verb Vectors with Nominal Fillers and Aspectual Features

For the remaining experiments (paths 3 and 4 in Fig. 3) we preprocessed the sentences from the SdeWaC corpus with the *Mate Dependency Parser*[8] [62] to determine subjects and objects (accusative, dative, and prepositional) for each verb and, in addition, to determine their aspectual features, which [9] suggested as a means of distinguishing aspectual verb classes. To that end we collected structures in the sentences such as adverbial fillers in dependent or governing positions, which distinguish the aspectual behaviors of the verbs being investigated. The aspectual features are:

1. verb in imperative form
2. verb complex with *aufhören/stoppen* ('to stop/to finish') as governing verbs,
3. verb complex with *überzeugen* ('to convince') as governing verb,
4. matrix verb with time adverbials for durations, like *minutenlang* ('for minutes'), *in einer Minute* ('in a minute'),
5. matrix verb with time units, like *Minute* ('minute'), *Jahrhundert* ('century'),
6. matrix verbs with *seit* ('since'), combined with unit of time,
7. matrix verb with adverbials *sorgfältig/mit Sorgfalt* ('careful/with care'),
8. matrix verb with adverbials *absichtlich/mit Absicht* ('on purpose'),
9. matrix verb with adverbials *fast/beinahe* ('almost').

We generated vectors for each feature combination (subjects, direct objects, dative objects, prepositional objects, and adverbials) in order to determine which combination of fillers has the best predictive power concerning the aspectual verb classes defined by Vendler.

### 4.6 Classification of Verb Vectors with Nominal Fillers and Aspectual Features with Reduced Dimensionality

Finally (path 4 in Fig. 3), we combined the informed distributional method based on parsed input with the dimensionality reduction based on cluster analysis. We constructed the verb vectors as described in Sect. 4.3 and clustered the nouns as described in Sect. 4.4. Then we reassembled the verb vectors using the generated noun classes from the noun clustering sub-workflow. The verb vectors could then be reduced to 39 or fewer dimensions (up to nine aspectual features complemented by ten clusters for each argument position).

## 5 Results

First we give the results of the classification based on raters associations. We compared the verbs' vectors by their cosine similarity. For the classes *state*, *accomplishment* and *accomplishment with an affected subject*, mostly verbs of

[8] See: https://code.google.com/p/mate-tools/.

| verb pairs | | cosine | verb pairs | | cosine |
|---|---|---|---|---|---|
| mitteilen - | *übermitteln* | .90 | übermitteln - | *verlängern* | .97 |
| - | *zersägen* | .90 | - | *zersägen* | .97 |
| - | *hämmern* | .90 | - | *hämmern* | .96 |
| - | *herstellen* | .88 | - | eingehen auf | .96 |
| - | eingehen auf | .89 | - | *verhindern* | .95 |
| - | *verlängern* | .87 | - | *herstellen* | .92 |
| - | *schneiden* | .85 | - | *mitteilen* | .90 |
| schneiden - | *zersägen* | .89 | zersägen - | *herstellen* | .98 |
| - | *herstellen* | .88 | - | *übermitteln* | .97 |
| - | *übermitteln* | .88 | - | *hämmern* | .96 |
| - | *hämmern* | .87 | - | *verlängern* | .96 |
| - | *mitteilen* | .85 | - | *verhindern* | .95 |
| - | eingehen auf | .85 | - | eingehen auf | .92 |
| hämmern - | eingehen auf | .97 | verhindern - | *verlängern* | .99 |
| - | *verlängern* | .97 | - | *zersägen* | .95 |
| - | *übermitteln* | .96 | - | *übermitteln* | .95 |
| - | *zersägen* | .96 | - | *hämmern* | .95 |
| - | *verhindern* | .95 | - | eingehen auf | .94 |
| - | *herstellen* | .92 | - | *herstellen* | .87 |
| verlängern - | *verhindern* | .99 | herstellen - | *zersägen* | .98 |
| - | eingehen auf | .97 | - | *übermitteln* | .92 |
| - | *übermitteln* | .97 | - | *hämmern* | .92 |
| - | *hämmern* | .97 | - | *verlängern* | .88 |
| - | *zersägen* | .96 | - | *mitteilen* | .88 |
| - | *herstellen* | .88 | - | *schneiden* | .88 |

**Fig. 4.** Verb pairs and their cosine values within the class *Accomplishments*.

the same class as the stimulus verbs have the highest cosine values. This also holds (albeit to a slightly lower degree) for the *achievement* class. The *activity* class was distracted by associations of different aspectual classes.

First, the cosine values of the verb pairs within the *accomplishment* class are given in Fig. 4. The verbs inside the boxes and in italics belong to the same verb class as the stimulus verb.

The accomplishments form a coherent group. To each target verb, almost exclusively verbs from the same verb class are assigned. In addition, the cosine values are mostly very high. Only the activity verb *eingehen auf* 'to respond to so./sth.' falls out of the line of the cosine lists. Since this verb achieves high cosine values with almost all accomplishment verbs our manual classification as an activity verb is clearly not confirmed by the raters. Figure 5 below displays the cosine lists of the class *accomplishments with an affected subject*:

Again, the target verbs show the highest cosine values with verbs from their own class. The cosine values are constantly high, in most cases clearly above .90. An exception is *erörtern* 'to debate'. Although the highest cosine value is held by *aufessen* 'to eat up', which is an *accomplishment with affected subject*-verb as

| verb pairs | | cosine | verb pairs | | cosine |
|---|---|---|---|---|---|
| untersuchen - | *nachprüfen* | .99 | nachprüfen - | *untersuchen* | .99 |
| - | *bedenken* | .96 | - | *bedenken* | .98 |
| - | *essen* | .92 | - | *essen* | .93 |
| - | übersehen | .84 | - | übersehen | .88 |
| - | *aufessen* | .71 | - | *aufessen* | .74 |
| - | *erörtern* | .48 | - | *erörtern* | .50 |
| bedenken - | *nachprüfen* | .98 | essen - | *bedenken* | .96 |
| - | *untersuchen* | .96 | - | *nachprüfen* | .93 |
| - | *essen* | .96 | - | *untersuchen* | .92 |
| - | übersehen | .90 | - | *aufessen* | .85 |
| - | *aufessen* | .81 | - | übersehen | .83 |
| - | *erörtern* | .55 | - | fehlen | .59 |
| aufessen - | *erörtern* | .87 | erörtern - | *aufessen* | .87 |
| - | *essen* | .85 | - | herstellen | .79 |
| - | *bedenken* | .81 | - | zersägen | .76 |
| - | *nachprüfen* | .74 | - | übermitteln | .70 |
| - | übersehen | .72 | - | hämmern | .68 |
| - | *untersuchen* | .71 | - | schneiden | .68 |

**Fig. 5.** Verb pairs and their cosine values within the class *Accomplishments with an affected subject.*

well, the five remaining verbs with high cosine values are pure accomplishments. This could be an indication that the raters associated *erörtern* 'debate' strongly with pure *accomplishments* that is, to a verb class which does not express affectedness of the subject. The high cosine values of the achievement verb *übersehen* 'overlook' within the cosine lists of all *accomplishment with an affected subject* verbs might indicate that an activity is associated with *übersehen* which affects the subject and has an effect on the object as well. This might be the case with an ongoing activity within a time span which includes the event of overlooking something. The cosine lists of the achievement verbs are given in Fig. 6 below.

*Verlieren* 'to lose', *vergehen* 'to go by/pass/to disappear', *anfangen* 'to begin', *richten auf* 'to focus/direct towards' and *orientieren an* 'to be geared to' exhibit consistent cosine lists since they consist exclusively of achievement verbs. In addition, the cosine values are constantly high. *Einschlafen* 'to fall asleep' has a consistent cosine list as well, however the activity verb *laufen* 'to walk/to run' has the highest value. *Übersehen* 'to overlook' has a less consistent cosine list. The four highest values are achieved by verbs of the class *accomplishment with an affected subject*, suggesting a strong associated semantic similarity of textitübersehen 'to overlook' with that verb class (see above). However, this verb clearly fails the test of accomplishmentship as becomes obvious by the contrast in acceptability in **er übersah die Ampel in einer Sekunde* 'he overlooked the traffic light in one second' and *er durchquerte den Dschungel in einem Jahr* 'he

| verb pairs | | cosine | verb pairs | | cosine |
|---|---|---|---|---|---|
| verlieren - | *richten auf* | .94 | einschlafen - | *laufen* | .72 |
| - | *vergehen* | .76 | - | *orientieren an* | .57 |
| - | *ansteigen* | .72 | - | *vergehen* | .55 |
| - | *orientieren an* | .69 | - | *verlieren* | .52 |
| - | *anfangen* | .61 | - | *richten auf* | .49 |
| - | *einschlafen* | .52 | - | *anfangen* | .44 |
| vergehen - | *anfangen* | .90 | anfangen - | *vergehen* | .90 |
| - | *orientieren an* | .86 | - | *orientieren an* | .84 |
| - | *richten auf* | .82 | - | *richten auf* | .79 |
| - | *verlieren* | .76 | - | *verlieren* | .61 |
| - | *einschlafen* | .55 | - | *einschlafen* | .44 |
| - | *ansteigen* | .41 | - | *ansteigen* | .41 |
| abweichen - | betreffen | .87 | ansteigen - | *richten auf* | .78 |
| - | existieren | .79 | - | herstellen | .73 |
| - | folgen aus | .65 | - | *verlieren* | .72 |
| - | müssen | .64 | - | zersägen.69 | |
| - | halten für | .60 | - | erörtern | .61 |
| - | verlängern | .58 | - | hämmern | .59 |
| richten auf - | *verlieren* | .94 | orientieren an - | *vergehen* | .86 |
| - | *vergehen* | .82 | - | *anfangen* | .84 |
| - | *anfangen* | .79 | - | *richten auf* | .79 |
| - | *orientieren an* | .79 | - | *verlieren* | .69 |
| - | *ansteigen* | .78 | - | *einschlafen* | .57 |
| - | *einschlafen* | .49 | - | *ansteigen* | .54 |
| übersehen - | bedenken | .90 | | | |
| - | nachprüfen | .88 | | | |
| - | untersuchen | .84 | | | |
| - | essen | .83 | | | |
| - | aufessen | .72 | | | |
| - | erörtern | .48 | | | |

**Fig. 6.** Verb pairs and their cosine values within the class *Achievements*.

crossed the jungle in one year'. The latter sentence contains a typical accomplishment verb. The same holds for *ansteigen* 'to increase/to rise'. This verb exhibits strong similarities with accomplishment verbs in its cosine list, and is apparently interpreted as expressing an end of state in the sense that something is increasing to a certain degree. No achievement verb is in the cosine list of *abweichen* 'to deviate', which clearly is assigned to the class of state verbs. The cosines of the activity verbs are given in Fig. 7 below:

In this case, the cosine lists do not confirm our manual classification. *Laufen* 'to run/walk' just exhibits some semantic similarity with the achievement verb

| verb pairs | | cosine | verb pairs | | cosine |
|---|---|---|---|---|---|
| laufen | – einschlafen | .72 | eingehen auf | – verlängern | .97 |
| | - übersehen | .30 | | - hämmern | .97 |
| | - mitteilen | .29 | | - übermitteln | .96 |
| | - orientieren | .15 | | - verhindern | .94 |
| | - ansteigen | .12 | | - zersägen | .92 |
| | - anfangen | .05 | | mitteilen | .89 |

**Fig. 7.** Verb pairs and their cosine values within the class *Activity*.

| verb pairs | | cosine | verb pairs | | cosine |
|---|---|---|---|---|---|
| existieren - | *betreffen* | .96 | betreffen - | *existieren* | .96 |
| - | *müssen* | .88 | - | *folgen aus* | .88 |
| - | *folgen aus* | .82 | - | abweichen | .87 |
| - | abweichen | .79 | - | *müssen* | .79 |
| - | *fehlen* | .70 | - | *halten für* | .72 |
| - | *halten für* | .69 | - | *fehlen* | .70 |
| müssen - | *existieren* | .88 | halten für - | *müssen* | .77 |
| - | *betreffen* | .79 | - | *betreffen* | .72 |
| - | *halten für* | .77 | - | *existieren* | .69 |
| - | *fehlen* | .71 | - | *folgen aus* | .62 |
| - | *folgen aus* | .68 | - | abweichen | .60 |
| - | abweichen | .64 | - | *fehlen* | .53 |
| folgen aus - | *existieren* | .82 | fehlen - | *folgen aus* | .88 |
| - | *betreffen* | .88 | - | *müssen* | .71 |
| - | *fehlen* | .88 | - | *existieren* | .70 |
| - | *müssen* | .68 | - | *betreffen* | .70 |
| - | abweichen | .65 | - | essen | .59 |
| - | halten für | .62 | - | abweichen | .54 |

**Fig. 8.** Verb pairs and their cosine values within the class *State*.

*einschlafen* 'to fall asleep' (see above). As shown above, the second activity verb *eingehen auf* 'to respond to so./sth.' that raters' associations assign this verb to the *accomplishments* class.

The cosine values of the verb pairs within the state class are given in Fig. 8. The highest cosine values pertain to verbs from the same class as the target verb. The cosine lists of *existieren* 'to exist' and *betreffen* 'to concern' are closely related since the respective cosine values are far above .90 and their sets of semantically related verbs are almost identical. *Halten für* 'to believe someone/something to be' has the lowest values in its cosine list. However, its list of semantic relations is consistent since the four highest cosine values are held by state verbs, only disrupted by the achievement verb *abweichen* 'to deviate'. This verb is within the cosine lists of *existieren* 'to exist', *betreffen* 'to concern' and *folgen aus* 'to follow from' and *müssen* 'to have to/must' *abweichen* 'to deviate', too. This could be an indication for a multiple class membership of *abweichen* 'to deviate' viz. to *states* and *achievements.*

We carried out a hierarchical, agglomerative Ward clustering analysis with the Euclidean distance metric on the matrix of cosine values. In addition, the probabilities of the clustering were calculated by multistep-multiscale bootstrap resampling [63] (R-package *pvclust,* [64]). The result of multistep-multiscale bootstrap resampling is displayed in Fig. 9. Relevant are the AU (Approximately Unbiased) probability values (left numbers).

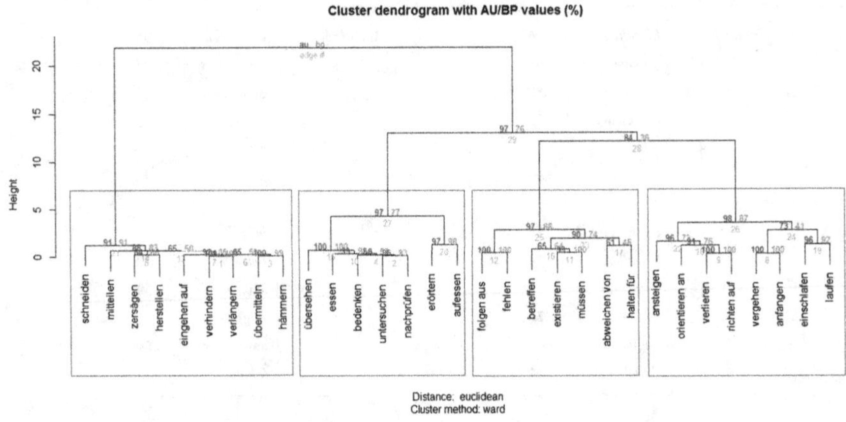


**Fig. 9.** Hierarchical clustering using Ward's method with the cosine values as input, showing the probability values at each of the clustering steps.

Four clusters with high probability values can clearly be distinguished and they correspond almost perfectly with the classes *accomplishments*, *accomplishments with an affected subject*, *states* and *achievements* of the amalgamation of Vendler's and Dowty's classifications. The activity class is not represented which confirms the cosine hierarchies from above. Just four verbs are misclassifications, which means that there is a high degree of agreement. The four verb classes of the cluster analysis and their probabilities are given below (misclassifications/dubious classifications are marked with an asterisk):

1. **accomplishments**: *schneiden* ('to cut'), *hämmern* ('to hammer'), *mitteilen* ('to tell/to inform'), *zersägen* ('to saw into pieces'), *eingehen auf** ('to respond to so./sth.'), *verhindern* ('to prevent'), *verlängern* ('to extend'), *übermitteln* ('to communicate/to forward'), $p = .91$
2. **accomplishments with affected subject**: *übersehen** ('to overlook'), *essen* ('to eat'), *bedenken* ('to consider'),*untersuchen* (to examine'), *nachprüfen* ('to ascertain/to check'), *erörtern* ('to debate'), *aufessen* ('eat up'), $p = .97$
3. **achievements**: *ansteigen** ('to increase/to rise'), *orientieren an** ('to orientate'),*verlieren* ('to lose'), *richten auf* ('to focus/to direct towards'), *vergehen*

('to go (by)/to pass/to disappear'), *anfangen* ('to begin'), *einschlafen* ('to fall asleep'), *laufen** ('to walk/to run'), $p = .98$
4. **states**: *folgen aus* ('to follow from'), *fehlen* ('to lack'), *betreffen* ('to concern'), *existieren* ('to exist'), *müssen* ('must'), *abweichen von** ('to deviate'), *halten für* ('to take so./sth. for so./ sth.'), $p = .97$

A comparison of this classification against the 35 verb-Gold Standard (Vendler + 1) in [1] and [14] yielded .81 accuracy. To determine the significance values for the accuracy level for the classification in five classes, we calculated Cohen's kappa. Kappa values above .81 are characterized as almost perfect agreement and therefore highly significant. The association-based classification's accuracy of the association bases classification has $\kappa = .76$, which is a substantial agreement.

The results of the classification experiments in the distributional frameworks are given in reverse order (from path 4 on the right to path 1 on the left of Fig. 3, because the method described in 4.6 was the starting point of our study.

### 5.1 Results of the Classification of Verbs Using Dimension Reduced Nominal Fillers and Aspectual Features

The workflow is a slightly modified version of the workflow in [15]. Thus, the results were practically the same: Feature combinations exclusively comprising aspect features yielded high accuracy values (see Fig. 10).

Input to the classification were vectors with 39 dimensions (each 10 for subjects, direct objects, and prepositional objects and 9 for the adverbial features reflecting the aspectual behaviour). Taking the classification with five aspectual verb classes as the gold standard, ten noun classes per argument position clearly outperform the approaches with fewer features. Additionally, counting every noun token leads to better results than counting only the noun types. Medium length vectors (2000 dimensions), constructed on the basis of a medium context width (window size of five elements) achieve the best outcomes; the verb vectors of the KMeansLloyd noun clustering in particular show the best performance. Figure 10 depicts the accuracy of feature combinations and is subject to the following result description.

The combinations *aspect/subject/direct object* and *aspect/ subject/ direct object/ prepositional object* outperform the remaining feature combinations with .95 accuracy, and .94 accuracy respectively. With the two feature combinations described above we reached kappa values higher than .90. The feature combinations *aspect/direct object/prepositional object* with .88 accuracy, $\kappa = .84$, and *aspect/prepositional object with* .86 accuracy, $\kappa = .81$, also achieve almost perfect agreements. Substantial agreements, with above .61, can be observed with the combinations *aspect/subject/prepositional object*, .84 accuracy, $\kappa = .78$, *aspect/direct object*, .92 accuracy, $\kappa = .75$, and *aspect/subject*, .82 accuracy, $\kappa = .75$. None of the feature combinations without aspectual features achieves a satisfactory result. The single features achieve only fair agreements: *Aspect* achieves .57 accuracy, $\kappa = .34$, *subject* achieves .52, $\kappa = .27$, and *direct object* and *prepositional object* achieve .51 accuracy and $\kappa = .24$ each. Figure 10 below gives the results of process chain 4.

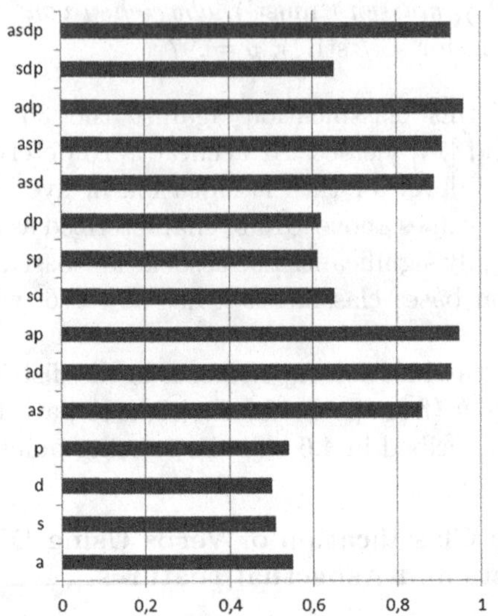


**Fig. 10.** Results of process chain 4 (Accuracy; a = aspectual features, s = Subject features, d = accusative object features, p = prepositional object features); see text for further explanations (figure taken from [2]).

### 5.2 Results of the Classification of Verbs Using Nominal Fillers and Aspectual Features (No Dimension Reduction)

To reduce the complexity of our workflow, we classified the verbs using feature vectors where all nominal fillers were taken into account instead of clustering them into groups (processing chain 3 in Fig. 3).

Instead of the 39-dimensional vectors in processing chain 4, we obtained vectors with almost 40000 dimensions (11257 subjects, 12450 direct objects, 16196 prepositional objects, 9 for adverbial fillers).

For the most part, the results were comparable to the results of processing chain 4 (see Fig. 11): Employing all nominal and adverbial fillers (marked as *asdp* in Fig. 11), we achieved .92 accuracy. In comparison with the *+cluster*-workflow we achieved the same accuracy value when we left out the adverbial fillers (*sdp*), but an even worse value when we left out the objects (*as*). This is not an overly surprising result because the adverbial fillers were limited to only nine dimensions. Within very high-dimensional vectors they should lose ground. We see here a first indication that the paradigm "the more the merrier" fits well with our results. We consistently achieved better results when we normalized the vectors by cosine. Without length normalization accuracy apparently decreases (at least .07, see Fig. 11, last bar).

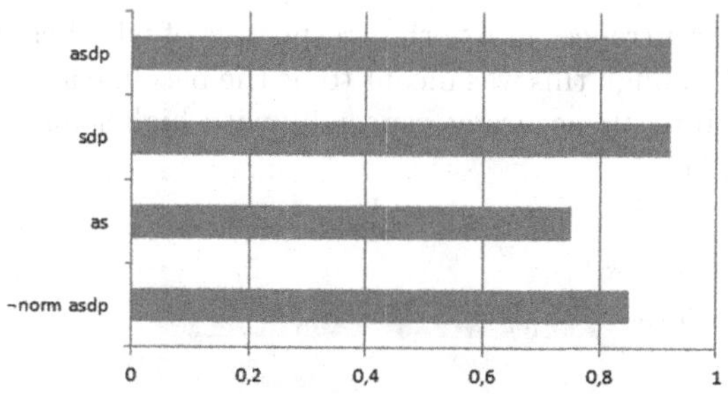


**Fig. 11.** Results of process chain 3 (Accuracy; a = aspectual features, s = Subject features, d = accusative object features, p = prepositional object features, norm = normalized); see text for further explanations (figure taken from [2]).

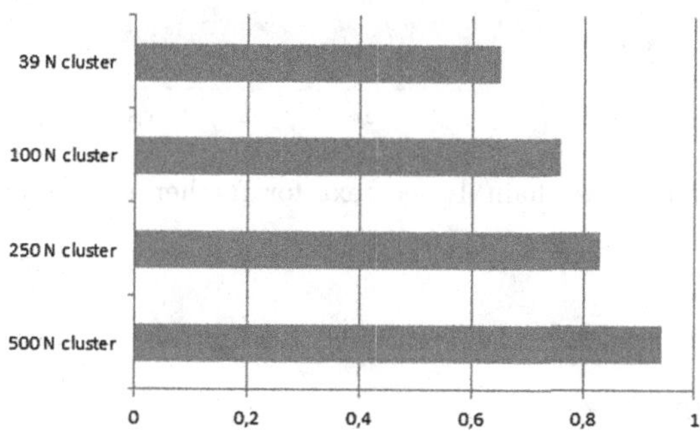


**Fig. 12.** Results of process chain 2; see text for further explanations (figure taken from [2]).

### 5.3 Results of the Classification of Verbs Using Dimension Reduced Co-Occurrences

In the third experiment (path 2 in Fig. 3) we left out the parsing step. Within process chain 2 we built verb vectors from co-occurrences of nouns that were clustered as illustrated above. Firstly, we generated 39 clusters to provide the same dimensionality as in process chain 4, which gave us a very poor result (see Fig. 12, first bar). By increasing the number of clusters, the results became better, cumulating in .90 accuracy for 500 clusters. Here again, the maxim seems to be "the more the merrier". Consequently, we should try to expand the number of clusters to the number of features. That is actually what we did in process chain 1, which will be described in the next section.

### 5.4 Results for the Classification of Verbs Using Pure Co-occurrences

In the last experiment, we classified the verbs without parsing and without clustering the noun fillers. Instead, we built the vectors by simply collecting the most frequent co-occurrences of a verb, irrespective of whether they are nominal elements or not. Although this was meant to be the baseline analysis, we obtained excellent results up to .98 accuracy, especially with higher dimensionality of the vectors (see Fig. 13).

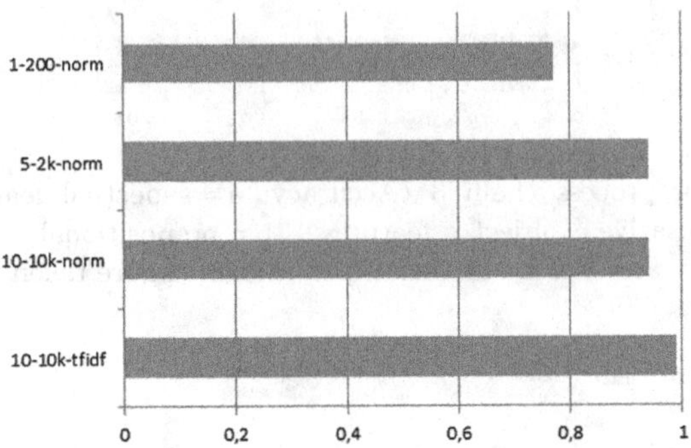


**Fig. 13.** Results of process chain 1; see text for further explanations (figure taken from [2]).

## 6 Conclusion

The present study provides evidence that aspectual verb classes, i.e. a Vendler + 1 classification, can be inferred from raters' associations. The agreement of the association-based classification with the Gold Standard from [1] was substantial. Human associations thus to a high degree reflect the classificatory concepts in [1] that is, the abstract semantic properties of verb aspect. We interpret the results as an indication, that these abstract semantic properties seem to be powerful criteria for a classification of verbs in the mental lexicon. Note however, that the activity class was surprisingly not represented in the classification since this class was polluted by a couple of non-activity verbs. As an interesting fact it turned out that the judgments of a group of 35 raters exhibited a similar degree of agreement with the Gold Standard as the data from the approximately 880,000,000 word sDeWaC corpus. We interpret this result as an indication that raters' associations are pertinent for verb classification. Our study confirms in principle the findings of [10,11] and [12] who achieved plausible verb classifications from human associations. An interesting point in the analysis in [10] was the detection of unexpected verb-verb relations. An interesting point in [10] analysis was the detection of unexpected verb-verb relations. In our study some unexpected relations came to light, as well, for instance *eingehen auf* 'respond to so./sth.' which was rated to be an accomplishment verb. This might be a hint of multiple class membership and is a topic of future research.

Both substantial and even excellent agreements were achieved in the classifications utilizing usage based data within the distributional framework [2].

We observed that two out of our four models outperformed the remaining ones and achieved excellent agreements between the automatically inferred aspectual classes and the Vendler + 1 gold standard classification: (i) a model within an *informed* distributional framework, considering structured, language theoretically well grounded (and thus restricted) context material that is, clustered nouns in the argument positions of verbs in combination with aspectual features and (ii) a model within a *non informed* framework, considering large amounts of data, i.e. completely unstructured co-occurrence material of verbs. This outcome can be interpreted as a manifestation of the principle 'the more, the merrier'. On the one hand, preprocessed linguistic information, i.e. small units of linguistic information, were used for the construction of verb vectors (*informed distributional*). The resulting verb vectors of the latter model have a small dimensionality, however a lot of preprocessing steps were necessary. On the other hand, as much pure data as possible was included in the induction, leading to high dimensional verb vectors (*non informed* distributional). This model needs relatively few preprocessing steps, which means that the experiment's workflow is easy to design. When combining the two approaches, that is using noun clusters and aspectual features in a (restricted) distributional framework or left out the clustering of noun arguments in a (restricted) *informed* distributional framework, the quality of classification decreased.

Which distributional model is preferable depends on the aims and preconditions of the analysis. When a very large set of verbs has to be classified, one might run into trouble with the very high dimensionalities of the verb vectors, making analysis slow, if not impossible. In that case the *informed* distributional method which requires preprocessing tools like parsers would be preferable. The choice of the method thus depends, in general, on the amount of data that have to be analyzed and on the availability of preprocessing tools for the language which is being studied.

The results of the present study fit well into theories of language acquisition. To begin with, we achieved very satisfying classification results within an unsupervised approach, which mirrors the situation in language acquisition. Taking [22,23] and [24] as point of departure, *frame compliance* is an essential strategy in language acquisition used by young children to interpret sentences.

In order to classify verbs into classes, a task which is mastered quite late in the acquisition process [25,26], children need to build up knowledge about sentence types, for instance about transitivity properties of sentences, and this knowledge is utilized to learn verb classes [65,66]. At the beginning of the acquisition process knowledge of sentence types is sometimes presumed to be item based [20] meaning that it depends on specific verbs and their contexts, while other studies provide evidence of a linguistic maturation process: A constant development of linguistic knowledge over time. Our study provides evidence for Tomasello's item based approach. Starting with unstructured contexts of verbs, learners identify very early item based prototypical verb/arguments structures and subsequently in the course of the acquisition process they use context materials to come to analogies. When learners recognize a context, they classify a new verb according to that context which is the environment of a previous learned and eventually previously classified verb. The classification based on associations brings to light that in order to manage the task of classifying verbs, linguistic experience is required: The more language learners build up linguistic knowledge and manage to identify arguments of verbs and other verb dependent elements in the sentence, the more they build up the structural knowledge of sentences types which in turn is a prerequisite in order to induce verbs classes from their contexts. The association task demonstrated that aspectual verb classes are an implicit entity in human's mental lexicon.

In summary, the results of this study show that, for German, the Vendler + 1 typology can be inferred in a unsupervised approach from raters' associations and in a supervised approach from the linguistic contexts of verbs. Employing the supervised approach, we found that both classification frameworks that is, the informed distributional subcategorization-frame-based framework and the non informed window-based framework performed almost on a par, while the association based classification performed slightly weaker - and did not discriminate the activity class - but performed nevertheless satisfying that is, we got additional evidence in favor of the Vendler + 1 classification.

## References

1. Richter, M., van Hout, R.: A classification of German verbs using empirical language data and concepts of Vendler and Dowty. Sprache und Datenverarbeitung (Int. J. Lang. Data Process.) **38**, 81–117 (2016)
2. Hermes, J., Richter, M., Neuefeind, C.: Supervised classification of aspectual verb classes in German: subcategorization-frame-based vs window-based approach: a comparison. In: Proceedings of 10th International Conference on Agents and Artificial Intelligence, ICAART 2018, pp. 653–662 (2018)
3. Harris, Z.: Distributional structure. Word **10**, 146–162 (1954)
4. Rubenstein, H., Goodenough, J.B.: Contextual correlates of synonymy. Commun. ACM **8**, 627–633 (1965)
5. Schütze, H., Pedersen, J.: A vector model for syntagmatic and paradigmatic relatedness, pp. 104–113 (1993)
6. Landauer, T.K., Dumais, S.T.: A solution to Plato's problem: the latent semantic analysis theory of acquisition, induction, and representation of knowledge. Psychol. Rev. **104**, 211–240 (1997)
7. Pantel, P.: Inducing ontological co-occurrence vectors. In: Proceedings of the 43rd Annual Meeting on Association for Computational Linguistics, ACL 2005, Stroudsburg, PA, USA, pp. 125–132. Association for Computational Linguistics (2005)
8. Turney, P.D., Pantel, P.: From frequency to meaning: vector space models of semantics. J. Artif. Int. Res. **37**, 141–188 (2010)
9. Vendler, Z.: Linguistics in philosophy: G - Reference. Information and Interdisciplinary Subjects Series. Cornell University Press, Ithaca (1967)
10. Schulte im Walde, S., Melinger, A.: Identifying semantic relations and functional properties of human verb associations. In: Proceedings of the Joint Conference on Human Language Technology and Empirical Methods in Natural Language Processing, pp. 612–619 (2005)

11. Schulte im Walde, S.: Human verb associations as the basis for gold standard verb classes: validation against GermaNet and FrameNet. In: Proceedings of the 5th Conference on Language Resources and Evaluation, pp. 825–830 (2006)
12. Schulte im Walde, S.: Can human verb associations help identify salient features for semantic verb classification? In: Proceedings of the 10th Conference on Computational Natural Language Learning, pp. 69–76 (2006)
13. Joachims, T.: Text categorization with support vector machines: learning with many relevant features. In: Nédellec, C., Rouveirol, C. (eds.) ECML 1998. LNCS, vol. 1398, pp. 137–142. Springer, Heidelberg (1998). https://doi.org/10.1007/BFb0026683
14. Richter, M., Hermes, J.: Classification of German verbs using nouns in argument positions and aspectual features. In: NetWordS 2015 Word Knowledge and Word Usage, pp. 177–181 (2015)
15. Hermes, J., Richter, M., Neuefeind, C.: Automatic induction of German aspectual verb classes in a distributional framework. In: Proceedings of the International Conference of the German Society for Computational Linguistics and Language Technology, (GSCL 2015), pp. 122–129 (2015)
16. Næss, A. (ed.): Prototypical Tranisitivity: Typological Studies in Language 72. Benjamins, Amsterdam (2007)
17. Siegel, E.V., McKeown, K.R.: Learning methods to combine linguistic indicators: improving aspectual classification and revealing linguistic insights. Comput. Linguist. **26**, 595–628 (2000)
18. Krifka, M.: Nominal reference, temporal constitution, and quantification in event semantics. In: Bartsch, R., van Benthem, J., van Emde Boas, P. (eds.) Semantics and Contextual Expressions, pp. 75–115. Foris (1989)
19. Van Orman Quine, W.: Word and Object. MIT press, Cambridge (1960)
20. Tomasello, M.: Do young children have adult syntactic competence? Cognition **74**, 209–253 (2000)
21. Goldberg, A.E.: Constructions: A Construction Grammar Approach to Argument Structure. University of Chicago Press, Chicago (1995)
22. Naigles, L.G., Fowler, A., Helm, A.: Developmental shifts in the construction of verb meanings. Cogn. Dev. **7**, 403–427 (1992)
23. Naigles, L., Fowler, A., Helm, A.: Syntactic bootstrapping from start to finish with special reference to down syndrome. In: Beyond Names for Things: Young Children's Acquisition of Verbs, pp. 299–330 (1995)
24. Naigles, L., Gleitman, L., Gleitman, H.: Children acquire word meaning components from syntactic evidence. In: Language and Cognition: A Developmental Perspective, Norwood, NJ, Ablex, vol. 5, pp. 104–140 (1993)
25. Wittek, A.: Learning the Meaning of Change-of-State Verbs: A Case Study of German Child Language, vol. 17. Walter de Gruyter, Berlin (2002)
26. Richter, M., van Hout, R.: Interpreting resultative sentences in German: stages in L1 acquisition. Linguistics **51**, 117–144 (2013)
27. Dowty, D.: Word Meaning and Montague Grammar. D. Reidel, Dordrecht (1979)
28. Dowty, D.: Thematic proto-roles and argument selection. Language **67**, 547–619 (1991)
29. Rothstein, S.: Structuring Events: A Study in the Semantics of Aspect. Explorations in Semantics. Wiley, Hoboken (2004)
30. Fernando, T.: A finite-state approach to events in natural language semantics. J. Log. Comput. **14**, 79–92 (2004)

31. Gruender, S.: An algorithm from adverbial aspect shift. In: Proceedings of the 22nd International Conference on Computer Linguistics (Coling 2008), pp. 289–296 (2008)
32. Klein, W.: How time is encoded. In: The Expression of Time, pp. 39–82. Mouton de Gruyter, Berlin (2009)
33. Siegel, E.V.: Learning methods for combining linguistic indicators to classify verb. In: Proceedings of the 2nd Conference on Empirical Methods in Natural Language Processing, EMNLP. Brown University, Providence (1997). cmp-lg/9707015
34. Klavans, J.L., Chodorow, M.: Degrees of stativity: the lexical representation of verb aspect. In: Proceedings of the 14th Conference on Computational Linguistics, COLING 1992, Stroudsburg, PA, USA, vol. 4, pp. 1126–1131. Association for Computational Linguistics (1992)
35. Zarcone, A., Lenci, A.: Computational models of event type classification in context. In: Proceedings of the 6th International Conference on Language Resources and Evaluation, Marrakech, Morocco, pp. 1232—1238 (2008)
36. Friedrich, A., Palmer, A.: Automatic prediction of aspectual class of verbs in context. In: Proceedings of the 52nd Annual Meeting of the Association for Computational Linguistics (Volume 2: Short Papers), Baltimore, Maryland, 517–523. Association for Computational Linguistics(2014)
37. Dorr, B.J., Jones, D.A.: Role of word sense disambiguation in lexical acquisition: predicting semantics from syntactic cues. In: Proceedings of the 16th International Conference on Computational Linguistics, COLING 1996, 5–9 August 1996, pp. 322–327. Center for Sprogteknologi, Copenhagen (1996)
38. Merlo, P., Stevenson, S.: Automatic verb classification based on statistical distributions of argument structure. Comput. Linguist. **27**, 373–408 (2001)
39. Joanis, E., Stevenson, S., James, D.: A general feature space for automatic verb classification. Natural Lang. Eng. **14**, 337–367 (2008)
40. Vlachos, A., Korhonen, A., Ghahramani, Z.: Unsupervised and constrained Dirichlet process mixture models for verb clustering. In: Proceedings of the Workshop on Geometrical Models of Natural Language Semantics, GEMS 2009, Stroudsburg, PA, USA, pp. 74–82. Association for Computational Linguistics (2009)
41. Schulte im Walde, S., Brew, C.: Inducing German semantic verb classes from purely syntactic subcategorisation information. In: Proceedings of the 40th Annual Meeting on Association for Computational Linguistics, ACL 2002, Stroudsburg, PA, USA, pp. 223–230. Association for Computational Linguistics (2002)
42. Schulte im Walde, S.: Experiments on the choice of features for learning verb classes. In: Proceedings of the Tenth Conference on European Chapter of the Association for Computational Linguistics, EACL 2003, Stroudsburg, PA, USA, vol. 1, pp. 315–322. Association for Computational Linguistics (2003)
43. Schulte im Walde, S.: Experiments on the automatic induction of German semantic verb classes. Comput. Linguist. **32**, 159–194 (2006)
44. Smith, C.: The Parameter of Aspect. Kluwer, Dordrecht (1991)
45. Verkuyl, H.J.: Aspectual composition: surveying the ingredients. In: Verkuyl, H.J., de Swart, H., van Hout, A. (eds.) Perspectives on Aspect. SITP, vol. 32, pp. 19–39. Springer, Dordrecht (2005). https://doi.org/10.1007/1-4020-3232-3_2
46. Pustejovsky, J.: The syntax of event structure. Cognition **41**, 47–81 (1991)
47. Bach, E.: The algebra of events. Linguist. Philos. **9**, 5–16 (1986)
48. Jackendoff, R.: Semantic Interpretation in Generative Grammar. MIT press, Cambridge (1972)
49. Lakoff, G.: Irregularity in Syntax. Rinehart and Winstons, New York (1970)

50. Von Wright, G.H.: Norm and Action. Routledge and Kegan Paul, London (1963)
51. Jackendoff, R.: Semantics and Cognition. MIT press, Cambridge (1983)
52. Levin, B., Rapoport, T.R.: Lexical subordination. In: Papers from the 24th Regional Meeting of the Chicago Linguistic Society, pp. 275–289 (1992)
53. Pulman, S.G.: Aspectual shift as type coercion. Trans. Phil. Soc. **95**(2), 279–317 (1997)
54. Hirschfeld, G., Bien, H., de Vries, M., Lüttmann, H., Schwall, J.: Open-source software to conduct online rating studies. Behav. Res. Methods **42**, 542–546 (2010)
55. Salton, G., Wong, A., Yang, C.: A vector space model for automatic indexing. Commun. ACM **18**, 613–620 (1975)
56. Schumacher, H.: Verben in Feldern: Valenzwörterbuch zur Syntax und Semantik deutscher Verben, vol. 1. Walter de Gruyter, Berlin (1986)
57. Faaß, G., Eckart, K.: SdeWaC – a corpus of parsable sentences from the web. In: Gurevych, I., Biemann, C., Zesch, T. (eds.) GSCL 2013. LNCS (LNAI), vol. 8105, pp. 61–68. Springer, Heidelberg (2013). https://doi.org/10.1007/978-3-642-40722-2_6
58. Hermes, J., Schwiebert, S.: Classification of text processing components: the tesla role system. In: Fink, A., Lausen, B., Seidel, W., Ultsch, A. (eds.) Advances in Data Analysis, Data Handling and Business Intelligence. STUDIES CLASS, pp. 285–294. Springer, Heidelberg (2009). https://doi.org/10.1007/978-3-642-01044-6_26
59. Levy, J.P., Bullinaria, J.A.: Learning lexical properties from word usage patterns: which context words should be used? In: French, R.M., Sougné, J.P. (eds.) Connectionist Models of Learning, Development and Evolution. PERSPECT.NEURAL, pp. 273–282. Springer, London (2001). https://doi.org/10.1007/978-1-4471-0281-6_27
60. Lund, K., Burgess, C.: Hyperspace analogue to language (HAL): a general model semantic representation. In: Brain and Cognition, vol. 30, p. 265 (1996)
61. Lowe, W., McDonald, S.: The direct route: mediated priming in semantic space. In: Proceedings of the Annual Conference of the Cognitive Science Society (CogSci 2000) (2000)
62. Bohnet, B.: Very high accuracy and fast dependency parsing is not a contradiction. In: Proceedings of the 23rd International Conference on Computational Linguistics, COLING 2010, Stroudsburg, PA, USA, pp. 89–97. Association for Computational Linguistics (2010)
63. Shimodaira, H.: Approximately unbiased tests of region using multistep-mulitscale bootstrap resampling. Ann. Stat. **32**, 2616–2641 (2004)
64. Suzuki, R., Shimodaira, H.: Pvclust: an R package for assessing the uncertainty in hierarchical clustering. Bioinformatics **22**, 1540–1542 (2006)
65. Brooks, P., Tomasello, M.: How children constrain their argument structure constructions. Language **75**, 720–738 (1999)
66. Brooks, P., Tomasello, M., Dodson, K., Lewis, L.: Young children's overgeneralizations with fixed transitivity verbs. Child Dev. **70**, 1325–1337 (1999)

# Linguistic Information in Word Embeddings

Ali Basirat(✉) and Marc Tang

Department of Linguistics and Philology, Uppsala University, Uppsala, Sweden
{Ali.Basirat,Marc.Tang}@lingfil.uu.se

**Abstract.** We study the presence of linguistically motivated information in the word embeddings generated with statistical methods. The nominal aspects of uter/neuter, common/proper, and count/mass in Swedish are selected to represent respectively grammatical, semantic, and mixed types of nominal categories within languages. Our results indicate that typical grammatical and semantic features are easily captured by word embeddings. The classification of semantic features required significantly less neurons than grammatical features in our experiments based on a single layer feed-forward neural network. However, semantic features also generated higher entropy in the classification output despite its high accuracy. Furthermore, the count/mass distinction resulted in difficulties to the model, even though the quantity of neurons was almost tuned to its maximum.

**Keywords:** Neural network · Nominal classification · Swedish
Word embedding

## 1 Introduction

The vector representation of words, known as word embeddings or word vectors, have shown great impact on the natural language processing tasks [1,2]. In this representation, each word is associated with a vector in such a way that word similarities are reflected through vector similarities [3]. Studies on word embeddings in natural language processing show that word similarities are captured by word vectors, e.g., the vectors associated with similar words are clustered together [4–6]. However, further research is required to understand which types of linguistic information (e.g., semantic or syntactic) are encoded in these vectors. Several evaluation metrics and tools are used to study the information encoded into word embeddings [4–8]. This study investigates the presence of deep linguistic information about the nominal classes in the word embeddings.

The nominal classification refers to how a language classify nouns of the lexicon. In the narrow sense, the most frequent grammaticalized system of nominal classification is grammatical gender [9–11], e.g., all nouns in German are affiliated to either masculine, feminine, or neuter. However, in a broader view, nominal classification may also refer to how nouns may be divided into categories


J. van den Herik and A. P. Rocha (Eds.): ICAART 2018, LNAI 11352, pp. 492–513, 2019.
https://doi.org/10.1007/978-3-030-05453-3_23

according to different semantic and/or syntactic criterion, i.e., count/mass and common/proper [12].

We further develop previous studies on Swedish and study different types of nominal classifications with regard to the syntactic and semantic information encoded to their word vectors [8]. A series of new experiments are done using simulated annealing and neural network to assess the required amount of neurons for different classification tasks. We also enforce the focus on the word embedding methods and their evaluation metrics. As a research question, we aim at evaluating the performance of word embeddings combined with different settings of classifiers on the task of nominal classification. A linear discriminant analysis and a feed-forward neural network tuned with simulated annealing is used for this aim. Three binary nominal features in Swedish are selected: uter/neuter (i.e., grammatical gender), count/mass, and proper/common nouns. These distinctions represent three different types of nominal classification in the broad sense.

First, grammatical gender is a typically grammaticalized feature, which is reflected in language via grammatical agreement with other elements of a phrase. For instance, in Swedish, the article and the adjective varies in terms of form depending on the grammatical gender (uter or neuter) of the following nouns, c.f., *ett stor-t äpple* (a.SG.NEUT big.SG.NEUT apple.SG.NEUT) 'a big apple' and *en stor-∅ häst* (a.SG.UTER big.SG.UTER horse.SG.UTER) 'a big horse'. The grammatical gender of a noun in Swedish is considered as a static nominal feature of the noun. The grammatical gender of a noun in Swedish is consistently marked within the sentence and it does not vary according to the context of the word.

Second, the categorization of common and proper nouns (proper names) is considered as a static semantic feature. Common nouns generally refer to classes of things (e.g., *book*, *desk*) while proper nouns designate particular individual entities such as *London*, *Tokyo*, among others [12, p.149]. To be more precise in terms of definition, proper nouns do not necessarily refer to only one specific individual. For instance, the proper name *Smith* may be given to different people (or even objects) which do not share any property or quality in common. On the other hand, common nouns refers to a set of entities which share specific properties. Common nouns may thus not be used in the same arbitrary way of proper nouns. As an example, naming a desk as a *book* in English would not be semantically valid, since the properties of a desk do not concord with the intrinsic semantic content of the noun *book* (e.g., a book is something that you can read). Nouns are either common or proper and do not fluctuate between the two categories. Hence, the common/proper distinction is defined as semantically static. Few exceptions of conversion are attested but they are context specific [13, p.58], thus we do not consider them in the current paper.

Finally, the count/mass distinction is generally considered as a mix of syntactic and semantic nominal features [14], as "the brain differentiates between count and mass nouns not only at the syntactic level but also at the semantic level" [15]. Count nouns refer semantically to objects which represent a discrete entity and may be counted, e.g., *computer*, *book* in English. On the other hand, mass nouns (also named non-count nouns) commonly indicate uncountable mass and are not specified as how to individuate or divide them, e.g., *water*, *milk* in English. With regard to morpho-syntax, mass nouns typically cannot occur in the plural form if a language possess grammatical number (among other criteria). Yet, the category of count/mass is more versatile than static syntactic and semantic nominal features such as uter/neuter or common/proper. First, nouns undergo more frequently conversion between count and mass, e.g., *coffee* may refer to the liquid category as a mass or as a countable entity in container, c.f., *The coffee is good* and *I want one more coffee* [13, p.51]. Second, overt plural marking does not always concord with the count/mass distinction [16,17]. For instance, the mass noun *luggage* in English has a count interpretation but behave as a mass noun since it only occurs in the singular form [18].

Previous studies on nominal categories in Swedish have shown that the count/mass distinction is harder to identify than the uter/neuter and proper/common categories. Our study aims at further testing the performance of different classifiers with different parameters (e.g., different amount of neurons) and investigates if the performance of classification may be enhanced with a specific setting. The structure of this paper is as follow. Section 2 presents a literature review of the word embedding and the three nominal features approached in our research question. Section 3 explains the architecture of the selected models of word embeddings and classifier. Section 4 lists the setting of our experiments. Section 5 details how the various types of classifiers performed with regard to the three nominal features involved in our study. In Sect. 6, we provide a summary to the performance of the classifier.

## 2 Literature Review

In this section, we review the literature of the word embedding and the nominal classes such as grammatical gender, common/proper, and count/mass distinction.

### 2.1 Word Embedding

This section reviews the literature of word embeddings and their evaluation methods. First, we provide a brief introduction on the word embedding methods. Then, we study different evaluation metrics used for assessing word embeddings.

Word embedding is referred to as the process of embedding words into a vectors space. Words as the most basic elements of syntax are associated with vectors as the most basic elements of a vectors space. In this view, word embedding is seen as a bridge between syntax (more generally linguistics) and linear algebra (more generally mathematics). The association between words and vectors is done in such a way that the similarities between words are reflected through the similarities between vectors. In other words, similar words are associated with similar vectors. The vectors associated with words are called *word embeddings*, or *word vectors* and the vector space is called the *distributional semantic space* or the *semantic space* for short.

**Methods.** The word embedding methods can be divided into two major classes:

- the methods that are developed in the area of distributional semantics [3,7, 19–23]
- the methods that are developed in the area of language modelling [1,24]

It is shown that both classes of methods are connected to each other [25]. In both classes, word embeddings are created through the application of dimensionality reduction techniques on a high dimensional vector space that models the contextual environments of words. The dimensions of the high dimensional vector space correspond to a set of contextual features (e.g. words, and syntactic categories of words) and its vectors correspond to a set of words in a language. The word vectors in this high dimensional vector space are called the *contextual word vectors*. The contextual word vectors are formed by accumulating the occurrence of words with different contextual features.

Different techniques of dimensionality reduction is used for generating word embeddings. Principal component analysis is among the popular methods of dimensionality reduction which is extensively used to reduce the dimensionality of contextual word vectors [7,20,21,23]. The other dimensionality reduction methods, used for this aim, are the restricted Boltzmann Machine [26,27], the auto-encoders [24], the mixture models [28,29], and the non-linear methods [27,30]. `GloVe` [22] formulates the problem of dimensionality reduction as a regression problem. `HPCA` [23] uses the singular value decomposition to estimate the principal components of a sample matrix of the contextual word vectors. `HPCA` ignores the centring step in PCA in order to take the advantage of the data sparsity. `RSV` [7] uses the same approach to compute the principal components. However, it performs the mean subtraction step to centre the column vectors around their mean. `RSV` is able to generate a set of word embeddings faster than other methods and the vectors generated by `RSV` are as good as other word embedding methods. In this paper, we use `RSV` for generating word embeddings.

**Evaluation.** Different evaluation metrics are used to asses the information captured by a set of word embeddings. The evaluation metrics used in the literature can be classified into three groups:

- The word similarity metrics
- The word analogy metrics
- The application-based metrics

The word similarity metrics evaluate a set of word embeddings with regard to the correlation between similar vectors and similar words. These metrics often use a dictionary that affiliates similar words to each other. For example, the words with the same meanings are affiliated with each other. The correlation between the vectors associated with similar words is used as the evaluation metric. A high value of correlation obtained from a set of word embeddings and a dictionary indicates that the word embeddings could capture the similarities encoded into the dictionary. The word similarity benchmark in [4] is a tool that evaluates a set of word embeddings with regard to several word similarity dictionaries.

The word analogy metrics are on the basis of test sets of analogy questions of the form "$a$ is to $b$ as $c$ is to $d$", where $a$, $b$, and $c$ are known words and $d$ is an unknown word which is asked. For example, an analogy question is "*saw* is to *see* as *returned* is to $d$" and the word $d$ is expected to be *return*. An analogy question corresponds to an equation in a semantic vector space representing the word vectors associated with the words in the question [5]. The analogy question "$a$ is to $b$ as $c$ is to $d$" corresponds to the equation

$$v_b - v_a = v_d - v_c \tag{1}$$

where $v_x$ is the vector associated with the word $x$. This equation suggests that the answer to an analogy question as above is the word associated with the vector with greatest cosine similarity to $y = v_b - v_a + v_c$. Given this, a set of word embeddings is evaluated with regard to the number of analogy questions that are answered correctly.

The application based metrics measure the meaningfulness of word embeddings to a task (e.g. machine translation,parsing, and part-of-speech tagging). In these evaluation metric, a set of word embeddings is used for training a learning model in an application. These embeddings are then evaluated with regard to their contributions in the learning process. `vceval` [6] is a framework consisting of several standard NLP tasks (applications) used for evaluating a set of word embeddings. This framework makes use of basic neural network architectures for the tasks. The performance of a neural network trained with a set of word embeddings on a task is reported as the evaluation result of the word embeddings with regard to the task.

This paper address a novel evaluation on word embeddings on the basis of the presence of rich linguistic information such as the lexical and morpho-syntactic features in the word embeddings. We use a dictionary consisting of words affiliated with their lexical and morpho-syntactic features. The words in this dictionary are replaced with their corresponding embeddings. This result in a list of word embeddings labelled with a set of lexical and morpho-syntactic features. This list addresses a standard classification problem in which the word embeddings are the observations and the features are the classes. We tackle the classification problem by a basic feed-forward neural network. The final accuracy of the neural network on a test set is considered as the evaluation metric for word embeddings.

The similarities and differences between evaluation metric introduced in this paper and the other metrics are as follows. Similar to the word similarity metrics, we use a dictionary for evaluating word embeddings. However, unlike the word similarity metrics that directly relates words with other, we relate words with their lexical and morpho-syntactic features. Another difference between the word similarity metric and the proposed metric is in the nature of the evaluation results. The word similarities report the correlations between the word embeddings as the evaluation results but we report the accuracy of a classifier as the evaluation results. Our evaluation metric is similar to the application based metrics in the way that the word embeddings are evaluated with regard to their contribution to a task (i.e. the task of predicting the lexical and morpho-syntactic features of the words associated with words embeddings). In this sense, the evaluation metric introduced in this paper is more close to the application-based evaluation metrics.

## 2.2 Nominal Categories

In this section we provide the theoretical definition of grammatical gender, common/proper, and count/mass distinction along with examples of each category. Furthermore, we list the difficulties predicted by the linguistic knowledge in terms of classification task.

**Grammatical Gender.** Nominal classification refers to how languages classify nouns of their lexicon. Such process reflects cognitive and cultural facets of the human mind [31–33]. Among languages of the world, grammatical gender is one of the most common systems of nominal classification [9]. For instance, in German, every noun of the lexicon is assigned to either masculine, feminine, or neuter gender. Gender languages are commonly found in Africa, Europe, Australia, and Oceania, while their presence is attested but non-continuous in the Pacific, Asia and Americas [34, p.78].

The formal definition of grammatical gender involves grammatical agreement between a noun and other syntactic units within a sentence. To be more precise, all nouns of the lexicon are assigned to certain classes. For instance, a language has two gender classes if two classes of nouns can be differentiated by the agreement they take [35]. As an example in French, *bus* 'bus' is masculine and *voiture* 'car' is feminine. Thus, the masculine and feminine gender classes are distinguished via the grammatical agreement on the articles, adjectives, and verbs, c.f., *un nouveau bus* (one.MASC new.MASC bus.MASC) 'A new bus' and *une nouvelle voiture* (one.FEM new.FEM car.FEM) 'A new car'. Likewise in Swedish, all nouns of the lexicon are labeled with the uter or neuter gender classes [36, p.198], which are mirrored through grammatical agreement (see examples in Sect. 1).

The grammatical agreement of gender relates to their main functions of facilitating referent tracking in discourse [32,37,38], as the agreement pattern provides transparent information. However, gender assignment is considered as much more opaque [9, p.57]. By way of illustration, it is relatively complex to explain why bus is masculine and car is feminine in French, whereas both nouns are affiliated to the feminine gender in Hindi. With regard to Swedish, contradictory observation occur. While grammatical gender is commonly considered as arbitrary [39,40], several semantic principles are attested, i.e., nouns referring to human and non-human animates tend to be affiliated to the uter gender, while inanimates are more likely to be neuter [41]. Moreover, nouns pointing at concrete or countable entities are generally uter while abstract or mass nouns are favored by the neuter gender [42].

As a summary, we expect that word embedding can easily capture the grammatical gender of nouns, since grammatical agreement provides consistent syntactic clues within the linguistic context of nouns. Due to this reason, grammatical gender is considered as a typically grammaticalized feature in our analysis.

**Common/Proper Nouns.** Nevertheless, not all categorization of nouns are marked by agreement marking. For instance, the distinction between common and proper nouns is mostly based on semantics. Common nouns indicate referents which share certain properties, while proper nouns name specific and individual referents [12, p.149]. As an example for common nouns, one of the inherent properties of a *clock* is 'a device which can indicate time'. Proper nouns, on the other hand, are not restricted by such intrinsic properties. By way of illustration, any person, animal, and object may be named after *Smith.* The distinction between common and proper nouns is realized via capitalization in languages such as English. However, such marking is only represented in the writing system, which is an additional invention of language. Moreover, the rules of capitalization of proper nouns are not consistent in a cross-language manner. For instance, English capitalizes names of the months (e.g., *December*) while Swedish does not, whereas German capitalizes nouns altogether.

Similar observations are made in terms of syntax, as no consistent criterion is available to differentiate between common and proper nouns. As an example, in English, proper nouns generally appear as bare forms but the same situation may occur for common nouns, e.g., *Jeff is a good man, coffee may wake you up.* Moreover, the use of definite articles may be preferred for specific types of proper nouns, e.g., *the United States.* Furthermore, the use of article with proper nouns is not universal cross-linguistically. By way of illustration, country names are used with the definite article in French, e.g., *la Chine* (the.FEM China), while in English it is not required (e.g., *China*). These observations support the fact that the classification of common and proper nouns is indeed a relevant issue for machine translation [43], sentiment analysis [44], topic tracking [45], web data search [46], case restoration [47], among others topics [48].

**Count/Mass Distinction.** The third main sub-categorization of nouns we apply in this study is the contrast between count and mass nouns. Count nouns are generally defined as entities which can be individuated and counted, while mass nouns refer to referents whose parts are not considered as discrete units [12, p.156]. For instance, a piece of a cake is still cake, however, a piece of a desk is not a desk. The reflection of the cognitive principle of individuation have been studied with regard to its connection to human cognition and how such cognitive concept is reflected through language [14,49–51]. As an example, morphological marking of grammatical number has been attested as one of the main linguistic realization of count/mass marking [13,52].

In terms of syntax, in languages with grammatical number, count nouns may bear singular and grammatical plural marking (c.f., *the book is here* and *the books are here* in English), while mass nouns solely occur in singular (c.f., the furniture is new, *the furnitures are new). Moreover, only count nouns can apply indefinite articles (c.f., *a table* and **a luggage*), among other syntactic criteria [50]. With regard to semantics, count and mass nouns may be distinguished on the basis of cumulativity [49], divisibility [53], and specificity [13, p.51–53]. Mass nouns are unspecified as how to be cumulated and divided, while count nouns are specified for how to be cumulated or divided. For instance, *coffee* may be counted in terms of cup, glass, barrel, brand, among other measure terms [54, p.9], with no intrinsic specification. On the opposite, count nouns such as *book* can inherently be counted by the mean of cardinal numbers and cannot be divided.

Nevertheless, even though both syntactic and semantic criteria are available to differentiate between count and mass nouns, the fact that nouns may undergo conversion (shift) and migrate to the other category represents a challenge for classification tasks [13]. As an example, *beer* in English may be used as a mass noun when referring to a type of drink, e.g., *I like beer.* Yet, the same word form can also be employed as a count noun when referring to 'a pint of beer', e.g., *I would like to have two beers.* Such conversion is extremely productive and common within languages of the world [14, p.14] and represents one of the major difficulty of identifying count and mass nouns in terms of computational linguistics [55]. Thus, we expect that the word embedding model is capable of retrieving the syntactic information of count and mass nouns to encode it into the word vectors; but also that the conversion between count and mass nouns may represent a source of difficulty for the classification task. For instance, previous studies have shown that a single layer feed-forward neural network could not interpret the count/mass feature of Swedish nouns at a high accuracy level due to frequent cross-category conversion [8]. Our study applies a similar methodology and further investigates the effect of neuron quantity on the performance of feed-forward neural network with regard to the classification of nominal features such as grammatical gender, common/proper, and count/mass.

## 3 Methodology

Swedish was chosen due to the contradictory observation attested on grammatical gender assignment and tracking (see Sect. 2.2). For each classification task, a classifier is trained on a set of word vectors that are labeled with their corresponding nominal classes, i.e., uter/neuter, common/proper, count/mass. The process is divided into three steps: vector generation (word embedding), data labeling, and classification.

First, a corpus of word-segmented raw sentences is fed to a word embedding model, which assigns a vector to each word in the corpus. This process is done in such a way that semantic similarities of words are modeled by the correlation between their corresponding vectors, i.e., words that are semantically similar are consequently assigned to similar vectors.

Second, a dictionary is used to associated a subset of word vectors with their corresponding nominal classes. We combine each noun from the dictionary with its vector extracted from the corpus. The output is a list of word vectors labeled with nominal classes. This list is then partitioned into train, and test sets.

Third, we train a classifier based on the pairs of word vectors and nominal classes. The classifier takes a single word vector as input and predicts the nominal class of its associated word. The train data obtained in the previous step is used to train the classifier, and the test set is used to evaluate the classification model.

The evaluation of the classifier is based of the performance of word vectors on each of the nominal classification tasks. For instance, a high accuracy of classification implies that the information about the nominal classes can be captured into the word vectors. In the following section, we elaborate the detailed settings for the three steps mentioned above: Word embedding, data labeling, and classification.

## 4 Experimental Settings

The word vectors are extracted via RSV (Real-valued Syntactic Word Vectors) model for word embedding [7]. RSV generates a set of word vectors from an unlabeled data in three major steps: First, a co-occurrence matrix is built based on the co-occurrence frequency of words. The components of this matrix are the frequency of seeing words in the domain of different context words. each column is associated with a word and the rows are associated with contexts. Each column forms a high dimensional word vector that describes the word with respect to its occurrence frequency in different contexts. Second, the high dimensional column vectors are transformed to match the Gaussian distribution with zero mean. Third, the low dimensional data is obtained from the top $K$ right singular vectors of the transformed co-occurrence matrix. During these three steps, the RSV model can be tuned according to the following parameters:

- Context type: the context of a word may refer to the preceding words (symmetric), following words or include both directions (asymmetric).
- Context size: how many words does the system count in the context. As an example, the most popular setting is one preceding word.
- Dimensionality: the quantity of dimensions the model may use to represent the word vectors. The amount of dimensions is generally positively correlated to the accuracy, but negatively correlated with the processing time and memory.

Within our experiments, context type and context size are set as the immediate preceding word [7], while the number of dimensions is set to 50.

Two types of classifiers are included in our experiments: linear discriminant analysis, and neural network. The purpose of this selection is to assess if the nominal classes are linearly separable. Linear discriminant analysis (LDA) is a linear generative classifier that fits a Gaussian distributions on the training data and predict the test data classes through the likelihood ratio of the data given the distributions. Neural network (NN) is a non-linear discriminative classifier that make no assumption on the data distribution. It searches for a boundary between the data points with regard to their classes in such a way that the classification accuracy is minimized. LDA is more simple in terms of structure and processing time but it may be less accurate depending on the complexity of the task. On the other hand, neural network is a more elaborate type of classifier but also more costly in terms of processing.

We use a feed-forward neural network, which consists of an input layer, a hidden layer, and an output layer. The size of the input layer is as big as the dimensionality of word embeddings, 50. The output layer consists of two neurons, equal to the number of classes in each of the nominal classification tasks. The size of the hidden layer is set in two ways: First, the size of the hidden layer is set to 100, regardless of the classification task. Second, the size of the hidden layer is set with regard to the performance of the neural network on the classification tasks. This is formulated as an optimization problem whose objective is to minimize the errors made by the neural network on each of the classification tasks. We use half of the training data for this purpose. We use 80% of this portion for training the neural network and 20% for validating it. This partitioning is done in such as way that the relative ratio of the classes in each part is equal to the overall rate of the classes in the entire training data. Given a neural network setting with one hidden layer consisting of $0 < h \leq 300$ neurons, the simulated annealing uses the training data to train the neural network. It then uses the validation set to compute the performance of the neural network. The error rate of the neural network on the validation set is used as the objective of the simulated annealing to be minimized. The output of the simulated annealing is the optimal number of neurons ($h^*$) in the hidden layer of the neural network. The neural network with $h^*$ neurons in its hidden layer (i.e. one hidden layer with $h^*$ neurons) is finally evaluated on the test set used for other classifiers.

Our computational model is fed with data that originate from the Swedish Language Bank (Språkbanken) at the University of Gothenburg.[1] The corpus of raw sentences is compiled by Språkbanken and includes data from Swedish Wikipedia (available at Wikipedia Monolingual Corpora, Swedish web news corpora (2001–2013) and Swedish Wikipedia corpus). The OpenNLP sentence splitter and tokenizer are used for normalizing the raw corpus.[2] All numbers are replaced with a NUMBER token and uppercase letters are converted to lowercase forms. Due to the high ratio of compound nouns in Swedish [56–58], we only involve nouns which have more than 100 occurrences in the corpus.

The information on nominal categories is extracted from the SALDO (Swedish Associative Thesaurus version 2) dictionary. The categorization of SALDO are rather extensive [59, p.27]. As an example, some nouns are affiliated to neither *uter* nor *neuter* but rather to a third type *vacklande* due to speaker variation. In our study, we only incorporate the relevant categories, since the amount of tokens in these peripheral categories is minimal. Nouns that are not in word vectors' vocabulary set are also filtered out, which results in the overview in Table 1.

The annotation of grammatical gender and common/proper nouns is rather straightforward in SALDO, whereas the count/mass distinction is not a category

[1] spraakbanken.gu.se/eng/resources/corpus.

[2] opennlp.apache.org.

**Table 1.** Nominal features in Swedish based on SALDO [8].

| Category | Quantity | Example |
|---|---|---|
| Uter | 13540 | *bok* 'book' |
| Neuter | 5518 | *hus* 'house' |
| Count | 16181 | *kontor* 'office' |
| Mass | 3085 | *bagage* 'luggage' |
| Comon | 18549 | *bord* 'table' |
| Proper | 3142 | *Alyssa* |

transparently specified in the dictionary. We therefore follow the formal syntactic definition and consider that only count nouns have plural inflection [50,51].

## 5 Results

The performance of the classifiers are evaluated based on the *Rand index* [60] (accuracy) and *F-score* [61]. The Rand index refers to the accuracy of the model and is calculated by dividing the total number of correctly retrieved tokens by the total number of retrieved tokens. Moreover, we apply the rule of majority label prediction, called *Zero rule*, since the investigated nominal categories are numerically unbalanced (e.g., 84% common nouns vs 16% proper nouns). Our baseline of accuracy for each classification task is thus equal to relative size of the larger class, i.e., 71.0% for grammatical gender prediction, 84.0% for count/mass prediction, and 85.5% for common/proper noun prediction. Moreover, we also measure the detailed performance on a category-internal scale, so that we can assess if one of the nominal sub-category represents more difficulties for the classifier. For instance, if uter nouns are harder or easier to identify. Hence, we generate the two values of *precision* and *recall*. Precision evaluates how many tokens are correct among all the output of the classifier, whereas recall quantifies how many tokens are correctly retrieved among all the expected correct output. The two measures assess different facets of the output, and merged into the F-score, which is equal to the harmonic mean of the precision and recall, $2\frac{\text{recall}\times\text{precision}}{\text{recall}+\text{precision}}$.

Furthermore, two figures are provided for every classification task. First, we display how the noun classes are clustered in the distributional semantic space formed by the word vectors [8]. This representation is expected to demonstrate visually the performance of word embedding when capturing information related to the relevant nominal category. Second, we show the histogram of the entropy of the neural network's output for nominal sub-category. The entropy measures the uncertainty involved in the neural network's output to identify the noun classes, it thus show how certain is the classifier when processing the classification task.

### 5.1 Grammatical Gender

The results obtained from the neural networks are represented in Table 2 two columns, NN, and SA-NN. The column NN represents the results obtained from the neural network architecture with 100 hidden units and the SA-NN represents the results obtained from the neural network architecture tuned by simulated annealing. The optimal size of the hidden layer for this task is 125 (i.e. the tuned neural network (SA-NN) has 125 neurons in its hidden layer). The neural networks reach higher accuracies (Rand index) than LDA, as they are able to identify correctly the grammatical gender of more than 93% of the nouns in the test set. Such performance is conjointly higher than our baseline accuracy, which is 71.0%. A comparison between NN and SA-NN shows that both settings result in almost the same performance, although the SA-NN setting uses smaller number of neurons in its hidden layer. The tuned neural network results in relatively higher value of f-score when it faces the neuter nouns.

**Table 2.** The performance of LDA, the neural network (NN), and the neural network tuned by simulated annealing (SA-NN) on the grammatical gender prediction.

| | LDA | NN | SA-NN |
|---|---|---|---|
| Accuracy | 92.7 | 93.6 | 93.7 |
| Uter recall | 94.8 | 96.3 | 96.5 |
| Uter precision | 94.8 | 95.0 | 94.6 |
| Uter f-score | 94.8 | 95.6 | 95.5 |
| Neuter recall | 87.9 | 87.4 | 87.3 |
| Neuter precision | 87.9 | 90.1 | 91.4 |
| Neuter f-score | 87.9 | 88.7 | 89.4 |

Table 2 shows that the word vectors could encode the information about the grammatical genders of the nouns and they are almost linearly separable with respect to the grammatical genders of the nouns. Such statement is supported by the semantic space of neural network in Fig. 1. The uter nouns (black) and the neuter nouns (red) are forming two clusters which only overlap at a small area. As expected, this intermediary zone is precisely where most of the errors generated by the neural network (green and blue) are located. Moreover, the classifiers had more difficulties identifying neuter nouns. For instance, neural network could interpret uter nouns with higher f-score (95.6%) compared to neuter nouns (88.7%).

Figure 2 shows the histogram of the entropy of the neural network's outputs. The top left histogram, the neuter nouns are classified as neuter, and the bottom right histogram, the uter nouns are classified as uter, are skewed toward left. This left skewness in the histograms show that the classifier predicts the correct grammatical genders with high confidence. This confirms that the information about the grammatical genders of the nouns are captured by the word

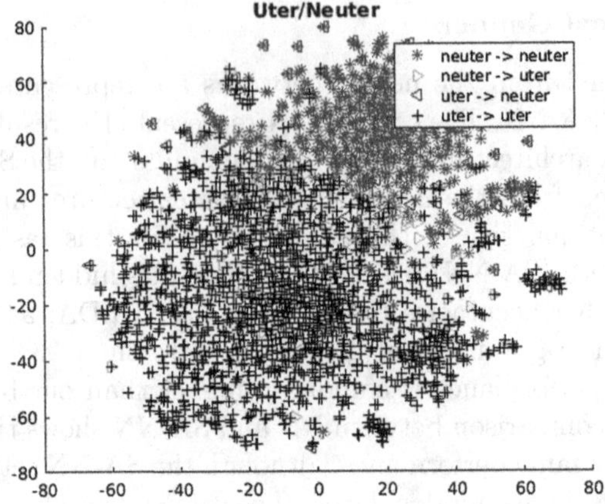


**Fig. 1.** tSNE representation of the word vectors with regard to their grammatical genders associated predicted by the neural network consisting of one hidden layer with 100 neurons [8]. (Color figure online)

vectors. We also see that the histogram of the entropy of the neural network's outputs for the erroneous items, i.e., the top right and the bottom left graphs, are skewed toward right. This displays the uncertainty involved in the neural network's outputs and indicates the lack of information in the erroneous word vectors. The analysis of the output's entropy thus demonstrate that with regard to grammatical gender, the neural network was interpreting the grammatical gender of nouns with high accuracy, with exception to some outliers for which the entropy was unusually high. Further explanation is provided in the following Section.

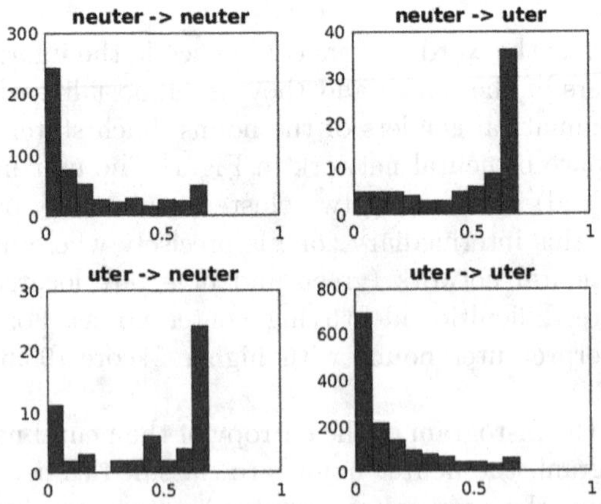


**Fig. 2.** The histogram of the entropy of the neural network's outputs with regard to grammatical genders. The neural network has one hidden layer with 100 neurons [8].

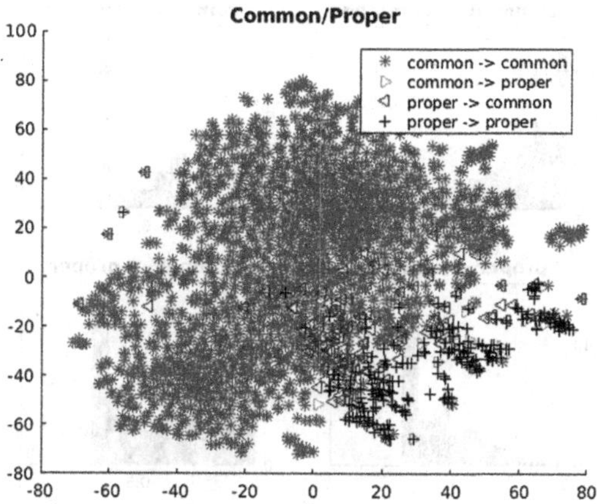


**Fig. 3.** tSNE representation of the word vectors associated with the proper noun and common noun categories by the neural network consisting of one hidden layer with 100 neurons [8].

### 5.2 Common/Proper Nouns

The optimal size of the hidden layer obtained by the simulated annealing algorithm for this task is 24. As shown in Table 3, all classifiers outperform our baseline accuracy (85.5%). In terms of accuracy, the neural networks are more accurate than LDA. However, most of this achievement is due to the unbalance data distribution which biases the neural networks toward the bigger population. In term of f-scores, we see that the results obtained from LDA are comparable to the results obtained from the neural networks. The relatively high value of f-scores obtained by LDA on the proper nouns show that the word vectors should be linearly separable with regard to this nominal classification. This statement is supported by the results obtained from the tuned neural network (SA-NN). We see that the tuned network result in substantially higher values of f-score on the identification of both common and proper nouns although the network has a smaller hidden layer (24 versus 100). The higher values of f-score obtained from a simpler neural network with a small hidden layer confirms that the data is to a large extent linearly separable.

The above conclusion about the linear separability of proper versus common nouns is supported by the visualisation of the word vectors with regard to their proper noun versus common noun categories. Figure 3 represents the data distribution in a two dimensional space. We see that the proper nouns are clustered in the bottom-right area of the semantic space. A major part of this area is linearly separable from the remaining vectors in the semantics; the vectors associated with common nouns. A certain part of proper nouns are merged into the common nouns, thus, hard to identify. In this case, the recall of the proper nouns is significantly improved if we use quadratic discriminant analysis (QDA) instead

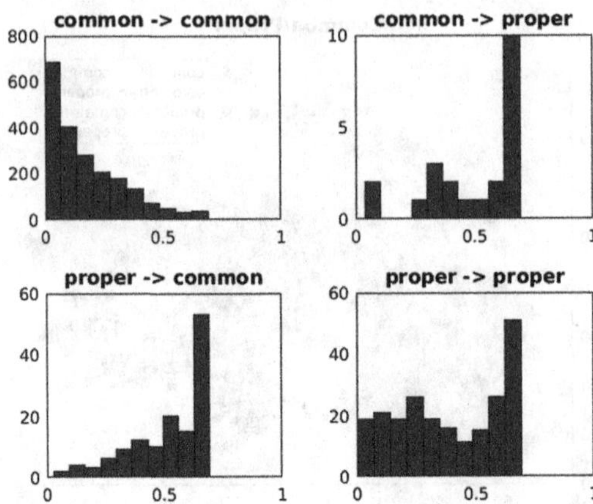


**Fig. 4.** The histogram of the entropy of the neural network's outputs with regard to the proper noun versus common noun classification. The neural network has one hidden layer with 100 neurons [8].

of the linear discriminant analysis. However, this improvement is together with a dramatic decrease on the recall of the common nouns. In our experiments with QDA, we obtained the f-score of 93.3% on the common nouns and the f-score of 71.4% on the proper nouns which are smaller than LDA and the neural networks.

Furthermore, the histogram of the entropy of the neural network's outputs in Fig. 4 displays less confidence in the outputs of the neural network when facing proper nouns as its inputs. In comparison with Fig. 2, we observe a higher amount of uncertainty in the classifier's performance which demonstrates that less information can be captured in word vectors with regard to the common/proper noun nominal category.

**Table 3.** The performance of LDA, the neural network (NN), and the neural network tuned by simulated annealing (SA-NN) on the classification between common versus proper nouns.

| | LDA | NN | SA-NN |
|---|---|---|---|
| Accuracy | 93.4 | 95.2 | 95.1 |
| Common noun recall | 96.8 | 98.9 | 98.7 |
| Common noun precision | 95.5 | 93.9 | 95.7 |
| Common noun f-score | 96.1 | 96.3 | 97.2 |
| Proper noun recall | 73.4 | 62.4 | 74.2 |
| Proper noun precision | 79.9 | 91.0 | 90.4 |
| Proper noun f-score | 76.5 | 74.3 | 81.5 |

### 5.3 Count/Mass Distinction

In this experiment, the neural network tuned by the simulated annealing algorithm has 294 neurons is its hidden layer. This value is very close to maximum number of the hidden layer size, 300. As shown in Table 4, the accuracy obtained from the classifiers are below our baseline, 85.5%. As we mentioned before, our baseline uses the Zero rule for classification which simply predicts the majority class, i.e., count noun in this case. So, it will completely unable to predict the minority class of mass nouns. The baseline's recall for the mass nouns, however, is 0.0% since all the mass nouns are classified as count noun. This is similar to the results obtained from the neural network, resulting in the high precision 99.0% on the count nouns but very small precision on the mass nouns. This basically shows that the neural network's prediction on the mass nouns is almost always wrong, i.e., mass nouns are always classified as count noun by the neural network. However we see that the LDA's recall on the mass nouns (76.9%) is significantly higher than the baseline's recall (0.0%) and the neural network's recall (7.1%). This is because of the generative nature of LDA that always give a chance to all classes, regardless of their size, to appear in the prediction task. However, this might not always work well specially when the data is not properly distributed with regard to the classes. In this case, the classifier will result in a small value of precision, as we see for LDA's precision on the mass nouns. In general, the weak performance of the classifiers on the count/mass classification task shows that the word vectors have almost no information about this feature of the nouns. We see that a very large hidden layer also is not helpful to classify between the mass versus count nouns. This difficult in the classification between mass and count nouns is because of the migration of words between the two classes (see Sect. 2.2) which allows a noun to be count or mass depending on its syntactic environment. This dynamic behavior of nouns results in a big overlap between the two classes of word vectors associated with count and mass nouns and makes the word vectors ineffective for this task. The overlap between the

**Table 4.** The performance of LDA, the neural network (NN), and the neural network tuned by simulated annealing (SA-NN) on the classification between count versus mass nouns.

| | LDA | NN | SA-NN |
|---|---|---|---|
| Accuracy | 74.8 | 82.8 | 79.2 |
| Count noun recall | 74.3 | 99.0 | 95.2 |
| Count noun precision | 93.7 | 83.2 | 81.2 |
| Count noun f-score | 82.9 | 90.4 | 87.6 |
| Mass noun recall | 76.9 | 7.2 | 24.9 |
| Mass noun precision | 39.1 | 61.4 | 60.7 |
| Mass noun f-score | 51.8 | 12.7 | 35.3 |

two classes of word vectors is seen in Fig. 5. We see that mass nouns and the count nouns appear everywhere in the semantic space.

Our observation in terms of general accuracy is also supported by the histogram of the entropy of the neural network's outputs in Fig. 6. First of all, the classifier is very uncertain about the identification of count versus mass nouns. This shows that few relevant information could be found in the distribution of word vectors and its decisions rely highly on chance. This uncertainty is seen is the four scenarios shown in Fig. 6. We equally observe that the amount of uncertainty involved in the classifier's decisions on the mass nouns that are correctly classifies as mass noun is higher than the count nouns that are correctly

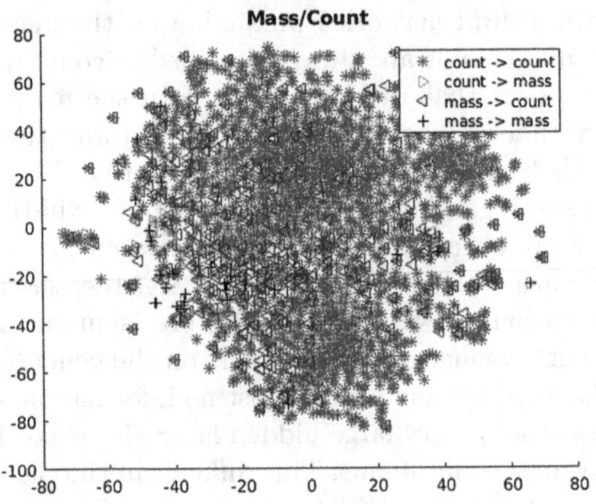


**Fig. 5.** tSNE representation of the word vectors associated with the mass nouns and count nouns by the neural network consisting of one hidden layer with 100 neurons [8].

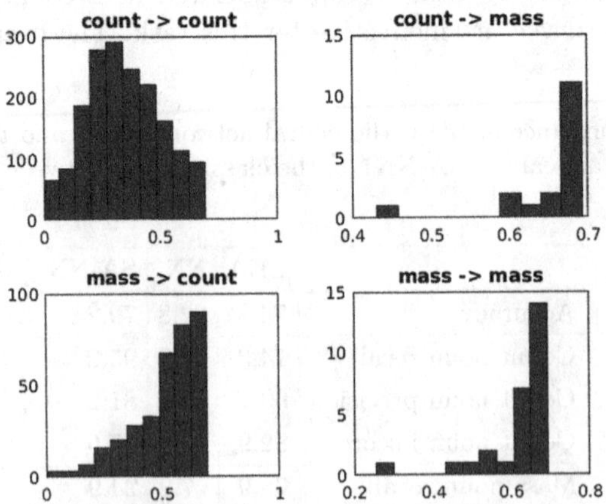


**Fig. 6.** The histogram of the entropy of the neural network's outputs with regard to the proper noun versus common noun classification. The neural network has one hidden layer with 100 neurons [8].

classified as count noun. This can be due to the fact that the likelihood of migration (shift) from mass category to count category is higher than the migration from the count category to mass category [13, p.57–58].

## 6 Concluding Discussion

Through the application of a neural network tuned with the simulated annealing algorithm, we are able to demonstrate which types of nominal features can be captured by word embeddings and how their loading and accuracy vary between each other. We show that both grammatical (uter/neuter) and semantic (common/proper) properties of nouns may be identified with high precision through word embedding. Moreover, the semantic properties of words are relatively easier to retrieve via word embeddings as the neural network trained for the classification between proper and common nouns requires five times fewer neurons than the neural network trained for the classification between the grammatical properties (24 vs 125). Yet, the analysis of entropy provides opposite insights: The entropy of the classifier was higher for common/proper categorization than for uter/neuter distinction, even though their general performance was similar. Further experiments are thus required to scrutinize the correlation of neuron quantity and classifier entropy with the general performance of classification. On the other hand, the count/mass categorization represented difficulties for the classifiers. Setting the hidden layer size near its maximum could not improve the performance either. We thus follow previous studies and suspect that two factors are plausible as explanation: First, the complex semantic and grammatical aspects of count and mass nouns may create difficulty to the word embeddings' classification. Second, the high occurrence of conversion across count and mass nouns may also generate noise in word embeddings. Under such assumption, the application of word embeddings would be considered as adequate for static nominal features such as grammatical genders or semantic features, but less appropriate for fluctuating properties such as count/mass. We speculate that conversion is the main source of complication as the error analysis of previous studies point out the importance of polysemy with regard to classification task, i.e., most of the errors encountered in uter/neuter and common/proper classifications were also due to cases where a singular word form shares two (or more) different entries that belong to two distinct nominal classes [8]. Further experiments with different word embeddings structures (e.g., GloVe and word2vec) along with different types of contexts are therefore required to verify which of the two factors has a stronger influence on the performance of classification.

**Acknowledgements.** Our work on this paper was fully collaborative; the order of the authors names is alphabetical and does not reflect any asymmetry in contribution. We are grateful for the fruitful discussion with the audience of the Special Session on Natural Language Processing in Artificial Intelligence at the 10th International Conference on Agents and Artificial Intelligence in Funchal, Madeira. We would like to express our gratitude to our colleagues Linnea Öberg, Karin Koltay, Rima Haddad, and

Josefin Lindgren for their comments and support. We also appreciate the constructive comments from the anonymous referees. We are fully responsible for any remaining errors.

## References

1. Collobert, R., Weston, J., Bottou, L., Karlen, M., Kavukcuoglu, K., Kuksa, P.: Natural language processing (almost) from scratch. J. Mach. Learn. Res. **12**, 2493–2537 (2011)
2. Chen, D., Manning, C.: A fast and accurate dependency parser using neural networks. In: Proceedings of the 2014 Conference on Empirical Methods in Natural Language Processing (EMNLP), pp. 740–750 (2014)
3. Sahlgren, M.: The word-space model. Ph.D. thesis, Stockholm University (2006)
4. Faruqui, M., Dyer, C.: Community evaluation and exchange of word vectors at wordvectors.org. In: Proceedings of the 52nd Annual Meeting of the Association for Computational Linguistics: System Demonstrations, Baltimore, USA. Association for Computational Linguistics, June 2014
5. Mikolov, T., Yih, W.T., Zweig, G.: Linguistic regularities in continuous space word representations. In: Proceedings of the 2013 Conference of the North American Chapter of the Association for Computational Linguistics: Human Language Technologies, Atlanta, Georgia, pp. 746–751. Association for Computational Linguistics, June 2013
6. Nayak, N., Angeli, G., Manning, C.D.: Evaluating word embeddings using a representative suite of practical tasks. In: Proceedings of the 1st Workshop on Evaluating Vector Space Representations for NLP, Berlin, Germany. Association for Computational Linguistics, August 2016
7. Basirat, A., Nivre, J.: Real-valued syntactic word vectors (RSV) for greedy neural dependency parsing. In: Proceedings of the 21st Nordic Conference on Computational Linguistics (NoDaLiDa), Gothenburg, Sweden, pp. 20–28. Association for Computational Linguistics, May 2017
8. Basirat, A., Tang, M.: Lexical and morpho-syntactic features in word embeddings: a casestudy of nouns in Swedish. In: Proceedings of the 10th International Conference on Agents and Artificial Intelligence (ICAART), Madeira, vol. 2, January 2018
9. Corbett, G.G.: Gender. Cambridge University Press, Cambridge (1991)
10. Seifart, F.: Nominal classification. Lang. Linguist. Compass **4**(8), 719–736 (2010)
11. Corbett, G.G.: Number of genders. In: Dryer, M.S., Haspelmath, M. (eds.) The World Atlas of Language Structures Online. Max Planck Institute for Evolutionary Anthropology, Leipzig (2013)
12. Delahunty, G.P., Garvey, J.J.: The English Language: From Sound to Sense. Parlor press, West Lafayette (2010)
13. Gillon, B.S.: The lexical semantics of English count and mass nouns. In: Viegas, E. (ed.) Breadth and Depth of Semantic Lexicons, vol. 10, pp. 19–37. Springer, Dordrecht (1999). https://doi.org/10.1007/978-94-017-0952-1_2
14. Doetjes, J.: Count/mass distinctions across languages. In: Maienborn, C., Heusinger, K.V., Portner, P. (eds.) Semantics: An International Handbook of Natural Language Meaning, Part III, pp. 2559–2580.Mouton de Gruyter, Berlin (2012)
15. Chiarelli, V., El Yagoubi, R., Mondini, S., Bisiacchi, P., Semenza, C.: The syntactic and semantic processing of mass and count nouns: an ERP study. PLoS ONE **6**(10), e25885 (2011)

16. Corbett, G.G.: Number. Cambridge University Press, Cambridge (2000)
17. Dryer, M.S.: Coding of nominal plurality. In: Haspelmath, M., Dryer, M.S., Gil, D., Comrie, B. (eds.) The Word Atlas of Language Structures, pp. 138–141. Oxford University Press, Oxford (2005)
18. Pelletier, F.J., Schubert, L.K.: Mass expressions. In: Gabbay, D., Guenther, F. (eds.) Handbook of Philosophical Logic. Volume IV: Topics in the Philosophy of Language, pp. 327–408. Reidel, Dordrecht (1989)
19. Schütze, H.: Dimensions of meaning. In: Proceedings of the 1992 ACM/IEEE Conference on Supercomputing, pp. 787–796. IEEE Computer Society Press (1992)
20. Lund, K., Burgess, C.: Producing high-dimensional semantic spaces from lexical co-occurrence. Behav. Res. Methods Instrum. Comput. **28**(2), 203–208 (1996)
21. Landauer, T.K., Dumais, S.T.: A solution to Plato's problem: the latent semantic analysis theory of acquisition, induction, and representation of knowledge. Psychol. Rev. **104**(2), 211 (1997)
22. Pennington, J., Socher, R., Manning, C.D.: Glove: global vectors for word representation. In: Proceedings of the 2014 Conference on Empirical Methods in Natural Language Processing (EMNLP), vol. 14, pp. 1532–1543 (2014)
23. Lebret, R., Collobert, R.: Word embeddings through Hellinger PCA. In: Proceedings of the 2014 Conference on Empirical Methods in Natural Language Processing (EMNLP), Gothenburg, Sweden, pp. 482–490. Association for Computational Linguistics, April 2014
24. Mikolov, T., Chen, K., Corrado, G., Dean, J.: Efficient estimation of word representations in vector space. In: Proceedings of Workshop at International Conference on Learning Representations (ICLR) (2013)
25. Levy, O., Goldberg, Y.: Neural word embedding as implicit matrix factorization. In: Advances in Neural Information Processing Systems, pp. 2177–2185 (2014)
26. Dahl, G., Adams, R., Larochelle, H.: Training restricted Boltzmann machines on word observations. In: Langford, J., Pineau, J. (eds.) Proceedings of the 29th International Conference on Machine Learning (ICML-12), ICML 2012, New York, NY, USA, pp. 679–686. Omnipress, July 2012
27. Hinton, G.E., Salakhutdinov, R.R.: Reducing the dimensionality of data with neural networks. Science **313**(5786), 504–507 (2006)
28. Hofmann, T.: Probabilistic latent semantic indexing. In: Proceedings of the 22nd Annual International ACM SIGIR Conference on Research and Development in Information Retrieval, pp. 50–57. ACM (1999)
29. Blei, D.M., Ng, A.Y., Jordan, M.I.: Latent Dirichlet allocation. J. Mach. Learn. Res. **3**(Jan), 993–1022 (2003)
30. Roweis, S.T., Saul, L.K.: Nonlinear dimensionality reduction by locally linear embedding. Science **290**(5500), 2323–2326 (2000)
31. Aikhenvald, A.Y.: Round women and long men: shape, size, and the meanings of gender in New Guinea and beyond. Anthropol. Linguist. **54**(1), 33–86 (2012)
32. Contini-Morava, E., Kilarski, M.: Functions of nominal classification. Lang. Sci. **40**, 263–299 (2013)
33. Kemmerer, D.: Categories of object concepts across languages and brains: the relevance of nominal classification systems to cognitive neuroscience. Lang. Cogn. Neurosci. **32**(4), 401–424 (2017)
34. Aikhenvald, A.Y.: Classifiers: A Typology of Noun Categorization Devices. Oxford University Press, Oxford (2000)
35. Senft, G.: Systems of Nominal Classification. Cambridge University Press, Cambridge (2000)

36. Bohnacker, U.: Nominal phrases. In: Josefsson, G., Platzack, C., Hkansson, G. (eds.) The Acquisition of Swedish Grammar, pp. 195–260. John Benjamins, Amsterdam (2004)
37. Dixon, R.M.W.: Noun class and noun classification. In: Craig, C. (ed.) Noun Classes and Categorization, pp. 105–112. John Benjamins, Amsterdam (1986)
38. Nichols, J.: The origin of nominal classification. In: Proceedings of the Fifteenth Annual Meeting of the Berkeley Linguistics Society, pp. 409–420 (1989)
39. Andersson, A.B.: Second language learners' acquisition of grammatical gender in Swedish. Ph.D. dissertation, University of Gothenburg, Gothenburg (1992)
40. Teleman, U., Hellberg, S., Andersson, E.: Svenska Akademiens Grammatik, vol. 2. Norstedts, Stockholm (1999). Ord. [The Swedish Academy Grammar, Part 2: Words]
41. Dahl, O.: Elementary gender distinctions. In: Unterbeck, B., Rissanen, M. (eds.) Gender in Grammar and Cognition, pp. 577–593. Mouton de Gruyter, Berlin (2000)
42. Fraurud, K.: Proper names and gender in Swedish. In: Unterbeck, B., Rissanen, M., Nevalainen, T., Saari, M. (eds.) Gender in Grammar and Cognition, pp. 167–220. Mouton de Gruyter, Berlin (2000)
43. Lopez, A.: Statistical machine translation. ACM Comput. Surv. **40**(3), 1–49 (2008)
44. Pang, B., Lee, L.: Opinion mining and sentiment analysis. Found. Trends Inf. Retr. **2**(1–2), 1–135 (2008)
45. Petrovic, S., Osborne, M., Lavrenko, V.: Streaming first story detection with application to Twitter. In: Human Language Technologies: The 2010 Annual Conference of the North American Chapter of the Association for Computational Linguistics, pp. 181–189 (2010)
46. Baeza-Yates, R., Ribeiro-Neto, B.: Modern Information Retrieval: The Concepts and Technology Behind Search. Addison Wesley Longman Limited, Essex (2011)
47. Baldwin, T., Joseph, M.P.A.K.: Restoring punctuation and casing in English text. In: Nicholson, A., Li, X. (eds.) AI 2009. LNCS (LNAI), vol. 5866, pp. 547–556. Springer, Heidelberg (2009). https://doi.org/10.1007/978-3-642-10439-8_55
48. Preiss, J., Stevenson, M.: Distinguishing common and proper nouns. In: Second Joint Conference on Lexical and Computational Semantics: Proceedings of the Main Conference and the Shared Task: Semantic Textual Similarity, vol. 1, pp. 80–84 (2013)
49. Quine, W.V.O.: Word and Object. MIT Press, Cambridge (1960)
50. Chierchia, G.: Plurality of mass nouns and the notion of semantic parameter. In: Rothstein, S. (ed.) Events and Grammar, pp. 53–104. Kluwer, Dordrecht (1998)
51. Chierchia, G.: Mass nouns, vagueness and semantic variation. Synthese **174**(1), 99–149 (2010)
52. Borer, H.: Structuring Sense, Part I. Oxford University Press, Oxford (2005)
53. Cheng, C.Y.: Response to Moravcsik. In: Hintikka, J., Moravczik, J., Suppes, P. (eds.) Approaches to Natural Language, pp. 286–288. D. Reidel, Dordrecht (1973)
54. Kilarski, M.: The place of classifiers in the history of linguistics. Hist. Linguist. **41**(1), 33–79 (2014)
55. Katz, G., Zamparelli, R.: Quantifying count/mass elasticity. In: Proceedings of the 29th West Coast Conference on Formal Linguistics, pp. 371–379 (2012)
56. Carter, D., Kaja, J., Neumeyer, L., Rayner, M., Weng, F., Wirn, M.: Handling compound nouns in a Swedish speech-understanding system. In: Proceedings of the Fourth International Conference on Spoken Language, vol. 1, pp. 26–29 (1996)
57. Ostling, R., Wirn, M.: Compounding in a Swedish blog corpus. In: Acta Universitatis Stockholmiensis, pp. 45–63 (2013)

58. Ullman, E., Nivre, J.: Paraphrasing Swedish compound nouns in machine translation. In: MWE@ EACL, pp. 99–103 (2014)
59. Borin, L., Forsberg, M., Lnngren, L.: The hunting of the BLARK - SALDO, a freely available lexical database for Swedish language technology. Studia Linguistica Upsaliensia, pp. 21–32 (2008)
60. Rand, W.M.: Objective criteria for the evaluation of clustering methods. J. Am. Stat. Assoc. **66**(336), 846–850 (1971)
61. Ting, K.M.: Precision and recall. In: Sammut, C., Webb, G.I. (eds.) Encyclopedia of Machine Learning, pp. 781–781. Springer, Boston (2010). https://doi.org/10.1007/978-0-387-30164-8

# Author Index

Printed in the United States
By Bookmasters